TEACHER'S ANSWER KEY

To Accompany

LEGAL RESEARCH AND CITATION STUDENT LIBRARY EXERCISES

Second Edition

By

LARRY L. TEPLY

Professor of Law
Creighton University

AMERICAN CASEBOOK SERIES

St. Paul, Minn.
WEST PUBLISHING CO.
1986

COPYRIGHT © 1986

by

WEST PUBLISHING CO.
50 West Kellogg Boulevard
P.O. Box 64526
St. Paul, Minnesota 55164-0526

ALL RIGHTS RESERVED

ISBN 0-314-26683-6

TABLE OF CONTENTS

Page

SUGGESTIONS FOR INSTRUCTORS - v

LIBRARY EXERCISE ANSWERS

1. Citing Case Names: Parties Cited, Omissions, Geographic Terms, Procedural Phrases, Business Firms, and Other Case Name Modifications - 1
2. United States Reports - 37
3. Parallel Citation of United States Reports - - - - - - - - - - - - 45
4. Supreme Court Reporter - 54
5. Lawyers' Edition of U.S. Supreme Court Reports - - - - - - - - - - 63
6. Early United States Reports - - - - - - - - - - - - - - - - - - - 76
7. Federal Reporter - 84
8. Federal Supplement - 101
9. Federal Rules Decisions - 111
10. Federal Cases - 122
11. Official State Court Reports - - - - - - - - - - - - - - - - - - - 130
12. West's Regional Reporters - 139
13. California Reporter - 156
14. New York Supplement - 166
15. American Law Reports Annotated - - - - - - - - - - - - - - - - - - 176
16. Annotations in U.S. Supreme Court Reports, Lawyers' Edition - - - 193
17. English Reports, Full Reprint - - - - - - - - - - - - - - - - - - 204
18. Law Reports - 213
19. West's Digests: Key Number Digests in West's Reporter Volumes - - 220
20. West's Digests: Finding Cases from Known Topics and Key Numbers - 230
21. West's Digests: Descriptive Word Indexes - - - - - - - - - - - - - 238
22. Lawyers Co-operative's Digests - - - - - - - - - - - - - - - - - - 249
23. Shepard's Case Citations: Subsequent History - - - - - - - - - - 256
24. Shepard's Case Citations: Subsequent Treatment - - - - - - - - - 272
25. West's Words and Phrases - 285
26. Tables of Cases and Popular Name Tables - - - - - - - - - - - - - 299
27. American Jurisprudence Second - - - - - - - - - - - - - - - - - - 310
28. Corpus Juris Secundum - 315
29. Topic Method of Search in Legal Encyclopedias - - - - - - - - - - 320

30.	Legal Periodicals	332
31.	<u>Index to Legal Periodicals</u>: Articles	338
32.	<u>Index to Legal Periodicals</u>: Case Notes and Comments	346
33.	Texts and Treatises	352
34.	Restatements of the Law	363
35.	United States Constitution	372
36.	<u>United States Treaties and Other International Agreements</u>	377
37.	<u>United States Statutes at Large</u>	384
38.	<u>United States Code Annotated</u>	389
39.	State Statutes	407
40.	<u>Code of Federal Regulations</u>	413
41.	Federal Administrative Decisions	413
42.	Federal Rules of Civil Procedure	420
43.	Legislative History of Federal Statutes	426
44.	<u>United States Attorney General Opinions</u>	437
45.	Formulating WESTLAW Search Requests	438
46.	Formulating LEXIS Search Requests	440

SUGGESTIONS FOR INSTRUCTORS

Before assignments are made from these materials, instructors should consider the following suggestions about the use of these library exercises:

1. <u>Requirement that Students Read the General Instructions for the Library Exercises</u>. Pages v and vi in the Student Library Exercise book contain "General Instructions" on how the Library Exercises are used. They also address several commonly asked questions concerning the use of problem numbers, answer-sheet format, citation form, typeface, retention of copies of the answer sheets, typing requirements, and permissible cooperation among students. It is strongly suggested that these two pages be included in the students' initial assignment.

2. <u>Assignment of Problem Numbers and Establishing a Procedure for Changing Problem Numbers When Students Encounter Difficulties Completing an Exercise</u>. As explained in the General Instructions, students should be assigned an individual problem number (a number from one to six hundred) that will direct them to their individual problem within each library exercise. In order to complete an exercise, the students should examine the instructions at the beginning of the exercise and then find their individual problem in the six columns of numbers under the heading "Problem #." The student would use the same procedure for each subsequent exercise. If a source needed to complete an exercise is unavailable or a change is necessary for some other reason, the student should use a different problem number for that exercise only.

In order for this system to operate, the instructor must prior to the first assignment (a) assign each student a problem number and (b) establish a procedure for students to use to select a different problem number when difficulties are encountered. One easy way of assigning problem numbers is to post a photocopy of the class list with a problem number written beside each name.

As the General Instructions note, one possible procedure for assigning alternate problem numbers is student self-reassignment through the addition (or subtraction) of a specified number to (from) your assigned problem number. This approach is the one recommended. For example, you should announce that if the student cannot complete their assigned problem in an exercise for some reason, they should add <u>105</u> to their problem number and do that problem instead. Thus, as the General Instructions illustrate, if a student's assigned problem number is 344 and that student is unable to complete one of the exercises because a needed book is unavailable, the student would add 105 to 344 and do problem number 449 for this exercise. In this situation, the student should clearly indicate on their answer sheet which problem number you used and the reason for the change, as shown in the General Instructions. If by adding the number you have designated (e.g, 105), the student still has trouble, the student should add 1 more, and so on. In the above example, the student would do problem number 450 and so on. Note that you want to have students with problem numbers in the 500's <u>subtract</u> the number instead (because only 600 numbers are used).

If a self-reassignment procedure is not used, the instructor should designate who is authorized to reassign problem numbers (e.g., the instructor, the library staff, student assistants), how the changes are to be recorded, if at all (e.g., on sheets listing the student's problem number, the number to which the student was reassigned, and the reason for reassignment), and when the authorized persons will be available for making reassignments.

3. <u>A Uniform System of Citation</u>. The citations contained in the answer keys are based upon the latest available (9th) printing of <u>A Uniform System of Citation</u> (13th ed. 1981). If the students' citations are to conform to the <u>USOC</u>, it is recommended that the students be asked to purchase a copy of this manual.

A word of caution concerning the <u>USOC</u> is in order. Its authors have continued to update each printing of the <u>USOC</u> without issuing a new edition.

While most of these changes are minor, you should be aware that those changes may account for minor differences between the answer key and the students' answers.

4. <u>Standard Operating Instructions</u>. You should note that in absence of an instructor's announcement that students should do otherwise, the General Instructions establish the following procedures:

(a) The students are instructed to retain the same problem number throughout all the library exercises.

(b) The exercises in most cases do not specify a particular form. In absence of specific instructions, the students are instructed that the citations should conform to the rules set forth in <u>A Uniform System of Citation</u>. The students are told, however, not include the subsequent history of a case in their citations unless they are specifically instructed to do so.

Furthermore, unless otherwise instructed, the students are told to use Memo/Brief form as their principal method of citation. They are instructed to indicate in their answers the Law Review form <u>unless</u> (1) the only difference between the Memo/Brief and Law Review form is the underlining of the <u>entire</u> case name in the Memo/Brief form or (2) when the only difference between the Law Review form and the Memo/Brief form is the use of large and small capitals in the Law Review form (as opposed to ordinary roman type).

Unless otherwise instructed, the students are told to indicate italics by single underlining.

(c) The students are directed to place their name and problem number at the top right-hand corner of the answer sheet.

(d) Unless otherwise instructed, the students are directed not to use a cover sheet or folder for their answers.

(e) In absence of specific permission or instructions from the instructor, the students are told that their answers should be typewritten. You will find that typewritten answers aid significantly in the speed and accuracy of correction.

(f) Unless otherwise stated, students are told that they are permitted to discuss the assignments with other students; however, the final written work must reflect the student's own individual work. In any event, students will find that overlap of answer sheets for any given group of students will be minimal.

(g) Unless otherwise instructed, students are directed to retain the handwritten answers from which their answers were typed or a photocopy of their answer sheet. The students are informed that, if their answer sheets are misplaced, they must be able to supply the instructor with copy of their answers.

5. <u>Administrative Details</u>. It is suggested that the following administrative details also be considered:

(a) where and when the assignments are to be handed in;

(b) what penalty, if any, will be assessed for late papers;

(c) how requests for extensions of a due date for an assignment are to be handled;

(d) under what circumstances, if any, handwritten assignments will be accepted;

(e) how corrected answer sheets will be returned;

(f) when questions concerning the returned assignment will be entertained and what supporting material (e.g., a photocopy of the relevant page), if any, must be presented by the student requesting a grade change; and

(g) where changes in assignments or other instructions will be posted.

6. **Coordination with Library Staff**. It is recommended that the instructor inform the library staff of the assignment so that they can plan for extraordinarily heavy use of the library. The exercises generate a large number of books for reshelving. Furthermore, it is important to review the availability of the books needed to complete the exercises. For example, before assigning Library Exercise 41 (Federal Administrative Decisions), it should be determined whether the library contains Federal Trade Commission Decisions. Consulting with the library staff is an easy way to determine this information. If the resources are particularly limited, it would be appropriate to place the needed materials on reserve.

7. **Library Rules**. It is recommended that the students be reminded of the library rules.

8. **Assignment Sequence**. The Student Library Exercises are arranged in order of treatment in the Programmed Text. The following table shows the corresponding library exercises for each chapter of that text:

Programmed Text	Library Exercises
1. Introduction to Legal Research and Citation	None
2. Case Reporting and Citation	Ex. 1
3. Federal Court Decisions	Ex. 2-10
4. State Court Decisions	Ex. 11-14
5. Annotated, Special Subject, and English Reporters	Ex. 15-18
6. Digests	Ex. 19-22
7. Shepard's Case Citations and Case History	Ex. 23-24
8. Words and Phrases, Case and Popular Name Tables, and Other "Case-Finding" Secondary Sources	Ex. 25-34
9. U.S. Constitution, Treaties, and Federal Statutes	Ex. 35-38
10. State Constitutions, Statutes, and Municipal Ordinances	Ex. 39
11. Administrative Regulations and Decisions, Presidential Documents, Court Rules, and Rules of Evidence, Practice, and Procedure	Ex. 40-42
12. Legislative History, Attorney General Opinions, and Finding Other Secondary Sources Useful for Interpreting Particular Statutes	Ex. 43-44
13. Law Dictionaries, Briefs, Records, Oral Arguments, Form Books, and Other Practice Aids	None
14. WESTLAW Computer-Assisted Legal Research	Ex. 45
15. LEXIS Computer-Assisted Legal Research	Ex. 46

9. **Review and Grading of Answers**. The second edition of the Programmed Text has introduced a Quick-Reference Abbreviation system to assist students in recognizing and correcting errors. It is suggested that this system be used in reviewing the students' answers. A complete listing of those abbreviations is given in a Table at the beginning of the Student Library Exercise book. The answer key also notes the ones that are particularly relevant to an exercise.

It is recommended that instructors choose from two principal approaches to grading the library exercises: (1) a "major error-minor error" point system or (2) a "pass/re-do" system.

(a) **"Major Error-Minor Error" Point System**. Under this system, errors made by students are divided into major errors and minor errors. Minor errors include improper spacing, omission of periods, misspelled words, typographical errors. All other errors (e.g., omission of parallel citations, improper designation of the court of decision, failure to abbreviate words in case names) are major ones.

A maximum point value could then be assigned for each exercise (e.g., two or three points for case or statutory citations, one point for informational errors). Each major error would be worth one point. Three or four minor errors could be made equivalent to one major error or minor errors could be disregarded. Thus, a student's grade might be 10/12, indicating that the student made the equivalent of two major errors and received ten of the possible twelve points.

To illustrate how this system would work, consider the following example:

Assume that the correct answer for an exercise is:

M/B: <u>State v. Craig</u>, 48 N.J. Super. 276, 137 A.2d 430 (App. Div. 1958).

A correct answer is worth 2 points.

This answer:

<u>State v. Craig</u>, 48 N.J. Super. 276, 137 A.2d 430 (1958) is worth 1 point (App. Div. omitted).

This answer:

<u>State v. Craig</u>, 48 N.J. Super. 276, 137 A.2d 430 (App. Div. 1959) is worth 1 point (year incorrect) (unless it is apparent that it was a typing error).

This answer:

<u>New Jersey v. Craig</u>, 50 N.J. Super. 197 (1958). is worth 0 points (wrong vol., wrong page, A.2d cite omitted, wrong case name).

This answer:

<u>Smith v. Jones</u>, 10 Neb. 143, 292 N.W. 408 (1907). is worth 0 points (wrong case cited).

This answer:

<u>State V. Craig</u>, 48 N.J. Super. 276, 137 A.2d 430 (App. Div. 1958). is worth 2 points (minor error, "v." apparently mistyped as a capital "V," assuming that you have decided not to deduct points for minor errors).

(b) "Pass/Re-Do" System. Under this system, the instructor sets a maximum number of errors that a student cannot exceed. If that number is exceeded, the assignment would have to be redone using a new problem number until a satisfactory minimum level of performance is achieved. It is strongly recommended that if this system is adopted, the student's knowledge be tested at the end of the course by means of an examination covering legal research methods and legal citation.

10. <u>Errors and Suggestions for Further Improvements</u>. The author welcomes notification of errors in the materials as well as any suggestions that instructors may want to offer concerning further improvements of these materials.

LIBRARY EXERCISE 1. CITING CASE NAMES: PARTIES CITED, OMISSIONS, GEOGRAPHIC TERMS, PROCEDURAL PHRASES, BUSINESS FIRMS, AND OTHER CASE NAME MODIFICATIONS.

INSTRUCTOR'S NOTE: The purpose of this exercise is to give students practice in citing case names in proper form. To complete this exercise, students must find in the library the volume of the South Western Reporter Second listed for your problem number below. Note that all the volumes listed are from second series (S.W.2d). For their answer, the students are to cite the name of the case that begins on each of the listed pages ((a)-(f)) in that volume in proper form. They are specifically instructed not to rely on the form of citation used by the publisher in running head for their answer. For purposes of correcting this exercise, all the CN (CASE NAME) Quick-Reference Abbreviations will be useful. Of those, the more frequently used ones will be:

    CASE NAME 1. CITE THE FIRST-LISTED ACTION ONLY. [CN 1]
    CASE NAME 7. DO NOT OMIT ANY PORTION OF A PARTNERSHIP NAME. [CN 7]
    CASE NAME 8. DO NOT OMIT THE FIRST-LISTED RELATOR. [CN 8]
    CASE NAME 12. RETAIN GIVEN NAMES AND INITIALS IN DESIGNATIONS OF BUSINESS FIRMS (CORPORATE OR PARTNERSHIP NAMES). [CN 12]
    CASE NAME 13. OMIT "INC.," "LTD.," AND SIMILAR TERMS WHEN THE CITED NAME ALSO CONTAINS "CO.," "BROS.," "ASS'N," OR SIMILAR TERMS THAT CLEARLY INDICATE THAT THE PARTY IS A BUSINESS FIRM. [CN 13]
    CASE NAME 14. OMIT "CO." WHEN THE CITED PARTY IS A RAILROAD OR RAILWAY COMPANY, EXCEPT WHEN THE FULL NAME IN THE OFFICIAL REPORT IS "RAILROAD CO." OR "RAILWAY CO." [CN 14]
    CASE NAME 15. SPECIAL RULES APPLY TO GEOGRAPHIC TERMS. [CN 15]
    (a) PREPOSITIONAL PHRASES OF LOCATION [CN 15(a)]
    (b) GEOGRAPHIC TERMS FOLLOWING "TOWN OF," "CITY OF," AND SIMILAR TERMS [15(b)]
    (c) GEOGRAPHIC TERMS NOT INTRODUCED BY A PREPOSITION [CN 15(c)]
    CASE NAME 16. OMIT "CITY OF," "TOWN OF," AND LIKE EXPRESSIONS WHEN THEY DO NOT BEGIN A PARTY'S OR RELATOR'S NAME. [CN 16]
    CASE NAME 17. OMIT "STATE OF," "PEOPLE OF," AND "COMMONWEALTH OF" EXCEPT WHEN DECISIONS OF THE COURTS OF THAT STATE ARE CITED, IN WHICH CASE RETAIN ONLY "STATE," "PEOPLE," OR "COMMONWEALTH." [CN 17]
    CASE NAME 19. SPECIAL RULES APPLY TO PROCEDURAL PHRASES. [CN 20]
    (a) OMIT PROCEDURAL PHRASES WHEN ADVERSARY PARTIES ARE NAMED. [CN 20(a)]
    (b) OMIT PROCEDURAL PHRASES AFTER THE FIRST ONE. [CN 20(b)]
    CASE NAME 24. ALWAYS ABBREVIATE "COMPANY," "CORPORATION," "LIMITED," "INCORPORATED," "NUMBER," AND "AND" IN CASE NAMES. [CN 24]
    CASE NAME 25. ALWAYS ABBREVIATE "ON RELATION OF" AND SIMILAR TERMS TO "EX REL." AND "IN THE MATTER OF" AND SIMILAR TERMS TO "IN RE." [CN 25]
    CASE NAME 28. WHEN INITIALS OF INDIVIDUALS ARE INCLUDED IN A CASE NAME, THE INITIALS SHOULD BE CLOSED UP. [CN 28]
    CASE NAME 31. IN LAW REVIEW FOOTNOTES, ALL GEOGRAPHIC WORDS IN THE NAMES OF RAILROADS, EXCEPT FOR THE FIRST WORD, SHOULD BE ABBREVIATED TO THE INITIAL LETTER OR TO RECOGNIZED ABBREVIATIONS UNLESS THEY COMPLETE THE NAME OF A STATE, CITY, OR OTHER ENTITY BEGUN BY THE FIRST WORD. CLOSE UP SINGLE CAPITALS. [CN 31]
    CASE NAME 32. USE THE USOC-REQUIRED ABBREVIATIONS FOR CASE NAMES IN LAW REVIEW FOOTNOTES. [CN 32]
    CASE NAME 33. IN LAW REVIEW FOOTNOTES, FORM PLURALS OF ABBREVIATED WORDS BY ADDING AN "S" INSIDE THE PERIOD (UNLESS OTHERWISE INDICATED). [CN33]
    CASE NAME 34. IN LAW REVIEW FOOTNOTES, DO NOT ABBREVIATE THE FIRST WORD OF A PARTY'S NAME, INCLUDING A RELATOR. HOWEVER, IT IS PERMISSIBLE TO ABBREVIATE OTHER WORDS WITH EIGHT OR MORE LETTERS (NOT LISTED ABOVE) IF (1) SUBSTANTIAL SPACE IS SAVED AND (2) THE RESULT IS UNAMBIGUOUS. [CN 34]
    CASE NAME 35. IN LAW REVIEW FOOTNOTE CITATIONS, CASES (EXCEPT FOR PROCEDURAL PHRASES) APPEAR IN ORDINARY ROMAN TYPE. PROCEDURAL PHRASES ALWAYS APPEAR IN ITALICS (SINGLE UNDERSCORING). [CN 35]

1 170 236 344 485 592 693   (a) 129 (b) 285 (c) 481 (d) 621 (e) 640 (f) 850
(a) James Reynolds and Carol Reynolds, Husband and Wife, Appellants, v. City of Independence, Missouri, Respondent.
M/B: Reynolds v. City of Independence

EXERCISE 1.   CITING CASE NAMES   (CONTINUED)

(b) Nina Smock Hill, Plaintiff-Respondent and Cross-Appellant, v. Mercantile First National Bank of Doniphan, Defendant-Appellant, v. Michael Smock, Third Party Defendant-Respondent.
M/B: Hill v. Mercantile First National Bank
LR: Hill v. Mercantile First Nat'l Bank
(c) In the Matter of the Estate of L.W. Izer, Deceased.
M/B: In re Estate of Izer
LR: In re Estate of Izer
(d) The Outlet Company and Baxter Gentry, Appellants, v. International Security Group, Inc. and Richard Medlin, Appellees.
M/B: Outlet Co. v. International Security Group, Inc.
LR: Outlet Co. v. International Sec. Group, Inc.
(e) James Lee Parker, Appellant, v. The State of Texas, Appellee.
M/B: Parker v. State
(f) Don Gaston & Son, Inc., d/b/a Don Gaston Construction Co., Plaintiff-Appellant, v. Vic Koepke Excavating & Grading Company, Defendant-Respondent.
M/B: Don Gaston & Son v. Vic Koepke Excavating & Grading Co.

2 171 237 345 486 593   692   (a) 209 (b) 420 (c) 470 (d) 525 (e) 803 (f) 926
(a) R. Marshall Downs, Appellant, v. City of Fort Worth, et al., Appellees.
M/B: Downs v. City of Fort Worth
(b) Margie Graves, Plaintiff-Appellant, v. Anchor Wire Corporation of Tennessee, Defendant-Appellee.
M/B: Graves v. Anchor Wire Corp.
(c) State of Texas ex rel. Sam D. Millsap, Jr., Criminal District Attorney, Bexar County, Petitioner, v. R. Robert Lozano, Judge County Court at Law No. 6, Bexar County, Respondent.
M/B: State ex rel. Millsap v. Lozano
LR: State ex rel. Millsap v. Lozano
(d) The Estate of Herbert Kaiser, Appellant, v. Myrvin H. Gifford, Appellee.
M/B: Estate of Kaiser v. Gifford
(e) Commonwealth of Kentucky, Movant, v. George Goforth, Respondent.
M/B: Commonwealth v. Goforth
(f) Roy E. Thomas Construction Company and Roy E. Thomas, Individually, Appellants, v. Robert J. Arbs and Wife, Martha J. Arbs, Appellees.
M/B: Ray E. Thomas Construction Co. v. Arbs
LR: Ray E. Thomas Constr. Co. v. Arbs

3 172 238 346 487 594   691   (a) 423 (b) 485 (c) 498 (d) 717 (e) 784 (f) 857
(a) Thomas E. Crane and John H. Crane, Plaintiffs-Appellants, v. Centerre Bank of Columbia as Trustee, et al., Defendants-Respondents.
M/B: Crane v. Centerre Bank
(b) In the Estate of John H. English, Deceased.
M/B: In re Estate of English
LR: In re Estate of English
(c) State ex rel. Robert O'Blennis, Relator, v. The Honorable George Adolf and the Honorable William Nicholls, Judges of the Circuit Court of the City of St. Louis, Mo., Respondents.
M/B: State ex rel. O'Blennis v. Adolf
LR: State ex rel. O'Blennis v. Adolf
(d) W.H. McCrory & Co., Inc. Appellant, v. Contractors Equipment and Supply Company, Appellee.
M/B: W.H. McCrory & Co. v. Contractors Equipment & Supply Co.
LR: W.H. McCrory & Co. v. Contractors Equip. & Supply Co.
(e) Russell D. Daves, Appellant, v. The State Bar of Texas, Appellee.
M/B: Daves v. State Bar
(f) Sonny Medford d/b/a Medford Electric, Inc., Appellant, v. Wholesale Electric Supply Company, Inc., Appellee.
M/B: Medford v. Wholesale Electric Supply Co.
LR: Medford v. Wholesale Elec. Supply Co.

4 173 239 347 488 595   690   (a) 358 (b) 465 (c) 473 (d) 517 (e) 672 (f) 897
(a) Jonathan D. Johnston, Gary D. Plummer, John Gundy, Robert Dale Allen, Robert M. Russell, Kevin Nielsen, Burt H. McGhee, Jr., Dwight Roy Ketcher, Bobby D. Clark, Travola Marvin Garlin, Rollins G. Hoge, Alan Lee Slate, Thomas L. Leek, Appellants, v. City of Fort Smith, Arkansas, Appellee.

EXERCISE 1.   CITING CASE NAMES   (CONTINUED)

M/B: Johnston v. City of Fort Smith
(b) Estate of Myrtle G. Kennedy, Deceased, Roberta H. Long, Administratrix, Respondent, v. Joseph B. Menard and Mary E. Menard, Appellants.
M/B: Estate of Kennedy v. Menard
(c) Lonnie Katzenberger, Claimant-Appellant, v. John Gill d/b/a Snow Hill Constr. Co., Employer-Respondent.
M/B: Katzenberger v. Gill
(d) State of Tennessee, Plaintiff-Appellee, v. Stephen Leon Williams, Defendant-Appellant.
M/B: State v. Williams
(e) Southern Farm Bureau Casualty Insurance Company, Appellant, v. Francisco Aguirre, Appellee.
M/B: Southern Farm Bureau Casualty Insurance Co. v. Aguirre
LR: Southern Farm Bureau Casualty Ins. Co. v. Aguirre
(f) Wright Way Spraying Service, Petitioner, v. Jack C. Butler, Respondent.
M/B: Wright Way Spraying Service v. Butler
LR: Wright Way Spraying Serv. v. Butler

5 174 240 348 489 596   689   (a) 45 (b) 78 (c) 399 (d) 599 (e) 647 (f) 830
(a) Richard Lynn d/b/a Kansas City Excursion, Appellant, v. Director of Revenue, Respondent.
M/B: Lynn v. Director of Revenue
(b) State of Missouri, ex rel., Donna Sue Amato, Relator, v. The Honorable Patrick Clifford, Judge of the Associate Circuit Court, St. Louis County, Missouri, Division 39, Respondent.
M/B: State ex rel. Amato v. Clifford
LR: State ex rel. Amato v. Clifford
(c) Jack Evans et ux., Petitioner, v. J. Stiles, Inc., Respondent.
M/B: Evans v. J. Stiles, Inc.
(d) Owen County Rural Electric Cooperative Corporation, Appellant, v. Public Service Commission of Kentucky, Campbell County Fiscal Court, Consolidated Foods Corporation, and the Union Light, Heat and Power Company, Appellees.
M/B: Owen County Rural Electric Cooperative Corp. v. Public Service Commission
LR: Owen County Rural Elec. Coop. Corp. v. Public Serv. Comm'n
(e) In the Interest of R.K.W.
M/B: In re R.K.W.
LR: In re R.K.W.
(f) Curtis L. Mann, Trustee of the Bankruptcy Estate of David E. Goodman, Plaintiff-Appellant, v. United Missouri Bank of Kirkwood, Defendant-Respondent.
M/B: Mann v. United Missouri Bank
LR: Mann v. United Mo. Bank

6 175 241 349 490 597   688   (a) 182 (b) 198 (c) 307 (d) 446 (e) 757 (f) 827
(a) Deborah Kay Fitts, Appellant, v. The City of Beaumont, Texas, Appellee.
M/B: Fitts v. City of Beaumont
(b) Insituform of North America, Inc., Plaintiff/Appellant, v. Miller Insituform, Inc., Defendant/Appellee.
M/B: Insituform of North America, Inc. v. Miller Insituform, Inc.
LR: Insituform of N. Am., Inc. v. Miller Insituform, Inc.
(c) In the matter of the Estate of Betty Jo Hodges, Deceased, Joyce Long, Executrix, Appellant, v. Thomas W. Wilkie III, Appellee.
M/B: Estate of Hodges v. Wilkie
(d) Third National Bank in Nashville, Plaintiff-Appellant, v. James T. McCord and Roberta McCord, et al., Defendants-Appellees.
M/B: Third National Bank v. McCord
LR: Third Nat'l Bank v. McCord
(e) State ex rel. Stephen C. Scott, Relator, v. Ellen S. Roper, Judge, Division 3, Circuit Court of Boon county, Respondent.
M/B: State ex rel. Scott v. Roper
LR: State ex rel. Scott v. Roper
(f) Arkansas Medical Society, Appellant, v. Arkansas Medical Society, Appellee.
M/B: Arkansas Medical Society v. Arkansas Medical Society
LR: Arkansas Medical Soc'y v. Arkansas Medical Soc'y

EXERCISE 1.   CITING CASE NAMES   (CONTINUED)

7 176 242 350 491 598   687   (a) 268 (b) 374 (c) 410 (d) 444 (e) 560 (f) 713
(a) Citizens Bank of Smithville, Appellant, v. R.M. Lair, Respondent.
M/B: Citizens Bank v. Lair
(b) James E. Alm, Appellant and Cross-Appellee, v. Aluminum Company of
America, et al., Appellees and Cross-Appellant.
M/B: Alm v. Aluminum Co. of America
LR: Alm v. Aluminum Co. of Am.
(c) Majorie Grissom Bauer, Appellant, v. Estate of Roger B. Bauer, Deceased,
Appellee.
M/B: Bauer v. Estate of Bauer
(d) Ex parte Jack Eugene Burroughs.
M/B: Ex parte Burroughs
LR: Ex parte Burroughs
(e) Gary Baumgardner, Appellant, v. Commonwealth of Kentucky, Appellee.
M/B: Baumgardner v. Commonwealth
(f) Glenn H. Hall, Appellant, v. American Freight System, Inc. Appellee.
M/B: Hall v. American Freight System
LR: Hall v. American Freight Sys.

8 177 243 351 492 599   686   (a) 87 (b) 101 (c) 226 (d) 469 (e) 543 (f) 799
(a) Sam Tucker, Administrator of the Estate of Robert L. Tucker,
Plaintiff-Appellant, v. Metropolitan Government of Nashville and Davidson
County, Tennessee; Metropolitan Board of Hospitals; Metropolitan Nashville
General Hospital; Vanderbilt Hospital, and D.R. Doyle, M.D.,
Defendants-Appellees.
M/B: Tucker v. Metropolitan Government
LR: Tucker v. Metropolitan Gov't
(b) Estate of L.W. Stonecipher et al., Petitioners, v. Estate of Thomas L.
Butts et al., Respondents.
M/B: Estate of Stonecipher v. Estate of Butts
(c) Dallas Bank of Trust Company, Appellant, v. Commonwealth Development
Corporation, American Industries Investments, Inc., and Forty-Five Fifteen
Corporation, Appellees.
M/B: Dallas Bank & Trust Co. v. Commonwealth Development Corp.
LR: Dallas Bank & Trust Co. v. Commonwealth Dev. Corp.
(d) Charles Lewis McClure, Appellant, v. Commonwealth of Kentucky, Appellee.
M/B: McClure v. Commonwealth
(e) State of Missouri, Plaintiff-Respondent, v. John William Smith, a/k/a,
John Arthur Maxim, Defendant-Appellant.
M/B: State v. Smith
(f) D & M Construction Company, Maryland Casualty Company Appellants, v. Steve
Archer and Robert Schwitzer, Appellees.
M/B: D & M Construction Co. v. Archer
LR: D & M Constr. Co. v. Archer

9 178 244 352 493 600   586   (a) 24 (b) 40 (c) 137 (d) 229 (e) 429 (f) 934
(a) Albert C. Edmonds, Appellant, v. Commonwealth of Kentucky.
M/B: Edmonds v. Commonwealth
(b) C. G. Campbell & Son, Inc., Appellant, v. Comdeq Corporation, d/b/a
Kentucky Food Service Equipment Division, Appellee.
M/B: C.G. Campbell & Son v. Comdeq Corp.   (c) Kearney M. Albaugh et al.,
Appellants, v. State Bank of La Vernia, Appellee.
M/B: Albaugh v. State Bank
(d) Robert J. Loyd and Iris June Loyd, Husband and Wife, et al., Appellants,
v. Southwest Arkansas Utilities Corporation.
M/B: Loyd v. Southwest Arkansas Utilities Corp.
LR: Loyd v. Southwest Ark. Utils. Corp.
(e) Louise C. Taliaferro, Employee-Respondent, v. Barnes Hospital,
Employer-Appellant.
M/B: Taliaferro v. Barnes Hospital
LR: Taliaferro v. Barnes Hosp.
(f) Railroad Commission of Texas, Appellant, v. R. J. Palmer, Appellee.
M/B: Railroad Commission v. Palmer
LR: Railroad Comm'n v. Palmer

10 179 245 353 494 501   684   (a) 252 (b) 440 (c) 624 (d) 876 (e) 903 (f) 929

EXERCISE 1.   CITING CASE NAMES   (CONTINUED)

(a) Don Venhaus, County Judge, Appellant, v. State of Arkansas, ex rel., Floyd J. Lofton, Appellee.
M/B: Venhaus v.State
(b) State ex rel. State Highway Commission, Plaintiff-Appellant, v. Edward F. Merkel, et al., Exceptions of Inland Container Corporation, Defendant-Respondent.
M/B: State ex rel. State Highway Commission v. Merkel
LR: State ex rel. State Highway Comm'n
(c) Emmy Austin and William L. Austin, Sr., As Next of Kin of William L. Austin, Jr., Deceased, Plaintiffs-Appellants, v. City of Memphis, Tennessee, County of Shelby, et al., Defendants-Appellees.
M/B: Austin v. City of Memphis
(d) In the Matter of Patrick L. Morrissey, Deceased [consolidated on appeal with Bucher v. St. Louis Union Trust Co., listed second in the case title].
M/B: In re Morrissey
LR: In re Morrissey
(e) City of Columbia, Missouri, A Municipal Corporation, Plaintiff/Appellant, v. L.D. and Anna Baurichter, Defendants/Appellants, Anderson Heirs, Defendants/Appellants, Fred and Mabel Coats, et al. Defendants/Respondents.
M/B: City of Columbia v. Baurichter
(f) Watkins Investment Company, d/b/a Radio Station KRFG, Plaintiff-Respondent, v. William B. Tanner Company, Inc., Defendant-Appellant.
M/B: Watkins Investment Co. v. William B. Tanner Co.
LR: Watkins Inv. Co. v. William B. Tanner Co.

11 180 246 354 495 502   683   (a) 173 (b) 180 (c) 318 (d) 741 (e) 763 (f) 928
(a) Mark D. Hixson, Kamal Shuja, James M. Cullen and Raymond Blair, Appellants, v. Pride of Texas Distributing Co., Inc. Appellee.
M/B: Hixson v. Pride Distributing Co.
LR: Hixson v. Pride Distrib. Co.
(b) The City of Denton, Texas & Frances Melton, Appellants, v. Michael Van Page and Ida Louise Page, Appellees.
M/B: City of Denton v. Page
(c) State of Missouri, ex rel., Dave Kolb and Janet Kolb, Appellants, v. County Court of St. Charles County, Missouri, et al., Respondents.
M/B: State ex rel. Kolb v. County Court
LR: State ex rel. Kolb v. County Court
(d) In re The Estate of Josephine Eva Caples. [consolidated with Marasovich v. Caples, listed second in the case title]
M/B: In re Estate of Caples
LR: In re Estate of Caples
(e) Michael D. O'Grady, Appellant, v. Gerald D. Hines, Inc. d/b/a Gerald D. Hines Interests, Appellee.
M/B: O'Grady v. Gerald D. Hines, Inc.
(f) Carolyn Mae Chandler, Petitioner, v. State of Arkansas, Respondent.
M/B: Chandler v. State

12 181 247 355 496 503   682   (a) 236 (b) 366 (c) 567 (d) 634 (e) 803 (f) 906
(a) George Young, Petitioner, v. C.E. Hodde d/b/a Aggieland Harley-Davidson et al., Respondents.
M/B: Young v. Hodde
(b) National Bank of Texas, Appellant, v. First National Bank of Round Rock, Appellee.
M/B: National Bank v. First National Bank
LR: National Bank v. First Nat'l Bank
(c) Tony O'Neal Govan, Appellant, v. The State of Texas, Appellee.
M/B: Govan v. State
(d) Damon L. Guthrie, Appellant, v. Republic National Life Insurance Company, Appellee.
M/B: Guthrie v. Republic National Life Insurance Co.
LR: Guthrie v. Republic Nat'l Life Ins. Co.
(e) Robert A. Sanders, Respondent, v. Daniel International Corporation, Appellant.
M/B: Sanders v. Daniel International Corp.
LR: Sanders v. Daniel Int'l Corp.
(f) In re Estate of Louis Frank Montesi [consolidated with Montesi v. Estate of Montesi, listed second in the case title].

EXERCISE 1.   CITING CASE NAMES   (CONTINUED)

M/B: In re Estate of Montesi
LR: In re Estate of Montesi

13 182 248 356 497 504   680   (a) 153 (b) 362 (c) 365 (d) 420 (e) 709 (f) 909
(a) John O'Flaherty, et al., Appellants, v. State Tax Commission of Missouri, Respondent.
M/B: O'Flaherty v. State Tax Commission
LR: O'Flaherty v. State Tax Comm'n
(b) In the Matter of the Estate of Mark Dowdy, Deceased [consolidated with J.B. v. Dowdy, listed second in the case title].
M/B: In re Dowdy
LR: In re Dowdy
(c) C.M. Brown & Associates, Inc., Plaintiff/Appellant, v. William D. King, Defendant/Respondent.
M/B: C.M. Brown & Associates v. King
LR: C.M. Brown & Assocs. v. King
(d) State of Missouri, Respondent, v. Dorothy V. Hood, Appellant.
M/B: State v. Wood
(e) Cephus Merrick Smith et al., Appellants, v. Lorraine E. Boone, Guardian, Appellee.
M/B: Smith v. Boone
(f) Arkansas Commission on Pollution Control and Ecology, Appellant, v. Land Developers, Inc. Appellee.
M/B: Arkansas Commission on Pollution Control & Ecology v. Land Developers, Inc.
LR: Arkansas Comm'n on Pollution Control & Ecology v. Land Developers, Inc.
Note: Pursuant to Rule 10.2.1 (long case names), a student may omit "& Ecology" from the citation since "& Ecology" is not necessary for identification.

14 183 249 357 498 505   679   (a) 15 (b) 370 (c) 416 (d) 544 (e) 740 (f) 779
(a) Ex parte David Wayne Griffin.
M/B: Ex parte Griffin
LR: Ex parte Griffin
(b) Edward Lawton and Thea Lawton, Plaintiffs-Respondents, v. The Jewish Hospital of St. Louis, Defendant-Appellant.
M/B: Lawton v. Jewish Hospital
LR: Lawton v. Jewish Hosp.
(c) Berniece M. Thornbrugh and Robert W. Thornbrugh and Maxine Thornbrugh, Plaintiffs-Appellants, v. Homer E. Poulin, Individually, Homer Edmond Poulin, Trustee of Poulin Trust, and Ozark Concrete Company, a Corporation, Defendants-Respondents.
M/B: Thornbrugh v. Poulin (d) Edward Lee LeBlanc, Appellant, v. The State of Texas, Appellee.
M/B: LeBlanc v. State
(e) American Petrofina, Inc., American Petrofina Company of Texas, and American Petrofina Marketing, Inc., Appellants.
M/B: American Petrofina, Inc. v. PPG Industries
LR: American Petrofina, Inc. v. PPG Indus.
(f) Liberty Enterprises, Inc., Appellant, v. Moore Transportation Company, Inc., and Fort Worth Pipe Company, Appellees.
M/B: Liberty Enterprises v. Moore Transportation Co.
LR: Liberty Enters. v. Moore Transp. Co.

15 184 250 358 499 506   678   (a) 61 (b) 205 (c) 225 (d) 443 (e) 661 (f) 800
(a) State of Tennessee, Upon Relation of Rollin W. Wyrick, W.J. Haren, James Rogers and Ralph Benjamin, Relators, who are citizens and residents of the City of Rockwood, Roane County, Tennessee, Appellants, v. William R. Wright, Appellee.
M/B: State ex rel. Wyrick v. Wright
LR: State ex rel. Wyrick v. Wright
(b) Renee McCracken Williams, et al., Appellants, v. Steves Industries, Inc. D/B/A Ingram Equipment Company, Appellee.
M/B: Williams v. Steves Industries
LR: Williams v. Steves Indus.
(c) The Second Injury Fund of the State of Texas, Appellant, v. Walter Johnson, et ux., Appellees.

EXERCISE 1.   CITING CASE NAMES   (CONTINUED)

M/B: Second Injury Fund v. Johnson
(d) Modern Auto Company, Inc., Plaintiff-Respondent, v. Vernon Bell, Defendant-Appellant.
M/B: Modern Auto Co. v. Bell
(e) State National Bank of El Paso, Appellant, v. Farah Manufacturing Company, Inc., Appellee.
M/B: State National Bank v. Farah Manufacturing Co.
LR: State Nat'l Bank v. Farah Mfg. Co.
(f) Phillip Rolli, Appellant, v. Commonwealth of Kentucky, Appellee.
M/B: Rolli v. Commonwealth

16 185 251 359 500 507   677   (a) 147 (b) 293 (c) 449 (d) 669 (e) 781 (f) 881
(a) Ex parte James Aubrey Snow.
M/B: Ex parte Snow
LR: Ex parte Snow
(b) Arkansas State Nurses Association, Appellant, v. Arkansas State Medical Board, Appellee.
M/B: Arkansas State Nurses Association v. Arkansas State Medical Board
LR: Arkansas State Nurses Ass'n v. Arkansas State Medical Bd.
(c) Super Flea Market of Chattanooga, Inc., et al., Plaintiffs-Appellants, v. Martha B. Olsen, Commissioner of Revenue, State of Tennessee, et al., Defendants-Appellees.
M/B: Super Flea Market, Inc. v. Olsen
LR: Super Flea Mkt., Inc. v. Olsen
Note: "Inc." may be properly omitted form the above citations.
(d) Commercial Credit Equipment Corporation, Appellant, v. Charlie West and Dee Allen, Appellees.
M/B: Commercial Credit Equipment Corp. v. West
LR: Commercial Credit Equip. Corp. v. West
(e) Joseph N. Self, Appellant, v. The State of Texas, Appellee.
M/B: Self v. State
(f) Commonwealth of Kentucky, Appellant, v. Wilbur Hite Littrell, Appellee.
M/B: Commonwealth v. Littrell

17 186 252 360 401 508   676   (a)   1 (b) 159 (c) 231 (d) 375 (e) 448 (f) 693
(a) Alice E. Williams, Appellant, v. A.B. Chance Company and Liberty Mutual Insurance Company, Respondents.
M/B: Williams v. A.B. Chance Co.
(b) Caldwell County, Texas, et al., Appellants, v. Citizens State Bank of Luling, Texas, Appellee.
M/B: Caldwell County v. Citizens State Bank
(c) James K. Burrell, Appellant, v. Electric Plant Board of the City of Franklin, Kentucky, Appellee.
M/B: Burrell v. Electric Plant Board
LR: Burrell v. Electric Plant Bd.
(d) The State of Texas ex. rel. Bill R. Turner, District Attorney, Brazos County, Petitioner, v. W.T. McDonald, Jr., Judge, 85th Judicial District Court of Brazos County, Respondent.
M/B: State ex rel. Turner v. McDonald
LR: State ex rel. Turner v. McDonald
(e) In the Matter of A.M.B., a Minor.
M/B: In re A.M.B.
LR: In re A.M.B.
(f) C.H. Leavell & Company, et al., Appellants, v. The Leavell Company, Appellee.
M/B: C.H. Leavell & Co. v. Leavell Co.

18 187 253 361 402 509   675   (a) 92 (b) 245 (c) 293 (d) 376 (e) 481 (f) 845
(a) J.S. Samland, et al., Respondents, v. J. White Transportation Co., Inc., et al., Appellants.
M/B: Samland v. J. White Transportation Co.
LR: Samland v. J. White Transp. Co.
(b) Texas Employers' Insurance Association, Appellant, v. Juan S. Garza, Appellee.
M/B: Texas Employers' Insurance Association v. Garza
LR: Texas Employers' Ins. Ass'n v. Garza
(c) Cancido Ozuna Gonzales, Appellant, v. The City of Lancaster, Appellee.

EXERCISE 1.   CITING CASE NAMES   (CONTINUED)

M/B: Gonzales v. City of Lancaster
(d) Shirley Basham, Appellant, v. Commonwealth of Kentucky, Appellee.
M/B: Basham v. Commonwealth
(e) Mattie Mae Paul, Plaintiff-Appellant, v. Insurance Company of North America, Defendant-Appellee.
M/B: Paul v. Insurance Co. of North America
LR: Paul v. Insurance Co. of N. Am.
(f) Arkansas Department of Health, Appellant, v. Dorothy L. Huntley, Appellee.
M/B: Arkansas Department of Health v. Huntley
LR: Arkansas Dep't of Health v. Huntley

19 188 254 362 403 510   674   (a) 139 (b) 293 (c) 437 (d) 737 (e) 781 (f) 953
(a) In the Matter of the Estate of Gilford Willard, Deceased. Melba H. Peters, May Jane Hofmann and the Estate of Walter B. Bathke, Petitioners-Appellants.
M/B: In re Estate of Willard
LR: In re Estate of Willard
(b) In re Estate of Charles Robert Wardell, Sr., ex rel., Charles Robert Wardell, Jr., Plaintiff-Appellant, v. Charlotte Mae Wardell Dailey, Defendant-Appellant.
M/B: Estate of Wardell ex rel. Wardell v. Dailey
LR: Estate of Wardell ex rel. Wardell v. Dailey
(c) Ford Motor Credit Company, Appellant, First State Bank of Smithville, Texas, Appellee.
M/B: Ford Motor Credit Co. v. First State Bank
(d) Naomi Merritt Gosnell, Plaintiff-Appellant, v. Ashland Chemical, Inc., Ashland Oil, Inc., BASF Wyandotte Corporation, Wyandotte Paint Products Company, Exxon Corporation, Spraylat Corporation, Defendants-Appellees.
M/B: Gosnell v. Ashland Chemical, Inc.
LR: Gosnell v. Ashland Chem., Inc.
(e) Insurance Company of North America, Appellant, v. Cypress Bank, Appellee.
M/B: Insurance Co. of North America v. Cypress Bank
LR: Insurance Co. of N. Am. v. Cypress Bank
(f) Eric J. Gavel a/k/a Allen Osborne, Movant, v. Commonwealth of Kentucky, Respondent.
M/B: Gavel v. Commonwealth

20 189 255 363 404 511   673   (a) 218 (b) 236 (c) 291 (d) 334 (e) 512 (f) 858
(a) First National Bank of Kerrville, Appellant, v. Estate of Rubelle Hackworth, Lena Rabensburg and Mattie B. Denson, Appellees.
M/B: First National Bank v. Estate of Hackworth
LR: First Nat'l Bank v. Estate of Hackworth
(b) Glen Young, Appellant, v. Kilroy Oil Company of Texas, Inc., et al., Appellees.
M/B: Young v. Kilroy Oil Co.
(c) W.W. Rodgers and Sons Produce Company and W.W. Rodgers and Sons Trucks, Inc., Relators, v. The Honorable H. Dee Johnson, Respondent.
M/B: W.W. Rodgers & Sons Produce v. Johnson
(d) Texas General Indemnity Company, Appellant, v. Yvonne Strait and Texas Industrial Accident Board, Appellees.
M/B: Texas General Indemnity Co. v. Strait
LR: Texas Gen. Indem. Co. v. Strait
(e) In re Anne Marie O'Donohue Rockwell.
M/B: In re Rockwell
LR: In re Rockwell
(f) Imperial Utility Corporation, Appellant, v. Benson Cytron, Respondent.
M/B: Imperial Utility Corp. v. Cytron
LR: Imperial Util. Corp. v. Cytron

21 190 256 364 405 512   672   (a) 349 (b) 394 (c) 470 (d) 769 (e) 852 (f) 922
(a) State of Missouri, ex rel., and William S. Rhodes, et al., Plaintiffs-Respondents (Cross-Appellants), v. City of Springfield, Springfield, Missouri, et al., Defendants-Appellants, and State of Missouri, ex rel., and William S. Rhodes, et al., Relators-Respondents, (Cross-Appellants), v. William E. Robinett, et al., Respondents-Appellants.
M/B: State ex rel. Rhodes v. City of Springfield
LR: State ex rel. Rhodes v. City of Springfield

EXERCISE 1.   CITING CASE NAMES   (CONTINUED)

(b) In the Matter of Williams, Terry and Janienne, Petitioners.
M/B: In re Williams
LR: In re Williams
(c) Ex parte Armando C. Acosta.
M/B: Ex parte Acosta
LR: Ex parte Acosta
(d) James B. Flowers, Plaintiff-Appellee, v. South Central Bell Telephone Company, Defendant-Appellant.
M/B: Flowers v. South Central Bell Telephone Co.
LR: Flowers v. South Cent. Bell Tel. Co.
(e) Necati Alkas, Ind., d/b/a Contract Design and J.M. Heaner, Appellants, v. United Savings Association of Texas, Inc. and Los Campeones, Inc., Appellees.
M/B: Alkas v. United Savings Association
LR: Alkas v. United Sav. Ass'n
(f) In re Beverly Hills Fire Litigation.
M/B: In re Beverly Hills Fire Litigation
LR: In re Beverly Hills Fire Litig.

22 191 257 365 406 513   671   (a) 591 (b) 644 (c) 757 (d) 801 (e) 812 (f) 941
(a) W.D. Lawther and Phylas S. Lawther, Appellants, v. Super X Drugs of Texas, Inc., and Walgreen Texas Company, Appellees.
M/B: Lawther v. Super X Drugs, Inc.
(b) In the Interest of Suzanne Soliz, a Child.
M/B: In re Soliz
LR: In re Soliz
(c) Stanley Lackey and Susan Lackey, Appellants, v. State of Arkansas, Appellee.
M/B: Lackey v. State
(d) Browning-Ferris Industries of Kansas City, Inc. Appellant, v. Sue Dance, et al., Respondents.
M/B: Browning-Ferris Industries v. Dance
LR: Browning-Ferris Indus. v. Dance
(e) Billy J. Evans, Plaintiff-Appellant-Respondent, v. Missouri Utilities Company and Hartford Accident and Indemnity Company, Defendants-Respondents-Appellants.
M/B: Evans v. Missouri Utilities Co.
LR: Evans v. Missouri Utils. Co.
(f) Kathy Diane Price Tanner and Highlands Insurance Company, Appellants, v. BDK Production Company, Inc., et al., Appellees.
M/B: Tanner v. BDK Production Co.
LR: Tanner v. BDK Prod. Co.

23 192 258 366 407 514   670   (a) 319 (b) 494 (c) 828 (d) 857 (e) 882 (f) 954
(a) Railroad Commission of Texas, Appellant, v. Home Transportation Company, et al., Appellees.
M/B: Railroad Commission v. Home Transportation Co.
LR: Railroad Comm'n v. Home Transp. Co.
(b) State ex rel. Honorable Gene McNary, et al., Relators, v. Honorable Samuel J. Hais, Associate Circuit Judge, St. Louis County, Respondent.
M/B: State ex rel. McNary v. Hais
LR: State ex rel. McNary v. Hais
(c) Jerry Jackson, Appellant, v. Commonwealth of Kentucky, Appellee.
M/B: Jackson v. Commonwealth
(d) Finney Company, Inc., Movant, v. Monarch Construction Co., Inc., Respondent.
M/B: Finney Co. v. Monarch Construction Co.
LR: Finney Co. v. Monarch Constr. Co.
(e) State of Missouri, Respondent, v. Henry B. Johnson, Appellant.
M/B: State v. Johnson
(f) Vernon E. Tyler, Appellant, v. Citizens Home Bank of Greenfield, Missouri, Respondent.
M/B: Tyler v. Citizens Home Bank

24 193 259 367 408 515   669   (a)   3 (b) 251 (c) 519 (d) 736 (e) 779 (f) 875
(a) Appleby Road Street Improvement District, Appellant, v. James W. Powell et al., Appellees.
M/B: Appleby Road Street Improvement District v. Powell

EXERCISE 1.   CITING CASE NAMES   (CONTINUED)
LR: Appleby Rd. St. Improvement Dist. v. Powell
(b) State of Missouri, ex rel. Robert L. Hicks, Relator-Appellant, v. Village of Bel-Ridge, Respondent.
M/B: State v. Village of Bel-Ridge
(c) Harold McQueen, Appellant, v. Commonwealth of Kentucky, Appellee.
M/B: McQueen v. Commonwealth
(d) Ernest Espinoza, Appellant, v. The State of Texas, Appellee.
M/B: Espinoza v. State
(e) Printing Center of Texas, Inc., Appellant, v. Supermind Publishing Co., Inc., Appellee.
M/B: Printing Center v. Supermind Publishing Co.
(f) Leo Thompson, Appellant, v. Arkansas Social Services, Appellee.
M/B: Thompson v. Arkansas Social Services
LR: Thompson v. Arkansas Social Servs.

25 194 260 368 409 516   668   (a)   1 (b) 37 (c) 252 (d) 533 (e) 569 (f) 641
(a) Estate of Robert D. Ingram Deceased and First National Bank of Stuttgart, Appellants, v. Oscar Kochtitzky, Appellee.
M/B: Estate of Ingram v. Kochtitzky
(b) Arkansas Power & Light Company, Appellant, v. Cleo J. Melkovitz and Martha A. Melkovitz, his wife, Herbert C. Rule and Elizabeth D. Rule, his wife; and Robert J. Conrad, Trustee of the Prudential Insurance Company of America, Appellees.
M/B: Arkansas Power & Light Co. v. Melkovitz
(c) State of Missouri, Plaintiff-Respondent, v. Carolyn Jean Davison, Defendant-Appellant.
M/B: State v. Davison
(d) First National Bank of Brinkley, Arkansas, Appellant, V.M.K. Frey and Eileen Patricia Frey, Appellees.
M/B: First National Bank v. Frey
LR: First Nat'l Bank v. Frey
(e) Commonwealth of Kentucky, by and on relation of Ronald G. Geary, Secretary of the Revenue Cabinet, Appellant, v. William Johnson, Master Commissioner, Franklin Circuit Court, Appellee.
M/B: Commonwealth ex rel. Geary v. Johnson
LR: Commonwealth ex rel. Geary v. Johnson
(f) State of Mo. ex rel., Warren Hooker, et al., Respondents, v. City of St. Charles, et al., Appellants.
M/B: State ex rel. Hooker v. City of St. Charles
LR: State ex rel. Hooker v. City of St. Charles

26 195 261 369 410 517   667   (a) 250 (b) 299 (c) 347 (d) 743 (e) 773 (f) 885
(a) Walter H. Stephens, Appellant, v. Henry S. Miller Company, Appellee.
M/B: Stephens v. Henry S. Miller Co.
(b) Kenneth Lee Chennault, Appellant, v. The State of Texas, Appellee.
M/B: Chennault v. State
(c) In the Matter of B.J.N., a Minor Child.
M/B: In re B.J.N.
LR: In re B.J.N.
(d) Phillip Nelson and Alice Nelson, Appellants, v. City of Chester, Illinois, a Municipal Corporation, Russell A. Helmers and Dale G. Volle, Respondents.
M/B: Nelson v. City of Chester
(e) Roger Miller, Appellant, v. The State of Texas, Appellee.
M/B: Miller v. State
(f) Red Bird Bank of Dallas, John R. Payne, and Harry S. Scaling, Appellants, v. Crocker National Bank, Appellee.
M/B: Red Bird Bank v. Crocker National Bank
LR: Red Bird Bank v. Crocker Nat'l Bank

27 196 262 370 411 518   666   (a) 11 (b) 48 (c) 61 (d) 213 (e) 416 (f) 613
(a) State of Missouri, Plaintiff-Respondent, v. Rayfield Britton, Defendant-Appellant.
M/B: State v. Britton
(b) Betty C. Poore, Plaintiff-Appellant, v. Magnavox Company of Tennessee, Defendant-Appellee.
M/B: Poore v. Magnavox Co.

EXERCISE 1.   CITING CASE NAMES   (CONTINUED)

(c) D. Clyde Haga, Plaintiff-Appellant, v. Blanc & West Lumber Company, Inc., and Adrian Blanc, Defendants-Appellees.
M/B: Haga v. Blanc & West Lumber Co.
LR: Haga v. Blanc & W. Lumber Co.
(d) Edward Joseph Dryden, Jr., Appellant, v. City National Bank of Laredo, Appellee.
M/B: Dryden v. City National Bank
LR: Dryden v. City Nat'l Bank
(e) Wine and Spirits Specialty, Inc., Plaintiff-Respondent, v. Edward D. Daniel, Director, Department of Public Safety, James A. Franklin, Jr., Supervisor, Division of Liquor Control, Defendants-Appellants, Missouri Wine and Spirits Association, Inc., Intervenor-Defendant-Appellant.
M/B: Wine & Spirits Specialty, Inc. v. Daniel
(f) Ex parte Ramiro Fernando Martinez-Velasco.
M/B: Ex parte Martinez-Velasco
LR: Ex parte Martinez-Velasco

28 197 263 371 412 519   665   (a)   87 (b) 132 (c) 133 (d) 208 (e) 278 (f) 324
(a) State of Tennessee, Plaintiff-Appellee, v. Gary Bradford Cone, Defendant-Appellant.
M/B: State v. Cone
(b) David McDavid Pontiac, Inc., Appellant, v. Francis Nix, Appellee.
M/B: David McDavid Pontiac, Inc. v. Nix
(c) City of Heath, Texas, Appellant, v. Gilbert L. King, et al., Appellee.
M/B: City of Heath v. King
(d) Munis A. Syed, d/b/a Ruby Switch Ranch, Appellant, v. Haufler Equipment Company, Appellee.
M/B: Syed v. Haufler Equipment Co.
LR: Syed v. Haufler Equip. Co.
(e) L.L. Cole & Son, Inc. and Estate of Richard L. Cole, Appellant, v. Rickey Hickman, Appellee.
M/B: L.L. Cole & Son v. Hickman
(f) In re Christian R. Mentrup, Respondent.
M/B: In re Mentrup
LR: In re Mentrup

29 198 264 372 413 520   664   (a) 625 (b) 698 (c) 734 (d) 805 (e) 830 (f) 851
(a) Denver Sample, Plaintiff-Appellant, v. Monsanto Chemical Co., Defendant-Respondent.
M/B: Sample v. Monsanto Chemical Co.
LR: Sample v. Monsanto Chem. Co.
(b) In the Matter of the Estate of Zeboim Cartter Patten, Deceased, Appellee v. Thomas H. Batchelor, et al., Appellants v. Hamilton Bankshares, Inc., et al.
M/B: Estate of Patten v. Batchelor
(c) Charles Everett Reynolds, Appellant, v. The State of Texas, Appellee.
M/B: Reynolds v. State
(d) Jose S. Cortez and Wife Idolina G. Cortez, Appellants, v. Brownsville National Bank and Paul Y. Cunningham, Appellees.
M/B: Cortez v. Brownsville National Bank
LR: Cortez v. Brownsville Nat'l Bank
(e) Blaeser Development Corporation of Texas, Appellant, v. W.C. Aldridge, d/b/a A-Abco Lawn Sprinklers, Appellee.
M/B: Blaeser Development Corp. v. Aldridge
LR: Blaeser Dev. Corp. v. Aldridge
(f) In the Interest of C.D., A Child.
M/B: In re C.D.
LR: In re C.D.

30 199 265 373 414 521   663   (a)   37 (b) 196 (c) 420 (d) 685 (e) 761 (f) 776
(a) J.V. Harrison Truck Lines, Inc., Appellant, v. Jackie Howard Larson, et al, Appellee.
M/B: J.V. Harrison Truck Lines v. Larson
(b) Central Maloney, Inc. and Aetna Casualty & Surety Company, Appellants, v. Charles Wayne York, Appellee.
M/B: Central Maloney, Inc. v. York

EXERCISE 1.   CITING CASE NAMES   (CONTINUED)

(c) In the matter of the Estate of Errington R. Curtis, Deceased [consolidated on appeal with Carnahan v. Curtis, listed second in the case title].
M/B: In re Estate of Curtis
LR: In re Estate of Curtis
(d) First National Bank of Irving, Appellant, v. H.C. Shockley, Appellee.
M/B: First National Bank v. Shockley
LR: First Nat'l Bank v. Shockley
(e) Peggy Piper, Appellant, v. The Singer Company, Inc., d/b/a Earle C. Clements Job Corps Center and Kentucky Unemployment Insurance Commission, Appellees.
M/B: Piper v. Singer Co.
(f) State of Missouri, Respondent, v. David Michael Thrasher, Appellant.
M/B: State v. Thrasher

31 200 266 374 415 522   662   (a) 129 (b) 141 (c) 396 (d) 693 (e) 709 (f) 928
(a) Tarrant County Ice Sports, Inc., Michael Counts, Richard Noonan and Chris Castro, Appellants, v. Equitable General Life Insurance Company of Oklahoma, Appellee.
M/B: Tarrant County Ice Sports, Inc. v. Equitable General Life Insurance Co.
LR: Tarrant County Ice Sports, Inc. v. Equitable Gen. Life Ins. Co.
(b) In the Interest of Shawn Leonard Mark Van Hersh, A Child.
M/B: In re Van Hersh
LR: In re Van Hersh
(c) Marian Nichols, d/b/a Marian Nichols Interiors, Appellant, v. William A. Taylor, Inc., a Corporation, Appellee.
M/B: Nichols v. William A. Taylor, Inc.
(d) Dickson Distributing Company, Appellant, v. Dana LeJune, Appellee.
M/B: Dickson Distributing Co. v. LeJune
LR: Dickson Distrib. Co. v. LeJune
(e) Purolator Armored, Inc., Appellant, v. The Railroad Commission of Texas, et al., Appellees.
M/B: Purolator Armored, Inc. v. Railroad Commission
LR: Purolator Armored, Inc. v. Railroad Comm'n
(f) State of Missouri ex rel. Gus T. Handge & Son Painting Co., Respondent, v. Tri-State Construction Co., et al., Appellant.
M/B: State ex rel. Gus T. Handge & Son Painting Co. v. Tri-State Construction Co.
LR: State ex rel. Gus T. Handge & Son Painting Co. v. Tri-State Constr. Co.

32 101 267 375 416 523   661   (a)   2 (b) 285 (c) 433 (d) 567 (e) 657 (f) 740
(a) Elmer Godsey, Appellant, v. Commonwealth of Kentucky, Appellee.
M/B: Godsey v. Commonwealth
(b) Gloria Cartusciello, Executrix of the Estate of Michael Cartusciello, Appellant, v. Allied Life Insurance Company of Texas, Appellee.
M/B: Cartusciello v. Allied Life Insurance Co.
LR: Cartusciello v. Allied Life Ins. Co.
(c) Arkansas Louisiana Gas Company and United States Fidelity & Guaranty Company, Appellants, v. Jerry Grooms, Appellee.
M/B: Arkansas Louisiana Gas Co. v. Grooms
LR: Arkansas La. Gas Co. v. Grooms
(d) C.A. Bianco, Inc., et al., Plaintiffs-Appellants, v. Emil E. Hoechst, et al., Defendants-Respondents.
M/B: C.A. Bianco, Inc. v. Hoechst
(e) In the Estate of Lyle Murphy, Deceased [consolidate on appeal with Murphy v. Murphy, listed second in the case title].
M/B: Estate of Murphy
(f) Ex Parte Mickey Robbins.
M/B: Ex parte Robbins
LR: Ex parte Robbins

33 102 268 376 417 524   660   (a) 58 (b) 144 (c) 265 (d) 404 (e) 471 (f) 584
(a) Jay Kelly Pinkerton, Appellant, v. The State of Texas, Appellee.
M/B: Pinkerton v. State
(b) Ex Parte Jodie M. Ditmer, Relator.
M/B: Ex parte Ditmer
LR: Ex parte Ditmer

EXERCISE 1.   CITING CASE NAMES   (CONTINUED)

(c) Dan Calvert and Sandra Calvert and Earl Calvert, Jr., Respondents, v. Safeco Insurance Company of America, Appellant.
M/B: Calvert v. Safeco Insurance Co. of America
LR: Calvert v. Safeco Ins. Co. of Am.
(d) Lewis G. Duke and Margaret Duke, Respondents, v. Gulf & Western Manufacturing Co., Appellant.
M/B: Duke v. Gulf & Western Manufacturing Co.
LR: Duke v. Gulf & W. Mfg. Co.
(e) In the Interest of D.L.H. and J.L.H., Minors [consolidated on appeal with McClure v. J.A.H., listed second in the case title].
M/B: In re D.L.H.
LR: In re D.L.H.
(f) Joe Moody Machinery Company, Appellant, v. The First National Bank of Fort Worth, Appellee.
M/B: Joe Moody Machinery Co. v. First National Bank
LR: Joe Moody Mach. Co. v. First Nat'l Bank

34 103 269 377 418 525   659   (a) 201 (b) 227 (c) 714 (d) 775 (e) 827 (f) 869
(a) Vondle Lee Hamilton, Appellant, v. Commonwealth of Kentucky, Appellee.
M/B: Hamilton v. Commonwealth
(b) Timothy Henderson, et al., Plaintiffs-Appellants, v. Terminal Railroad Association of St. Louis, Defendant-Respondent.
M/B: Henderson v. Terminal Railroad Association
LR: Henderson v. Terminal R.R. Ass'n
(c) Trinity River Authority, et al., Appellants, v. Carla Leigh Williams, et al., Appellees.
M/B: Trinity River Authority v. Williams
LR: Trinity River Auth. v. Williams
(d) State ex rel. Eagle Bank and Trust Company, by Larry Roderman, President, Relator, v. Honorable James S. Corcoran, Judge, 22nd Judicial Circuit of Missouri, Respondent.
M/B: State ex rel. Eagle Bank & Trust Co. v. Corcoran
LR: State ex rel. Eagle Bank & Trust Co. v. Corcoran
(e) Ex parte Billy Ray Jordan.
M/B: Ex parte Jordan
LR: Ex parte Jordan
(f) William G. Priest and William G. Priest, Jr., Appellants, v. First Mortgage Company of Texas, Inc., Appellee.
M/B: Priest v. First Mortgage Co.

35 104 270 378 419 526   658   (a) 17 (b) 70 (c) 186 (d) 218 (e) 323 (f) 665
(a) Commercial Bank of St. Louis County, Plaintiff-Respondent, v. Ray S. James, Defendant-Appellant, and City of Olivette, Defendant-Respondent.
M/B: Commercial Bank v. James
(b) Norma Burtrum, Personal Representative of the Estate of Loren Webb, Plaintiff-Respondent, v. U-Haul Company of Southern Missouri, Defendant-Appellant.
M/B: Burtrum v. U-Haul Co.
(c) Kansas City Southern Railway Company, Appellant, v. Benny K. Chaffin, Appellee.
M/B: Kansas City Southern Railway v. Chaffin
LR: Kansas City S. Ry. v. Chaffin
(d) Rhodessa Development Company, Appellants, v. J.M. Simpson, Appellee.
M/B: Rhodessa Development Co. v. Simpson
LR: Rhodessa Dev. Co. v. Simpson
(e) Joe Aldrich, Sr., et al., Appellants, v. State of Texas ex rel. Emma Cox, et al., Appellees.
M/B: Aldrich v. State ex rel. Cox
LR: Aldrich v. State ex rel. Cox
(f) Matrix, Inc., Appellant, v. Provident American Insurance Co., et al., Appellee.
M/B: Matrix, Inc. v. Provident American Insurance Co.
LR: Matrix, Inc. v. Provident Am. Ins. Co.

36 105 271 379 420 527   657   (a) 207 (b) 425 (c) 494 (d) 583 (e) 636 (f) 824
(a) American Trucking Associates, Inc.; Transcon Lines, Inc.; Diamond Transportation System, Inc.; Rollins Leasing Corporation; Commercial Carriers,

EXERCISE 1.   CITING CASE NAMES   (CONTINUED)

Inc., On Behalf of Themselves and All Other Similarly Situated Taxpayers; Arkansas Bus and Truck Association Inc.; and Jones Truck Lines, Inc. On behalf of Themselves & All Other Similarly Situated Taxpayers, Appellants, v. Henry C. Gray, Director, Arkansas Highway and Transportation Department; David Soloman; Ron Herrod; Patsy Lee Thomasson; Raymond Pritchett, Jr.; Bobby Hopper; Members of the Arkansas State Highway Commission; Roy L. Johnson, Chief of the Arkansas Highway Police Division of the Arkansas Highway & Transportation Department; Charles D. Ragland, Commissioner of Revenues, Revenue Division, Arkansas Department of Finance & Administration; Jimmie Lou Fisher, Treasurer of the State of Arkansas; Mahlon Martin, Director, Arkansas Department of Finance & Administration, Appellees.
M/B: American Trucking Associations v. Gray
LR: American Trucking Ass'ns v. Gray
(b) In the Matter of Pamela I. Hamilton [consolidated on appeal with State v. Hamilton, listed second in the case title].
M/B: In re Hamilton
LR: In re Hamilton
(c) Texas Farm Products Company, Appellant, v. Paul Stock, Appellee.
M/B: Texas Farm Products Co. v. Stock
LR: Texas Farm Prods. Co. Stock
(d) Commonwealth of Kentucky, Movant, v. Robert Preston Karnes, Respondent.
M/B: Commonwealth v. Karnes
(e) In re the Estate of Margaret M. Pettit, Deceased, Andrew Culbertson and Alex Culbertson, Appellants-Cross-Respondents, v. Arnold D. Levine, Personal Representative, William F. Culbertson and Frederick X. Culbertson, Respondents-Cross-Appellants, Mercantile Trust Company, N.A., Personal Representative.
M/B: Estate of Pettit v. Levine
(f) Amoco Production Company, Inc., et al., Appellants, v. Terry Thompson and Ideal Lease Service, Inc., Appellees.
M/B: Amoco Production Co. v. Thompson
LR: Amoco Prod. Co. v. Thompson

37 106 272 380 421 528   656   (a) 107 (b) 470 (c) 589 (d) 612 (e) 740 (f) 836
(a) City of Houston, Appellant, v. Public Utility Commission of Texas, et al., Appellees.
M/B: City of Houston v. Public Utility Commission
LR: City of Houston v. Public Util. Comm'n
Note: "PUC" is also correct.
(b) Ex parte Jerry Wayne Mason.
M/B: Ex parte Mason
LR: Ex parte Mason
(c) Oak Forest Bank of Houston, Appellant, v. Harlingen State Bank, Appellee.
M/B: Oak Forest Bank v. Harlingen State Bank
(d) Texas General Indemnity Company, Appellant, v. Richard N. Watson, Appellee.
M/B: Texas General Indemnity Co. v. Watson
LR: Texas Gen. Indem. Co. v. Watson
(e) David Edward Faught, Appellant, v. Commonwealth of Kentucky, Appellee.
M/B: Faught v. Commonwealth
(f) State of Tennessee, ex rel. W.B. Lockert, Jr., et al., Plaintiffs-Appellees, v. Gentry Crowell, Secretary of State of the State of Tennessee, et al., Defendants-Appellants, and Tennessee Voters' Council, Defendants-Intervenors.
M/B: State ex rel. Lockert v. Crowell
LR: State ex rel. Lockert v. Crowell

38 107 273 381 422 529   655   (a) 110 (b) 327 (c) 506 (d) 515 (e) 638 (f) 845
(a) In re Alleged Incompetency of Edna E. Richard [consolidated on appeal with Richard v. Richard].
M/B: In re Richard
LR: In re Richard
(b) Bluebonnet Express, Inc., Appellant, v. Employers Insurance of Wausau, Appellee.
M/B: Bluebonnet Express, Inc. v. Employers Insurance
LR: Bluebonnet Express, Inc. v. Employers Ins.
Note: "Inc." may be omitted in the above citations.

EXERCISE 1. CITING CASE NAMES   (CONTINUED)

(c) Greg Allen Ivey, Appellant, v. Commonwealth of Kentucky, Appellee.
M/B: Ivey v. Commonwealth
(d) National Garment Company, a Corporation, Plaintiff-Appellant, v. City of Paris, Missouri, A Municipal Corporation, and Gates Energy Products, Inc., A Corporation, Defendants-Respondents.
M/B: National Garment Co. v. City of Paris
(e) Jewish Hospital of St. Louis, Relator, v. The Hon. Gary M. Gaertner, Judge, Division One, Circuit Court of the City of St. Louis, Missouri, Respondent.
M/B: Jewish Hospital v. Gaertner
LR: Jewish Hosp. v. Gaertner
(f) David P. Arst and Maxine E. Arst, his Wife, Plaintiffs-Appellants, v. Max Barken, Inc., Defendant-Respondent, Third-Party Plaintiff, v. Reitz & Jens, Inc., and the Freeman Contracting Company, Inc. Third-Party Defendants.
M/B: Arst v. Max Barken, Inc.

39 108 274 382 423 530   653   (a)   35 (b)   93 (c) 377 (d) 436 (e) 539 (f) 703
(a) Ex parte Victor Marek.
M/B: Ex parte Marek
LR: Ex parte Marek
(b) Houston General Insurance Company, Appellant, v. Ralph Owens and Ralph Owens Trucking Company, Inc., Appellees.
M/B: Houston General Insurance Co. v. Owens
LR: Houston Gen. Ins. Co. v. Owens
(c) Walter L. Williams, Appellant, v. Texas Employers' Insurance Association, Appellee.
M/B: Williams v. Texas Employers' Insurance Association
LR: Williams v. Texas Employers' Ins. Ass'n
(d) Ronald Dale Danford, Appellant, v. The State of Texas, Appellee.
M/B: Danford v. State
(e) International Bank of Commerce of Laredo, the City of Laredo, Union National Bank, Appellants, v. Union National Bank of Laredo, the City of Laredo, International Bank of Commerce of Laredo, Appellees.
M/B: International Bank of Commerce v. Union National Bank
LR: International Bank of Commerce v. Union Nat'l Bank
(f) State ex rel. City of St. Louis, Relator, v. Hon. Arthur Litz, Circuit Judge, (City of Berkeley, et al.), Respondent.
M/B: State ex rel. City of St. Louis v. Litz
LR: State ex rel. City of St. Louis v. Litz

40 109 275 383 424 531   652   (a) 202 (b) 252 (c) 515 (d) 655 (e) 851 (f) 856
(a) Citizens Bank & Trust of Rock Port, Missouri, Plaintiff-Respondent, v. Elmer Mitchell, Defendant-Appellant.
M/B: Citizens Bank & Trust v. Mitchell
(b) In re Estate of Yolanda Y. Patterson and Teneille Y. Patterson, Minors [consolidated on appeal with Hawthorne v. Patterson, listed second in the case title].
M/B: In re Estate of Patterson
LR: In re Estate of Patterson
(c) Beacon National Insurance Company, Appellant, v. R.C. Byrd, Appellee.
M/B: Beacon National Insurance Co. v. Byrd
LR: Beacon Nat'l Ins. Co. v. Byrd
(d) Kenneth Wade Perry, Movant, v. Commonwealth of Kentucky, ex rel. Sheryl Kessinger, Respondent.
M/B: Perry v. Commonwealth ex rel. Kessinger
LR: Perry v. Commonwealth ex rel. Kessinger
(e) James K. Bale and B.A. Guilfoil, Movants, v. Mammoth Cave Production Credit Association, Respondent.
M/B: Bale v. Mammoth Cave Production Credit Association
LR: Bale v. Mammoth Cave Prod. Credit Ass'n
(f) Leonard E. Gilliam, Movant, v. Commonwealth of Kentucky, Respondent.
M/B: Gilliam v. Commonwealth

41 110 276 384 425 532   651   (a) 31 (b) 232 (c) 525 (d) 613 (e) 616 (f) 851
(a) Ricky D. Peters, Appellant, v. The State of Texas, Appellee.
M/B: Peters v. State

EXERCISE 1.   CITING CASE NAMES   (CONTINUED)

(b) Gibson Lumber Company, Plaintiff-Appellant, v. Neely Coble Company, Inc., Mack Trucks, Inc., and Leon B. Batson, Deputy Sheriff for Davidson County, Tennessee, Defendants-Appellees.
M/B: Gibson Lumber Co. v. Neely Coble Co.
(c) In the Matter of T.C.M. and B.J.M., Petitioners-Respondents, and J.M.M., Respondent-Appellant.
M/B: In re T.C.M.
LR: In re T.C.M.
(d) Clarence Bollmann, Plaintiff-Respondent, v. Certain-Teed Products Corp. and Aetna Casualty & Surety Co., Defendants-Appellants, and Travelers Insurance Company, Defendant-Respondent.
M/B: Bollmann v. Certain-Teed Products Corp.
LR: Bollmann v. Certain-Teed Prods. Corp.
(e) Terry Braxton, Plaintiff-Respondent, v. United States Fire Insurance Company, Defendant-Appellant.
M/B: Braxton v. United States Fire Insurance Co.
LR: Braxton v. United States Fire Ins. Co.
(f) Mortgageamerica Corporation, Appellant, v. The American National Bank of Austin, Appellee.
M/B: Mortgageamerica Corp. v. American National Bank
LR: Mortgageamerica Corp. v. American Nat'l Bank

42 111 277 385 426 533   650   (a)   68 (b) 312 (c) 467 (d) 623 (e) 879 (f) 938
(a) Ex parte Earnest Lee Smith.
M/B: Ex parte Smith
LR: Ex parte Smith
(b) Noreen Kastner, et al., Appellants, v. Beech Aircraft Corporation, Respondents.
M/B: Kastner v. Beech Aircraft Corp.
(c) Southwestern Bell Telephone Company, Appellant, v. Debbie Baker, Appellee.
M/B: Southwestern Bell Telephone Co. v. Baker
LR: Southwestern Bell Tel. Co. v. Baker
(d) State of Missouri, ex rel. The School District of Springfield R-12, and Kenneth W. Draft, Treasurer of the School District of Springfield R-12, Plaintiffs, v. Gene Wickliffe, Collector of Revenue, Greene County, Missouri, and Carol Langsford, Treasurer, Green County, Missouri, Ernest E. Frisch, Jr., Auditor, Greene County, Missouri, Defendants.
M/B: State ex rel. School District R-12 v. Wickliffe
LR: State ex rel. School Dist. R-12 v. Wickliffe
Note: Pursuant to Rule 10.2.1 (long case names), a student may omit "R-12" from the citation since "R-12" is not necessary for identification.
(e) Pan American Bank of Brownsville, Appellant, v. William B. Nowland and George K. Wilcox, Jr., Trustee, Appellees.
M/B: Pan American Bank v. Nowland
LR: Pan Am. Bank v. Nowland
(f) Carlos I. Miro, Appellant, v. Allied Finance Company, Appellee.
M/B: Miro v. Allied Finance Co.
LR: Miro v. Allied Fin. Co.

43 112 278 386 427 534   649   (a) 198 (b) 456 (c) 524 (d) 561 (e) 791 (f) 812
(a) Craig Cook, Larry White, and Albert Gruneisen, Movants, v. Commonwealth of Kentucky, Respondent.
M/B: Cook v. Commonwealth
(b) Calvin L. Caulfield, Appellant, v. George K. Baum Y. Company, Inc., Respondents.
M/B: Caulfield v. George K. Baum & Co.
(c) Jesse Newman, Appellant, v. Twin City State Bank, et al., Respondents.
M/B: Newman v. Twin City State Bank
(d) State of Missouri ex rel. J.W. Martin (Relator), v. Honorable William J. Peters, Judge Circuit Court of Jackson County, Sixteenth Judicial Circuit and Mickey Gill, Sheriff Buchanan County, Missouri (Respondents).
M/B: State ex rel. Martin v. Peters
LR: State ex rel. Martin v. Peters
(e) Miles Homes of Texas, Inc., Eileen Franks and Insilco Corp., Appellants, v. Ray Brubaker and wife, Gwen Brubaker, Appellees.
M/B: Miles Homes, Inc. v. Brubaker

EXERCISE 1.   CITING CASE NAMES   (CONTINUED)

(f) Citizens National Bank of Temple, Appellant, v. James E. Baggerly, Appellee.
M/B: Citizens National Bank v. Baggerly
LR: Citizens Nat'l Bank v. Baggerly

44 113 279 387 428 535   648   (a) 351 (b) 542 (c) 568 (d) 763 (e) 800 (f) 858
(a) In the Interest of S.D.S. And R.L.F., Jr., Children.
M/B: In re S.D.S.
LR: In re S.D.S.
(b) Billy K. Banks, Appellant, v. Board of Education of Letcher County, Kentucky; and Jack M. Burkich, Individually and as Superintendent of the Letcher County Schools, Appellees.
M/B: Banks v. Board of Education
LR: Banks v. Board of Educ.
(c) State of Missouri ex rel. State Highway Commission of Missouri, Plaintiff-Respondent.
M/B: State ex rel. State Highway Commission v. Recker
LR: State ex rel. State Highway Comm'n v. Recker
(d) Marian Dodds and Dona Manley, a/k/a Mrs. John D. Manley, III, Both Individually and d/b/a Centipede Shoe Fashions, Appellants, v. Charles Jourdan Boutique, Inc., Appellee.
M/B: Dodds v. Charles Jourdan Boutique, Inc.
Note: "Inc." may be omitted from the above citation.
(e) Bank of Cabot, Appellant, v. Mark Ray, Appellee.
M/B: Bank of Cabot v. Ray
(f) Dennis Paul Alvey, Movant, v. Commonwealth of Kentucky, Respondent.
M/B: Alvey v. Commonwealth

45 114 280 388 429 536   646   (a) 17 (b) 177 (c) 246 (d) 347 (e) 717 (f) 765
(a) Popeye's Famous Fried Chicken and Continental Insurance Company, Appellants, v. Linda Willis, Appellee.
M/B: Popeye's Famous Fried Chicken v. Willis
(b) Larry Jerome Dodson, Appellant, v. The State of Texas, Appellee.
M/B: Dodson v. State
(c) First National Bank of Mercedes, Texas, Appellant, v. La Sara Grain Company, et al., Appellee.
M/B: First National Bank v. La Sara Grain Co.
LR: First Nat'l Bank v. La Sara Grain Co.
(d) Kentucky Bar Association, Complainant, v. Douglas E. Johnson, Respondent.
M/B: Kentucky Bar Association v. Johnson
LR: Kentucky Bar Ass'n v. Johnson
(e) South Central Bell Telephone Company, Movant, v. Commonwealth of Kentucky, ex rel. Steven L. Beshear, Attorney General, et al., Respondents.
M/B: South Central Bell Telephone Co. v. Commonwealth ex rel. Beshear
LR: South Cent. Bell Tel. Co. v. Commonwealth ex rel. Beshear
(f) Collettee Bass, Appellant, v. Nooney Company, a corporation, and Otis Elevator Company, a corporation, Respondents.
M/B: Bass v. Nooney Co.

46 115 281 389 430 537   645   (a) 70 (b) 91 (c) 149 (d) 204 (e) 310 (f) 346
(a) The Estate of Evelyn S. Linck, Deceased [consolidated on appeal with Arterburn v. Carr, listed second in the case title].
M/B: Estate of Linck
(b) Thomas J. Phipps, Appellant, v. The School District of Kansas City, Missouri, Respondent.
M/B: Phipps v. School District
LR: Phipps v. School Dist.
(c) James Hall, Plaintiff-Respondent, v. County of New Madrid, Defendant-Appellant.
M/B: Hall v. County of New Madrid
(d) State of Missouri, ex rel. Doris E. Shannon, Plaintiff, v. The Honorable James Clifford Crouch, Judge of the Circuit Court, 38th Judicial Circuit, Defendant.
M/B: State ex rel. Shannon v. Crouch
LR: State ex rel. Shannon v. Crouch
(e) Ex parte George Washington Smith.
M/B: Ex parte Smith

EXERCISE 1.   CITING CASE NAMES   (CONTINUED)

LR: Ex parte Smith
(f) Robert R. Evans, M.D., Movant, v. Commonwealth of Kentucky, Respondent.
and Leo J. Thomas, D.M.D., Movant, v. Commonwealth of Kentucky, Respondent.
M/B: Evans v. Commonwealth

47 116 282 390 431 538   640   (a) 137 (b) 222 (c) 343 (d) 362 (e) 619 (f) 781
(a) State of Missouri, ex rel. Robert E. Payton and Betty A. Payton,
Respondents, v. City of Riverside, Missouri and David E. Brenner, Mayor, et
al., Appellants.
M/B: State ex rel. Payton v. City of Riverside
LR: State ex rel. Payton v. City of Riverside
(b) Jimmie Motley and husband, George Motley, Plaintiffs-Appellants, v. Fluid
Power of Memphis, Inc. and Clippard Instrument Laboratory, Inc.,
Defendants-Appellees.
M/B: Motley v. Fluid Power, Inc.
(c) Railroad Commission of Texas, et al., Appellants, v. Exxon Corporation,
Appellee.
M/B: Railroad Commission v. Exxon Corp.
LR: Railroad Comm'n v. Exxon Corp.
(d) Port Terminal Railroad Association, Appellant, v. Oleta R. Sweet,
Appellee.
M/B: Port Terminal Railroad Association v. Sweet
LR: Port Terminal R.R. Ass'n v. Sweet
(e) Ex parte Jerry Lynn Girnus.
M/B: Ex parte Girnus
LR: Ex parte Girnus
(f) David Crockett Spriggs, Jr., Appellants, v. The State of Texas, State.
M/B: Spriggs v. State

48 117 283 391 432 539   641   (a) 108 (b) 193 (c) 451 (d) 477 (e) 780 (f) 927
(a) Flossie Taylor, et al., Plaintiffs-Appellants, v. F.W. Woolworth Company,
a corp., Defendant-Respondent.
M/B: Taylor v. F.W. Woolworth Co.
(b) State of Missouri, Respondent, v. Cornelius Anderson, Appellant.
M/B: State v. Anderson
(c) Kathy Patton and Charles Jenkins, Appellants, v. Bank of St. Louis,
Respondent.
M/B: Patton v. Bank of St. Louis
(d) State of Missouri, ex rel. Ray Bernsen, Plaintiff-Appellant, v. City of
Florissant, et al., Defendants-Respondents.
M/B: State ex rel. Bernsen v. City of Florissant
LR: State ex rel. Bernsen v. City of Florissant
(e) J. C. Nichols Company, Plaintiff-Respondent, v. Lula M. Powell,
Defendant-Appellant.
M/B: J.C. Nichols Co. v. Powell
(f) Ex parte Ronald Edwin Wilkinson [consolidated on appeal with Ex parte
Williams, listed second in the case title].
M/B: Ex parte Wilkinson
LR: Ex parte Wilkinson

49 118 284 392 433 540   642   (a)   1 (b) 160 (c) 336 (d) 504 (e) 820 (f) 907
(a) John Dull & Company, Appellant, v. Life of Nebraska Insurance Company,
Appellee.
M/B: John Dull & Co. v. Life Insurance Co.
LR: John Dull & Co. v. Life Ins. Co.
(b) Turner, Collie & Braden, Inc., Petitioner, v. Brookhollow, Inc., et al.,
Respondents.
M/B: Turner, Collie & Braden, Inc. v. Brookhollow, Inc.
(c) L.M. Medlock et al., Appellants, v. Arkansas State Highway Commission et
al., Appellees.
M/B: Medlock v. Arkansas State Highway Commission
LR: Medlock v. Arkansas State Highway Comm'n
(d) Matthew Thomas McBrayer, Appellant, v. The State of Texas, Appellee.
M/B: McBrayer v. State
(e) Wade T. Verges, Appellant, v. Lomas & Nettleton Financial Corporation,
Appellee.
M/B: Verges v. Lomas & Nettleton Financial Corp.

EXERCISE 1.   CITING CASE NAMES   (CONTINUED)
LR: Verges v. Lomas & Nettleton Fin. Corp.
(f) State of Missouri, ex rel. Homer E. Sayad, et al., Plaintiffs, v. Thomas
E. Zych, et al., Defendants.
M/B: State ex rel. Sayad v. Zych
LR: State ex rel. Sayad v. Zych

50 119 285 393 434 541   643   (a)   46 (b) 195 (c) 222 (d) 526 (e) 592 (f) 737
(a) State of Missouri, ex rel., State Highway Commission of Missouri, Respondent, v. Ted H. Lock, et al., Appellants.
M/B: State ex rel. State Highway Commission v. Lock
LR: State ex rel. State Highway Comm'n v. Lock
(b) In re Patrick Ganne [consolidated on appeal with Williams v. State, listed second in the case title].
M/B: In re Ganne
LR: In re Ganne
(c) Curtis Glenn Hammond, Appellant, v. The Estate of Almeda Childress Rimmer, Deceased, Appellee.
M/B: Hammond v. Estate of Rimmer
(d) W.M. Bashlin Company, Appellant, v. James Smith and Janet Smith, and Arkansas Power and Light Company, Appellees.
M/B: W.M. Bashlin Co. v. Smith
(e) Commonwealth of Kentucky, Appellant, v. Sherry Gail Barber, Appellee.
M/B: Commonwealth v. Barber
(f) Carlton Lynch, Appellant, v. The State of Texas, Appellee.
M/B: Lynch v. State

51 120 286 394 435 542   644   (a) 148 (b) 292 (c) 355 (d) 533 (e) 615 (f) 815
(a) Bennie Williams, Appellant, v. Citizens State Bank of Hempstead, Appellee.
M/B: Williams v. Citizens State Bank
(b) Glen Pillow and Terry Dicus, d/b/a Pillow and Dicus Farm, Appellants, v. Thermogas Company of Walnut Ridge, Appellee.
M/B: Pillow v. Thermogas Co.
(c) Junior Wayne Pedigo, Appellant, v. Commonwealth of Kentucky, Appellee.
M/B: Pedigo v. Commonwealth
(d) Sam Bradley Realty Company and Doris Williford, Appellants, v. William D. McNair and Wife, Doris Ann McNair, Appellees.
M/B: Sam Bradley Realty Co. v. McNair
(e) Gerald Boyd and Patsy Boyd, his wife, Appellants, v. Greene County, Arkansas, Appellee.
M/B: Boyd v. Greene County
(f) In the Matter of Darrin Keith Edwards, Appellant.
M/B: In re Edwards
LR: In re Edwards

52 121 287 395 436 543   647   (a)   5 (b)   8 (c) 477 (d) 539 (e) 625 (f) 866
(a) Louis B. Hughes, et al., Appellant, v. Houston Northwest Medical Center, et al., Appellee.
M/B: Hughes v. Houston Northwest Medical Center
Note: A student may abbreviate "Northwest" to "N.W." in the LR form.
(b) Susan Parrish, Appellant, v. State of Texas, Appellee.
M/B: Parrish v. State
(c) Revere Copper and Brass, Inc., Appellant, v. Thearman E. Talley, Jr., Employee, Appellee.
M/B: Revere Copper & Brass, Inc. v. Talley
(d) State ex rel. Bagnell Investment Company, Inc., Relators, v. Hon. Drew W. Luten, Jr., Judge, Circuit Court of St. Louis County, Respondent.
M/B: State ex rel. Bagnell Investment Co. v. Luten
LR: State ex rel. Bagnell Inv. Co. v. Luten
(e) John M. and Mary Ann Bishop, Plaintiffs-Respondents, v. United Missouri Bank of Carthage, Defendant-Appellant.
M/B: Bishop v. United Missouri Bank
LR: Bishop v. United Mo. Bank
(f) Marilyn Piva, Respondent, v. General American Life Insurance Company, Appellant.
M/B: Piva v. General American Life Insurance Co.
LR: Piva v. General Am. Life Ins. Co.

EXERCISE 1.   CITING CASE NAMES   (CONTINUED)

53 122 288 396 437 544   654   (a)   31 (b)   68 (c)   367 (d)   376 (e)   835 (f)   889
(a) First State Bank of Frankston, Appellant, v. Allen Ray Hughes, Appellee.
M/B: First State Bank v. Hughes
(b) Ex parte Joe Glenn Gray.
M/B: Ex parte Gray
LR: Ex parte Gray
(c) Charles L. Friedman and Karen L. Friedman, Plaintiffs-Appellants, v.
Edward L. Bakewell, Inc. and Nancy Bardenheier, Defendants-Respondents.
M/B: Friedman v. Edward L. Bakewell, Inc.
(d) State of Missouri, Plaintiff-Respondent, v. Elwin Pierre Adams,
Defendant-Appellant.
M/B: State v. Adams
(e) Robert B. Ferguson, et al., Appellants, v. Tanner Development Company, et
al., Appellees.
M/B: Ferguson v. Tanner Development Co.
LR: Ferguson v. Tanner Dev. Co.
(f) State ex rel. George Morasch, II, Relator, v. Honorable William M.
Kimberlin, Judge, Circuit Court, Cass County, Respondent.
M/B: State ex rel. Morasch v. Kimberlin
LR: State ex rel. Morasch v. Kimberlin

54 123 289 397 438 545   639   (a)   86 (b)   286 (c)   545 (d)   700 (e)   786 (f)   825
(a) State of Missouri ex rel. State Highway Commission of Missouri,
Plaintiff-Respondent, v. Theodore F. Koziatek, et al., Exceptions of Faith
Hospital Association, a Corporation, Defendant-Appellant.
M/B: State ex rel. State Highway Commission v. Koziatek
LR: State ex rel. State Highway Comm'n v. Koziatek
(b) Frank L. Courtin and Nettie E. Courtin, Plaintiffs-Respondents, v. McGraw
Construction Co. and Robert McGraw Defendants-Appellants.
M/B: Courtin v. McGraw Construction Co.
LR: Courtin v. McGraw Constr. Co.
(c) Board of Education of Bellevue, Kentucky, Movant, v. Richard Rothfuss,
Respondent.
M/B: Board of Education v. Rothfuss
LR: Board of Educ. v. Rothfuss
(d) Ex parte Kenneth L. Henson.
M/B: Ex parte Henson
LR: Ex parte Henson
(e) R.B. Williams, Appellant, v. Commonwealth of Kentucky, Appellee.
M/B: Williams v. Commonwealth
(f) A.A. Weber, Appellant, v. Missouri State Highway Commission, Cannon
Drainage District, Holt County, Missouri, County Court of Holt County, Missouri, and Fortescue Special Road District, Respondents.
M/B: Weber v. Missouri State Highway Commission
LR: Weber v. Missouri State Highway Comm'n

55 124 290 398 439 546   638   (a)   108 (b)   218 (c)   272 (d)   557 (e)   905 (f)   908
(a) Sammy V. Rodriguez, et ux., Appellants, v. Jim Walter Homes, Inc.,
Appellee.
M/B: Rodriguez v. Jim Walter Homes, Inc.
(b) County Commissioners Court of Dallas County, Texas, Appellant, v. Roger G.
Williams et. al., Appellees.
M/B: County Commissioners Court v. Williams
LR: County Comm'rs Court v. Williams
(c) Danny Pevlor, Appellant, v. Commonwealth of Kentucky, Appellee.
M/B: Pevlor v. Commonwealth
(d) Lower Colorado River Authority, et al., Appellants, v. Texas Department of
Water Resources, et al., Appellee.
M/B: Lower Colorado River Authority v. Texas Department of Water Resources
LR: Lower Colo. River Auth. v. Texas Dep't of Water Resources
(e) Ex parte Bobbie Louis Thomas.
M/B: Ex parte Thomas
LR: Ex parte Thomas
(f) Texas General Indemnity Co., Appellant, v. Miguel S. Moreno, Appellee.
M/B: Texas General Idemnity Co. v. Moreno
LR: Texas Gen. Idem. Co. v. Moreno

EXERCISE 1.   CITING CASE NAMES   (CONTINUED)

56 125 291 399 440 547   637   (a)   84 (b)   94 (c) 251 (d) 373 (e) 903 (f) 943
(a) Harold Alderson, Appellant, v. Clark Oil & Refining Corporation, et al., Respondents.
M/B: Alderson v. Clark Oil & Refining Corp.
LR: Alderson v. Clark Oil & Ref. Corp.
(b) State of Missouri ex rel. George R. "Buzz" Westfall, Plaintiff, v. Honorable Robert Lee Campbell, Judge, Circuit Court, St. Louis County, Missouri, Defendant.
M/B: State ex rel. Westfall v. Campbell
LR: State ex rel. Westfall v. Campbell
(c) Sandra K. Hyde, Appellant, v. City of Columbia, Missouri; Nate Brown, Tribune Publishing Co., d/b/a Columbia Daily Tribune: Walter Potter, Missourian Publishing Assn., Inc. d/b/a Columbia Missourian, Respondents.
M/B: Hyde v. City of Columbia
(d) The First National Bank of St. Charles, Appellant, v. Chemical Products, Inc., Paul McDowell, Leona McDowell, Donald Gaston and Travelers Indemnity Company, Respondents.
M/B: First National Bank v. Chemical Products, Inc.
LR: First Nat'l Bank v. Chemical Prods., Inc.
(e) Westland Oil Development Corporation et al., Petitioners, v. Gulf Oil Corporation et al., Respondents.
M/B: Westland Oil Development Corp. v. Gulf Oil Corp.
LR: Westland Oil Dev. Corp. v. Gulf Oil Corp.
(f) Ex parte Joe Williams.
M/B: Ex parte Williams
LR: Ex parte Williams

57 126 292 400 441 548   636   (a) 484 (b) 530 (c) 648 (d) 706 (e) 828 (f) 896
(a) City of Humble, et al., Appellants, v. Metropolitan Transit Authority, et al., Appellees.
M/B: City of Humble v. Metropolitan Transit Authority
LR: City of Humble v. Metropolitan Transit Auth.
(b) Royal Indemnity Co., et al., Appellants, v. Little Joe's Catfish Inn, Inc., et al., Appellees.
M/B: Royal Idemnity Co. v. Little Joe's Catfish Inn
LR: Royal Idem. Co. Little Joe's Catfish Inn
(c) Aldean Henderson, Appellant, v. Commonwealth of Kentucky, Appellee.
M/B: Henderson v. Commonwealth
(d) State of Tennessee, ex rel. Brooks McLemore, Attorney General and Reporter for the State of Tennessee, Plaintiff-Appellee, v. Clarksville School of Theology, Dr. W. Roy Stewart, President, Clarksville School of Theology, Ernestine King Stewart, Roy Machen, George H.W. Phillipp, and Frank G. Ester, Individually and as Officers of Administration, Clarksville School of Theology, Defendants-Appellants.
M/B: State ex rel. McLemore v. Clarksville School of Theology
LR: State ex rel. McLemore v. Clarksville School of Theology
(e) Ex parte Chester B. Hovermale, Relator.
M/B: Ex parte Hovermale
LR: Ex parte Hovermale
(f) J. T. Nelson Company, Inc., Appellant, v. James A. Comstock and Charles A. Witherspoon, Appellees.
M/B: J.T. Nelson Co. v. Comstock

58 127 293 301 442 549   635   (a)   51 (b)   98 (c) 268 (d) 554 (e) 615 (f) 658
(a) State of Missouri, Respondent, v. Stanley E. Wade, Appellant, State of Missouri, Respondent, v. Stanley E. Wade, Appellant.
M/B: State v. Wade
(b) General Insurance Company of America, Plaintiff-Appellee, v. Larry D. Crawford, et al., Defendants-Appellants.
M/B: General Insurance Co. of America v. Crawford
LR: General Ins. Co. of Am. v. Crawford
(c) Madison Bank and Trust, et al., Appellants, v. First National Bank of Huntsville, Arkansas, et al., Appellees.
M/B: Madison Bank & Trust v. First National Bank
LR: Madison Bank & Trust v. First Nat'l Bank
(d) Ex parte Bruce Everett.
M/B: Ex parte Everett

21

EXERCISE 1.   CITING CASE NAMES   (CONTINUED)

LR: Ex parte Everett
(e) Don M. Smart, Appellant, v. Tower Land and Investment Company, Appellee.
M/B: Smart v. Tower Land & Investment Co.
LR: Smart v. Tower Land & Inv. Co.
(f) Jim C. Morris and Melinda Morris, Appellant, v. Chaunce A. Beane & Company Inc., d/b/a Beane & Company and C. A. Beane, Individually, Appellees.
M/B: Morris v. Chaunce A. Beane & Co.

59 128 294 302 443 550   634   (a)   2 (b) 153 (c) 234 (d) 249 (e) 286 (f) 815
(a) Bank of Texas, Appellant, v. John Childs, et al., Appellees.
M/B: Bank of Texas v. Childs
(b) La Verne O'Bryan, Appellant, v. Commonwealth of Kentucky, Appellee.
M/B: O'Bryan v. Commonwealth
(c) State Bank of Fisk, Plaintiff-Appellant, v. Omega Electronics, Inc., Defendant, and Morris Adams, Gaylen E. Sanders, Joseph Warbington, Joyce Moore, and James R. Ross, Defendants-Respondents.
M/B: State Bank v. Omega Electronics, Inc.
LR: State Bank v. Omega Elecs., Inc.
(d) John W. Coots, Jr., et al., Respondents-Plaintiffs, v. J. A. Tobin Construction Co., Appellant-Defendant.
M/B: Coots v. J.A. Tobin Construction Co.
LR: Coots v. J.A. Tobin Constr. Co.
(e) State of Tennessee, Appellee, v. Jack Wimberly, Appellant.
M/B: State v. Wimberly
(f) Ex parte Stephen A. McWilliams.
M/B: Ex parte McWilliams
LR: Ex parte McWilliams

60 129 295 303 444 551   633   (a)   73 (b) 161 (c) 366 (d) 488 (e) 733 (f) 761
(a) Commonwealth of Kentucky, Appellant, v. Bobby G. Hammond, Appellee.
M/B: Commonwealth v. Hammond
(b) State of Missouri, Respondent, v. Kelly Younger, Appellant.
M/B: State v. Younger
(c) Janice Attwood, Individually and As Mother and Next Friend of Richard Breck Attwood, Appellant, v. The Estate of Richard Breckenridge Attwood, Appellee.
M/B: Attwood v. Estate of Attwood
(d) Bernard Wajtasiak, Appellee, v. Morgan County, Tennessee, Appellant.
M/B: Wajtasiak v. Morgan County
(e) State ex rel. Jimmie L. Milham, D. O., Plaintiff, v. Honorable John Rickhoff, Judge, Circuit Court, St. Louis County, Defendant.
M/B: State ex rel. Milham v. Rickhoff
LR: State ex rel. Milham v. Rickhoff
(f) Max D. Lunceford, d/b/a Town and Country Discount, Appellee, v. John K. King, Commissioner of Revenue of the State of Tennessee, Appellant.
M/B: Lunceford v. King

61 130 296 304 445 552   632   (a)   6 (b) 227 (c) 323 (d) 621 (e) 885 (f) 950
(a) Teresa Dell (Vaughn) Thompson, Appellant, v. St. Joseph County Club, Respondent.
M/B: Thompson v. St. Joseph Country Club
(b) Lincoln National Life Insurance Company, Appellant, v. State of Texas, et al., Appellees.
M/B: Lincoln National Life Insurance Co. v. State
LR: Lincoln Nat'l Life Ins. Co. v. State
(c) In re Estate of Mona Beets Miles [consolidated on appeal with Miles v. Burrus, listed second in the case title].
M/B: In re Estate of Miles
LR: In re Estate of Miles
(d) Ex parte Cecil Dale McFarland.
M/B: Ex parte McFarland
LR: Ex parte McFarland
(e) River and Beach Land Corporation and Chulavista Land Investment Co., Inc., Appellants, v. W. H. O'Donnell, Trustee, and Joe G. Sanders, Trustee, Appellees.
M/B: River & Beach Land Corp. v. O'Donnell

EXERCISE 1.   CITING CASE NAMES   (CONTINUED)

(f) The Bank of Woodson, Appellant, v. Robert Stewart, State Banking Commissioner, et al., Appellees.
M/B: Bank of Woodson v. Stewart

62 131 297 305 446 553   631   (a)   1 (b)   73 (c) 103 (d) 410 (e) 825 (f) 893
(a) John H. Kellensworth, Jr., Appellant, v. State of Arkansas, Appellee.
M/B: Kellensworth v. State
(b) State of Missouri ex rel. Missouri Highway and Transportation Commission, (formerly the State Highway Commission of Missouri), Plaintiff-Appellant, v. Bank of St. Ann, et al., Exceptions of Bernard W. Dugan, et al., Defendants-Respondents.
M/B: State ex rel. Missouri Highway & Transportation Commission v. Bank of St. Ann
LR: State ex rel. Missouri Highway & Transp. Comm'n v. Bank of St. Ann
Note: "Missouri" should not be abbreviated in the LR form because it is the first word of the relator's name, see Rule 10.2.2.
(c) City of Lake Ozark, Missouri, Appellant, v. Walter L. Prewitt, et al., Respondents.
M/B: City of Lake Ozark v. Prewitt
(d) American City Bank of Tullahoma, Plaintiff-Appellee, v. Western Auto Supply Company, Defendant-Appellant.
M/B: American City Bank v. Western Auto Supply Co.
(e) Ex parte Wesley Wayne Miller.
M/B: Ex parte Miller
LR: Ex parte Miller
(f) Arthur E. Wehmeier, Plaintiff-Appellant, v. The Public School Retirement System of Missouri, Defendant-Respondent.
M/B: Wehmeier v. Public School Retirement System
LR: Wehmeier v. Public School Retirement Sys.

63 132 298 306 447 554   629   (a) 201 (b) 324 (c) 524 (d) 645 (e) 816 (f) 943
(a) Derek Jackson, et al., Appellants, v. Waco Independent School District, et al., Appellees.
M/B: Jackson v. Waco Independent School District
LR: Jackson v. Waco Indep. School Dist.
(b) Otis Creamer, Appellant, v. Commonwealth of Kentucky, Appellee.
M/B: Creamer v. Commonwealth
(c) J. Herbert Francisco, Respondent, v. The Kansas City Star Company, Appellant.
M/B: Francisco v. Kansas City Star Co.
(d) State of Missouri ex rel. James Darwin Hutson, Plaintiff, v. The Honorable Flake L. McHaney, Circuit Judge, Thirty-fifth Judicial Circuit Defendant.
M/B: State ex rel. Hutson v. McHaney
LR: State ex rel. Hutson v. McHaney
(e) Henry Dennis, Appellant, v. The State of Texas, Appellee.
M/B: Dennnis v. State
(f) Ex parte Danny Orona Ybarra, Appellant.
M/B: Ex parte Ybarra
LR: Ex parte Ybarra

64 133 299 307 448 555   628   (a) 329 (b) 497 (c) 582 (d) 637 (e) 887 (f) 941
(a) City of Waldo, Appellant, v. Peggy Poetker, et al., Appellees.
M/B: City of Waldo v. Poetker
(b) First National Bank in Dallas as Executor of the Estate of Louis J. Hexter, Deceased, et al., Appellants, v. Texas Federal Savings & Loan Association, Appellee.
M/B: First National Bank v. Texas Federal Savings & Loan Association
LR: First Nat'l Bank v. Texas Fed. Sav. & Loan Ass'n
(c) Mad Butcher, Inc., & Continental Insurance Company, Appellants, v. Carl Parker, Appellee.
M/B: Mad Butcher, Inc. v. Parker
(d) State ex rel. James O. Stoffer, et al., Relators, v. The Honorable Weldon W. Moore, Judge, 25th Judicial Circuit, et al., Respondents.
M/B: State ex rel. Stoffer v. Moore
LR: State ex rel. Stoffer v. Moore
(e) William H. Meredith, Appellant, v. Commonwealth of Kentucky, Appellee.
M/B: Meredith v. Commonwealth

EXERCISE 1.   CITING CASE NAMES   (CONTINUED)

(f) Katie Davis, Respondent, v. Bi-State Development Agency, Appellant.
M/B: Davis v. Bi-State Development Agency
LR: Davis v. Bi-State Dev. Agency

65 134 300 308 449 556   627   (a) 166 (b) 382 (c) 567 (d) 741 (e) 868 (f) 882
(a) Charles Edward Aliff, Appellant, v. The State of Texas, Appellee.
M/B: Aliff v. State
(b) James Knight, Petitioner, v. International Harvester Credit Corporation, et al., Respondents.
M/B: Knight v. International Harvester Credit Corp.
(c) Francis E. Bourland and Shelby J. Bourland, Husband and Wife, Appellants, v. Title Insurance Company of Minnesota, Appellee.
M/B: Bourland v. Title Insurance Co.
LR: Bourland v. Title Ins. Co.
(d) John L. Shook, Appellant, v. Republic National Bank of Dallas, Appellee.
M/B: Shook v. Republic National Bank
LR: Shook v. Republic Nat'l Bank
(e) Robert D. Green, et al., Appellants, v. City of Lubbock, et al., Appellees.
M/B: Green v. City of Lubbock
(f) State ex rel., Missouri Public Service Co., Relator-Appellant, v. Charles J. Fraas, et al., Defendants-Respondents.
M/B: State ex rel. Missouri Public Service Co. v. Fraas
LR: State ex rel. Missouri Pub. Serv. Co. v. Fraas
Note: "Missouri" should not be abbreviated in the LR form because it is the first word of the relator's name, see Rule 10.2.2.

66 135 201 309 450 557   626   (a) 30 (b) 422 (c) 478 (d) 817 (e) 850 (f) 912
(a) Norbert Lee Peltier and Larry Moore Pape, Appellant, v. The State of Texas, Appellee.
M/B: Peltier v. State
(b) State of Missouri, ex rel. E. G. Turri, Plaintiff, v. The Honorable James H. Keet, Jr., Judge of the Circuit Court of Greene County, Missouri, Div. 3, Defendant.
M/B: State ex rel. Turri v. Keet
LR: State ex rel. Turri v. Keet
(c) Fretz Construction Company, Petitioner, v. Southern National Bank of Houston, Respondent.
M/B: Fretz Construction Co. v. Southern National Bank
LR: Fretz Constr. Co. v. Southern Nat'l Bank
(d) Ex parte Ben Smiley, Relator.
M/B: Ex parte Smiley
LR: Ex parte Smiley
(e) Flournoy Production Company, Appellant, v. John G. Kain & Wife, Catherine Douglas Kain, Appellees.
M/B: Flournoy Production Co. v. Kain
LR: Flournoy Prod. Co. v. Kain
(f) Earl F. Jones, et ux., Appellant, v. Tarrant Utility Co., Appellee
M/B: Jones v. Tarrant Utility Co.
LR: Jones v. Tarrant Util. Co.

67 136 202 310 451 558   625   (a) 1 (b) 151 (c) 192 (d) 581 (e) 731 (f) 874
(a) Jordan Ford, Inc. Appellant, v. Dave W. Alsbury and M. Jayne Alsbury, Appellees.
M/B: Jordan Ford, Inc. v. Alsbury
(b) In the Matter of the Application of James G. George, Applicant.
M/B: In re George
LR: In re George
(c) Connie Sue Alexander, Respondent, v. Pin Oaks Nursing Home, Appellant.
M/B: Alexander v. Pin Oaks Nursing Home
(d) Mark Marshall, Appellant, v. Commonwealth of Kentucky, Appellee.
M/B: Marshall v. Commonwealth
(e) Ex parte Anthony Mark Prejean.
M/B: Ex parte Prejean
LR: Ex parte Prejean
(f) State of Missouri, Respondent, v. Roy F. Van Horn, Appellant.
M/B: State v. Van Horn

EXERCISE 1.   CITING CASE NAMES   (CONTINUED)

68 137 203 311 452 559   624   (a)   11 (b) 453 (c) 474 (d) 573 (e) 886 (f) 933
(a) State of Missouri, Respondent, v. Charles David Patterson, Appellant.
M/B: State v. Patterson
(b) State ex rel. National Advertising Company, Appellant, v. State Highway Commission of the State of Missouri, Respondent.
M/B: State ex rel. National Advertising Co. v. State Highway Commission
LR: State ex rel. National Advertising Co. v. State Highway Comm'n
Note: "National" should not be abbreviated in the LR form because it is the first word of the relator's name, see Rule 10.2.2.
(c) The First National Bank of Kansas City, and Sam C. Sherwood, John D. Petterson, Loren J. Duensing, Trustees Under the Last Will and Testament of Margery M. Smith, Deceased, Plaintiffs-Respondents, v. Mary Hearne Christopher, Defendant-Appellant, and the Unknown and Unborn Heirs, Grantees or Successors of Margery M. Smith, Deceased; of Madeleine Smith, Deceased; and of Mary Hearne Christopher, Defendants-Respondents.
M/B: First National Bank v. Christopher
LR: First Nat'l Bank v. Christopher
(d) Ex parte John Jackson Wray, III, Appellant, v. The State of Texas, Appellee.
M/B: Wray v. State
(e) City of Carthage, Plaintiff-Respondent, v. Fairview Realty and Development Company, A Missouri Corporation, Defendant-Appellant.
M/B: City of Carthage v. Fairview Realty & Development Co.
LR: City of Carthage v. Fairview Realty & Dev. Co.
(f) Kilgore Federal Savings & Loan Association, Appellant, v. Richard Donnelly & William P. Donnelly, III, Appellees.
M/B: Kilgore Federal Savings & Loan Association v. Donnelly
LR: Kilgore Fed. Sav. & Loan Ass'n v. Donnelly

69 138 204 312 453 560   623   (a) 448 (b) 699 (c) 745 (d) 797 (e) 843 (f) 895
(a) Naomi Lisby, Guardian of the Estate of Lewis F. Richardson, an Incompetent, Appellant, v. Estate of Willette R. Richardson (Charlsye Green Administratrix), Appellee.
M/B: Lisby v. Estate of Richardson
(b) International Harvester Company, Appellant, v. Pedro Zavala and Fisher Controls Company, Appellees.
M/B: International Harvester Co. v. Zavala
(c) Edward J. Hale, et al., Appellants, v. City of Los Fresnos, et al., Appellees.
M/B: Hale v. City of Los Fresnos
(d) Patsy Ann Stanford, et vir., Appellants, v. Dairy Queen Products of Texas, et al., Appellees.
M/B: Stanford v. Dairy Queen Products
LR: Stanford v. Dairy Queen Prods.
(e) 555, Inc., and Atlo Distributing Company, Appellants, v. Leon Barlow, Appellee.
M/B: 555, Inc. v. Barlow
(f) Jeffrey Lamont Cardine, Appellant, v. Commonwealth of Kentucky, Appellee.
M/B: Cardine v. Commonwealth

70 139 205 313 454 561   622   (a) 36 (b) 319 (c) 482 (d) 535 (e) 736 (f) 844
(a) State of Tennessee, on relation of James Edward Inman, a resident of Shelby County, Tennessee; and Bench and Bar, a non-profit corporation organized under the Tennessee General Corporation Act, Plaintiffs-Appellants, v. Ray L. Brock, Jr., William H. D. Fones, Robert E. Cooper, Joseph W. Henry, and William J. Harbison, and Thomas H. Shriver, District Attorney General for the Tenth Judicial Circuit, Davidson County, Tennessee, Defendants-Appellees.
M/B: State ex rel. Inman v. Brock
LR: State ex rel. Inman v. Brock
(b) In the Interest of L. A. H., a Minor.
M/B: In re L.A.H.
LR: In re L.A.H.
(c) Ex parte Dewayne Donnel Williams.
M/B: Ex parte Williams
LR: Ex parte Williams

EXERCISE 1.   CITING CASE NAMES   (CONTINUED)

(d) James A. Blackwell and Shirley Moseley, Plaintiffs-Appellees, v. The Quarterly County Court of Shelby County, Tennessee, Its Chairman and Members, and Shelby County, Tennessee, Defendants-Appellants.
M/B: Blackwell v. Quarterly County Court
(e) Three-O-Three Investments, Inc., Plaintiff-Respondent, v. Gene R. Moffitt, John S. Evans James H. Block, Allen J. Block, d/b/a Summit Development Co. Defendants-Appellants.
M/B: Three-O-Three Investments, Inc. v. Moffitt
LR: Three-O-Three Invs., Inc. v. Moffitt
(f) The Estate of O. C. McWhorter et al., Petitioners, v. Evie Wooten, Respondent.
M/B: Estate of McWhorter v. Wooten

71 140 206 314 455 562   620   (a)   5 (b) 157 (c) 181 (d) 362 (e) 648 (f) 732
(a) State of Missouri, Respondent, v. Michael Williams, Appellant.
M/B: State v. Williams
(b) James N. Grace, D/B/A Grace Pest Control, Appellant, v. Structural Pest Control Board of Texas, et al., Appellees.
M/B: Grace v. Structural Pest Control Board
LR: Grace v. Structural Pest Control Bd.
(c) Joe M. Poteet, Appellant, v. The City of Palestine, Appellee.
M/B: Poteet v. City of Palestine
(d) In the Matter of Marvin L. Maloney, Respondent.
M/B: In re Maloney
LR: In re Maloney
(e) Joe D. Browning and Browning Associates, Inc., Appellants, v. Aviation Office of America and Trinity Universal Insurance Company, Appellees.
M/B: Browning v. Aviation Office of America
LR: Browning v. Aviation Office of Am.
(f) First City National Bank of Houston, Trustee, et al., Appellants, v. G.P. Hardy, Jr., et al., Appellees.
M/B: First City National Bank v. Hardy
LR: First City Nat'l Bank v. Hardy

72 141 207 315 456 563   619   (a) 199 (b) 725 (c) 814 (d) 873 (e) 904 (f) 910
(a) Connecticut General Life Insurance Company, Appellant, v. Kathern Lee Tommie and Edith Jones, Appellees.
M/B: Connecticut General Life Insurance Co. v. Tommie
LR: Connecticut Gen. Life Ins. Co. v. Tommie
(b) C. E. H., a juvenile, Movant, v. Commonwealth of Kentucky, Respondent.
M/B: C.E.H. v. Commonwealth
(c) Olga Despotis, Plaintiff-Respondent, v. City of Sunset Hills, Defendant-Appellant.
M/B: Despotis v. City of Sunset Hills
(d) State of Missouri ex rel. Jon E. DeGraffenreid, Plaintiff, v. The Honorable James H. Keet, Jr., Judge of the Circuit Court of Greene County, Missouri, Defendant.
M/B: State ex rel. DeGraffenreid v. Keet
LR: State ex rel. DeGraffenreid v. Keet
(e) In the Matter of the Estate of Helen Louise Kamer, Incompetent [consolidated on appeal with Ahr v. Kranung, listed second in the case title].
M/B: In re Kamer
LR: In re Kamer
(f) Charles E. Lawson, Appellant, v. Estate of Randall D. Slaybaugh, Respondent.
M/B: Lawson v. Estate of Slaybaugh

73 142 208 316 457 564   618   (a) 229 (b) 280 (c) 288 (d) 502 (e) 543 (f) 591
(a) Earl Williams, Plaintiff-Respondent-Appellant, v. United Insurance Company of America, Defendant-Appellant-Respondent.
M/B: Williams v. United Insurance Co. of America
LR: Williams v. United Ins. Co. of Am.
(b) In re Estate of Mary Bennett, Deceased, Grace White, et al., Appellants, v. Walter L. Mulvania, et al., Respondents.
M/B: Estate of Bennett v. Mulvania

EXERCISE 1.   CITING CASE NAMES   (CONTINUED)

(c) Commerce Bank of Lebanon, a corporation, Plaintiff-Respondent, v.
Halladale A Corporation, a corporation, Larry Mahan, Beverly Ann Mahan, Larry
G. Mahan, Trustee, Milton D. Mahan and Harold D. Mahan, Defendants-Appellants.
M/B: Commerce Bank v. Halladale A Corp.
(d) Russell Rives, d/b/a Beech Street Auto Salvage, Plaintiff-Appellant, v.
City of Clarksville, Tennessee, Defendant-Appellee.
M/B: Rives v. City of Clarksville
(e) Big Three Industries, Inc., Petitioner, v. Railroad Commission of Texas et
al., Respondents.
M/B: Big Three Industries v. Railroad Commission
LR: Big Three Indus. v. Railroad Comm'n
(f) Gregory Keith Kohlheim, Appellant, v. Commonwealth of Kentucky, Appellee.
M/B: Kohlheim v. Commonwealth

74 143 209 317 458 565   617   (a)   61 (b) 262 (c) 329 (d) 479 (e) 731 (f) 767
(a) Roosevelt Small, Appellant, v. Commonwealth of Kentucky, Appellee.
M/B: Small v. Commonwealth
(b) Ex parte Christopher L. Tipton.
M/B: Ex parte Tipton
LR: Ex parte Tipton
(c) Janis Pierce Wilson, Appellant, v. Teacher Retirement System of Texas,
Appellee.
M/B: Wilson v. Teacher Retirement System
LR: Wilson v. Teacher Retirement Sys.
(d) Mary L. Word, Appellant, v. City of St. Louis, Respondent.
M/B: Word v. City of St. Louis
(e) The Citizens National Bank in Abilene, et al., Appellants, v. Cattleman's
Production Credit Association, Appellee.
M/B: Citizens National Bank v. Cattleman's Production Credit Association
LR: Citizens Nat'l Bank v. Cattleman's Prod. Credit Ass'n
(f) Jim Walter Homes, Inc., Appellant, v. Charles E. White, et ux., Appellees.
M/B: Jim Walter Homes, Inc. v. White

75 144 210 318 459 566   616   (a)   39 (b) 373 (c) 452 (d) 587 (e) 600 (f) 679
(a) Charles Scott, Appellant, v. Commonwealth of Kentucky, Appellee.
M/B: Scott v. Commonwealth
(b) Clara Campbell, Appellant, v. Beneficial Finance Company of Dallas and
Raymond Bernard Johnson, Appellees.
M/B: Campbell v. Beneficial Finance Co.
LR: Campbell v. Beneficial Fin. Co.
(c) Kenneth Jensen d/b/a Jensen Welding, Appellant, v. First City National
Bank, Appellee.
M/B: Jensen v. First City National Bank
LR: Jensen v. First City Nat'l Bank
(d) State of Missouri ex rel. Carol Jane Morris Robinson, Plaintiff, v. The
Honorable James Clifford Crouch, Judge of the Circuit Court of Christian
County, Missouri, Defendant.
M/B: State ex rel. Robinson v. Crouch
LR: State ex rel. Robinson v. Crouch
(e) Cora Pauline Blackburn, Plaintiff-Appellee, v. Allied Chemical Corporation
and the Travelers Insurance Company, Defendants-Appellants.
M/B: Blackburn v. Allied Chemical Corp.
LR: Blackburn v. Allied Chem. Corp.
(f) Luis Fuentes, Appellant, v. City of Kingsville, Appellee.
M/B: Fuentes v. City of Kingsville

76 145 211 319 460 567   615   (a)   1 (b) 164 (c) 293 (d) 309 (e) 574 (f) 869
(a) Commonwealth of Kentucky, Appellant, v. William C. Johnson, Appellee.
M/B: Commonwealth v. Johnson
(b) Estate of Otha Faye McQuaid Claveria, Petitioner, v. Patricio Claveria,
Respondent.
M/B: Estate of Claveria v. Claveria
(c) Ex parte Joellen Finn, Relator.
M/B: Ex parte Finn
LR: Ex parte Finn
(d) Texas Utilities Fuel Company, Appellant, v. First National Bank in Dallas
et al., Appellees.

EXERCISE 1.   CITING CASE NAMES   (CONTINUED)

M/B: <u>Texas Utilities Fuel Co. v. First National Bank</u>
LR: Texas Utils. Fuel Co. v. First Nat'l Bank
(e) David T. Jordan, Appellant-Respondent, v. Robert Half Personnel Agencies of Kansas City, Inc. and Donald Apple, Respondents-Appellants.
M/B: <u>Jordan v. Robert Half Personnel Agencies, Inc.</u>
(f) George S. Khalaf, Appellant, v. United Business Investments, Inc., Appellee.
M/B: <u>Khalaf v. United Business Investments, Inc.</u>
LR: Khalaf v. United Business Invs., Inc.

77 146 212 320 461 568   621   (a) 12 (b) 22 (c) 451 (d) 539 (e) 731 (f) 889
(a) Henry Ketcher, et al., Appellants, v. Mayor and the City Council of North Little Rock, Arkansas, et al., Appellees.
M/B: <u>Ketcher v. Mayor of North Little Rock</u>
LR: Ketcher v. Mayor of N. Little Rock
Note: "City Council" should be omitted because only the first-listed party should be cited, see example in Rule 10.2.1(a) ("Mayor of Baltimore," <u>not</u> "Mayor & City Counsel of Baltimore"). "Ketcher v. Mayor" is incorrect because prepositional phrases of location are not omitted when their omission would leave only one word in the name of the party ("Mayor").
(b) Clayton Warner, Appellant, v. Commonwealth of Kentucky, Appellee.
M/B: <u>Warner v. Commonwealth</u>
(c) Bayliss McInnis, et al., Appellants, v. Corpus Christi National Bank, et al., Appellees.
M/B: <u>McInnis v. Corpus Christi National Bank</u>
LR: McInnis v. Corpus Christi Nat'l Bank
(d) Carla Watson Stearns, Appellant, v. Be-Mac Transport Company, Inc., Respondent.
M/B: <u>Stearns v. Be-Mac Transport Co.</u>
LR: Stearns v. Be-Mac Transp. Co.
(e) L. B. Pete, Plaintiff-Appellant, v. Cumberland County, Tennessee, et al., Defendants-Appellees.
M/B: <u>Pete v. Cumberland County</u>
(f) Tommy Barrett d/b/a Barrett Real Estate, Appellant, v. Land Mart of America, Inc. Appellee.
M/B: <u>Barrett v. Land Mart of America, Inc.</u>
LR: Barrett v. Land Mart of Am., Inc.

78 147 213 321 462 569   614   (a) 227 (b) 429 (c) 563 (d) 695 (e) 701 (f) 903
(a) Kelton R. Brown, Appellant, v. Summerlin Associates, Inc., Appellee.
M/B: <u>Brown v. Summerlin Associates</u>
LR: Brown v. Summerlin Assocs.
(b) Ex parte Donald Dee Collier.
M/B: <u>Ex parte Collier</u>
LR: <u>Ex parte Collier</u>
(c) Contractors Supply Company, Respondent, v. Labor and Industrial Relations Commission, Division of Employment Security and James Tyrone Thomas, Appellants.
M/B: <u>Contractors Supply Co. v. Labor & Industrial Relations Commission</u>
LR: Contractors Supply Co. v. Labor & Indus. Relations Comm'n
(d) Arkansas State Highway Commission, Appellant, v. Marvin A. Pearrow et ux., Appellees.
M/B: <u>Arkansas State Highway Commission v. Pearrow</u>
LR: Arkansas State Highway Comm'n v. Pearrow
(e) David Wayne Duncan, Appellant, v. Commonwealth of Kentucky Appellee.
M/B: <u>Duncan v. Commonwealth</u>
(f) Railroad Commission of Texas et al., Appellants, v. United Parcel Service, Inc., Appellee.
M/B: <u>Railroad Commission v. United Parcel Service</u>
LR: Railroad Comm'n v. United Parcel Serv.

79 148 214 322 463 570   613   (a) 431 (b) 440 (c) 716 (d) 793 (e) 800 (f) 833
(a) Scott Davidson and Brian Davidson, Juveniles Under the Age of 14 Years, Appellants, v. Commonwealth of Kentucky, Appellees.
M/B: <u>Davidson v. Commonwealth</u>

EXERCISE 1.   CITING CASE NAMES   (CONTINUED)

(b) State of Missouri ex rel. John Ashcroft, Attorney General, Plaintiff-Appellant, v. Marketing Unlimited of America, Inc., d/b/a Handicapped Assistance League of America, Inc. et al., Defendants-Respondents.
M/B: State ex rel. Ashcroft v. Marketing Unlimited of America, Inc.
LR: State ex rel. Ashcroft v. Marketing Unlimited of Am., Inc.
(c) Barbara B. (Busby) Bridges, Plaintiff-Respondent, v. First National Bank in St. Louis, Defendant-Appellant.
M/B: Bridges v. First National Bank
LR: Bridges v. First Nat'l Bank
(d) Barney Stagner, Individually et al. v. Friendswood Development Company, Inc. et al.
M/B: Stagner v. Friendswood Development Co.
LR: Stagner v. Friendswood Dev. Co.
(e) Basin, Inc. Appellant, v. Railroad Commission of Texas et al., Appellees.
M/B: Basin, Inc. v. Railroad Commission
LR: Basin, Inc. v. Railroad Comm'n
(f) Bernard A. Baltz and Margaret Baltz, his wife, Appellants, v. Security Bank of Paragould, Paragould, Arkansas, Appellee.
M/B: Baltz v. Security Bank

80 149 215 323 464 571   612   (a) 257 (b) 503 (c) 766 (d) 799 (e) 866 (f) 935
(a) City of Fort Worth, Appellant, v. Edwin Bewley et al., Appellee.
M/B: City of Fort Worth v. Bewley
(b) Eagle Trucking Company et al., Petitioners, v. Texas Bitulithic Company et al., Respondents.
M/B: Eagle Trucking Co. v. Texas Bitulithic Co.
(c) Commonwealth of Kentucky, Appellant, v. Glenn "Sonny" Hurd, Appellee.
M/B: Commonwealth v. Hurd
(d) First Security Bank of Brookfield, Missouri, Plaintiff-Respondent, v. Fastwich, Inc., and John H. Smith, II, Defendants-Appellants, and Gary D. Smith, Cheryl J. Smith and Carolyn S. Smith, Defendants.
M/B: First Security Bank v. Fastwich, Inc.
LR: First Sec. Bank v. Fastwich, Inc.
(e) State of Missouri ex rel. State Highway Commission of Missouri, Plaintiff-Respondent, v. Select Properties, Inc., et al., Exceptions of Lambert Realty & Development Corp., Defendant-Appellant.
M/B: State ex rel. State Highway Commission v. Select Properties, Inc.
LR: State ex rel. State Highway Comm'n v. Select Properties, Inc.
(f) Ex parte Joe Nathan Lightfoot.
M/B: Ex parte Lightfoot
LR: Ex parte Lightfoot

81 150 216 324 465 572   611   (a)   1 (b) 860 (c) 869 (d) 897 (e) 911 (f) 928
(a) In the Matter of Gerald H. Lowther.
M/B: In re Lowther
LR: In re Lowther
(b) Salvador Ortiz, Appellant, v. O. J. Beck & Sons, Inc. Appellee.
M/B: Ortiz v. O.J. Beck & Sons
(c) Della Faye Gilbert, Appellant, v. Fireside Enterprises, Inc., d/b/a Fireside Lodge of Dallas, Appellee.
M/B: Gilbert v. Fireside Enterprises
LR: Gilbert v. Fireside Enters.
(d) Evelyn Sell et al., Appellants, v. C. B. Smith Volkswagen, Inc., et al., Appellees.
M/B: Sell v. C.B. Smith Volkswagen, Inc.
(e) Railroad Commission of Texas, Appellant, v. Lone Star Gas Company, a Division of Enserch Corporation, Appellee.
M/B: Railroad Commission v. Lone Star Gas Co.
LR: Railroad Comm'n v. Lone Star Gas Co.
(f) Connecticut General Life Insurance Company, Appellant, v. Gray W. Shelton et ux., Appellee.
M/B: Connecticut General Life Insurance Co. v. Shelton
LR: Connecticut Gen. Life Ins. Co. v. Shelton

82 151 217 325 466 573   610   (a) 217 (b) 681 (c) 744 (d) 807 (e) 922 (f) 935
(a) Roy Arnold Fairchild, Appellant, v. Insurance Company of North America, Appellee.

EXERCISE 1.   CITING CASE NAMES   (CONTINUED)

M/B: Fairchild v. Insurance Co. of North America
LR: Fairchild v. Insurance Co. of N. Am.
(b) In the Matter of the Estate of Frank W. Mitchell, Deceased.
M/B: In re Estate of Mitchell
LR: In re Estate of Mitchell
(c) Kenneth Coalson et al., Relators, v. City Council of Victoria, Texas, Respondent.
M/B: Coalson v. City Council
(d) Daniel Saldana, Jr., Appellant, v. Houston General Insurance Company, Appellee.
M/B: Saldana v. Houston General Insurance Co.
LR: Saldana v. Houston Gen. Ins. Co.
(e) Commonwealth of Kentucky, Appellant, v. George Boarman, Appellee.
M/B: Commonwealth v. Boarman
(f) Pearl Miller, Appellant, v. Board of Education of Hardin County, Kentucky; Charlie Akins, individually and in his official capacity as Superintendent and Secretary of the Board of Education of Hardin County, Kentucky; and J. Russell Hargan, Elizabeth Bland, Bill Logsdon, Kenneth Hayden, and Johnny Simpson, all individually and in their official capacities as members of the Board of Education of Hardin County, Kentucky, Appellees.
M/B: Miller v. Board of Education
LR: Miller v. Board of Educ.

83 152 218 326 467 574   608   (a) 51 (b) 374 (c) 405 (d) 576 (e) 722 (f) 819
(a) The Owensboro National Bank, Movant, v. Sam Crisp, Respondent.
M/B: Owensboro National Bank v. Crisp
LR: Owensboro Nat'l Bank v. Crisp
(b) Hubert W. Barrett, Appellant, v. Commonwealth of Kentucky, Appellee.
M/B: Barrett v. Commonwealth
(c) State ex rel. Sharon Lynn McClintock, Relator-Petitioner, v. Honorable Gary R. Black, Sr., Circuit Judge, 24th Judicial Circuit, St. Francois County, Respondent.
M/B: State ex rel. McClintock v. Black
LR: State ex rel. McClintock v. Black
(d) Kenneth Abney, Plaintiff-Appellant, v. Farmers Mutual Insurance Company of Sikeston, Defendant-Respondent.
M/B: Abney v. Farmers Mutual Insurance Co.
LR: Abney v. Farmers Mut. Ins. Co.
(e) Estate of W. Thomas Bolton, Deceased, Appellant, v. Alton Coats et al., Appellees.
M/B: Estate of Bolton v. Coats
(f) In the Matter of J. A. L.
M/B: In re J.A.L.
LR: In re J.A.L.

84 153 219 327 468 575   607   (a) 421 (b) 507 (c) 677 (d) 832 (e) 856 (f) 857
(a) Gregory McClain, Appellant, v. Commonwealth of Kentucky, Appellee, and Albert Sullivan, Appellant, v. Commonwealth of Kentucky, Appellee.
M/B: McClain v. Commonwealth
(b) Ex parte Harvey Joseph Duffy, Jr.
M/B: Ex parte Duffy
LR: Ex parte Duffy
(c) The Southern Company, Inc., Appellant, v. James Graham and Verdie Mae Graham D/B/A Graham Drive-In, Appellees.
M/B: Southern Co. v. Graham
(d) Patrick Petrovich, Appellant, v. Orscheln Brothers Truck Lines, Inc., and Insurance Company of North America, Respondents.
M/B: Petrovich v. Orscheln Brothers Truck Lines
LR: Petrovich v. Orscheln Bros. Truck Lines
(e) State Bank of Desoto, Respondent, v. Joseph Newman and Sho-Me Builders, Appellants.
M/B: State Bank v. Newman
(f) May Department Stores Company et al., Plaintiffs-Respondents, v. County of St. Louis, Missouri et al., Defendants-Appellants.
M/B: May Department Stores Co. v. County of St. Louis
LR: May Dep't Stores v. County of St. Louis

EXERCISE 1.   CITING CASE NAMES   (CONTINUED)

85 154 220 328 469 576   606   (a) 169 (b) 578 (c) 696 (d) 725 (e) 732 (f) 792
(a) Charles Reeves Wonn, Appellant, v. Commonwealth of Kentucky, Appellee.
M/B: Wonn v. Commonwealth
(b) Gomer Evans, Appellant, v. Arkansas Racing Commission and Oaklawn Jockey Club, Inc., Appellees.
M/B: Evans v. Arkansas Racing Commission
LR: Evans v. Arkansas Racing Comm'n
(c) First State Bank of Corpus Christi et al., Appellant, v. Arthur E. Ake, Appellee.
M/B: First State Bank v. Ake
(d) Texas General Indemnity Company, Appellant, v. Billie Dougharty et al, Appellees.
M/B: Texas General Indemnity Co. v. Dougharty
LR: Texas Gen. Indem. Co. v. Dougharty
(e) Dorothy Marshall Wehmeyer, Appellant, v. A. J. Marshall & Sons, a partnership, Appellee.
M/B: Wehmeyer v. A.J. Marshall & Sons
(f) In re the Estate of Pearl I. Horton, Deceased [consolidated on appeal with Shuey v. Willard, listed second in the case title].
M/B: In re Estate of Horton
LR: In re Estate of Horton

86 155 221 329 470 577   605   (a) 43 (b) 501 (c) 506 (d) 749 (e) 800 (f) 955
(a) Michael Allen Waugh, Appellant, v. Commonwealth of Kentucky, Appellee.
M/B: Waugh v. Commonwealth
(b) Elizabeth H. Stanfill, Plaintiff-Appellant, v. City of Richmond Heights, Missouri, and Ronald Murray, Defendants-Respondents.
M/B: Stanfill v. City of Richmond Heights
(c) State ex rel. Fred O. Whaley, Petitioner, v. Hon. Carl R. Gaertner, Judge, Circuit Court of the City of St. Louis, Respondent.
M/B: State ex rel. Whaley v. Gaertner
LR: State ex rel. Whaley v. Gaertner
(d) Mack Financial Corporation, Appellant, v. Donald Chrestman d/b/a Wheatley Diesel Service and Danny Goodman, Appellees.
M/B: Mack Financial Corp. v. Chrestman
LR: Mack Fin. Corp. v. Chrestman
(e) Richard Henderson, Respondent, v. St. Louis Housing Authority, Appellant.
M/B: Henderson v. St. Louis Housing Authority
LR: Henderson v. St. Louis Hous. Auth.
(f) In the Matter of S.E.C., a child, Appellant.
M/B: In re S.E.C.
LR: In re S.E.C.

87 156 222 330 471 578   604   (a) 221 (b) 396 (c) 415 (d) 511 (e) 623 (f) 791
(a) Estate of B. E. Griffin, Deceased et al., Appellants, v. Mrs. B. F. Sumner et vir., Appellees.
M/B: Estate of Griffin v. Sumner
(b) Clarence S. Gipson, Appellant, v. Southwest Oil company of San Antonio, Inc., Appellee.
M/B: Gipson v. Southwest Oil Co.
(c) State Banking Board et al., Appellants, v. Valley National Bank et al., Appellees.
M/B: State Banking Board v. Valley National Bank
LR: State Banking Bd. v. Valley Nat'l Bank
(d) Westwood Independent School District, Appellant, v. Southern Clay Products, Inc., Appellee.
M/B: Westwood Independent School District v. Southern Clay Products, Inc.
LR: Westwood Indep. School Dist. v. Southern Clay Prods., Inc.
(e) State of Missouri ex rel. Missouri Public Service Company, Appellant, v. A. Robert Pierce, Jr., Chairman, Commissioners Fain, Sprague, Jones and Mulvaney, As Members of and Constituting the Public Service Commission of Missouri, Respondents.
M/B: State ex rel. Missouri Public Service Co.
LR: State ex rel. Missouri Pub. Serv. Co.
Note: "Missouri" should not be abbreviated in the LR form because it is the first word of the relator's name, see Rule 10.2.2.

EXERCISE 1.   CITING CASE NAMES   (CONTINUED)

(f) L. R. Stevenson, Plaintiff-Respondent, v. First National Bank of Callaway County, a Missouri Banking Corporation, Defendant-Appellant.
M/B: <u>Stevenson v. First National Bank</u>
LR: <u>Stevenson v. First Nat'l Bank</u>

88 157 223 331 472 579   603   (a) 37 (b) 335 (c) 793 (d) 829 (e) 930 (f) 931
(a) State Highway Commission of Missouri, Respondent, v. William and Marlene Bodine, Appellants.
M/B: <u>State Highway Commission v. Bodine</u>
LR: <u>State Highway Comm'n v. Bodine</u>
(b) Grady E. Wooldridge, Appellant, v. The Groos National Bank, Appellee.
M/B: <u>Wooldridge v. Groos National Bank</u>
LR: <u>Wooldridge v. Groos Nat'l Bank</u>
(c) In the Interest of T. E. T.
M/B: <u>In re T.E.T.</u>
LR: <u>In re T.E.T.</u>
(d) The State Bar of Texas, Relator, v. Honorable Wyatt H. Heard, Judge, Respondent.
M/B: <u>State Bar v. Heard</u>
(e) State ex rel. Council Apartments, Inc., a Mo. Corp., Relator, v. George C. Leachman, Collector of Revenue, St. Louis County, Respondent.
M/B: <u>State ex rel. Council Apartments v. Leachman</u>
LR: <u>State ex rel. Council Apartments v. Leachman</u>
(f) In re Estate of J. Roger DeWitt et al., Appellants, v. State of Missouri, Respondent.
M/B: <u>Estate of DeWitt v. State</u>

89 158 224 332 473 580   602   (a) 118 (b) 150 (c) 327 (d) 400 (e) 609 (f) 874
(a) Twin City Fire Insurance Company, Appellant, v. Donald Wayne Brown, Appellee.
M/B: <u>Twin City Fire Insurance Co. v. Brown</u>
LR: <u>Twin City Fire Ins. Co. v. Brown</u>
(b) Richard Earl Compton, Movant, v. Commonwealth of Kentucky, Respondent. and Chester Eugene Compton, Movant, v. Commonwealth of Kentucky, Respondent.
M/B: <u>Compton v. Commonwealth</u>
(c) The First National Bank of Marshall, Texas Trustee, Appellant, v. J. W. Beavers Jr. and Mildred L. Bowden, Appellees.
M/B: <u>First National Bank v. Beavers</u>
LR: <u>First Nat'l Bank v. Beavers</u>
(d) Ex parte Henry Gayle Jones.
M/B: <u>Ex parte Jones</u>
LR: <u>Ex parte Jones</u>
(e) Arkansas State Highway Commission, Appellant, v. First Pyramid Life Insurance Company of America, Appellee.
M/B: <u>Arkansas State Highway Commission v. First Pyramid Life Insurance Co. of America</u>
LR: <u>Arkansas State Highway Comm'n v. First Pyramid Life Ins. Co. of Am.</u>
(f) State of Missouri ex rel. Clifford J. Stutz, Sr., Relator, v. The Honorable Robert Lee Campbell, Judge of the Circuit Court of St. Louis County, Missouri, Division No. 15, Respondent.
M/B: <u>State ex rel. Stutz v. Campbell</u>
LR: <u>State ex rel. Stutz v. Campbell</u>

90 159 225 333 474 581   601   (a) 186 (b) 191 (c) 280 (d) 717 (e) 766 (f) 923
(a) Railroad Commission of Texas et al. v. Champion International Corporation et al. v. Champion International Corporation et al.
M/B: <u>Railroad Commission v. Champion International Corp.</u>
LR: <u>Railroad Comm'n v. Champion Int'l Corp.</u>
(b) S. S. S. Water Systems, Inc., Appellant, v. The City of Granite Shoals, Texas, Appellee.
M/B: <u>S.S.S. Water Systems v. City of Granite Shoals</u>
LR: <u>S.S.S. Water Sys. v. City of Granite Shoals</u>
(c) Shelia Wilson, Appellant, v. Commonwealth of Kentucky, Appellee.
M/B: <u>Wilson v. Commonwealth</u>
(d) State of Texas ex rel., James F. Hury, Jr., District Attorney of Galveston County, Petitioner, v. Don B. Morgan, Judge of 56th District Court, Galveston County, Respondent.

EXERCISE 1.   CITING CASE NAMES   (CONTINUED)

M/B: State ex rel. Hury v. Morgan
LR: State ex rel. Hury v. Morgan
(e) In the Interest of S. R. M. a child.
M/B: In re S.R.M.
LR: In re S.R.M.
(f) John A. Lindsey, Appellant, v. Smith and Johnson, Inc., Appellee.
M/B: Lindsey v. Smith & Johnson, Inc.

91 160 226 334 475 582   600   (a) 358 (b) 457 (c) 601 (d) 660 (e) 695 (f) 850
(a) Clinton Foshee et al., Appellants, v. Republic National Bank of Dallas, Trustee, Appellee.
M/B: Foshee v. Republic National Bank
LR: Foshee v. Republic Nat'l Bank
(b) Terry Lee Gully, Movant, v. Commonwealth of Kentucky, Respondent.
M/B: Gully v. Commonwealth
(c) State of Missouri, at the relation of Gary Rybolt and Pat Rybolt, husband and wife, Relators-Appellants, v. Amy Easley, David Horner, Dale Kennedy, Roland Walker, and Robert Spiva, being all the members of the Boone County Board of Adjustment and Boone County, Missouri, Respondents-Respondents.
M/B: State ex rel. Rybolt v. Easley
LR: State ex rel. Rybolt v. Easley
(d) City of Kansas City, Missouri, Appellant-Respondent, v. Milrey Development Company, George W. Miller, Neal O. Reyburn and A. C. Bay, Respondents-Appellants.
M/B: City of Kansas City v. Milrey Development Co.
LR: City of Kansas City v. Milrey Dev. Co.
(e) In the Matter of Michael O'Brien, a person alleged to be mentally ill.
M/B: In re O'Brien
LR: In re O'Brien
(f) Texas Municipal Power Agency, Appellant, v. Tony R. Berger et al., Appellees.
M/B: Texas Municipal Power Agency v. Berger
LR: Texas Mun. Power Agency v. Berger

92 161 227 335 476 583   599   (a) 121 (b) 427 (c) 545 (d) 655 (e) 841 (f) 900
(a) Rolen R. Rains, Appellant, v. Mercantile national Bank at Dallas and Jerry J. Aills, Appellees.
M/B: Rains v. Mercantile National Bank
LR: Rains v. Mercantile Nat'l Bank
(b) Farm Bureau Mutual Insurance Company of Arkansas, Inc., Appellant, v. Laura Mae Fuqua, Appellee.
M/B: Farm Bureau Mutual Insurance Co. v. Fuqua
LR: Farm Bureau Mut. Ins. Co. v. Fuqua
(c) State of Tennessee ex rel. Collier et al., Appellants, v. City of Pigeon Forge et al., Appellees.
M/B: State ex rel. Collier v. City of Pigeon Forge
LR: State ex rel. Collier v. City of Pigeon Forge
(d) Lloyd A. Merbitz, Appellant, v. Great National Life Insurance Company, Appellee.
M/B: Merbitz v. Great National Life Insurance Co.
LR: Merbitz v. Great Nat'l Life Ins. Co.
(e) R. A. M., a juvenile, Appellant, v. The State of Texas, Appellee.
M/B: R.A.M. v. State
(f) Johnny Marshall Smith, Appellant, v. Commonwealth of Kentucky, Appellee.
M/B: Smith v. Commonwealth

93 162 228 336 477 584   598   (a) 11 (b) 503 (c) 528 (d) 640 (e) 660 (f) 783
(a) Donoho & Sons, Inc., Appellant, v. Aetna Insurance Company, Appellee.
M/B: Donoho & Sons v. Aetna Insurance Co.
LR: Donoho & Sons v. Aetna Ins. Co.
(b) Carl L. Huff et al., Apps., Plaintiffs-Appellants, v. Union Electric Company, Defendant-Respondent.
M/B: Huff v. Union Electric Co.
LR: Huff v. Union Elec. Co.
(c) In the Matter of the Estate of Eunice Viola Soper, Incompetent [consolidated on appeal with Acardia Valley Bank v. Black, listed second in the the case title].

EXERCISE 1.   CITING CASE NAMES   (CONTINUED)

M/B: In re Estate of Soper
LR: In re Estate of Soper
(d) H. P. Duckett, Appellant, v. Civil Service Commission of the City of Houston, Appellee.
M/B: Duckett v. Civil Service Commission
LR: Duckett v. Civil Serv. Comm'n
(e) K. W. M., Appellant, v. The State of Texas, Appellee.
M/B: K.W.M. v. State
(f) Outdoor Advertising Association of Tennessee, Inc., et al., Plaintiffs-Appellants, v. Eddie Shaw, Commissioner of Transportation, State of Tennessee, Defendant-Appellee.
M/B: Outdoor Advertising Association v. Shaw
LR: Outdoor Advertising Ass'n v. Shaw

94 163 229 337 478 585   597   (a) 434 (b) 510 (c) 724 (d) 783 (e) 861 (f) 871
(a) Patricio Claveria, Appellant, v. Estate of Otha Faye McQuaid Claveria, Appellee.
M/B: Claveria v. Estate of Claveria
(b) Dianne Thompson, Appellant, v. United Services Automobile Association, Appellee.
M/B: Thompson v. United Services Automobile Association
LR: Thompson v. United Servs. Auto. Ass'n
(c) State ex rel. Reginald Jordon, Relator, v. Hon. Richard J. Mehan, Judge, Twenty Second Judicial Circuit, Respondent.
M/B: State ex rel. Jordon v. Mehan
LR: State ex rel. Jordon v. Mehan
(d) First National Bank in Weatherford, Texas, Appellant, v. Exxon Corporation et al, Appellees.
M/B: First National Bank v. Exxon Corp.
LR: First Nat'l Bank v. Exxon Corp.
(e) H. F. Barraclough and Donna Barraclough, Appellants, v. Arkansas Power and Light Company, Appellee.
M/B: Barraclough v. Arkansas Power & Light Co.
(f) Christo A. Weltscheff, M.D., Respondent, v. Medical Center of Independence, Inc., a General Not For Profit Corporation also known as Medical Center of Independence, Appellant.
M/B: Weltscheff v. Medical Center

95 164 230 338 479 586   596   (a) 150 (b) 240 (c) 397 (d) 716 (e) 796 (f) 824
(a) Regal Construction Company, Appellant, v. Phill Hansel et ux, Appellees.
M/B: Regal Construction Co. v. Hansel
LR: Regal Constr. Co. v. Hansel
(b) In re Estate of George T. Roots, Deceased.
M/B: In re Estate of Roots
LR: In re Estate of Roots
(c) Commonwealth of Kentucky, Appellant, v. E. G. Bertram III, Appellee.
M/B: Commonwealth v. Bertram
(d) Mary B. Wallin et al., Appellants, v. Insurance Company of North America and Federal Guaranty Life Insurance Company, Appellees.
M/B: Wallin v. Insurance Co. of North America
LR: Wallin v. Insurance Co. of N. Am.
(e) State of Tennessee ex rel. Eddie Shaw, Commissioner, Department of Transportation, Petitioner, v. Bonnie Gorman et al., Respondents.
M/B: State ex rel. Shaw v. Gorman
LR: State ex rel. Shaw v. Gorman
(f) Third National Bank in Nashville, Trustee Under the Will of Goodloe Cockrill, Deceased, Plaintiff-Appellee, v. First American National Bank of Nashville, Executor of the Estate of Sterling B. Cockrill, Deceased, and Executor of the Estate of Mary Harris Cockrill, Deceased, Jane Douglas Cockrill Moore, Katherine Peyton Cockrill, Individually and Executrix of the Estate of Calvin Cockrill, Deceased, Peyton Cockrill Davis, Defendants-Appellees.
M/B: Third National Bank v. First American National Bank
LR: Third Nat'l Bank v. First Am. Nat'l Bank

96 165 231 339 480 587   594   (a) 163 (b) 449 (c) 545 (d) 723 (e) 898 (f) 908

EXERCISE 1.   CITING CASE NAMES   (CONTINUED)

(a) United Savings Association of Texas, Appellant, v. L. Alvis Vandygriff,
Savings and Loan Commissioner of Texas, et al., Appellees.
M/B: United Savings Association v. Vandygriff
LR: United Sav. Ass'n v. Vandygriff
(b) Ex parte Walter Moore, Jr. and Steven Blaine Moore.
M/B: Ex parte Moore
LR: Ex parte Moore
(c) W. Howell Cocke, Jr. et ux, Appellants, v. Pacific Gulf Development
Corporation et al., Appellees.
M/B: Cocke v. Pacific Gulf Development Corp.
LR: Cocke v. Pacific Gulf Dev. Corp.
(d) W. Warren Graham and wife, Barbara G. Graham, Plaintiffs-Appellees, v.
First American National Bank, Defendant-Appellant.
M/B: Graham v. First American National Bank
LR: Graham v. First Am. Nat'l Bank
(e) Leslie Beecham, Appellant, v. Commonwealth of Kentucky, Appellee.
M/B: Beecham v. Commonwealth
(f) State ex rel. George R. Westfall, Relator, v. Hon. Donald L. Mason, Judge,
16th Judicial Circuit, Respondent.
M/B: State ex rel. Westfall v. Mason
LR: State ex rel. Westfall v. Mason

97 166 232 340 481 588   593   (a)   84 (b)   193 (c)   731 (d)   749 (e)   869 (f)   923
(a) Dealers Transport Company, Appellant, v. Marilyn Joyce Thomspon, James R.
Yocom, Commissioner of Labor and Custodian of the Special Fund, and Workmen's
Compensation Board, Appellees.
M/B: Dealers Transport Co. v. Thompson
LR: Dealers Transp. Co. v. Thompson
(b) In the Matter of Sheryl Ann Trapp, Dee Ann Trapp, and Duane Edwin Trapp.
Robert Emery Trapp, Father, Linda Mae Trapp, Mother and Appellant, David L.
and Judy E. Bridgeman, Intervenors-Respondents.
M/B: In re Trapp
LR: In re Trapp
(c) Hugh Robison Farm Machinery, Inc. and Security State Bank of Navasota,
Texas, Appellants, v. Henry Wied, Appellee.
M/B: Hugh Robison Farm Machinery, Inc. v. Wied
LR: Hugh Robison Farm Mach., Inc. v. Wied
(d) Jim Walter Homes, Inc. Appellants, v. Ervin and Gladys Foster, Appellee.
M/B: Jim Walter Homes, Inc. v. Foster
(e) Frank Jones, Appellant, v. Commonwealth of Kentucky, Appellee.
M/B: Jones v. Commonwealth
(f) J. B. Herbison, d/b/a J. B. Herbison Painting Contractor, Appellee, v.
Employers Insurance Company of Alabama, Incorporated
M/B: Herbison v. Employers Insurance Co.
LR: Herbison v. Employers Ins. Co.

98 167 233 341 482 589   592   (a)   35 (b)   38 (c)   134 (d)   285 (e)   432 (f)   670
(a) In the Interest of D. N. S., a child.
M/B: In re D.N.S.
LR: In re D.N.S.
(b) Rodolfo Partida, Appellant, v. Park North General Hospital et al.,
Appellees.
M/B: Partida v. Park North General Hospital
LR: Partida v. Park N. Gen. Hosp.
(c) Robert E. Martin, III, Appellant, v. Commonwealth of Kentucky, Appellee.
M/B: Martin v. Commonwealth
(d) State ex rel. Board of Public Utilities of the City of Springfield,
Missouri, and Del Caywood, Denton Smith, Nancy Hoflund, J. David Lages, Ransom
Ellis, N. L. McCartney, Russell Harthcock and William E. Hoyer, individually
and as members of the Board of Public Utilities, Relators.
M/B: State ex rel. Board of Public Utilities v. Crow
LR: State ex rel. Board of Pub. Utils. v. Crow
Note: "Board" should not be abbreviated in the LR form because it is the
first word of the relator's name, see Rule 10.2.2.
(e) Leonard Anderson, Appellant, v. Texas General Indemnity Company, Appellee.
M/B: Anderson v. Texas General Indemnity Co.
LR: Anderson v. Texas Gen. Indem. Co.

EXERCISE 1.   CITING CASE NAMES   (CONTINUED)

(f) Jim Walter Homes, Inc., Appellant, v. Richard P. Smith et ux., Appellees.
M/B: Jim Walter Homes, Inc. v. Smith

99 168 234 342 483 590   590   (a) 173 (b) 241 (c) 563 (d) 783 (e) 878 (f) 946
(a) Marcelino B. Cavazos, Appellant, v. The Fidelity & Casualty Company of New York, Appellee.
M/B: Cavazos v. Fidelity & Casualty Co.
(b) Vera McEntire, Appellant, v. Estate of J. L. McEntire, Deceased, James C. McEntire, Executor, and Pine Bluff National Bank, Appellees.
M/B: McEntire v. Estate of McEntire
(c) Community Public Service Company, Appellant, v. L. J. Andrews, Appellee.
M/B: Community Public Service Co. v. Andrews
LR: Community Pub. Serv. Co. v. Andrews
(d) Liberty Mutual Insurance Company, Appellant, v. United State Fire Insurance Company, Appellee.
M/B: Liberty Mutual Insurance Co. v. United States Fire Insurance Co.
LR: Liberty Mut. Ins. Co. v. United States Fire Ins. Co.
(e) Commonwealth of Kentucky, Movant, v. William Lee Burris, Respondent.
M/B: Commonwealth v. Burris
(f) T. P. S., Appellant, v. State of Texas, Appellee.
M/B: T.P.S. v. State

100 169 235 343 484 591   588   (a) 46 (b) 50 (c) 199 (d) 489 (e) 602 (f) 877
(a) William K. Young, Plaintiff-Appellant, v. United States Fidelity & Guaranty Co., a Corporation, Defendant-Respondent.
M/B: Young v. United States Fidelity & Guaranty Co.
LR: Young v. United States Fidelity & Guar. Co.
(b) In the Matter of the Estate of Elbert C. Fields, Deceased.
M/B: In re Estate of Fields
LR: In re Estate of Fields
(c) Efton A. Stanfield, Appellant, v. National Electrical Contractors Association, Inc., et al., Respondents.
M/B: Stanfield v. National Electrical Contractors Association
LR: Stanfield v. National Elec. Contractors Ass'n
(d) State of Missouri ex rel. Maryland Heights Concrete Contractors, Inc., Relator, v. The Honorable Franklin R. Ferriss, Respondent.
M/B: State ex rel. Maryland Heights Concrete Contractors, Inc. v. Ferriss
LR: State ex rel. Maryland Heights Concrete Contractors, Inc. v. Ferriss
Note: "Maryland" should not be abbreviated in the LR form because it is the first word of the relator's name, see Rule 10.2.2.
(e) The University of Texas System, Appellant, v. Yvonne Schieffer, Appellee.
M/B: University of Texas System v. Schieffer
LR: University of Tex. Sys. v. Schieffer
(f) Paul M. Watson and wife Ruth Watson v. United American Bank in Knoxville.
M/B: Watson v. United American Bank
LR: Watson v. United Am. Bank

LIBRARY EXERCISE 2. UNITED STATES REPORTS.

INSTRUCTOR'S NOTE: This Exercise teaches students how to find a case in the official reporter of U.S. Supreme Court decisions from a known citation and gives them practice in citing that case in proper form. The students are required to find the case that begins on the page listed below in the designated volume of United States Reports and to cite the case to United States Reports only. (Note that the volume of United States Reports used to complete this Exercise also is used to complete Exercise 3). In addition to other CN (Case Name) Quick-Reference Abbreviations, the following are especially relevant to this and the next exercise:

    CASE NAME 6. "COMMISSIONER OF INTERNAL REVENUE" SHOULD BE CITED AS "COMMISSIONER." [CN 6]
    CASE NAME 26. ABBREVIATE A PARTY'S NAME WHEN THE FULL NAME OF THE PARTY CAN BE SHOWN BY WIDELY RECOGNIZED INITIALS (WITHOUT PERIODS). [CN 26]
    CASE NAME 27. DO NOT ABBREVIATE UNITED STATES. [CN 27]

1 131 201 305 404 503   135 U.S. 342
Yale Lock Manufacturing Company v. Berkshire National Bank (May 5, 1890)
M/B: Yale Lock Manufacturing Co. v. Berkshire National Bank, 135 U.S. 342 (1890).
LR: Yale Lock Mfg. Co. v. Berkshire Nat'l Bank, 135 U.S. 342 (1890).

2 132 202 306 405 504   343 U.S. 214
Ray, Chairman of the State Democratic Executive Committee of Alabama, v. Blair (April 3, 1952)
M/B: Ray v. Blair, 343 U.S. 214 (1952).

3 133 203 307 406 505   333 U.S. 591
Commissioner of Internal Revenue v. Sunnen (April 5, 1948)
M/B: Commissioner v. Sunnen, 333 U.S. 591 (1948).

4 134 204 308 407 506   346 U.S. 119
Securities & Exchange Commission v. Ralston Purina Co. (June 8, 1953)
M/B: SEC v. Ralston Purina Co., 346 U.S. 119 (1953).

5 135 205 309 408 507   434 U.S. 159
United States v. New York Telephone Co. (December 7, 1977)
M/B: United States v. New York Telephone Co., 434 U.S. 159 (1977).
LR: United States v. New York Tel. Co., 434 U.S. 159 (1977).

6 136 206 310 409 508   322 U.S. 238
Hazel-Atlas Glass Co. v. Hartford-Empire Co. (May 15, 1944)
M/B: Hazel-Atlas Glass Co. v. Hartford-Empire Co., 322 U.S. 238 (1944).

7 137 207 311 410 509   252 U.S. 308
Panama Railroad Company v. Toppin (March 15, 1920)
M/B: Panama Railroad v. Toppin, 252 U.S. 308 (1920).
LR: Panama R.R. v. Toppin, 252 U.S. 308 (1920).

8 138 208 312 411 510   379 U.S. 378
United States v. First National City Bank (January 18, 1965)
M/B: United States v. First National City Bank, 379 U.S. 378 (1965).
LR: United States v. First Nat'l City Bank, 379 U.S. 378 (1965).

9 139 209 313 412 511   336 U.S. 176
Wisconsin Electric Power Co. v. United States (February 14, 1949)
M/B: Wisconsin Electric Power Co. v. United States, 336 U.S. 176 (1949).
LR: Wisconsin Elec. Power Co. v. United States, 336 U.S. 176 (1949).

10 140 210 314 413 512   334 U.S. 219
Mandeville Island Farms, Inc. et al. v. American Crystal Sugar Co. (May 10, 1948)
M/B: Mandeville Island Farms v. American Crystal Sugar Co., 334 U.S. 219 (1948).

11 141 211 315 414 513   378 U.S. 1
Malloy v. Hogan, Sheriff (June 15, 1964)

EXERCISE 2. UNITED STATES REPORTS   (CONTINUED)

M/B: Malloy v. Hogan, 378 U.S. 1 (1964).

12 142 212 316 415 514   257 U.S. 308
State of Oklahoma v. State of Texas, United States, Intervener (December 12, 1921)
M/B: Oklahoma v. Texas, 257 U.S. 308 (1921).

13 143 213 317 416 515   297 U.S. 288
Ashwander et al. v. Tennessee Valley Authority et al. (February 17, 1936)
M/B: Ashwander v. TVA, 297 U.S. 288 (1936).

14 144 214 318 417 516   317 U.S. 217
Fisher, Receiver, v. Whiton, Executrix, et al. (December 7, 1942)
M/B: Fisher v. Whiton, 317 U.S. 217 (1942).

15 145 215 319 418 517   328 U.S. 293
Securities & Exchange Commission v. W.J. Howey Co. et al. (May 27, 1946)
M/B: SEC v. W.J. Howey Co., 328 U.S. 293 (1946).

16 146 216 320 419 518   247 U.S. 231
Ex parte Simons, Petitioner (June 3, 1918)
M/B: Ex parte Simons, 247 U.S. 231 (1918).
LR: Ex parte Simons, 247 U.S. 231 (1918).

17 147 217 321 420 519   219 U.S. 121
Assaria State Bank v. Dolley, Bank Commissioner of the State of Kansas (January 3, 1911)
M/B: Assaria State Bank v. Dolley, 219 U.S. 121 (1911).

18 148 218 322 421 520   299 U.S. 248
Landis et al. v. North American Co. (December 7, 1936)
M/B: Landis v. North American Co., 299 U.S. 248 (1936).
LR: Landis v. North Am. Co., 299 U.S. 248 (1936).

19 149 219 323 422 521   332 U.S. 407
Priebe & Sons, Inc. v. United States (November 17, 1947)
M/B: Priebe & Sons v. United States, 332 U.S. 407 (1947).

20 150 220 324 423 522   146 U.S. 338
United States v. Dunnington; Dunnington v. United States (December 8, 1892)
M/B: United States v. Dunnington, 146 U.S. 338 (1892).

21 151 221 325 424 523   251 U.S. 146
Hamilton, Collector of Internal Revenue for the Collection District of Kentucky, v. Kentucky Distilleries & Warehouse Company (December 15, 1919)
M/B: Hamilton v. Kentucky Distilleries & Warehouse, 251 U.S. 146 (1919).
Note: The students should not cite Dryfoos v. Edwards for this problem. The Dryfoos case was consolidated with the Hamilton case on appeal and is listed second.

22 152 222 326 425 524   351 U.S. 105
National Labor Relations Board v. Babcock & Wilcox Co. (April 30, 1956)
M/B: NLRB v. Babcock & Wilcox Co., 351 U.S. 105 (1956).

23 153 223 327 426 525   385 U.S. 276
Woodby v. Immigration and Naturalization Service (December 12, 1966)
M/B: Woodby v. Immigration & Naturalization Service, 385 U.S. 276 (1966).
LR: Woodby v. Immigration & Naturalization Serv., 385 U.S. 276 (1966).
Note: "INS" may be a widely enough recognized abbreviation for the Immigration & Naturalization Service to be proper and should also be counted as correct.

24 154 224 328 427 526   149 U.S. 273
United States v. Mock (May 1, 1893)
M/B: United States v. Mock, 149 U.S. 273 (1893).

EXERCISE 2.   UNITED STATES REPORTS   (CONTINUED)

25 155 225 329 428 527   301 U.S. 402
United States et al. v. American Sheet & Tin Plate Co. et al. (May 17, 1937)
M/B: United States v. American Sheet & Tin Plate Co., 301 U.S. 402 (1937).

26 156 226 330 429 528   312 U.S. 410
Equitable Life Insurance Co. of Iowa v. Halsey, Stuart & Co. (March 3, 1941)
M/B: Equitable Life Insurance Co. v. Halsey, Stuart & Co., 312 U.S. 410 (1941).
LR: Equitable Life Ins. Co. v. Halsey, Stuart & Co., 312 U.S. 410 (1941).

27 157 227 331 430 529   258 U.S. 483
Federal Trade Commission v. Winsted Hosiery Company (April 24, 1922)
M/B: FTC v. Winsted Hosiery Co., 258 U.S. 483 (1922).

28 158 228 332 431 530   297 U.S. 500
Terminal Warehouse Co. v. Pennsylvania Railroad Co. et al. (March 2, 1936)
M/B: Terminal Warehouse v. Pennsylvania Railroad, 297 U.S. 500 (1936).
LR: Terminal Warehouse v. Pennsylvania R.R., 297 U.S. 500 (1936).

29 159 229 333 432 531   328 U.S. 193
Butz, Secretary of Agriculture, et al. v. Glover Livestock Commission Co., Inc. (March 28, 1973)
M/B: Butz v. Glover Livestock Commission Co., 328 U.S. 193 (1973).
LR: Butz v. Glover Livestock Comm'n Co., 328 U.S. 193 (1973).

30 160 230 334 433 532   349 U.S. 1
Granville-Smith v. Granville-Smith (April 11, 1955)
M/B: Granville-Smith v. Granville-Smith, 349 U.S. 1 (1955).

31 161 231 335 434 533   118 U.S. 271
Mullan & Another v. United States (May 10, 1886)
M/B: Mullan v. United States, 118 U.S. 271 (1886).

32 162 232 336 435 534   282 U.S. 481
Russian Volunteer Fleet v. United States (February 24, 1931)
M/B: Russian Volunteer Fleet v. United States, 282 U.S. 481 (1931).

33 163 233 337 436 535   314 U.S. 212
United States v. Kansas Flour Mills Corporation (December 8, 1941)
M/B: United States v. Kansas Flour Mills Corp., 314 U.S. 212 (1941).

34 164 234 338 437 536   243 U.S. 210
Hawkins v. Bleakly, Auditor of the State of Iowa, et al. (March 6, 1917)
M/B: Hawkins v. Bleakly, 243 U.S. 210 (1917).

35 165 235 339 438 537   367 U.S. 687
American Automobile Association v. United States (June 19, 1961)
M/B: American Automobile Association v. United States, 367 U.S. 687 (1961).
LR: American Auto. Ass'n v. United States, 367 U.S. 687 (1961).
Note: "AAA" may be widely enough known to be an acceptable abbreviation of "American Automobile Association" and should be accepted as correct.

36 166 236 340 439 538   333 U.S. 683
Federal Trade Commission v. Cement Institute et al. (April 26, 1948)
M/B: FTC v. Cement Institute, 333 U.S. 683 (1948).
LR: FTC v. Cement Inst., 333 U.S. 683 (1948).

37 167 237 341 440 539   380 U.S. 300
American Ship Building Co. v. National Labor Relations Board (March 29, 1965)
M/B: American Ship Building Co. v. NLRB, 380 U.S. 300 (1965).
LR: American Ship Bldg. Co. v. NLRB, 380 U.S. 300 (1965).

38 168 238 342 441 540   369 U.S. 404
National Labor Relations Board v. Walton Manufacturing Co. et al. (April 9, 1962)
M/B: NLRB v. Walton Manufacturing Co., 369 U.S. 404 (1962).
LR: NLRB v. Walton Mfg. Co., 369 U.S. 404 (1962).

EXERCISE 2. UNITED STATES REPORTS   (CONTINUED)

39 169 239 343 442 541   206 U.S. 158
Yates v. Jones National Bank (May 13, 1907)
M/B: Yates v. Jones National Bank, 206 U.S. 158 (1907).
LR: Yates v. Jones Nat'l Bank, 206 U.S. 158 (1907).

40 170 240 344 443 542   210 U.S. 339
Bobbs-Merrill Company, v. Straus et al. doing business as R. H. Macy & Company (June 1, 1908)
M/B: Bobbs-Merrill Co. v. Straus, 210 U.S. 339 (1908).

41 171 241 345 444 543   382 U.S. 323
Katchen v. Landy, Trustee in Bankruptcy (January 17, 1966)
M/B: Katchen v. Landy, 382 U.S. 323 (1966).

42 172 242 346 445 544   373 U.S. 221
National Labor Relations Board v. Erie Resistor Corp. et al. (May 13, 1963)
M/B: NLRB v. Erie Resistor Corp., 373 U.S. 221 (1963).

43 173 243 347 446 545   365 U.S. 624
United States v. Virginia Electric & Power Co. (April 3, 1961)
M/B: United States v. Virginia Electric & Power Co., 365 U.S. 624 (1961).
LR: United States v. Virginia Elec. & Power Co., 365 U.S. 624 (1961).

44 174 244 348 447 546   317 U.S. 217
Fisher, Receiver, v. Whiton, Executrix, et al. (December 7, 1942)
M/B: Fisher v. Whiton, 317 U.S. 217 (1942).

45 175 245 349 448 547   296 U.S. 459
Radio Corporation of America v. Raytheon Manufacturing Co. (December 23, 1935)
M/B: Radio Corp. of America v. Raytheon Manufacturing Co., 296 U.S. 459 (1935).
LR: Radio Corp. of Am. v. Raytheon Mfg. Co., 296 U.S. 459

46 176 246 350 449 548   345 U.S. 427
Calmar Steamship Corp. v. Scott et al. (April 27, 1953)
M/B: Calmar Steamship Corp. v. Scott, 345 U.S. 427 (1953).
LR: Calmar S.S. Corp. v. Scott, 345 U.S. 427 (1953).

47 177 247 351 450 549   340 U.S. 474
Universal Camera Corp. v. National Labor Relations Board (February 26, 1951)
M/B: Universal Camera Corp. v. NLRB, 340 U.S. 474 (1951).

48 178 248 352 451 550   358 U.S. 242
International. Boxing Club of New York, Inc., et al. v. United States (January 12, 1959)
M/B: International Boxing Club v. United States, 358 U.S. 242 (1959).

49 179 249 353 452 551   359 U.S. 500
Beacon Theatres, Inc. v. Westover, U.S. District Judge, et al. (May 25, 1959)
M/B: Beacon Theatres v. Westover, 359 U.S. 500 (1959).

50 180 250 354 453 552   234 U.S. 245
United States v. First National Bank of Detroit, Minnesota (June 8, 1914)
M/B: United States v. First National Bank, 234 U.S. 245 (1914).
LR: United States v. First Nat'l Bank, 234 U.S. 245 (1914).

51 181 251 355 454 553   272 U.S. 321
United States v. One Ford Coupe Automobile (November 22, 1926)
M/B: United States v. One Ford Coupe Automobile, 272 U.S. 321 (1926).
LR: United States v. One Ford Coupe Auto., 272 U.S. 321 (1926).

52 182 252 356 455 554   362 U.S. 458
Maryland and Virginia Milk Producers Association, Inc., v. United States (May 2, 1960)
M/B: Maryland & Virginia Milk Producers Association, v. United States, 362 U.S. 458 (1960).

EXERCISE 2. UNITED STATES REPORTS   (CONTINUED)

LR: Maryland & Va. Milk Producers Ass'n, v. United States, 362 U.S. 458 (1960).

53 183 253 357 456 555   257 U.S. 85
Pennsylvania Railroad Company v. Weber, Surviving Partner of Jacoby and Weber, Copartners, Trading Under the Firm Name of W.F. Jacoby & Company (November 7, 1921)
M/B: Pennsylvania Railroad v. Weber, 257 U.S. 85 (1921).
LR: Pennsylvania R.R. v. Weber, 257 U.S. 85 (1921).

54 184 254 358 457 556   359 U.S. 231
Glus v. Brooklyn Eastern District Terminal (April 20, 1959)
M/B: Glus v. Brooklyn Eastern District Terminal, 359 U.S. 231 (1959).
LR: Glus v. Brooklyn E. Dist. Terminal, 359 U.S. 231 (1959).

55 185 255 359 458 557   250 U.S. 153
Public Service Company of Northern Illinois v. Corboy, Drainage Commissioner of the Calumet Ditch (June 2, 1919)
M/B: Public Service Co. v. Corboy, 250 U.S. 153 (1919).
LR: Public Serv. Co. v. Corboy, 250 U.S. 153 (1919).
Note: "PSC" might be a widely enough known abbreviation of "Public Service Co." and should be accepted as correct.

56 186 256 360 459 558   252 U.S. 538
Estate of P.D. Beckwith, Inc. v. Commissioner of Patents (April 19, 1920)
M/B: Estate of P.D. Beckwith, Inc. v. Commissioner of Patents, 252 U.S. 538 (1920).

57 187 257 361 460 559   256 U.S. 170
Marcus Brown Holding Company, Inc. v. Feldman et al. (April 18, 1921)
M/B: Marcus Brown Holding Co. v. Feldman, 256 U.S. 170 (1921).

58 188 258 362 461 560   220 U.S. 428
Diamond Rubber Company of New York v. Consolidated Rubber Tire Company (April 10, 1911)
M/B: Diamond Rubber Co. v. Consolidated Rubber Tire Co., 220 U.S. 428 (1911).

59 189 259 363 462 561   334 U.S. 624
United States v. John J. Felin & Co., Inc. (June 14, 1948)
M/B: United States v. John J. Felin & Co., 334 U.S. 624 (1948).

60 190 260 364 463 562   175 U.S. 178
Coudert, Administrator, v. United States (November 20, 1899)
M/B: Coudert v. United States, 175 U.S. 178 (1899).

61 191 261 365 464 563   303 U.S. 283
Saint Paul Mercury Indemnity Co. v. Red Cab Company (February 28, 1938)
M/B: Saint Paul Mercury Indemnity Co. v. Red Cab Co., 303 U.S. 283 (1938).
LR: Saint Paul Mercury Indem. Co. v. Red Cab Co., 303 U.S. 283 (1938).

62 192 262 366 465 564   244 U.S. 332
Erie Railroad Company v. Stone et al., Partners, Doing Business Under the Name of Stone & Noble (June 4, 1917)
M/B: Erie Railroad v. Stone, 244 U.S. 332 (1917).
LR: Erie R.R. v. Stone, 244 U.S. 332 (1917).

63 193 263 367 466 565   336 U.S. 220
Daniel, Attorney General, et al. v. Family Security Life Insurance Co. et al. (February 28, 1949)
M/B: Daniel v. Family Security Life Insurance Co., 336 U.S. 220 (1949).
LR: Daniel v. Family Sec. Life Ins. Co., 336 U.S. 220 (1949).

64 194 264 368 467 566   383 U.S. 715
United Mine Workers of America v. Gibbs (March 28, 1966)
M/B: United Mine Workers v. Gibbs, 383 U.S. 715 (1966) OR UMW v. Gibbs, 383 U.S. 715 (1966).

EXERCISE 2. UNITED STATES REPORTS   (CONTINUED)

65 195 265 369 468 567   343 U.S. 90
Lilly et al. v. Commissioner of Internal Revenue (March 10, 1952)
M/B: Lilly v. Commissioner, 343 U.S. 90 (1952).

66 196 266 370 469 568   262 U.S. 361
Houston Coal Company v. United States (June 4, 1923)
M/B: Houston Coal Co. v. United States, 262 U.S. 361 (1923).

67 197 267 371 470 569   321 U.S. 126
B. F. Goodrich Co. v. United States (January 31, 1944)
M/B: B.F. Goodrich Co. v. United States, 321 U.S. 126 (1944).

68 198 268 372 471 570   339 U.S. 186
United States et al. v. United States Smelting Refining & Mining Co. et al. (March 27, 1950)
M/B: United States v. United States Smelting Refining & Mining Co., 339 U.S. 186 (1950).
LR: United States v. United States Smelting Ref. & Mining Co., 339 U.S. 186 (1950).

69 199 269 373 472 571   310 U.S. 354
Ex Parte Bransford, County Treasurer of Pima County, Arizona, etc. (May 20, 1940)
M/B: Ex parte Bransford, 310 U.S. 354 (1940).
LR: Ex parte Bransford, 310 U.S. 354 (1940).

70 200 270 374 473 572   288 U.S. 152
Atlantic City Electric Co. v. Commissioner of Internal Revenue (February 6, 1933)
M/B: Atlantic City Electric Co. v. Commissioner, 288 U.S. 152 (1933).
LR: Atlantic City Elec. Co. v. Commissioner, 288 U.S. 152 (1933).

71 101 271 375 474 573   273 U.S. 83
Public Utilities Commission of Rhode Island et al. v. Attleboro Steam & Electric Company (January 3, 1927)
M/B: Public Utilities Commission v. Attleboro Steam & Electric Co., 273 U.S. 83 (1927).
LR: Public Utils. Comm'n v. Attleboro Steam & Elec. Co., 273 U.S. 83 (1927).
Note: "PUC" is probably a widely enough known abbreviation of "Public Utilities Commission" to be acceptable and should be considered correct.

72 102 272 376 475 574   263 U.S. 1
Frese, Administratrix of Frese, v. Chicago, Burlington & Quincy Railroad Company (October 15, 1923)
M/B: Frese v. Chicago, Burlington & Quincy Railroad, 263 U.S. 1 (1923).
LR: Frese v. Chicago, B. & Q.R.R., 263 U.S. 1 (1923).

73 103 273 377 476 575   270 U.S. 59
Millers' Indemnity Underwriters v. Nellie Boudreaux Braud and Ed. J. Braud (February 1, 1926)
M/B: Millers' Indemnity Underwriters v. Braud, 270 U.S. 59 (1926).
LR: Millers' Indem. Underwriters v. Braud, 270 U.S. 59 (1926).

74 104 274 378 477 576   332 U.S. 194
Securities & Exchange Commission v. Chenery Corporation et al. (June 23, 1947)
M/B: SEC v. Chenery Corp., 332 U.S. 194 (1947).

75 105 275 379 478 577   171 U.S. 220
Ely's Administrator v. United States (May 31, 1898)
M/B: Ely's Administrator v. United States, 171 U.S. 220 (1898).
LR: Ely's Adm'r v. United States, 171 U.S. 220 (1898).

76 106 276 380 479 578   133 U.S. 67
Schrader v. Manufacturers' National Bank of Chicago (January 20, 1890)
M/B: Schrader v. Manufacturers' National Bank, 133 U.S. 67 (1890).
LR: Schrader v. Manufacturers' Nat'l Bank, 133 U.S. 67 (1890).

EXERCISE 2.   UNITED STATES REPORTS   (CONTINUED)

77 107 277 381 480 579   322 U.S. 31
United States et al. v. Marshall Transport Co. et al. (May 1, 1944)
M/B: United States v. Marshall Transport Co., 322 U.S. 31 (1944).
LR: United States v. Marshall Transp. Co., 322 U.S. 31 (1944).

78 108 278 382 481 580   308 U.S. 256
United States v. Sponenbarger et al. (December 4, 1939)
M/B: United States v. Sponenbarger, 308 U.S. 256 (1939).

79 109 279 383 482 581   263 U.S. 103
Des Moines National Bank v. Fairweather, Mayor; et al. (November 12, 1923)
M/B: Des Moines National Bank v. Fairweather, 263 U.S. 103 (1923).
LR: Des Moines Nat'l Bank v. Fairweather, 263 U.S. 103 (1923).

80 110 280 384 483 582   342 U.S. 437
Perkins v. Benguet Consolidated Mining Co. et al. (March 3, 1952)
M/B: Perkins v. Benguet Consolidated Mining Co., 342 U.S. 437 (1952).
LR: Perkins v. Benguet Consol. Mining Co., 342 U.S. 437 (1952).

81 111 281 385 484 583   258 U.S. 365
Exporters of Manufacturers' Products, Inc. v. Butterworth-Judson Company
(April 10, 1922)
M/B: Exporters of Manufacturers' Products, Inc. v. Butterworth-Judson Co.,
258 U.S. 365 (1922).
LR: Exporters of Mfrs' Prods., Inc. v. Butterworth-Judson Co., 258 U.S. 365
(1922).

82 112 282 386 485 584   166 U.S. 601
United States v. Greathouse (April 19, 1897)
M/B: United States v. Greathouse, 166 U.S. 601 (1897).

83 113 283 387 486 585   330 U.S. 545
Walling, Wage and Hour Administrator, v. General Industries Co. (March 31,
1947)
M/B: Walling v. General Industries Co., 330 U.S. 545 (1947).
LR: Walling v. General Indus. Co., 330 U.S. 545 (1947).

84 114 284 388 487 586   276 U.S. 467
Alaska Packers Association v. Industrial Accident Commission et al. (April 9,
1928)
M/B: Alaska Packers Association v. Industrial Accident Commission, 276 U.S.
467 (1928).
LR: Alaska Packers Ass'n v. Industrial Accident Comm'n, 276 U.S. 467 (1928).

85 115 285 389 488 587   266 U.S. 503
Farmers & Mechanics National Bank of Fort Worth, Texas v. Wilkinson, Trustee,
and the United States (January 5, 1925)
M/B: Farmers & Mechanics National Bank v. Wilkinson, 266 U.S. 503 (1925).
LR: Farmers & Mechanics Nat'l Bank v. Wilkinson, 266 U.S. 503 (1925).

86 116 286 390 489 588   312 U.S. 195
Armour & Company v. Alton Railroad Co. et al. (February 3, 1941)
M/B: Armour & Co. v. Alton Railroad, 312 U.S. 195 (1941).
LR: Armour & Co. v. Alton R.R., 312 U.S. 195 (1941).

87 117 287 391 490 589   253 U.S. 300
Ex Parte Peterson, As Receiver of the Interstate Coal Company, Inc.,
Petitioner (June 1, 1920)
M/B: Ex parte Peterson, 253 U.S. 300 (1920).
LR: Ex parte Peterson, 253 U.S. 300 (1920).

88 118 288 392 491 590   261 U.S. 140
Minnesota Commercial Men's Association v. Benn, Executrix of Benn (February
19, 1923)
M/B: Minnesota Commercial Men's Association v. Benn, 261 U.S. 140 (1923).
LR: Minnesota Commercial Men's Ass'n v. Benn, 261 U.S. 140 (1923).

EXERCISE 2. UNITED STATES REPORTS   (CONTINUED)

89 119 289 393 492 591   295 U.S. 295
Realty Associates Securities Corp. et al. v. O'Connor et al. (April 29, 1935)
M/B: Realty Associates Securities Corp. v. O'Connor, 295 U.S. 295 (1935).
LR: Realty Assocs. Sec. Corp. v. O'Connor, 295 U.S. 295 (1935).

90 120 290 394 493 592   291 U.S. 227
Clark's Ferry Bridge Co. v. Public Service Commission of Pennsylvania
(February 5, 1934)
M/B: Clark's Ferry Bridge Co. v. Public Service Commission, 291 U.S. 227 (1934).
LR: Clark's Ferry Bridge Co. v. Public Serv. Comm'n, 291 U.S. 227 (1934).
Note: "PSC" is also correct.

91 121 291 395 494 593   316 U.S. 4
Schipps-Howard Radio, Inc. v. Federal Communications Commission (April 6, 1942)
M/B: Schipps-Howard Radio, Inc. v. FCC, 316 U.S. 4 (1942).

92 122 292 396 495 594   302 U.S. 556
Lanasa Fruit Steamship & Importing Co. v. Universal Insurance Co. (January 10, 1938)
M/B: Lanasa Fruit Steamship & Importing Co. v. Universal Insurance Co., 302 U.S. 556 (1938).
LR: Lanasa Fruit S.S. & Importing Co. v. Universal Ins. Co., 302 U.S. 556 (1938).

93 123 293 397 496 595   355 U.S. 587
United States v. R. F. Ball Construction Co., Inc., et al. (March 3, 1958)
M/B: United States v. R.F. Ball Construction Co., 355 U.S. 587 (1958).
LR: United States v. R.F. Ball Constr. Co., 355 U.S. 587 (1958).

94 124 294 398 497 596   308 U.S. 241
National Labor Relations Board v. Newport News Shipbuilding & Dry Dock Co.
(December 4, 1939)
M/B: NLRB v. Newport News Shipbuilding & Dry Dock Co. 308 U.S. 241 (1939).

95 125 295 399 498 597   277 U.S. 258
Jenkins, Receiver, et al. v. National Surety Company (May 14, 1928)
M/B: Jenkins v. National Surety Co., 277 U.S. 258 (1928).
LR: Jenkins v. National Sur. Co., 277 U.S. 258 (1928).

96 126 296 400 499 598   251 U.S. 108
Evans, Sole Surviving Receiver of the Citizens & Screven County Bank, v.
National Bank of Savannah (December 8, 1919)
M/B: Evans v. National Bank, 251 U.S. 108 (1919).

97 127 297 301 500 599   201 U.S. 344
York Manufacturing Company v. Cassell (April 2, 1906)
M/B: York Manufacturing Co. v. Cassell, 201 U.S. 344 (1906).
LR: York Mfg. Co. v. Cassell, 201 U.S. 344 (1906).

98 128 298 302 401 600   267 U.S. 233
A. B. Small Company v. American Sugar Refining Company (March 2, 1925)
M/B: A.B. Small Co. v. American Sugar Refining Co., 267 U.S. 233 (1925).
LR: A.B. Small Co. v. American Sugar Ref. Co., 267 U.S. 233 (1925).

99 129 299 303 402 501   408 U.S. 204
Mancusi, Correctional Superintendent v. Stubbs (June 26, 1972)
M/B: Mancusi v. Stubbs, 408 U.S. 204 (1972).

100 130 300 304 403 502   376 U.S. 86
United States v. Wiesenfeld Warehouse Co. (February 17, 1964)
M/B: United States v. Wiesenfeld Warehouse Co., 376 U.S. 86 (1964).
LR: United States v. Wiesenfeld Warehouse Co., 376 U.S. 86 (1964).

LIBRARY EXERCISE 3. PARALLEL CITATION OF UNITED STATES REPORTS.

INSTRUCTOR'S NOTE: The students are required to find the case that begins on the page listed for their problem number in the designated volume of United States Reports and to cite that case using a parallel citation to all three Supreme Court reporters. They are to use the appropriate volume of Shepard's Citations to find the parallel citations. If the appropriate Shepard's volume is unavailable, they are to use the "Table of Cases" in one of the Supreme Court digests to find the parallel citations. (Note that the citation below is to a different page in the same volume that the students used to complete Exercise 2.)

The following two Quick-Reference FED Abbreviations are particularly relevant to this exercise:

FEDERAL COURT CITATION 4. IF PARALLEL CITATIONS TO U.S. SUPREME COURT DECISIONS ARE USED, FOLLOW THE TRADITIONAL PRACTICE OF CITING UNITED STATES REPORTS FIRST, WEST'S SUPREME COURT REPORTER SECOND, AND THE LAWYERS' EDITION THIRD. [FED 4]

FEDERAL COURT CITATION 5. ABBREVIATE WEST'S SUPREME COURT REPORTER TO "S. Ct." AND THE LAWYERS' EDITION TO "L. Ed." OR "L. Ed. 2d." [FED 5]

1 131 201 305 404 503   135 U.S. 100
Leisy v. Hardin (April 28, 1890)
M/B: Leisy v. Hardin, 135 U.S. 100, 10 S. Ct. 681, 34 L. Ed. 128 (1890).

2 132 202 306 405 504   343 U.S. 579
Youngstown Sheet & Tube Co. et al. v. Sawyer (June 2, 1952)
M/B: Youngstown Sheet & Tube Co. v. Sawyer, 343 U.S. 579, 72 S. Ct. 863, 96 L. Ed. 1153 (1952).

3 133 203 307 406 505   333 U.S. 364
United States v. United States Gypsum Co. et al. (March 8, 1948)
M/B: United States v. United States Gypsum Co., 333 U.S. 364, 68 S. Ct. 525, 92 L. Ed. 746 (1948).

4 134 204 308 407 506   346 U.S. 537
Theatre Enterprises, Inc. v. Paramount Film Distributing Corp. et al. (January 4, 1954)
M/B: Theatre Enterprises v. Paramount Film Distributing Corp., 346 U.S. 537 (1954).
LR: Theatre Enterprises v. Paramount Film Distrib. Corp., 346 U.S. 537 (1954).

5 135 205 309 408 507   434 U.S. 246
Quilloin v. Walcott et vir (January 10, 1978)
M/B: Quilloin v. Walcott, 434 U.S. 246, 98 S. Ct. 549, 54 L. Ed. 2d 511 (1978).

6 136 206 310 409 508   322 U.S. 137
Allen Calculators, Inc. v. National Cash Register Co. et al. (May 1, 1944)
M/B: Allen Calculators, Inc. v. National Cash Register Co., 322 U.S. 137, 64 S. Ct. 905, 88 L. Ed. 1188 (1944).

7 137 207 311 410 509   252 U.S. 416
State of Missouri v. Holland, United States Game Warden (April 19, 1920)
M/B: Missouri v. Holland, 252 U.S. 416, 40 S. Ct. 382, 64 L. Ed. 641 (1920).

8 138 208 312 411 510   379 U.S. 294
Katzenbach, Acting Attorney General, et al. v. McClung et al. (December 14, 1964)
M/B: Katzenbach v. McClung, 379 U.S. 294, 85 S. Ct. 377, 13 L. Ed. 2d 290 (1964).

9 139 209 313 412 511   336 U.S. 525
H. P. Hood & Sons, Inc. v. Du Mond, Commissioner of Agriculture and Markets (April 4, 1949)

EXERCISE 3.   PARALLEL CITATION OF UNITED STATES REPORTS   (CONTINUED)

M/B: H.P. Hood & Sons v. Du Mond, 336 U.S. 525, 69 S. Ct. 657, 93 L. Ed. 865 (1949).

10 140 210 314 413 512   334 U.S. 653
Central Greyhound Lines, Inc. v. Mealey et al. (June 14, 1948)
M/B: Central Greyhound Lines v. Mealey, 334 U.S. 653, 68 S. Ct. 1260, 92 L. Ed. 1633 (1948).

11 141 211 315 414 513   378 U.S. 158
United States v. Penn-Olin Chemical Co. et al. (June 22, 1964)
M/B: United States v. Penn-Olin Chemical Co., 378 U.S. 158, 84 S. Ct. 1710, 12 L. Ed. 2d 775 (1964).
LR: United States v. Penn-Olin Chem. Co., 378 U.S. 158, 84 S. Ct. 1710, 12 L. Ed. 2d 775 (1964).

12 142 212 316 415 514   257 U.S. 377
American Column & Lumber Company et al. v. United States (December 19, 1921)
M/B: American Column & Lumber Co. v. United States, 257 U.S. 377, 42 S. Ct. 114, 66 L. Ed. 284 (1921).

13 143 213 317 416 515   297 U.S. 537
Wright et al. v. Central Kentucky Natural Gas Co. et al. (March 16, 1936)
M/B: Wright v. Central Kentucky Natural Gas Co., 297 U.S. 537, 56 S. Ct. 578, 80 L. Ed. 850 (1936).
LR: Wright v. Central Ky. Natural Gas Co., 297 U.S. 537, 56 S. Ct. 578, 80 L. Ed. 850 (1936).

14 144 214 318 417 516   317 U.S. 341
Parker, Director of Agriculture, et al. v. Brown (January 4, 1943)
M/B: Parker v. Brown, 317 U.S. 341, 63 S. Ct. 307, 87 L. Ed. 315 (1943).

15 145 215 319 418 517   328 U.S. 408
Prudential Insurance Company v. Benjamin, Insurance Commissioner (June 3, 1946)
M/B: Prudential Insurance Co. v. Benjamin, 328 U.S. 408, 66 S. Ct. 1142, 90 L. Ed. 1342 (1946).
LR: Prudential Ins. Co. v. Benjamin, 328 U.S. 408, 66 S. Ct. 1142, 90 L. Ed. 1342 (1946).

16 146 216 320 419 518   247 U.S. 251
Hammer, United States Attorney for the Western District of North Carolina v. Dagenhart et al. (June 3, 1918)
M/B: Hammer v. Dagenhart, 247 U.S. 251, 38 S. Ct. 529, 62 L. Ed. 1101 (1918).

17 147 217 321 420 519   219 U.S. 346
Muskrat v. United States; Brown and Gritts v. United States (January 23, 1911)
M/B: Muskrat v. United States, 219 U.S. 346, 31 S. Ct. 250, 55 L. Ed. 246 (1911).

18 148 218 322 421 520   299 U.S. 304
United States v. Curtiss-Wright Export Corp. et al. (December 21, 1936)
M/B: United States v. Curtiss-Wright Export Corp., 299 U.S. 304, 57 S. Ct. 216, 81 L. Ed. 255 (1936).

19 149 219 323 422 521   332 U.S. 689
United States v. Sullivan, Trading as Sullivan's Pharmacy (January 19, 1948)
M/B: United States v. Sullivan, 332 U.S. 689, 68 S. Ct. 331, 92 L. Ed. 297 (1948).

20 150 220 324 423 522   146 U.S. 183
Cook v. Hart (November 21, 1892)
M/B: Cook v. Hart, 146 U.S. 183, 13 S. Ct. 40, 36 L. Ed. 934 (1892).

21 151 221 325 424 523   251 U.S. 417
United States v. United States Steel Corporation et al. (March 1, 1920)
M/B: United States v. United States Steel Corp., 251 U.S. 417, 40 S. Ct. 293, 64 L. Ed. 343 (1920).

EXERCISE 3. PARALLEL CITATION OF UNITED STATES REPORTS   (CONTINUED)

22 152 222 326 425 524   351 U.S. 345
Cecil Reginald Jay v. John P. Boyd, District Director, Immigration and
Naturalization Service (June 11, 1956)
M/B: Jay v. Boyd, 351 U.S. 345, 76 S. Ct. 919, 100 L. Ed. 1242 (1956).

23 153 223 327 426 525   385 U.S. 493
Garrity et al. v. New Jersey (January 16, 1967)
M/B: Garrity v. New Jersey, 385 U.S. 493, 87 S. Ct. 616, 17 L. Ed. 2d 562
(1967).

24 154 224 328 427 526   149 U.S. 481
Bibb v. Allen (May 10, 1893)
M/B: Bibb v. Allen, 149 U.S. 481, 13 S. Ct. 950, 37 L. Ed. 819 (1893).

25 155 225 329 428 527   301 U.S. 548
Steward Machine Co. v. Davis, Collector of Internal Revenue (May 24, 1937)
M/B: Steward Machine Co. v. Davis, 301 U.S. 548, 57 S. Ct. 883, 81 L. Ed.
1279 (1937).
LR: Steward Mach. Co. v. Davis, 301 U.S. 548, 57 S. Ct. 883, 81 L. Ed. 1279
(1937).

26 156 226 330 429 528   312 U.S. 100
United States v. Darby (February 3, 1941)
M/B: United States v. Darby, 312 U.S. 100, 61 S. Ct. 451, 85 L. Ed. 609
(1941).

27 157 227 331 430 529   258 U.S. 495
Stafford et al., Copartners, d/b/a Stafford Brothers, et al. v. Wallace,
Secretary of Agriculture, et al.; Burton et al. v. Clyne, United States
District Attorney for the Northern District of Illinois (May 1, 1922)
M/B: Stafford v. Wallace, 258 U.S. 495, 42 S. Ct. 397, 66 L. Ed. 735 (1922).

28 158 228 332 431 530   297 U.S. 1
United States v. Butler et al., Receivers of Hoosac Mills Corp. (January 6,
1936)
M/B: United States v. Butler, 297 U.S. 1, 56 S. Ct. 312, 80 L. Ed. 477
(1936).

29 159 229 333 432 531   411 U.S. 677
Frontiero et vir v. Richardson, Secretary of Defense, et al. (May 14, 1973)
M/B: Frontiero v. Richardson, 411 U.S. 677, 93 S. Ct. 1764, 36 L. Ed. 2d 583
(1973).

30 160 230 334 433 532   349 U.S. 294
Brown et al. v. Board of Education of Topeka et al. (May 31, 1955)
M/B: Brown v. Board of Education, 349 U.S. 294, 75 S. Ct. 753, 99 L. Ed. 1083
(1955).
LR: Brown v. Board of Educ., 349 U.S. 294, 75 S. Ct. 753, 99 L. Ed. 1083
(1955).

31 161 231 335 434 533   118 U.S. 356
Yick Wo v. Hopkins, Sheriff; Wo Lee v. Hopkins, Sheriff (May 10, 1886)
M/B: Yick Wo v. Hopkins, 118 U.S. 356, 6 S. Ct. 1064, 30 L. Ed. 220 (1886).

32 162 232 336 435 534   282 U.S. 555
Story Parchment Company v. Paterson Parchment Paper Company et al. (February
24, 1931)
M/B: Story Parchment Co. v. Paterson Parchment Paper Co., 282 U.S. 555, 51 S.
Ct. 248, 75 L. Ed. 544 (1931).

33 163 233 337 436 535   314 U.S. 488
Morton Salt Co. v. G.S. Suppriger Co. (January 5, 1942)
M/B: Morton Salt Co. v. G.S. Suppriger Co., 314 U.S. 488, 62 S. Ct. 402, 86
L. Ed. 363 (1942).

34 164 234 338 437 536   243 U.S. 502

EXERCISE 3.   PARALLEL CITATION OF UNITED STATES REPORTS   (CONTINUED)

Motion Picture Patents Company v. Universal Film Manufacturing Company et al. (April 9, 1917)
M/B: Motion Picture Patents Co. v. Universal Film Manufacturing Co., 243 U.S. 502, 37 S. Ct. 416, 61 L. Ed. 871 (1917).
LR: Motion Picture Patents Co. v. Universal Film Mfg. Co., 243 U.S. 502, 37 S. Ct. 416, 61 L. Ed. 871 (1917).

35 165 235 339 438 537   367 U.S. 497
Poe et al. v. Ullman, States Attorney (June 19, 1961)
M/B: Poe v. Ullman, 367 U.S. 497, 81 S. Ct. 1752, 6 L. Ed. 2d 989 (1961).

36 166 236 340 439 538   333 U.S. 287
United States v. Line Material Co. et al. (March 8, 1948)
M/B: United States v. Line Material Co., 333 U.S. 287, 68 S. Ct. 550, 92 L. Ed. 701 (1948).

37 167 237 341 440 539   380 U.S. 479
Dombrowski et al. v. Pfister, Chairman, Joint Legislative Committee on Unamerican Activities of the Louisiana Legislature, et al. (April 26, 1965)
M/B: Dombrowski v. Pfister, 380 U.S. 479, 85 S. Ct. 1116, 14 L. Ed. 2d 22 (1965).

38 168 238 342 441 540   369 U.S. 186
Baker et al. v. Carr et al. (March 26, 1962)
M/B: Baker v. Carr, 369 U.S. 186, 82 S. Ct. 691, 7 L. Ed. 2d 663 (1962).

39 169 239 343 442 541   206 U.S. 46
Kansas v. Colorado et al. Defendants, and the United States, Intervenor (May 13, 1907)
M/B: Kansas v. Colorado, 206 U.S. 46, 27 S. Ct. 655, 51 L. Ed. 956 (1907).

40 170 240 344 443 542   210 U.S. 405
Continental Paper Bag Company v. Eastern Paper Bag Company (June 1, 1908)
M/B: Continental Paper Bag Co. v. Eastern Paper Bag Co., 210 U.S. 405, 28 S. Ct. 748, 52 L. Ed. 1122 (1908).

41 171 241 345 444 543   382 U.S. 172
Walker Process Equipment, Inc. v. Food Machinery & Chemical Corp. (December 6, 1965)
M/B: Walker Process Equipment, Inc. v. Food Machinery & Chemical Corp., 382 U.S. 172, 86 S. Ct. 347, 15 L. Ed. 2d 247 (1965).
LR: Walker Process Equip., Inc. v. Food Mach. & Chem. Corp., 382 U.S. 172, 86 S. Ct. 347, 15 L. Ed. 2d 247 (1965).

42 172 242 346 445 544   373 U.S. 341
Silver, d/b/a Municipal Securities Co., et al. v. New York Stock Exchange (May 20, 1963)
M/B: Silver v. New York Stock Exchange, 373 U.S. 341, 83 S. Ct. 1246, 10 L. Ed. 2d 389 (1963).
LR: Silver v. New York Stock Exch., 373 U.S. 341, 83 S. Ct. 1246, 10 L. Ed. 2d 389 (1963).

43 173 243 347 446 545   365 U.S. 320
Tampa Electric Co. v. Nashville Coal Co. et al. (February 27, 1961)
M/B: Tampa Electric Co. v. Nashville Coal Co., 365 U.S. 320, 81 S. Ct. 623, 5 L. Ed. 2d 580 (1961).
LR: Tampa Elec. Co. v. Nashville Coal Co., 365 U.S. 320, 81 S. Ct. 623, 5 L. Ed. 2d 580 (1961).

44 174 244 348 447 546   317 U.S. 111
Wickard, Secretary of Agriculture, et al. v. Filburn (November 9, 1942)
M/B: Wickard v. Filburn, 317 U.S. 111, 63 S. Ct. 82, 87 L. Ed. 122 (1942).

45 175 245 349 448 547   296 U.S. 287
United States v. Constantine (December 9, 1935)
M/B: United States v. Constantine, 296 U.S. 287, 56 S. Ct. 223, 80 L. Ed. 233 (1935).

EXERCISE 3.   PARALLEL CITATION OF UNITED STATES REPORTS   (CONTINUED)

46 176 246 350 449 548   345 U.S. 22
United States v. Kahriger (March 9, 1953)
M/B: United States v. Kahriger, 345 U.S. 22, 73 S. Ct. 510, 97 L. Ed. 754 (1953).

47 177 247 351 450 549   340 U.S. 349
Dean Milk Co. v. City of Madison et al. (January 15, 1951)
M/B: Dean Milk Co. v. City of Madison, 340 U.S. 349, 71 S. Ct. 295, 95 L. Ed. 329 (1951).

48 178 248 352 451 550   358 U.S. 534
Youngstown Sheet & Tube Co. v. Bowers, Tax Commissioner of Ohio (February 24, 1959)
M/B: Youngstown Sheet & Tube Co. v. Bowers, 358 U.S. 534, 79 S. Ct. 383, 3 L. Ed. 2d 490 (1959).

49 179 249 353 452 551   359 U.S. 207
Klor's, Inc. v. Broadway-Hale Stores, Inc., et al. (April 6, 1959)
M/B: Klor's, Inc. v. Broadway-Hale Stores, 359 U.S. 207, 79 S. Ct. 705, 3 L. Ed. 2d 741 (1959).

50 180 250 354 453 552   234 U.S. 600
Eastern States Retail Lumber Dealers' Association et al. v. United States; McBride, Individually and as President of the Retail Lumbermen's Association v. United States (June 22, 1914)
M/B: Eastern States Retail Lumber Dealers' Association v. United States, 234 U.S. 600, 34 S. Ct. 951, 58 L. Ed. 1490 (1914).
LR: Eastern States Retail Lumber Dealers' Ass'n v. United States, 234 U.S. 600, 34 S. Ct. 951, 58 L. Ed. 1490 (1914).

51 181 251 355 454 553   272 U.S. 476
United States v. General Electric Company et al. (November 23, 1926)
M/B: United States v. General Electric Co., 272 U.S. 476, 47 S. Ct. 192, 71 L. Ed. 362 (1926).
LR: United States v. General Elec. Co., 272 U.S. 476, 47 S. Ct. 192, 71 L. Ed. 362 (1926).

52 182 252 356 455 554   362 U.S. 29
United States v. Parke, Davis & Co. (February 29, 1960)
M/B: United States v. Parke, Davis & Co., 362 U.S. 29, 80 S. Ct. 503, 4 L. Ed. 2d 505 (1960).

53 183 253 357 456 555   257 U.S. 441
Federal Trade Commission v. Beech-Nut Packing Company (January 3, 1922)
M/B: FTC v. Beech-Nut Packing Co., 257 U.S. 441, 42 S. Ct. 150, 66 L. Ed. 307 (1922).

54 184 254 358 457 556   359 U.S. 520
Bibb, Director, Department of Public Safety of Illinois, et al. v. Navajo Freight Lines, Inc., et al. (May 25, 1959)
M/B: Bibb v. Navajo Freight Lines, 359 U.S. 520, 79 S. Ct. 962, 3 L. Ed. 2d 1003 (1959).

55 185 255 359 458 557   250 U.S. 300
United States v. Colgate & Company (June 2, 1919)
M/B: United States v. Colgate & Co., 250 U.S. 300, 39 S. Ct. 465, 63 L. Ed. 992 (1919).

56 186 256 360 459 558   252 U.S. 85
United States v. A. Schrader's Son, Inc. (March 1, 1920)
M/B: United States v. A. Schrader's Son, 252 U.S. 85, 40 S. Ct. 251, 64 L. Ed. 471 (1920).
Note: A student may decide that "Son" in "A. Schrader's Son" does not sufficiently convey that the party is a business entity and thus may properly include "Inc." in the citation and should receive credit for doing so.

EXERCISE 3. PARALLEL CITATION OF UNITED STATES REPORTS   (CONTINUED)

57 187 257 361 460 559   256 U.S. 208
Frey & Son, Incorporated v. Cudahy Packing Company (April 18, 1921)
M/B: <u>Frey & Son v. Cudahy Packing Co.</u>, 256 U.S. 208, 41 S. Ct. 451, 65 L. Ed. 892 (1921).

58 188 258 362 461 560   220 U.S. 373
Dr. Miles Medical Company v. John D. Park & Sons Company (April 3, 1911)
M/B: <u>Dr. Miles Medical Co. v. John D. Park & Sons</u>, 220 U.S. 373, 31 S. Ct. 376, 55 L. Ed. 502 (1911).

59 189 259 363 462 561   334 U.S. 495
United States v. Columbia Steel Co. et al. (June 7, 1948)
M/B: <u>United States v. Columbia Steel Co.</u>, 334 U.S. 495, 68 S. Ct. 1107, 92 L. Ed. 1533 (1948).

60 190 260 364 463 562   175 U.S. 211
Addyston Pipe and Steel Company v. United States (December 4, 1899)
M/B: <u>Addyston Pipe & Steel Co. v. United States</u>, 175 U.S. 211, 20 S. Ct. 96, 44 L. Ed. 136 (1899).

61 191 261 365 464 563   303 U.S. 177
South Carolina State Highway Department et al. v. Barnwell Brothers, Inc., et al. (February 14, 1938)
M/B: <u>South Carolina State Highway Department v. Barnwell Brothers</u>, 303 U.S. 177, 58 S. Ct. 510, 82 L. Ed. 734   (1938).
LR: South Carolina State Highway Dep't v. Barnwell Bros., 303 U.S. 177, 58 S. Ct. 510, 82 L. Ed. 734   (1938).

62 192 262 366 465 564   244 U.S. 310
Seaboard Air Line Railway v. Blackwell (June 4, 1917)
M/B: <u>Seaboard Air Line Railway v. Blackwell</u>, 244 U.S. 310, 37 S. Ct. 640, 61 L. Ed. 1160 (1917).
LR: Seaboard Air Line Ry. v. Blackwell, 244 U.S. 310, 37 S. Ct. 640, 61 L. Ed. 1160 (1917).
<u>Note</u>: "Air" and "Line" are not abbreviated because they are not geographic words (Rule 10.2.2).

63 193 263 367 466 565   336 U.S. 460
United States v. Women's Sportswear Manufacturers Association et al. (March 28, 1949)
M/B: <u>United States v. Women's Sportswear Manufacturers Association</u>, 336 U.S. 460, 69 S. Ct. 714, 93 L. Ed. 805 (1949).
LR: United States v. Women's Sportswear Mfrs. Ass'n, 336 U.S. 460, 69 S. Ct. 714, 93 L. Ed. 805 (1949).

64 194 264 368 467 566   383 U.S. 190
Idaho Sheet Metal Works, Inc. v. Wirtz, Secretary of Labor (February 24, 1966)
M/B: <u>Idaho Sheet Metal Works v. Wirtz</u>, 383 U.S. 190, 86 S. Ct. 737, 15 L. Ed. 2d 694   (1966).

65 195 265 369 468 567   343 U.S. 306
Zorach et al. v. Clauson et al., Constituting the Board of Education of the City of New York, et al. (April 28, 1952)
M/B: <u>Zorach v. Clauson</u>, 343 U.S. 306, 72 S. Ct. 679, 96 L. Ed. 954 (1952).

66 196 266 370 469 568   262 U.S. 390
Meyer v. State of Nebraska (June 4, 1923)
M/B: <u>Meyer v. Nebraska</u>, 262 U.S. 390, 43 S. Ct. 625, 67 L. Ed. 1042 (1923).

67 197 267 371 470 569   321 U.S. 573
Follett v. Town of McCormick (March 27, 1944)
M/B: <u>Follett v. Town of McCormick</u>, 321 U.S. 573, 64 S. Ct. 717, 88 L. Ed. 938 (1944).

68 198 268 372 471 570   339 U.S. 485
United States v. National Association of Real Estate Boards et al. (May 8, 1950)

EXERCISE 3.   PARALLEL CITATION OF UNITED STATES REPORTS   (CONTINUED)

M/B: <u>United States v. National Association of Real Estate Boards</u>, 339 U.S. 485, 70 S. Ct. 711, 94 L. Ed. 1007 (1950).
LR: United States v. National Ass'n of Real Estate Bds., 339 U.S. 485, 70 S. Ct. 711, 94 L. Ed. 1007 (1950).

69 199 269 373 472 571   310 U.S. 150
United States v. Socony-Vacuum Oil Co., Inc., et al. (May 6, 1940)
M/B: <u>United States v. Socony-Vacuum Oil Co.</u>, 310 U.S. 150, 60 S. Ct. 811, 84 L. Ed. 1129 (1940).

70 200 270 374 473 572   288 U.S. 344
Appalachian Coals, Inc., et al. v. United States (March 13, 1933)
M/B: <u>Appalachian Coals, Inc. v. United States</u>, 288 U.S. 344, 53 S. Ct. 471, 77 L. Ed. 825 (1933).

71 101 271 375 474 573   273 U.S. 392
United States v. Trenton Potteries Company et al. (February 21, 1927)
M/B: <u>United States v. Trenton Potteries Co.</u>, 273 U.S. 392, 47 S. Ct. 377, 71 L. Ed. 700 (1927).

72 102 272 376 475 574   263 U.S. 255
Craig v. Hecht, United States Marshal for the Southern District of New York (November 19, 1923)
M/B: <u>Craig v. Hecht</u>, 263 U.S. 255, 44 S. Ct. 103, 68 L. Ed. 293 (1923).

73 103 273 377 476 575   270 U.S. 593
Moore, President of the Odd-Lot Cotton Exchange of New York v. New York Cotton Exchange et al. (April 12, 1926)
M/B: <u>Moore v. New York Cotton Exchange</u>, 270 U.S. 593, 46 S. Ct. 367, 70 L. Ed. 750 (1926).
LR: Moore v. New York Cotton Exch., 270 U.S. 593, 46 S. Ct. 367, 70 L. Ed. 750 (1926).

74 104 274 378 477 576   332 U.S. 392
International Salt Co., Inc. v. United States (November 10, 1947)
M/B: <u>International Salt Co. v. United States</u>, 332 U.S. 392, 68 S. Ct. 12, 92 L. Ed. 20 (1947).

75 105 275 379 478 577   171 U.S. 604
Anderson v. United States (October 24, 1898)
M/B: <u>Anderson v. United States</u>, 171 U.S. 604, 19 S. Ct. 50, 43 L. Ed. 300 (1898).

76 106 276 380 479 578   133 U.S. 375
Quebec Steamship Co. v. Merchant (March 3, 1890)
M/B: <u>Quebec Steamship Co. v. Merchant</u>, 133 U.S. 375, 10 S. Ct. 397, 33 L. Ed. 656 (1890).
LR: Quebec S.S. Co. v. Merchant, 133 U.S. 375, 10 S. Ct. 397, 33 L. Ed. 656 (1890).

77 107 277 381 480 579   322 U.S. 607
Addison, et al. v. Holly Hill Fruit Products, Inc. (June 5, 1944)
M/B: <u>Addison v. Holly Hill Fruit Products, Inc.</u>, 322 U.S. 607, 64 S. Ct. 1215, 88 L. Ed. 1488 (1944).
LR: Addison v. Holly Hill Fruit Prods., Inc., 322 U.S. 607, 64 S. Ct. 1215, 88 L. Ed. 1488 (1944).

78 108 278 382 481 580   308 U.S. 188
United States v. Borden Company et al. (December 4, 1939)
M/B: <u>United States v. Borden Co.</u>, 308 U.S. 188, 60 S. Ct. 182, 84 L. Ed. 181 (1939).

79 109 279 383 482 581   263 U.S. 444
Tidal Oil Co. et al. v. Flanagan (January 7, 1924)
M/B: <u>Tidal Oil Co. v. Flanagan</u>, 263 U.S. 444, 44 S. Ct. 197, 68 L. Ed. 382 (1924).

EXERCISE 3.   PARALLEL CITATION OF UNITED STATES REPORTS   (CONTINUED)

80 110 280 384 483 582   342 U.S. 371
United States v. New Wrinkle, Inc. et al. (February 4, 1952)
M/B: United States v. New Wrinkle, Inc., 342 U.S. 371, 72 S. Ct. 350, 96 L.
Ed. 417 (1952).

81 111 281 385 484 583   258 U.S. 451
United Shoe Machinery Corporation et al. v. United States (April 17, 1922)
M/B: United Shoe Machinery Corp. v. United States, 258 U.S. 451, 42 S. Ct.
363, 66 L. Ed. 708 (1922).
LR: United Shoe Mach. Corp. v. United States, 258 U.S. 451, 42 S. Ct. 363, 66
L. Ed. 708 (1922).

82 112 282 386 485 584   166 U.S. 489
Electric Company v. Dow (April 19, 1897)
M/B: Electric Co. v. Dow, 166 U.S. 489, 17 S. Ct. 645, 41 L. Ed. 1088 (1897).

83 113 283 387 486 585   330 U.S. 743
Bruce's Juices, Inc. v. American Can Co. (April 7, 1947)
M/B: Bruce's Juices, Inc. v. American Can Co., 330 U.S. 743, 67 S. Ct. 1015,
91 L. Ed. 1219 (1947).

84 114 284 388 487 586   276 U.S. 311
Swift & Company et al. v. United States (March 19, 1928)
M/B: Swift & Co. v. United States, 276 U.S. 311, 48 S. Ct. 311, 72 L. Ed. 587
(1928).

85 115 285 389 488 587   266 U.S. 17
Terminal Railroad Association of St. Louis et al. v. United States et al.
(October 13, 1924)
M/B: Terminal Railroad Association v. United States, 266 U.S. 17, 45 S. Ct.
5, 69 L. Ed. 150 (1924).
LR: Terminal R.R. Ass'n v. United States, 266 U.S. 17, 45 S. Ct. 5, 69 L. Ed.
150 (1924).

86 116 286 390 489 588   312 U.S. 600
United States v. Cooper Corporation et al. (March 31, 1941)
M/B: United States v. Cooper Corp., 312 U.S. 600, 61 S. Ct. 742, 85 L. Ed.
1071 (1941).

87 117 287 391 490 589   253 U.S. 421
Federal Trade Commission v. Gratz et al., Copartners doing business under the
Firm Name and Style of Warren, Jones & Gratz, et al. (June 7, 1920)
M/B: FTC v. Gratz, 253 U.S. 421, 40 S. Ct. 572, 64 L. Ed. 993 (1920).

88 118 288 392 491 590   261 U.S. 463
Federal Trade Commission v. Sinclair Refining Company; Federal Trade
Commission v. Standard Oil Company (New Jersey); Federal Trade Commission v.
Gulf Refining Company; Federal Trade Commission v. Maloney Oil & Manufacturing
Company (April 9, 1923)
M/B: FTC v. Sinclair Refining Co., 261 U.S. 463, 43 S. Ct. 450, 67 L. Ed. 746
(1923).
LR: FTC v. Sinclair Ref. Co., 261 U.S. 463, 43 S. Ct. 450, 67 L. Ed. 746
(1923).

89 119 289 393 492 591   295 U.S. 555
Louisville Joint Stock Land Bank v. Radford (May 27, 1935)
M/B: Louisville Joint Stock Land Bank v. Radford, 295 U.S. 555, 55 S. Ct.
854, 79 L. Ed. 1593 (1935).

90 120 290 394 493 592   291 U.S. 491
Landress v. Phoenix Mutual Life Insurance Co. et al. (March 5, 1934)
M/B: Landress v. Phoenix Mutual Life Insurance Co., 291 U.S. 491, 54 S. Ct.
461, 78 L. Ed. 934 (1934).
LR: Landress v. Phoenix Mut. Life Ins. Co., 291 U.S. 491, 54 S. Ct. 461, 78
L. Ed. 934 (1934).

91 121 291 395 494 593   316 U.S. 114

EXERCISE 3.   PARALLEL CITATION OF UNITED STATES REPORTS   (CONTINUED)

Goldstein et al. v. United States (April 27, 1942)
M/B: Goldstein v. United States, 316 U.S. 114, 62 S. Ct. 1000, 86 L. Ed. 1312 (1942).

92 122 292 396 495 594   302 U.S. 379
Nardone et al. v. United States (December 20, 1937)
M/B: Nardone v. United States, 302 U.S. 379, 58 S. Ct. 275, 82 L. Ed. 314 (1937).

93 123 293 397 496 595   355 U.S. 96
Benanti v. United States (December 9, 1957)
M/B: Benanti v. United States, 355 U.S. 96, 78 S. Ct. 155, 2 L. Ed. 2d 126 (1957).

94 124 294 398 497 596   308 U.S. 321
Weiss et al. v. United States (December 11, 1939)
M/B: Weiss v. United States, 308 U.S. 321, 60 S. Ct. 269, 84 L. Ed. 298 (1939).

95 125 295 399 498 597   277 U.S. 438
Olmstead et al. v. United States; Green et al. v. Same; McInnis v. Same (June 4, 1928)
M/B: Olmstead v. United States, 277 U.S. 438, 48 S. Ct. 564, 72 L. Ed. 944 (1928).

96 126 296 400 499 598   251 U.S. 385
Silverthorne Lumber Company, Inc., et al. v. United States (January 26, 1920)
M/B: Silverthorne Lumber Co. v. United States, 251 U.S. 385, 40 S. Ct. 182, 64 L. Ed. 319 (1920).

97 127 297 301 500 599   201 U.S. 43
Hale v. Henkel (March 12, 1906)
M/B: Hale v. Henkel, 201 U.S. 43, 26 S. Ct. 370, 50 L. Ed. 652 (1906).

98 128 298 302 401 600   267 U.S. 132
Carroll et al. v. United States (March 2, 1925)
M/B: Carroll v. United States, 267 U.S. 132, 45 S. Ct. 280, 69 L. Ed. 543 (1925).

99 129 299 303 402 501   408 U.S. 169
Healy et al. v. James et al. (June 26, 1972)
M/B: Healy v. James, 408 U.S. 169, 92 S. Ct. 2338, 33 L. Ed. 2d 266 (1972).

100 130 300 304 403 502   376 U.S. 254
New York Times Co. v. Sullivan (March 9, 1964)
M/B: New York Times Co. v. Sullivan, 376 U.S. 254, 84 S. Ct. 710, 11 L. Ed. 2d 686 (1964).

LIBRARY EXERCISE 4. SUPREME COURT REPORTER.

INSTUCTOR'S NOTE: The students are asked to assume that they know the <u>United States Reports</u> citation of a case, but only the <u>Supreme Court Reporter</u> is available. They are to locate the <u>Supreme Court Reporter</u> volume that covers the volume of <u>United States Reports</u> listed for their problem number. The volumes of <u>United States Reports</u> covered by a given <u>Supreme Court Reporter</u> volume are printed on the outside binding. Using the Table of "Supreme Court Reporter References" in the front of the volume, they are to locate the page at which the case is reported. If they cannot locate the reference table, they are to check for it at the end of the volume. If the table has been deleted during the binding process, they then are to use the appropriate volume of <u>Shepard's Citations</u> to find the <u>Supreme Court Reporter</u> citation. For purposes of this exercise only, the case is to be cited to the <u>Supreme Court Reporter</u> without parallel citations.

The following two Quick-Reference Codes are particularly relevant to this exercise:

FEDERAL COURT CITATION 4. IF PARALLEL CITATIONS TO U.S. SUPREME COURT DECISIONS ARE USED, FOLLOW THE TRADITIONAL PRACTICE OF CITING <u>UNITED STATES REPORTS</u> FIRST, WEST'S <u>SUPREME COURT REPORTER</u> SECOND, AND THE <u>LAWYERS' EDITION</u> THIRD. [FED 4]

FEDERAL COURT CITATION 5. ABBREVIATE WEST'S <u>SUPREME COURT REPORTER</u> TO "S. Ct." AND THE <u>LAWYERS' EDITION</u> TO "L. Ed." OR "L. Ed. 2d." [FED 5]

1 128 210 322 411 590   106 U.S. 95
Brown v. State of Colorado (November 20, 1882)
M/B: <u>Brown v. Colorado</u>, 1 S. Ct. 342 (1882).

2 129 211 323 412 591   106 U.S. 558
Citizens Against Rent Control/Coalition for Fair Housing, et al., Appellants v. City of Berkeley, California (Dec. 14, 1981)
M/B: <u>Citizens Against Rent Control v. City of Berkeley</u>, 102 S. Ct. 434 (1981).
Note: "Coalition for Fair Housing" is not included in the running head and also is an entity different from "Citizens Against Rent Control." Based on Rule 10.2.1, it has been omitted from the citation. ("In long case names, omit words not necessary for identification; the running head . . . may serve as a guide.")

3 130 212 324 413 592   107 U.S. 265
Ex parte Wall (April 16, 1883)
M/B: <u>Ex parte Wall</u>, 2 S. Ct. 569 (1883).
LR: <u>Ex parte</u> Wall, 2 S. Ct. 569 (1883).

4 131 213 325 414 593   107 U.S. 512
State of Minnesota, Petitioner, v. Clover Leaf Creamery Company et al. (Jan. 21, 1981)
M/B: <u>Minnesota v. Clover Leaf Creamery Co.</u>, 101 S. Ct. 715 (1981).

5 132 214 326 415 594   109 U.S. 336
Keyes v. United States (November 26, 1883)
M/B: <u>Keyes v. United States</u>, 3 S. Ct. 202 (1883).

6 133 215 327 416 595   109 U.S. 527
Hatzlachh Supply Co., Inc., Petitioner, v. United States (Jan. 21, 1980)
M/B: <u>Hatzlachh Supply Co. v. United States</u>, 100 S. Ct. 647 (1980).

7 134 216 328 417 596   111 U.S. 43
Ex parte Virginia (March 17, 1884)
M/B: <u>Ex parte Virginia</u>, 4 S. Ct. 333 (1884).
LR: <u>Ex parte</u> Virginia, 4 S. Ct. 333 (1884).

8 135 217 329 418 597   110 U.S. 131
State of California, Plaintiff, v. State of Arizona and the United States (Feb. 22, 1979)
M/B: <u>California v. Arizona</u>, 99 S. Ct. 919 (1979).

EXERCISE 4. SUPREME COURT REPORTER   (CONTINUED)

9 136 218 330 419 598   112 U.S. 150
City of Fort Scott v. Hickman   (November 3, 1884)
M/B: City of Fort Scott v. Hickman, 5 S. Ct. 56 (1884).

10 137 219 331 420 599   114 U.S. 417
Ex parte Wilson (March 30, 1885)
M/B: Ex parte Wilson, 5 S. Ct. 935 (1885).
LR: Ex parte Wilson, 5 S. Ct. 935 (1885).

11 138 220 332 421 600   115 U.S. 683
Louisville Gas Co. v. Citizens' Gas-Light Co. (December 7, 1885)
M/B: Louisville Gas Co. v. Citizens' Gas-Light Co., 6 S. Ct. 265 (1885).

12 139 221 333 422 501   119 U.S. 513
Eldred v. Bell Telephone Co. of Missouri (December 20, 1886)
M/B: Eldred v. Bell Telephone Co., 7 S. Ct. 296 (1886).
LR: Eldred v. Bell Tel. Co., 7 S. Ct. 296 (1886).

13 140 222 334 423 502   435 U.S. 6
Michael Lee Simpson and Tommy Wayne Simpson, Petitioners v. United States;
Michael Lee Simpson, Petitioner v. United States (February 28, 1978)
M/B: Simpson v. United States, 98 S. Ct. 909 (1978).

14 141 223 335 424 503   128 U.S. 129
Asher v. State of Texas (October 29, 1888)
M/B: Asher v. Texas, 9 S. Ct. 1 (1888).

15 142 224 336 425 504   132 U.S. 131
Cross et al. v. State of North Carolina   (November 11, 1889)
M/B: Cross v. North Carolina, 10 S. Ct. 47 (1889).

16 143 225 337 426 505   137 U.S. 624
Ex parte Converse (January 5, 1891)
M/B: Ex parte Converse, 11 S. Ct. 191 (1891).
LR: Ex parte Converse, 11 S. Ct. 191 (1891).

17 144 226 338 427 506   143 U.S. 621
United States v. State of Texas   (February 29, 1892)
M/B: United States v. Texas, 12 S. Ct. 488 (1892).

18 145 227 339 428 507   147 U.S. 486
In re Hawkins (January 30, 1893)
M/B: In re Hawkins, 13 S. Ct. 512 (1893).
LR: In re Hawkins, 13 S. Ct. 512 (1893).

19 146 228 340 429 508   151 U.S. 303
Hickory v. United States   (January 15, 1894)
M/B: Hickory v. United States, 14 S. Ct. 334 (1894).

20 147 229 341 430 509   156 U.S. 1
United States v. E. C. Knight Co. et al. (January 21, 1895)
M/B: United States v. E.C. Knight Co., 15 S. Ct. 249 (1895).

21 148 230 342 431 510   162 U.S. 1
United States v. State of Texas   (March 16, 1896)
M/B: United States v. Texas, 16 S. Ct. 725 (1896).

22 149 231 343 432 511   166 U.S. 150
Henderson Bridge Co. v. Commonwealth of Kentucky (March 15, 1897)
M/B: Henderson Bridge Co. v. Kentucky, 17 S. Ct. 532 (1897).

23 150 232 344 433 512   168 U.S. 90
Turner v. People of State of New York   (October 18, 1897)
M/B: Turner v. New York, 18 S. Ct. 38 (1897).

24 151 233 345 434 513   460 U.S. 370

EXERCISE 4. SUPREME COURT REPORTER   (CONTINUED)

Hillsboro National Bank, Petitioner v. Commissioner of Internal Revenue. United States, Petitioner v. Bliss Dairy, Inc. (March 7, 1983)
M/B: Hillsboro National Bank v. Commissioner, 103 S. Ct. 1134 (1983).
LR: Hillsboro Nat'l Bank v. Commissioner, 103 S. Ct. 1134 (1983).

25 152 234 346 435 514   178 U.S. 327
Mutual Life Insurance Company of New York, Petitioner v. Nellie Phinney, Executrix of Guy C. Phinney, Deceased (May 28, 1900)
M/B: Mutual Life Insurance Co. v. Phinney, 20 S. Ct. 906 (1900).
LR: Mutual Life Ins. Co. v. Phinney, 20 S. Ct. 906 (1900).

26 153 235 347 436 515   180 U.S. 471
H. Drusilla Mitchell v. First National Bank of Chicago (March 5, 1901)
M/B: Mitchell v. First National Bank, 21 S. Ct. 418 (1901).
LR: Mitchell v. First Nat'l Bank, 21 S. Ct. 418 (1901).

27 154 236 348 437 516   183 U.S. 191
Wilson Brothers, a Corporation, and Jacob Kahn, Henry Kahn, Jacob Wohlbach, Copartners under the Name of Kahn Brothers & Company, and A. W. Becker, Harry L. Mayer, Joseph Mayer, and Henry B. Mayer, Copartners under the Firm Name of Becker, Mayer & Company v. Cassius B. Nelson (December 9, 1901)
M/B: Wilson Brothers v. Nelson, 22 S. Ct. 74 (1901).
LR: Wilson Bros. v. Nelson, 22 S. Ct. 74 (1901).

28 155 237 349 438 517   187 U.S. 553
Lone Wolf, Principal Chief of the Kiowas, et al. v. Ethan A. Hitchcock, Secretary of the Interior, et al. (January 5, 1903)
M/B: Lone Wolf v. Hitchcock, 23 S. Ct. 216 (1903).
Note: Students should not cite United States v. Sampson (which appears on the same page of the Supreme Court Reporter but corresponds to 187 U.S. 436--a different U.S. citation).

29 156 238 350 439 518   192 U.S. 243
Commercial National Bank of Portland, Plff. in Err., v. Henry Weinhard; Commercial National Bank of Portland, Plff. in Err., v. George H. Williams (January 18, 1904)
M/B: Commercial National Bank v. Weinhard, 24 S. Ct. 253 (1904).
LR: Commercial Nat'l Bank v. Weinhard, 24 S. Ct. 253 (1904).

30 157 239 351 440 519   197 U.S. 394
Middletown National Bank v. Toledo, Ann Arbor & Northern Michigan Railway Company et al. (April 3, 1905)
M/B: Middletown National Bank v. Toledo, Ann Arbor & Northern Michigan Railway, 25 S. Ct. 462 (1905).
LR: Middletown Nat'l Bank v. Toledo, A.A. & N.M. Ry., 25 S. Ct. 462 (1905).

31 158 240 352 441 520   202 U.S. 1
State of Louisiana, Complainant, v. State of Mississippi (March 5, 1906)
M/B: Louisiana v. Mississippi, 26 S. Ct. 408 (1906).

32 159 241 353 442 521   204 U.S. 522
Eau Claire National Bank, Plff. in Err., v. Ralph W. Jackman, as Trustee of the Estate of John H. Young, a Bankrupt (February 25, 1907)
M/B: Eau Claire National Bank v. Jackman, 27 S. Ct. 391 (1907).
LR: Eau Claire Nat'l Bank v. Jackman, 27 S. Ct. 391 (1907).

33 160 242 354 443 522   209 U.S. 211
General Oil Company, Plff. in Err., v. John H. Cain, Inspector of Coal Oil, Carbon Oil, Petroleum, Kerosene Oil, Gasolene, etc., for the County of Shelby and City of Memphis, Tenn. (March 23, 1908)
M/B: General Oil Co. v. Cain, 28 S. Ct. 475 (1908).

34 161 243 355 444 523   212 U.S. 354
Gustave A. Jahn et al. v. Steamship Folmina, William Van Eyken, Claimant (February 23, 1909)
M/B: Jahn v. Steamship Folmina, 29 S. Ct.363 (1909).

EXERCISE 4. SUPREME COURT REPORTER   (CONTINUED)

Note: "Steamship" is not abbreviated in the LR form because it is the first word of the cited party.

35 162 244 356 445 524   216 U.S. 531
Interstate Commerce Commission, Appt., v. Delaware, Lackawanna & Western Railroad Company (March 7, 1910)
M/B: ICC v. Delaware, Lackawanna & Western Railroad, 30 S. Ct. 415 (1910).
LR: ICC v. Delaware, L. & W.R.R., 30 S. Ct. 415 (1910).

36 163 245 357 446 525   220 U.S. 462
Shawnee Severage & Drainage Company, Appt., v. Frank P. Stearns, as Mayor of the City of Shawnee; John Lain et al., Members of the City Council of the City of Shawnee, et al. (April 10, 1911)
M/B: Shawnee Severage & Drainage Co. v. Stearns, 31 S. Ct. 452 (1911).

37 164 246 358 447 526   224 U.S. 1
Sidney Henry et al. v. A. B. Dick Company (March 11, 1912)
M/B: Henry v. A.B. Dick Co., 32 S. Ct. 364 (1912).

38 165 247 359 448 527   229 U.S. 523
J. Butler Studley, Trustee in Bankruptcy of the Collver Tours Company, Appt., v. Boylston National Bank of Boston (June 9, 1913)
M/B: Studley v. Boylston National Bank, 33 S. Ct. 806 (1913).
LR: Studley v. Boylston Nat'l Bank, 33 S. Ct. 806 (1913).

39 166 248 360 449 528   231 U.S. 222
Isidor Straus and Nathan Straus, Composing the Firm of R. H. & Macy & Company, Plffs. in Err., v. American Publishers' Association et al. (December 1, 1913)
M/B: Straus v. American Publishers' Association, 34 S. Ct. 84 (1913).
LR: Straus v. American Publishers' Ass'n, 34 S. Ct. 84 (1913).
Note: Students should not cite United States v. Daniels (which is on the same page as the Straus case in the Supreme Court Reporter) but corresponds to a different United States Reports citation (231 U.S 218).

40 167 249 361 450 529   236 U.S. 247
Mutual Film Company, Appt., v. Industrial Commission of Ohio et al. (February 23, 1915)
M/B: Mutual Film Co. v. Industrial Commission, 35 S. Ct. 393 (1915).
LR: Mutual Film Co. v. Industrial Comm'n, 35 S. Ct. 393 (1915).
Note: Students should not cite Mutual Film Corp. v. Hodges (which is on the same page) but is a different Supreme Court case (corresponding to 236 U.S. 248, not 236 U.S. 247).

41 168 250 362 451 530   241 U.S. 22
G. & C. Merriam Company, Appt., v. Arthur J. Saalfield, Saalfield Publishing Company, and George W. Ogilvie (April 17, 1916)
M/B: G. & C. Merriam Co. v. Saalfield, 36 S. Ct. 477 (1916).

42 169 251 363 452 531   242 U.S. 568
Frank W. Merrick, John W. Haarer, and Grant Fellows, Appts., v. N. W. Halsey & Company et al., and the Weis Fibre Container Corporation (January 22, 1917)
M/B: Merrick v. N.W. Halsey & Co., 37 S. Ct. 227 (1917).

43 170 252 364 453 532   245 U.S. 603
Gardiner v. William S. Butler & Co., Inc., et al. (February 4, 1918)
M/B: Gardiner v. William S. Butler & Co., 38 S. Ct. 214 (1918).

44 171 253 365 454 533   249 U.S. 454
Barbour v. State of Georgia   (April 14, 1919)
M/B: Barbour v. Georgia, 39 S. Ct. 316 (1919).

45 172 254 366 455 534   252 U.S. 465
United States v. Simpson (April 19, 1920)
M/B: United States v. Simpson, 40 S. Ct. 364 (1920).

46 173 255 367 456 535   256 U.S. 296
People of State of New York v. State of New Jersey et al. (May 2, 1921)

EXERCISE 4. SUPREME COURT REPORTER   (CONTINUED)

M/B: New York v. New Jersey, 41 S. Ct. 492 (1921).

47 174 256 368 457 536   423 U.S. 336
Thermtron Products, Inc., and Larry Dean Newhard, Petitioners v. H. David Hermansdorfer, Judge, United States District Court for the Eastern District of Kentucky (January 20, 1976)
M/B: Thermtron Products, Inc. v. Hermansdorfer, 96 S. Ct. 584 (1976).
LR: Thermtron Prods., Inc. v. Hermansdorfer, 96 S. Ct. 584 (1976).

48 175 257 369 458 537   261 U.S. 428
Keller et al., Public Utilities Commission of District of Columbia v. Potomac Electric Power Co., Inc., et al. (April 9, 1923)
M/B: Keller v. Potomac Electric Power Co., 43 S. Ct. 445 (1923).
LR: Keller v. Potomac Elec. Power Co., 43 S. Ct. 445 (1923).

49 176 258 370 459 538   265 U.S. 269
Nassau Smelting & Refining Works, Limited v. Brightwood Bronze Foundry Co. (May 26, 1924)
M/B: Nassau Smelting & Refining Works, v. Brightwood Bronze Foundry Co., 44 S. Ct. 506 (1924).
LR: Nassau Smelting & Ref. Works, v. Brightwood Bronze Foundry Co., 44 S. Ct. 506 (1924).

50 177 259 371 460 539   268 U.S. 295
Coronado Coal Co. et al. v. United Mine Workers of America et al. (May 25, 1925)
M/B: Coronado Coal Co. v. United Mine Workers, 45 S. Ct. 551 (1925) OR Coronado Coal Co. v. UMW, 45 S. Ct. 551 (1925).

51 178 260 372 461 540   269 U.S. 328
State of New Jersey v. Sargent, Atty. Gen., et al. (Jan. 4, 1926)
M/B: New Jersey v. Sargent, 46 S. Ct. 122 (1926).

52 179 261 373 462 541   430 U.S. 349
Daniel Wilbur Gardner, Petitioner, v. State of Florida (March 22, 1977)
M/B: Gardner v. Florida, 97 S. Ct. 1197 (1977).

53 180 262 374 463 542   276 U.S. 358
Corona Cord Tire Co. v. Dovan Chemical Corporation (April 9, 1928)
M/B: Corona Cord Tire Co. v. Dovan Chemical Corp., 48 S. Ct. 380 (1928).
LR: Corona Cord Tire Co. v. Dovan Chem. Corp., 48 S. Ct. 380 (1928).

54 181 263 375 464 543   278 U.S. 300
United Fuel Gas Co., et al. v. Railroad Commission of Kentucky et al. (January 2, 1929)
M/B: United Fuel Gas Co. v. Railroad Commission, 49 S. Ct. 150 (1929).
LR: United Fuel Gas Co. v. Railroad Comm'n, 49 S. Ct. 150 (1929).

55 182 264 376 465 544   280 U.S. 218
Corn Exchange Bank v. Coler, Commissioner of Public Welfare of City of New York (Jan. 6, 1930)
M/B: Corn Exchange Bank v. Coler, 50 S. Ct. 94 (1930).
LR: Corn Exch. Bank v. Coler, 50 S. Ct. 94 (1930).

56 183 265 377 466 545   284 U.S. 263
Marine Transit Corporation v. Dreyfus et al. (Jan. 4. 1932)
M/B: Marine Transit Corp. v. Dreyfus, 52 S. Ct. 166 (1932).

57 184 266 378 467 546   288 U.S. 436
Porter et al. v. Commissioner of Internal Revenue (March 13, 1933)
M/B: Porter v. Commissioner, 53 S. Ct. 451 (1933).

58 185 267 379 468 547   291 U.S. 610
Ex parte Baldwin et al. (March 10, 1934)
M/B: Ex parte Baldwin, 54 S. Ct. 551 (1934).
LR: Ex parte Baldwin, 54 S. Ct. 551 (1934).

EXERCISE 4. SUPREME COURT REPORTER   (CONTINUED)

59 186 268 380 469 548   293 U.S. 322
Herring v. Commissioner of Internal Revenue (two cases) (December 3, 1934)
M/B: Herring v. Commissioner, 55 S. Ct.179 (1934).

60 187 269 381 470 549   282 U.S. 379
Educational Films Corporation of America v. Ward, Attorney General of New York, et al. (January 12, 1931)
M/B: Educational Films Corp. of America v. Ward, 51 S. Ct. 170 (1931).
LR: Educational Films Corp. of Am. v. Ward, 51 S. Ct. 170 (1931).

61 188 270 382 471 550   297 U.S. 227
Palmer Clay Products Co. v. Brown (February 10, 1936)
M/B: Palmer Clay Products Co. v. Brown, 56 S. Ct. 450 (1936).
LR: Palmer Clay Prods. Co. v. Brown, 56 S. Ct. 450 (1936).

62 189 271 383 472 551   300 U.S. 414
Dugas v. American Surety Co. of New York (March 29, 1937)
M/B: Dugas v. American Surety Co., 57 S. Ct. 515 (1937).
LR: Dugas v. American Sur. Co., 57 S. Ct. 515 (1937).

63 190 272 384 473 552   304 U.S. 126
Guaranty Trust Co. of New York v. United States (April 25, 1938)
M/B: Guaranty Trust Co. v. United States, 58 S. Ct. 785 (1938).

64 191 273 385 474 553   306 U.S. 346
Milk Control Board of Pennsylvania v. Eisenberg Farm Products (February 27, 1939)
M/B: Milk Control Board v. Eisenberg Farm Products, 59 S. Ct. 528 (1939).
LR: Milk Control Bd. v. Eisenberg Farm Prods., 59 S. Ct. 528 (1939).

65 192 274 386 475 554   309 U.S. 94
James Stewart & Co., Inc. v. Sadrakula (January 29, 1940)
M/B: James Stewart & Co. v. Sadrakula, 60 S. Ct. 431 (1940).

66 193 275 387 476 555   311 U.S. 570
Railroad Commission of Texas et al. v. Rowan & Nichols Oil Co. (January 6, 1941)
M/B: Railroad Commission v. Rowan & Nichols Oil Co., 61 S. Ct. 343 (1941).
LR: Railroad Comm'n v. Rowan & Nichols Oil Co., 61 S. Ct. 343 (1941).

67 194 276 388 477 556   316 U.S. 174
State Tax Commission of Utah v. Aldrich et al. (April 27, 1942)
M/B: State Tax Commission v. Aldrich, 62 S. Ct. 1008 (1942).
LR: State Tax Comm'n v. Aldrich, 62 S. Ct. 1008 (1942).

68 195 277 389 478 557   319 U.S. 598
Oklahoma Tax Commission v. United States (three cases) (June 14, 1943)
M/B: Oklahoma Tax Commission v. United States, 63 S. Ct. 1284 (1943).
LR: Oklahoma Tax Comm'n v. United States, 63 S. Ct. 1284 (1943).

69 196 278 390 479 558   321 U.S. 158
Prince v. Commonwealth of Massachusetts (January 31, 1944)
M/B: Prince v. Massachusetts, 64 S. Ct. 438 (1944).

70 197 279 391 480 559   324 U.S. 401
Malinski et al. v. People of State of New York (March 26, 1945)
M/B: Malinski v. New York, 65 S. Ct. 781 (1945).

71 198 280 392 481 560   328 U.S. 331
Pennekamp et al. v. State of Florida (June 3, 1946)
M/B: Pennekamp v. Florida, 66 S. Ct. 1029 (1946).

72 199 281 393 482 561   331 U.S. 752
Aircraft & Diesel Equipment Corporation v. Hirsch et al. (June 16, 1947)
M/B: Aircraft & Diesel Equipment Corp. v. Hirsch, 67 S. Ct. 1493 (1947).
LR: Aircraft & Diesel Equip. Corp. v. Hirsch, 67 S. Ct. 1493 (1947).

EXERCISE 4. SUPREME COURT REPORTER   (CONTINUED)

73 200 282 394 483 562   335 U.S. 106
United States v. Congress of Industrial Organizations et al. (June 21, 1948)
M/B: United States v. Congress of Industrial Organizations, 68 S. Ct. 1349 (1948) OR United States v. CIO, 68 S. Ct. 1349 (1948).
LR: United States v. Congress of Indus. Orgs., 68 S. Ct. 1349 (1948) OR United States v. CIO, 68 S. Ct. 1349 (1948).

74 101 283 395 484 563   336 U.S. 422
National Carbide Corporation v. Commissioner of Internal Revenue; Air Reduction Sales Co. v. Commissioner of Internal Revenue; Pure Carbonic, Inc. v. Commissioner of Internal Revenue (March 28, 1949)
M/B: National Carbide Corp. v. Commissioner, 69 S. Ct. 726 (1949).

75 102 284 396 485 564   339 U.S. 707
United States v. State of Texas (June 5, 1950)
M/B: United States v. Texas, 70 S. Ct. 918 (1950).

76 103 285 397 486 565   340 U.S. 602
Spector Motor Service, Inc. v. O'Connor (March 26, 1951)
M/B: Spector Motor Service v. O'Connor, 71 S. Ct. 508 (1951).
LR: Spector Motor Serv. v. O'Connor, 71 S. Ct. 508 (1951).

77 104 286 398 487 566   343 U.S. 99
Buck et al. v. People of State of California (March 10, 1952)
M/B: Buck v. California, 72 S. Ct. 502 (1952).

78 105 287 399 488 567   345 U.S. 981
State of Nebraska v. State of Wyoming, and the State of Colorado, Impleaded Defendant, The United States of America, Intervenor (June 15, 1953)
M/B: Nebraska v. Wyoming, 73 S. Ct. 1041 (1953).

79 106 288 400 489 568   347 U.S. 128
Irvine v. People of State of California (February 8, 1954)
M/B: Irvine v. California, 74 S. Ct. 381 (1954).

80 107 289 301 490 569   349 U.S. 435
Federal Power Commission v. The State of Oregon, The Fish Commission of Oregon, The Oregon State Game Commission (June 6, 1955)
M/B: FPC v. Oregon, 75 S. Ct. 832 (1955).

81 108 290 302 491 570   351 U.S. 79
American Airlines, Incorporated, Petitioner, v. North American Airlines, Incorporated (April 23, 1956)
M/B: American Airlines v. North American Airlines, 76 S. Ct. 600 (1956).
LR: American Airlines v. North Am. Airlines, 76 S. Ct. 600 (1956).

82 109 291 303 492 571   354 U.S. 234
Paul M. Sweezy, Appellant, v. State of New Hampshire by Louis C. Wyman, Attorney General (June 17, 1957)
M/B: Sweezy v. New Hampshire, 77 S. Ct. 1203 (1957).

83 110 292 304 493 572   357 U.S. 63
Walter W. Flora v. United States of America (June 16, 1958)
M/B: Flora v. United States, 78 S. Ct. 1079 (1958).

84 111 293 305 494 573   359 U.S. 171
Service Storage & Transfer Co., Inc., Petitioner, v. Commonwealth of Virginia (March 30, 1959)
M/B: Service Storage & Transfer Co. v. Virginia, 79 S. Ct. 714 (1959).

85 112 294 306 495 574   361 U.S. 147
Eleazar Smith, Appellant, v. People of the State of California (December 14, 1959)
M/B: Smith v. California, 80 S. Ct. 215 (1959).

86 113 295 307 496 575   363 U.S. 278

EXERCISE 4. SUPREME COURT REPORTER   (CONTINUED)

Commissioner of Internal Revenue, Petitioner, v. Mose Duberstein et al.; Alden D. Stanton et al., Petitioners, v. United States of America (June 13, 1960)
M/B: Commissioner v. Duberstein, 80 S. Ct. 1190 (1960).

87 114 296 308 497 576   430 U.S. 564
United States, Petitioner, v. Martin Linen Supply Company et al. (April 4, 1977)
M/B: United States v. Martin Linen Supply Co., 97 S. Ct. 1349 (1977).

88 115 297 309 498 577   368 U.S. 157
John Burrell Garner et al., Petitioners, v. State of Louisiana; Mary Briscoe et al., Petitioners, v. State of Louisiana; Jannette Hoston, Petitioners, et al. v. State of Louisiana (December 11, 1961)
M/B: Garner v. Louisiana, 82 S. Ct. 248 (1961).

89 116 298 310 499 578   370 U.S. 626
William Link, Petitioner, v. Wabash Railroad Company (June 25, 1962)
M/B: Link v. Wabash Railroad, 82 S. Ct. 1386 (1962).
LR: Link v. Wabash R.R., 82 S. Ct. 1386 (1962).

90 117 299 311 500 579   371 U.S. 132
Chester A. Pearlman, Trustee, Petitioner, v. Reliance Insurance Company (December 3, 1962)
M/B: Pearlman v. Reliance Insurance Co., 83 S. Ct. 232 (1962).
LR: Pearlman v. Reliance Ins. Co., 83 S. Ct. 232 (1962).

91 118 300 312 401 580   374 U.S. 174
United States, Appellant, v. The Singer Manufacturing Company (June 17, 1963)
M/B: United States v. Singer Manufacturing Co., 83 S. Ct. 1773 (1963).
LR: United States v. Singer Mfg. Co., 83 S. Ct. 1773 (1963).

92 119 201 313 402 581   378 U.S. 478
Danny Escobedo, Petitioner, v. State of Illinois (June 22, 1964)
M/B: Escobedo v. Illinois, 84 S. Ct. 1758 (1964).

93 120 202 314 403 582   379 U.S. 241
Heart of Atlanta Motel, Inc., Appellant, v. United States et al. (December 14, 1964)
M/B: Heart of Atlanta Motel v. United States, 85 S. Ct. 348 (1964).

94 121 203 315 404 583   390 U.S. 341
Federal Trade Commission, Petitioner, v. Fred Meyer, Inc., et al. (March 18, 1968)
M/B: FTC v. Fred Meyer, Inc., 88 S. Ct. 904 (1968).

95 122 204 316 405 584   393 U.S. 297
United States, Petitioner, v. The Donruss Company (January 13, 1969)
M/B: United States v. Donruss Co., 89 S. Ct. 501 (1969).

96 123 205 317 406 585   395 U.S. 352
Paulette Boudreaux Rodrigue et al., Petitioners, v. Aetna Casualty and Surety Company et al. (June 9, 1969)
M/B: Rodrigue v. Aetna Casualty & Surety Co., 89 S. Ct. 1835 (1969).
LR: Rodrigue v. Aetna Casualty & Sur. Co., 89 S. Ct. 1835 (1969).

97 124 206 318 407 586   404 U.S. 528
Trbovich, Petitioner, v. United Mine Workers of America et al. (January 17, 1972)
M/B: Trbovich v. United Mine Workers, 92 S. Ct. 630 (1972) OR Trbovich v. UMW, 92 S. Ct. 630 (1972).

98 125 207 319 408 587   416 U.S. 21
The California Bankers Association, Appellant, v. George P. Shultz, Secretary of the Treasury, et al.; George P. Schultz, Secretary of the Treasury, et al., Appellants, v. The California Bankers Association, et al.; Fortney H. Stark, Jr., et al., Appellants, v. George P. Shultz et al. (April 1, 1974)
M/B: California Bankers Association v. Shultz, 94 S. Ct. 1494 (1974).

EXERCISE 4. SUPREME COURT REPORTER   (CONTINUED)

LR: California Bankers Ass'n v. Shultz, 94 S. Ct. 1494 (1974).

99 126 208 320 409 588   418 U.S. 656
United States, Appellant, v. The Connecticut National Bank, et al. (June 26, 1974)
M/B: United States v. Connecticut National Bank, 94 S. Ct. 2788 (1974).
LR: United States v. Connecticut Nat'l Bank, 94 S. Ct. 2788 (1974).

100 127 209 321 410 589   420 U.S. 395
Chemehuevi Tribe of Indians et al.,Petitioners, v. Federal Power Commission et al.; Arizona Public Service Company et al., Petitioners, v. Chemehuevi Tribe of Indians et al.; Federal Power Commission, Petitioner, v. Chemehuevi Tribe of Indians et al. (March 3, 1975)
M/B: Chemehuevi Tribe of Indians v. FPC, 95 S. Ct. 1066 (1975).

LIBRARY EXERCISE 5. LAWYERS' EDITION OF U.S. SUPREME COURT REPORTS.

INSTRUCTOR'S NOTE: Students are required to find the page[s] listed below in the designated volume of Lawyers' Edition of United States Reports. They are to assume that they have quoted the language on the page[s] given with their problem number. They are required to cite the case and the quotation to United States Reports using the star paging in the Lawyers' Edition. For example, if the student's problem was "46 L. Ed. 2d 525 'The position adopted by the Court of Appeals would mean that two subcontractors who committed similar acts and caused similar damage could be subjected to widely disparate penalties,'" the proper answer would be United States v. Bornstein, 423 U.S. 303, 315-16 (1976) (memo/brief form) or United States v. Bornstein, 423 U.S. 303, 315-16 (1976) (law review form).

Note that when the quoted portion of the case extends over more than one page in United States Reports, the students must give inclusive page numbers, separated by a hyphen (315-16). They should retain the last two digits but other repetitious digits should be deleted. The quotations below indicate the star paging in brackets for your information.

Note that the Lawyers' Edition omits the period after the "v" in the case citation. The period is required for proper Blue Book form.

In a few instances, a separate opinion of one of the Justices has been quoted for this exercise. It would be correct to include an an explanatory parenthetical containing that information (e.g., concurring opinion) at the end of the citation. See Rule 10.6. Such an indication is not required of the students for this exercise.

1 142 220 365 409 517   1 L. Ed. 2d 489   "[495] In short, Congress in § 2 was referring to a group of [496] unions already defined and constituted under the § 3 procedures."
Pennsylvania Railroad Company and Brotherhood of Railroad Trainmen, Petitioners, v N. P. Ruchlik, Individually and on Behalf of and as Representative of Other Employees of the Pennsylvania Railroad (February 25, 1957)
M/B: Pennsylvania Railroad v. Ruchlik, 352 U.S. 480, 495-96 (1957).
LR: Pennsylvania R.R. v. Ruchlik, 352 U.S. 480, 495-96 (1957).

2 143 221 366 410 518   1 L. Ed. 2d 742   "[174] No special threat [175] to appellees arises from the . . . assertion of Commission jurisdiction to regulate Alleghany."
Alleghany Corporation et al., Appellants, v Breswick & Company et al., as Common Stockholders of Alleghany Corp., etc. (April 22, 1957)
M/B: Alleghany Corp. v. Breswick & Co., 353 U.S. 151, 174-75 (1957).

3 144 222 367 411 519   2 L. Ed. 2d 477   "[543] There the question, much mooted, was whether [544] the federal policy conflicted with the state policy fixing the price of milk which the United States purchased."
Public Utilities Commission of the State of California, Appellant, v United States of America (March 3, 1958)
M/B: Public Utilities Commission v. United States, 355 U.S. 534, 543-44 (1958).
LR: Public Utils. Comm'n v. United States, 355 U.S. 534, 543-44 (1958).
Note: "PUC" is probably a widely enough recognized abbreviation to be used in this citation and should be considered to be correct.

4 145 223 368 412 520   2 L. Ed. 2d 1129   "[41] [W]e find it unnecessary to decide whether the respondent was a transferee within the meaning [42] of § 311 because we hold that the Kentucky statutes govern the question of the beneficiary's liability."
Commissioner of Internal Revenue, Petitioner, v Jean F. Stern, Transferee (June 9, 1958)
M/B: Commissioner v. Stern, 357 U.S. 39, 41-42 (1958).

5 146 224 369 413 521   3 L. Ed. 2d 32   "[61] [T]he taxpayers in this case have met those conditions and should be allowed the claimed deductions. [62] The meaning of 'home' was expressly left undecided in Flowers."

EXERCISE 5. LAWYERS' EDITION OF U.S. SUPREME COURT REPORTS   (CONTINUED)

James E. Peurifoy, Paul V. Stines, Betty O. Stines, et al., Petitioners, v
Commissioner of Internal Revenue (November 10, 1958)
M/B: Peurifoy v. Commissioner, 358 U.S. 59, 61-62 (1958).

6 147 225 370 414 522   3 L. Ed. 2d 999   "[512] Clearly these conspiracy
allegations stated a cause of action triable as of right by [513] a jury."
Beacon Theatres, Inc., Petitioner, v Hon. Harry C. Westover, Judge of the
United States District Court of the Southern District of California, Central
Division, et al. (May 25, 1959)
M/B: Beacon Theatres v. Westover, 359 U.S. 500, 512-13 (1959).

7 148 226 371 415 523   4 L. Ed. 2d 8   "[25] The equipment then had to be
moved for a similar operation [26] on the second car."
Henry J. Harris, Petitioner, v Pennsylvania Railroad Company (October 19,
1959)
M/B: Harris v. Pennsylvania Railroad, 361 U.S. 15, 25-26 (1959).
LR: Harris v. Pennsylvania R.R., 361 U.S. 15, 25-26 (1959).

8 149 227 372 416 524   4 L. Ed. 2d 725   "[294] The State [295] in which
the respondent is incorporated prohibits unfair or deceptive practices in the
insurance business there or 'in any other state.'"
Federal Trade Commission, Petitioner, v Travelers Health Association (March
28, 1960)
M/B: FTC v. Travelers Health Association, 362 U.S. 293, 294-95 (1960).
LR: FTC v. Travelers Health Ass'n, 362 U.S. 293, 294-95 (1960).

9 150 228 373 417 525   5 L. Ed. 2d 4   "[303] [T]he United States
instituted proceedings to [304] redeem the property pursuant to ... 28 U.S.C.
§ 2410(c)."
United States, Appellant, v John Hancock Mutual Life Insurance Co., George
Hetzel and Grace Marie Hetzel (November 7, 1960)
M/B: United States v. John Hancock Mutual Life Insurance Co., 364 U.S. 301,
303-04 (1960).
LR: United States v. John Hancock Mut. Life Ins. Co., 364 U.S. 301, 303-04
(1960).

10 151 229 374 418 526   5 L. Ed. 2d 600-01   "[348] Congress [349] did not
want patentees to be barred from prosecuting their claims for direct
infringement."
Aro Manufacturing Co., Inc., et al., Petitioners, v Convertible Top
Replacement Co., Inc. (February 27, 1961)
M/B: Aro Manufacturing Co. v. Convertible Top Replacement Co., 365 U.S. 336,
348-49 (1961).
LR: Aro Mfg. Co. v. Convertible Top Replacement Co., 365 U.S. 336, 348-49
(1961).

11 152 230 375 419 527   6 L. Ed. 2d 53   "[726] The highest court of
Delaware has thus construed this [727] legislative enactment as authorizing
discriminatory classifications based exclusively on color."
William H. Burton, Appellant, v Wilmington Parking Authority et al. (April 17,
1961)
M/B: Burton v. Wilmington Parking Authority, 365 U.S. 715, 726-27 (1961).
LR: Burton v. Wilmington Parking Auth., 365 U.S. 715, 726-27 (1961).

12 153 231 376 420 528   6 L. Ed. 2d 1115   "[695] To interpret its careful
consideration of the problem otherwise is to [696] accuse the Congress of
engaging in sciamachy."
American Automobile Association, Petitioner, v United States (June 19, 1961)
M/B: American Automobile Association v. United States, 367 U.S. 687, 695-96
(1961).
LR: American Auto. Ass'n v. United States, 367 U.S. 687, 695-96 (1961).
Note: "AAA" is probably a widely enough recognized abbreviation of "American
Automobile Association" to be acceptable and full credit should be given for
an answer using that abbreviation.

13 154 232 377 421 529   7 L. Ed. 2d 631   "[142] [T]he Court issued a writ
of mandamus ordering a district [143] judge to issue a bench warrant which he

EXERCISE 5. LAWYERS' EDITION OF U.S. SUPREME COURT REPORTS   (CONTINUED)

had refused to do, in the purported exercise of his discretion, for a person under an indictment returned by a properly constituted grand jury."
Fong Foo et al., Petitioners, v United States (No. 64) (March 19, 1962)
M/B: Fong Foo v. United States, 369 U.S. 141, 142-43 (1964).

14 155 233 378 422 530   7 L. Ed. 2d 329   "[340] [T]he term 'reorganization' means 'the acquisition by one corporation, [341] in exchange solely for all or a part of its voting stock, of at least 80[%] of the . . . stock of another corporation.'"
Grover D. Turnbow et al., Petitioners, v Commissioner of Internal Revenue (December 18, 1961)
M/B: Turnbow v. Commissioner, 368 U.S. 337, 340-41 (1961).

15 156 234 379 423 531   8 L. Ed. 2d 190   "[675] The Court of Appeals for the Second Circuit [676] affirmed the Tax Court's orders sustaining the Commissioner's deficiency determination."
The Hanover Bank, Executor, et al., Petitioners, v Commissioner of Internal Revenue (May 21, 1962)
M/B: Hanover Bank v. Commissioner, 369 U.S. 672, 675-76 (1962).

16 157 235 380 424 532   8 L. Ed. 2d 740   "[633] Petitioner voluntarily chose this attorney as his representative in the action, and he cannot now avoid the consequences of the acts or omissions of this freely selected [634] agent."
William Link, Petitioner, v Wabash Railroad Company (June 25, 1962)
M/B: Link v. Wabash Railroad, 370 U.S. 626, 633-34 (1962).
LR: Link v. Wabash R.R., 370 U.S. 626, 633-34 (1962).

17 158 236 381 425 533   9 L. Ed. 2d 567   "[35] The charge in the indictment was in the exact language of the statute, and, in specifying the conduct covered by the charge, the indictment did [36] nothing more than state the price the defendant was alleged to have collected."
United States, Appellant, v National Dairy Products Corp. et al. (February 18, 1963)
M/B: United States v. National Dairy Products Corp., 372 U.S. 29, 35-36 (1963).
LR: United States v. National Dairy Prods. Corp., 372 U.S. 29, 35-36 (1963).

18 159 237 382 426 534   9 L. Ed. 2d 640   "[138] The Government's theories would [139] force upon an accrual-basis taxpayer a cash basis for advance payments in disregard of the federal statute which explicitly authorizes income tax returns to be based upon sound accrual accounting methods."
Mark E. Schlude et al., Petitioners, v Commissioner of Internal Revenue (February 18, 1963)
M/B: Schlude v. Commissioner, 372 U.S. 128, 138-39 (1963).

19 160 238 383 427 535   10 L. Ed. 2d 293   "[200] Congress restricted the full deduction under § 23(k) to bad [201] debts incurred in the taxpayer's trade or business and provided that 'nonbusiness' bad debts were to be deducted as short-term capital losses."
A. J. Whipple et al., Petitioners, v Commissioner of Internal Revenue (May 13, 1963)
M/B: Whipple v. Commissioner, 373 U.S. 193, 200-01 (1963).

20 161 239 384 428 536   10 L. Ed. 2d 775   "[89] [T]he state law creditor, asserting that the [90] assignment under which he claimed was a mortgage within the predecessor to § 6323, insisted upon priority over the federal lien."
United States, Petitioner, v Pioneer American Insurance Company et al. (June 10, 1963)
M/B: United States v. Pioneer American Insurance Co., 374 U.S. 84, 89-90 (1963).
LR: United States v. Pioneer Am. Ins. Co., 374 U.S. 84, 89-90 (1963).

EXERCISE 5. LAWYERS' EDITION OF U.S. SUPREME COURT REPORTS   (CONTINUED)

21 162 240 385 429 537   11 L. Ed. 2d 593   "[172] Under the labor agreement, however, the 'upgraded' helper does not immediately acquire permanent seniority [173] as a journeyman."
Donald I. Tilton et al., Petitioners, v Missouri Pacific Railroad Co. (February 17, 1964)
M/B: Tilton v. Missouri Pacific Railroad, 376 U.S. 169, 172-73 (1964).
LR: Tilton v. Missouri Pac. R.R., 376 U.S. 169, 172-73 (1964) OR Tilton v. Missouri P.R.R., 376 U.S. 169, 172-73 (1964).

22 163 241 386 430 538   11 L. Ed. 2d 358   "[316] New York law . . . does not require any such express promise by the agent in order to create a valid agency for receipt of [317] process."
National Equipment Rental, Ltd., Petitioner, v Steve Szukhent et al. (January 6, 1964)
M/B: National Equipment Rental, Ltd. v. Szukhent, 375 U.S. 311, 316-17 (1964).
LR: National Equip. Rental, Ltd. v. Szukhent, 375 U.S. 311, 316-17 (1964).

23 164 242 387 431 539   12 L. Ed. 2d 694   "[77] We hold that the constitutional privilege [78] against self-incrimination protects a state witness against incrimination under federal as well as state law."
William Murphy and John Moody, Sr., Petitioners, v Waterfront Commission of New York Harbor (June 15, 1964)
M/B: Murphy v. Waterfront Commission, 378 U.S. 52, 77-78 (1964).
LR: Murphy v. Waterfront Comm'n, 378 U.S. 52, 77-78 (1964).

24 165 243 388 432 540   12 L. Ed. 2d 784   "[168] This is the first case reaching this Court . . . that directly involves the validity under § 7 of the joint participation of two corporations in the [169] creation of a third as a new domestic producing organization."
United States, Appellant, v Penn-Olin Chemical Co. et al. (June 22, 1964)
M/B: United States v. Penn-Olin Chemical Co., 378 U.S. 158, 168-69 (1964).
LR: United States v. Penn-Olin Chem. Co., 378 U.S. 158, 168-69 (1964).

25 166 244 389 433 541   13 L. Ed. 2d 861   "[307] No one would deny that an employer is free to shut down his enterprise temporarily [308] for reasons of renovation or lack of profitable work unrelated to his collective bargaining situation."
American Ship Building Company, Petitioner, v National Labor Relations Board (March 29, 1965)
M/B: American Ship Building Co. v. NLRB, 380 U.S. 300, 307-08 (1965).
LR: American Ship Bldg. Co. v. NLRB, 380 U.S. 300, 307-08 (1965).

26 167 245 390 434 542   13 L. Ed. 2d 915   "[386] The Commission, [387] on the other hand, submits that the misrepresentation of any fact so long as it materially induces a purchaser's decision to buy is a deception prohibited by § 5."
Federal Trade Commission, Petitioner, v Colgate-Palmolive Co. et al. (April 5, 1965)
M/B: FTC v. Colgate-Palmolive Co., 380 U.S. 374, 386-87 (1965).

27 168 246 391 435 543   14 L. Ed. 2d 245   "[97] [T]he more compelling inference is that Congress intended [98] the inquiry into the project's effect on commerce to include, but not be limited to, effect on downstream navigability."
Federal Power Commission, Petitioner, v Union Electric Company (May 3, 1965)
M/B: FPC v. Union Electric Co., 381 U.S. 90, 97-98 (1965).
LR: FPC v. Union Elec. Co., 381 U.S. 90, 97-98 (1965).

28 169 247 392 436 544   14 L. Ed. 2d 129   "[643] The regulation thus indicates that [644] the question to be asked is whether the mine operators have a significant investment in the coal in place."
Paragon Jewel Coal Company, Inc., Petitioner, v Commissioner of Internal Revenue (No. 134) (April 28, 1965)
M/B: Paragon Jewel Coal Co. v. Commissioner, 380 U.S. 624, 643-44 (1965).

EXERCISE 5.   LAWYERS' EDITION OF U.S. SUPREME COURT REPORTS   (CONTINUED)

29 170 248 393 437 545   15 L. Ed. 2d 298   "[242] It established that the term 'connecting lines' [243] extends beyond physical connection to encompass lines participating in a through route."
Western Pacific Railroad Company et al., Appellants, v United States et al. (December 7, 1965)
M/B: <u>Western Pacific Railroad v. United States</u>, 382 U.S. 237, 242-43 (1965).
LR: Western Pac. R.R. v. United States, 382 U.S. 237, 242-43 (1965) OR Western P.R.R., 382 U.S. 237, 242-43 (1965).

30 171 249 394 438 546   15 L. Ed. 2d 224   "[155] [T]he Commission's analysis of the merger was fatally defective because the Commission had not determined whether [156] the merger violated § 7 of the Clayton Act."
Seaboard Air Line Railroad Company et al., Appellants, v United States et al. (No. 425) (November 22, 1965)
M/B: <u>Seaboard Air Line Railroad v. United States</u>, 382 U.S. 154, 155-56 (1965).
LR: Seaboard Air Line R.R. v. United States, 382 U.S. 154, 155-56 (1965).
Note: "Air" and "Line" are not abbreviated because they are not geographic terms.

31 172 250 395 439 547   16 L. Ed. 2d 243-44   "[747] The defendants moved to dismiss [748] the indictment on the ground it did not charge an offense under the laws of the United States."
United States, Appellant, v Herbert Guest et al. (March 28, 1966)
M/B: <u>United States v. Guest</u>, 383 U.S. 745, 747-48 (1966).

32 173 251 396 440 548   16 L. Ed. 2d 344   "[45] § 9 appears firmly anchored to the assumption that the Sherman Act will deter any attempts . . . to preserve [the] price level by conspiring to raise prices at which liquor is sold elsewhere [46] in the country."
Joseph E. Seagram & Sons, Inc., et al, Appellants, v Donald S. Hostetter, etc., et al. (April 19, 1966)
M/B: <u>Joseph E. Seagram & Sons v. Hostetter</u>, 384 U.S. 35, 45-46 (1966).

33 174 252 397 441 549   17 L. Ed. 2d 255   "[144] This unreliability in [145] turn undermines the security of the prime contractor's performance."
United States, Petitioner, v Acme Process Equipment Company (December 5, 1966)
M/B: <u>United States v. Acme Process Equipment Co.</u>, 385 U.S. 138, 144-45 (1966).
LR: United States v. Acme Process Equip. Co., 385 U.S. 138, 144-45 (1966).

34 175 253 398 442 550   17 L. Ed. 2d 379   "[297] He was [298] also under a federal indictment for embezzling union funds."
James R. Hoffa, Petitioner, v United States (No. 32) (December 12, 1966)
M/B: <u>Hoffa v. United States</u>, 385 U.S. 293, 297-98 (1966).

35 176 254 399 443 551   55 L. Ed. 2d 237   "[225] After a jury of 5 persons had been selected [226] and sworn, petitioner moved that the court impanel a jury of 12 persons."
Claude D. Ballew, Petitioner, v State of Georgia (March 21, 1978)
M/B: <u>Ballew v. Georgia</u>, 435 U.S. 223, 225-26 (1978).

36 177 255 400 444 552   18 L. Ed. 2d 857   "[410] There is no Commission power to compel the railroads to do so, and it is argued that from this we [411] should derive a congressional intent that the ICC may not compel the railroads to furnish services to motor carriers in any circumstances."
American Trucking Associations, Inc., et al., Appellants, v Atchison, Topeka, and Santa Fe Railway Company et al. (No. 57) (May 29, 1967)
M/B: <u>American Trucking Associations v. Atchison, Topeka, & Santa Fe Railway</u>, 387 U.S. 397, 410-11 (1967).
LR: American Trucking Ass'ns v. Atchison, T. & S.F. Ry., 387 U.S. 397, 410-11 (1967).

37 178 256 301 445 553   19 L. Ed. 2d 443   "[239] In holding that this Florida law . . . conflicts with the Supremacy Clause of the Constitution [240] we but follow the unbroken rule that has come down through the years."

EXERCISE 5. LAWYERS' EDITION OF U.S. SUPREME COURT REPORTS   (CONTINUED)

Minnie E. Nash, Petitioner, v Florida Industrial Commission et al. (December 5, 1967)
M/B: Nash v. Florida Industrial Commission, 389 U.S. 235, 239-40 (1967).
LR: Nash v. Florida Indus. Comm'n, 389 U.S. 235, 239-40 (1967).

38 179 257 302 446 554   19 L. Ed. 2d 793   "[6] Several [7] bills were then introduced combining the grant of borrowing power with various provisions to prohibit territorial expansion, and one of these bills was eventually enacted as the TVA amendments of 1959."
Edward J. Hardin, as Mayor of Tazewell, Tennessee, et al., Petitioners, v Kentucky Utilities Company (No. 40) (January 16, 1968)
M/B: Hardin v. Kentucky Utilities Co., 390 U.S. 1, 6-7 (1968).
LR: Hardin v. Kentucky Utils. Co., 390 U.S. 1, 6-7 (1968).

39 180 258 303 447 555   20 L. Ed. 2d 584   "[274] [C]ounsel's affidavit pointed to the following evidence as tending to show a participation by Cities in the al-[275]leged conspiracy to boycott his attempts to resell the Iranian oil to which he allegedly had access under his contract."
First National Bank of Arizona, etc., Petitioner, v Cities Service Co. (May 20, 1968)
M/B: First National Bank v. Cities Service Co., 391 U.S. 253, 274-75 (1968).
LR: First Nat'l Bank v. Cities Serv. Co., 391 U.S. 253, 274-75 (1968).

40 181 259 304 448 556   20 L. Ed. 2d 453   "[86] [T]he Internal Revenue Service had ruled that shareholders who sold rights would realize [87] ordinary income in the amount of the sales price."
Commissioner of Internal Revenue, Petitioner, v Irving Gordon et ux. (No. 760) (May 20, 1968)
M/B: Commissioner v. Gordon, 391 U.S. 83, 86-87 (1968).

41 182 260 305 449 557   21 L. Ed. 2d 352   "[209] Since in all relevant aspects the transactions here were American, not Korean, we hold that they are not 'export trade' [210] within the meaning of the Webb-Pomerene Act."
United States, Appellant, v Concentrated Phosphate Export Association, Inc., et al. (November 25, 1968)
M/B: United States v. Concentrated Phosphate Export Association, 393 U.S. 199, 209-10 (1968).
LR: United States v. Concentrated Phosphate Export Ass'n, 393 U.S. 199, 209-10 (1968).

42 183 261 306 450 558   21 L. Ed. 2d 482   "[278] If HUD's [279] power is not so limited, the Authority argues, HUD would be free to impair its contractual obligations to the Authority through unilateral action."
Joyce C. Thorpe, Petitioner, v Housing Authority of the City of Durham (January 13, 1969)
M/B: Thorpe v. Housing Authority, 393 U.S. 268, 278-79 (1969).
LR: Thorpe v. Housing Auth., 393 U.S. 268, 278-79 (1969).

43 184 262 307 451 559   22 L. Ed. 2d 375-76   "[405] [A]n employer who pays compensation [406] benefits to the representative of a deceased employee may be subrogated to the rights of the representative [407] against third persons."
Federal Marine Terminals, Inc., Petitioner, v Burnside Shipping Co., Ltd. (April 1, 1969)
M/B: Federal Marine Terminals v. Burnside Shipping Co., 394 U.S. 404, 405-07 (1969).

44 185 263 308 452 560   22 L. Ed. 2d 715   "[765] They [766] generally provide a guide to action that the agency may be expected to take in future cases."
National Labor Relations Board, Petitioner, v Wyman-Gordon Company (April 23, 1969)
M/B: NLRB v. Wyman-Gordon Co., 394 U.S. 759, 765-66 (1969).

45 186 264 309 453 561   23 L. Ed. 2d 76   "[26] The [27] text and legislative history of the Marihuana Tax Act plainly disclose a similar congressional purpose."

EXERCISE 5. LAWYERS' EDITION OF U.S. SUPREME COURT REPORTS   (CONTINUED)

Timothy F. Leary, Petitioner, v United States (May 19, 1969)
M/B: Leary v. United States, 395 U.S. 6, 26-27 (1969).

46 187 265 310 454 562   23 L. Ed. 2d 363   "[353] The state statute would have allowed recovery [354] for additional elements of damage."
Paulette Boudreaux Rodrigue et al., Petitioners, v Aetna Casualty and Surety Company et al. (June 9, 1969)
M/B: Rodrigue v. Aetna Casualty & Surety Co., 395 U.S. 352, 353-54 (1969).
LR: Rodrigue v. Aetna Casualty & Sur. Co., 395 U.S. 352, 353-54 (1969).

47 188 266 311 455 563   24 L. Ed. 2d 261   "[59] The experts . . . testified that they had been doubtful that radiant heat would solve the problem of [60] the cold joint."
Anderson's-Black Rock, Inc., Petitioner, v Pavement Salvage Co., Inc. (December 8, 1969)
M/B: Anderson's-Black Rock, Inc. v. Pavement Salvage Co., 369 U.S. 57, 59-60 (1969).

48 189 267 312 456 564   24 L. Ed. 2d 727   "[529] [T]he provisions of the charter of Northern Pacific Railroad Company which are urged to bar this merger were directed only to [530] the operations of the federal corporation, not to the operation of the railroad."
United States, Appellant, v Interstate Commerce Commission et al. (No. 28) (February 2, 1970)
M/B: United States v. ICC, 396 U.S. 491, 529-30 (1970).

49 190 268 313 457 565   25 L. Ed. 2d 583   "[578] This is not such a borderline [579] case."
Fred W. Woodward et al., Petitioners, v Commissioner of Internal Revenue (April 20, 1970)
M/B: Woodward v. Commissioner, 397 U.S. 572, 578-79 (1970).

50 191 269 314 458 566   25 L. Ed. 2d 376   "[365] [C]ivil labels and good [366] intentions do not themselves obviate the need for criminal due process safeguards in juvenile courts."
In The Matter of Samuel Winship, Appellant (March 31, 1970)
M/B: In re Winship, 397 U.S. 358, 365-66 (1970).
LR: In re Winship, 397 U.S. 358, 365-66 (1970).

51 192 270 315 459 567   26 L. Ed. 2d 305   "[329] The Brantley case presented a situation where a defendant's appeal from a conviction for a [330] lesser included offense ultimately led to retrial and conviction on the greater offense."
Earl Price, Petitioner, v State of Georgia (June 15, 1970)
M/B: Price v. Georgia, 398 U.S. 323, 329-30 (1970).

52 193 271 316 460 568   26 L. Ed. 2d 590   "[236] [T]he effect of the sentence imposed here required appellant to be [237] confined for 101 days beyond the maximum period of confinement fixed by the statute."
Willie E. Williams, Appellant, v State of Illinois (June 29, 1970)
M/B: Williams v. Illinois, 399 U.S. 235, 236-37 (1970).

53 194 272 317 461 569   27 L. Ed. 2d 663   "[28] Nor may the State penalize petitioner solely because he personally, as the committee suggests, [29] 'espouses illegal aims.'"
In The Matter of Application of Martin Robert Stolar (February 23, 1971)
M/B: In re Stolar, 401 U.S. 23, 28-29 (1971).
LR: In re Stolar, 401 U.S. 23, 28-29 (1971).

54 195 273 318 462 570   27 L. Ed. 2d 747   "[151] The principle of prudent restraint we invoke today is [152] nothing new."
Lelia Mae Sanks et al., Appellants, v State of Georgia et al. (February 23, 1971)
M/B: Sanks v. Georgia, 401 U.S. 144, 151-52 (1971).

55 196 274 319 463 571   28 L. Ed. 2d 376   "[626] It is settled that courts should give great weight to any reasonable construction of a regulatory

EXERCISE 5. LAWYERS' EDITION OF U.S. SUPREME COURT REPORTS   (CONTINUED)

statute [627] adopted by the agency charged with the enforcement of that statute."
Investment Company Institute et al., Petitioners, v William B. Camp, Comptroller of the Currency, et al. (No. 61) (April 5, 1971)
M/B: Investment Co. Institute v. Camp, 401 U.S. 617, 626-27 (1971).
LR: Investment Co. Inst. v. Camp, 401 U.S. 617, 626-27 (1971).

56 197 275 320 464 572   28 L. Ed. 2d 262   "[496] It is a time-honored [497] maxim of the Anglo-American common-law tradition that a court possessed of jurisdiction generally must exercise it."
State of Ohio, Plaintiff, v Wyandotte Chemicals Corporation et al. (March 23, 1971)
M/B: Ohio v. Wyandotte Chemicals Corp., 401 U.S. 493, 496-97 (1971).
LR: Ohio v. Wyandotte Chems. Corp., 401 U.S. 493, 496-97 (1971).

57 198 276 321 465 573   29 L. Ed. 2d 527   "[353] The payment [354] was made during the taxable year."
Commissioner of Internal Revenue, Petitioner, v Lincoln Savings and Loan Association (June 14, 1971)
M/B: Commissioner v. Lincoln Savings & Loan Association, 403 U.S. 345, 353-54 (1971).
LR: Commissioner v. Lincoln Sav. & Loan Ass'n, 403 U.S. 345, 353-54 (1971).

58 199 277 322 466 574   29 L. Ed. 2d 82   "[524] [T]he Commission concluded that no standby charge should [525] be imposed on either party to the interconnection."
Gainesville Utilities Department et al., Petitioners, v Florida Power Corporation (No. 464) (May 24, 1971)
M/B: Gainesville Utilities Department v. Florida Power Corp., 402 U.S. 515, 524-25 (1971).
LR: Gainesville Utils. Dep't v. Florida Power Corp., 402 U.S. 515, 524-25 (1971).

59 200 278 323 467 575   30 L. Ed. 2d 719   "[563] The court did not . . . consider the constitutionality of § 501(c)(3) 'as [564] a whole.'"
United States, Appellant, v Christian Echoes National Ministry, Inc. (January 24, 1972)
M/B: United States v. Christian Echoes National Ministry, Inc., 404 U.S. 561 (1972).
LR: United States v. Christian Echoes Nat'l Ministry, Inc., 404 U.S. 561 (1972).

60 101 279 324 468 576   30 L. Ed. 2d 580   "[423] '[O]wnership of this quantity of stock suffices to [424] provide access to inside information.'"
Reliance Electric Company, Petitioner, v Emerson Electric Company (January 11, 1972)
M/B: Reliance Electric Co. v. Emerson Electric Co., 404 U.S. 418, 423-24 (1972).
LR: Reliance Elec. Co. v. Emerson Elec. Co., 404 U.S. 418, 423-24 (1972).

61 102 280 325 469 577   31 L. Ed. 2d 619   "[704] Petitioner . . . asserted a claim against an additional [705] party that had virtually no relationship to the claim or relief sought."
T. R. Grubbs, dba T. R. Grubbs Tire & Appliance, Petitioner, v General Electric Credit Corporation (April 18, 1972)
M/B: Grubbs v. General Electric Credit Corp., 405 U.S. 699, 704-05 (1972).
LR: Grubbs v. General Elec. Credit Corp., 405 U.S. 699, 704-05 (1972).

62 103 281 326 470 578   31 L. Ed. 2d 779   "[175] Courts are powerless to prevent [176] the social opprobrium suffered by these hapless children, but the Equal Protection Clause does enable us to strike down discriminatory laws relating to status of birth."
Willie Mae Weber, Petitioner, v Aetna Casualty & Surety Company et al. (April 24, 1972)
M/B: Weber v. Aetna Casualty & Surety Co., 406 U.S. 164, 175-76 (1972).
LR: Weber v. Aetna Casualty & Sur. Co., 406 U.S. 164, 175-76 (1972).

EXERCISE 5. LAWYERS' EDITION OF U.S. SUPREME COURT REPORTS   (CONTINUED)

63 104 282 327 471 579   32 L. Ed. 2d 701   "[215] [T]he cause is remanded to the [216] Special Master for further proceedings."
Commonwealth of Pennsylvania, Plaintiff, v State of New York et al. (June 19, 1972)
M/B: Pennsylvania v. New York, 407 U.S. 206, 215-16 (1972).

64 105 283 328 472 580   32 L. Ed. 2d 264   "[502] They also contend that the Michigan statute conflicts with or is [503] pre-empted by federal law."
Lake Carriers' Association et al., Appellants, v Ralph A. MacMullan et al. (May 30, 1972)
M/B: Lake Carriers' Association v. MacMullan, 406 U.S. 498, 502-03 (1972).
LR: Lake Carriers' Ass'n v. MacMullan, 406 U.S. 498, 502-03 (1972).

65 106 284 329 473 581   33 L. Ed. 2d 127   "[543] The Board ordered the company [544] to rescind its no-distribution rule."
Central Hardware Company, Petitioner, v National Labor Relations Board et al. (June 22, 1972)
M/B: Central Hardware Co. v. NLRB, 407 U.S. 539, 543-44 (1972).

66 107 285 330 474 582   33 L. Ed. 2d 353   "[244] The words 'cruel and unusual' certainly include penalties [245] that are barbaric."
William Henry Furman, Petitioner. v State of Georgia (No. 69-5003) (June 29, 1972)
M/B: Furman v. Georgia, 408 U.S. 238, 244-45 (1972).

67 108 286 331 475 583   34 L. Ed. 2d 429   "[222] [T]he policy of § 7 would not be frustrated by a holding that an employee could . . . knowingly waive his § 7 right to resign from the union and to return to work [223] without sanction."
National Labor Relations Board, Petitioner, v Granite State Joint Board, Textile Workers Union of America, Local 1029, AFL-CIO (December 7, 1972)
M/B: NLRB v. Granite State Joint Board, 409 U.S. 213, 222-23 (1972).
LR: NLRB v. Granite State Joint Bd., 409 U.S. 213, 222-23 (1972).

68 109 287 332 476 584   34 L. Ed. 2d 535   "[300] We declined to hold that Congress intended to oust completely the antitrust laws and supplant them with the self-regulatory scheme authorized [301] by the Exchange Act."
Thomas Ricci, Petitioner, v Chicago Mercantile Exchange et al. (January 9, 1973)
M/B: Ricci v. Chicago Mercantile Exchange, 409 U.S. 289, 300-01 (1973).
LR: Ricci v. Chicago Mercantile Exch., 409 U.S. 289, 300-01 (1973).

69 110 288 333 477 585   35 L. Ed. 2d 305   "[288] At trial, he endeavored to develop two [289] grounds of defense."
Leon Chambers, Petitioner, v State of Mississippi (February 21, 1973)
M/B: Chambers v. Mississippi, 410 U.S. 284, 288-89 (1973).

70 111 289 334 478 586   35 L. Ed. 2d 240   "[246] Charges are fixed that nonowning railroads must pay [247] owning railroads for boxcars of the latter that are on the tracks of the former."
United States et al., Appellants, v Florida East Coast Railway Company et al. (January 22, 1973)
M/B: United States v. Florida East Coast Railway, 410 U.S. 224, 246-47 (1973).
LR: United States v. Florida E.C. Ry., 410 U.S. 224, 246-47 (1973).

71 112 290 335 479 587   61 L. Ed. 2d 421   "[118] The court concluded that the investigations and the speech were clearly within the [119] ambit of the Clause."
Ronald R. Hutchinson, Petitioner, v William Proxmire and Morton Schwartz (June 26, 1979)
M/B: Hutchinson v. Proxmire, 443 U.S. 111, 118-19 (1979).

72 113 291 336 480 588   36 L. Ed. 2d 573   "[660] 'Congress did not, however, intend criminal penalties for people who [661] failed to comply with a non-existent regulatory program.'"

EXERCISE 5. LAWYERS' EDITION OF U.S. SUPREME COURT REPORTS   (CONTINUED)

United States, Petitioner, v Pennsylvania Industrial Chemical Corporation (May 14, 1973)
M/B: United States v. Pennsylvania Industrial Chemical Corp., 411 U.S. 655, 660-61 (1973).
LR: United States v. Pennsylvania Indus. Chem. Corp., 411 U.S. 655, 660-61 (1973).

73 114 292 337 481 589   37 L. Ed. 2d 453   "[51] The two films in question, 'Magic Mirror' and 'It All Comes Out in the End,' depict sexual conduct characterized [52] by the Georgia Supreme Court as 'hard core pornography' leaving 'little to the imagination.'"
Paris Adult Theatre I et al., Petitioners, v Lewis R. Slaton, District Attorney, Atlanta Judicial Circuit, et al. (June 21, 1973)
M/B: Paris Adult Theatre I v. Slaton, 413 U.S. 49, 51-52 (1973).

74 115 293 338 482 590   37 L. Ed. 2d 41   "[415] The judgment of the [416] Court of Claims on this issue is reversed and the case is remanded for further proceedings."
United States, Petitioner, v Chicago, Burlington & Quincy Railroad Company (June 4, 1973)
M/B: United States v. Chicago, Burlington & Quincy Railroad, 412 U.S. 401, 415-16 (1973).
LR: United States v. Chicago, B. & Q.R.R., 412 U.S. 401, 415-16 (1973).

75 116 294 339 483 591   38 L. Ed. 2d 383   "[159] [E]ver since 1789, Congress has granted this Court the power to intervene in State litigation [160] only after 'the highest court of a State in which a decision in the suit could be had' has rendered a 'final judgment or decree.'"
North Dakota State Board of Pharmacy, Petitioner, v Snyder's Drug Stores, Inc. (December 5, 1973)
M/B: North Dakota State Board of Pharmacy v. Snyder's Drug Stores, 414 U.S. 156, 159-60 (1973).
LR: North Dakota State Bd. of Pharmacy v. Snyder's Drug Stores, 414 U.S. 156, 159-60 (1973).

76 117 295 340 484 592   38 L. Ed. 2d 514   "[292] From the outset, Congress has provided that suits between citizens of different States are maintainable in the district courts only if the 'matter in controversy' [293] exceeds the statutory minimum, now set at $10,000."
H. Keith Zahn et al., Petitioners, v International Paper Company (December 17, 1973)
M/B: Zahn v. International Paper Co., 414 U.S. 291, 292-93 (1973).

77 118 296 341 485 593   54 L. Ed. 2d 264   "[90] However, the House and Senate initially [91] differed on the significance that should be given the convenience-of-the employer doctrine for purposes of § 119."
Commissioner of Internal Revenue, Petitioner, v Robert J. Kowalski et ux. (November 29, 1977)
M/B: Commissioner v. Kowalski, 434 U.S. 77, 90-91 (1977).

78 119 297 342 486 594   39 L. Ed. 2d 23   "[588] Objection to permitting recovery for loss of society often centers upon the fear that such damages are somewhat speculative and that factfinders will return [589] excessive verdicts."
Sea-Land Services, Inc., Petitioner, v Helen Stein Gaudet, Administratrix of the Estate of Awtrey C. Gaudet, Sr. (January 21, 1974)
M/B: Sea-Land Services v. Gaudet, 414 U.S. 573, 588-89 (1974).
LR: Sea-Land Servs. v. Gaudet, 414 U.S. 573, 588-89 (1974).

79 120 298 343 487 595   40 L. Ed. 2d 220   "[390] We do not suggest that where there is doubt as to local law and where the certification procedure is available, [391] resort to it is obligatory."
Lehman Brothers, Petitioners, v Jacob Schein et al. (No. 73-439) (April 29, 1974)
M/B: Lehman Brothers v. Schein, 416 U.S. 386, 390-91 (1974).
LR: Lehman Bros. v. Schein, 416 U.S. 386, 390-91 (1974).

EXERCISE 5. LAWYERS' EDITION OF U.S. SUPREME COURT REPORTS   (CONTINUED)

80 121 299 344 488 596   53 L. Ed. 2d 413   "[368] Indeed, the one-year statute of limitations . . . could [369] under some circumstances directly conflict with the timetable for administrative action expressly established in the 1972 Act."
Occidental Life Insurance Company of California, Petitioner, v Equal Employment Opportunity Commission (June 20, 1977)
M/B: Occidental Life Insurance Co. v. EEOC, 432 U.S. 355, 368-69 (1977).
LR: Occidental Life Ins. Co. v. EEOC, 432 U.S. 355, 368-69 (1977).

81 122 300 345 489 597   41 L. Ed. 2d 543   "[9] There is no disagreement [10] as to the allocation of depreciation between construction and maintenance."
Commissioner of Internal Revenue, Petitioner, v Idaho Power Company (June 24, 1974)
M/B: Commissioner v. Idaho Power Co., 418 U.S. 1, 9-10 (1974).

82 123 201 346 490 598   41 L. Ed. 2d 248   "[471] In furtherance of its [472] long-range responsibilities the Reorganization Court enjoined secured creditors from selling collateral to reduce their claims."
George P. Baker et al., Petitioners, v Gold Seal Liquors, Inc. (June 17, 1974)
M/B: Baker v. Gold Seal Liquors, Inc., 417 U.S. 467, 471-72 (1974).

83 124 202 347 491 599   42 L. Ed. 2d 405   "[221] Petitioners therefore [222] are able to state that the requirements . . . are satisfied."
American Radio Association, AFL-CIO, et al., Petitioners, v Mobile Steamship Association, Inc., et al. (December 17, 1974)
M/B: American Radio Association v. Mobile Steamship Association, 419 U.S. 215, 221-22 (1974).
LR: American Radio Ass'n v. Mobile S.S. Ass'n, 419 U.S. 215, 221-22 (1974).

84 125 203 348 492 600   42 L. Ed. 2d 460   "[292] The testimony thus presented the carriers' maximum potential exposure, [293] leaving considerable leeway for predicting what was likely if applications were granted."
Bowman Transportation, Inc., Appellant, v Arkansas-Best Freight System, Inc., et al. (No. 73-1055) (December 23, 1974)
M/B: Bowman Transportation v. Arkansas-Best Freight System, 419 U.S. 281, 292-93 (1974).
LR: Bowman Transp. v. Arkansas-Best Freight Sys., 419 U.S. 215, 292-93 (1974).

85 126 204 349 493 501   43 L. Ed. 2d 181   "[262] A single employee confronted by an employer [263] investigating whether certain conduct deserves discipline may be too fearful or inarticulate to relate accurately the incident being investigated, or too ignorant to raise extenuating factors."
National Labor Relations Board, Petitioner, v J. Weingarten, Inc. (February 19, 1975)
M/B: NLRB v. J. Weingarten, Inc., 420 U.S. 251, 262-63 (1975).

86 127 205 350 494 502   43 L. Ed. 2d 126   "[190] Suspending or changing demurrage charges [191] may increase the transportation charges."
Interstate Commerce Commission, Appellant, v Oregon Pacific Industries, Inc., et al. (February 19, 1975)
M/B: ICC v. Oregon Pacific Industries, 420 U.S. 184, 190-91 (1975).
LR: ICC v. Oregon Pac. Indus., 420 U.S. 184, 190-91 (1975).

87 128 206 351 495 503   44 L. Ed. 2d 649   "[7] This phrase might also merely mean ... that the time limit established by [8] this provision ... runs from the date of the last voluntary payment."
Intercounty Construction Corporation et al., Petitioners, v Noah C.A. Walter, Etc., et al. (June 16, 1975)
M/B: Intercounty Construction Corp. v. Walter, 422 U.S. 1, 7-8 (1975).
LR: Intercounty Constr. Corp. v. Walter, 422 U.S. 1, 7-8 (1975).

88 129 207 352 496 504   44 L. Ed. 2d 271   "[421] Even failing [422] those alternatives, a firm may be able to liquidate under supervision of one of the self-regulatory organizations, or the district court, without danger of loss to customers."

EXERCISE 5. LAWYERS' EDITION OF U.S. SUPREME COURT REPORTS   (CONTINUED)

Securities Investor Protection Corporation, Petitioner, v James C. Barbour et al. (May 19, 1975)
M/B: Securities Investor Protection Corp. v. Barbour, 421 U.S. 412, 421-22 (1975).
Note: "SIPC" may be widely enough known to be correct.

89 130 208 353 497 505   45 L. Ed. 2d 494   "[699] This case [700] focuses . . . on the potential secondary market in mutual-fund shares."
United States, Appellant, v National Association of Securities Dealers, Inc., et al. (June 26, 1975)
M/B: United States v. National Association of Securities Dealers, 422 U.S. 694, 699-700 (1975).
LR: United States v. National Ass'n of Sec. Dealers, 422 U.S. 694, 699-700 (1975).

90 131 209 354 498 506   45 L. Ed. 2d 189   "[285] The District Court, therefore, properly [286] concluded that the acquisition and merger in this case were not within the coverage of § 7 of the Clayton Act."
United States, Appellant, v American Building Maintenance Industries (June 24, 1975)
M/B: United States v. American Building Maintenance Industries, 422 U.S. 271, 285-86 (1975).
LR: United States v. American Bldg. Maintenance Indus., 422 U.S. 271, 285-86 (1975).

91 132 210 355 499 507   46 L. Ed. 2d 176   "[35] Under the Motor Carrier Act [of] 1935, [36] . . . only a properly certificated carrier may haul freight in interstate or foreign commerce."
Transamerican Freight Lines, Inc., Petitioner, v Brada Miller Freight Systems, Inc., et al. (November 12, 1975)
M/B: Transamerican Freight Lines v. Brada Miller Freight Systems, 423 U.S. 28, 35-36 (1975).
LR: Transamerican Freight Lines v. Brada Miller Freight Sys., 423 U.S. 28, 35-36 (1975).

92 133 211 356 500 508   46 L. Ed. 2d 550   "[343] Neither the propriety of the removal nor the jurisdiction of the court [344] was questioned by respondent in the slightest."
Thermtron Products, Inc. and Larry Dean Newhard, Petitioners, v H. David Hermansdorfer, Judge, United States District Court for the Eastern District of Kentucky (January 20, 1976)
M/B: Thermtron Products, Inc. v. Hermansdorfer, 423 U.S. 336, 343-44 (1976).
LR: Thermtron Prods., Inc. v. Hermansdorfer, 423 U.S. 336, 343-44 (1976).

93 134 212 357 401 509   47 L. Ed. 2d 456   "[754] 'Embodied [755] in the words 'cases' and 'controversies' are two complementary but somewhat different limitations.'"
Harold Franks and Johnnie Lee, Petitioners, v Bowman Transportation Company, Inc., et al. (March 24, 1976)
M/B: Franks v. Bowman Transportation Co., 424 U.S. 747, 754-55 (1976).
LR: Franks v. Bowman Transp. Co., 424 U.S. 747, 754-55 (1976).

94 135 213 358 402 510   47 L. Ed. 2d 291   "[629] Here the Government seized respondent's property [630] and contends that it has absolutely no obligation to prove that the seizure has any basis in fact no matter how severe or irreparable the injury."
Commissioner of Internal Revenue, Petitioner, v Samuel Shapiro et ux. (March 8, 1976)
M/B: Commissioner v. Shapiro, 424 U.S. 614, 629-30 (1976).

95 136 214 359 403 511   71 L. Ed. 2d 415   "[556] [T]he court [of appeals] correctly [557] noted that the certificate of deposit is not expressly excluded from the definition since it is not currency and it has a maturity exceeding nine months." Marine Bank, Petitioner, v Samuel Weaver, et ux. (March 8, 1982)
M/B: Marine Bank v. Weaver, 455 U.S. 551, 556-57 (1982).

EXERCISE 5. LAWYERS' EDITION OF U.S. SUPREME COURT REPORTS   (CONTINUED)

96 137 215 360 404 512   72 L. Ed. 2d 801   "[219] These arguments do not apply [220] with the same force to classifications imposing disabilities on the minor children of such illegal entrants."
James Plyler, Superintendent of the Tyler Independent School District and its Board of Trustees et al., Appellants, v J. and R. Doe et al. (No. 80-1538) (June 15, 1982)
M/B: Plyer v. Doe, 457 U.S. 202, 219-20 (1982).

97 138 216 361 405 513   73 L. Ed. 2d 847   "[387] [T]he fact that the prohibitions of § 1981 [388] encompass private as well as governmental action does not suggest that the statute reaches more than purposeful discrimination, whether public or private."
General Building Contractors Association, Inc., Petitioner v Pennsylvania et al. (June 29, 1982)
M/B: General Building Contractors Association v. Pennsylvania, 458 U.S. 375, 387-88 (1982).
LR: General Bldg. Contractors Ass'n v. Pennsylvania, 458 U.S. 375, 387-88 (1982).

98 139 217 362 406 514   74 L. Ed. 2d 304   "[121] Given the broad powers of states under the [t]wenty-first [a]mendment, judicial deference to the legislative exercise of zoning powers by a city council or other legislative zoning body is especially appropriate in the area of liquor [122] regulation."
John J. Larkin et al., Appellants v Grendel's Den, Inc. (December 13, 1982)
M/B: Larkin v. Grendel's Den, Inc., 459 U.S. 116, 121-22 (1982).

99 140 218 363 407 515   75 L. Ed. 2d 153   "[394] As long as the payment itself was not negated by a refund to the corporation, the change in character of the funds in the hands of the [395] State does not require the corporation to recognize income."
Hillsboro National Bank, Petitioner v Commissioner of Internal Revenue (March 7, 1983)
M/B: Hillsboro National Bank v. Commissioner, 460 U.S. 370, 394-95 (1983).
LR: Hillsboro Nat'l Bank v. Commissioner, 460 U.S. 370, 394-95 (1983).

100 141 219 364 408 516   76 L. Ed. 2d 289   "[743] States have only a [744] negligible interest, if any, in having insubstantial claims adjudicated by their courts, particularly in the face of the strong federal interest in vindicating the rights protected by the national labor laws." Bill Johnson's Restaurants, Inc., Petitioner v National Labor Relations Board (May 31, 1983).
M/B: Bill Johnson's Restaurants, Inc. v. NLRB, 461 U.S. 731, 743-44 (1983).
Note: "Inc." may be omitted from the above citation.

LIBRARY EXERCISE 6. EARLY UNITED STATES REPORTS.

INSTRUCTOR'S NOTE: The students are required to cite the case that begins on the page listed in the volume of United States Reports designated for their problem number. Note that the page listed, which is the page that should be used in the citation of the case, is the star page when the pagination in United States Reports differs from that of the original report. For this Exercise, students are allowed to use the year of the term of the court if the date of decision is not given with the opinion in United States Reports. If the student uses the Lawyers' Edition to find the year of decision (for cases beginning with the December 1854 Term), the year used by the student may be one year later than the year listed in the answers below.

The following Quick-Reference Abbreviations are particularly relevant to this exercise:

CASE NAME 9. DO NOT ALTER THE ORDER OF A PARTY'S NAME GIVEN AT THE BEGINNING OF THE OFFICIAL REPORTER. [CN 9]
CASE NAME 19. OMIT "THE" WHEN IT IS THE FIRST WORD OR A PARTY'S NAME EXCEPT WHEN CITING A POPULAR NAME, THE NAME OF THE OBJECT OF AN IN REM ACTION, OR "THE KING" OR "THE QUEEN." [CN 19]
FEDERAL COURT CITATION 6. USE THE STAR PAGING IN THE EARLY UNITED STATES REPORTS VOLUMES IN THE CITATIONS OF OPINIONS IN THESE VOLUMES. [FED 6]
FEDERAL COURT CITATION 7. INCLUDE A PARENTHETICAL INDICATION OF THE NOMINATIVE REPORTER'S NAME AND THE VOLUME NUMBER OF HIS SERIES IN CITATIONS OF THE FIRST NINETY VOLUMES OF UNITED STATES REPORTS. PLACE THE PARENTHETICAL BETWEEN THE "U.S." AND THE CITED PAGE NUMBER AND ABBREVATE THE NOMINATIVE REPORTER'S NAME, AS APPROPRIATE. [FED 7]

1 199 232 316 493 589   50 U.S. 356
George S. Gaines, Francis S. Lyon and his Wife, Sarah Lyon, James Davenport, Goodman G. Griffen and his Wife, Willey Ann Griffin, George Frederick Glover, Ann Gaines Glover, Louisa Davenport Glover, Mary Thompson, and Mary A. Glover, Appellants, v. Isaac W. Nicolson, Powhatan B. Thermond, Lewis B. Barnes, John T. Moseley, S. M. Goode, and John Hilman
M/B: Gaines v. Nicolson, 50 U.S. (9 How.) 356 (1850).

2 200 233 317 494 590   73 U.S. 719
Gaines v. De la Croix
M/B: Gaines v. De la Croix, 73 U.S. (6 Wall.) 719 (1867).

3 101 234 318 495 591   65 U.S. 553
Myra Clark Gaines, Appellant, v. Duncan H. Hennen
M/B: Gaines v. Hennen, 65 U.S. (24 How.) 53 (1860).

4 102 235 319 496 592   7 U.S. 337
United States v. Grundy and Thornburgh
M/B: United States v. Grundy, 7 U.S. (3 Cranch) 37 (1806).

5 103 236 320 497 593   37 U.S. 264
James Galloway, Junior, Appellant, v. Henry R. Finley and David Barr, Appellees
M/B: Galloway v. Finley, 37 U.S. (12 Pet.) 264 (1838).

6 104 237 321 498 594   85 U.S. 350
Galpin v. Page
M/B: Galpin v. Page, 85 U.S. (18 Wall.) 350 (1873).

7 105 238 322 499 595   29 U.S. 332
William T. Galt and others, Appellants, v. James Galloway, Jr., and others, Appellees
M/B: Galt v. Galloway, 29 U.S. (4 Pet.) 332 (1830).

8 106 239 323 500 596   51 U.S. 270
Charles Barnard, Abel Adams, George M. Barnard, and Charles Larkin, Plaintiffs in Error, v. Joseph Adams, Andrew H. Bennet, and Joseph Fletcher
M/B: Barnard v. Adams, 51 U.S. (10 How.) 270 (1850).

9 107 240 324 401 597   57 U.S. 451

EXERCISE 6.   EARLY UNITED STATES REPORTS   (CONTINUED)

Louis D. Gamache, Samuel and Leonore Gamache, by Guardian, Wilson Primm, Louis Primm, John Cavenden, and Abby P. True, Plaintiffs in Error, v. Francois X. Piquignot, and the Inhabitants of the Town of Carondelet
M/B: Gamache v. Piquignot, 57 U.S. (16 How.) 451 (1853).

10 108 241 325 402 598   74 U.S. 506
Ex parte McCardle
M/B: Ex parte McCardle, 74 U.S. (7 Wall.) 506 (1868).
LR: Ex parte McCardle, 74 U.S. (7 Wall.) 506 (1868).

11 109 242 326 403 599   44 U.S. 707
Lessee of Daniel W. Gantly et al., Plaintiff, v. William G. and George W. Ewing, Defendants
M/B: Lessee of Gantly v. Ewing, 44 U.S. (3 How.) 707 (1845).

12 110 243 327 404 600   88 U.S. 36
Gardner v. Brown
M/B: Gardner v. Brown, 88 U.S. (21 Wall.) 36 (1874).

13 111 244 328 405 501   27 U.S. 58
William A. Gardner v. John C. Collins et al.
M/B: Gardner v. Collins, 27 U.S. (2 Pet.) 58 (1829).

14 112 245 329 406 502   45 U.S. 131
Hugh A. Garland, Plaintiff in Error, v. George M. Davis, Defendant
M/B: Garland v. Davis, 45 U.S. (4 How.) 131 (1846).

15 113 246 330 407 503   61 U.S. 6
Josiah Garland, Plaintiff in Error, v. Robert H. Wynn, Executor and Devisee of William Wynn, Deceased
M/B: Garland v. Wynn, 61 U.S. (20 How.) 6 (1857).

16 114 247 331 408 504   33 U.S. 75
Reuben M. Garnett et al., Heirs of Reuben Garnett, deceased, Appellants, v. Henry Jenkins et al.
M/B: Garnett v. Jenkins, 33 U.S. (8 Pet.) 75 (1834).

17 115 248 332 409 505   36 U.S. 226
State of Rhode Island v. State of Massachusetts
M/B: Rhode Island v. Massachusetts, 36 U.S. (11 Pet.) 226 (1837).

18 116 249 333 410 506   56 U.S. 272
John Garrow, Thomas Y. How, Jr., James Seymour, and George Miller, Appellants, v. Amos Davis, George M. Pickerling, William McCrillis, and Ephraim Paulk
M/B: Garrow v. Davis, 56 U.S. (15 How.) 272 (1853).

19 117 250 335 411 507   31 U.S. 761
Pierre Gassies, Plaintiff in error, v. Jean Gassies Ballon, Defendant in error
M/B: Gassies v. Ballon, 31 U.S. (6 Pet.) 761 (1832).

20 118 251 335 412 508   89 U.S. 308
Gavinzel v. Crump
M/B: Gavinzel v. Crump, 89 U.S. (22 Wall.) 308 (1874).

21 119 252 336 413 509   80 U.S. 434
Clinton et al. v. Englebrecht
M/B: Clinton v. Englebrecht, 80 U.S. (13 Wall.) 434 (1871).

22 120 253 337 414 510   68 U.S. 81
Gaylords v. Kelshaw et al.
M/B: Gaylords v. Kelshaw, 68 U.S. (1 Wall.) 81 (1863).

23 121 254 338 415 511   16 U.S. 246
Gelston et al. v. Hoyt
M/B: Gelston v. Hoyt, 16 U.S. (3 Wheat.) 246 (1818).

24 122 255 339 416 512   25 U.S. 408

EXERCISE 6.   EARLY UNITED STATES REPORTS   (CONTINUED)

The General Interest Insurance Company, Plaintiffs in error, v. Ruggles, Defendant in error
M/B: <u>General Interest Insurance Co. v. Ruggles</u>, 25 U.S. (12 Wheat.) 408 (1827).
LR: General Interest Ins. Co. v. Ruggles, 25 U.S. (12 Wheat.) 408 (1827).

25 123 256 340 417 513   90 U.S. 150
Stickney, Assignee, v. Wilt
M/B: <u>Stickney v. Wilt</u>, 90 U.S. (23 Wall.) 150 (1874).

26 124 257 341 418 514   53 U.S. 407
Snead v. McCoull et al.
M/B: <u>Snead v. McCoull</u>, 53 U.S. (12 How.) 407 (1851).

27 125 258 342 419 515   74 U.S. 564
Generes v. Bonnemer
M/B: <u>Generes v. Bonnemer</u>, 74 U.S. (7 Wall.) 564 (1868).

28 126 259 343 420 516   78 U.S. 193
Generes v. Campbell
M/B: <u>Generes v. Campbell</u>, 78 U.S. (11 Wall.) 193 (1870).

29 127 260 344 421 517   14 U.S. 408
The George, The Bothnea, and The Janstaff
M/B: <u>The George</u>, 14 U.S. (1 Wheat.) 408 (1816).

30 128 261 345 422 518   15 U.S. 290
Morgan's Heirs v. Morgan et al.
M/B: <u>Morgan's Heirs v. Morgan</u>, 15 U.S. (2 Wheat.) 290 (1817).

31 129 262 346 423 519   79 U.S. 259
Germain v. Mason
M/B: <u>Germain v. Mason</u>, 79 U.S. (12 Wall.) 259 (1870).

32 130 263 347 424 520   73 U.S. 231
Mason v. Eldred et al.
M/B: <u>Mason v. Eldred</u>, 73 U.S. (6 Wall.) 231 (1867).

33 131 264 348 425 521   87 U.S. 201
The Lottawanna
M/B: <u>The Lottawanna</u>, 87 U.S. (20 Wall.) 201 (1873).

34 132 265 349 426 522   77 U.S. 304
Gunnell v. Bird
M/B: <u>Gunnell v. Bird</u>, 77 U.S. (10 Wall.) 304 (1869).

35 133 266 350 427 523   19 U.S. 453
Hughes v. Blake
M/B: <u>Hughes v. Blake</u>, 19 U.S. (6 Wheat.) 453 (1821).

36 134 267 351 428 524   22 U.S. 1
Gibbons, appellant, v. Ogden, respondent
M/B: <u>Gibbons v. Ogden</u>, 22 U.S. (9 Wheat.) 1 (1824).

37 135 268 352 429 525   41 U.S. 315
John A. Gibson and Kinchen A. Martin, Plaintiffs in error, v. Beverly Chew, Defendant in error
M/B: <u>Gibson v. Chew</u>, 41 U.S. (16 Pet.) 315 (1842).

38 136 269 353 430 526   75 U.S. 314
Gibson v. Chouteau
M/B: <u>Gibson v. Chouteau</u>, 75 U.S. (8 Wall.) 314 (1868).

39 139 270 354 431 527   49 U.S. 402
John West, Appellant, v. Joseph Smith and Ellen, his wife
M/B: <u>West v. Smith</u>, 49 U.S. (8 How.) 402 (1850).

EXERCISE 6.   EARLY UNITED STATES REPORTS   (CONTINUED)

40 138 271 355 432 528   81 U.S. 244
Gibson v. Warden
M/B: Gibson v. Warden, 81 U.S. (14 Wall.) 244 (1871).

41 139 272 356 433 529   87 U.S. 571
Gillette v. Bullard
M/B: Gillette v. Bullard, 87 U.S. (20 Wall.) 571 (1874).

42 140 273 357 434 530   70 U.S. 713
Gilman v. Philadelphia
M/B: Gilman v. Philadelphia, 70 U.S. (3 Wall.) 713 (1865).

43 141 274 358 435 531   67 U.S. 510
Gilman v. The City of Sheboygan
M/B: Gilman v. City of Sheboygan, 67 U.S. (2 Black) 510 (1862).

44 142 275 359 436 532   71 U.S. 409
Gilman v. Lockwood
M/B: Gilman v. Lockwood, 71 U.S. (4 Wall.) 409 (1866).

45 143 276 360 437 533   35 U.S. 298
Benjamin I. Gilman, Plaintiff in error, v. Peter G. Rives
M/B: Gilman v. Rives, 35 U.S. (10 Pet.) 298 (1836).

46 144 277 361 438 534   72 U.S. 545
The Bird of Paradise
M/B: The Bird of Paradise, 72 U.S. (5 Wall.) 545 (1866).

47 145 278 362 439 535   66 U.S. 595
Glasgow et al. v. Hortiz et al.
M/B: Glasgow v. Hortiz, 66 U.S. (1 Black) 595 (1861).

48 146 279 363 440 536   86 U.S. 41
The Wenona
M/B: The Wenona, 86 U.S. (19 Wall.) 41 (1873).

49 147 280 364 441 537   84 U.S. 123
Goddard v. Foster
M/B: Goddard v. Foster, 84 U.S. (17 Wall.) 123 (1872).

50 148 281 365 442 538   37 U.S. 178
Joseph S. Clarke and Richard S. Briscoe, Appellants, v. William G. W. White, Appellee
M/B: Clarke v. White, 37 U.S. (12 Pet.) 178 (1838).

51 149 282 366 443 539   62 U.S. 248
Thomas Maguire, Claimant of the Steamer Goliah, Appellant, v. Stephen Card, Libellant
M/B: Maguire v. Card, 62 U.S. (21 How.) 248 (1858).

52 150 283 367 444 540   11 U.S. 339
Locke v. United States
M/B: Locke v. United States, 11 U.S. (7 Cranch) 339 (1813).

53 151 284 368 445 541   58 U.S. 478
The State of Florida, Complainant, v. The State of Georgia
M/B: Florida v. Georgia, 58 U.S. (17 How.) 478 (1854).

54 152 285 369 446 542   7 U.S. 268
Gordon v. Caldoleugh et al.
M/B: Gordon v. Caldoleugh, 7 U.S. (3 Cranch) 268 (1806).

55 153 286 370 447 543   76 U.S. 203
Star of Hope
M/B: Star of Hope, 76 U.S. (9 Wall.) 203 (1869).

56 154 287 371 448 544   83 U.S. 314

EXERCISE 6. <u>EARLY UNITED STATES REPORTS</u>   (CONTINUED)

Walker v. Whitehead
M/B: <u>Walker v. Whitehead</u>, 83 U.S. (16 Wall.) 314 (1872).

57 155 288 372 449 545   28 U.S. 33
Alexander Gordon and others v. Francis B. Ogden
M/B: <u>Gordon v. Ogden</u>, 28 U.S. (3 Pet.) 33 (1830).

58 156 289 373 450 546   69 U.S. 591
Read v. Bowman
M/B: <u>Read v. Bowman</u>, 69 U.S. (2 Wall.) 591 (1864).

59 157 290 374 451 547   40 U.S. 284
William M. Gwin, Marshal of the Southern District of Mississippi, Plaintiff in error, v. James H. Breedlove, Defendant in error
M/B: <u>Gwin v. Breedlove</u>, 40 U.S. (15 Pet.) 284 (1841).

60 158 291 375 452 548   82 U.S. 187
Gould v. Rees
M/B: <u>Gould v. Rees</u>, 82 U.S. (15 Wall.) 187 (1872).

61 159 292 376 453 549   73 U.S. 441
The Grace Girdler
M/B: <u>The Grace Girdler</u>, 73 U.S. (6 Wall.) 441 (1867).

62 160 293 377 454 550   21 U.S. 642
Anderson Childress, Executor of Joel Childress, Plaintiff in error v. Emory and McCleur, Executors of John G. Comegys, surviving partner of William Cochran & Comegys, Defendants in error
M/B: <u>Childress v. Emory</u>, 21 U.S. (8 Wheat.) 642 (1823).

63 161 294 378 455 551   12 U.S. 462
Alexander and others v. Pendleton
M/B: <u>Alexander v. Pendleton</u>, 12 U.S. (8 Cranch) 462 (1814).

64 162 295 379 456 552   60 U.S. 126
Romelius L. Baker and Jacob Henrici, Trustee of the Harmony Society of Beaver County, Pennsylvania, and others, Appellants, v. Joshua Nachtrieb
M/B: <u>Baker v. Nachtrieb</u>, 60 U.S. (19 How.) 126 (1856).

65 163 296 380 457 553   85 U.S. 623
Grant v. Strong
M/B: <u>Grant v. Strong</u>, 85 U.S. (18 Wall.) 623 (1873).

66 164 297 381 458 554   2 U.S. 419
Chisholm, executor, v. Georgia
M/B: <u>Chisholm v. Georgia</u>, 2 U.S. (2 Dall.) 419 (1793).

67 165 298 382 459 555   23 U.S. 473
J. Manro and others v. Joseph Almeida and the goods, chattels and credits of the said Almeida
M/B: <u>Manro v. Almeida</u>, 23 U.S. (10 Wheat.) 473 (1825).

68 166 299 383 460 556   42 U.S. 169
James C. Bell and Robert Grant, Plaintiffs in error, v. Matthias Bruen
M/B: <u>Bell v. Bruen</u>, 42 U.S. (1 How.) 169 (1843).

69 167 300 384 461 557   26 U.S. 351
Montgomery Bell, Plaintiff in error, v. James Morrison, Anthony Butler and Jonathan Taylor, Defendants in error
M/B: <u>Bell v. Morrison</u>, 26 U.S. (1 Pet.) 351 (1828).

70 168 201 385 462 558   38 U.S. 263
William B. Bend v. Jesse Hoyt
M/B: <u>Bend v. Hoyt</u>, 38 U.S. (13 Pet.) 263 (1839).

71 169 202 386 463 559   19 U.S. 204
Anderson v. Dunn

EXERCISE 6.   EARLY UNITED STATES REPORTS   (CONTINUED)

M/B: Anderson v. Dunn, 19 U.S. (6 Wheat.) 204 (1821).

72 170 203 387 464 560   47 U.S. 279
The United States, Plaintiffs in error, v. A. Hodge and Levi Pearce
M/B: United States v. Hodge, 47 U.S. (6 How.) 279 (1848).

73 171 204 388 465 561   62 U.S. 394
Francis Martin, Administrator of Dennis T. Donovan, Deceased, Plaintiff in
Error, v. Christian Imhsen
M/B: Martin v. Imhsen, 62 U.S. (21 How.) 394 (1858).

74 172 205 389 466 562   60 U.S. 252
John Bell, Plaintiff in error, v. Columbus C. Hearne, Samuel R. Hearne, and
Samuel H. Dockery
M/B: Bell v. Hearne, 60 U.S. (19 How.) 252 (1856).

75 173 206 390 467 563   4 U.S. 14
Cooper v. Telfair
M/B: Cooper v. Telfair, 4 U.S. (4 Dall.) 14 (1800).

76 174 207 391 468 564   8 U.S. 384
Young v. Bank of Alexandria
M/B: Young v. Bank of Alexandria, 8 U.S. (4 Cranch) 384 (1808).

77 175 208 392 469 565   61 U.S. 162
William B. Grant, William Bradstreet, William L. Flitner, Peter Grant, in his
own right and as Administrator of Thomas Grant, deceased, Elizabeth F. Grant,
Administratrix, William S. Grant and George Bacon, Administrators of the
Estate of Samuel C. Grant, deceased, owners of the American Ship
Constellation, Libellants and Appellants, v. Cornelius Poillon, Richard
Poillon, James L. Varick, impleaded with H. Johnson, Hicks, Bailey, William Y.
Clark, Dean W. W. Hinchen, C. H. Clark, and D. D. Miller, Respondents and
Appellees
M/B: Grant v. Poillon, 61 U.S. (20 How.) 162 (1857).

78 176 209 393 470 566   88 U.S. 354
Hotchkiss v. National Banks
M/B: Hotchkiss v. National Banks, 88 U.S. (21 Wall.) 354 (1874).

79 177 210 394 471 567   3 U.S. 305
Hunter v. Fairfax's Devisee
M/B: Hunter v. Fairfax's Devisee, 3 U.S. (3 Dall.) 305 (1796).

80 178 211 395 472 568   5 U.S. 137
William Marbury v. James Madison, Secretary of State of the United States
M/B: Marbury v. Madison, 5 U.S. (1 Cranch) 137 (1803).

81 179 212 396 473 569   6 U.S. 187
Church v. Hubbart
M/B: Church v. Hubbart, 6 U.S. (2 Cranch) 187 (1804).

82 180 213 397 474 570   9 U.S. 173
Kempe's Lessee v. Kennedy et al.
M/B: Kempe's Lessee v. Kennedy, 9 U.S. (5 Cranch) 173 (1809).

83 181 214 398 475 571   10 U.S. 53
O'Neale v. Thornton
M/B: O'Neale v. Thornton, 10 U.S. (6 Cranch) 53 (1810).

84 182 215 399 476 572   13 U.S. 456
Pratt and others, original Complainants, v. Thomas Law and William Campbell,
original Defendants
M/B: Pratt v. Law, 13 U.S. (9 Cranch) 456 (1815).

85 183 216 400 477 573   18 U.S. 116
McClung v. Ross
M/B: McClung v. Ross, 18 U.S. (5 Wheat.) 116 (1820).

EXERCISE 6.   EARLY UNITED STATES REPORTS   (CONTINUED)

LR: McClung v. Ross, 18 U.S. (5 Wheat.) 116 (1820).

86 184 217 301 478 574   24 U.S. 78
Brooks v. Marbury
M/B: Brooks v. Marbury, 24 U.S. (11 Wheat.) 78 (1826).

87 185 218 302 479 575   30 U.S. 248
Lessee of John Fisher, Plaintiff in error, v. William Cockerell, Defendant in error
M/B: Lessee of Fisher v. Cockerell, 30 U.S. (5 Pet.) 248 (1831).

88 186 219 303 480 576   32 U.S. 171
John Holmes, Michael O'Mealy, Richard Caton, Hugh Thompson and William Slater, Appellants, v. Daniel Trout, William Moreland, Walter Moreland, Jeremiah Trout, Jacob Overpeck and William Buchannan, Appellees
M/B: Holmes v. Trout, 32 U.S. (7 Pet.) 171 (1833).

89 187 220 304 481 577   34 U.S. 86
William Caldwell, Isaac Caldwell and Samuel Brents, Appellants, v. Sarah and George Carrington's Heirs
M/B: Caldwell v. Carrington's Heirs, 34 U.S. (9 Pet.) 86 (1835).

90 188 221 305 482 578   39 U.S. 77
William A. Carr, Appellant, v. Samuel H. Duval and others, Appellees
M/B: Carr v. Duval, 39 U.S. (14 Pet.) 77 (1840).

91 189 222 306 483 579   43 U.S. 65
Ex parte Barry
M/B: Ex parte Barry, 43 U.S. (2 How.) 65 (1844).
LR: Ex parte Barry, 43 U.S. (2 How.) 65 (1844).

92 190 223 307 484 580   52 U.S. 232
Richard C. Stockton, Appellant, v. James C. Ford
M/B: Stockton v. Ford, 52 U.S. (11 How.) 232 (1850).

93 191 224 308 485 581   54 U.S. 115
David D. Mitchell, Plaintiff in error, v. Manuel X. Harmony
M/B: Mitchell v. Harmony, 54 U.S. (13 How.) 115 (1851).

94 192 225 309 486 582   55 U.S. 79
David B. Herman, Plaintiff in error, v. James Phalen; Same v. Same
M/B: Herman v. Phalen, 55 U.S. (14 How.) 79 (1852).

95 193 226 310 487 583   63 U.S. 144
John C. Hale, Plaintiff in error, v. William H. Gaines and Maria Gaines his wife, Albert Belding, Henry Belding, and George Belding, Heirs and Legal Representatives of Ludovious Belding, deceased, Defendants
M/B: Hale v. Gaines, 63 U.S. (22 How.) 144 (1859).

96 194 227 311 488 584   74 U.S. 32
The Georgia
M/B: The Georgia, 74 U.S. (7 Wall.) 32 (1868).

97 195 228 312 489 585   61 U.S. 372
Charles W. Gazzam, Plaintiff in Error, v. Lessee of Elam Phillips and Mary his wife, and Ashbey W. Etheridge
M/B: Gazzam v. Lessee of Phillips, 61 U.S. (20 How.) 372 (1857).

98 196 229 313 490 586   51 U.S. 627
Merritt M. Robinson and Marguerite his wife, Aurore Gayoso, Fernando Gayoso, and Felicite Gayoso, Appellants, v. Wm. J. Minor, James C. Wilkins, and Henry Chotard, Executors of the Last Will and Testament of Katharine Minor, deceased, Frances Chotard, Katharine L. Wilkins, and Wm. J. Minor
M/B: Robinson v. Minor, 51 U.S. (10 How.) 627 (1850).

99 197 230 314 491 587   45 U.S. 336
Benjamin D. Harris, Plaintiff in error, v. James Robinson, Defendant in error

EXERCISE 6.   EARLY UNITED STATES REPORTS   (CONTINUED)

M/B: Harris v. Robinson, 45 U.S. (4 How.) 336 (1846).

100 198 231 315 492 588   37 U.S. 511
Manuel Garcia, Plaintiff in error, v. Samuel Lee
M/B: Garcia v. Lee, 37 U.S. (12 Pet.) 511 (1838).

LIBRARY EXERCISE 7. FEDERAL REPORTER.

INSTRUCTOR'S NOTE: The students are required to cite the following two cases that begin on the pages listed below in the designated volumes of the Federal Reporter Second.

The following Quick-Reference Abbreviations are particularly relevant to this exercise:

FEDERAL COURT CITATION 9. DECISIONS OF U.S. COURTS OF APPEALS SHOULD BE CITED TO THE FEDERAL REPORTER. . . . BE SURE TO USE THE PROPER ABBREVIATION OF THE FEDERAL REPORTER (F., F.2d) AND FEDERAL CASES (F. Cas.). [FED 9]

FEDERAL COURT CITATION 11. CITE THE DECISIONS OF THE VARIOUS SPECIALIZED FEDERAL COURTS TO THE FEDERAL REPORTER OR THE FEDERAL SUPPLEMENT IF THEY HAVE BEEN PUBLISHED THEREIN. OTHERWISE, CITE TO THE APPROPRIATE OFFICIAL REPORTER OR SERVICE. BE SURE TO USE THE PROPER ABBREVIATION OF THE FEDERAL REPORTER (F.2d) OR THE FEDERAL SUPPLEMENT (F. Supp.). [FED 11]

FEDERAL COURT CITATION 12. IN CITATIONS OF DECISIONS OF THE U.S. COURTS OF APPEALS AND THE OLD CIRCUIT COURTS OF APPEALS, INCLUDE A PARENTHETICAL INDICATION OF THE CIRCUIT AND DATE. BE SURE TO USE THE PROPER ABBREVIATION OF THE CIRCUIT (1st Cir., D.C. Cir., Fed. Cir.). [FED 12]

FEDERAL COURT CITATION 14. INCLUDE THE APPROPRIATE ABBREVIATED NAME OF A SPECIALIZED FEDERAL COURT IN THE CITATION IF IT IS NOT INDICATED BY THE NAME OF THE REPORTER CITED. [FED 14]

1 150 235 311 460 525   277 F.2d 177   116 F.2d 273
(a) Black Panther Company, Inc. v. Cook Chemical Company (United States Court of Customs and Patent Appeals April 6, 1960)
M/B: Black Panther Co. v. Cook Chemical Co., 277 F.2d 177 (C.C.P.A. 1960).
LR: Black Panther Co. v. Cook Chem. Co., 277 F.2d 177 (C.C.P.A. 1960).

(b) Doggett v. Peek et al. (Circuit Court of Appeals, Fifth Circuit Dec. 11, 1940)
M/B: Doggett v. Peek, 116 F.2d 273 (5th Cir. 1940).

2 151 236 312 461 526   421 F.2d 602   65 F.2d 191
(a) Earl Leroy Blackburn, Appellee, v. Roger B. Copinger, Warden, Maryland State Penitentiary, Appellant (United States Court of Appeals, Fourth Circuit February 20, 1970)
M/B: Blackburn v. Copinger, 421 F.2d 602 (4th Cir. 1970).

(b) Doggett v. Burnet, Commissioner of Internal Revenue (Court of Appeals of the District of Columbia April 10, 1933)
M/B: Doggett v. Burnet, 65 F.2d 191 (D.C. Cir. 1933).

3 152 237 313 462 527   151 F.2d 392   262 F.2d 19
(a) Blackford et al. v. Powell et al.; Guaranty Trust Co. of New York et al. v. Seaboard Air Line Ry. Co. et al. (Circuit Court of Appeals, Fourth Circuit October 11, 1945)
M/B: Blackford v. Powell, 151 F.2d 392 (4th Cir. 1945).

(b) Harry Carlisle, Appellant, v. William P. Rogers, Attorney General of the United States, Appellee (United States Court of Appeals District of Columbia Circuit May 15, 1958)
M/B: Carlisle v. Rogers, 262 F.2d 19 (D.C. Cir. 1958).

4 153 238 314 463 528   205 F.2d 13   413 F.2d 381
(a) Blackmon v. Lee, Deputy Administrator, Civil Aeronautics Administration, et al. (United States Court of Appeals District of Columbia Circuit May 14, 1953)
M/B: Blackmon v. Lee, 205 F.2d 13 (D.C. Cir. 1953).

(b) Cornelius H. Doherty, Sr., et al., Appellants, v. Virginia Fairall et al., Appellees (United States Court of Appeals District of Columbia Circuit April 14, 1969)
M/B: Doherty v. Fairall, 413 F.2d 381 (D.C. Cir. 1969).

5 154 239 315 464 529   176 F.2d 498   169 F.2d 965

EXERCISE 7. FEDERAL REPORTER   (CONTINUED)

(a) Blackner et al. v. McDermott (United States Court of Appeals Tenth Circuit August 11, 1949)
M/B: Blackner v. McDermott, 176 F.2d 498 (10th Cir. 1949).

(b) Doherty v. Stoner et al. (United States Court of Appeals District of Columbia Circuit September 7, 1948)
M/B: Doherty v. Stoner, 169 F.2d 965 (D.C. Cir. 1948).

6 155 240 316 465 530   304 F.2d 623   176 F.2d 449
(a) Jakov Blagaic, Plaintiff-Petitioner, v. W.T. Flagg, District Director, Chicago District, Immigration and Naturalization Service, Defendant-Respondent (United States Court of Appeals Seventh Circuit June 15, 1962)
M/B: Blagaic v. Flagg, 304 F.2d 623 (7th Cir. 1962).

(b) Doing et al. v. Riley (United States Court of Appeals Fifth Circuit July 22, 1949)
M/B: Doing v. Riley, 176 F.2d 449 (5th Cir. 1949).

7 156 241 317 466 531   261 F.2d 631   127 F.2d 13
(a) Lewis F. Blagg, Appellant, v. Irving I. Bass, Trustee in Bankruptcy of the Estate of Lewis F. Blagg, Bankrupt, Appellee (United States Court of Appeals Ninth Circuit December 11, 1958)
M/B: Blagg v. Bass, 261 F.2d 631 (9th Cir. 1958).

(b) Dillon et al. v. Evansville Refining Co., Inc. (Circuit Court of Appeals, Seventh Circuit April 3, 1942)
M/B: Dillon v. Evansville Refining Co., 127 F.2d 13 (7th Cir. 1942).
LR: Dillon v. Evansville Ref. Co., 127 F.2d 13 (7th Cir. 1942).

8 157 242 318 467 532   322 F.2d 397   91 F.2d 860
(a) Patricia Blau, Petitioner, v. Subversive Activities Control Board, Respondent (United States Court of Appeals District of Columbia Circuit June 6, 1963)
M/B: Blau v. Subversive Activities Control Board, 322 F.2d 397 (D.C. Cir. 1963).
LR: Blau v. Subversive Activities Control Bd., 322 F.2d 397 (D.C. Cir. 1963).

(b) Doll v. Scott Paper Co. et al. (Circuit Court of Appeals, Third Circuit August 5, 1937)
M/B: Doll v. Scott Paper Co., 91 F.2d 860 (3d Cir. 1937).

9 158 243 319 468 533   81 F.2d 198   184 F.2d 245
(a) Blaydes v. Barnes (Circuit Court of Appeals, Fourth Circuit January 6, 1936)
M/B: Blaydes v. Barnes, 81 F.2d 198 (4th Cir. 1936).

(b) Dollar et al. v. Land, Chairman, United States Maritime Commission, et al. (United States Court of Appeals District of Columbia Circuit July 17, 1950)
M/B: Dollar v. Land, 184 F.2d 245 (D.C. Cir. 1950).

10 159 244 320 469 534   149 F.2d 770   154 F.2d 307
(a) Bleecker v. Drury (Circuit Court of Appeals, Second Circuit May 28, 1945)
M/B: Bleecker v. Drury, 149 F.2d 770 (2d Cir. 1945).

(b) Dollar et al. v. Land et al. (United States Court of Appeals District of Columbia March 18, 1946)
M/B: Dollar v. Land, 154 F.2d 307 (D.C. Cir. 1946).

11 160 245 321 470 535   164 F.2d 481   130 F.2d 860
(a) Bledsoe v. Johnston, Warden (Circuit Court of Appeals, Ninth Circuit January 12, 1948)
M/B: Bledsoe v. Johnston, 164 F.2d 481 (9th Cir. 1948).

(b) Super Mold Corporation of California v. Bacon et al. (Circuit Court of Appeals, Ninth Circuit September 12, 1942)
M/B: Super Mold Corp. v. Bacon, 130 F.2d 860 (9th Cir. 1942).

EXERCISE 7. FEDERAL REPORTER   (CONTINUED)

12 161 246 322 471 536   110 F.2d 566   323 F.2d 882
(a) Blevins et al. v. Sun Oil Co. et al. (Circuit Court of Appeals, Fifth
Circuit March 28, 1940)
M/B: Blevins v. Sun Oil Co., 110 F.2d 566 (5th Cir. 1940).

(b) Albert E. Domanski, Plaintiff-Appellee, v. Anthony J. Celebrezze,
Secretary of Health, Edcuation and Welfare, Defendant-Appellant (United States
Court of Appeals Sixth Circuit November 4, 1963)
M/B: Domanski v. Celebrezze, 323 F.2d 882 (6th Cir. 1963).

13 162 247 323 472 537   416 F.2d 949   321 F.2d 463
(a) Calvin C. Campbell, Plaintiff-Appellant, v. Louie L. Wainwright, Director,
Division of Corrections, State of Florida, Defendant-Appellee (United States
Court of Appeals Fifth Circuit October 6, 1969)
M/B: Campbell v. Wainwright, 416 F.2d 949 (5th Cir. 1969).

(b) Janis Osvald Dombrovskis et al., Plaintiffs-Appellants, v. P. A. Esperdy,
District Director, Immigration and Naturalization Service, United States
Department of Justice, Defendant-Appellee (United States Court of Appeals
Second Circuit August 7, 1963)
M/B: Dombrovskis v. Esperdy, 321 F.2d 463 (2d Cir. 1963).

14 163 248 324 473 538   208 F.2d 457   114 F.2d 91
(a) Campbell v. Walker (United States Court of Appeals Fifth Circuit December
9, 1953)
M/B: Campbell v. Walker, 208 F.2d 457 (5th Cir. 1953).

(b) Dombrowski v. Beu et al. (Circuit Court of Appeals, Ninth Circuit July 26,
1940)
M/B: Dombrowski v. Beu, 114 F.2d 91 (9th Cir. 1940).

15 164 249 325 474 539   118 F.2d 7   49 F.2d 849
(a) Campbell Co. v. Commercial Shirt Co. (Circuit Court of Appeals, Second
Circuit February 3, 1941)
M/B: Campbell Co. v. Commercial Shirt Co., 118 F.2d 7 (2d Cir. 1941).

(b) Domenech v. Havemeyer et al. (Circuit Court of Appeals, First Circuit
April 28, 1931)
M/B: Domenech v. Havemeyer, 49 F.2d 849 (1st Cir. 1931).

16 165 250 326 475 540   275 F.2d 166   232 F.2d 112
(a) Guy F. Campbell and American Machine and Foundry Company, Appellants, v.
Robert C. Watson, Commissioner of Patents, Appellee (United States Court of
Appeals District of Columbia Circuit January 28, 1960)
M/B: Campbell v. Watson, 275 F.2d 166 (D.C. Cir. 1960).

(b) John A. Domenico, doing business as Denver Vegetable Gardens, Appellants,
v. James P. Mitchell, Secretary of Labor, United States Department of Labor,
Appellee (United States Court of Appeals Tenth Circuit March 19, 1956)
M/B: Domenico v. Mitchell, 232 F.2d 112 (10th Cir. 1956).

17 166 251 327 476 541   427 F.2d 131   422 F.2d 831
(a) Calvin C. Campbell, Plaintiff-Appellant, v. Honorable J. E. Weatherford,
County Judge, Nassau County, Florida, Defendant-Appellee (United States Court
of Appeals, Fifth Circuit May 20, 1970)
M/B: Campbell v. Weatherford, 427 F.2d 131 (5th Cir. 1970).

(b) Robert K. Domer, Petitioner-Appellant, v. P. G. Smith, Warden, United
States Penitentiary, Terre Haute, Indiana, Respondent-Appellee (United States
Court of Appeals Seventh Circuit December 10, 1969)
M/B: Domer v. Smith, 422 F.2d 831 (7th Cir. 1969).

18 167 252 328 477 542   241 F.2d 661   342 F.2d 219
(a) Herbert Campos, Appellant, v. Carl E. Olson, also known as Carl "Bobo"
Olson; Sid E. Flaherty and Sid Flaherty Promotional Enterprises, a
Corporation, Appellees (United States Court of Appeals Ninth Circuit February
15, 1957)

EXERCISE 7.   FEDERAL REPORTER   (CONTINUED)

M/B: Campos v. Olson, 241 F.2d 661 (9th Cir. 1957).

(b) Frank P. Domeracki, Appellant, v. Gulf Oil Corporation (United States Court of Appeals Third Circuit March 4, 1965)
M/B: Domeracki v. Gulf Oil Corp., 342 F.2d 219 (3d Cir. 1965).

19 168 253 329 478 543   170 F.2d 606   426 F.2d 800
(a) Canada v. Jones, Warden (United States Court of Appeals Eighth Circuit November 17, 1948)
M/B: Canada v. Jones, 170 F.2d 606 (8th Cir. 1948).

(b) William B. Donlavey, Petitioner-Appellant, v. S. Lamont Smith, Warden, Georgia State Prison, Beidsville, Georgia, Respondent-Appellee (United States Court of Appeals, Fifth Circuit April 30, 1970)
M/B: Donlavey v. Smith, 426 F.2d 800 (5th Cir. 1970).

20 169 254 330 479 544   421 F.2d 1065   320 F.2d 24
(a) Burlee Carroll, Petitioner-Appellant, v. Dr. George J. Beto, Director, Texas Department of Corrections, Respondent-Appellee (United States Court of Appeals, Fifth Circuit January 27, 1970)
M/B: Carroll v. Beto, 421 F.2d 1065 (5th Cir. 1970).

(b) D. S. Donley, Appellant, v. La Verne H. Christopher, Executrix of the Estate of H. Ward Christopher, E. Alex Phillips, Joseph A. Phillips, Kenneth P. Milliken and Sylvia Milliken Blair, Appellees (United States Court of Appeals Tenth Circuit July 16, 1963)
M/B: Donley v. Christopher, 320 F.2d 24 (10th Cir. 1963).

21 170 255 331 480 545   402 F.2d 62   323 F.2d 850
(a) Willard Wilson Wood, Appellant, v. Olin G. Blackwell, Warden, United States Penitentiary, Atlanta, Georgia, Appellee (United States Court of Appeals Fifth Circuit October 24, 1968)
M/B: Wood v. Blackwell, 402 F.2d 62 (5th Cir. 1968).

(b) William B. Donnell, Petitioner, v. E. V. Nash, Warden, Missouri State Penitentiary, Respondent (United States Court of Appeals Eighth Circuit October 22, 1963)
M/B: Donnell v. Nash, 323 F.2d 850 (8th Cir. 1963).

22 171 256 332 481 546   379 F.2d 329   194 F.2d 164
(a) Clifford Darrell Carroll, Appellant, v. Dr. George J. Beto, Director, Texas Department of Corrections, Appellee (United States Court of Appeals Fifth Circuit June 22, 1967)
M/B: Carroll v. Beto, 379 F.2d 329 (5th Cir. 1967).

(b) Donnelly v. Guthrie (United States Court of Appeals Fifth Circuit February 7, 1952)
M/B: Donnelly v. Guthrie, 194 F.2d 164 (5th Cir. 1952).

23 172 257 333 482 547   347 F.2d 96   775 F.2d 1349
(a) Charles Ray Carroll, Appellant, v. Otto C. Boles, Warden of the West Virginia State Penitentiary, Appellee United States Court of Appeals Fourth Circuit June 11, 1965)
M/B: Carroll v. Boles, 347 F.2d 96 (4th Cir. 1965).

(b) Carolyn R. Young, Individually and As Next Friend of Her Minor Child, Nikiya A. Young, and as Community Survivor of David A. Young, Deceased, Plaintiff-Appellee Cross-Appellant, v. The City of Killeen, Texas, etc. et al., Defendants-Cross Appellees   (Nov. 8, 1985)
M/B: Young v. City of Killeen, 775 F.2d 1349 (5th Cir. 1985).

24 173 258 334 483 548   361 F.2d 903   180 F.2d 1019
(a) Robert Louis Carroll, Appellant, v. Sherman H. Crouse, Warden, Appellee (United States Court of Appeals Tenth Circuit June 7, 1966)
M/B: Carroll v. Crouse, 361 F.2d 903 (10th Cir. 1966).

EXERCISE 7. FEDERAL REPORTER   (CONTINUED)

(b) Donnelly v. Steele (United States Court of Appeals Eighth Circuit March 30, 1950)
M/B: Donnelly v. Steele, 180 F.2d 1019 (8th Cir. 1950).

25 174 259 335 484 549   222 F.2d 508   154 F.2d 38
(a) G. W. Carroll, Appellant, v. George Funk and Lydia Funk, Appellees (United States Court of Appeals Ninth Circuit May 9, 1955)
M/B: Carroll v. Funk, 222 F.2d 508 (9th Cir. 1955).

(b) Donnelly Garment Co. et al. v. Dubinsky et al. (Circuit Court of Appeals, Eighth Circuit March 11, 1946)
M/B: Donnelly Garment Co. v. Dubinsky, 154 F.2d 38 (8th Cir. 1946).

26 175 260 336 485 550   336 F.2d 425   123 F.2d 215
(a) V. H. Carroll, Trustee Holliman Drilling Company, a corporation, Appellant, v. Lorena Morris Holliman, Appellee (United States Court of Appeals Tenth Circuit August 21, 1964)
M/B: Carroll v. Holliman, 336 F.2d 425 (10th Cir. 1964).

(b) Donnelly Garment Co. v. National Labor Relations Board (Donnelly Garment Worker's Union et al., Interveners) (Circuit Court of Appeals, Eighth Circuit November 6, 1941)
M/B: Donnelly Garment Co. v. NLRB, 123 F.2d 215 (8th Cir. 1941).

27 176 261 337 486 551   333 F.2d 363   190 F.2d 409
(a) D. B. Clarke, d/b/a Thunderbird Aviation Company, Appellant, v. Continental Motors Corporation, Appellee (United States Court of Appeals Fifth Circuit June 24, 1964)
M/B: Clarke v. Continental Motors Corp., 333 F.2d 363 (5th Cir. 1964).

(b) Donnely et al. v. Mavar Shrimp & Oyster Co., Inc. et al. (United States Court of Appeals Fifth Circuit July 17, 1951)
M/B: Donnely v. Mavar Shrimp & Oyster Co., 190 F.2d 409 (5th Cir. 1951).

28 177 262 338 487 552   106 F.2d 598   232 F.2d 185
(a) Clarke v. Gold Dust Corporation (Circuit Court of Appeals, Third Circuit August 10, 1939)
M/B: Clarke v. Gold Dust Corp., 106 F.2d 598 (3d Cir. 1939).

(b) Isadore Donner, Plaintiff-Appellant, v. David H. Levine et al., Defendants-Appellees (United States Court of Appeals Second Circuit April 6, 1956)
M/B: Donner v. Levine, 232 F.2d 185 (2d Cir. 1956).

29 178 263 339 488 553   91 F.2d 12   328 F.2d 817
(a) Clarke v. Gold Dust Corporation (Circuit Court of Appeals, Third Circuit June 23, 1937)
M/B: Clarke v. Gold Dust Corp., 91 F.2d 12 (3d Cir. 1937).

(b) Donner Corporation and H. L. Brown, Appellants, v. Union Producing Company et al., Appellees (United States Court of Appeals Fifth Circuit February 28, 1964)
M/B: Donner Corp. v. Union Producing Co., 328 F.2d 817 (5th Cir. 1964).

30 179 264 340 489 554   374 F.2d 550   168 F.2d 229
(a) Johnny Lee Clarke, Appellant, v. T. Ralph Grimes, Sheriff, Fulton County, Georgia, Appellee (United States Court of Appeals Fifth Circuit March 24, 1967)
M/B: Clarke v. Grimes, 374 F.2d 550 (5th Cir. 1967).

(b) Donovan v. Shell Oil Co., Inc. (Circuit Court of Appeals, Fourth Circuit May 7, 1948)
M/B: Donovan v. Shell Oil Co., 168 F.2d 229 (4th Cir. 1948).

31 180 265 341 490 555   403 F.2d 687   285 F.2d 714

EXERCISE 7. FEDERAL REPORTER   (CONTINUED)

(a) John Randolph Clarke, Petitioner-Appellant, v. C. Murray Henderson, Warden, Tennessee State Penitentiary, Respondent-Appellee (United States Court of Appeals Sixth Circuit November 27, 1968)
M/B: Clarke v. Henderson, 403 F.2d 687 (6th Cir. 1968).

(b) Thomas F. Donovan, Assignee, Intervenor, Appellant, v. Wilson Sporting Goods Co., Defendant. Appellee (United State Court of Appeals First Circuit January 5, 1961)
M/B: Donovan v. Wilson Sporting Goods Co., 285 F.2d 714 (1st Cir. 1961).

32 181 266 342 491 556   119 F.2d 204   326 F.2d 941
(a) Clarke v. Huff (United States Court of Appeals for the District of Columbia March 31, 1941)
M/B: Clarke v. Huff, 119 F.2d 204 (D.C. Cir. 1941).

(b) Nettie Lou Dooly, Executrix of the Estate of B. A. Dooly, Deceased, et al., Appellants, v. Thomas Payne et al., Appellees (United States Court of Appeals Fifth Circuit January 21, 1964)
M/B: Dooly v. Payne, 326 F.2d 941 (5th Cir. 1964).

33 182 267 343 492 557   427 F.2d 1322   195 F.2d 764
(a) John Randolph Clarke, Petitioner-Appellant, v. W. S. Neil, Warden, Tennessee State Penitentiary, Respondent-Appellee (United States Court of Appeals, Sixth Circuit June 12, 1970)
M/B: Clarke v. Neil, 427 F.2d 1322 (6th Cir. 1970).

(b) Door v. Donaldson, Postmaster General (United States Court of Appeals District of Columbia Circuit January 31, 1952)
M/B: Door v. Donaldson, 195 F.2d 764 (D.C. Cir. 1952).

34 183 268 344 493 558   584 F.2d 48   369 F.2d 505
(a) Merther Treadway, Appellant, v. Joseph A. Califano, Jr., Secretary of the Department of Health, Education and Welfare, Appellee (United States Court of Appeals, Fourth Circuit October 5, 1978)
M/B: Treadway v. Califano, 584 F.2d 48 (4th Cir. 1978).

(b) Leopold Joseph Doran, Appellant, v. Lawrence E. Wilson, Warden, San Quentin Prison, Appellee (United States Court of Appeals Ninth Circuit December 5, 1966)
M/B: Doran v. Wilson, 369 F.2d 505 (9th Cir. 1966).

35 184 269 345 494 559   174 F.2d 89   170 F.2d 721
(a) Skelly Oil Co. et al. v. Phillips Petroleum Co. (United States Court of Appeals Tenth Circuit March 28, 1949)
M/B: Skelly Oil Co. v. Phillips Petroleum Co., 174 F.2d 89 (10th Cir. 1949).

(b) Doreau v. Marshall, Secretary of State (United States Court of Appeals Third Circuit August 23, 1948)
M/B: Doreau v. Marshall, 170 F.2d 721 (3d Cir. 1948).

36 185 270 346 495 560   236 F.2d 412   295 F.2d 496
(a) Louis B. Cline et al., Appellants, v. Carlisle Rountree, Ind., etc., Appellee (United States Court of Appeals Sixth Circuit August 1, 1956)
M/B: Cline v. Rountree, 236 F.2d 412 (6th Cir. 1956).

(b) Joseph Dores, Individually and as Administrator of the Estate of Victoria Dores, Deceased, Appellant, v. T. V. Anderson and Jesse L. Neal, etc., et al., Appellees (United States Court of Appeals Fifth Circuit October 24, 1961)
M/B: Dores v. Anderson, 295 F.2d 496 (5th Cir. 1961).

37 186 271 347 496 561   61 F.2d 889   355 F.2d 488
(a) The Cockatoo (Circuit Court of Appeals, Second Circuit August 23, 1932)
M/B: The Cockatoo, 61 F.2d 889 (2d Cir. 1932).

(b) Charles Dorf, Plaintiff-Appellee, v. John J. Relles, Defendant-Appellant (United States Court of Appeals Seventh Circuit January 13, 1966)
M/B: Dorf v. Relles, 355 F.2d 488 (7th Cir. 1966).

EXERCISE 7. FEDERAL REPORTER   (CONTINUED)

38 187 272 348 497 562   375 F.2d 889   430 F.2d 558
(a) Hubert L. Cockrell and Mrs. Hubert L. Cockrell, Appellants, v. George A. Ferrier and Melton Truck Lines, Appellees (United States Court of Appeals Fifth Circuit April 18, 1967)
M/B: Cockrell v. Ferrier, 375 F.2d 889 (5th Cir. 1967).

(b) Ron Dorfman, Joel Snyder, Association of Working Press, Incorporated, Writer's Guild of America, East, Chicago Unit, Chicago Newspaper Guild, on behalf of themselves and all other persons and organizations similarly situated, Plaintiffs-Appellants, v. John Meiszner, United States Marshal, and Thomas A. Foran, United States Attorney for the Northern District of Illinois, Defendants-Appellees (United States Court of Appeals, Seventh Circuit June 19, 1970)
M/B: Dorfman v. Meiszner, 430 F.2d 558 (7th Cir. 1970).

39 188 273 349 498 563   413 F.2d 256   414 F.2d 1168
(a) Leroy Morris Cockrell and Ivy Dell Cockrell, Petitioners, v. E. J. Oberhauser and Iverna Carter, Respondents (United States Court of Appeals Ninth Circuit June 6, 1969)
M/B: Cockrell v. Oberhauser, 413 F.2d 256 (9th Cir. 1969).

(b) Richard Dorfmann et al., TM/B:A Tenth Street Limited Partnership, Appellees, v. Russell B. Boozer et al., Appellants (United States Court of Appeals District of Columbia Circuit June 16, 1969)
M/B: Dorfmann v. Boozer, 414 F.2d 1168 (D.C. Cir. 1969).

40 189 274 350 499 564   396 F.2d 438   180 F.2d 45
(a) Margie J. Elliott and Lon Elliott, wife and husband, Appellants, v. Alpac Corporation, a Nevada Corporation, d/b/a Glaser Beverages, Appellee (United States Court of Appeals Ninth Circuit May 31, 1968)
M/B: Elliott v. Alpac Corp., 396 F.2d 438 (9th Cir. 1968).

(b) Marzall, Commissioner of Patents v. Fox (United States Court of Appeals District of Columbia Circuit (February 6, 1950)
M/B: Marzall v. Fox, 180 F.2d 45 (D.C. Cir. 1950).

41 190 275 351 500 565   282 F.2d 913   245 F.2d 201
(a) Empire Petroleum Company, Appellant, v. Sinclair Pipeline Company, Appellee (United States Court of Appeals Tenth Circuit August 23, 1960)
M/B: Empire Petroleum Co. v. Sinclair Pipeline Co., 282 F.2d 913 (10th Cir. 1960).

(b) William A. Dorney, Appellant, v. Mabel P. Dorney, Appellee (United States Court of Appeals Fourth Circuit May 27, 1957)
M/B: Dorney v. Dorney, 245 F.2d 201 (4th Cir. 1957).

42 191 276 352 401 566   235 F.2d 860   373 F.2d 619
(a) A. V. Falcone and R. K. Millstein, Appellants, v. Josef Washington Hall et al., Appellees (United States Court of Appeals District of Columbia Circuit July 5, 1956)
M/B: Falcone v. Hall, 235 F.2d 860 (D.C. Cir. 1956).

(b) Susie Dornton, and Frederick Dornton, her husband, and Frederick Dornton, Individually, Appellants, v. Estelle M. Darby, Appellee (United States Court of Appeals Fifth Circuit March 8, 1967)
M/B: Dornton v. Darby, 373 F.2d 619 (5th Cir. 1967).

43 192 277 353 402 567   19 F.2d 357   148 F.2d 857
(a) Chism Mail Box Co. et al. v. S. H. Couch Co. (Circuit Court of Appeals, First Circuit May 17, 1927)
M/B: Chism Mail Box Co. v. S.H. Couch Co., 19 F.2d 357 (1st Cir. 1927).

(b) Dorsey v. Gill, General Superintendent, D. C. Penal Institutions (United States Court of Appeals District of Columbia February 26, 1945)
M/B: Dorsey v. Gill, 148 F.2d 857 (D.C. Cir. 1945).

EXERCISE 7. FEDERAL REPORTER   (CONTINUED)

44 193 278 354 403 568   202 F.2d 180   254 F.2d 373
(a) Fibreboard Products, Inc. v. Townsend (United States Court of Appeals
Ninth Circuit February 2, 1953)
M/B: Fibreboard Products, Inc. v. Townsend, 202 F.2d 180 (9th Cir. 1953).
LR: Fibreboard Prods., Inc. v. Townsend, 202 F.2d 180 (9th Cir. 1953).

(b) J. K. Dorsett, Jr., As Executor Under the Will of J. K. Dorsett, Appellant
and Cross-Appellee, v. W. T. Shore, J. H. McAden, S. Y. McAden, Mrs. S. J.
Cothran, Estate of Sallie J. McAden, and Miss Susan Bynum, respective
shareholders in Merchants and Farmers National Bank, objectors and exceptors,
in behalf of themselves and all other shareholders in said Bank, Appellees and
Cross-Appellants (United States Court of Appeals Fourth Circuit March 11,
1957)
M/B: Dorsett v. Shore, 254 F.2d 373 (4th Cir. 1957).

45 194 279 355 404 569   181 F.2d 1008   195 F.2d 567
(a) Fruehauf Trailer Co. v. Myers (United States Court of Appeals Ninth
Circuit March 24, 1950)
M/B: Fruehauf Trailer Co. v. Myers, 181 F.2d 1008 (9th Cir. 1950).

(b) Dorsey v. Dorsey (United States Court of Appeals District of Columbia
Circuit March 13, 1952)
M/B: Dorsey v. Dorsey, 195 F.2d 567 (D.C. Cir. 1952).

46 195 280 356 405 570   268 F.2d 391   57 F.2d 407
(a) Fruit Industries, Inc., Appellant, v. Stella Petty, as Administratrix of
the Estate of Julius E. Petty, deceased, et al., Appellees (United States
Court of Appeals Fifth Circuit June 29, 1959)
M/B: Fruit Industries v. Petty, 268 F.2d 391 (5th Cir. 1959).
LR: Fruit Indus. v. Petty, 268 F.2d 391 (5th Cir. 1959).

(b) Dorsey v. Gotwals et al. (Court of Appeals of the District of Columbia
February 8, 1932)
M/B: Dorsey v. Gotwals, 57 F.2d 407 (D.C. Cir. 1932).

47 196 281 357 406 571   346 F.2d 82   173 F.2d 405
(a) Jack Frost, Appellant, v. Nathanael Davis et al., Appellees (United States
Court of Appeals Fifth Circuit May 20, 1965)
M/B: Frost v. Davis, 346 F.2d 82 (5th Cir. 1965).

(b) Dorsey v. Kingsland, Commissioner of Patents (United States Court of
Appeals District of Columbia Circuit January 26, 1949)
M/B: Dorsey v. Kingsland, 173 F.2d 405 (D.C. Cir. 1949).

48 197 282 358 407 572   199 F.2d 460   294 F.2d 678
(a) Frost v. Saluski (United States Court of Appeals Seventh Circuit October
27, 1952)
M/B: Frost v. Saluski, 199 F.2d 460 (7th Cir. 1952).

(b) Charles Alden Dorsey, d/b/a Dorsey Insurance Agency, Appellant, v. State
Farm Insurance Company, Appellees (United States Court of Appeals Fifth
Circuit October 6, 1961)
M/B: Dorsey v. State Farm Insurance Co., 294 F.2d 678 (5th Cir. 1961).
LR: Dorsey v. State Farm Ins. Co., 294 F.2d 678 (5th Cir. 1961).

49 198 283 359 408 573   112 F.2d 119   195 F.2d 69
(a) Fruit Treating Corporation et al. v. Food Machinery Corporation (Circuit
Court of Appeals, Fifth Circuit May 27, 1940)
M/B: Fruit Treating Corp. v. Food Machinery Corp., 112 F.2d 119 (5th Cir.
1940).
LR: Fruit Treating Corp. v. Food Mach. Corp., 112 F.2d 119 (5th Cir. 1940).

(b) Dorzback v. Collison, Collector of Internal Revenue (United States Court
of Appeals Third Circuit March 18, 1952)
M/B: Dorzback v. Collison, 195 F.2d 69 (3d Cir. 1952).

50 199 284 360 409 574   355 F.2d 849   161 F.2d 839

EXERCISE 7. FEDERAL REPORTER   (CONTINUED)

(a) Louis Gee, Plaintiff-Appellant, v. Anthony J. Celebrezze, Secretary of Health, Education and Welfare of the United States, Defendant-Appellee (United States Court of Appeals Seventh Circuit January 20, 1966)
M/B: Gee v. Celebrezze, 355 F.2d 849 (7th Cir. 1966).

(b) Dossett et al. v. Porter (Circuit Court of Appeals Sixth Circuit May 26, 1947)
M/B: Dossett v. Porter, 161 F.2d 839 (6th Cir. 1947).

51 200 285 361 410 575   290 F.2d 666   430 F.2d 1299
(a) Nate Gellman, Burt Horwitz and Peter Podany, individually and as co-partners doing business as Gellman Brothers, Petitioners, v. Federal Trade Commission, Respondent (United States Court of Appeals Eighth Circuit May 26, 1961)
M/B: Gellman v. FTC, 290 F.2d 666 (8th Cir. 1961).

(b) Theodore Dostal and David Gass, Plaintiffs-Appellants, v. Carl B. Stokes, Mayor of the City of Cleveland, Clarence L. James, Jr., Law Director, Joseph McManamon, Safety Director, Patrick J. Gerity, Michael J. Blackwell, Harry Leisman, Larry Todd, John McNulty and William J. Blakemore, Defendants-Appellees (United States Court of Appeals, Sixth Circuit August 7, 1970)
M/B: Dostal v. Stokes, 430 F.2d 1299 (6th Cir. 1970).

52 101 286 362 411 576   82 F.2d 427   318 F.2d 453
(a) General Baking Co. v. Commander-Larabee Corporation (Court of Customs and Patent Appeals March 23, 1936)
M/B: General Baking Co. v. Commander-Larabee Corp., 82 F.2d 427 (C.C.P.A. 1936).

(b) Bennie Doster, Petitioner-Appellant, v. William H. Bannan, Warden, et al., State Prison of Southern Michigan, Ingham County Circuit Court, Louis E. Coash, Circuit Judge, Respondents-Appellees (United States Court of Appeals Sixth Circuit June 15, 1963)
M/B: Doster v. Bannan, 318 F.2d 453 (6th Cir. 1963).

53 102 287 363 412 577   132 F.2d 790   394 F.2d 178
(a) Gilcrease Oil Co. v. Cosby et al. (Circuit Court of Appeals, Fifth Circuit January 20, 1943)
M/B: Gilcrease Oil Co. v. Cosby, 132 F.2d 790 (5th Cir. 1943).

(b) Pierre E. Dostert, Appellant, v. Stephen Bradford Crowley, Jr., Katherine P. Crowley, Elizabeth H. Allen, and Barry H. Helfand, Appellees (United States Court of Appeals Fourth Circuit April 11, 1968)
M/B: Dostert v. Crowley, 394 F.2d 178 (4th Cir. 1968).

54 103 288 364 413 578   295 F.2d 698   583 F.2d 19
(a) Paul Ginsburg, Appellant, v. Horace Stern and Patrick N. Bolsinger (United States Court of Appeals Third Circuit October 19, 1961)
M/B: Ginsburg v. Stern, 295 F.2d 698 (3d Cir. 1961).

(b) Merchants National Bank, Executor of the Estate of Marian A. Burdick, Plaintiff, Appellee, v. United States of America, Defendant, Appellant (United States Court of Appeals, First Circuit August 21, 1978)
M/B: Merchants National Bank v. United States, 583 F.2d 19 (1st Cir. 1978).
LR: Merchants Nat'l Bank v. United States, 583 F.2d 19 (1st Cir. 1978).

55 104 289 365 414 579   159 F.2d 330   328 F.2d 97
(a) Godfrey et al. v. Powell et al. (Circuit Court of Appeals, Fifth Circuit February 5, 1947)
M/B: Godfrey v. Powell, 159 F.2d 330 (5th Cir. 1947).

(b) Dewey Doucet et al., Appellants, v. Stanley H. Middleton, Appellee (United States Court of Appeals Fifth Circuit February 7, 1964)
M/B: Doucet v. Middleton, 328 F.2d 97 (5th Cir. 1964).

56 105 290 366 415 580   180 F.2d 220   362 F.2d 263

EXERCISE 7. FEDERAL REPORTER   (CONTINUED)

(a) Godfrey v. Smyth, Collector of Internal Revenue (United States Court of Appeals Ninth Circuit January 21, 1950)
M/B: Godfrey v. Smyth, 180 F.2d 220 (9th Cir. 1950).

(b) Mary U. Doucet and Semar Doucet, Appellants, v. The Travelers Insurance Company and A. W. Dunn, Appellees (United States Court of Appeals Fifth Circuit June 10, 1966)
M/B: Doucet v. Travelers Insurance Co., 362 F.2d 263 (5th Cir. 1966).
LR: Doucet v. Travelers Ins. Co., 362 F.2d 263 (5th Cir. 1966).

57 106 291 367 416 581   426 F.2d 1388   194 F.2d 834
(a) Marion Goad, Plaintiff-Appellant, v. Robert Finch, Secretary of Health, Education & Welfare, Defendant-Appellee (United States Court of Appeals, Sixth Circuit June 1, 1970)
M/B: Goad v. Finch, 426 F.2d 1388 (6th Cir. 1970).

(b) Doucette v. Vincent et al. (United States Court of Appeals First Circuit February 5, 1952)
M/B: Doucette v. Vincent, 194 F.2d 834 (1st Cir. 1952).

58 107 292 368 417 582   317 F.2d 47   405 F.2d 867
(a) Vernelle W. Gober, Appellee, v. Revlon, Inc., Appellant (United States Court of Appeals Fourth Circuit March 28, 1963)
M/B: Gober v. Revlon, Inc., 317 F.2d 47 (4th Cir. 1963).

(b) Rose Marie Dougal and Elva Mae Brokenshire v. Gerald C. Williams and Jacquesonia Varner, also known as Jacqueso Varner (United States Court of Appeals Third Circuit January 17, 1969)
M/B: Dougal v. Williams, 405 F.2d 867 (3d Cir. 1969).

59 108 293 369 418 583   351 F.2d 905   115 F.2d 479
(a) Vernon E. Goodson, Appellant, v. C. C. Peyton, Superintendent of the Virginia State Penitentiary, Appellee (United States Court of Appeals Fourth Circuit October 25, 1965)
M/B: Goodson v. Peyton, 351 F.2d 905 (4th Cir. 1965).

(b) Miller v. Commissioner of Internal Revenue (Circuit Court of Appeals, Ninth Circuit November 13, 1940)
M/B: Miller v. Commissioner, 115 F.2d 479 (9th Cir. 1940).

60 109 294 370 419 584   341 F.2d 908   396 F.2d 128
(a) Irvin Goodspeed, Appellant, v. Dr. George J. Beto, Director, Texas Department of Corrections, Appellee (United States Court of Appeals Fifth Circuit February 4, 1965)
M/B: Goodspeed v. Beto, 341 F.2d 908 (5th Cir. 1965).

(b) Chester Clifton Doughty, Appellant, v. Dr. George J. Beto, Director, Texas Department of Corrections, Appellee (United States Court of Appeals Fifth Circuit June 19, 1968)
M/B: Doughty v. Beto, 396 F.2d 128 (5th Cir. 1968).

61 110 295 371 420 585   340 F.2d 227   358 F.2d 711
(a) J. C. Guerra et al., Appellants, v. F. C. Gonzalez et al., Appellees (United States Court of Appeals Fifth Circuit January 15, 1965)
M/B: Guerra v. Gonzalez, 340 F.2d 227 (5th Cir. 1965).

(b) Natalie A. Douglas, Administratrix, Plaintiff, Appellant, v. Clayton E. Brown, Defendant, Appellee (United States Court of Appeals First Circuit April 13, 1966)
M/B: Douglas v. Brown, 358 F.2d 711 (1st Cir. 1966).

62 111 296 372 421 586   261 F.2d 952   110 F.2d 911
(a) Jacques Arthur Gubbels, Appellant, v. Richard C. Hoy, as District Director, Immigration and Naturalization Service, Los Angeles, California, Appellee (United States Court of Appeals Ninth Circuit November 14, 1958)
M/B: Gubbels v. Hoy, 261 F.2d 952 (9th Cir. 1958).

EXERCISE 7. FEDERAL REPORTER   (CONTINUED)

(b) Douglas v. King, Warden (Circuit Court of Appeals, Eighth Circuit April 8, 1940)
M/B: Douglas v. King, 110 F.2d 911 (8th Cir. 1940).

63 112 297 373 422 587   384 F.2d 886   357 F.2d 320
(a) Martin Guerrero, Jr., Appellant, v. Dr. George J. Beto, Director, Texas Department of Corrections, Appellee (United States Court of Appeals Fifth Circuit November 7, 1967)
M/B: Guerrero v. Beto, 384 F.2d 886 (5th Cir. 1967).

(b) Odus Douglas, Petitioner-Appellant, v. E. L. Maxwell, Warden, Ohio Penitentiary, Respondent-Appellee (United States Court of Appeals Sixth Circuit March 11, 1966)
M/B: Douglas v. Maxwell, 357 F.2d 320 (6th Cir. 1966).

64 113 298 374 423 588   257 F.2d 22   386 F.2d 684
(a) Oscar Guest, as Administrator of the Estate of Callie W. Beane, deceased, Appellant, v. Dr. C. S. Breedin and St. Mary's Hospital and Training School for Nurses, a corporation, Appellees (United States Court of Appeals Fourth Circuit July 16, 1958)
M/B: Guest v. Breedin, 257 F.2d 22 (4th Cir. 1958).

(b) Donnell Douglas, Appellant, v. Maurice H. Sigler, Warden, Nebraska Penal Complex, Appellee (United States Court of Appeals Eighth Circuit November 28, 1967)
M/B: Douglas v. Sigler, 386 F.2d 684 (8th Cir. 1967).

65 114 299 375 424 589   175 F.2d 626   311 F.2d 182
(a) Factor v. Fox, Warden (United States Court of Appeals Sixth Circuit July 5, 1949)
M/B: Factor v. Fox, 175 F.2d 626 (6th Cir. 1949).

(b) Hubert Gene Douglas, Virginia Doulgas, and Allstate Insurance Company, a corporation, Appellants, v. Union Carbide Corporation, a corporation, Appellee (United States Court of Appeals Fourth Circuit December 7, 1962)
M/B: Douglas v. Union Carbide Corp., 311 F.2d 182 (4th Cir. 1962).

66 115 300 376 425 590   115 F.2d 873   353 F.2d 30
(a) Dixwell v. Scott & Co., Limited (Circuit Court of Appeals, First Circuit December 3, 1940)
M/B: Dixwell v. Scott & Co., 115 F.2d 873 (1st Cir. 1940).

(b) R. D. Douglas, Jr., Appellee, v. W. Willard Wirtz, Secretary of Labor of the United States Department of Labor, Appellant (United States Court of Appeals Fourth Circuit October 8, 1965)
M/B: Douglas v. Wirtz, 353 F.2d 30 (4th Cir. 1965).

67 116 201 377 426 591   406 F.2d 1035   287 F.2d 500
(a) Roy J. Dixon, Appellant, v. John W. Gardner, Secretary of Health, Education and Welfare (Wilbur J. Cohen, Successor), Appellee (United States Court of Appeals Fourth Circuit February 5, 1969)
M/B: Dixon v. Gardner, 406 F.2d 1035 (4th Cir. 1969).

(b) Prentiss Douglass, Trustee in Bankruptcy of the Commercial Plumbing & Heating Company, Inc., Plaintiff-Appellee v. Carrie D. Pugh, Defendant-Appellant (United States Court of Appeals Sixth Circuit March 6, 1961)
M/B: Douglass v. Pugh, 287 F.2d 500 (6th Cir. 1961).

68 117 202 378 427 592   261 F.2d 233   282 F.2d 256
(a) S. D. Dick, Appellant, v. H. E. Moore, Warden, Texas Department of Corrections, Appellee (United States Court of Appeals Fifth Circuit December 5, 1958)
M/B: Dick v. Moore, 261 F.2d 233 (5th Cir. 1958).

(b) Earnestine Dove et al., Appellants, v. Lee Parham et al., Appellees (two cases) (United States Court of Appeals Eighth Circuit August 30, 1960)

EXERCISE 7. FEDERAL REPORTER   (CONTINUED)

M/B: Dove v. Parham, 282 F.2d 256 (8th Cir. 1960).

69 118 203 379 428 593   245 F.2d 317   343 F.2d 210
(a) Edward S. Dickenson, Appellant, v. Colonel James W. Davis, Commandant,
United States Disciplinary Barracks, Fort Leavenworth, Kansas, Appellee
(United States Court of Appeals Tenth Circuit May 16, 1957)
M/B: Dickenson v. Davis, 245 F.2d 317 (10th Cir. 1957).

(b) Charles H. Dove, Jr., Appellant, v. C. C. Peyton, Superintendent of the
Virginia State Penitentiary, Appellee (United States Court of Appeals Fourth
Circuit March 5, 1965)
M/B: Dove v. Peyton, 343 F.2d 210 (4th Cir. 1965).

70 119 204 380 429 594   168 F.2d 305   389 F.2d 882
(a) Derounian v. Stokes (Circuit Court of Appeals, Tenth Circuit May 11, 1948)
M/B: Derounian v. Stokes, 168 F.2d 305 (10th Cir. 1948).

(b) E. L. Dow, Appellant, v. Glen O. Baird, Roy Lee Shaffer and Leslie
Davison, Appellees (United States Court of Appeals Tenth Circuit March 1,
1968)
M/B: Dow v. Baird, 389 F.2d 882 (10th Cir. 1968).

71 120 205 381 430 595   171 F.2d 696   139 F.2d 42
(a) De Santa v. Nehi Corporation (United States Court of Appeals Second
Circuit December 3, 1948)
M/B: De Santa v. Nehi Corp., 171 F.2d 696 (2d Cir. 1948).

(b) Dow Chemical Co. v. Kavanagh, Collector of Internal Revenue (Circuit Court
of Appeals, Sixth Circuit November 30, 1943)
M/B: Dow Chemical Co. v. Kavanagh, 139 F.2d 42 (6th Cir. 1943).
LR: Dow Chem. Co. v. Kavanagh, 139 F.2d 42 (6th Cir. 1943).

72 121 206 382 431 596   219 F.2d 271   197 F.2d 807
(a) Juelene Howell Deshotels, etc., Appellant, v. Liberty Mutual Insurance
Company, Appellee (United States Court of Appeals, Fifth Circuit February 11,
1955)
M/B: Deshotels v. Liberty Mutual Insurance Co., 219 F.2d 271 (5th Cir. 1955).
LR: Deshotels v. Liberty Mut. Ins. Co., 219 F.2d 271 (5th Cir. 1955).

(b) Dow Chemical Co. v. Skinner et al. (United States Court of Appeals, Sixth
Circuit April 15, 1952)
M/B: Dow Chemical Co. v. Skinner, 197 F.2d 807 (6th Cir. 1952).
LR: Dow Chem. Co. v. Skinner, 197 F.2d 807 (6th Cir. 1952).

73 122 207 383 432 597   225 F.2d 235   337 F.2d 93
(a) Pauline Des Isles, formerly known as Pauline M. Dinsmore, Appellant, v.
Harry Evans and I. Evans, d/b/a Sea Gull Pool & Cabana Club, Appellees (United
States Court of Appeals Fifth Circuit August 23, 1955)
M/B: Des Isles v. Evans, 225 F.2d 235 (5th Cir. 1955).

(b) J. Patrick Dowd, Appellant, v. Bryan Webb, Margaret H. Webb, Charles J.
Hesse, Jr., Michael J. Stavola, Stanley Savage, John Doe, Individuals and
Beacon Stables, a Partnership (United States Court of Appeals Third Circuit
October 8, 1964)
M/B: Dowd v. Webb, 337 F.2d 93 (3d Cir. 1964).

74 123 208 384 433 598   200 F.2d 614   189 F.2d 637
(a) Des Isles v. Evans et al. (United States Court of Appeals, Fifth Circuit
December 17, 1952)
M/B: Des Isles v. Evans, 200 F.2d 614 (5th Cir. 1952).

(b) Dowdy et al. v. Hawfield (United States Court of Appeals for the District
of Columbia Circuit March 1, 1951)
M/B: Dowdy v. Hawfield, 189 F.2d 637 (D.C. Cir. 1951).

75 124 209 385 434 599   198 F.2d 550   386 F.2d 809

EXERCISE 7.   FEDERAL REPORTER   (CONTINUED)

(a) Des Marais et al. v. Beckman (United States Court of Appeals Ninth Circuit August 14, 1952)
M/B: Des Marais v. Beckman, 198 F.2d 550 (9th Cir. 1952).

(b) Eileen Dowell, Plaintiff-Appellee, v. John W. Gardner, Secretary of Health, Education and Welfare, Defendant-Appellant (United States Court of Appeals Sixth Circuit November 30, 1967)
M/B: Dowell v. Gardner, 386 F.2d 809 (6th Cir. 1967).

76 125 210 386 435 600   342 F.2d 754   166 F.2d 214
(a) Roland G. Desmarais, Administrator, etc., Plaintiff, Appellant, v. Herbert A. Gentle et al., Defendants, Appellees (United States Court of Appeals First Circuit March 11, 1965)
M/B: Desmarais v. Gentle, 342 F.2d 754 (1st Cir. 1965).

(b) Dowell, Inc. v. Jowers et al. (Circuit Court of Appeals, Fifth Circuit February 18, 1948)
M/B: Dowell, Inc. v. Jowers, 166 F.2d 214 (5th Cir. 1948).

77 126 211 387 436 501   375 F.2d 742   265 F.2d 521
(a) George R. Desmond, Trustee, Plaintiff, Appellant, v. Marilyn J. Moffie, Defendant, Appellee (United States Court of Appeals First Circuit April 13, 1967)
M/B: Desmond v. Moffie, 375 F.2d 742 (1st Cir. 1967).

(b) Dowell, Inc., et al., Appellants, v. J. B. Lyons et al., Appellees (United States Court of Appeals Sixth Circuit April 9, 1959)
M/B: Dowell, Inc. v. Lyons, 265 F.2d 521 (6th Cir. 1959).

78 127 212 388 437 502   582 F.2d 604   238 F.2d 633
(a) Southland Royalty Company v. The United States (United States Court of Claims July 14, 1978)
M/B: Southland Royalty Co. v. United States, 582 F.2d 604 (Ct. Cl. 1978).

(b) Dowell, Inc., and R. L. Ashcraft, Appellants, v. J. B. Lyons, J. W. Greene, and John F. Greene, Trading and d.b.a. Virgin Oil Company, Appellees (United States Court of Appeals Sixth Circuit December 5, 1956)
M/B: Dowell, Inc. v. Lyons, 238 F.2d 633 (6th Cir. 1956).

79 128 213 389 438 503   188 F.2d 177   313 F.2d 596
(a) Desper v. Starved Rock Ferry Co. (United States Court of Appeals Seventh Circuit March 20, 1951)
M/B: Desper v. Starved Rock Ferry Co., 188 F.2d 177 (7th Cir. 1951).

(b) Thomas W. Dower and Nordic Development Corporation, Appellants, v. Thomas J. Bomar, Trustee for Kitimat Corporation, Appellee (United States Court of Appeals Fifth Circuit February 13, 1963)
M/B: Dower v. Bomar, 313 F.2d 596 (5th Cir. 1963).

80 129 214 390 439 504   377 F.2d 864   329 F.2d 684
(a) Leo Desrosiers, Plaintiff-Appellant, v. American Cyanamid Company, Defendant-Appellee, and International Chemical Workers Union A.F.L.-C.I.O. Local No. 436, Defendant (United States Court of Appeals Second Circuit May 26, 1967)
M/B: Desrosiers v. American Cyanamid Co., 377 F.2d 864 (2d Cir. 1967).

(b) Robert K. Dower, Appellant, v. United Air Lines, Inc., a Corporation, Appellee (United States Court of Appeals Ninth Circuit March 16, 1964)
M/B: Dower v. United Air Lines, 329 F.2d 684 (9th Cir. 1964).

81 130 215 391 440 505   143 F.2d 907   327 F.2d 660
(a) Des Rosiers v. Ford Motor Co. (Circuit Court of Appeals, First Circuit July 20, 1944)
M/B: Des Rosiers v. Ford Motor Co., 143 F.2d 907 (1st Cir. 1944).

EXERCISE 7.   FEDERAL REPORTER   (CONTINUED)

(b) Sammy Joe Downey, Appellant, v. J. C. Taylor, Warden, United States Penitentiary, Leavenworth, Kansas, Appellee (United States Court of Appeals Tenth Circuit February 4, 1964)
M/B: Downey v. Taylor, 327 F.2d 660 (10th Cir. 1964).

82 131 216 392 441 506   122 F.2d 852   408 F.2d 343
(a) Detroit Edison Co. v. Ewing (Circuit Court of Appeals, Sixth Circuit October 6, 1941)
M/B: Detroit Edison Co. v. Ewing, 122 F.2d 852 (6th Cir. 1941).

(b) Richard Francis Downie, Petitioner-Appellant, v. John C. Burke, Respondent-Appellee (United States Court of Appeals Seventh Circuit March 6, 1969)
M/B: Downie v. Burke, 408 F.2d 343 (7th Cir. 1969).

83 132 217 393 442 507   152 F.2d 422   193 F.2d 760
(a) Detroit Edison Co. v. Knowles (Circuit Court of Appeals, Sixth Circuit December 13, 1945)
M/B: Detroit Edison Co. v. Knowles, 152 F.2d 422 (6th Cir. 1945).

(b) Downie et al. v. Powers et al. (United States Court of Appeals Tenth Circuit December 20, 1951)
M/B: Downie v. Powers, 193 F.2d 760 (10th Cir. 1951).

84 133 218 394 443 508   186 F.2d 297   162 F.2d 654
(a) Deupree v. Levinson et al. (United States Court of Appeals Sixth Circuit December 22, 1950)
M/B: Deupree v. Levinson, 186 F.2d 297 (6th Cir. 1950).

(b) Downing v. Howard et al. (Circuit Court of Appeals, Third Circuit June 24, 1947)
M/B: Downing v. Howard, 162 F.2d 654 (3d Cir. 1947).

85 134 219 395 444 509   107 F.2d 26   234 F.2d 830
(a) Devine v. Sanford, Warden (Circuit Court of Appeals, Fifth Circuit October 31, 1939)
M/B: Devine v. Sanford, 107 F.2d 26 (5th Cir. 1939).

(b) James B. Doyle, Appellant, v. Oliver A. Fox, J. E. Patterson and Corey Gabrielson, Appellees (United States Court of Appeals Ninth Circuit June 12, 1956)
M/B: Doyle v. Fox, 234 F.2d 830 (9th Cir. 1956).

86 135 220 396 445 510   423 F.2d 32   107 F.2d 337
(a) George Devine, Appellant, v. Lester Pope, Appellee (United States Court of Appeals Ninth Circuit March 13, 1970)
M/B: Devine v. Pope, 423 F.2d 32 (9th Cir. 1970).

(b) Doyle et al. v. Loring et al. (Circuit Court of Appeals, Sixth Circuit November 10, 1939)
M/B: Doyle v. Loring, 107 F.2d 337 (6th Cir. 1939).

87 136 221 397 446 511   123 F.2d 962   112 F.2d 155
(a) Devine v. Pollard (Circuit Court of Appeals, Fifth Circuit December 5, 1941)
M/B: Devine v. Pollard, 123 F.2d 962 (5th Cir. 1941).

(b) Doyne et al. v. Saettele et al. (Circuit Court of Appeals, Eighth Circuit May 22, 1940)
M/B: Doyne v. Saettele, 112 F.2d 155 (8th Cir. 1940).

88 137 222 398 447 512   287 F.2d 687   209 F.2d 26
(a) George Raymond Devine, Appellant, v. Tracy A. Hand, Warden, Kansas State Penitentiary, Appellee (United State Court of Appeals Tenth Circuit January 24, 1961)
M/B: Devine v. Hand, 287 F.2d 687 (10th Cir. 1961).

EXERCISE 7.   FEDERAL REPORTER   (CONTINUED)

(b) Dragna v. Landon et al. (United States Court of Appeals Ninth Circuit December 19, 1953)
M/B: <u>Dragna v. Landon</u>, 209 F.2d 26 (9th Cir. 1953).

89 138 223 399 448 513   242 F.2d 828   309 F.2d 161
(a) Dr. V. J. Devine, Appellant and Cross-Appellee, v. James S. Patteson, Jr., Appellee and Cross-Appellant (United States Court of Appeals Sixth Circuit March 29, 1957)
M/B: <u>Devine v. Patteson</u>, 242 F.2d 828 (6th Cir. 1957).

(b) Joe Dragich and Van Camp Sea Food Company, Inc., Appellants, v. Nikola Strika, Appellee (United States Court of Appeals Ninth Circuit September 26, 1962)
M/B: <u>Dragich v. Strika</u>, 309 F.2d 161 (9th Cir. 1962).

90 139 224 400 449 514   247 F.2d 604   411 F.2d 1142
(a) Melville Diamond, as the Administrator of the Estate of P. M. Diamond as owner of the 23-foot Higgins Speedboat, Official Number 18J1555, Appellant, v. Deborah Beutel and Marion D. Hopwood, Appellees (United States Court of Appeals Fifth Circuit August 8, 1957)
M/B: <u>Diamond v. Beutel</u>, 247 F.2d 604 (5th Cir. 1957).

(b) James R. Berry and Lucille Berry, Plaintiffs-Appellees, v. Bert Allen, James R. Watts, William P. Lusk and Joe Jones, Defendants-Appellants (United States Court of Appeals Sixth Circuit June 20, 1969)
M/B: <u>Berry v. Allen</u>, 411 F.2d 1142 (6th Cir. 1969).

91 140 225 301 450 515   627 F.2d 1032   475 F.2d 918
(a) C. F. Williams and Jeanne V. Williams, Appellants, v. Commissioner of Internal Revenue, Appellee (United States Court of Appeals, Tenth Circuit July 11, 1980)
M/B: <u>Williams v. Commissioner</u>, 627 F.2d 1032 (10th Cir. 1980).

(b) Philip Berrigan, Daniel J. Berrigan, Appellants, v. Maurice Sigler, Chairman of the Board of Parole, and all members of the said Board of Parole (all of whom have their offices at room 354 HOLC Building), et al. (United States Court of Appeals, District of Columbia Circuit January 17, 1973)
M/B: <u>Berrigan v. Sigler</u>, 475 F.2d 918 (D.C. Cir. 1973).

92 141 226 302 451 516   411 F.2d 565   428 F.2d 693
(a) Jerry S. Diamond, Appellant, v. Peter J. Pitchess, Sheriff, et al., Appellees (United States Court of Appeals Ninth Circuit April 29, 1969)
M/B: <u>Diamond v. Pitchess</u>, 411 F.2d 565 (9th Cir. 1969).

(b) John Bershad, Plaintiff-Appellee, v. Bernard P. McDonough, Defendant-Appellant (United States Court of Appeals, Seventh Circuit June 11, 1970)
M/B: <u>Bershad v. McDonough</u>, 428 F.2d 693 (7th Cir. 1970).

93 142 227 303 452 517   221 F.2d 264   446 F.2d 649
(a) Oscar K. Diamond and Helen J. Diamond, Plaintiffs, v. Walter R. Sturr, Collector of Internal Revenue, Defendant (United States Court of Appeals Second Circuit March 28, 1955)
M/B: <u>Diamond v. Sturr</u>, 221 F.2d 264 (2d Cir. 1955).

(b) Joseph 13X Bethea, Petitioner-Appellant, v. J. J. Clark, Warden, Respondent-Appellee (United States Court of Appeals Fifth Circuit August 12, 1971)
M/B: <u>Bethea v. Clark</u>, 446 F.2d 649 (5th Cir. 1971).

94 143 228 304 453 518   13 F.2d 588   444 F.2d 113
(a) Dodge v. Allsion et al. (Circuit Court of Appeals, Third Circuit June 14, 1926)
M/B: <u>Dodge v. Allsion</u>, 13 F.2d 588 (3d Cir. 1926).

EXERCISE 7.   FEDERAL REPORTER   (CONTINUED)

(b) Freddie Freeman, Plaintiff-Petitioner, v. W. T. Stone, Superintendent, Defendant-Respondent (United States Court of Appeals Ninth Circuit June 14, 1971)
M/B: Freeman v. Stone, 444 F.2d 113 (9th Cir. 1971).

95 144 229 305 454 519   255 F.2d 246   445 F.2d 1163
(a) Melvin A. Dodge, Appellant, v. Vassar A. Anderson et al., Appellees (United States Court of Appeals Fifth Circuit May 21, 1958)
M/B: Dodge v. Anderson, 255 F.2d 246 (5th Cir. 1958).

(b) Joseph X. Bethea, Appellant, v. Joseph J. Reid, Agent, Federal Bureau of Investigation, Newark, New Jersey, et al., Appellees (United States Court of Appeals, Third Circuit July 27, 1971)
M/B: Bethea v. Reid, 445 F.2d 1163 (3d Cir. 1971).

96 145 230 306 455 520   355 F.2d 485   441 F.2d 495
(a) Kermit Slone, Plaintiff-Appellee, v. John W. Gardner, Secretary of Health, Education and Welfare, Defendant-Appellant (United States Court of Appeals Sixth Circuit February 2, 1966)
M/B: Slone v. Gardner, 355 F.2d 485 (6th Cir. 1966).

(b) Edward Bethell, Plaintiff-Appellee, v. Veronica M. Peace, Defendant-Appellant (United States Court of Appeals, Fifth Circuit April 26, 1971)
M/B: Bethell v. Peace, 441 F.2d 495 (5th Cir. 1971).

97 146 231 307 456 521   102 F.2d 703   396 F.2d 432
(a) Dodge et al. v. Dodge et al. (Circuit Court of Appeals, First Circuit March 25, 1939)
M/B: Dodge v. Dodge, 102 F.2d 703 (1st Cir. 1939).

(b) George J. Beto, Director, Texas Department of Corrections, Appellant, v. Richard Allen Martin, Appellee (United States Court of Appeals Fifth Circuit May 14, 1968)
M/B: Beto v. Martin, 396 F.2d 432 (5th Cir. 1968).

98 147 232 308 457 522   266 F.2d 52   442 F.2d 393
(a) Lucy E. Dodson, Appellant, v. Travelers Insurance Company, Appellee (United States Court of Appeals Eighth Circuit April 21, 1959)
M/B: Dodson v. Travelers Insurance Co., 266 F.2d 52 (8th Cir. 1959).
LR: Dodson v. Travelers Ins. Co., 266 F.2d 52 (8th Cir. 1959).

(b) James E. Bush, Appellant, v. William B. Robinson (Warden), County Jail, Allegheny (County of Allegheny)--Dismissed 5M/B:22M/B:70 (United States Court of Appeals Third Circuit April 15, 1971)
M/B: Bush v. Robinson, 442 F.2d 393 (3d Cir. 1971).

99 148 233 309 458 523   255 F.2d 118   434 F.2d 1009
(a) John Doe, an Attorney, Appellant, v. Samuel L. Rosenberry, David L. Benetar, Samuel M. Chapin, Horace S. Manges, Alexander Caldwell Neave, Stuart N. Scott, W. Mason Smith, Jr., David Teitelbaum, Stephen P. Duggan, Jr., Joseph E. Dyer, John A. Gifford, James H. Halpin, Roger Bryant Hunting, Murray Foster Johnson, Carlyle E. Maw, F. W. H. Adams, Ernest J. Ellenwood, John D. Garrison, Edgar M. Souza and Harris B. Steinberg, Appellees (United States Court of Appeals Second Circuit May 8, 1958)
M/B: Doe v. Rosenberry, 255 F.2d 118 (2d Cir. 1958).

(b) Raymond J. Butler, Petitioner, v. Allan L. Robbins, Warden, Maine State Prison, Respondent (United States Court of Appeals First Circuit November 18, 1970)
M/B: Butler v. Robbins, 434 F.2d 1009 (1st Cir. 1970).

100 149 234 310 459 524   625 F.2d 1291   360 F.2d 118
(a) Earman Oil Company, Inc. and Courtesy House, Inc., Florida Corporations, Plaintiffs-Appellants, v. Burroughs Corporation, a Michigan Corporation, Defendant-Appellee (United States Court of Appeals, Fifth Circuit September 19, 1980)

EXERCISE 7. FEDERAL REPORTER   (CONTINUED)

M/B: Earman Oil Co. v. Burroughs Corp., 625 F.2d 1291 (5th Cir. 1980).

(b) Robert L. Butler, Petitioner-Appellant, v. John C. Burke, Warden, Wisconsin State Prison, Respondent-Appellee (United States Court of Appeals Seventh Circuit April 15, 1966)
M/B: Butler v. Burke, 360 F.2d 118 (7th Cir. 1966).

LIBRARY EXERCISE 8.   FEDERAL SUPPLEMENT.

INSTRUCTOR'S NOTE: This exercise teaches how to use the "Table of Cases Reported" in the front of the Federal Supplement. They are to find that table in the front of the volume listed for their problem number and to use it to find and cite the designated case in proper form. For this and the next exercise, the following Quick-Reference Abbreviations are particulary relevant:

   FEDERAL COURT CITATION 10. CITE FEDERAL DISTRICT COURT OPINIONS TO THE FEDERAL REPORTER, THE FEDERAL SUPPLEMENT, FEDERAL RULES DECISIONS, THE BANKRUPTCY REPORTER, OR FEDERAL CASES IF THEREIN. BE SURE TO USE THE PROPER ABBREIVIATIONS FOR THESE REPORTERS: F., F.2d, F. Supp., F.R.D., Bankr., AND F. Cas. [FED 10]
   FEDERAL COURT CITATION 11. CITE THE DECISIONS OF THE VARIOUS SPECIALIZED FEDERAL COURTS TO THE FEDERAL REPORTER OR THE FEDERAL SUPPLEMENT IF THEY HAVE BEEN PUBLISHED THEREIN. OTHERWISE, CITE TO THE APPROPRIATE OFFICIAL REPORTER OR SERVICE. BE SURE TO USE THE PROPER ABBREVIATION OF THE FEDERAL REPORTER (F.2d) OR THE FEDERAL SUPPLEMENT (F. Supp.). [FED 11]
   FEDERAL COURT CITATION 13. IN CITATIONS OF FEDERAL DISTRICT COURT DECISIONS, INDICATE THE APPROPRIATELY ABBREVIATED DISTRICT AND STATE PARENTHETICALLY. DO NOT INDICATE THE DIVISION WITHIN THE DISTRICT. CLOSE UP ADJOINING CAPITAL LETTERS UNLESS THE SECOND CAPITAL LETTER IS PART OF A LONGER ABBREVIATION. [FED 13]
   FEDERAL COURT CITATION 14. INCLUDE THE APPROPRIATELY ABBREVIATED NAME OF A SPECIALIZED FEDERAL COURT IN THE CITATION IF IT IS NOT INDICATED BY THE NAME OF THE REPORTER CITED. [FED 14]

1 116 211 335 450 555   210 Allen
Charles J. Allen, Jr., and American Crankshaft Company, Plaintiffs, v. Standard Cranshaft & Hydraulic Company, Inc., Parts Warehouse, Inc,. and Homer H. Brackett, Defendants   (W.D. North Carolina Nov. 7, 1962)
M/B: Allen v. Standard Crankshaft & Hydraulic Co., 210 F. Supp. 844 (W.D.N.C. 1962).

2 117 212 336 451 556   208 Titcomb
A. Shepard Titcomb, Plaintiff, v. Norton Company, Defendant (D. Connecticut Oct. 8, 1959)
M/B: Titcomb v. Norton Co., 208 F. Supp. 9 (D. Conn. 1959).

3 118 213 337 452 557   207 Randall
Alvin Randall, Sr., administrator of the Succession of Alvin Randall, Jr., Complainant, v. William A. Bisso, Defendant (E.D. Louisiana June 14, 1962)
M/B: Randall v. Bisso, 207 F. Supp. 89 (E.D. La. 1962).

4 119 214 338 453 558   204 Becken Co.
A. C. Becken Co., an Illinois corporation, Plaintiff, v. The Gemex Corporation, a New Jersey corporation, Defendant (N.D. Illinois, E.D. April 12, 1962)
M/B: A.C. Becken Co. v. Gemex Corp., 204 F. Supp. 28 (N.D. Ill. 1962).

5 120 215 339 454 559   490 Hanson
Lowell Hanson and Carol Hanson, Plaintiffs, v. Gerald Cushman, Chris P. Christensen, Burl Glendenning, William J. Sieter, Eugene Paslov and Patrick M. Coady, Individually and in their official capacity, Defendants (W.D. Michigan, S.D. March 24, 1980)
M/B: Hanson v. Cushman, 490 F. Supp. 109 (W.D. Mich. 1980).

6 121 216 340 455 560   202 Nickel Rim Mines
Nickel Rim Mines Limited, Plaintiff, v. Universal-Cyclops Steel Corporation, Defendant (D.New Jersey February 9, 1962)
M/B: Nickel Rim Mines v. Universal-Cyclops Steel Corp., 202 F. Supp. 170 (D.N.J. 1962).

7 122 217 341 456 561   470 Anderson
Edward Lee Anderson and Irene Moore Anderson, Plaintiffs, v. Pamlico Chemical Company, Incorporated, Defendant (E.D. North Carolina November 22, 1977)
M/B: Anderson v. Pamlico Chemical Co., 470 F. Supp. 12 (E.D.N.C. 1977).
LR: Anderson v. Pamlico Chem. Co., 470 F. Supp. 12 (E.D.N.C. 1977).

EXERCISE 8.   FEDERAL SUPPLEMENT   (CONTINUED)

8 123 218 342 457 562   200 Stancil
Rosa L. Stancil, Administratrix of the Estate of George Ben Stancil, deceased, Plaintiff, v. United States of America, Defendant and Third-Party Plaintiff (E.D. Virginia December 8, 1961)
M/B: Stancil v. United States, 200 F. Supp. 36 (E.D. Va. 1961).

9 124 219 343 458 563   199 Falcon Sales Co.
Falcon Sales Company, J. J. Murphy & Co. v. United States (United States Customs Court October 18, 1961)
M/B: Falcon Sales Co. v. United States, 199 F. Supp. 97 (Cust. Ct. 1961).

10 125 220 344 459 564   198 Wiley
Frank W. Wiley, Plaintiff, v. Arthur S. Flemming (Substituted by The Honorable Abraham A. Ribicoff), Secretary of Health, Education, and Welfare, Defendant (D. Oregon September 15, 1961)
M/B: Wiley v. Flemming, 198 F. Supp. 705 (D. Or. 1961).

11 126 221 345 460 565   197 Rota-Carb
Rota-Carb Corporation, a New York Corporation, and Bernard Harmon, Plaintiffs, v. Frye Manufacturing Company, an Iowa Corporation, Defendant (S.D. Iowa July 18, 1961)
M/B: Rota-Carb Corp. v. Frye Manufacturing Co., 197 F. Supp. 54 (S.D. Iowa 1961).
LR: Rota-Carb Corp. v. Frye Mfg. Co., 197 F. Supp. 54 (S.D. Iowa 1961).

12 127 222 346 461 566   471 Pharmaceutical Manufacturers Ass'n
Pharmaceutical Manufacturers Association v. Donald Kennedy, Commission of Food and Drugs, Leonard D. Schaeffer, Administrator Health Care Financing Administration, Joseph A. Califano, Jr., Secretary of Health, Education and Welfare, United States of America (D. Maryland May 21, 1979)
M/B: Pharmaceutical Manufacturers Association v. Kennedy, 471 F. Supp. 1224 (D. Md. 1979).
LR: Pharmaceutical Mfrs. Ass'n v. Kennedy, 471 F. Supp. 1224 (D. Md. 1979).

13 128 223 347 462 567   195 Miller
William C. Miller, Plaintiff, v. Abraham A. Ribicoff, as Secretary of Health, Education and Welfare, United States of America, Defendant (W.D. South Carolina July 3, 1961)
M/B: Miller v. Ribicoff, 195 F. Supp. 534 (W.D.S.C. 1961).

14 129 224 348 463 568   493 Parker
Barry T. Parker, James S. Cafiero, Donald Di Francesco, John H. Doresey, Wayne Dumont, Jr., John H. Ewing, Walter E. Foran, S. Thomas Gagliano, Garrett W. Hagedorn, Brian T. Kennedy, Lee B. Laskin, James J. Vreeland, Jr., James H. Wallwork, Members of the Senate of the State of New Jersey and Individually; and Ralph Fucetola, Clarence A. Haverly, Richard Mahon, John Rice and Barbara Tauriello, Individually, Plaintiffs, v. Joseph P. Merlino, Eugene J. Bedell, John P. Caufield, Frank J. Dodd, Bernard J. Dwyer, Angelo J. Errichetti, David J. Friedland, Matthew Feldman, Frank X. Graves, John T. Gregorio, William J. Hamilton, Francis X. Herbert, Joseph Hirkala, Wynona A. Lipman, Joseph A. Maressa, William Vincent Musto, Carmen A. Orechio, Steven P. Perskie, Frank E. Rodgers, Anthony Scardino, Jr., Walter N. Sheil, John M. Skevin, Charles B. Yates and Raymond J. Zane, Members of the Senate of the State of new Jersey; and the Senate of the State of New Jersey and the State of New Jersey, Defendants (D. New Jersey June 13, 1980)
M/B: Parker v. Merlino, 493 F. Supp. 381 (D.N.J. 1980).

15 130 225 349 464 569   205 Lipp
Morris J. Lipp v. National Screen Service Corporation (E.D. Pennsylvania May 31, 1961)
M/B: Lipp v. National Screen Service Corp., 205 F. Supp. 180 (E.D. Pa. 1961).
LR: Lipp v. National Screen Serv. Corp., 205 F. Supp. 180 (E.D. Pa. 1961).

16 131 226 350 465 570   258 Denton
Sylvester Jeff Denton, Plaintiff, v. Blair Campbell Ellis and Humble Oil & Refining Company, Defendants (E.D. North Carolina September 1, 1966)

EXERCISE 8. FEDERAL SUPPLEMENT   (CONTINUED)

M/B: Denton v. Ellis, 258 F. Supp. 223 (E.D.N.C. 1966).

17 132 227 351 466 571   259 Silver
Norman Silver, Plaintiff, v. The Sloop Silver Cloud, her engines, tackle, apparel, etc., and A. LeComte Company, Inc., and all other persons lawfully intervening for their interest in said sloop, Defendants (S.D. New York August 23, 1966)
M/B: Silver v. The Sloop Silver Cloud, 259 F. Supp. 187 (S.D.N.Y. 1966).

18 133 228 352 467 572   260 McDonald
Truman Eldin McDonald v. J. D. Middlebrooks, Warden, Louisisana State Penitentiary (E.D. Louisiana November 14, 1966)
M/B: McDonald v. Middlebrooks, 260 F. Supp. 563 (E.D. La. 1966).

19 134 229 353 468 573   261 Stockwell
Ernest Stockwell, Petitioner, v. Harold R. Swenson, Warden, Respondent (W.D. Missouri November 3, 1966)
M/B: Stockwell v. Swenson, 261 F. Supp. 77 (W.D. Mo. 1966).

20 135 230 354 469 574   262 Paley
Lewis A. Paley, Plaintiff, v. Morris O. Wolk, Michael E. Rogers, Edward L. Brenner and John T. Connor, Defendants (N.D. Illinois, E.D. December 29, 1965)
M/B: Paley v. Wolk, 262 F. Supp. 640 (N.D. Ill. 1965).

21 136 231 355 470 575   263 Wagner
In the Matter of Bernard Wagner, Plaintiff, v. J. F. Maroney, Superintendent, State Correctional Institution, Pittsburgh, Pennsylvania, N. Welch, Deputy Superintendent, State Correctional Institution, Pittsburgh, Pennsylvania, A. T. Prasse, Commissioner of Correctional Institution of State of Pennsylvania, Attorney General of the State of Pennsylvania, Defendants (W.D. Pennsylvania January 27, 1967)
M/B: Wagner v. Maroney, 263 F. Supp. 377 (W.D. Pa. 1967).

22 137 232 356 471 576   264 Crowder
Ruth Crowder, Mother and Next Friend of Walter Paul Crowder and David Douglas Crowder, Minors, Plaintiff, v. Gordons Transports, Inc., a Corporation, Defendant (W.D. Arkansas February 21, 1967)
M/B: Crowder v. Gordons Transports, 264 F. Supp. 137 (W.D. Ark. 1967).
LR: Crowder v. Gordons Transps., 264 F. Supp. 137 (W.D. Ark. 1967).

23 138 233 357 472 577   265 Weaver
Robert Theordore Weaver, Petitioner, v. United States of America, Respondent (E.D. Missouri, E.D. January 11, 1967)
M/B: Weaver v. United States, 265 F. Supp. 131 (E.D. Mo. 1967).

24 139 234 358 473 578   266 Sanders
Edgar M. Sanders, as General Secretary Treasurer of Journeymen Barbers, Hairdressers, Cosmetologists and Proprietors International Union of America, AFL-CIO, Plaintiff, v. Daniel De Lucia and Adolph Rosenbaum, individually and as President and Secretary Treasurer, respectively of Barbers, Hairdressers and Beauty Culturists Union, Independent, Local 1, Anthony Franco and Joseph Visconti, individually and as President and Secretary Treaurer, respectively of Barbers, Hairstylists and Beauty Culturists Union, Independent, Local 2, Louis Palude and George Pelletiere, individually and as President and Secretary Treasurer, respectively of Barber, Hairstylists and Beauty Culturists Union Independent, Local 3, and John Restivo and Ben Carbone, individually and as President and Secretary Treasurer respectively, of Barbers, Hairstylists and Beauty Culturists Union, Independent, Local 4, Defendants (S.D. New York May 1, 1967)
M/B: Sanders v. De Lucia, 266 F. Supp. 852 (S.D.N.Y. 1967).

25 140 235 359 474 579   267 Sugarman
Harry Sugarman, Petitioner, v. Jack B. Forbragd, Fred E. Norman, Food and Drug Officers, Respondents (N.D. California May 11, 1967)
M/B: Sugarman v. Forbragd, 267 F. Supp. 817 (N.D. Cal. 1967).

26 141 236 360 475 580   494 Moore

EXERCISE 8. FEDERAL SUPPLEMENT   (CONTINUED)

Richard A. Moore, Petitioner, v. David Scurr, Warden, Iowa State Penitentiary, Respondent (S.D. Iowa, C.D. August 28, 1980)
M/B: Moore v. Scurr, 494 F. Supp. 1042 (S.D. Iowa 1980).

27 142 237 361 476 581   269 Unruh
Paul E. Unruh, Plaintiff, v. Stewart L. Udall, Secretary of the Interior of the United States, and Individually, J. R. Penny, formerly Nebada State Director, Bureau of Land Management, U.S. Department of the Interior, and Individually, Nolan F. Keil, Nevada State Director, Bureau of Land Management, U.S. Department of the Interior, and Individually, Val B. Richman, District Manager, Carson City Office, Bureau of Land Management, U.S. Department of the Interior, and Individually, and Wesley Laverne Edwards, Individually, Defendants (D. Nevada June 1967)
M/B: Unruh v. Udall, 269 F. Supp. 97 (D. Nev. 1967).

28 143 238 362 477 582   472 Leon Industries
Leon Industries, Inc., Sigma Chemical Company, Plaintiffs, v. I.C.N. Pharmaceuticals, Defendant (E.D. Missouri, E.D. July 19, 1979)
M/B: Leon Industries v. I.C.N. Pharmaceuticals, 472 F. Supp. 1241 (E.D. Mo. 1979).
LR: Leon Indus. v. I.C.N. Pharmaceuticals, 472 F. Supp. 1241 (E.D. Mo. 1979).

29 144 239 363 478 583   271 Kapral
Andrew Kapral et al., Plaintiffs, v. Alan H. Jepson et al., Defendants (D. Connecticut May 31, 1967)
M/B: Kapral v. Jepson, 271 F. Supp. 74 (D. Conn. 1967).

30 145 240 364 479 584   272 Abee
Eldon Abee, Administrator of the Estate of Andrew Bert Weigel, Jr., a/k/a/ Andrew B. Weigel, Jr., Deceased, Plaintiff, v. James Stamm and Milton J. Sokolovich, Defendants (W.D. Pennsylvania August 30, 1967)
M/B: Abee v. Stamm, 272 F. Supp. 406 (W.D. Pa. 1967).

31 146 241 365 480 585   312 Abramson
Fred B. Abramson, Plaintiff, v. Nytronics, Inc., et al., Defendants (S.D. New York April 3, 1970)
M/B: Abramson v. Nytronics, Inc., 312 F. Supp. 519 (S.D.N.Y. 1970).

32 147 242 366 481 586   313 Scott
William D. Scott, Petitioner, v. Commanding Officer, Commander Thomas M. Volatile, Armed Forces Examining Entrance Station, Philadelphia, Pennsylvania and Secretary of Defense, The Pentagon, Arlington, Virginia, Respondents (E.D. Pennsylvania February 20, 1970)
M/B: Scott v. Volatile, 313 F. Supp. 193 (E.D. Pa. 1970).

33 148 243 367 482 587   314 Zanoviak
Sophie Zanoviak v. Robert H. Finch, Secretary, Department of Health, Education, and Welfare (W.D. Pennsylvania July 31, 1970)
M/B: Zanoviak v. Finch, 314 F. Supp. 1152 (W.D. Pa. 1970).

34 149 244 368 483 588   315 Lovan
James Taylor Lovan, Petitioner, v. John W. Wingo, Warden, Kentucky State Penitentiary, Respondent (W.D. Kentucky January 6, 1970)
M/B: Lovan v. Wingo, 315 F. Supp. 656 (W.D. Ky. 1970).

35 150 245 369 484 589   316 Runyon
Bill C. Runyon, Petitioner, v. J.D. Cox, Superintendent, Virginia State Penitentiary, Respondent (W.D. Virginia August 14, 1970)
M/B: Runyon v. Cox, 316 F. Supp. 1338 (W.D. Va. 1970).

36 151 246 370 485 590   317 Ross
Delores Ross, a minor, by her Next Friend, Mary Alice Benjamin, et al., Plaintiffs, United States of America, Plaintiff-Intervenor, v. Robert Eckels, as President of the Board of Trustees of the Houston Independent School District, et al., Defendants (S.D. Texas May 30, 1970)
M/B: Ross v. Eckels, 317 F. Supp. 512 (S.D. Tex. 1970).

EXERCISE 8. FEDERAL SUPPLEMENT   (CONTINUED)

37 152 247 371 486 591   318 Stone
John Gilbert Stone, Plaintiff, v. Hal B. Jennings, Jr., et al., Defendants (S.D. New York July 29, 1970)
M/B: Stone v. Jennings, 318 F. Supp. 1379 (S.D.N.Y. 1970).

38 153 248 372 487 592   319 Tucker
Edythe F. Tucker, Plaintiff, v. Joseph M. Burton, Clerk D. C. Court of General Sessions and Household Finance Corporation of Suitland, Defendants (District of Columbia November 12, 1970)
M/B: Tucker v. Burton, 319 F. Supp. 567 (D.D.C.1970).

39 154 249 373 488 593   320 Callaway
Luke Callaway v. M. E. Kirkland, J. E. Edmonds, and the Clayton County Board of Education (N.D. Georgia December 29, 1970)
M/B: Callaway v. Kirkland, 320 F. Supp. 1135 (N.D. Ga. 1970).

40 155 250 374 489 594   321 Pitts
F. W. Pitts, G. Graham Segars, Marion M. Gandy, Robert K. Bass, Walter G. Wofford, Guss Hoffmeyer, A. R. Mims, George L. Timmons, A. T. J. Morrison, Harrell L. Gardner, and Edward E. Saleeby, proposed organizers of The First National Bank of Hartsville, a national banking association in the process of formation, Plaintiffs, v. William B. Camp, Comptroller of the Currency of the United States, Defendant (D. South Carolina October 15, 1970)
M/B: Pitts v. Camp, 321 F. Supp. 407 (D.S.C. 1970).

41 156 251 375 490 595   322 Walsh
Joseph H. and Anne M. Walsh, Plaintiffs, v. United States of America, Defendant (E.D. New York November 18, 1970)
M/B: Walsh v. United States, 322 F. Supp. 613 (E.D.N.Y. 1970).

42 157 252 376 491 596   323 Clark
Peter F. Clark et al., Plaintiffs, v. Kraftco Corporation et al., Defendants (S.D. New York February 25, 1971)
M/B: Clark v. Kraftco Corp., 323 F. Supp. 358 (S.D.N.Y. 1971).

43 158 253 377 492 597   360 Schonfeld
Frank Schonfeld, Individually and as Secretary-Treasurer of District Council 9, International Brotherhood of Painters and Allied Trades, AFL-CIO, Plaintiff, v. John Penza, as Chairman and member, et al., Defendants (S.D. New York December 7, 1972)
M/B: Schonfeld v. Penza, 360 F. Supp. 1228 (S.D.N.Y. 1972).

44 159 254 378 493 598   362 Von Brimer
Michael J. Von Brimer et al., Co-executors of the Estate of Joseph W. Von Brimer, Deceased, Plaintiffs, v. Whirlpool Corporation, Defendants (N.D. California August 20, 1973)
M/B: Von Brimer v. Whirlpool Corp., 362 F. Supp. 1182 (N.D. Cal. 1973).

45 160 255 379 494 599   363 Garrett
Joseph Garrett, Plaintiff, v. Elliot L. Richardson, Secretary of Health, Education, and Welfare, Defendant (D. South Carolina August 15, 1973)
M/B: Garrett v. Richardson, 363 F. Supp. 83 (D.S.C. 1973).

46 161 256 380 495 600   364 Wuillamey
Marianne Wuillamey et al., Plaintiffs, v. David A. Werblin and Richard J. Sullivan, Defendants (D. New Jersey August 27, 1973)
M/B: Wuillamey v. Werblin, 364 F. Supp. 237 (D.N.J. 1973).

47 162 257 381 496 501   365 Sims
M. O. Sims, et al., Plaintiffs, R. E. Farr, et al., Intervening Plaintiffs, United States of America, Plaintiff and Amicus Curiae, v. Mabel Amos, Secretary of State of the State of Alabama, et al., Defendants, Pierre Pelham, et al., Individually and as members of the Joint Legislative Committee of the Legislature of Alabama, etc., et al., Intervening Defendants (M.D. Alabama August 3, 1973)
M/B: Sims v. Amos, 365 F. Supp. 215 (M.D. Ala. 1973).

EXERCISE 8. FEDERAL SUPPLEMENT   (CONTINUED)

48 163 258 382 497 502   366 Newhall
Edward R. Newhall v. John Boyle, Sheriff of Hampshire County as he is custodian of the House of Correction at Northampton, Mass. (D. Massachusetts November 20, 1973)
M/B: <u>Newhall v. Boyle</u>, 366 F. Supp. 871 (D. Mass. 1973).

49 164 259 383 498 503   134 Woodard
Carl L. Woodard, Plaintiff, v. Gary Campbell, Director of Internal Revenue, Defendant, United States of America, Intervenor-Defendant (S.D. Indiana August 8, 1955)
M/B: <u>Woodard v. Campbell</u>, 134 F. Supp. 258 (S.D. Ind. 1955).

50 165 260 384 499 504   82 Sutherland Paper Co.
Sutherland Paper Co. v. Grant Paper Box Co. et al. (W.D. Pennsylvania January 25, 1949)
M/B: <u>Sutherland Paper Co. v. Grant Paper Box Co.</u>, 82 F. Supp. 250 (W.D. Pa. 1949).

51 166 261 385 500 505   81 Loroco Industries
Loroco Industries, Inc., v. Steele et al. (W.D. Missouri, W.D. November 26, 1948)
M/B: <u>Loroco Industries v. Steele</u>, 81 F. Supp. 146 (W.D. Mo. 1948).
LR: Loroco Indus. v. Steele, 81 F. Supp. 146 (W.D. Mo. 1948).

52 167 262 386 401 506   80 Zalkind
Zalkind v. Scheinman et al. (Guide System & Supply Co., Inc., Third-Party Defendant) (S.D. New York March 8, 1948)
M/B: <u>Zalkind v. Scheinman</u>, 80 F. Supp. 299 (S.D.N.Y. 1948).

53 168 263 387 402 507   79 O'Connor
O'Connor v. Yardley Golf Club (E.D. Pennsylvania July 21, 1947)
M/B: <u>O'Connor v. Yardley Golf Club</u>, 79 F. Supp. 264 (E.D. Pa. 1947).

54 169 264 388 403 508   78 Lo Bue
Lo Bue v. United States et al. (E.D. New York June 10, 1948)
M/B: <u>Lo Bue v. United States</u>, 78 F. Supp. 86 (E.D.N.Y. 1948).

55 170 265 389 404 509   77 Wright
Wright v. Johnston, Warden (N.D. California April 23, 1948)
M/B: <u>Wright v. Johnston</u>, 77 F. Supp. 687 (N.D. Cal. 1948).

56 171 266 390 405 510   474 Mardirosian
Aram H. Mardirosian, Plaintiff, v. The American Institute of Architects, and Seymour Auerbach, Defendants (District of Columbia June 25, 1979)
M/B: <u>Mardirosian v. American Institute of Architects</u>, 474 F. Supp. 628 (D.D.C. 1979).
LR: Mardirosian v. American Inst. of Architects, 474 F. Supp. 628 (D.D.C. 1979).

57 172 267 391 406 511   75 Mahon
Mahon v. Bennett et al. (W.D. Missouri, W.D. January 8, 1948)
M/B: <u>Mahon v. Bennett</u>, 75 F. Supp. 666 (W.D. Mo. 1948).

58 173 268 392 407 512   613 Warren
Alvin Warren and Alfred Warren, Plaintiffs, v. Halstead Industries, Inc., Defendant (M.D. North Carolina April 26 1985)
M/B: <u>Warren v. Halstead Industries</u>, 613 F. Supp. 499 (M.D.N.C. 1985).
LR: Warren v. Halstead Indus., 613 F. Supp. 499 (M.D.N.C. 1985).

59 174 269 393 408 513   3 Monamotor Oil
Monamotor Oil Co. v. Johnson, State Treasurer, et al. (S.D. Iowa, W.D. March 29, 1933)
M/B: <u>Monamotor Oil Co. v. Johnson</u>, 3 F. Supp. 189 (S.D. Iowa 1933).

60 175 270 394 409 514   72 Worel

EXERCISE 8.   FEDERAL SUPPLEMENT   (CONTINUED)

Worel et al. v. Ooms, Commissioner of Patents (District of Columbia July 9, 1947)
M/B: Worel v. Ooms, 72 F. Supp. 273 (D.D.C. 1947).

61 176 271 395 410 515   71 Alley
Alley v. Clark, Attorney General (E.D. New York May 1, 1947)
M/B: Alley v. Clark, 71 F. Supp. 521 (E.D.N.Y. 1947).

62 177 272 396 411 516   614 Stokes
Charles Stokes, Plaintiff, v. Bechtel North American Power Corporation, Bechtel Power Corporation, Pacific Gas & Electric, Code III, Doe Companies One through Twenty-Five, inclusive, and Does One through Twenty-Five, inclusive, Defendants
M/B: Stokes v. Bechtel North American Power Corp., 614 F. Supp. 732 (N.D. Cal. 1985).
LR: Stokes v. Bechtel N. Am. Power Corp., 614 F. Supp. 732 (N.D. Cal. 1985).

63 178 273 397 412 517   1 Flynn
Flynn v. Templeton et al. (W.D. New York August 8, 1932)
M/B: Flynn v. Templeton, 1 F. Supp. 238 (W.D.N.Y. 1932).

64 179 274 398 413 518   2 Harp
Harp v. United States (W.D. Arkansas February 5, 1932)
M/B: Harp v. United States, 2 F. Supp. 32 (W.D. Ark. 1932).

65 180 275 399 414 519   73 Weaver
Weaver et al. v. Marcus et al. (W.D. Virginia September 9, 1947)
M/B: Weaver v. Marcus, 73 F. Supp. 736 (W.D. Va. 1947).

66 181 276 400 415 520   615 Texasgulf
Texasgulf Inc. and Texasgulf Aviation, Inc., Plaintiffs, v. Colt Electronics Co., Inc., Phoenix Aerospace, Inc., the Garrett Corporation, Lockheed Corporation, and the United States of America, Defendants. (S.D. New York Nov. 16, 1984)
M/B: Texasgulf Inc. v. Colt Electronics Co., 615 F. Supp. 648 (S.D.N.Y. 1984).
LR: Texasgulf Inc. v. Colt Elecs. Co., 615 F. Supp. 648 (S.D.N.Y. 1984).

67 182 277 301 416 521   135 Mitchell
Henry Mitchell, Plaintiff, v. United States of America, Defendant (D. New Jersey November 10, 1955)
M/B: Mitchell v. United States, 135 F. Supp. 289 (D.N.J. 1955).

68 183 278 302 417 522   136 Mattheis
Valorus Joe Mattheis, Plaintiff, v. Howard W. Hoyt, James Tolhuizen, Martin Goodman, K. T. Meyer, Ray Robinson, Pat Untermeyer, Arthur Marchand, N. R. Sachs, R. F. Gallagher, T. R. Pol, P. H. Norworth, V. A. Jirsa, and Male Publishing Corporation, Defendants (W.D. Michigan, S.D. November 30, 1955)
M/B: Mattheis v. Hoyt, 136 F. Supp. 119 (W.D. Mich. 1955).

69 184 279 303 418 523   495 Ward
Thomas Joseph Ward, Plaintiff, v. Ken Connor, Sr., Arlene Doe, Ken Connor, Jr., Phil Doe, John Doe, Robert S. Mandelkorn, Eugenia Mandelkorn, Richard Roe, Mary Roe, Lyle Mosier, Judy Kimes, Reverend Dean, Alan Tate Wood, Dee Anderson, Marty Berg, Father Marty O'Rourke, Ted Morgan, Rose Morgan, Father Martin Conroy, Jeff Yeslein, Jack McConeghy, Betty McConeghy, Jo Munchouer, and Sister Maria Victoria, Defendants (E.D. Virginia April 18, 1980)
M/B: Ward v. Connor, 495 F. Supp. 434 (E.D. Va. 1980).

70 185 280 304 419 524   138 Ferenz
Caroline B. Ferenz, Plaintiff, v. Oveta Culp Hobby, Secretary of Health, Education and Welfare, Defendant (W.D. Pennsylvania October 4, 1955)
M/B: Ferenz v. Hobby, 138 F. Supp. 446 (W.D. Pa. 1955).

71 186 281 305 420 525   139 Vanderveer
Jewell W. Vanderveer, Plaintiff, v. Erie Malleable Iron Company, Defendant (W.D. Pennsylvania March 28, 1956)

EXERCISE 8. FEDERAL SUPPLEMENT   (CONTINUED)

M/B: <u>Vanderveer v. Erie Malleable Iron Co.</u>, 139 F. Supp. 340 (W.D. Pa. 1956).

72 187 282 306 421 526   140 Bierman
Al Bierman and William Miller, Plaintiffs, v. Samuel Marcus and Milmar Estate, Inc., a corporation organized under the laws of the State of New Jersey, Defendants (D. New Jersey March 12, 1956)
M/B: <u>Bierman v. Marcus</u>, 140 F. Supp. 66 (D.N.J. 1956).

73 188 283 307 422 527   141 Buffa
Nick Buffa, Plaintiff, v. General Motors Corporation, a Delaware corporation, Defendant, and J. A. Utley Company, a corporation, Third-Party Defendant (E.D. Michigan, S.D. June 20, 1956)
M/B: <u>Buffa v. General Motors Corp.</u>, 141 F. Supp. 803 (E.D. Mich. 1956).

74 189 284 308 423 528   142 Garden Homes
Garden Homes, Inc., v. Norman P. Mason, Commissioner, Federal Housing Administration (D. New Hampshire March 23, 1956)
M/B: <u>Garden Homes, Inc. v. Mason</u>, 142 F. Supp. 744 (D.N.H. 1956).

75 190 285 309 424 529   143 Harrison
Herbert Miles Harrison, Plaintiff, v. United Fruit Company, Defendant (S.D. New York July 31, 1956)
M/B: <u>Harrison v. United Fruit Co.</u>, 143 F. Supp. 598 (S.D.N.Y. 1956).

76 191 286 310 425 530   144 Muller
A. F. Muller v. Lyke Coastwise Line, Inc. et al. (S.D. Texas February 29, 1940)
M/B: <u>Muller v. Lyke Coastwise Line</u>, 144 F. Supp. 135 (S.D. Tex. 1940).

77 192 287 311 426 531   145 Stookey
Kenneth W. Stookey and The Gas Machinery Company, Plaintiffs, v. Robert C. Watson, Commissioner of Patents, Defendant (District of Columbia July 26, 1956)
M/B: <u>Stookey v. Watson</u>, 145 F. Supp. 101 (D.D.C. 1956).

78 193 288 312 427 532   6 Century Indemnity
Century Indemnity Co. v. New York Tank Barge Co. (E.D. New York December 4, 1933)
M/B: <u>Century Indemnity Co. v. New York Tank Barge Co.</u>, 6 F. Supp. 280 (E.D.N.Y. 1933).
LR: Century Indem. Co. v. New York Tank Barge Co., 6 F. Supp. 280 (E.D.N.Y. 1933).

79 194 289 313 428 533   147 Wilt
Pauline Wilt v. Norman H. Smack (E.D. Pennsylvania January 7, 1957)
M/B: <u>Wilt v. Smack</u>, 147 F. Supp. 700 (E.D. Pa. 1957).

80 195 290 314 429 534   148 Whittenberg
Donald E. Whittenberg et al., Plaintiff, v. United States of America, Defendant (S.D. Texas December 12, 1956)
M/B: <u>Whittenberg v. United States</u>, 148 F. Supp. 353 (S.D. Tex. 1956).

81 196 291 315 430 535   85 Russick
Russick et al. v. Hicks (W.D. Michigan, S.D. August 31, 1949)
M/B: <u>Russick v. Hicks</u>, 85 F. Supp. 281 (W.D. Mich. 1949).

82 197 292 316 431 536   84 In re Bush
In re Bush (District of Columbia June 21, 1949)
M/B: <u>In re Bush</u>, 84 F. Supp. 873 (D.D.C. 1949).
LR: <u>In re</u> Bush, 84 F. Supp. 873 (D.D.C. 1949).

83 198 293 317 432 537   83 Lowe
Lowe v. United States (W.D. Missouri, W.D. March 17, 1949)
M/B: <u>Lowe v. United States</u>, 83 F. Supp. 128 (W.D 1949).

84 199 294 318 433 538   475 Sexe

EXERCISE 8.   FEDERAL SUPPLEMENT   (CONTINUED)

Elmer A. Sexe and Arlene Sexe, Plaintiffs, v. Husky Oil Company, Defendant (D. Montana August 24, 1979)
M/B: Sexe v. Husky Oil Co., 475 F. Supp. 135 (D. Mont. 1979).

85 200 295 319 434 539   146 Tague
Sidney Tague, individually, and as Administrator of the Estate of Harry Tague, deceased, Plaintiff, v. Harry Balaban, Elmer Balaban, John Balaban, H & E Balaban Corporation, a corporation fo the State of Illinois, Joseph H. Feulner, Balaban & Katz Corporation, a corporation of the State of Delaware, Twentieth Century-Fox Film Corporation, a corporation of the State of New York, Paramount Film Distributing Corporation, a corporation of the State of New York, Warner Bros. Pictures Distributing Corporation, a corporation of the State of Delaware, and Loew's Inc., a corporation fo the State of Delaware, Defendants (N.D. Illinois, E.D. November 6, 1956)
M/B: Tague v. Balaban, 146 F. Supp. 356 (N.D. Ill. 1956).

86 101 296 320 435 540   7 Rosenstadt
Rosenstadt & Waller, Inc., v. United States (Court of Claims June 4, 1934)
M/B: Rosenstadt & Waller, Inc. v. United States, 7 F. Supp. 287 (Ct. Cl. 1934).

87 102 297 321 436 541   8 Utah Radio
Utah Radio Products Co. et al. v. Boudette et al. (D. Massachusetts August 7, 1934)
M/B: Utah Radio Products Co. v. Boudette, 8 F. Supp. 5 (D. Mass. 1934).
LR: Utah Radio Prods. Co. v. Boudette, 8 F. Supp. 5 (D. Mass. 1934).

88 103 298 322 437 542   9 Whitehall Lunch Club
Whitehall Lunch Club v. United States (Court of Claims December 3, 1934)
M/B: Whitehall Lunch Club v. United States, 9 F. Supp. 132 (Ct. Cl. 1934).

89 104 299 323 438 543   10 Acme, Inc.
Acme, Inc., v. Besson, U.S. Dist. Atty (D. New Jersey March 12, 1935)
M/B: Acme, Inc. v. Besson, 10 F. Supp. 1 (D.N.J. 1935).

90 105 300 324 439 544   19 In re Beachley
In re Beachley (D. Maryland April 29, 1937)
M/B: In re Beachley, 19 F. Supp. 104 (D. Md. 1937).
LR: In re Beachley, 19 F. Supp. 104 (D. Md. 1937).

91 106 201 325 440 545   20 Apex Hosiery
Apex Hosiery Co. v. Leader et al. (E.D. Pennsylvania June 5, 1937)
M/B: Apex Hosiery Co. v. Leader, 20 F. Supp. 138 (E.D. Pa. 1937).

92 107 202 326 441 546   21 Edison Light
Edison Light & Power Co. v. Driscoll et al. (M.D. Pennsylvania October 18, 1937)
M/B: Edison Light & Power Co. v. Driscoll, 21 F. Supp. 1 (M.D. Pa. 1937).

93 108 203 327 442 547   22 Evale
Evale v. Tremaine, Comptroller of State of New York, et al. (W.D. New York February 5, 1938)
M/B: Evale v. Tremaine, 22 F. Supp. 171 (W.D.N.Y. 1938).

94 109 204 328 443 548   23 Sampson
Sampson v. Welch, Formerly Collector of Internal Revenue (S.D. California April 30, 1938)
M/B: Sampson v. Welch, 23 F. Supp. 271 (S.D. Cal. 1938).

95 110 205 329 444 549   29 Heal
Heal v. Wood et al. (W.D. Washington, N.D. October 6, 1939)
M/B: Heal v. Wood, 29 F. Supp. 509 (W.D. Wash. 1939).

96 111 206 330 445 550   28 Gray
Gray v. Swope, Warden (W.D. Washington, S.D. August 30, 1939)
M/B: Gray v. Swope, 28 F. Supp. 822 (W.D. Wash. 1939).

EXERCISE 8. FEDERAL SUPPLEMENT   (CONTINUED)

97 112 207 331 446 551   27 Standard Rice
Standard Rice Co., Inc., v. Scofield, Collector of Internal Revenue (W.D. Texas May 20, 1939)
M/B: Standard Rice Co. v. Scofield, 27 F. Supp. 854 (W.D. Tex. 1939).

98 113 208 332 447 552   26 Shields
Shields v. Shields (W.D. Missouri January 20, 1939)
M/B: Shields v. Shields, 26 F. Supp. 211 (W.D. Mo. 1939).

99 114 209 333 448 553   25 Ripperger
Ripperger v. Allyn et al. (S.D. New York June 27, 1938)
M/B: Ripperger v. Allyn, 25 F. Supp. 554 (S.D.N.Y. 1938).

100 115 210 334 449 554   24 Bahr Starting Gate Corp.
Bahr Starting Gate Corporation v. Dade Park Jockey Club (W.D. Kentucky September 28, 1938)
M/B: Bahr Starting Gate Corp. v. Dade Park Jockey Club, 24 F. Supp. 709 (W.D. Ky. 1938).

LIBRARY EXERCISE 9. FEDERAL RULES DECISIONS.

INSTRUCTOR'S NOTE: The students are required to cite the case that begins on the page listed below in the designated volume of Federal Rules Decisions.

1 112 225 304 488 519   1 F.R.D. 679
Dairy Engineering Corporation, Limited, et al. v. De-Raef Corporation et al. (W.D. Missouri, W.D. March 17, 1941)
M/B: Dairy Engineering Corp. v. De-Raef Corp., 1 F.R.D. 679 (W.D. Mo. 1941).
LR: Dairy Eng'g Corp. v. De-Raef Corp., 1 F.R.D. 679 (W.D. Mo. 1941).

2 113 226 305 489 520   102 F.R.D. 172
Roger Taylor, Plaintiff v. Belger Cartage Service, Inc., et al., Defendants (W.D. Missouri, W.D. May 23, 1984)
M/B: Taylor v. Belger Cartage Service, 102 F.R.D. 172 (W.D. Mo. 1984).
LR: Taylor v. Belger Cartage Serv., 102 F.R.D. 172 (W.D. Mo. 1984).

3 114 227 306 490 521   2 F.R.D. 405
Malcom v. Cities Service Co. et al. (D. Delaware 1942)
M/B: Malcom v. Cities Service Co., 2 F.R.D. 405 (D. Del. 1942).
LR: Malcom v. Cities Serv. Co., 2 F.R.D. 405 (D. Del. 1942).

4 115 228 307 491 522   80 F.R.D. 449
Burt Printing Co., Inc., Plaintiff, v. Middle East Media Corporation, Defendant (S.D. New York November 9, 1978)
M/B: Burt Printing Co. v. Middle East Media Corp., 80 F.R.D. 449 (S.D.N.Y. 1978).
LR: Burt Printing Co. v. Middle E. Media Corp., 80 F.R.D. 449 (S.D.N.Y. 1978).

5 116 229 308 492 523   81 F.R.D. 490
Patricia P. Perry, Individually and on behalf of all other persons similarly situated, Plaintiff, v. Beneficial Finance Co. of New York, Inc. (W.D. New York January 22, 1979)
M/B: Perry v. Beneficial Finance Co., 81 F.R.D. 490 (W.D.N.Y. 1979).
LR: Perry v. Beneficial Fin. Co., 81 F.R.D. 490 (W.D.N.Y. 1979).

6 117 230 309 493 524   4 F.R.D. 325
Parker v. Transcontinental & Western Air, Inc. (W.D. Missouri, W.D. November 15, 1944)
M/B: Parker v. Transcontinental & Western Air, Inc., 4 F.R.D. 325 (W.D. Mo. 1944).
LR: Parker v. Transcontinental & W. Air, Inc., 4 F.R.D. 325 (W.D. Mo. 1944).

7 118 231 310 494 525   5 F.R.D. 126
Winslow et al. v. National Electric Products Corporation (W.D. Pennsylvania February 1, 1946)
M/B: Winslow v. National Electric Products Corp., 5 F.R.D. 126 (W.D. Pa. 1946).
LR: Winslow v. National Elec. Prods. Corp., 5 F.R.D. 126 (W.D. Pa. 1946).

8 119 232 311 495 526   6 F.R.D. 340
Panhandle Eastern Pipe Line Co. v. Parish et ux. (Toklan Royalty Corporation et al., Interveners) (D. Kansas January 6, 1947)
M/B: Panhandle Eastern Pipe Line v. Parish, 6 F.R.D. 340 (D. Kan. 1947).
LR: Panhandle E. Pipe Line v. Parish, 6 F.R.D. 340 (D. Kan. 1947).

9 120 233 312 496 527   7 F.R.D. 239
Raylite Electric Corporation v. Noma Electric Corporation (S.D. New York December 23, 1946)
M/B: Raylite Electric Corp. v. Noma Electric Corp., 7 F.R.D. 239 (S.D.N.Y. 1946).
LR: Raylite Elec. Corp. v. Noma Elec. Corp., 7 F.R.D. 239 (S.D.N.Y. 1946).

10 121 234 313 497 528   8 F.R.D. 99
Associated Transport, Inc., et al. v. Riss & Co., Inc. (N.D. Ohio, E.D. February 5, 1948)
M/B: Associated Transport v. Riss & Co., 8 F.R.D. 99 (N.D. Ohio 1948).
LR: Associated Transp. v. Riss & Co., 8 F.R.D. 99 (N.D. Ohio 1948).

EXERCISE 9. FEDERAL RULES DECISIONS   (CONTINUED)

11 122 235 314 498 529   9 F.R.D. 590
Barnhart et al. v. John B. Rogers Producing Co. (W.D. Pennsylvania January 6, 1950)
M/B: Barnhart v. John B. Rogers Producing Co., 9 F.R.D. 590 (W.D. Pa. 1950).

12 123 236 315 499 530   10 F.R.D. 381
Air King Products Co., Inc., v. Hazeltine Research, Inc. (E.D. New York June 29, 1950)
M/B: Air King Products Co. v. Hazeltine Research, Inc., 10 F.R.D. 381 (E.D.N.Y. 1950).
LR: Air King Prods. Co. v. Hazeltine Research, Inc., 10 F.R.D. 381 (E.D.N.Y. 1950).

13 124 237 316 500 531   105 F.R.D. 83
Delma R. Layton and Roy E. Layton v. Blue Giant Equipment Company of Canada, Ltd., Stokvis Multition Corporation, Equipment Company of America, and Lift Parts Manufacturing Company v. Anderson, Clayton & Company (Feb. 19, 1985)
M/B: Layton v. Blue Giant Equipment Co. of Canada, 105 F.R.D. 83 (E.D. Pa. 1985).
LR: Layton v. Blue Giant Equip. Co. of Can., 105 F.R.D. 83 (E.D. Pa. 1985).

14 125 238 317 401 532   11 F.R.D. 553
Lopinsky v. Hertz Drive-Ur-Self System, Inc., et al. (S.D. New York April 27, 1951)
M/B: Lopinsky v. Hertz Drive-Ur-Self System, 11 F.R.D. 553 (S.D.N.Y. 1951).
LR: Lopinsky v. Hertz Drive-Ur-Self Sys., 11 F.R.D. 553 (SDNY. 1951).

15 126 239 318 402 533   12 F.R.D. 346
National Cash Register Co. v. Realty & Industrial Corp. et al. (D. New Jersey December 12, 1951)
M/B: National Cash Register Co. v. Realty & Industrial Corp., 12 F.R.D. 346 (D.N.J. 1951).
LR: National Cash Register Co. v. Realty & Indus. Corp., 12 F.R.D. 346 (D.N.J. 1951).

16 127 240 319 403 534   13 F.R.D. 96
Mitchell v. Public Service Coordinated Transport et al. (D. New Jersey September 29, 1952)
M/B: Mitchell v. Public Service Coordinated Transport, 13 F.R.D. 96 (D.N.J. 1952).
LR: Mitchell v. Public Serv. Coordinated Transp., 13 F.R.D. 96 (D.N.J. 1952).

17 128 241 320 404 535   14 F.R.D. 351
Ex parte Sparrow (N.D. Alabama, S.D. May 19, 1953)
M/B: Ex parte Sparrow, 14 F.R.D. 351 (N.D. Ala. 1953).
LR: Ex parte Sparrow, 14 F.R.D. 351 (N.D. Ala. 1953).

18 129 242 321 405 536   15 F.R.D. 385
Empire Industries, Inc. v. Mastic Tile Corp. of America (S.D. New York April 14, 1954)
M/B: Empire Industries v. Mastic Tile Corp. of America, 15 F.R.D. 385 (S.D.N.Y. 1954).
LR: Empire Indus. v. Mastic Tile Corp. of Am., 15 F.R.D. 385 (S.D.N.Y. 1954).

19 130 243 322 406 537   16 F.R.D. 472
Security Mutual Casualty Company, a corporation, and Aetna Casualty and Surety Company of Hartford, Connecticut, a corporation, Plaintiffs, v. Sylvester Rich, doing business as Rich and Company, Defendant (W.D. Pennsylvania December 8, 1954)
M/B: Security Mutual Casualty Co. v. Rich, 16 F.R.D. 472 (W.D. Pa. 1954).
LR: Security Mut. Casualty Co. v. Rich, 16 F.R.D. 472 (W.D. Pa. 1954).

20 131 244 323 407 538   107 F.R.D. 215
In re Asbestos School Litigation (E.D. Pennsylania March 28, 1985)
M/B: In re Asbestos School Litigation, 107 F.R.D. 215 (E.D. Pa. 1985).
LR: In re Asbestos School Litig., 107 F.R.D. 215 (E.D. Pa. 1985).

EXERCISE 9. FEDERAL RULES DECISIONS   (CONTINUED)

21 132 245 324 408 539   17 F.R.D. 277
The Connecticut Mutual Life Insurance Company, Plaintiff, v. Paul V. Shields et al., Defendants, and six related cases (S.D. New York March 30, 1955)
M/B: Connecticut Mutual Life Insurance Co. v. Shields, 17 F.R.D. 277 (S.D.N.Y. 1955).
LR: Connecticut Mut. Life Ins. Co. v. Shields, 17 F.R.D. 277 (S.D.N.Y. 1955).

22 133 246 325 409 540   18 F.R.D. 347
Enger-Kress Company, Plaintiff, v. Amity Leather Products Co. and Armour and Company, Defendants (E.D. Wisconsin December 2, 1955)
M/B: Enger-Kress Co. v. Amity Leather Products Co., 18 F.R.D. 347 (E.D. Wis. 1955).
LR: Enger-Kress Co. v. Amity Leather Prods. Co., 18 F.R.D. 347 (E.D. Wis. 1955).

23 134 247 326 410 541   19 F.R.D. 115
Bank of America, National Trust and Savings Association, Enterprise Productions, Inc. and Sunset Securities Co., Plaintiffs, v. Loew's International Corporation, Defendant (S.D. New York March 1, 1956)
M/B: Bank of America v. Loew's International Corp., 19 F.R.D. 115 (S.D.N.Y. 1956).
LR: Bank of Am. v. Loew's Int'l Corp., 19 F.R.D. 115 (S.D.N.Y. 1956).

24 135 248 327 411 542   20 F.R.D. 228
Overseas Exchange Corporation, Plaintiff, v. Inwood Motors, Inc., Defendant and Third-Party Plaintiff, Esco Packers & Supply Co., Inc., Third-Party Defendant (S.D. New York Dec. 31, 1956)
M/B: Overseas Exchange Corp. v. Inwood Motors, 20 F.R.D. 228 (S.D.N.Y. 1956).
LR: Overseas Exch. Corp. v. Inwood Motors, 20 F.R.D. 228 (S.D.N.Y. 1957).

25 136 249 328 412 543   21 F.R.D. 372
Antonio Atella, Plaintiff, v. General Electric Company, Defendant and Third-Party Plaintiff, Hartwell Company, Inc., and R. W. Short, Inc., Third-Party Defendants (D. Rhode Island December 19, 1957)
M/B: Atella v. General Electric Co., 21 F.R.D. 372 (D.R.I. 1957).
LR: Atella v. General Elec. Co., 21 F.R.D. 372 (D.R.I. 1957).

26 137 250 329 413 544   22 F.R.D. 238
Howard Jamison, Administrator of the Estate of Earl B. Benner, Deceased, Plaintiff, v. Pennsylvania Salt Manufacturing Company, Inc., Defendant (W.D. Pennsylvania June 20, 1958)
M/B: Jamison v. Pennsylvania Salt Manufacturing Co., 22 F.R.D. 238 (W.D. Pa. 1958).
LR: Jamison v. Pennsylvania Salt Mfg. Co., 22 F.R.D. 238 (W.D. Pa. 1958).

27 138 251 330 414 545   23 F.R.D. 281
Forrest A. Wonneman, Plaintiff, v. Stratford Securities Co., Inc., Samuel P. Lewis, Joseph Schwartz, Pauline Edith Lewis, Sidney B. Josephson, R. Snow, General Oil & Industries, Inc., Charles E. Graham, Jr., Moses Siegel, Sam Hoffman and James A. Carney, d/b/a/ Corporate Registrar and Transfer Company, Defendants (S.D. New York April 8, 1959)
M/B: Wonneman v. Stratford Securities Co., 23 F.R.D. 281 (S.D.N.Y. 1959).
LR: Wonneman v. Stratford Sec. Co., 23 F.R.D. 281 (S.D.N.Y. 1959).

28 139 252 331 415 546   24 F.R.D. 205
Yonkers Contracting Company, Inc., Plaintiff, v. Maine Turnpike Authority, Defendant (D. Maine October 17, 1958)
M/B: Yonkers Contracting Co. v. Maine Turnpike Authority, 24 F.R.D. 205 (D. Me. 1958).
LR: Yonkers Contracting Co. v. Maine Turnpike Auth., 24 F.R.D. 205 (D. Me. 1958).

29 140 253 332 416 547   79 F.R.D. 98
Black Grievance Committee, Ulysses Miles, Alfred Murray, Henri P. Freeland, Robert Parrish, Joanne Bond, George Wright, William Hand, Calvin Brown, on behalf of themselves and all other similarly situated v. Philadelphia Electric Company (E.D. Pennsylvania June 14, 1978)

EXERCISE 9. FEDERAL RULES DECISIONS   (CONTINUED)

M/B: Black Grievance Committee v. Philadelphia Electric Co., 79 F.R.D. 98 (E.D. Pa. 1978).
LR: Black Grievance Comm. v. Philadelphia Elec. Co., 79 F.R.D. 98 (E.D. Pa. 1978).

30 141 254 333 417 548   26 F.R.D. 113
Sharon Steel Corp., Plaintiff, v. Travelers Indemnity Co., Defendant (N.D. Ohio, E.D. September 13, 1960)
M/B: Sharon Steel Corp. v. Travelers Indemnity Co., 26 F.R.D. 113 (N.D. Ohio 1960).
LR: Sharon Steel Corp. v. Travelers Indem. Co., 26 F.R.D. 113 (N.D. Ohio 1960).

31 142 255 334 418 549   106 F.R.D. 1
Roper Corporation, Plaintiff, v. Litton Systems, Inc., Defendant (N.D. Illinois, E.D. Dec. 12, 1984)
M/B: Roper v. Litton Systems, 106 F.R.D. 1 (N.D. Ill. 1984).
LR: Roper v. Litton Sys., 106 F.R.D. 1 (N.D. Ill. 1984).

32 143 256 335 419 550   27 F.R.D. 243
United States of America, Plaintiff, v. Carter Products, Inc., and American Home Products Corporation, Defendants (S.D. New York March 29, 1961)
M/B: United States v. Carter Products, Inc., 27 F.R.D. 243 (S.D.N.Y. 1961).
LR: United States v. Carter Prods., Inc., 27 F.R.D. 243 (S.D.N.Y. 1961).

33 144 257 336 420 551   28 F.R.D. 368
Raul International Corporation, Plaintiff, v. Nu-Era Gear Corporation, Defendant (S.D. New York May 24, 1961)
M/B: Raul International Corp. v. Nu-Era Gear Corp., 28 F.R.D. 368 (S.D.N.Y. 1961).
LR: Raul Int'l Corp. v. Nu-Era Gear Corp., 28 F.R.D. 368 (S.D.N.Y. 1961).

34 145 258 337 421 552   29 F.R.D. 138
Fred K. Wagoner, Jack R. Wagoner, Donald L. Wagoner and Howard R. Wagoner, co-partners, doing business under the firm name and style of Wagoner Construction Company, Plaintiffs, v. Mountain Savings and Loan Association, a corporation, and Donald E. Barnes, Defendants (D. Colorado December 8, 1961)
M/B: Wagoner v. Mountain Savings & Loan Association, 29 F.R.D. 138 (D. Colo. 1961).
LR: Wagoner v. Mountain Sav. & Loan Ass'n, 29 F.R.D. 138 (D. Colo. 1961).

35 146 259 338 422 553   82 F.R.D. 122
Leroy C. Gipson, Jr., d/b/a/ Burlington Home Builders, and L. G. Bass River, Inc., a New Jersey corporation, Plaintiff, v. Township of Bass River, a municipal corporation, Ronald Criss, Donald Mickens, William McLennon, Thurman Seay, Jeanette Snyder, Individually, and John Doe and Richard Roe, unknown defendants, Defendants (D. New Jersey April 5, 1979)
M/B: Gipson v. Township of Bass River, 82 F.R.D. 122 (D.N.J. 1979).

36 147 260 339 423 554   31 F.R.D. 256
Jerome Gross, Plaintiff, v. JFD Manufacturing Co., Inc., Defendant (E.D. New York Sept. 27, 1962)
M/B: Gross v. JFD Manfacturing Co., 31 F.R.D. 256 (E.D.N.Y. 1962).
LR: Gross v. JFD Mfg. Co., 31 F.R.D. 256 (E.D.N.Y. 1962).

37 148 261 340 424 555   32 F.R.D. 365
Mellon National Bank & Trust Company, Executor of the Estate of Jacob Casale, Deceased, et al. v. Nationwide Mutual Insurance Company et al. (W.D. Pennsylvania Dec. 4, 1962)
M/B: Mellon National Bank & Trust Co. v. Nationwide Mutual Insurance Co., 32 F.R.D. 365 (W.D. Pa. 1962).
LR: Mellon Nat'l Bank & Trust Co. v. Nationwide Mut. Ins. Co., 32 F.R.D. 365 (W.D. Pa. 1962).

38 149 262 341 425 556   32 F.R.D. 335
Louise Vann et al., Plaintiffs, v. Housing Authority of Kansas City, Missouri et al., Defendants (W. D. Missouri, W.D. Aug. 12, 1980)

EXERCISE 9. FEDERAL RULES DECISIONS   (CONTINUED)

M/B: Vann v. Housing Authority, 32 F.R.D. 335 (W.D. Mo. 1980).
LR: Vann v. Housing Auth., 32 F.R.D. 335 (W.D. Mo. 1980).

39 150 263 342 426 557   33 F.R.D. 335
Willis Johnson Moss v. Associated Transport, Inc. (E.D. Tennessee May 15, 1963)
M/B: Moss v. Associated Transport, 33 F.R.D. 335 (E.D. Tenn. 1963).
LR: Moss v. Associated Transp., 33 F.R.D. 335 (E.D. Tenn. 1963).

40 151 264 343 427 558   35 F.R.D. 373
Charles E. Stemler, Plaintiff, v. Wenham Transportation, Inc., and Billy Dean Bell and Robert L. Cook, Defendant (W. D. Pennsylvania June 30, 1964)
M/B: Stemler v. Wenham Transportation, 35 F.R.D. 373 (W.D. Pa. 1964).
LR: Stemler v. Wenham Transp., 35 F.R.D. 373 (W.D. Pa. 1964).

41 152 265 344 428 559   36 F.R.D. 434
Reserve Life Insurance Company, Plaintiff v. Davis Hospital, Inc., Defendant (W. D. North Carolina, Stateville Division Jan. 11, 1965)
M/B: Reserve Life Insurance Co. v. Davis Hospital, 36 F.R.D. 434 (W.D.N.C. 1965).
LR: Reserve Life Ins. Co. v. Davis Hosp., 36 F.R.D. 434 (W.D.N.C. 1965).

42 153 266 345 429 560   37 F.R.D. 51
Trabon Engineering Corporation, an Ohio corporation, Plaintiff, v. Eaton Manufacturing Company, an Ohio corporation, Defendant (N. D. Ohio, E. D. Dec. 9, 1964)
M/B: Trabon Engineering Corp. v. Eaton Manufacturing Co., 37 F.R.D. 51 (N.D. Ohio 1964).
LR: Trabon Eng'g Corp. v. Eaton Mfg. Co., 37 F.R.D. 51 (N.D. Ohio 1964).

43 154 267 346 430 561   38 F.R.D. 482
Merit Finance Company, Inc. of Kingsport, a Corporation, Plaintiff, v. Service Finance Company, Inc. of Greenwood, a Corporation, and E. H. Beshers, Defendants (D. South Carolina, Greenwood Division Dec. 6, 1965)
M/B: Merit Finance Co. v. Service Finance Co., 38 F.R.D. 482 (D.S.C. 1965).
LR: Merit Fin. Co. v. Service Fin. Co., 38 F.R.D. 482 (D.S.C. 1965).

44 155 268 347 431 562   39 F.R.D. 309
Interstate Commerce Commission, Plaintiff, v. St. Paul Transportation Co., Inc., a corporation, and Robert L. Wilkinson, an individual, Defendants (D. Minnesota Fourth Division Feb. 9, 1966)
M/B: ICC v. St. Paul Transportation Co., 39 F.R.D. 309 (D. Minn. 1966).
LR: ICC v. St. Paul Transp. Co., 39 F.R.D. 309 (D. Minn. 1966).

45 156 269 348 432 563   40 F.R.D. 8
Mrs. Melba J. Craven, Administratrix of Donald Price Craven, Deceased, Plaintiff, v. Associated Transport, Inc., Green Construction of Indiana, Inc., William R. Lewis and Clarence Earl Norris, Defendants (D. South Carolina, Anderson Division April 5, 1966)
M/B: Craven v. Associated Transport, 40 F.R.D. 8 (D.S.C. 1966).
LR: Craven v. Associated Transp., 40 F.R.D. 8 (D.S.C. 1966).

46 157 270 349 433 564   41 F.R.D. 279
Oscar Gruss & Son, Plaintiff, v. Lumbermens Mutual Casualty Company, Defendant and Third-Party Plaintiff, v. Isidor Buchmann, Third-Party Defendant   (S.D. New York 1966)
M/B: Oscar Gruss & Son v. Lumbermens Mutual Casualty Co., 41 F.R.D. 279 (S.D.N.Y. 1966).
LR: Oscar Gruss & Son v. Lumbermens Mut. Casualty Co., 41 F.R.D. 279 (S.D.N.Y. 1966).

47 158 271 350 434 565   42 F.R.D. 398
United Insurance Company of America v. V. W. Rudy, Inc., Bertram W. Rudy (a/k/a B. W. Rudy), Chestnut Avenue Apartments, Inc., and Harry L. Haeberle (E. D. Pennsylvania July 17, 1967)
M/B: United Insurance Co. of America v. V.W. Rudy, Inc., 42 F.R.D. 398 (E.D. Pa. 1967).

EXERCISE 9. FEDERAL RULES DECISIONS   (CONTINUED)

LR: United Ins. Co. of Am. v. V.W. Rudy, Inc., 42 F.R.D. 398 (E.D. Pa. 1967).

48 159 272 351 435 566   88 F.R.D. 44
Outdoor Sports Industries, Inc., Plaintiff, v. Telvest, Inc., Telco Marketing Services, Inc., Libco Corporation, and Clyde Engle, Defendants (N. D. Illinois, E. D. Sept. 4, 1980)
M/B: Outdoor Sports Industries v. Telvest, Inc., 88 F.R.D. 44 (N.D. Ill. 1980).
LR: Outdoor Sports Indus. v. Telvest, Inc., 88 F.R.D. 44 (N.D. Ill. 1980).

49 160 273 352 436 567   43 F.R.D. 374
Johnnie Banks v. Hanover Steamship Corporation, Defendant and Third-Party Defendant; Alexander J. Korzun v. N. Y. Stoomv. Maats Nederland, Defendant and Third-Party Plaintiff, v. Jarka Corporaiton of Baltimore, Third-Party Defedant; Oscar H. Sebree, James Wallace and William Walker v. Grace Lines, Inc., Defendant and Third-Party Plaintiff, v. The Cottman Company, Third-Party Defendant (D. Maryland Dec. 8, 1967)
M/B: Banks v. Hanover Steamship Corp., 43 F.R.D. 374 (D. Md. 1967).
LR: Banks v. Hanover S.S. Corp., 43 F.R.D. 374 (D. Md. 1967).

50 161 274 353 437 568   44 F.R.D. 453
Fullerform Continuous Pipe Corporation, an Arizona corporation; R. Fuller and C. V. Cherry, Jr., Co-Partners, doing business under the style and firm name of R. Fuller Co.; Pascal & Ludwig, Inc., a California corporation; Fullerform, Inc., an Arixona corporation, Plaintiffs, v. American Pipe and Construction Co.; American Concerte Pipe Co.; United Concrete Pipe Corporation, Martin-Marietta Corporation, Hydro Conduit Corporation; Six Points Lumber & Supply Company, a corporation, doing business under the sytle and firm name of O'Malley-Gannaway Concrete Pipe Co.; Arizona Concrete Pipe Co.; Arizona Concrete Pipe Association, Defendants (D. Arizona April 25, 1968)
M/B: Fullerform Continuous Pipe Corp. v. American Pipe & Construction Co., 44 F.R.D. 453 (D. Ariz. 1968).
LR: Fullerform Continuous Pipe Corp. v. American Pipe & Constr. Co., 44 F.R.D. 453 (D. Ariz. 1968).

51 162 275 354 438 569   45 F.R.D. 375
Struthers Scientific and International Corporation, Plaintiff, v. General Foods Corporation, Defendant (S.D. Texas October 1, 1968)
M/B: Struthers Scientific & International Corp. v. General Foods Corp., 45 F.R.D. 375 (S.D. Tex. 1968).
LR: Struthers Scientific & Int'l Corp. v. General Foods Corp., 45 F.R.D. 375 (S.D. Tex. 1968).

52 163 276 355 439 570   46 F.R.D. 465
American Steel Works, a Missouri corporation, Plaintiff, v. Hurley Construction Company, a Minnesota corporation and Cadillac Plastic Company, an Illinois corporation, Defendants (D. Minnesota February 14, 1969)
M/B: American Steel Works v. Hurley Construction Co., 46 F.R.D. 465 (D. Minn. 1969).
LR: American Steel Works v. Hurley Constr. Co., 46 F.R.D. 465 (D. Minn. 1969).

53 164 277 356 440 571   47 F.R.D. 278
Charles LaRocca, Plaintiff, v. State Farm Mutual Automobile Insurance Company, Defendant (W.D. Pennsylvania March 11, 1969)
M/B: LaRocca v. State Farm Mutual Automobile Insurance Co., 47 F.R.D. 278 (W.D. Pa. 1969).
LR: LaRocca v. State Farm Mut. Auto. Ins. Co., 47 F.R.D. 278 (W.D. Pa. 1969).

54 165 278 357 441 572   48 F.R.D. 404
Sylvia L. Brinson Roberson v. Great American Insurance Companies of New York (N.D. Georgia March 31, 1969)
M/B: Roberson v. Great American Insurance Cos., 48 F.R.D. 404 (N.D. Ga. 1969).
LR: Roberson v. Great Am. Ins. Cos., 48 F.R.D. 404 (N.D. Ga. 1969).

55 166 279 358 442 573   83 F.R.D. 556

EXERCISE 9. FEDERAL RULES DECISIONS   (CONTINUED)

Rockwell International Corporation, acting by and through its Collins Radio Group v. KND Corporation (N.D. Texas (July 27, 1979)
M/B: Rockwell International Corp. v. KND Corp., 83 F.R.D. 556 (N.D. Tex. 1979).
LR: Rockwell Int'l Corp. v. KND Corp., 83 F.R.D. 556 (N.D. Tex. 1979).

56 167 280 359 443 574   49 F.R.D. 271
Agnes Phyllis Hess, Administratrix of the Estate of Richard W. Hess, Deceased, Plaintiff, v. Pittsburgh Steel Foundry & Machine Co., A Division of Textron, Inc., the Aetna Casualty & Surety Company, the Osborn Manufacturing Company and Master Chemcial Corporation, Defendants (W.D. Pennsylvania April 9, 1970)
M/B: Hess v. Pittsburgh Steel Foundry & Machine Co., 49 F.R.D. 271 (W.D. Pa. 1970).
LR: Hess v. Pittsburgh Steel Foundry & Mach. Co., 49 F.R.D. 271 (W.D. Pa. 1970).

57 168 281 360 444 575   50 F.R.D. 179
John R. Corbett v. Free Press Association, Inc. (D. Vermont June 17, 1970)
M/B: Corbett v. Free Press Association, 50 F.R.D. 179 (D. Vt. 1970).
LR: Corbett v. Free Press Ass'n, 50 F.R.D. 179 (D. Vt. 1970).

58 169 282 361 445 576   51 F.R.D. 512
Ashland Oil & Refining Co., Plaintiff, v. Hooker Chemical Corp., Defendant (S.D. Ohio October 14, 1970)
M/B: Ashland Oil & Refining Co. v. Hooker Chemical Corp., 51 F.R.D. 512 (S.D. Ohio 1970).
LR: Ashland Oil & Ref. Co. v. Hooker Chem. Corp., 51 F.R.D. 512 (S.D. Ohio 1970).

59 170 283 362 446 577   52 F.R.D. 139
Alex L. Kallay et al., Plaintiffs, v. Community National Life Insurance Company et al., Defendants (N.D. Oklahoma March 26, 1971)
M/B: Kallay v. Community National Life Insurance Co., 52 F.R.D. 139 (N.D. Okla. 1971).
LR: Kallay v. Community Nat'l Life Ins. Co., 52 F.R.D. 139 (N.D. Okla. 1971).

60 171 284 363 447 578   53 F.R.D. 531
Dale Electronics, Inc. v. R.C.L. Electronics, Inc., on behalf of itself and as representative of others similarly situated. (D. New Hampshire December 7, 1971)
M/B: Dale Electronics, Inc. v. R.C.L. Electronics, Inc., 53 F.R.D. 531 (D.N.H. 1971).
LR: Dale Elecs., Inc. v. R.C.L. Elecs., Inc., 53 F.R.D. 531 (D.N.H. 1971).

61 172 285 364 448 579   84 F.R.D. 46
Eva Lou Gray v. John Jovino Company, Inc. (E.D. Tennessee June 1, 1979)
M/B: Gray v. John Jovino Co., 84 F.R.D. 46 (E.D. Tenn. 1979).

62 173 286 365 449 580   85 F.R.D. 597
Steven J Glusband, As Receiver for Morgan, Harris & Scott, Ltd., Harrison Prescott, Inc., and Eur American Currency Corpoaration, Plaintiffs, v. Euro-Swiss International Corporation, Trimble, Coven & Goldman, P.C., Bernard J Coven, Henry W. Trimble, Jr., and Morris Goldman, Defendants (S.D. New York November 30, 1979)
M/B: Glusband v. Euro-Swiss International Corp., 85 F.R.D. 597 (S.D.N.Y. 1979).
LR: Glusband v. Euro-Swiss Int'l Corp., 85 F.R.D. 597 (S.D.N.Y. 1979).

63 174 287 366 450 581   54 F.R.D. 524
Spartanics, Ltd., Plaintiff, v. Dynetics Engineering Corporation, Defendant (N.D. Illinois January 14, 1972)
M/B: Spartanics, Ltd. v. Dynetics Engineering Corp., 54 F.R.D. 524 (N.D. Ill. 1972).
LR: Spartanics, Ltd. v. Dynetics Eng'g Corp., 54 F.R.D. 524 (N.D. Ill. 1972).

64 175 288 367 451 582   55 F.R.D. 475

EXERCISE 9. FEDERAL RULES DECISIONS   (CONTINUED)

Marvyn Gould, Executor of the Estate of J. Donald Rogasner, and J. David
Pincus, on behalf of themselves and all others similarly situated, Plaintiffs,
Mary S. McCord and Charles T. McCord, Jr., Intervening Plaintiffs, v. American
Hawaiian Steamship Company et al., Defendants (D. Delaware June 20, 1972)
M/B: Gould v. American Hawaiian Steamship Co., 55 F.R.D. 475 (D. Del. 1972).
LR: Gould v. American Hawaiian S.S. Co., 55 F.R.D. 475 (D. Del. 1972).

65 176 289 368 452 583   89 F.R.D. 346
Torin Corporation, Plaintiff, v. Philips Industries, Inc. (S.D. Ohio, W.D.
January 20, 1981)
M/B: Torin Corp. v. Philips Industries, 89 F.R.D. 346 (S.D. Ohio 1981).
LR: Torin Corp. v. Philips Indus., 89 F.R.D. 346 (S.D. Ohio 1981).

66 177 290 369 453 584   56 F.R.D. 21
James Davis, Administrator of the Estate of Dorothea Davis, Deceased v. Lower
Bucks Hospital (E.D. Pennsylvania August 14, 1972)
M/B: Davis v. Lower Bucks Hospital, 56 F.R.D. 21 (E.D. Pa. 1972).
LR: Davis v. Lower Bucks Hosp., 56 F.R.D. 21 (E.D. Pa. 1972).

67 178 291 370 454 585   57 F.R.D. 503
Willie Blacks v. Mosley Machinery Company, Inc. (E.D. Pennsylvania December
13, 1972)
M/B: Blacks v. Mosley Machinery Co., 57 F.R.D. 503 (E.D. Pa. 1972).
LR: Blacks v. Mosley Mach. Co., 57 F.R.D. 503 (E.D. Pa. 1972).

68 179 292 371 455 586   90 F.R.D. 589
Commonwealth of Pennsylvania and Raymond Williams, et al. v. Local Union 542,
International Union of Operating Engineers, et al (E.D. Pennsylvania June 8,
1981)
M/B: Pennsylvania v. Local Union 542, International Union of Operating
Engineers, 190 F.R.D. 589 (E.D. Pa. 1981) OR Pennsylvania v. Local Union 542,
IUOE, 190 F.R.D. 589 (E.D. Pa. 1981).
LR: Pennsylvania v. Local Union 542, Int'l Union of Operating Eng'rs, 190
F.R.D. 589 (E.D. Pa. 1981) OR Pennsylvania v. Local Union 542, IUOE, 190
F.R.D. 589 (E.D. Pa. 1981).

69 180 293 372 456 587   58 F.R.D. 570
Leon Weisfeld, on behalf of himself and all other common and Class A
stockholders of Spartans Industries, Inc., Plaintiff, v. Spartans Industries,
Inc., et al., Defendants (S.D. New York December 29, 1972)
M/B: Weisfeld v. Spartans Industries, 58 F.R.D. 570 (S.D.N.Y. 1972).
LR: Weisfeld v. Spartans Indus., 58 F.R.D. 570 (S.D.N.Y. 1972).

70 181 294 373 457 588   91 F.R.D. 267
Swann Oil, Inc., Plaintiff, v. M/S Vassilis, her engines, tackle, apparel,
etc., et al., Defendants (E.D. North Carolina August 28, 1981)
M/B: Swann Oil, Inc. v. M/S Vassilis, 91 F.R.D. 267 (E.D.N.C. 1981).

71 182 295 374 458 589   59 F.R.D. 577
Martin M. Sigel, Individually and on behalf of all others similarly situated,
Plaintiffs, v. General Development Corporation, Defendants (M.D. Florida May
11, 1973)
M/B: Sigel v. General Development Corp., 59 F.R.D. 577 (M.D. Fla. 1973).
LR: Sigel v. General Dev. Corp., 59 F.R.D. 577 (M.D. Fla. 1973).

72 183 296 375 459 590   92 F.R.D. 375
John Dutka, Kevin Lafferty, and Douglas Knight, Plaintiffs, v. Southern
Railway Company, Defendant (N.D. Georgia August 19, 1981)
M/B: Dutka v. Southern Railway, 92 F.R.D. 375 (N.D. Ga. 1981).
LR: Dutka v. Southern Ry., 92 F.R.D. 375 (N.D. Ga. 1981).

73 184 297 376 460 591   60 F.R.D. 671
James Griffin v. Jackson Parish School Board et al. (W.D. Louisiana September
19, 1973)
M/B: Griffin v. Jackson Parish School Board, 60 F.R.D. 671 (W.D. La. 1973).
LR: Griffin v. Jackson Parish School Bd., 60 F.R.D. 671 (W.D. La. 1973).

EXERCISE 9.   FEDERAL RULES DECISIONS   (CONTINUED)

74 185 298 377 461 592   94 F.R.D. 672
Ronald L. Monzo, Plaintiff, v. American Airlines, Inc., Defendant (S.D. New York July 2, 1982)
M/B: Monzo v. American Airlines, 94 F.R.D. 672 (S.D.N.Y. 1982).

75 186 299 378 462 593   86 F.R.D. 145
Michael Martino, McDonald's Drive-In of Appelton, Wisconsin, a Wisconsin Corporation, and McDonald's Drive-In of Manitowac, Wisconsin, a Wisconsin Corporation, Individually and on Behalf of All Other Persons of Corporations Similarly Situated, Plaintiffs, v. McDonald's System, Inc., an Illinois Corporation, and Franchise Realty Interstate Corporation, an Illinois Corporation, Defendants (N.D. Illinois March 5, 1980)
M/B: Martino v. McDonald's System, 86 F.R.D. 145 (N.D. Ill. 1980).
LR: Martino v. McDonald's Sys., 86 F.R.D. 145 (N.D. Ill. 1980).

76 187 300 379 463 594   61 F.R.D. 427
Richard H. Ralston et al., Plaintiffs, v. Volkswagenwerk, A.G., et al., Defendants (W.D. Missouri August 23, 1973)
M/B: Ralston v. Volkswagenwerk, A.G., 61 F.R.D. 427 (W.D. Mo. 1973).

77 188 201 380 464 595   62 F.R.D. 480
Johnnie R. Vaughn, Sr. v. Hartford Accident and Indemnity Company (E.D. Texas March 29, 1974)
M/B: Vaughn v. Hartford Accident & Indemnity Co., 62 F.R.D. 480 (E.D. Tex. 1974).
LR: Vaughn v. Hartford Accident & Indem. Co., 62 F.R.D. 480 (E.D. Tex. 1974).

78 189 202 381 465 596   98 F.R.D. 569
William B. May Co., Inc., Plaintiff, v. David Hyatt and Lillian L. Hyatt, Defendants (S.D. New York July 15, 1983)
M/B: William B. May Co. v. Hyatt, 98 F.R.D. 569 (S.D.N.Y. 1983).

79 190 203 382 466 597   100 F.R.D. 255
AM International, Inc., Plaintiff, v. Eastman Kodak Company, (N.D. Illinois October 21, 1981)
M/B: AM International, Inc. v. Eastman Kodak Co., 100 F.R.D. 255 (N.D. Ill. 1981).
LR: AM Int'l, Inc. v. Eastman Kodak Co., 100 F.R.D. 255 (N.D. Ill. 1981).

80 191 204 383 467 598   63 F.R.D. 662
Everco Industries, Inc., an Illinois corporation, Plaintiff, v. O.E.M. Products Company, Defendant (N.D. Illinois June 3, 1974)
M/B: Everco Industries v. O.E.M. Products Co., 63 F.R.D. 662 (N.D. Ill. 1974).
LR: Everco Indus. v. O.E.M. Prods. Co., 63 F.R.D. 662 (N.D. Ill. 1974).

81 192 205 384 468 599   99 F.R.D. 279
Art Wagner, et al. v. Central Louisiana Electric Company, Inc. and Washington-St. Tammany Electric Cooperative, Inc. (E.D. Louisiana August 26, 1983)
M/B: Wagner v. Central Louisiana Electric Co., 99 F.R.D. 279 (E.D. La. 1983).
LR: Wagner v. Central La. Elec. Co., 99 F.R.D. 279 (E.D. La. 1983).

82 193 206 385 469 600   101 F.R.D. 405
Roy James Saunders, et al., Plaintiffs, v. Jim Emes Petroleum Company, Inc., a West Virginia corporation, Defendant (W.D. Pennsylvania October 24, 1983)
M/B: Saunders v. Jim Emes Petroleum Co., 101 F.R.D. 405 (W.D. Pa. 1983).

83 194 207 386 470 501   64 F.R.D. 690
Daiflon, Inc., Plaintiff, v. Allied Chemical Corporation et al., Defendants (W.D. Oklahoma December 10, 1974)
M/B: Daiflon, Inc. v. Allied Chemical Corp., 64 F.R.D. 690 (W.D. Okla. 1974).
LR: Daiflon, Inc. v. Allied Chem. Corp., 64 F.R.D. 690 (W.D. Okla. 1974).

84 195 208 387 471 502   65 F.R.D. 375
Terrebonne Land Development Corporation, Plaintiff, v. The Superior Oil Company, Defendant (E.D. Louisiana November 8, 1974)

EXERCISE 9. FEDERAL RULES DECISIONS   (CONTINUED)

M/B: Terrebonne Land Development Corp. v. Superior Oil Co., 65 F.R.D. 375 (E.D. La. 1974).
LR: Terrebonne Land Dev. Corp. v. Superior Oil Co., 65 F.R.D. 375 (E.D. La. 1974).

85 196 209 388 472 503   75 F.R.D. 511
Charles W. Stallings, Phillip R. Robertson and Alfonso C. Tolbert, Plaintiffs, v. Container Corporation of America, Defendant (D. Delaware July 15, 1977)
M/B: Stallings v. Container Corp. of America, 75 F.R.D. 511 (D. Del. 1977).
LR: Stallings v. Container Corp. of Am., 75 F.R.D. 511 (D. Del. 1977).

86 197 210 389 473 504   76 F.R.D. 192
William H. Pendleton and Franne Nelson et al. v. Trans Union Systems Corp. t/a Philadelphia Credit Bureau, and t/a Credit Information Corporation of Philadelphia and the Federal Trade Commission (E.D. Pennsylvania September 7, 1977)
M/B: Pendleton v. Trans Union Systems Corp., 76 F.R.D. 192 (E.D. Pa. 1977).
LR: Pendleton v. Trans Union Sys. Corp., 76 F.R.D. 192 (E.D. Pa. 1977).

87 198 211 390 474 505   66 F.R.D. 105
Michel Chevalier and Jean Chevalier, his wife, Individually and on behalf of all members of a class of mortgagors similarly situated, et al. v. Baird Savings Association et al. (E.D. Pennsylvania March 4, 1975)
M/B: Chevalier v. Baird Savings Association, 66 F.R.D. 105 (E.D. Pa. 1975).
LR: Chevalier v. Baird Sav. Ass'n, 66 F.R.D. 105 (E.D. Pa. 1975).

88 199 212 391 475 506   97 F.R.D. 427
In re "Agent Orange" Product Liability Litigation (E.D. New York March 10, 1983)
M/B: In re "Agent Orange" Product Liability Litigation, 97 F.R.D. 427 (E.D.N.Y. 1983).
LR: In re "Agent Orange" Prod. Liab. Litig., 97 F.R.D. 427 (E.D.N.Y. 1983).

89 200 213 392 476 507   78 F.R.D. 190
Heinold Commodities, Inc., a corporation, Plaintiff, v. New York Mercantile Exchange, a corporation, et al. (S.D. New York February 27, 1978)
M/B: Heinold Commodities, Inc. v. New York Mercantile Exchange, 78 F.R.D. 190 (S.D.N.Y. 1978).
LR: Heinold Commodities, Inc. v. New York Mercantile Exch., 78 F.R.D. 190 (S.D.N.Y. 1978).

90 101 214 393 477 508   79 F.R.D. 671
Johnny Champagne, Plaintiff, v. Hygrade Food Products, Inc., et al. (E.D. Washington August 28, 1978)
M/B: Champagne v. Hygrade Food Products, Inc., 79 F.R.D. 671 (E.D. Wash. 1978).
LR: Champagne v. Hygrade Food Prods., Inc., 79 F.R.D. 671 (E.D. Wash. 1978).

91 102 215 394 478 509   69 F.R.D. 69
Robert Seiffer et al., Plaintiffs, v. Topsy's International, Inc., et al., Defendants (D. Kansas November 6, 1975)
M/B: Seiffer v. Topsy's International, Inc., 69 F.R.D. 69 (D. Kan. 1975).
LR: Seiffer v. Topsy's Int'l, Inc., 69 F.R.D. 69 (D. Kan. 1975).

92 103 216 395 479 510   104 F.R.D. 42
Abbott Laboratories and Abbott Laboratories International Co., Plaintiffs, v. Granite State Insurance Co., Defendant (N.D. Illinois E.D. November 5, 1984)
M/B: Abbott Laboratories v. Granite State Insurance Co., 104 F.R.D. 42 (N.D. Ill. 1984).
LR: Abbott Laboratories v. Granite State Ins. Co., 104 F.R.D. 42 (N.D. Ill. 1984).

93 104 217 396 480 511   103 F.R.D. 421
Carol J. Cody, Plaintiff, v. Marriott Corporation, Wolfrum Krupa, and Mark S. McCaw, Defendants (D. Massachusetts November 14, 1984)
M/B: Cody v. Marriott Corp., 103 F.R.D. 421 (D. Mass. 1984).

EXERCISE 9. FEDERAL RULES DECISIONS   (CONTINUED)

94 105 218 397 481 512   68 F.R.D. 583
Frances P. Daniels, mother, Plaintiff, v. Hadley Memorial Hospital et al., Defendants (District Court, District of Columbia September 12, 1975)
M/B: Daniels v. Hadley Memorial Hospital, 68 F.R.D. 583 (D.D.C. 1975).
LR: Daniels v. Hadley Memorial Hosp., 68 F.R.D. 583 (D.D.C. 1975).

95 106 219 398 482 513   96 F.R.D. 227
K. R. Jones v. Employers Insurance of Wausau (N.D. Georgia December 27, 1982)
M/B: Jones v. Employers Insurance, 96 F.R.D. 227 (N.D. Ga. 1982).
LR: Jones v. Employers Ins., 96 F.R.D. 227 (N.D. Ga. 1982).

96 107 220 399 483 514   72 F.R.D. 564
Henry J. Holt and Myrtis Holt, Plaintiffs, v. Ferdon Equipment Co. and Eaton Corporation, Defendants (D. New Jersey November 12, 1976)
M/B: Holt v. Ferdon Equipment Co., 72 F.R.D. 564 (D.N.J. 1976).
LR: Holt v. Ferdon Equip. Co., 72 F.R.D. 564 (D.N.J. 1976).

97 108 221 400 484 515   95 F.R.D. 391
William J. Gabriel, Sr., individually and as Administrator of the Estate of Carole An Gabriel, and Dorothea P. Gabriel, Plaintiffs, v. Kent General Hospital Incorporated, a corporation of the State of Delaware, Thomas Maxwell, M.D., William C. Kahler, William B. Tetreault, Diamond State Truck Brokers, Inc., a corporation of the State of Delaware, The City of Dover, a municipal corporation of the State of Delaware, Nationwide Mutual Insurance Company, a corporation of Ohio, and Diamond State Trucking Co., Inc., a corporation of the State of Delaware, Defendants (D. Delaware September 13, 1982)
M/B: Gabriel v. Kent General Hospital, 95 F.R.D. 391 (D. Del. 1982).
LR: Gabriel v. Kent Gen. Hosp., 95 F.R.D. 391 (D. Del. 1982).

98 109 222 301 485 516   71 F.R.D. 652
Linda Cobb, Plaintiff, v. Avon Products, Incorporated, Defendant (W.D. Pennsylvania July 26, 1976)
M/B: Cobb v. Avon Products, Inc., 71 F.R.D. 652 (W.D. Pa. 1976).
LR: Cobb v. Avon Prods., Inc., 71 F.R.D. 652 (W.D. Pa. 1976).

99 110 223 302 486 517   93 F.R.D. 512
James Shackelford v. Vermeer Manufacturing Company, et al. (W.D. Texas February 5, 1982)
M/B: Shackelford v. Vermeer Manufacturing Co., 93 F.R.D. 512 (W.D. Tex. 1982).
LR: Shackelford v. Vermeer Mfg. Co., 93 F.R.D. 512 (W.D. Tex. 1982).

100 111 224 303 487 518   77 F.R.D. 430
Sun First National Bank of Orlando, Plaintiff, v. Eldon Miller, et al. (S.D. New York January 9, 1978)
M/B: Sun First National Bank v. Miller, 77 F.R.D. 430 (S.D.N.Y. 1978).
LR: Sun First Nat'l Bank v. Miller, 77 F.R.D. 430 (S.D.N.Y. 1978).

LIBRARY EXERCISE 10. FEDERAL CASES.

INSTRUCTOR'S NOTE: This exercise requires the students to find and cite an early federal decision published in Federal Cases. The following three Quick-Reference Abbreviations are particularly relevant to this exercise:

FEDERAL COURT CITATION 15. DO NOT GIVE A PARALLEL CITATION TO THE ORIGINAL REPORT IF AN OPINION HAS BEEN REPRINTED IN WEST'S FEDERAL CASES. [FED 15]
FEDERAL COURT CITATION 16. ALWAYS INDICATE WEST'S FEDERAL CASE NUMBER PARENTHETICALLLY IN A CIATION TO FEDERAL CASES. [FED 16]
FEDERAL COURT CITATION 17. WHEN CITING THE OLD CIRCUIT COURTS IN FEDERAL CASES, INDICATE THE COURT (C.C.), THE DISTRICT, AND THE STATE PARENTHETICALLY. CIRCUIT COURT DECISIONS FROM THE DISTRICT OF COLUMBIA SHOULD BE CITED "D.C. CIR.," HOWEVER, NOT "C.C.D.C." [FED 17]

1 161 300 310 420 530   Abbe   6
Abbe v. Rood (Circuit Court, D. Michigan June, 1854)
M/B: Abbe v. Rood, 1 F. Cas. 7 (C.C.D. Mich. 1854) (No. 6).

2 162 201 311 421 531   Acker   26
Acker v. The Rainbow (District Court, S. D. New York Oct. 11, 1851)
M/B: Acker v. The Rainbow, 1 F. Cas. 45 (S.D.N.Y. 1851) (No. 26).

3 163 202 312 422 532   Ada   38
The Ada (District Court, D. Maine Sept. 12, 1849)
M/B: The Ada, 1 F. Cas. 72 (D. Me. 1849) (No. 38).

4 164 203 313 423 533   Babbitt   695
Babbitt v. Walbrun et al. (Circuit Court, W.D. Missouri April Term 1871)
M/B: Babbitt v. Walbrun, 2 F. Cas. 285 (C.C.W.D. Mo. 1871) (No. 695).

5 165 204 314 424 534   Backus   713
Backus v. The Marengo (Circuit Court, D. Michigan June, 1855)
M/B: Backus v. The Marengo, 2 F. Cas. 324 (C.C.D. Mich. 1855) (No. 713).

6 166 205 315 425 535   Bates   1102
Bates et al. v. The Natchez (E.D. Louisiana Nov. Term, 1854)
M/B: Bates v. The Natchez, 2 F. Cas. 1023 (E.D. La. 1854).

7 167 206 316 426 536   Bishop   1439
In re Bishop (Circuit Court, District of Columbia March 31, 1857)
M/B: In re Bishop, 3 F. Cas. 452 (D.C. Cir. 1857) (No. 1439).
LR: In re Bishop, 3 F. Cas. 452 (D.C. Cir. 1857) (No. 1439).

8 168 207 317 427 537   B.J. Willard   1454
The B. J. Willard (District Court, D. Pennsylvania May 7, 1879)
M/B: The B.J. Willard, 3 F. Cas. 492 (D. Pa. 1879) (No. 1454).

9 169 208 318 428 538   Berry   1358a
Berry v. The Montezuma (District Court, S.D. New York March 6, 1856)
M/B: Berry v. The Montezuma, 3 F. Cas. 290 (S.D.N.Y. 1856) (No. 1358a).

10 170 209 319 429 539   Brown   2026
Brown v. Piatt (Circuit Court, District of Columbia October Term, 1821)
M/B: Brown v. Piatt, 4 F. Cas. 425 (D.C. Cir. 1821) (No. 2026).

11 171 210 320 430 540   Brown   2033
Brown v. Whittemore (Circuit Court, D. Massachusetts May Term, 1872)
M/B: Brown v. Whittemore, 4 F. Cas. 437 (C.C.D. Mass. 1872) (No. 2033).

12 172 211 321 431 541   Burke   2157
In re Burke et al. (S.D. New York Nov. 21, 1876)
M/B: In re Burke, 4 F. Cas. 731 (S.D.N.Y. 1876) (No. 2157).
LR: In re Burke, 4 F. Cas. 731 (S.D.N.Y. 1876) (No. 2157).
Note: Case No. 2158 (D. Minn.), which has the same name as 2157 above; the Minnesota case (page 732) should not be cited.

13 173 212 322 432 542   Clover   2908

EXERCISE 10.   FEDERAL CASES   (CONTINUED)

The Clover (D. Massachusetts July, 1869)
M/B: The Clover, 5 F. Cas. 1095 (D. Mass. 1869) (No. 2908).

14 174 213 323 433 543 Cayuga 2537
The Cayuga (Circuit Court, E.D. New York June 18, 1870)
M/B: The Cayuga, 5 F. Cas. 329 (C.C.E.D.N.Y. 1870) (No. 2537).

15 175 214 324 434 544 Chacon 2568
Chacon v. Eighty-Nine Bales of Cochineal (Circuit Court, D. Virginia May Term, 1821)
M/B: Chacon v. Eighty-Nine Bales of Cochineal, 5 F. Cas. 390 (C.C.D. Va. 1821) (No. 2568).

16 176 215 325 435 545 Cooke 3170
In re Cooke et al. (District Court, E.D. Pennsylvania March 23, 1875)
M/B: In re Cooke, 6 F. Cas. 427 (E.D. Pa. 1875) (No. 3170).
LR: In re Cooke, 6 F. Cas. 427 (E.D. Pa. 1875) (No. 3170).

17 177 216 326 436 546 Cooke 3181
Cooke et al. v. Woodrow (Circuit Court, District of Columbia July Term, 1807)
M/B: Cooke v. Woodrow, 6 F. Cas. 449 (D.C. Cir. 1807) (No. 3170).

18 178 217 327 437 547 Corcoran 3227
Corcoran v. Dougherty (Circuit Court, District of Columbia May Term, 1832)
M/B: Corcoran v. Dougherty, 6 F. Cas. 543 (D.C. Cir. 1832) (No. 3227).

19 179 218 328 438 548 Delhi 3770
The Delhi (District Court, S.D. New York November Term, 1870)
M/B: The Delhi, 7 F. Cas. 413 (S.D.N.Y. 1870) (No. 3770).

20 180 219 329 439 549 Delight 3772
The Delight (District Court, S.D. New York April 1862)
M/B: The Delight, 7 F. Cas. 415 (S.D.N.Y. 1862) (No. 3772).

21 181 220 330 440 550 Delta 3778
The Delta (Circuit Court, S.D. New York July 17, 1863)
M/B: The Delta, 7 F. Cas. 449 (C.C.S.D.N.Y. 1863) (No. 3778).

22 182 221 331 441 551 Evans 4571
Evans v. Robinson (Circuit Court, D. Maryland 1813)
M/B: Evans v. Robinson, 8 F. Cas. 886 (C.C.D. Md. 1813) (No. 4571).

23 183 222 332 442 552 Fagan 4605
Fagan et al. v. The Pluto (Circuit Court, S.D. New York April 24, 1857)
M/B: Fagan v. The Pluto, 8 F. Cas. 951 (C.C.S.D.N.Y. 1857) (No. 4605).

24 184 223 333 443 553 Fairchild 4610
Fairchild v. Camac (Circuit Court, E.D. Pennsylvania October Term, 1819)
M/B: Fairchild v. Camac, 8 F. Cas. 953 (C.C.E.D Pa. 1819) (No.4610).

25 185 224 334 444 554 Flower 4891
Flower v. Parker et al. (Circuit Court, D. Massachusetts, October Term, 1823)
M/B: Flower v. Parker, 9 F. Cas. 323 (C.C.D. Mass. 1823) (No. 4891).

26 186 225 335 445 555 Focke 4894
Focke et al. v. Lawrence (Circuit Court, S.D. New York November 1852)
M/B: Focke v. Lawrence, 9 F. Cas. 329 (C.C.S.D.N.Y. 1852) (No. 4894).

27 187 226 336 446 556 Fowler   4997
In re Fowler et al. (S.D. New York May 1876)
M/B: In re Fowler, 9 F. Cas. 613 (S.D.N.Y. 1876) (No. 4997).
LR: In re Fowler, 9 F. Cas. 1018 (S.D.N.Y. 1876) (No. 4997).
Note: This case should not be confused with Case Nos. 4998 and 4999, which have the same name (pages 614 and 615, both D. Mass.)

28 188 227 337 447 557 Geib 5297
Geib v. Enterprise Co. (Circuit Court, D. Minnesota June 1870)

EXERCISE 10. FEDERAL CASES   (CONTINUED)

M/B: Geib v. Enter. Co., 10 F. Cas. 156 (C.C.D. Minn. 1870) (No. 5297).
LR: Geib v. Enterprise Co., 10 F. Cas. 156 (C.C.D. Minn. 1870) (No. 5297).

29 189 228 338 448 558 Gay   5281
Gay v. Lyons et al. (Circuit Court, E.D. Louisiana April Term, 1877)
M/B: Gay v. Lyons, 10 F. Cas. 112 (C.C.E.D. La. 1877) (No. 5281).

30 190 229 339 449 559 Georgetown   5342
Georgetown v. Baker (Circuit Court, District of Columbia April Term, 1822)
M/B: Georgetown v. Baker, 10 F. Cas. 231 (D.C. Cir. 1822) (No. 5342).

31 191 230 340 450 560 Hall   5919
Ex parte Hall (Circuit Court, D. Massachusetts 1842)
M/B: Ex parte Hall, 11 F. Cas. 196 (C.C.D. Mass. 1842) (No. 5919).
LR: Ex parte Hall, 11 F. Cas. 196 (C.C.D. Mass. 1842) (No. 5919).

32 192 231 341 451 561 Green   5761
Green v. Taylor et al. (Circuit Court, E.D. Virginia May 5, 1879)
M/B: Green v. Taylor, 10 F. Cas. 1120 (C.C.E.D. Va. 1879) (No. 5761).

33 193 232 342 452 562 Greene   5765
Greene v. Darling et al. (Circuit Court, D. Rhode Island November Term, 1828)
M/B: Greene v. Darling, 10 F. Cas. 1144 (C.C.D.R.I. 1828) (No. 5765).

34 194 233 343 453 563 Henry   6384
Henry v. Providence Tool Co. (Circuit Court, D. Rhode Island October 9, 1878)
M/B: Henry v. Providence Tool Co., 11 F. Cas. 1182 (C.C.D.R.I. 1878) (No. 6384).

35 195 234 344 454 564 Hill   6498
Hill v. Scott (Circuit Court, District of Columbia November Term, 1838)
M/B: Hill v. Scott, 12 F. Cas. 176 (D.C. Cir. 1838) (No. 6498).

36 196 235 345 455 565 Hinds   6516
In re Hinds et al. (District Court, N.D. New York October 29, 1869)
M/B: In re Hinds, 12 F. Cas. 202 (N.D.N.Y. 1869) (No. 6516).
LR: In re Hinds, 12 F. Cas. 202 (N.D.N.Y. 1869) (No. 6516).

37 197 236 346 456 566 Jewett   7307
In re Jewett et al. (Circuit Court, W.D. Wisconsin June 1877)
M/B: In re Jewett, 13 F. Cas. 591 (C.C.W.D. Wis. 1877) (No. 7307).
LR: In re Jewett, 13 F. Cas. 591 (C.C.W.D. Wis. 1877) (No. 7307).

38 198 237 347 457 567 Janeway   7208
In re Janeway (District Court, D. New Jersey October 18, 1870)
M/B: In re Janeway, 13 F. Cas. 348 (D.N.J. 1870) (No. 7208).
LR: In re Janeway, 13 F. Cas. 348 (D.N.J. 1870) (No. 7208).

39 199 238 348 458 568 Johnson   7416
Johnson v. Tompkins et al. (Circuit Court, E.D. Pennsylvania April Term, 1833)
M/B: Johnson v. Tompkins, 13 F. Cas. 840 (C.C.E.D. Pa. 1833) (No. 7416).

40 200 239 349 459 569 Kennedy   7708
Kennedy v. Washington (Circuit Court, District of Columbia May Term, 1829)
M/B: Kennedy v. Washington, 14 F. Cas. 330 (D.C. Cir. 1829) (No. 7708).

41 101 240 350 460 570 Keys   7747
Keys et al. v. The Ambassador (District Court, S.D. Ohio February Term, 1859)
M/B: Keys v. The Ambassador, 14 F. Cas. 436 (S.D. Ohio 1859) (No. 7747).

42 102 241 351 461 571 Kingston   7822
Kingston v. Kincaid et al. (Circuit Court, D. Pennsylvania October Term, 1806)
M/B: Kingston v. Kincaid, 14 F. Cas. 592 (C.C.D. Pa. 1806) (No. 7822).

43 103 242 352 462 572 Laski   8098
In re Laski (Circuit Court, W.D. Tennessee 1871)
M/B: In re Laski, 14 F. Cas. 1163 (C.C.W.D. Tenn. 1871) (No. 8098).

EXERCISE 10. FEDERAL CASES   (CONTINUED)

LR: In re Laski, 14 F. Cas. 1163 (C.C.W.D. Tenn. 1871) (No. 8098).

44 104 243 353 463 573   Kohlsaat   7918
In re Kohlsaat (S.D. New York 1878)
M/B: In re Kohlsaat, 14 F. Cas. 883 (S.D.N.Y. 1878) (No. 7918).
LR: In re Kohlsaat, 14 F. Cas. 883 (S.D.N.Y. 1878) (No. 7918).

45 105 244 354 464 574   Lowerre   8577
In re Lowerre (S.D. New York Sept. 14, 1867)
M/B: In re Lowerre., 15 F. Cas. 1030 (S.D.N.Y. 1867) (No. 8577).
LR: In re Lowerre, 15 F. Cas. 75 (S.D.N.Y. 1867) (No. 8577).

46 106 245 355 465 575   Maud Webster   9302
The Maude Webster. Chalmers et al. v. Howell (listed second) (S.D. New York Nov., 1876)
M/B: The Maude Webster, 16 F. Cas. 1157 (S.D.N.Y. 1876) (No. 9302).
Note: This case should not be confused with Case No. 9303, which has the same name (D. Me.).

47 107 246 356 466 576   Marsh   9120
Marsh v. United States (District Court, N.D. California December Term, 1857)
M/B: Marsh v. United States, 16 F. Cas. 820 (N.D. Cal. 1857) (No. 9120).

48 108 247 357 467 577   Marsh   9117
Marsh et al. v. The Minnie; Commins v. Same; Bee et al. v. Same; Smyzer v. Same (District Court, E.D. South Carolina 1858)
M/B: Marsh v. The Minnie, 16 F. Cas. 810 (E.D.S.C. 1858) (No. 9117).

49 109 248 358 468 578   Napoleon   10,011
The Napoleon (District Court, E.D. Wisconsin April 1877)
M/B: The Napoleon, 17 F. Cas. 1150 (E.D. Wis. 1877) (No. 10,011).

50 110 249 359 469 579   Narragansett   10,020
The Narragansett (District Court, S.D. New York September 1846)
M/B: The Narragansett, 17 F. Cas. 1169 (S.D.N.Y. 1846) (No. 10,020).

51 111 250 360 470 580   Neidlinger   10,086
Neidlinger et al. v. Insurance Co. of North America (District Court, E.D. New York January 1879)
M/B: Neidlinger v. Insurance Co. of North America, 17 F. Cas. 1293 (E.D.N.Y. 1879) (No. 10,086).
LR: Neidlinger v. Insurance Co. of N. Am., 17 F. Cas. 1293 (E.D.N.Y. 1879) (No. 10,086).

52 112 251 361 471 581   Parker   10,733
Parker v. Ferguson (Circuit Court, N.D. New York June Term, 1849)
M/B: Parker v. Ferguson, 18 F. Cas. 1126 (C.C.N.D.N.Y. 1849) (No. 10,733).

53 113 252 362 472 582   Osprey   10,606
The Osprey (District Court, D. Massachusetts Sept., 1854)
M/B: The Osprey, 18 F. Cas. 884 (D. Mass. 1854) (No. 10,606).
LR: The Osprey, 18 F. Cas. 884 (D. Mass. 1854) (No. 10,606).

54 114 253 363 473 583   Odorless Rubber Co.   10,438
Odorless Rubber Co. v. North Bennington Boot & Shoe Co. (Circuit Court, D. Connecticut June 16, 1876)
M/B: Odorless Rubber Co. v. North Bennington Boot & Shoe Co., 18 F. Cas. 592 (C.C.D. Conn. 1876) (No. 10,438).

55 115 254 364 474 584   Phelps   11,073
Phelps et al. v. The Camilla (Circuit Court, D. Maryland April Term, 1838)
M/B: Phelps v. The Camilla, 19 F. Cas. 441 (C.C.D. Md. 1838) (No. 11,073).

56 116 255 365 475 585   Philips   11,092
Philips et al. v. Crammond et al. (Circuit Court, D. Pennsylvania April Term, 1810)
M/B: Philips v. Crammond, 19 F. Cas. 497 (C.C.D. Pa. 1810) (No. 11,092).

EXERCISE 10.   FEDERAL CASES   (CONTINUED)

57 117 256 366 476 586   Plastic Slate-Roofing   11,209
Plastic Slate-Roofing Joint-Stock Co. et al. v. Moore (Circuit Court, D. Rhode
Island June 1872)
M/B: Plastic Slate-Roofing Joint-Stock Co. v. Moore, 19 F. Cas. 812
(C.C.D.R.I. 1872) (No. 11,209).

58 118 257 367 477 587   Pusey   11,477
In re Pusey (District Court, E.D. Michigan November 8, 1871)
M/B: In re Pusey, 20 F. Cas. 75 (E.D. Mich. 1871) (No. 11,477).
LR: In re Pusey, 20 F. Cas. 75 (E.D. Mich. 1871) (No. 11,477).

59 119 258 368 478 588   Richmond   11,796
The Richmond (N.D. Illinois April, 1854)
M/B: The Richmond, 20 F. Cas. 732 (N.D. Ill. 1854) (No. 11,796).
Note: This case should not be confused with several others with the same name
but different Federal Case Numbers (e.g., 11,797, 11,795a)

60 120 259 369 479 589   Ready Roofing   11,613
Ready Roofing Co. et al. v. Taylor et al. (Circuit Court, S.D. New York July
23, 1878)
M/B: Ready Roofing Co. v. Taylor, 20 F. Cas. 365 (C.C.S.D.N.Y. 1878) (No.
11,613).

61 121 260 370 480 590   Silver Moon   12,856
The Silver Moon (District Court, D. Maine February Term, 1870)
M/B: The Silver Moon, 22 F. Cas. 139 (D. Me. 1870) (12,856).

62 122 261 371 481 591   Stansfield   13,294
In re Stansfield (D. Nevada 1877)
M/B: In re Stansfield, 22 F. Cas. 1061 (D. Nev. 1877) (No. 13,294).
LR: In re Stansfield, 22 F. Cas. 1061 (D. Nev. 1877) (No. 13,294).

63 123 262 372 482 592   Smythe   13,134
Smythe v. Banks (Circuit Court, D. Pennsylvania April 1797)
M/B: Smythe v. Banks, 22 F. Cas. 710 (C.C.D. Pa. 1797) (No. 13,134).

64 124 263 373 483 593   Taylor   13,803
Taylor v. The Royal Saxon (Circuit Court, E.D. Pennsylvania July 11, 1849)
M/B: Taylor v. The Royal Saxon, 23 F. Cas. 797 (C.C.E.D. Pa. 1849) (13,803).

65 125 264 374 484 594   Swearinger   13,683
In re Swearinger et al. (District Court, D. Nevada December 13, 1877)
M/B: In re Swearinger, 23 F. Cas. 527 (D. Nev. 1877) (13,683).
LR: In re Swearinger, 23 F. Cas. 527 (D. Nev. 1877) (13,683).

66 126 265 375 485 595   Thorp   14,003
Thorp et al. v. The Defender   (S. D. Ohio   Oct. Term, 1860)
M/B: Thorp v. The Defender, 23 F. Cas. 1155 (S.D. Ohio 1860) (No. 14,003).

67 127 266 376 486 596   Tong Duck Chung   14,093
Tong Duck Chung v. Kelly (Circuit Court, D. Oregon April 1879)
M/B: Tong Duck Chung v. Kelly, 24 F. Cas. 46 (C.C.D. Or. 1879) (14,093).

68 128 267 377 487 597   Trigg   14,173
Trigg v. Conway et al. (Circuit Court, D. Arkansas April 1855)
M/B: Trigg v. Conway, 24 F. Cas. 196 (C.C.D. Ark. 1855) (No. 14,173).

69 129 268 378 488 598   Towanda   14,109
The Towanda (Circuit Court, E.D. Pennsylvania October 22, 1877)
M/B: The Towanda, 24 F. Cas. 74 (C.C.E.D. Pa. 1877) (14,109).

70 130 269 379 489 599   U.S. (v. Faw)   15,077
United States v. Faw (Circuit Court, District of Columbia November Term, 1807)
M/B: United States v. Faw, 25 F. Cas. 1052 (D.C. Cir. 1807) (No. 15,077).

71 131 270 380 490 600   U.S. (v. Fossat)   15,137

EXERCISE 10. FEDERAL CASES   (CONTINUED)

United States v. Fossat (Circuit Court, N.D. California June Term, 1857)
M/B: United States v. Fossat, 25 F. Cas. 1157 (C.C.N.D. Cal. 1857) (No. 15,137).

72 132 271 381 491 501   U.S. (v. Gadsby)   15,180
United States v. Gadsby (Circuit Court, District of Columbia January Term, 1802)
M/B: United States v. Gadsby, 25 F. Cas. 1236 (D.C. Cir. 1802) (No. 15,180).

73 133 272 382 492 502   U.S. (v. Keen)   15,511
United States v. Keen (Circuit Court, D. Massachusetts May Term, 1830)
M/B: United States v. Keen, 26 F. Cas. 693 (C.C.D. Mass. 1830) (No. 15,511).

74 134 273 383 493 503   U.S. (v. Hare)   15,304
United States v. Hare (Circuit Court, D. Maryland May 1818)
M/B: United States v. Hare, 26 F. Cas. 148 (C.C.D. Md. 1818) (15,304).

75 135 274 384 494 504   U.S. (v. Horn)   15,389
United States v. Horn (Circuit Court, S.D. New York November 10, 1862)
M/B: United States v. Horn, 26 F. Cas. 373 (C.C.S.D.N.Y. 1862) (No. 15,389).

76 136 275 385 495 505   U.S. (v. Queen)   16,109
United States v. Queen (Circuit Court, District of Columbia December Term, 1828)
M/B: United States v. Queen, 27 F. Cas. 673 (D.C. Cir. 1828) (No. 16,109).

77 137 276 386 496 506   U.S. (v. Reagan)   16,128
United States v. Reagan (District Court, D. Massachusetts 1872)
M/B: United States v. Reagan, 27 F. Cas. 717 (D. Mass. 1872) (16,128).

78 138 277 387 497 507   U.S. (v. Ringgold)   16,167
United States v. Ringgold (Circuit Court, District of Columbia November Term, 1837)
M/B: United States v. Ringgold, 27 F. Cas. 817 (D.C. Cir. 1837) (No. 16,167).

79 139 278 388 498 508   U.S. (v. Thompkins)   16,483
United States v. Thompkins (Circuit Court, District of Columbia June Term, 1812)
M/B: United States v. Thompkins, 28 F. Cas. 89 (D.C. Cir. 1812) (No. 16,483).

80 140 279 389 499 509   U.S. (v. Two Horses)   16,578
United States v. Two Horses (District of Court, E.D. New York May 1878)
M/B: United States v. Two Horses, 28 F. Cas. 294 (E.D.N.Y. 1878) (No. 16,578).

81 141 280 390 500 510   U.S. (v. Whiskey)   16,671
United States v. Whiskey (District Court, E.D. Pennsylvania March 15, 1870)
M/B: United States v. Whiskey, 28 F. Cas. 536 (E.D. Pa. 1870) (No. 16,671).

82 142 281 391 401 511   Warner   17,180
Warner v. Cronkhite (Circuit Court, E.D. Wisconsin September 1875)
M/B: Warner v. Cronkhite, 29 F. Cas. 243 (C.C.E.D. Wis. 1875) (No. 17,180).

83 143 282 392 402 512   Wall   17,093
Wall v. The Royal Saxon (E. D. Pennsylvania Feb. 4, 1848) (No. 17,093).
M/B: Wall v. The Royal Saxon, 29 F. Cas. 61 (E.D. Pa. 1848) (No. 17,093).

84 144 283 393 403 513   Watson   17,286
Watson et al. v. Insurance Co. of North America (Circuit Court, D. Pennsylvania April Term, 1811)
M/B: Watson v. Insurance Co. of North America, 29 F. Cas. 433 (C.C.D. Pa. 1811) (No. 17,286).
LR: Watson v. Insurance Co. of N. Am., 29 F. Cas. 433 (C.C.D. Pa. 1811) (No. 17,286).

85 145 284 394 404 514   Winans   17,861
Winans v. Eaton et al. (Circuit Court, N.D. New York September 1854)

EXERCISE 10. FEDERAL CASES   (CONTINUED)

M/B: Winans v. Eaton, 30 F. Cas. 262 (C.C.N.D.N.Y. 1854) (No. 17,861).

86 146 285 395 405 515   Works   18,046
Works v. Junction Railroad (Circuit Court, D. Ohio April 1853)
M/B: Works v. Junction Railroad, 30 F. Cas. 626 (C.C.D. Ohio 1853) (No. 18,046).
LR: Works v. Junction R.R., 30 F. Cas. 626 (C.C.D. Ohio 1853) (No. 18,046).

87 147 286 396 406 516   Winthrop   17,900
In re Winthrop (District Court, D. Massachusetts March 26, 1842)
M/B: In re Winthrop, 30 F. Cas. 375 (D. Mass. 1842) (No. 17,900).
LR: In re Winthrop, 30 F. Cas. 375 (D. Mass. 1842) (No. 17,900).

88 148 288 397 407 517   Einstein   4320
Einstein et al. v. Gourdin et al. (Circuit Court, S.D. Georgia November Term, 1877)
M/B: Einstein v. Gourdin, 8 F. Cas. 392 (C.C.S.D. Ga. 1877) (No. 4320).

89 149 288 398 408 518   Hattie   6216
The Hattie (District Court, S.D. New York December 1863)
M/B: The Hattie, 11 F. Cas. 825 (S.D.N.Y. 1863) (No. 6216).

90 150 289 399 409 519   Lowe   8565
Lowe v. The Benjamin (Circuit Court, E.D. Pennsylvania April 1847)
M/B: Lowe v. The Benjamin, 15 F. Cas. 1016 (C.C.E.D. Pa. 1847) (No. 8565).

91 151 290 400 410 520   Parker   10,751
Parker v. United States (Circuit Court, D. Pennsylvania October Term, 1809)
M/B: Parker v. United States, 18 F. Cas. 1179 (C.C.D. Pa. 1809) (No. 10,751).

92 152 291 301 411 521   Russell   12,165
Russell et al. v. Wiggin et al. (Circuit Court, D. Massachusetts May Term, 1842)
M/B: Russell v. Wiggin, 21 F. Cas. 68 (C.C.D. Mass. 1842) (No. 12,165).

93 153 292 302 412 522   Tallman   13,739
In re Tallman (District Court, S.D. New York April 1868)
M/B: In re Tallman, 23 F. Cas. 678 (S.D.N.Y. 1868) (No. 13,739).
LR: In re Tallman, 23 F. Cas. 678 (S.D.N.Y. 1868) (No. 13,739).

94 154 293 303 413 523   U.S. (v. The Good Friends)   15,227
United States v. The Good Friends (District Court, D. Delaware May 5, 1812)
M/B: United States v. The Good Friends, 25 F. Cas. 1355 (D. Del. 1812) (No. 15,227).

95 155 294 304 414 524   U.S. (v. Stott)   16,408
United States v. Stott (Circuit Court, District of Columbia April Term, 1825)
M/B: United States v. Stott, 27 F. Cas. 1349 (D.C. Cir. 1825) (No. 16,408).

96 156 295 305 415 525   Whitcomb   17,529
Ex parte Whitcomb (District Court, D. Massachusetts November 27, 1876)
M/B: Ex parte Whitcomb, 29 F. Cas. 962 (D. Mass. 1876) (No. 17,529).
LR: Ex parte Whitcomb, 29 F. Cas. 962 (D. Mass. 1876) (No. 17,529).

97 157 296 306 416 526   Whipple   17,513
In re Whipple (District Court, D. Massachusetts March 1875)
M/B: In re Whipple, 29 F. Cas. 929 (D. Mass. 1875) (No. 17,513).
LR: In re Whipple, 29 F. Cas. 929 (D. Mass. 1875) (No. 17,513).

98 158 297 307 417 527   Zenobia   18,209
The Zenobia (District Court, S.D. New York December 1847)
M/B: The Zenobia, 30 F. Cas. 922 (S.D.N.Y. 1847) (No. 18,209).

99 159 298 308 418 528   Thompson   13,938
In re Thompson (District Court, E.D. Michigan 1876)
M/B: In re Thompson, 23 F. Cas. 1021 (E.D. Mich. 1876) (No. 13,938).
LR: In re Thompson, 23 F. Cas. 1021 (E.D. Mich. 1876) (No. 13,938).

EXERCISE 10.   FEDERAL CASES   (CONTINUED)

100 160 299 309 419 529   Steam Stone Cutter   13,334
Steam Stone Cutter Co. v. Shortsleeves (Circuit Court, D. Vermont June 7, 1879)
M/B: Steam Stone Cutter Co. v. Shortsleeves, 22 F. Cas. 1168 (C.C.D. Vt. 1879) (No. 13,334).

LIBRARY EXERCISE 11. OFFICIAL STATE COURT REPORTS.

INSTRUCTOR'S NOTE: In this exercise, the students are required to find and cite the case that begins on the page listed below in the designated official state court reporter volume. Students are to use the National Reporter Blue Book to find the parallel West regional reporter citation when necessary. If the library does not have the designated state reporter, the students are instructed to note in their answer "official report not available" and to state the parallel West reporter citation (e.g., "158 N.W. 202") based upon the appropriate entry in the National Reporter Blue Book. If the National Reporter Blue Book is unavailable, students are to use the Table of Cases volume in the appropriate West state or regional digest or the appropriate state edition of Shepard's Citations to find the parallel citation.

The following Quick-Reference Abbreviations are particularly relevant to this exercise:

STATE COURT CITATION 1. CITE STATE COURT DECISIONS TO THE OFFICIAL REPORTER FIRST (IF IT IS STILL PUBLISHED) AND THEN TO THE PREFERRED UNOFFICIAL REPORTER OR REPORTERS. ALWAYS CITE THE OFFICIAL REPORT FIRST. [ST 1]
STATE COURT CITATION 3. IN REPORTER ABBREVIATIONS, CLOSE UP ADJACENT SINGLE CAPITALS. TREAT NUMERALS AND ORDINALS AS SINGLE CAPITALS. HOWEVER, DO NOT CLOSE UP SINGLE CAPITALS WITH LONGER ABBREVIATIONS. [ST 3]
STATE COURT CITATION 6. WHEN THE HIGHEST STATE COURT IS CITED, INDICATE ONLY THE ABBREVIATED NAME OF THE JURISDICTION IN THE PARENTHETICAL. WHEN THE REPORT IS THE SAME AS THE NAME OF THE JURISDICTION, ELIMINATE THE INDICATION OF THE JURISDICTION AS WELL. [ST 6]

1 200 222 394 417 576   102 Neb. 361
Paul B. Fitch v. State of Nebraska (April 12, 1918)
M/B: Fitch v. State, 102 Neb. 361, 167 N.W. 417 (1918).

2 101 223 395 418 577   103 Neb. 111
Charles Chandler, Appellant, v. L. E. Sipes, Appellee (January 20, 1919)
M/B: Chandler v. Sipes, 103 Neb. 111, 170 N.W. 604 (1919).

3 102 224 396 419 578   104 Neb. 465
Louise VonDorn, Appellant, v. Louis Rubin et al., Appellees (April 17, 1920)
M/B: VonDorn v. Rubin, 104 Neb. 465, 177 N.W. 653 (1920).

4 103 225 397 420 579   119 Neb. 153
Abie State Bank et al., Appellees, v. Arthur J. Weaver, Governor, et al., Appellants (December 7, 1929)
M/B: Abie State Bank v. Weaver, 119 Neb. 153, 227 N.W. 922 (1929).

5 104 226 398 421 580   120 Neb. 525
Elizabeth Brown Hogoboom v. State of Nebraska (January 7, 1931)
M/B: Hogoboom v. State, 120 Neb. 525, 234 N.W. 422 (1931).

6 105 227 399 422 581   121 Neb. 488
Peter Jensen, Trustee, Appellant v. A. Ballmer, Appellee (July 2, 1931)
M/B: Jensen v. Ballmer, 121 Neb. 488, 237 N.W. 613 (1931).

7 106 228 400 423 582   141 Neb. 538
Evelyn Nollett, Special Administratrix, Appellant v. Holland Lumber Company, Appellee 4 N.W.2d 554 (May 29, 1942)
M/B: Nollett v. Holland Lumber Co., 141 Neb. 538, 4 N.W.2d 554 (1942).

8 107 229 301 424 583   142 Neb. 736
Sue M. Crandall, Administratris, Appellee v. Charles F. Ladd et al., Appellants 7 N.W.2d 642 (January 15, 1943)
M/B: Crandall v. Ladd, 142 Neb. 736, 7 N.W.2d 642 (1943).

9 108 230 302 425 584   161 Neb. 404
Wesley Jones, Appellee v. Yankee Hill Brick Manufacturing Company et al., Appellants 73 N.W.2d 394 (December 9, 1955)
M/B: Jones v. Yankee Hill Brick Manufacturing Co., 161 Neb. 404, 73 N.W.2d 394 (1955).
LR: Jones v. Yankee Hill Brick Mfg. Co., 161 Neb. 404, 73 N.W.2d 394 (1955).

EXERCISE 11. OFFICIAL STATE COURT REPORTS   (CONTINUED)

10 109 231 303 426 585   179 Neb. 817
Safeway Stores, Incorporated, A Corporation, Appellant v. Nebraska Liquor Control Commission et al., Apellees 140 N.W.2d 668 (March 4, 1966)
M/B: Safeway Stores v. Nebraska Liquor Control Commission, 179 Neb. 817, 140 N.W.2d 668 (1966).
LR: Safeway Stores v. Nebraska Liquor Control Comm'n, 179 Neb. 817, 140 N.W.2d 668 (1966).

11 110 232 304 427 586   111 Kan. 577
The State of Kansas, Appellee v. Clarence Bolton, Appellant (1922)
M/B: State v. Bolton, 111 Kan. 577, 207 P. 653 (1922).

12 111 233 305 428 587   112 Kan. 708
The Central National Bank of Attica, Indiana, Appellant v. Max Engler and Bessie Engler, Appellees (1923)
M/B: Central National Bank v. Engler, 112 Kan. 708, 212 P. 656 (1923).
LR: Central Nat'l Bank v. Engler, 112 Kan. 708, 212 P. 656 (1923).

13 112 234 306 429 588   113 Kan. 513
Bertha Hoag et al., Appellants, v. The Kansas Independent Laundry Company, Appellee (1923)
M/B: Hoag v. Kansas Independent Laundry Co., 113 Kan. 513, 215 P. 295 (1923).
LR: Hoag v. Kansas Indep. Laundry Co., 113 Kan. 513, 215 P. 295 (1923).

14 113 235 307 430 589   134 Kan. 149
Milburn L. Holt, Widow of Julius E. Holt, Deceased, Appellee, v. The Peterson Construction Company et al., appellants 4 P.2d 428 (1931)
M/B: Holt v. Peterson Construction Co., 134 P. 149, 4 P.2d 428 (1931).
LR: Holt v. Peterson Constr. Co., 134 P. 149, 4 P.2d 428 (1931).

15 114 236 308 431 590   135 Kan. 100
The United Power and Light Corporation of Kansas, Appellant, v. Charles R. Murphy and Laura Murphy, Appellees 9 P.2d 658 (1932)
M/B: United Power & Light Corp. v. Murphy, 135 Kan. 100, 9 P.2d 658 (1932).

16 115 237 309 432 591   136 Kan. 591
Ferne Behler, Appellee, v. The Wichita Transportation Company, Appellant 16 P.2d 503 (1932)
M/B: Behler v. Wichita Transportation Co., 136 Kan. 591, 16 P.2d 503 (1932).
LR: Behler v. Wichita Transp. Co., 136 Kan. 591, 16 P.2d 503 (1932).

17 116 238 310 433 592   159 Kan. 520
Robert H. Ferguson, Appellee v. The Kansas City Public Service Company, Appellant 156 P.2d 869
M/B: Ferguson v. Kansas City Public Service Co., 159 Kan. 520, 156 P.2d 869 (1945).
LR: Ferguson v. Kansas City Pub. Serv. Co., 159 Kan. 520, 156 P.2d 869 (1945).

18 117 239 311 434 593   160 Kan. 258
Albert J. Bailey, Appellant v. The Mosby Hotel Company, Appellee 160 P.2d 701 (1945)
M/B: Bailey v. Mosby Hotel Co., 160 Kan. 258, 160 P.2d 701 (1945).
LR: Bailey v. Mosby Hotel Co, 160 Kan. 258, 160 P.2d 701 (1945).

19 118 240 312 435 594   288 Mo. 482
The State ex rel. Russel E. Burton, Appellant v. David Bagby, Probate Judge (June 23, 1921)
M/B: State ex rel. Burton v. Bagby, 288 Mo. 482, 232 S.W. 474 (1921).
LR: State ex rel. Burton v. Bagby, 288 Mo. 482, 232 S.W. 474 (1921).

20 119 241 313 436 595   289 Mo. 506
The State ex rel. John W. Calhoun, Judge of Circuit Court; John H. Conrades et al., Recievers of Blue Bird Manufacturing Company; Walton & Spencer Company, and Oscar Mandel et al., Comprising firm of Mandel & Schwarzmann v. George D. Reynolds et al., Judges of St. Louis Court of Appeals (July 22, 1921)

EXERCISE 11. OFFICIAL STATE COURT REPORTS   (CONTINUED)

M/B: State ex rel. Calhoun v. Reynolds, 289 Mo. 506, 233 S.W. 483 (1921).
LR: State ex rel. Calhoun v. Reynolds, 289 Mo. 506, 233 S.W. 483 (1921).

21 120 242 314 437 596   290 Mo. 143
The State ex rel. Ella Plummer, Appellant v. Frederick D. Garner, Governor, et al. (October 11, 1921)
M/B: State ex rel. Plummer v. Garner, 290 Mo. 143, 234 S.W. 53 (1921).
LR: State ex rel. Plummer v. Garner, 290 Mo. 143, 234 S.W. 53 (1921).

22 121 243 315 438 597   161 Minn. 269
Olaf Benson and Others v. Saffert-Gugisberg Cement Construction Company and Others (December 19, 1924)
M/B: Benson v. Saffert-Gugisberg Cement Construction Co., 161 Minn. 269, 201 N.W. 424 (1924).
LR: Benson v. Saffert-Gugisberg Cement Constr. Co., 161 Minn. 269, 201 N.W. 424 (1924).

23 122 244 316 439 598   162 Minn. 410
P. Anton Peterson and Another v. Peter S. Weberg (April 3, 1925)
M/B: Peterson v. Weberg, 162 Minn. 410, 203 N.W. 209 (1925).

24 123 245 317 440 599   163 Minn. 389
In Re Estate of Mary Weber, Deceased (June 5, 1925)
M/B: In re Estate of Weber, 163 Minn. 389, 204 N.W. 52 (1925).
LR: In re Estate of Weber, 163 Minn. 389. 204 N.W. 52 (1925).

25 124 246 318 441 600   184 Minn. 309
State Ex Rel. J. Walter Kollman v. John A. Johnson (October 16, 1931)
M/B: State ex rel. Kollman v. Johnson, 184 Minn. 309, 238 N.W. 490 (1931).
LR: State ex rel. Kollman v. Johnson, 184 Minn. 309, 238 N.W. 490 (1931).

26 125 247 319 442 501   287 Ill. 182
The Ayers National Bank of Jacksonville et al. Plaintiffs in Error, vs. William Barber et al. Defendants in Error (Opinion filed February 20, 1919 - Rehearing denied April 2, 1919)
M/B: Ayers National Bank v. Barber, 287 Ill. 182, 122 N.E. 533 (1919).
LR: Ayers Nat'l Bank v. Barber, 287 Ill. 182, 122 N.E. 533 (1919).

27 126 248 320 443 502   288 Ill. 304
The People ex rel. Samuel P. Thrasher, Appellant, vs. Jacob M. Eisenberg, Appellee (June 18, 1919)
M/B: People ex rel. Thrasher v. Eisenberg, 288 Ill. 304, 123 N.E. 532 (1919).
LR: People ex rel. Thrasher v. Eisenberg, 288 Ill. 304, 123 N.E. 532 (1919).

28 127 249 321 444 503   289 Ill. 315
The Spring Valley Coal Company, Plaintiff in Error, vs. The Industrial Commission et al. (Peter Sabatini, Defendant in Error) (October 27, 1919)
M/B: Spring Valley Coal Co. v. Industrial Commission, 289 Ill. 315, 124 N.E. 545 (1919).
LR: Spring Valley Coal Co. v. Industrial Comm'n, 289 Ill. 315, 124 N.E. 545 (1919).
Note: "(Sabatini)" may be appended to the above citations after the date to aid in identification of this case. See Rule 10.2.1(a) in the USOC.

29 128 250 322 445 504   348 Ill. 441
The People ex rel. Herman H. Seiler, by, etc., Petitioner, vs. Henry C. Hill, Warden, Respondent (April 23, 1932)
M/B: People ex rel. Seiler v. Hill, 348 Ill. 441, 181 N.E. 295 (1932).
LR: People ex rel. Seiler v. Hill, 348 Ill. 441, 181 N.E. 295 (1932).

30 129 251 323 446 505   349 Ill. 436
Seba J. Akker et al. Plaintiffs in Error, vs. The Cat Tail Drainage District, Defendant in Error (June 24, 1932)
M/B: Akker v. Cat Tail Drainage District, 349 Ill. 436, 182 N.E. 630 (1932).
LR: Akker v. Cat Tail Drainage Dist., 349 Ill. 436, 182 N.E. 630 (1932).

31 130 252 324 447 506   350 Ill. 200

EXERCISE 11. OFFICIAL STATE COURT REPORTS   (CONTINUED)

Czilli Czecz, Appellant, vs. The New Era Association, Appellee (October 22, 1932)
M/B: Czecz v. New Era Association, 350 Ill. 200, 182 N.E. 742 (1932).
LR: Czecz v. New Era Ass'n, 350 Ill. 200, 182 N.E. 742 (1932).

32 131 253 325 448 507   395 Ill. 348
The People of the State of Illinois, Defendant in Error vs. Raymond Belcher, Plaintiff in Error (November 20, 1946)
M/B: People v. Belcher, 395 Ill. 348, 70 N.E.2d 201 (1946).

33 132 254 326 449 508   382 Ill. 218
Chicago Park District, Appellant, vs. Frank Canfield, Appellee (January 21, 1943)
M/B: Chicago Park District v. Canfield, 382 Ill. 218, 47 N.E.2d 61 (1943).
LR: Chicago Park Dist. v. Canfield, 382 Ill. 218, 47 N.E.2d 61 (1943).

34 133 255 327 450 509   396 Ill. 404
Angeline DeBartolo, Appellee, vs. The Village of Oak Park, Appellant (January 22, 1947)
M/B: DeBartolo v. Village of Oak Park, 396 Ill. 404, 71 N.E.2d 693 (1947).

35 134 256 328 451 510   275 Pa. 542
Harmony Electric Co. v. Public Service Commission et al., Appellants (1923)
M/B: Harmony Electric Co. v. Public Service Commission, 275 Pa. 542, 119 A. 712 (1923).
LR: Harmony Elec. Co. v. Public Serv. Comm'n, 275 Pa. 542, 119 A. 712 (1923).
Note: "PSC" may be a widely enough recognized abbreviation of "Public Service Commission" to be acceptable in the above citations and thus should be accepted as correct.

36 135 257 329 452 511   276 Pa. 212
National Union Fire Insurance Co. v. Mellon National Bank, Appellant (1923)
M/B: National Union Fire Insurance Co. v. Mellon National Bank, 276 Pa. 212, 119 A. 910 (1923).
LR: National Union Fire Ins. Co. v. Mellon Nat'l Bank, 276 Pa. 212, 119 A. 910 (1923).

37 136 258 330 453 512   277 Pa. 184
First National Bank of Greencastle v. Baer et al., Appellants (1923)
M/B: First National Bank v. Baer, 277 Pa. 184, 120 A. 815 (1923).
LR: First Nat'l Bank v. Baer, 277 Pa. 184, 120 A. 815 (1923).

38 137 259 331 454 513   302 Pa. 254
Brown v. Victor Building Association, Appellant (1931)
M/B: Brown v. Victor Building Association, 302 Pa. 254, 153 A. 349 (1931).
LR: Brown v. Victor Bldg. Ass'n, 302 Pa. 254, 153 A. 349 (1931).

39 138 260 332 455 514   303 Pa. 156
Simrell et ux. v. Eschenbach, Appellant (1931)
M/B: Simrell v. Eschenbach, 303 Pa. 156, 154 A. 369 (1931).

40 139 261 333 456 515   304 Pa. 221
Hegarty et ux. v. Berger, Appellant (1931)
M/B: Hegarty v. Berger, 304 Pa. 221, 155 A. 484 (1931).

41 140 262 334 457 516   346 Pa. 584
Fiumara v. American Surety Company of New York, Appellant
M/B: Fiumara v. American Surety Co., 346 Pa. 584, 31 A.2d 283 (1943).
LR: Fiumara v. American Sur. Co., 346 Pa. 584, 31 A.2d 283 (1943).

42 141 263 335 458 517   347 Pa. 510
Commonwealth ex rel. Greenawalt, Appellant v. Greenawalt
M/B: Commonwealth ex rel. Greenawalt v. Greenawalt, 347 Pa. 510, 32 A.2d 757 (1943).
LR: Commonwealth ex rel. Greenawalt v. Greenawalt, 347 Pa. 510, 32 A.2d 757 (1943).

EXERCISE 11. OFFICIAL STATE COURT REPORTS   (CONTINUED)

43 142 264 336 459 518 348 Pa. 409
Commonwealth ex rel. Biglow vs. Ashe, Warden, et al. (1944)
M/B: Commonwealth ex rel. Biglow v. Ashe, 348 Pa. 409, 35 A.2d 340 (1944).
LR: Commonwealth ex rel. Biglow v. Ashe, 348 Pa. 409, 35 A.2d 340 (1944).

44 143 265 337 460 519 22 Fla. 627
R. E. O'Brien, Appellant, vs. E. E. Vaill, Appellee (1886)
M/B: O'Brien v. Vaill, 22 Fla. 627, 1 So. 137 (1886).

45 144 266 338 461 520 127 Va. 563
Boice v. Finance and Guaranty Corporation (March 18, 1920)
M/B: Boice v. Finance & Guaranty Corp., 127 Va. 563, 102 S.E. 591 (1920).
LR: Boice v. Finance & Guar. Corp., 127 Va. 563, 102 S.E. 591 (1920).
Note: "Finance" is not abbreviation in the LR form because it is the first word of the party's name.

46 145 267 339 462 521 128 Va. 517
Scott v. Albemarle Horse Show Association (November 18, 1920)
M/B: Scott v. Albemarle Horse Show Association, 128 Va. 517, 104 S.E. 842 (1920).
LR: Scott v. Albemarle Horse Show Ass'n, 128 Va. 517, 104 S.E. 842 (1920).

47 146 268 340 463 522 129 Va. 297
Stephen Putney Shoe Company, Inc., v. Ormsby's Administrator (January 28, 1921)
M/B: Stephen Putney Shoe Co. v. Ormsby's Administrator, 129 Va. 297, 105 S.E. 563 (1921).
LR: Stephen Putney Shoe Co. v. Ormsby's Adm'r, 129 Va. 297, 105 S.E. 563 (1921).

48 147 269 341 464 523 130 Va. 584
W. B. Addington, Administrator Etc., v. Guests River Coal Company (September 22, 1921)
M/B: Addington v. Guests River Coal Co., 130 Va. 584, 108 S.E. 695 (1921).

49 148 270 342 465 524 129 Wis. 245
Donner, Respondent, vs. Genz, Appellant (May 10-October 9, 1906)
M/B: Donner v. Genz, 129 Wis. 245, 109 N.W. 71 (1906).

50 149 271 343 466 525 130 Wis. 560
In Re Kingston's Estate (January 11-January 29, 1907)
M/B: In re Kingston's Estate, 130 Wis. 560, 110 N.W. 417 (1907).
LR: In re Kingston's Estate, 130 Wis. 560, 110 N.W. 417 (1907).

51 150 272 344 467 526 112 Ohio St. 284
Becker, Exr., v. Fisher et al.
M/B: Becker v. Fisher, 112 Ohio St. 284, 147 N.E. 744 (1925).

52 151 273 345 468 527 113 Ohio St. 377
Todor v. The State of Ohio
M/B: Todor v. State, 113 Ohio St. 377, 149 N.E. 326 (1925).

53 152 274 346 469 528 123 Ohio St. 378
Great Lakes Stages, Inc. v. Laing (1931)
M/B: Great Lakes Stages v. Laing, 123 Ohio St. 378, 175 N.E. 598 (1931).

54 153 275 347 470 529 124 Ohio St. 39
Breinig v. The State of Ohio (June 10, 1931)
M/B: Breinig v. State, 124 Ohio St. 39, 176 N.E. 674 (1931).

55 154 276 348 471 530 125 Ohio St. 291
The National Casualty Co. v. Bogart, Admx. (May 4, 1932)
M/B: National Casualty Co. v. Bogart, 125 Ohio St. 291, 181 N.E. 134 (1932).

56 155 277 349 472 531 126 Ohio St. 251
Industrial Commission of Ohio v. Palmer (March 1, 1933)
M/B: Industrial Commission v. Palmer, 126 Ohio St. 251, 185 N.E. 66 (1933).

EXERCISE 11.   OFFICIAL STATE COURT REPORTS   (CONTINUED)

LR: Industrial Comm'n v. Palmer, 126 Ohio St. 251, 185 N.E. 66 (1933).

57 156 278 350 473 532   144 Ohio St. 443
The Hower Corp., Appellant v. Vance et al., Appellees. Vance et al.,
Appellees v. The Hower Corp., Appellant (February 7, 1945)
M/B: Hower Corp. v. Vance, 144 Ohio St. 443, 59 N.E.2d 377 (1945).

58 157 279 351 474 533   145 Ohio St. 198
Stevens, Appellee, v. Industrial Commission of Ohio, Appellant (May 2, 1945)
M/B: Stevens v. Industrial Commission, 145 Ohio St. 198, 61 N.E.2d 198
(1945).
LR: Stevens v. Industrial Comm'n, 145 Ohio St. 198, 61 N.E.2d 198 (1945).

59 158 280 352 475 534   146 Ohio St. 288
Deering, Appellant v. Hirsch et al., Appellees (March 6, 1946)
M/B: Deering v. Hirsch, 146 Ohio St. 288, 65 N.E.2d 649 (1946).

60 159 281 353 476 535   147 Ohio St. 263
The State of Ohio, Appellant, v. Nevius, Appellee (1947)
M/B: State v. Nevius, 147 Ohio St. 263, 71 N.E.2d 258 (1947).

61 160 282 354 477 536   109 Or. 254
J. M. Dougan v. Van Riper, Klamath County Treasurer, et al. 198 Pac. 897
(1923)
M/B: Dougan v. Van Riper, 109 Or. 254, 198 P. 897 (1923).

62 161 283 355 478 537   110 Okla. 57
Knight v. Cecil (Feb. 24, 1925)
M/B: Knight v. Cecil, 110 Okla. 57, 235 P. 1107 (1925).

63 162 284 356 479 538   111 Okla. 282
State ex rel. Walcott, Bank Com'r v. Brown et al. (Sept. 15, 1925)
M/B: State ex rel. Walcott v. Brown, 111 Okla. 282, 239 P. 671 (1925).
LR: State ex rel. Walcott v. Brown, 111 Okla. 282, 239 P. 671 (1925).

64 163 285 357 480 539   114 Okla. 103
Sparks et al. v. Gallagher et al. (Dec. 15, 1925)
M/B: Sparks v. Gallagher, 114 Okla. 103, 243 P. 228 (1925).

65 164 286 358 481 540   116 Okla. 50
B. Kuppenheimer & Co. v. Levine et al. (Opinion filed Nov.12, 1924, Rehearing
denied Feb. 2, 1926)
M/B: B. Kuppenheimer & Co. v. Levine, 116 Okla. 50, 243 P. 182 (1924).
LR: First Nat'l Bank v. Shipley, 116 Okla. 55, 243 P. 186 (1925).

66 165 287 359 482 541   169 Okla. 336
Whittaker v. White et al. (Oct. 23, 1934)
M/B: Whittaker v. White, 169 Okla. 336, 37 P.2d 247 (1934).

67 166 288 360 483 542   170 Okla. 349
Home Bakery et al. v. Robinson Milling Co. (Jan. 22, 1935)
M/B: Home Bakery v. Robinson Milling Co. 170 Okla. 349, 40 P.2d 637 (1935).

68 167 289 361 484 543   171 Okla. 337
S. O. Maxey & Co. v. Crowl (April 2, 1935)
M/B: S.O. Maxey & Co. v. Crowl, 171 Okla. 337, 41 P.2d 254 (1935).

69 168 290 362 485 544   172 Okla. 221
Hannah v. Oklahoma State Highway Commission (May 14, 1935)
M/B: Hannah v. Oklahoma State Highway Commission, 172 Okla. 221, 45 P.2d 53
(1935).
LR: Hannah v. Oklahoma State Highway Comm'n, 172 Okla. 221, 45 P.2d 53
(1935).

70 169 291 363 486 545   180 Iowa 833
W. H. Hoopes & Sons, Appellee, v. F. H. Simpson Fruit Company, Appellant
(1917)

EXERCISE 11. OFFICIAL STATE COURT REPORTS   (CONTINUED)

M/B: W.H. Hoopes & Sons v. F.H. Simpson Fruit Co., 180 Iowa 833, 161 N.W. 629 (1917).

71 170 292 364 487 546   181 Iowa 1081
In Re Estate of William E. Ensign (December 10, 1917)
M/B: In re Estate of Ensign, 181 Iowa 1081, 165 N.W. 319 (1917).
LR: In re Estate of Ensign, 181 Iowa 1081, 165 N.W. 319 (1917).

72 171 293 365 488 547   182 Iowa 973
I. E. Harvey et al., Appellants, v. J. H. Kirton et al., Appellees (October 24, 1917)
M/B: Harvey v. Kirton, 182 Iowa 973, 164 N.W. 888 (1917).

73 172 294 366 489 548   183 Iowa 956
Louis Wokoun, Appellant v. G. H. Jameson et al., Appellees
M/B: Wokoun v. Jameson, 183 Iowa 956, 167 N.W. 676 (1918).

74 173 295 367 490 549   213 Iowa 800
J. F. Lineberger, Appellant v. Ray E. Johnson, Appellee
M/B: Lineberger v. Johnson, 213 Iowa 800, 239 N.W. 679 (1931).

75 174 296 368 491 550   214 Iowa 825
James Glass, Appellant, v. Hutchinson Ice Cream Company et al., Appellees
M/B: Glass v. Hutchinson Ice Cream Co., 214 Iowa 825, 243 N.W. 352 (1932).

76 175 297 369 492 551   215 Iowa 600
State of Iowa, Appelle v. J. A. Brown, Appellant
M/B: State v. Brown, 215 Iowa 600, 246 N.W. 258 (1933).

77 176 298 370 493 552   216 Iowa 688
W. I. Sargent, Appellee, v. Mechanics Insurance Company of Philadelphia, Appellant (March 14, 1933)
M/B: Sargent v. Mechanics Insurance Co., 216 Iowa 688, 247 N.W. 267 (1933).
LR: Sargent v. Mechanics Ins. Co., 216 Iowa 688, 247 N.W. 267 (1933).

78 177 299 371 494 553   223 Iowa 780
B. G. Engle, Assignee, Appellee, v. Lloyd A. Ungles, doing business under the name and style of Ungles Baking Company, Appellant (June 15, 1937)
M/B: Engle v. Ungles, 223 Iowa 780, 273 N.W. 879 (1937).

79 178 300 372 495 554   224 Iowa 439
George J. Carpenter et al., Plaintiffs, Appellants v. A. O. Lothringer, Administrator, et al., Defendants, Appellees, Clara Z. Baker et al., Intervenors, Appellees
M/B: Carpenter v. Lothringer, 224 Iowa 439, 275 N.W. 98 (1937).

80 179 201 373 496 555   225 Iowa 809
H. E. Peterson, Appellee v. De Luxe Cab Company et al., Appellants (October 18, 1938)
M/B: Peterson v. De Luxe Cab Co., 225 Iowa 809, 281 N.W. 737 (1938).

81 180 202 374 497 556   226 Iowa 712
Burdette L. Bowne, and Burdette L. Bowne, as Trustee, Appellants, v. W. B. Bonnfield et al., Appellees (April 4, 1939)
M/B: Bowne v. Bonnfield, 226 Iowa 712, 285 N.W. 144 (1939).

82 181 203 375 498 557   136 Md. 334
Safe Deposit and Trust Company, Substituted Trustee, et al., vs. Edgar Ellis and Isabella Ellis, His wife; Safe Deposit and Trust Company, Substituted Trustee, vs. Charles Wilkens, Jr.; Charles Wilkens, Jr., vs. Safe Deposit and Trust Company, Trustee (1920)
M/B: Safe Deposit & Trust Co. v. Ellis, 136 Md. 334, 110 A. 481 (1920).

83 182 204 376 499 558   137 Md. 349
Herbert W. Rydstrom vs. Queen Insurance Company of America (January 11th, 1921)

EXERCISE 11. OFFICIAL STATE COURT REPORTS   (CONTINUED)

M/B: Rydstrom v. Queen Insurance Co. of America, 137 Md. 349, 112 A. 586 (1921).
LR: Rydstrom v. Queen Ins. Co. of Am., 137 Md. 349, 112 A. 586 (1921).

84 183 205 377 500 559   138 Md. 446
Title Guaranty and Surety Company and City of Chicago vs. Edwin W. Poe et al., Receivers of the United Surety Company 138 Md. 446 (1921)
M/B: Title Guaranty & Surety Co. v. Poe, 138 Md. 446, 114 A. 481 (1921).
LR: Title Guar. & Sur. Co. v. Poe, 138 Md. 446, 114 A. 481 (1921).

85 184 206 378 401 560   139 Md. 450
Nichols vs. William C. Meyer 139 Md. 450
M/B: Nichols v. Meyer, 139 Md. 450, 115 A. 786 (1921).

86 185 207 379 402 561   140 Md. 45
In re William W. Paca, a Lunatic 140 Md. 450 (1922)
M/B: In re Paca, 140 Md. 450, 116 A. 847 (1922).
LR: In re Paca, 140 Md. 450, 116 A. 847 (1922).

87 186 208 380 403 562   159 Md. 370
A. Louella Burhans v. Edna May Burhans; A. Louella Burhans v. Dora E. Burhans (April 1930)
M/B: Burhans v. Burhans, 159 Md. 370, 150 A. 795 (1930).

88 187 209 381 404 563   160 Md. 407
John H. Sieling et al. v. State Roads Commission et al. (October 1930)
M/B: Sieling v. State Roads Commission, 160 Md. 407, 153 A. 614 (1930).
LR: Sieling v. State Rds. Comm'n, 160 Md. 407, 153 A. 614 (1930).

89 188 210 382 405 564   161 Md. 375
Frey & Son, Inc., v. W. Harry Magness (October 1931)
M/B: Frey & Son v. Magness, 161 Md. 375, 157 A. 400 (1931).

90 189 211 383 406 565   162 Md. 419
Sun Cab Company v. William W. Cloud et al. (January 1932)
M/B: Sun Cab Co. v. Cloud, 162 Md. 419, 159 A. 922 (1932).

91 190 212 384 407 566   163 Md. 353
State of Maryland v. Algie P. Gregg (October 1932)
M/B: State v. Gregg, 163 Md. 353, 163 A. 119 (1932).

92 191 213 385 408 567   164 Md. 381
Henry E. Crumlick v. Lucie J. Crumlick (January 1933)
M/B: Crumlick v. Crumlick, 164 Md. 381, 165 A. 189 (1933).

93 192 214 386 409 568   71 Colo. 410
The Siegel-Campion Live Stock Commission Co. v. Ardohain, et al. (May 1, 1922)
M/B: Siegel-Campion Live Stock Commission Co. v. Ardohain, 71 Colo. 410, 207 P. 82 (1922).
LR: Siegel-Campion Live Stock Comm'n Co. v. Ardohain, 71 Colo. 410, 207 P. 82 (1922).

94 193 215 387 410 569   72 Colo. 42
Zink v. Fry (July 3, 1922)
M/B: Zink v. Fry, 72 Colo. 42, 209 P. 510 (1922).

95 194 216 388 411 570   73 Colo. 356
Hathaway v. Bottenfield, Administratrix (May 7, 1923)
M/B: Hathaway v. Bottenfield, 73 Colo. 356, 215 P. 864 (1923).

96 195 217 389 412 571   74 Colo. 268
Dively v. People (December 3, 1923)
M/B: Dively v. People, 74 Colo. 268, 220 P. 991 (1923).

97 196 218 390 413 572   126 Wis. 216
Mackin, Administrator, Respondent, vs. Hobbs, Appellant (October 26-November 14, 1905)

EXERCISE 11.   OFFICIAL STATE COURT REPORTS   (CONTINUED)

M/B: Mackin v. Hobbs, 126 Wis. 216, 105 N.W. 305 (1905).

98 197 219 391 414 573   127 Wis. 451
J. H. Clark Company, Appellant, vs. Rice, Respondent (January 30-March 20, 1906)
M/B: J.H. Clark Co. v. Rice, 127 Wis. 451, 106 N.W. 231 (1906).

99 198 220 392 415 574   110 Ohio St. 636
Jamieson v. Davis, Agent (June 10, 1924)
M/B: Jamieson v. Davis, 110 Ohio St. 636, 144 N.E. 291 (1924).

100 199 221 393 416 575   111 Ohio St. 448
The State of Ohio v. Barger et al. (December 16, 1924)
M/B: State v. Barger, 111 Ohio St. 448, 145 N.E. 857 (1924).

LIBRARY EXERCISE 12.   WEST'S REGIONAL REPORTERS.

INSTRUCTOR'S NOTE: (a) For their citation listed, students are to find the case in the appropriate West regional reporter. For their answer to this part, they are required to cite the case using Shepard's Citations or the appropriate state or regional digest to find parallel citations when necessary. (b) The students should give the name of the law firm(s) and the last name of the individual attorney(s) who presented the case for the parties, as listed by West Publishing Co. (e.g., Horton (Appellant); Armitrage & Quigley, Quigley (Appellee); Wilson (Amicus Curiae). No special form is required. (c) In this part, the students are required to list the Digest Topics and Key Numbers for the first two headnotes (e.g., Searches and Seizures 7(1); Estoppel 116.) (d) Lastly, the students are to state the page number (e.g., 306) in the text of the opinion where the second headnote number can be located in the opinion.

The ST Quick-Reference Codes are relevant to this exercise.

1 121 241 331 421 521   11 S.E.2d 631
Stickley v. Givens, State Veterinarian (Supreme Court of Appeals of Virginia Nov. 25, 1940)
(a) M/B: Stickley v. Givens, 176 Va. 548, 11 S.E.2d 631 (1940).
(b) Wright (Appellant)
     Staples and Gibson (Appellees)
(c) Injunction 128
     Animals 29
(d) 636

2 122 242 332 422 522   10 S.E.2d 506
Buckle et al. v. Marshall et al. (Supreme Court of Appeals of Virginia Sept. 5, 1940)
(a) M/B: Buckle v. Marshall, 176 Va. 139, 10 S.E.2d 506 (1940).
(b) Vansant and Thompson (Appellants)
     Crews and Clement (Appellees)
(c) Appeal and Error 1019
     Trusts 218(1)
(d) 512

3 123 243 333 423 523   7 S.E.2d 394
Moore, Com'r of Roads and Revenues, v. Whaley et al. (Supreme Court of Georgia Feb. 15, 1940)
(a) M/B: Moore v. Whaley, 189 Ga. 647, 7 S.E.2d 394 (1940).
(b) Armistead (Plaintiff in Error)
     Poole, Pearce, Richardson & Graham and Poole (Defendnats in Error)
(c) Counties 39
     Counties 39
(d) 396

4 124 244 334 424 524   99 A.2d 860
Panzarella v. United States Rubber Co. (Supreme Court of Rhode Island Nov. 3, 1953)
(a) M/B: Panzarella v. United States Rubber Co., 81 R.I. 149, 99 A.2d 860 (1953).
(b) Kirshenbaum & Kireshenbaum and Weintraub (Petitioner)
     Carroll (Respondent)
(c) Workmen's Compensation 1538, 1676
     Workmen's Compensation 1752
(d) 863

5 125 245 335 425 525   146 S.E.2d 257
Claude Dickson, Petitioner, v. State of South Carolina and Ellis C. MacDougall, Director, Department of Corrections, Respondents (Supreme Court of South Carolina Jan. 11, 1966)
(a) M/B: Dickson v. State, 247 S.C. 153, 146 S.E.2d 257 (1966).
(b) Houck (Petitioner)
     McLeod and Latimer (Respondents)
(c) Habeas Corpus 54
     Habeas Corpus 25.1(9)
(d) 258

EXERCISE 12. WEST'S REGIONAL REPORTERS   (CONTINUED)

6 126 246 336 426 526   148 S.E.2d 149
William E. Hucks, Respondent, v. Green's Fuel of South Carolina and Hartford Accident & Indemnity Co., Appellants (Supreme Court of South Carolina April 25, 1966)
(a) M/B: <u>Hucks v. Green's Fuel</u>, 247 S.C. 457, 148 S.E.2d 149 (1966).
(b) Ray and McCutcheon (Appellants)
    Respondent not represented by counsel
(c) Workmen's Compensation 1302
    Estoppel 116
(d) 150

7 127 247 337 427 527   188 S.W.2d 564
Knight et al. v. Chicago Corporation et al. (Supreme Court of Texas June 13, 1945)
(a) M/B: <u>Knight v. Chicago Corp.</u>, 144 Tex. 98, 188 S.W.2d 564 (1945).
(b) Neel, King & Rachal, and Rachal, Neel, Moody, and Robertson (Petitioners)
    Vinson, Elkins, Weems & Francis and Morrow (Respondent); Small, Arney & Small, and Tarlton & Koch, and Koch (Respondents)
(c) Mines & Minerals 66
    Mines & Minerals 66
(d) 566

8 128 248 338 428 528   100 A.2d 630
Kotal v. Goldberg (Supreme Court of Pennsylvania Nov. 24, 1953)
(a) M/B: <u>Kotal v. Goldberg</u>, 375 Pa. 397, 100 A.2d 630 (1953).
(b) Schultz, Still, Smith, Kessler, Luria & Still, and Luria (Appellant)
    Lawyer, Rothbard, and Rothbard & Rothbard (Appellee)
(c) Trial 143, 143
    Trial 139(1)
(d) 633

9 129 249 339 429 529   190 S.W.2d 450
McHaney v. McHaney et al. (Supreme Court of Arkansas Nov. 19, 1945)
(a) M/B: <u>McHaney v. McHaney</u>, 209 Ark. 337, 190 S.W.2d 450 (1945).
(b) Rhine & Rhine (Appellant)
    Kirsch & Cathay and Beauchampt (Appellees)
(c) Principal and Agent 69(1)
    Principal and Agent 48
(d) 454

10 130 250 340 430 530   252 S.W.2d 809
Driver v. Kelley (Supreme Court of Arkansas Dec. 1, 1952)
(a) M/B: <u>Driver v. Kelley</u>, 221 Ark. 290, 252 S.W.2d 809 (1952).
(b) Bailey and Bailey (Appellant)
    Farish and Moore (Appellee)
(c) Deeds 210, 211(1, 4)
    Appeal & Error 1152
(d) 810

11 131 251 341 431 531   255 S.W.2d 961
Barnes v. Rebsamen Motors, Inc. et al. (Supreme Court of Arkansas March 16, 1953)
(a) M/B: <u>Barnes v. Rebsamen Motors</u>, 221 Ark. 791, 255 S.W.2d 961 (1953).
(b) Dixon (Appellant)
    Talley & Owen and Owen (Appellees)
(c) Infants 99
    Infants 98
(d) 962

12 132 252 342 432 532   250 S.W.2d 549
State for Use and Benefit of Lawrence County v. Hobbs, et al. (Supreme Court of Tennessee July 11, 1952)
(a) M/B: <u>State ex rel. Lawrence County v. Hobbs</u>, 194 Tenn. 323, 250 S.W.2d 549
    (1952).

EXERCISE 12. WEST'S REGIONAL REPORTERS   (CONTINUED)

       LR: State ex rel. Lawrence County v. Hobbs, 194 Tenn. 323, 250 S.W.2d
549
    (1952).
(b) Freemon (Appellants)
    Locke & Holtsford, Henry & Henry (Appellees)
(c) Appeal adn Error 507
    Appeal and Error 801(1)
(d) 551 (or 551-52)

13 133 253 343 433 533 168 N.W.2d 710
Nancy Boe, Plaintiff and Respondent, v. James Healy, Defendant and Appellant
(Supreme Court of South Dakota June 12, 1969)
(a) M/B: Boe v. Healy, 84 S.D. 155, 168 N.W.2d 710 (1969).
(b) Davenport Evans, Hurwitz & Smith and Wirt (Appellant)
    Patterson and Dickey (Respondent)
(c) Landlord & Tenant 164(1), 167(8)
    Landlord & Tenant 166(10)
(d) 713

14 134 254 344 434 534 167 N.W.2d 587
Loren Blackwell, Plaintiff in Error, v. State of Wisconsin, Defendant in Error
(two cases) (Supreme Court of Wisconsin May 9, 1969)
(a) M/B: Blackwell v. State, 42 Wis. 2d 615, 167 N.W.2d 587 (1969).
(b) McDermott (Plaintiff in Error)
    Warren, Platz, Madison, McCann, Gardner, and Jackson (Defendant in Error)
(c) Poisons 9
    Criminal Law 1162
(d) 590

15 135 255 345 435 535 179 N.W.2d 641
State of Wisconsin, Appellant, v. J.C. Penney Co., Respondent (Supreme Court
of Wisconsin Oct. 9, 1970)
(a) M/B: State v. J.C. Penney Co., 48 Wis. 2d 125, 179 N.W.2d 641 (1970).
(b) Warren, Jeffries (Appellant)
    Preloznik, Johnson (Amicus Curiae)
    Orr, Isaksen, Werner, Lathrop & Heaney and Totto (Respondent)
(c) Usury 18, 32
    Usury 32
(d) 646 (or 647-47)

16 136 256 346 436 536 388 P.2d 637
O.J. Connell, Jr., and Eldon Schwemmer, Appellants, v. The State Highway
Commission of Kansas, Appellee (Supreme Court of Kansas Jan. 25, 1964)
(a) M/B: Connell v. State Highway Commission, 192 Kan. 371, 388 P.2d 637
(1964).
      LR: Connell v. State Highway Comm'n, 192 Kan. 371, 388 P.2d 637 (1964).
(b) Ralston and Moss (Appellants)
    Bond, Henson, Lowe, and Bond (Appellee)
(c) Appeal and Error 66
    Appeal and Error 76(1)
(d) 641

17 137 257 347 437 537 387 P.2d 319
Star Realty Company and Palant International Realty, Inc.,
Plaintiffs-Appellees, v. H.A. Sellers and Laura H. Sellers,
Defendants-Appellants (Supreme Court of New Mexico Aug. 5, 1963)
(a) M/B: Star Realty Co. v. Sellers, 73 N.M. 207, 387 P.2d 319 (1963).
(b) Smith, Smith & Tharp (Appellants)
    Matteucci and Domenici (Appellees)
(c) Trial 395(5)
    Appeal & Error 1008(1)
(d) 320

18 138 258 348 438 538 386 P.2d 249
Orville G. Gray, Plaintiff-Appellant, v. International Service Insurance
Company, Defendant-Appellee (Supreme Court of New Mexico Oct. 28, 1963)

EXERCISE 12. WEST'S REGIONAL REPORTERS   (CONTINUED)

(a) M/B: Gray v. International Service Insurance Co., 73 N.M. 158, 386 P.2d 249 (1963).
     LR: Gray v. International Serv. Ins. Co., 73 N.M. 158, 386 P.2d 249 (1963).
(b) Chavez and Robins (Appellant)
     Shaffer & Butt (Appellee)
(c) Insurance 146.7(1)
     Insurance 146.7(8)
(d) 252

19 139 259 349 439 539   98 A.2d 55
Herr v. Herr (Supreme Court of New Jersey June 22, 1953)
(a) M/B: Herr v. Herr, 13 N.J. 79, 98 A.2d 55 (1953).
(b) Ruback (Lum, Fairlie & Foster)   (Appellant)
     Ryan (Ryan & Saros)   (Appellee)
(c) Frauds, Statute of 4
     Frauds, Statute of 129(1)
(d) 58

20 140 260 350 440 540   384 P.2d 256
Saradan Hanberry and Travelers Insurance Company, a corporation, Plaintiffs-Appellees, v. A.P. Fitzgerald, George Anderman and P.P. Glasebrook d/b/a Albuquerque Bus Company, and Jessie W. Harris, Defendants-Appellants (Supreme Court of New Mexico Aug. 26, 1963)
(a) M/B: Hanberry v. Fitzgerald, 72 N.M. 383, 384 P.2d 256 (1963).
(b) Oldaker, Miller, Oldaker (Appellants)
     Ortega (Appellee)
     Rodey, Dickason, Sloan, Akin & Robb, Larrabee (Appellee)
(c) Appeal & Error 948
     Evidence 538
(d) 259

21 141 261 351 441 541   91 N.E.2d 401
Johnston v. City of East Moline (Supreme Court of Illinois March 22, 1950)
(a) M/B: Johnston v. City of East Moline, 405 Ill. 460, 91 N.E.2d 401 (1950).
     LR: Johnston v. City of E. Moline, 405 Ill. 460, 91 N.E.2d 401 (1950).
(b) Stewart & Glockhoff (Appellant)
     Eagle & Eagle (Appellee)
(c) Automobiles 258, 282
     Negligence 59
(d) 403

22 142 262 352 442 542   93 N.E.2d 5
Nahas v. George (153 Ohio St. 574 Supreme Court of Ohio May 31, 1950)
(a) M/B: Nahas v. George, 153 Ohio St. 574, 93 N.E.2d 5 (1950).
(b) Brouse, McDowell, May, Bierce & Wortman (Appellant)
     Slabaugh, Guinther & Pflueger and Schwartz (Appellee)
(c) Partnership 319
     Partnership 298, 319
(d) 7 (or 7-8)

23 143 263 353 443 543   90 N.E.2d 908
McHale et al. v. Treworgy et al. (Supreme Juicial Court of Massachusetts March 2, 1950)
(a) M/B: McHale v. Treworgy, 325 Mass. 381, 90 N.E.2d 908 (1950).
(b) Cassidy (Plaintiffs)
     Harvey (Defendants)
(c) Appeal & Error 1009(6)
     Taxation 770
(d) 910

24 144 264 354 444 544   96 N.E.2d 739
Burns v. Merritt Engineering Co. et al. (Court of Appeals of New York Jan. 18, 1951)
(a) M/B: Burns v. Merritt Engineering Co., 302 N.Y. 131, 96 N.E.2d 739 (1951).

EXERCISE 12. WEST'S REGIONAL REPORTERS   (CONTINUED)

      LR: Burns v. Merritt Eng'g Co., 302 N.Y. 131, 96 N.E.2d 739 (1951).
- (b) Thill and Windelberg (Appellants)
  Goldstein (Landy, Brown, and Wiedersum) (Respondent)
- (c) Master and Servant 29
  Workmen's Compensation 788
- (d) 740

25 145 265 355 445 545   95 N.E.2d 685
Trattar el al. v. Rausch (154 Ohio St. 286 Supreme Court of Ohio Dec. 6, 1950)
- (a) M/B: <u>Tratttar v. Rausch</u>, 154 Ohio St. 286, 95 N.E.2d 685 (1950).
- (b) Rausch (pro. per.) (optional--may be listed by the student)
  Griswold, Leeper, Miller & Corry (Appellees)
- (c) Easements 1
  Easements 1
- (d) 688

26 146 266 356 446 546   190 So. 2d 334
Ralph D. Clark, Petitioner, v. Western Knapp Engineering Company and the Florida Industrial Commission, Respondents (Supreme Court of Florida Sept. 28, 1966)
- (a) M/B: <u>Clark v. Western Knapp Engineering Co.</u>, 190 So. 2d 334 (Fla. 1966).
  LR: <u>Clark v. Western Knapp Eng'g Co.</u>, 190 So. 2d 334 (Fla. 1966).
- (b) Inman (Petitioner)
  Gurney, Gurney & Handley, Sparks, Mears, and Garner (Respondents)
- (c) Workmen's Compensation 1939
  Workmen's Compensation 858
- (d) 335

27 147 267 357 447 547   179 So. 2d 324
Joseph H. Wilson, Jr. v. Robert Lowe (Supreme Court of Alabama Oct. 21, 1965)
- (a) M/B: <u>Wilson v. Lowe</u>, 278 Ala. 578, 179 So. 2d 324 (1965).
- (b) Courtney (Appellant)
  Alonzo, Pelham, and Kennamer (Appellee)
- (c) Municipal Corporations 213
  Municipal Corporations 213
- (d) 325

28 148 268 358 448 548   44 So. 2d 748
Jones v. Mullin et al. (Supreme Court of Alabama March 2, 1950)
- (a) M/B: <u>Jones v. Mullin</u>, 253 Ala. 331, 44 So. 2d 748 (1950).
- (b) Patterson & Patterson (Appellant)
  Smith & Smith and Ferrell (Appellees)
- (c) Jury 131(6)
  Witnesses 270(2)
- (d) 749

29 149 269 359 449 549   43 So. 2d 763
Dowling v. Canal Bank & Trust Co. et al. (Supreme Court of Louisiana Nov. 7, 1949)
- (a) M/B: <u>Dowling v. Canal Bank & Trust Co.</u>, 216 La. 372, 43 So. 2d 763 (1949).
- (b) Dowling, Danna, Dowling (Appellant)
  Sehrt (State Bank Com'r) Graham (Amicus Curiae)
  Monroe, Toler, Monroe & Lemann, Chaffe, McCall, Toler & Phillips (Appellees)
  Schillin, Yarrut, Reuter, Yarrut & Fishman (Certain Intervenors and (Appellees)
- (c) Banks & Banking 77(2)
  Banks & Banking 63 1/2
- (d) 770

30 150 270 360 450 550   30 N.W.2d 484
Rudolph v. Davis et al. (Supreme Court of Iowa Jan. 12, 1948)
- (a) M/B: <u>Rudolph v. Davis</u>, 239 Iowa 372, 30 N.W.2d 484 (1948).
- (b) Jones, Cambridge & Carl (Appellants)
  Rudolph & Rudolph, Dalton & Dalton, and Richards (Appellee)
- (c) Forcible Entry & Detainer 2

EXERCISE 12. WEST'S REGIONAL REPORTERS   (CONTINUED)

    Forcible Entry & Detainer 6(2)
(d) 486

31 151 271 361 451 551   29 N.W.2d 704
LeBaron Homes, Inc. v. Pontiac Housing Fund, Inc., et al. (Supreme Court of Michigan Dec. 3, 1947)
(a) M/B: <u>Le Baron Homes, Inc. v. Pontiac Housing Fund, Inc.</u>, 319 Mich. 310, 29 N.W.2d 704 (1947).
    LR: Le Baron Homes, Inc. v. Pontiac Hous. Fund, Inc., 319 Mich. 310, 29 N.W.2d 704 (1947).
(b) Heitsch (Appellant)
    Howlett & Hartman (Appellee)
    Porritt (Appellee)
(c) Equity 239
    Specific Performance 57
(d) 706

32 152 272 362 452 552   28 N.W.2d 363
Holl v. City of Merrill et al. (Supreme Court of Wisconsin July 1, 1947)
(a) M/B: <u>Holl v. City of Merrill</u>, 251 Wis. 203, 28 N.W.2d 363 (1947).
(b) Nienow (Appellant)
    Wurster & Curtis (Appellant)
    Schnabel (Respondent)
(c) Counties 142
    Municipal Corporations 692
(d) 365

33 153 273 363 453 553   31 N.W.2d 170
Welch v. Chippewa Sales Co. (Supreme Court of Wisconsin Feb. 17, 1948)
(a) M/B: <u>Welch v. Chippewa Sales Co.</u>, 252 Wis. 166, 31 N.W.2d 170 (1948).
(b) Stafford & Stafford (Pfiffner, of counsel) (Appellant)
    McPhee (Respondent)
(c) Injunction 136(1)
    Specific Performance 68
(d) 171

34 154 274 364 454 554   63 P.2d 693
Cook v. Hunt (Supreme Court of Oklahoma Oct. 27, 1936)
(a) M/B: <u>Cook v. Hunt</u>, 178 Okla. 477, 63 P.2d 693 (1936).
(b) Tillman & Tillman, Johnson and McNeil (Plaintiff in Error)
    Cornett and Wilson (Defendant in Error)
(c) Negligence 2
    Weapons 18(1)
(d) 694 (<u>or</u> 694-95)

35 155 275 365 455 555   62 P.2d 445
Peoples Bank & Trust Co. v. L. Romano Engineering Corporation et al. (Supreme Court of Washington Nov. 18, 1936)
(a) M/B: <u>Peoples Bank & Trust Co. v. L. Romano Engineering Corp.</u>, 188 Wash. 290, 62 P.2d 445 (1936).
    LR: Peoples Bank & Trust Co. v. L. Romano Eng'g Corp., 188 Wash. 290, 62 P.2d 445 (1936).
(b) Macbride and Williams (Appellant)
    Kennett (Respondent)
(c) Jury 13(18)
    Evidence 441(9)
(d) 447

36 156 276 366 456 556   61 P.2d 559
Welch et al. v. Holland, Chairman of County Election Board, et al. (Supreme Court of Oklahoma Oct. 9, 1936)
(a) M/B: <u>Welch v. Holland</u>, 177 Okla. 585, 61 P.2d 559 (1936).
(b) Jennings (Petitioners)
    Williamson and Hansen (Respondents)
(c) Statutes 76(2), 94(1)
    Statutes 76(4), 101(1)
(d) 561

EXERCISE 12. WEST'S REGIONAL REPORTERS   (CONTINUED)

37 157 277 367 457 557   59 P.2d 771
Vahlberg, County Treasurer, v. Porter (Supreme Court of Oklahoma July 14, 1936)
  (a) M/B: Vahlberg v. Porter, 177 Okla. 380, 59 P.2d 771 (1936).
  (b) Morris (Co. Atty.) & Logsdon (Asst. Co. Atty.) (Plaintiff in error)
       Gumm (Defendant in error)
       Green, Hasse, Cruce, Satterfield, & Grigsby, Bleakmore, Barry, Farmer,
       and Rainey, Flynn & Green (Amici curiae)
  (c) Taxation 491
       Taxation 550
  (d) 772 (or 772-73 or 773)

38 158 278 368 458 558   131 P. 843
Health v. Seattle Taxicab Co. (Supreme Court of Washington April 28, 1913)
  (a) M/B: Health v. Seattle Taxicab Co., 73 Wash. 177, 131 P. 843 (1913).
  (b) Birghtman & Tennant (Appellant)
       Longfellow & Fitzpatrick (Respondent)
  (c) Appeal & Error 1066
       Municipal Corporations 703
  (d) 844

39 159 279 369 459 559   132 P. 1170
Kjellander v. Kjellander (Supreme Court of Kansas June 7, 1913)
  (a) M/B: Kjellander v. Kjellander, 90 Kan. 112, 132 P. 1170 (1913).
  (b) Pile and Sheppard, Sheppard & Sheppard (Appellant)
       Burton and Disch (Appellee)
  (c) Appeal and Error 1
       Divorce 182
  (d) 1171

40 160 280 370 460 560   133 P. 118
McElroy v. Whitney (Supreme Court of Idaho June 11, 1913)
  (a) M/B: McElroy v. Whitney, 24 Idaho 210, 133 P. 118 (1913).
       LR: McElroy v. Whitney, 24 Idaho 210, 133 P. 118 (1913).
  (b) Ruick and Oppenheim (Appellant)
       Martin & Martin and McElroy (Respondent)
  (c) Executors & Administrators 255
       Executors & Administrators 256
  (d) 118

41 161 281 371 461 561   134 P. 807
White v. Reservation Electric Co. (Supreme Court of Washington Aug. 26, 1913)
  (a) M/B: White v. Reservation Electric Co., 75 Wash. 139, 134 P. 807 (1913).
       LR: White v. Reservation Elec. Co., 75 Wash. 139, 134 P. 807 (1913).
  (b) Englehart & Rigg (Appellant)
       Lee and Snively (Respondent)
  (c) Electricity 19
       Electricity 14
  (d) 808

42 162 282 372 462 562   45 N.E.2d 280
Gleason v. Mann (Supreme Judicial Court of Massachusetts Nov. 30, 1942)
  (a) M/B: Gleason v. Mann, 312 Mass. 420, 45 N.E.2d 280 (1942).
  (b) Ryan & Tashjian (Plaintiff)
       Fairhurst (Defendant)
  (c) Contracts 138(6), 346(7) and Pleading 258(3)
       Contracts 138(6)
  (d) 282

43 163 283 373 463 563   42 N.E.2d 627
Albers et al. v. Lamson et al. (Supreme Court of Illinois June 11, 1942)
  (a) M/B: Albers v. Lamson, 380 Ill. 35, 42 N.E.2d 627 (1942).
  (b) Moses, Kennedy, Stein & Bachrach and McGrath & Copeland
       (Bachrach & Moses, and Birkett (Appellees)
  (c) Constitutional Law 47
       Commerce 8(1)

EXERCISE 12.   WEST'S REGIONAL REPORTERS   (CONTINUED)

   (d)   630

44 164 284 374 464 564   39 N.E.2d 734
Zaring et al. v. Zaring et al. (Supreme Court of Indiana Feb. 26, 1942)
(a) M/B: Zaring v. Zaring, 219 Ind. 514, 39 N.E.2d 734 (1942).
(b) Clippinger and Little (Appellants)
    Henning (Appellees)
(c) Judges 25(1)
    Judges 25(1)
(d) 736

45 165 285 375 465 565   33 N.E.2d 282
Turner et al. v. United Mineral Lands Corporation et al. (Supreme Judicial Court of Massachusetts April 3, 1941)
(a) M/B: Turner v. United Mineral Lands Corp., 308 Mass. 531, 33 N.E.2d 282 (1941).
(b) Abrams, Palais, & Hinckley (Plaintiffs)
    Hall, Jones, & Gerould (Defendants)
(c) Corporations 665(1)
    Appeal and error 694(1)
(d) 284 (or 284-86)

46 166 286 376 466 566   36 N.E.2d 760
School City of East Chicago v. Sigler (Supreme Court of Indiana Oct. 7, 1941)
(a) M/B: School City v. Sigler, 219 Ind. 9, 36 N.E.2d 760 (1941).
(b) Twyman (Appellant)
    Lyddick & Thiel (Appellee)
(c) Appeal & Error 327(7)
    School & School Districts 55
(d) 762

47 167 287 377 467 567   236 A.2d 737
Albert G. Levy et al. v. Montgomery County et al. (Court of Appeals of Maryland Jan. 4, 1968)
(a) M/B: Levy v. Montgomery County, 248 Md. 346, 236 A.2d 767 (1968).
(b) Levy (in pro. per.)
    Linowes (Linowes & Blocher, Metz, Covington & Burling, and Hogan & Hartson on the brief) (Appellee)
    Cahoon (Malone on the brief) (Appellee)
(c) Zoning 539
    Zoning 539
(d) 739

48 168 288 378 468 568   234 A.2d 334
National Grange Mutual Insurance Company v. Wellington M. Churchill, James M. Cleary, Mitchell Walters, Natalle Walters, Al-Warren Ford, Inc. (Supreme Court of Vermont Oct. 3, 1967)
(a) M/B: National Grange Mutual Insurance Co. v. Churchill, 126 Vt. 428, 234 A.2d 334 (1967).
    LR: National Grange Mut. Ins. Co. v. Churchill, 126 Vt. 428, 234 A.2d 334 (1967).
(b) Webber & Costello (Plaintiff)
    Feen (Defendants)
(c) Evidence 264
    Insurance 437.1(5)
(d) 336

49 169 289 379 469 569   233 A.2d 828
New Hampshire Water Resources Board v. Lebanon Sand & Gravel, Inc. (Supreme Court of New Hampshire Oct. 6, 1967)
(a) M/B: New Hampshire Water Resources Board v. Lebanon Sand & Gravel, Inc., 108 N.H. 254, 233 A.2d 828 (1967).
    LR: New Hampshire Water Resources Bd. v. Lebanon Sand & Gravel, Inc., 108 N.H. 254, 233 A.2d 828 (1967).
(b) Pappagianis and Shapiro (Plaintiff)
    Upton, Sanders & Upton (Defendant)
(c) Navigable Waters 36(2)

EXERCISE 12. WEST'S REGIONAL REPORTERS   (CONTINUED)

      Navigable Waters 37(4)
(d)   831

50 170 290 380 470 570   231 A.2d 740
Nick D. Lardas, Appellant, Constance Lardas, James Lardas, Evangeline Lardas, Constantin Lardas and Sophie Lardas v. Underwriters Insurance Company, the Home Insurance Company, National Union Fire Insurance Company, Fidelity-Phenix Fire Insurance Company (Supreme Court of Pennsylvania June 29, 1967)
(a)   M/B: <u>Lardas v. Underwriters Insurance Co.</u>, 426 Pa. 47, 231 A.2d 740 (1967).
      LR: Lardas v. Underwriters Ins. Co., 426 Pa. 47, 231 A.2d 740 (1967).
(b)   Shorall, Shorall, Royston, Robb, Leonard, Edgecombe, Miller & Shorall (Appellant)
      Graffam, White, Jones & Gregg (Appellees)
(c)   Insurance 612(1), 622(2)
      Insurance 622(4)
(d)   742

51 171 291 381 471 571   237 A.2d 320
Peloso, Inc. v. George Peloso (Supreme Court of Rhode Island Jan. 17, 1968)
(a)   M/B: <u>Peloso, Inc. v. Peloso</u>, 103 R.I. 294, 237 A.2d 320 (1968).
(b)   Keenan, Rice & Dolan, Rice (Petitioner)
      Gunning & LaFazia, LaFazia (Respondent)
(c)   Workmen's Compensation 840
      Workmen's Compensation 803
(d)   323

52 172 292 382 472 572   239 A.2d 640
Dorothy S. MacDonald v. Edward P. Manning, Trustee et al. (Supreme Court of Rhode Island March 11, 1968)
(a)   M/B: <u>MacDonald v. Manning</u>, 103 R.I. 538, 239 A.2d 640 (1968).
(b)   Jordon, Hanson & Curran (Curran, of counsel) (Plaintiff)
      West, DeSimone, Allen (Defendants)
      Charleson & Carberry (guardian ad litem) Brill (persons in military service)
(c)   Wills 440, 442
      Charities 6
(d)   644

53 173 293 383 473 573   240 A.2d 60
Town of Plainfield v. Vernon A. Hood et al. (Supreme Court of New Hampshire March 29, 1968)
(a)   M/B: <u>Town of Plaintfield v. Hood</u>, 108 N.H. 502, 240 A.2d 60 (1968).
(b)   Nolin, Upton, Sanders & Upton, Upton (Plaintiff)
      Sulloway, Hollis, Godfrey & Soden, and Ransmeier (Amicus Curiae)
      Spanos & Spanos, Shulins & Duncan, Spanos, and Duncan (Defendants)
(c)   Towns 15, 28
      Nunicipal Corporations 61
(d)   63

54 175 294 384 474 574   146 A.2d 281
Estate of John William Richley, also known as J.W. Richley, Late of the City of York, York County, Pennsylvania, Deceased. Appeal of John William Richley Snyder and June F. Snyder (Supreme Court of Pennsylvania Nov. 25, 1958)
(a)   M/B: <u>Estate of Richley</u>, 394 Pa. 188, 146 A.2d 281 (1958).
(b)   Stetler and Gribben (Appellants)
      Ports, Fluhrer, Gerber, and Shelley (Appellee)
      Stock & Leader, Leader (Appellee)
      Markowitz & Kagen, Griffith, Garber (Appellee)
(c)   Gifts 47(2), 49(4)
      Gifts 49(4)
(d)   282

55 175 295 385 475 575   92 A.2d 222
Olan Mills, Inc. v. City of Sharon et al. (371 Pa. 609 Supreme Court of Pennsylvania Nov. 18, 1952)
(a)   <u>Olan Mills v. City of Sharon</u>, 371 Pa. 609, 92 A.2d 222 (1952).

EXERCISE 12. WEST'S REGIONAL REPORTERS   (CONTINUED)

(b) Cusick, Garvey, & Wiesen, Cusick & Madden (Appellant)
     Routman (City Sol.) (Appellee)
(c) Licenses 15(2)
     Licenses 7(1)
(d) 223

56 176 296 386 476 576 93 A.2d 349
Whippany Paperboard Co., Inc. v. Local No. 301, United Paperworkers of America, C.I.O., et al. (Supreme Court of New Jersey Dec. 22, 1952)
(a) M/B: Whippany Paperboard Co. v. Local No. 301, United Paperworkers, 11 N.J. 153, 93 A.2d 349 (1952).
(b) Oxfeld, Rothbard, Harris & Oxfeld, Rothbard (of counsel), Goldberger
     (on the brief) (Appellants)
     Handler, Lombardino and Berlin (cn the brief) (Respondent)
(c) Contempt 40
     Contempt 20
(d) 355

57 177 297 387 477 577 94 A.2d 385
Klein v. Sunbeam Corp. (Supreme Court of Delaware Dec. 31, 1952)
(a) M/B: Klein v. Sunbeam Corp., 47 Del. 526, 94 A.2d 385 (1952).
(b) Van Brundt & Snellenberg (of Killoran & Van Brunt) (Appellant)
     Anderson & Latchum (of Berl, Potter & Anderson) (Appellee)
(c) Corporations 662
     Corporations 642(4 1M/B:2)
(d) 388

58 178 298 388 478 578 95 A.2d 689
Cratty v. Samuel Aceto & Co. (Supreme Judicial Court of Maine March 17, 1953)
(a) M/B: Cratty v. Samuel Aceto & Co., 148 Me. 453, 95 A.2d 689 (1953).
(b) Cratty & Cratty (Plaintiff)
     Locke, Campbell, Reid & Hebert (Defendant)
(c) Pleading 420(2)
     Pleading 416
(d) 690

59 179 299 389 479 579 96 A.2d 246
Linkins v. State (Court of Appeals of Maryland April 17, 1953)
(a) M/B: Linkins v. State, 202 Md. 212, 96 A.2d 246 (1953).
(b) Kuhn (Appellant)
     Proctor (Asst. Atty. Gen.), Hollyday, Rollins (Atty. Gen. on brief)
     (Appellee)
(c) Criminal Law 1167(2)
     Robbery 19
(d) 247 (or 247-49)

60 180 300 390 480 580 97 A.2d 540
Balavich v. Yarnish et ux. (Supreme Judicial Court of Maine June 3, 1953)
(a) M/B: Balavich v. Yarnish, 149 Me. 1, 97 A.2d 540 (1953).
(b) Jacobson & Jacobson (Plaintiff)
     Berman & Berman (Defendant)
(c) New Trial 56
     New Trial 49
(d) 542

61 181 201 391 481 581 36 N.W.2d 507
O'Connor v. Burns, Potter & Co. (Supreme Court of Nebraska March 18, 1949)
(a) M/B: O'Connor v. Burns, Potter & Co., 151 Neb. 9, 36 N.W.2d 507 (1949).
(b) Ritchie (Appellant)
     Kennedy, Holland, DeLacy & Svoboda (Appellee)
(c) Trusts 1
     Trusts 30 1M/B:2(1)
(d) 517

62 182 202 392 482 582 37 N.W.2d 473
State ex rel. Frederick v.Zimmerman et al. (254 Wis. 600 Supreme Court of Wisconsin April 26, 1949)

EXERCISE 12.   WEST'S REGIONAL REPORTERS   (CONTINUED)

(a)   M/B: State ex rel. Frederick v. Zimmerman, 254 Wis. 600, 37 N.W.2d 473 (1949).
(b)   Callahan & Arnold and Grady (Plaintiff)
      Cannon & Meister and Meister (Defendant Gehl)
      Bender (Defendant Watson)
      La France, Baumblatt, Konnak and Whaley (Defendant Goodland)
      Fairchild (Atty. Gen.) and Honeck (Deputy Atty. Gen.) (for Zimmerman)
      Fisher, Reinholdt & Peickert (for Doudna)
      Corrigan, Lines, Spooner & Quarles (Quarles and Mann, of counsel) (Amicus curiae)
(c)   Constitutional law 24
      Constitutional law 19, 20
(d)   479

63 183 203 393 483 583   38 N.W.2d 863
Miller et ux. v. National Bank of Detroit et al. (Supreme Court of Michigan Sept. 8, 1949)
(a)   M/B: Miller v. National Bank, 325 Mich. 395, 38 N.W.2d 863 (1949).
(b)   Patterson and Patterson (Plaintiffs-Appellees)
      Dickinson, Wright, Davis, McKean & Cudlip (Rogers, of counsel)
      Phillips (Trustee, in pro per.)   (Defendant-Appellant)
      Pence - (Miller and others)
(c)   Trusts 57
      Trusts 57
(d)   866

64 184 204 394 484 584   39 N.W.2d 468
Hunter v. Neuville et al. (Supreme Court of Wisconsin Oct. 11, 1949)
(a)   M/B: Hunter v. Neuville, 255 Wis. 423, 39 N.W.2d 468 (1949).
(b)   O'Melia & Kay (Appellant)
      DeBardeleben and Debardeleben (of counsel) (Respondent)
(c)   Quieting title 10(2)
      Quieting title 10(2)
(d)   472

65 185 205 395 485 585   40 N.W.2d 252
Krepcik v. Interstate Transit Lines (152 Neb. 39 Supreme Court of Nebraska Dec. 12, 1949)
(a)   M/B: Krepcik v. Interstate Transit Lines, 152 Neb. 39, 40 N.W.2d 252 (1949).
(b)   Padley, Beatty, Clarke, Murphy & Morgan (Appellant)
      Hamer, Hamer, Holdrege, Matthai, and McIntosh (Appellee)
Note: Gothenberg and North Platte are cities in Nebraska.

66 186 206 396 486 586   201 P. 1029
Pickering v. Industrial Commission of Utah (Supreme Court of Utah Nov. 7, 1921)
(a)   M/B: Pickering v. Industrial Commission, 59 Utah 35, 201 P. 1029 (1921).
      LR: Pickering v. Industrial Comm'n, 59 Utah 35, 201 P. 1029 (1921).
(b)   Pierce, Critchlow & Marr (Plaintiff)
      Cluff & Robinson (Defendant)
(c)   Master & Servant 369
      Constitutional Law 70(3)
(d)   1030

67 187 207 397 487 587   202 P. 316
Sanditen v. Allied Refining Co. (Supreme Court of Oklahoma Nov. 29, 1921)
(a)   M/B: Sanditen v. Allied Refining Co., 84 Okla. 47, 202 P. 316 (1921).
      LR: Sanditen v. Allied Ref. Co., 84 Okla. 47, 202 P. 316 (1921).
(b)   Dennis (Plaintiff in Error)
      McCrory & Shackelford (Defendant in Error)
(c)   Set-off and counterclaim 52(1)
      Accord and satisfaction 10(1)
(d)   317

68 188 208 398 488 588   203 P. 920
Grolier Society v. Foster (Supreme Court of Kansas Jan. 7, 1922)

EXERCISE 12. WEST'S REGIONAL REPORTERS   (CONTINUED)
(a) M/B: Grolier Society v. Foster, 110 Kan. 306, 203 P. 920 (1922).
     LR: Grolier Soc'y v. Foster, 110 Kan. 306, 203 P. 920 (1922).
(b) Courtright & Clark (Appellant)
     Billings (Appellee)
(c) Parties 76(5)
     Parties 75(7)
(d) 921

69 189 209 399 489 589   204 P. 754
Harris v. United States Mexico Oil Co. (Supreme Court of Kansas Feb. 11, 1922)
(a) M/B: Harris v. United States Mexico Oil Co., 110 Kan. 532, 204 P. 754 (1922).
     LR: Harris v. United States Mex. Oil Co., 110 Kan. 532, 204 P. 754 (1922).
(b) Fry & Jackson (Appellant)
     Sheppard & Sheppard (Appellee)
(c) Corporations 28(1)
     Corporations 668(14)
(d) 757

70 190 210 400 490 590   206 P. 587
Yuma County v. Fidelity Title Guaranty Co. (Supreme Court of Arizona May 6, 1922)
(a) M/B: Yuma County v. Fidelity Title Guaranty Co., 24 Ariz. 33, 206 P. 587 (1922).
     LR: Yuma County v. Fidelity Title Guar. Co., 24 Ariz. 33, 206 P. 587 (1922).
(b) Ryan & Wupperman (Appellant)
     Coleman & Molloy (Appellee)
(c) District and prosecuting attorneys 3(5), 5(4)
     District and prosecuting attorneys 3(5), 5(6)
(d) 588

71 191 211 301 491 591   103 N.E.2d 527
Taber Crisp, Respondent, v. Checker Cab Co., a Wis. corporation, Appellant (10 Wis.2d 603 Supreme Court of Wisconsin June 7, 1960)
(a) M/B: Crisp v. Checker Cab Co., 10 Wis. 2d 603, 103 N.E.2d 527 (1960).
(b) Kivett & Kasdorf (Appellant) Clack and Swietlik (of counsel)
     Eisenberg & Kletzke (Respondent) Bernard (of counsel)
(c) Torts 27
     Judgment 181(33)
(d) 530

72 192 212 302 492 592   104 N.E.2d 669
Pokraka et al. v. Lummus Co. (Supreme Court of Indiana March 27, 1952)
(a) M/B: Pokraka v. Lummus Co., 230 Ind. 523, 104 N.E.2d 669 (1952).
(b) Sullivan (Appellants)
     Call, Gary, Riley, Reed, Murphy & McAtee, McAtee (Appellee)
(c) Appeal and Error 882(1)
     Appeal and Error 882(5)
(d) 671

73 193 213 303 493 593   105 N.E.2d 99
Chesher v. United States Casualty Co. (Court of Appeals of New York March 14, 1952)
(a) M/B: Chesher v. United States Casualty Co., 303 N.Y. 589, 105 N.E.2d 99 (1952).
(b) Lines and Osborn (Appellant)
     Maloney (Respondent)
(c) Insurance 435.8
     Insurance 435.8
(d) 100

74 194 214 304 494 594   106 N.E.2d 350
Ellman et al. v. De Ruiter (Supreme Court of Illinois May 22, 1952)
(a) M/B: Ellman v. De Ruiter, 412 Ill. 285, 106 N.E.2d 350 (1952).
(b) Sonnenschein, Berkson, Lautmann, Levinson & Morse (Ferguson, of

EXERCISE 12. WEST'S REGIONAL REPORTERS   (CONTINUED)

        counsel) (Appellant)
        Gomberg (Missner, of counsel) (Appellees)
(c)   Judgment 334
        Judgment 334
(d)   353

75 195 215 305 495 595   107 N.E.2d 3
Property Owners, Inc. et al. v. City of Anderson et al. (Supreme Court of Indiana July 23, 1952)
(a)   M/B: <u>Property Owners, Inc. v. City of Anderson</u>, 231 Ind. 78, 107 N.E.2d 3 (1952).
(b)   Jeffrey, Jeffrey, and DeArmond (Appellants)
        O'Neill (Welsh and Jones, of counsel)   (Appellees)
(c)   Appeal and Error 750(7)
        Appeal and Error 736
(d)   5

76 196 216 306 496 596   21 So. 2d 418
Emery et al. v. Orleans Levee Board. In re Emery et al. (Supreme Court of Louisiana Jan. 15, 1945)
(a)   M/B: <u>Emery v. Orleans Levee Board</u>, 207 La. 386, 21 So. 2d 418 (1945).
        LR: Emery v. Orleans Levee Bd., 207 La. 386, 21 So. 2d 418 (1945).
(b)   Richardson (Applicants)
        Darden & Wilkinson (Respondent)
(c)   Levees and flood control 13 1M/B:2
        Dedication 16(1)
(d)   421

77 197 217 307 497 597   22 So. 2d 417
Caudle v. Birmingham Electric Co. (Supreme Court of Alabama May 31, 1945)
(a)   M/B: <u>Caudle v. Birmingham Electric Co.</u>, 247 Ala. 34, 22 So. 2d 417 (1945).
        LR: Caudle v. Birmingham Elec. Co., 247 Ala. 34, 22 So. 2d 417 (1945).
(b)   Denson (Appellant)
        Lange, Simpson, Brantley & Robinson (Appellee)
(c)   Negligence 61(1)
        Negligence 61(2)
(d)   420

78 198 218 308 498 598   8 So. 2d 689
Texas Co. v. Fontenot, Director of Revenue (Supreme Court of Louisiana May 25, 1942)
(a)   M/B: <u>Texas Co. v. Fontenot</u>, 200 La. 753, 8 So. 2d 689 (1942).
(b)   Blish and Flory (Plaintiff-Appellant)
        Stanley, Smullin, and Gremillion (Defendant-Appellee)
(c)   Licenses 28, 29
        Licenses 29; Mines and minerals 79(1)
(d)   692

79 199 219 309 499 599   24 So. 2d 525
In re Ringling's Estate (Supreme Court of Florida, Division B Jan. 22, 1946)
(a)   M/B: <u>In re Ringling's Estate</u>, 156 Fla. 810, 24 So. 2d 525 (1946).
        LR: In re Ringling's Estate, 156 Fla. 810, 24 So. 2d 525 (1946).
(b)   Burket, Bisco, Mabry, Reaves, Carlton, Anderson & Fields (Petitioners)
        Kirk, Reeves, Reeves, Allen & Johnson (Respondent)
(c)   Appeal and Error 627(1)
        Appeal and Error 627(1)
(d)   525

80 200 220 310 500 600   25 So. 2d 625
Hemphill v. Tremont Lumber Co. (209 La. 885 Supreme Court of Louisiana Feb. 11, 1946)
(a)   M/B: <u>Hemphill v. Tremont Lumber Co.</u>, 209 La. 885, 25 So. 2d 625 (1946).
(b)   Long (Plaintiff, Appellant, Relator)
        Grisham, Davis & Leigh (Defendant)
(c)   Workmen's compensation 1939
        Workmen's compensation 1571

EXERCISE 12. WEST'S REGIONAL REPORTERS   (CONTINUED)

(d)   627 (or 627-29)

81 101 221 311 401 501   343 S.W.2d 869
City of Memphis et al. v. Sherwood Building Corporation et al. (Supreme Court
of Tennessee Jan. 19, 1961)
(a)   M/B: City of Memphis v. Sherwood Building Corp., 208 Tenn. 17, 343
S.W.2d 869 (1961).
      LR: City of Memphis v. Sherwood Bldg. Corp., 208 Tenn. 17, 343 S.W.2d
869 (1961).
(b)   Gianotti & Bartusch (Petitioners)
      Laughlin, Watson & Creson, Farnsworth, Burch, Porter,
      Johnson & Brown (Respondents)
(c)   Zoning 574
      Certiorari 64(1), 68
(d)   871

82 102 222 312 402 502   344 S.W.2d 153
Ex parte R.P. Davis, Jr. (Supreme Court of Texas Feb. 22, 1961)
(a)   M/B: Ex parte Davis, 161 Tex. 561, 344 S.W.2d 153 (1961).
      LR: Ex parte Davis, 161 Tex. 561, 344 S.W.2d 153 (1961).
(b)   Mayfield & Atkins (Relator)
      Moses & Truett, McKinney, Sneed & Vine, Troutman with
      Sneed & Vine (Respondent)
(c)   Habeas Corpus 29
      Divorce 311
(d)   155

83 103 223 313 403 503   345 S.W.2d 170
George L. Winger, Trustee, Respondent, v. General American Life Insurance
Company, Appellant (Supreme Court of Missouri, Division No. 1 Feb. 13, 1961)
(a)   M/B: Winger v. General American Life Insurance Co., 345 S.W.2d 170 (Mo.
1961).
      LR: Winger v. General Am. Life Ins. Co., 345 S.W.2d 170 (Mo. 1961).
(b)   Osdol, Magruder, Terrell, Hess, Van Osdol & Magruder,
      (Aschemeyer, of counsel) (Appellant)
      Barnett & Skeer, Skeet, Barnett (Respondent)
(c)   Appeal and Error 927(7), 989
      Insurance 378(1), 389(9), 392(1)
(d)   179

84 104 224 314 404 504   346 S.W.2d 3
State Property & Buildings Commission of the Commonwealth of Kentucky et al.,
Appellants, v. William H. Hays et al., Appellees (Court of Appeals of Kentucky
April 28, 1961)
(a)   M/B: State Property & Buildings Commission v. Hays, 346 S.W.2d 3 (Ky.
1961).
      LR: State Property & Bldgs. Comm'n v. Hays, 346 S.W.2d 3 (Ky. 1961).
(b)   Rubin, Breckinridge, McTyeire (Appellants)
      Jackson, Seiller (Appellees)
(c)   Counties 150(2)
      Statutes 120(4)
(d)   6

85 105 225 315 405 505   347 S.W.2d 233
Farrell E. Breshears, Eva M. Breshears, Edwin Breshears, Helen Breshears, Carl
Williams, Emma Williams, W. C. Williams, Gertrude E. Williams, Clarence
Powell, Ruby Shin, Clarence Crabtree, Verda May Crabtree, W. A. Thomas, Nora
Lay, Leo Tatum, William F. Watkins, Eva Watkins, Bob Shin, Bill Ed Moree, J.
W. Shockmann, Jane Shockmann, Respondents, v. Union Electric Company of
Missouri, a Corporation, Appellant, and Ada A. Stephens, Rettie Jones, Flora
Jones, Fred T. Harris, Claude Kays, Vesta Kays, Wilbur Boring, Lucile Boring,
Defendants (Supreme Court of Missouri June 12, 1961)
(a)   M/B: Breshears v. Union Electric Co., 347 S.W.2d 233 (Mo. 1961).
      LR: Breshears v. Union Elec. Co., 347 S.W.2d 233 (Mo. 1961).
(b)   Salveter, Kay (Woodbridge, of counsel) (Appellant)
      Miller, Brady, Junge, Neff (Repondents)
(c)   Trial 253(7)

EXERCISE 12. WEST'S REGIONAL REPORTERS   (CONTINUED)

      Trial 253(7)
(d)   237

86 106 226 316 406 506   348 S.W.2d 930
Ruby Mullikin, Administratrix of the Estate of Jacob Albert Demaree, Appellant, v. Jewish Hospital Association of Louisville, Kentucky, Appellee (Court of Appeals of Kentucky May 5, 1961)
(a)   M/B: <u>Mullikin v. Jewish Hospital Association</u>, 348 S.W.2d 930 (Ky. 1961).
      LR: Mullikin v. Jewish Hosp. Ass'n, 348 S.W.2d 930 (Ky. 1961).
(b)   Karem, Karem & Karem (Appellant)
      Dinning, McElwain, Dinning, Clarke & Winstead (Appellee)
(c)   Charities 45(2)
      Charities 45(2)
(d)   935

87 107 227 317 407 507   349 S.W.2d 416
Charles Parrinello, (Plaintiff) Respondent, v. Rulo Investment Company, Inc., (Defendant) Appellant (St. Louis Court of Appeals. Missouri. Sept. 19, 1961)
(a)   M/B: <u>Parrinello v. Rulo Investment Co.</u>, 349 S.W.2d 416 (Mo. Ct. App. 1961).
      LR: Parrinello v. Rulo Inv. Co., 349 S.W.2d 416 (Mo. Ct. App. 1961).
(b)   Heege & Heege (Appellant)
      Feigenbaum & Librach (Respondent)
(c)   Damages 216(3)
      Damages 216(3)
(d)   420

88 108 228 318 408 508   350 S.W.2d 446
Percy Sloss, (Plaintiff) Respondent, v. Farmers Mutual Automobile Insurance Company, (Defendant) Appellant (St. Louis Court of Appeals. Missouri. Oct. 17, 1961)
(a)   M/B: <u>Sloss v. Farmers Mutual Automobile Insurance Co.</u>, 350 S.W.2d 446 (Mo. Ct. App. 1961).
      LR: Sloss v. Farmers Mut. Auto. Ins. Co., 350 S.W.2d 446 (Mo. Ct. App. 1961).
(b)   McClintock & Medley, McClintock (Appellant)
      Carr (Respondent)
(c)   Reformation of Instruments 1
      Insurance 162
(d)   451

89 109 229 319 409 509   132 S.E.2d 263
First National Bank of Atlanta, Ex'r. v. State Highway Department of Georgia (Supreme Court of Georgia May 29, 1963)
(a)   M/B: <u>First National Bank v. State Highway Department</u>, 219 Ga. 144, 132 S.E.2d 263 (1963).
      LR: First Nat'l Bank v. State Highway Dep't, 219 Ga. 144, 132 S.E.2d 263 (1963).
(b)   Boykin (Plaintiff in Error)
      Cook, Goode, Summerour, Wiggins (Defendant in Error)
(c)   Eminent Domain 243(2)
      Constitutional Law 46(2)
(d)   266

90 110 230 320 410 510   133 S.E.2d 122
Neil F. Coker, Appellant, v. Nationwide Mutual Insurance Company, Respondent (Supreme Court of South Carolina Oct. 30, 1963)
(a)   M/B: <u>Coker v. Nationwide Mutual Insurance Co.</u>, 243 S.C. 170, 133 S.E.2d 122 (1963).
      LR: Coker v. Nationwide Mut. Ins. Co., 243 S.C. 170, 133 S.E.2d 122 (1963).
(b)   Rogers & Riggs (Appellant)
      Richardson & James (Respondent)
(c)   Pleading 22
      Municipal Corporations 742(1, 4)
(d)   124

EXERCISE 12. WEST'S REGIONAL REPORTERS   (CONTINUED)

91 111 231 321 411 511   134 S.E.2d 889
William Delardas, who sues, etc. v. Morgantown Water Commission et al.
(Supreme Coourt of Appeals of West Virginia March 3, 1964)
(a) M/B: Delardas v. Morgantwon Water Commission, 148 W. Va. 318, 134 S.E.2d 889 (1964).
     LR: Delardas v. Morgantwon Water Comm'n, 148 W. Va. 318, 134 S.E.2d 889 (1964).
(b) Cox (Plaintiff in Error)
     Jaco, Magro (Defendants in Error)
(c) Appeal and Error 23
     Appeal and Error 78(3)
(d) 890

92 112 232 322 412 512   135 S.E.2d 205
Foreman Manufacturing Comapny, Inc. v. W. A. Johnson, Commissioner of Revenue of North Carolina (Supreme Court of North Carolina March 25, 1964)
(a) M/B: Foreman Manufacturing Co. v. Johnson, 261 N.C. 504, 135 S.E.2d 205 (1964).
     LR: Foreman Mfg. Co. v. Johnson, 261 N.C. 504, 135 S.E.2d 205 (1964).
(b) Hall (Plaintiff-Appellee)
     Bruton, Barham, and Brady (Defendant-Appellant)
(c) Taxation 995
     Corporations 60
(d) 207

93 113 233 323 413 513   137 S.E.2d 319
T. B. McCarroll v. First Investment Company (Court of Appeals of Gerogia, Division No. 3 May 21, 1964)
(a) M/B: McCarroll v. First Investment Co., 109 Ga. App. 748, 137 S.E.2d 319 (1964).
     LR: McCarroll v. First Inv. Co., 109 Ga. App. 748, 137 S.E.2d 319 (1964).
(b) Newton (Plaintiff in Error)
     Lewis, Wylly & Javetz, Lewis (Defendant in Error)
(c) Bills and Notes 396
     Evidence 423(6)
(d) 320

94 114 234 324 414 514   136 S.E.2d 404
Bremen Products Company v. Ledbetter-Johnson Company et al. (Court of Appeals of Georgia, Division No. 2 April 25, 1964)
(a) M/B: Bremen Products Co. v. Ledbetter-Johnson Co., 109 Ga. App. 573, 136 S.E.2d 404 (1964).
     LR: Bremen Prods. Co. v. Ledbetter-Johnson Co., 109 Ga. App. 573, 136 S.E.2d 404 (1964).
(b) Roberts (Plaintiff in Error)
     Tisinger, Tisinger, Gilbert (Defendants in Error)
(c) Counties 129
     Counties 129
(d) 406

95 115 235 325 415 515   160 A.2d 694
Lenore Aneva Johnson, Administratrix of the Estate of Albert Leroy Johnson, Deceased, Appellant, v. Pennsylvania Railroad Company (Supreme Court of Pennsylvania May 4, 1960)
(a) M/B: Johnson v. Pennsylvania Railroad, 399 Pa. 436, 160 A.2d 694 (1960).
     LR: Johnson v. Pennsylvania R.R., 399 Pa. 436, 160 A.2d 694 (1960).
(b) House, Suckling (Appellant)
     Smith, Best & Horn, Smith, Golden (Appellee)
(c) Railroads 350(22)
     Railroads 328(1)
(d) 697

96 116 236 326 416 516   161 A.2d 843
Aetna Casualty & Surety Co. v. Eastern Trust & Banking Co. (Supreme Judicial Court of Maine May 17, 1960)

EXERCISE 12.   WEST'S REGIONAL REPORTERS   (CONTINUED)

(a) M/B: Aetna Casualty & Surety Co. v. Eastern Trust & Banking Co., 156 Me. 87, 161 A.2d 843 (1960).
    LR: Aetna Casualty & Sur. Co. v. Eastern Trust & Banking Co., 156 Me. 87, 161 A.2d 843 (1960).
(b) Locke, Campbell, Reid & Hebert (Plaintiff)
    Mitchell & Ballou (Defendant)
(c) Appeal and Error 893(2)
    Appeal and Error 1009(1), 1122(2)
(d) 845

97 117 237 327 417 517   162 A.2d 854
Gertrude Kulp Baesler, Individually and as Guardian ad litem of Bernard Kulp, Plaintiffs-Appellants, v. Globe Indemnity Co., a corporation of the State of New York, authorized to do business in New Jersey, Defendant-Respondent (Supreme Court of New Jersey June 28, 1960)
(a) M/B: Baesler v. Globe Indemnity Co., 33 N.J. 148, 162 A.2d 853 (1960).
    LR: Baesler v. Globe Indem. Co., 33 N.J. 148, 162 A.2d 853 (1960).
(b) Hull (Plaintiffs-Appellants)
    Doan (Stalter & Dines, on the brief) (Defendant-Respondent)
(c) Insurance 435.11
    Insurance 435.11
(d) 856

98 118 238 328 418 518   83 A.2d 355
Rapp v. Public Service Coordinated Transport, Inc. (Superior Court of New Jersey Appellate Division Sept. 11, 1951)
(a) M/B: Rapp v. Public Service Coordinated Transport, 15 N.J. Super. 305, 83 A.2d 355 (App. Div. 1951).
    LR: Rapp v. Public Serv. Coordinated Transp., 15 N.J. Super. 305, 83 A.2d 355 (App. Div. 1951).
(b) Rooney (Plaintiff-Respondent)
    Kirby and Freggens (Defendant-Appellant)
(c) Evidence 586(3)
    Electricity 19(12)
(d) 358

99 119 239 329 419 519   84 A.2d 511
In re Minichello's Estate (Supreme Court of Pennsylvania, Nov. 27, 1951)
(a) M/B: In re Minichello's Estate, 368 Pa. 639, 84 A.2d 511 (1951).
    LR: In re Minichello's Estate, 368 Pa. 639, 84 A.2d 511 (1951).
(b) Burke and James (Appellant)
    Carrozza (Lib. Nat'l Bank)
    Jones and Hyman (Jennie Minichello)
    Berger and Thalenfeld (Louis Minichello)
(c) Executors and Administrators 158
    Executors and Administrators 158
(d) 513

100 120 240 330 420 520   85 A.2d 102
Dickerson v. Dickerson Overseas Co. et al. (369 Pa. 244 Supreme Court of Pennsylvania Jan. 7, 1952)
(a) M/B: Dickerson v. Dickerson Overseas Co. 369 Pa. 244, 85 A.2d 102 (1952).
(b) Hannum, 3rd, Bonsall & Evans, Bayard & Frick (Appellants)
    Stevens, Stradley, Ronon, Stevens & Young, Goffman, Wolf, and Wolf, Block, Schorr, & Solis-Cohen (Appellee)
(c) Set-Off and Counterclaim 41
    Set-Off and Counterclaim 41
(d) 104

LIBRARY EXERCISE 13. CALIFORNIA REPORTER.

INSTRUCTOR'S NOTE: Using the "Table of Statutes Construed," which lists all statutes interpreted by cases reported in the volume, the students are required to find the case in the designated volume of West's California Reporter that construes the California Code provision listed below. For their answer, they are required to cite the case using the Table of Cases volumes accompanying West's California Digest or Pacific Digest to find parallel citations. If the appropriate Table of Cases volume is unavailable, they are to use Shepard's California Reporter Citations. If the California Reporter volume was bound without including the "Table of Statutes Construed," students are to check a duplicate copy; if the Table cannot be located, the students are to complete a different problem number.

1 157 240 329 411 516   Cal. Rptr. Vol. # 1   Bus. & Prof. § 24200(e)
Albert Vallerga et al., Appellants, v. Department of Alcoholic Beverage Control et al., Respondents (Dec. 23, 1959)
M/B: Vallerga v. Department of Alcoholic Beverage Control, 53 Cal. 2d 313, 347 P.2d 909, 1 Cal. Rptr. 494 (1959).

2 158 241 330 412 517   Cal. Rptr. Vol. # 2   Civ. Proc. § 32
Paul De Vries, Plaintiff and Respondent, v. James J. Brumback, Appellant (Feb. 19, 1960)
M/B: De Vries v. Brumback, 53 Cal. 2d 643, 349 P.2d 532, 2 Cal. Rptr. 764 (1960).

3 159 242 331 413 518   Cal. Rptr. Vol. # 3   Civ. Proc. § 614
James Davis, Plaintiff and Appellant, v. Stein Erickson, Chris Kuraisa, George Canon, Rudolph Gersick, Phillip Musso, Bente Larssen, and Doe Four, Defendants and Respondents (March 25, 1960)
M/B: Davis v. Erickson, 53 Cal. 2d 860, 350 P.2d 535, 3 Cal. Rptr. 567 (1960).

4 160 243 332 414 519   Cal. Rptr. Vol. # 4   Civ. § 2982(d)
General Motors Acceptance Corporation, a Corporation, Appellant, v. Ronald M. Kyle, Respondent (May 10, 1960)
M/B: General Motors Acceptance Corp. v. Kyle, 54 Cal. 2d 101, 351 P.2d 768, 4 Cal. Rptr. 496 (1960).
Note: "GMAC" may be a widely enough known abbreviation of "Genral Motors Acceptance Corp." to be acceptable and should be counted as correct.

5 161 244 333 415 520   Cal. Rptr. Vol. # 5   Welf. & Inst. § 2004
Tyson A. Pearson et al. Respondents, v. State Social Welfare Board, Appellant (May 20, 1960)
M/B: Pearson v. State Social Welfare Board, 54 Cal. 2d 184, 353 P.2d 33, 5 Cal. Rptr. 553 (1960).
LR: Pearson v. State Social Welfare Bd., 54 Cal. 2d 184, 353 P.2d 33, 5 Cal. Rptr. 553 (1960).

6 162 245 334 416 521   Cal. Rptr. Vol. # 6   Pub. Util. § 1002
Richfield Oil Corporation (a Corporation), Petitioner, v. Public Utilities Commission of the State of California, Respondent (July 1, 1960)
M/B: Richfield Oil Corp. v. Public Utilities Commission, 54 Cal. 2d 419, 354 P.2d 4, 6 Cal. Rptr. 548 (1960).
LR: Richfield Oil Corp. v. Public Utils. Comm'n, 54 Cal. 2d 419, 354 P.2d 4, 6 Cal. Rptr. 548 (1960).
Note: "PUC" may be a widely enough known abbreviation of "Public Utilities Commission" to be acceptable and should be counted as correct.

7 163 246 335 417 522   Cal. Rptr. Vol. # 7   Welf. & Inst. § 2353
Fifield Manor (a Corporation), Appellant, v. Sidney S. Finston et al., Respondents (September 6, 1960)
M/B: Fifield Manor v. Finston, 54 Cal. 2d 632, 354 P.2d 1073, 7 Cal. Rptr. 377 (1960).

8 164 247 336 418 523   Cal. Rptr. Vol. # 8   Pub. Res. § 4010
Argonaut Insurance Company (a Corporation), Petitioner, v. Industrial Accident Commission (October 27, 1960)

EXERCISE 13.   CALIFORNIA REPORTER   (CONTINUED)

M/B: <u>Argonaut Insurance Co. v. Industrial Accident Commission</u>, 54 Cal. 2d 740, 356 P.2d 182, 8 Cal. Rptr. 438 (1960).
LR: Argonaut Ins. Co. v. Industrial Accident Comm'n, 54 Cal. 2d 740, 356 P.2d 182, 8 Cal. Rptr. 438 (1960).

9 165 248 337 419 524   Cal. Rptr. Vol. # 9   Health & Safety § 11503
People, Respondent, v. Joseph Brown, Appellant (December 22, 1960)
M/B: <u>People v. Brown</u>, 55 Cal. 2d 64, 357 P.2d 1072, 9 Cal. Rptr. 816 (1960).

10 166 249 338 420 525   Cal. Rptr. Vol. # 10   Civ. Proc. § 657(4)
Fomco, Inc. (a Corporation), Respondent, v. Joe Maggio, Inc. (a Corporation) et al., Appellants (January 24, 1961)
M/B: <u>Fomco, Inc. v. Joe Maggio, Inc.</u>, 55 Cal. 2d 162, 358 P.2d 918, 10 Cal. Rptr. 462 (1961).

11 167 250 339 421 526   Cal. Rptr. Vol. # 11   Penal § 261(1)
People of the State of California, Respondent, v. Harold Joseph Golden, Appellant (February 9, 1961)
M/B: <u>People v. Golden</u>, 55 Cal. 2d 358, 359 P.2d 448, 11 Cal. Rptr. 80 (1961).

12 168 251 340 422 527   Cal. Rptr. Vol. # 12   Civ. §§ 1734-1736
James P. Aced, Respondent, v. Hobbs-Sesack Plumbing Co. (a Partnership), Appellant (April 6, 1961)
M/B: <u>Aced v. Hobbs-Sesack Plumbing Co.</u>, 55 Cal. 2d 573, 360 P.2d 897, 12 Cal. Rptr. 257 (1961).

13 169 252 341 423 528   Cal. Rptr. Vol. # 13   Bus. & Prof. § 23090
Hollywood Circle, Inc. (a Corporation), Appellant, v. Department of Alcoholic Beverage Control et al., Respondents (May 8, 1961)
M/B: <u>Hollywood Circle, Inc. v. Department of Alcoholic Beverage Control</u>, 55 Cal. 2d 728, 361 P.2d 712, 13 Cal. Rptr. 104 (1961).

14 170 253 342 424 529   Cal. Rptr. Vol. # 14   Penal § 647(4)
In re Holland Cregler, on Habeas Corpus (July 20, 1961)
M/B: <u>In re Cregler</u>, 56 Cal. 2d 308, 363 P.2d 305, 14 Cal. Rptr. 289 (1961).
LR: In re Cregler, 56 Cal. 2d 308, 363 P.2d 305, 14 Cal. Rptr. 289 (1961).

15 171 254 343 425 530   Cal. Rptr. Vol. # 15   Penal § 825
People, Plaintiff and Respondent, v. James P. Van Eyk, Defendant and Appellant (August 10, 1961)
M/B: <u>People v. Van Eyk</u>, 56 Cal. 2d 471, 364 P.2d 326, 15 Cal. Rptr. 150 (1961).

16 172 255 344 426 531   Cal. Rptr. Vol. # 16   Lab. § 4750
State Compensation Insurance Fund, Petitioner, v. Industrial Accident Commission of the State of California and Joseph Quick, Respondents (October 13, 1961)
M/B: <u>State Compensation Insurance Fund v. Industrial Accident Commission</u>, 56 Cal. 2d 681, 365 P.2d 415, 16 Cal. Rptr. 359 (1961).
LR: State Compensation Ins. Fund v. Industrial Accident Comm'n, 56 Cal. 2d 681, 365 P.2d 415, 16 Cal. Rptr. 359 (1961).

17 173 256 345 427 532   Cal. Rptr. Vol. # 17   Bus. & Prof. § 2392
Jack R. Magit, Plaintiff and Respondent, v. Board of Medical Examiners of the State of California, Defendant and Appellant (December 7, 1961)
M/B: <u>Magit v. Board of Medical Examiners</u>, 57 Cal. 2d 74, 366 P.2d 816, 17 Cal. Rptr. 488 (1961).

18 174 257 346 428 533   Cal. Rptr. Vol. # 18   Bus. & Prof. § 2552(b)
Herman Blumenthal, Plaintiff and Appellant, v. The Board of Medical Examiners, Defendant and Respondent (January 18, 1962)
M/B: <u>Blumenthal v. Board of Medical Examiners</u>, 57 Cal. 2d 228, 368 P.2d 101, 18 Cal. Rptr. 501 (1962).

19 175 258 347 429 534   Cal. Rptr. Vol. # 19   Pub. Util. § 1007

EXERCISE 13. CALIFORNIA REPORTER   (CONTINUED)

Golden Gate Scenic Steamship Lines, Inc., et al., Petitioners, v. The Public Utilities Commission of the State of California, Respondent; Russell G. Lewis, Real Party in Interest (March 1, 1962)
M/B: Golden Gate Scenic Steamship Lines v. Public Utilities Commission, 57 Cal. 2d 373, 369 P.2d 257, 19 Cal. Rptr. 657 (1962).
LR: Golden Gate Scenic S.S. Lines v. Public Utils. Comm'n, 57 Cal. 2d 373, 369 P.2d 257, 19 Cal. Rptr. 657 (1962).
Note: "PUC" may be a widely enough known abbreviation of "Public Utilities Commission" to be acceptable and should be counted as correct.

20 176 259 348 430 535   Cal. Rptr. Vol. # 20   Water § 31084
Howard C. Lattin et al., Plaintiffs and Appellants, v. Coachella Valley County Water District, Defendant and Respondent (April 4, 1962)
M/B: Lattin v. Coachella Valley County Water District, 57 Cal. 2d 499, 370 P.2d 332, 20 Cal. Rptr. 628 (1962).
LR: Lattin v. Coachella Valley County Water Dist., 57 Cal. 2d 499, 370 P.2d 332, 20 Cal. Rptr. 628 (1962).

21 177 260 349 431 536   Cal. Rptr. Vol. # 21   Penal § 1368
The People, Plaintiff and Appellant, v. Joseph O. Brock and Vera G. Brock, Defendants and Appellants (May 15, 1962)
M/B: People v. Brock, 57 Cal. 2d 644, 371 P.2d 296, 21 Cal. Rptr. 560 (1962).

22 178 261 350 432 537   Cal. Rptr. Vol. # 22   Civ. Proc. § 2042
The People, Plaintiff and Respondent, v. Charley Luther Pike and Richard D. Ceniceros, Defendants and Appellants (June 27, 1962)
M/B: People v. Pike, 58 Cal. 2d 70, 372 P.2d 656, 22 Cal. Rptr. 664 (1962).

23 179 262 351 433 538   Cal. Rptr. Vol. # 23   Veh. § 10851
The People, Plaintiff and Respondent, v. Harvey George Thomas, Defendant and Appellant (July 17, 1962)
M/B: People v. Thomas, 58 Cal. 2d 121, 373 P.2d 97, 23 Cal. Rptr. 161 (1962).

24 180 263 352 434 539   Cal. Rptr. Vol. # 24   Civ. Proc. § 348
Douglas Aircraft Company, Inc., Plaintiff and Respondent, v. Alan Cranston, as State Controller, Defendant and Appellant (October 2, 1962)
M/B: Douglas Aircraft Co. v. Cranston, 58 Cal. 2d 462, 374 P.2d 819, 24 Cal. Rptr. 851 (1962).

25 181 264 353 435 540   Cal. Rptr. Vol. # 25   Gov't § 1090
Owen Stigall, Jr., Plaintiff and Appellant, v. City of Taft et al., Defendants and Respondents (October 23, 1962)
M/B: Stigall v. City of Taft, 58 Cal. 2d 565, 375 P.2d 289, 25 Cal. Rptr. 441 (1962).

26 182 265 354 436 541   Cal. Rptr. Vol. # 26   Prob. § 202
Julian M. Sieroty and Alan Sieroty, as Executors of the Estate of Marc Silver, Deceased, Cross-Complainants and Appellants, v. Ethel E. Silver, Cross-Complainant and Cross-Appellant (December 4, 1962)
M/B: Sieroty v. Silver, 58 Cal. 2d 799, 376 P.2d 563, 26 Cal. Rptr. 635 (1962).

27 183 266 355 437 542   Cal. Rptr. Vol. # 27   Ins. § 530
Luciano A. Sabella et al., Plaintiffs and Appellants v. J. W. Wisler, Defendant and Appellant; National Union Fire Insurance Company, Defendant and Respondent (January 17, 1963)
M/B: Sabella v. Wisler, 59 Cal. 2d 21, 377 P.2d 889, 27 Cal. Rptr. 689 (1963).

28 184 267 356 438 543   Cal. Rptr. Vol. # 28   Penal § 1026
Department of Mental Hygiene, Plaintiff and Respondent, v. William A. Hawley, Defendant and Appellant (February 28, 1963)
M/B: Department of Mental Hygiene v. Hawley, 59 Cal. 2d 247, 379 P.2d 22, 28 Cal. Rptr. 718 (1963).

29 185 268 357 439 544   Cal. Rptr. Vol. # 29   Penal § 1239(b)

EXERCISE 13. CALIFORNIA REPORTER   (CONTINUED)

The People, Plaintiff and Respondent, v. Lawrence Akin Jackson, Defendant and Appellant (April 2, 1963)
M/B: People v. Jackson, 59 Cal. 2d 375, 379 P.2d 937, 29 Cal. Rptr. 505 (1963).

30 186 269 358 440 545   Cal. Rptr. Vol. # 30   Penal § 189
The People, Plaintiff and Respondent, v. Donald Floyd Ketchel, H. B. Sears, and Thomas Edward Sears, Defendants and Appellants (May 7, 1963)
M/B: People v. Ketchel, 59 Cal. 2d 503, 381 P.2d 394, 30 Cal. Rptr. 538 (1963).

31 187 270 359 441 546   Cal. Rptr. Vol. # 31   Educ. § 984(a)
Jay R. Jackson, Jr., a Minor, etc., Plaintiff and Appellant, v. Pasadena City School District et al., Defendants and Respondents (June 27, 1963)
M/B: Jackson v. Pasadena City School District, 59 Cal. 2d 876, 382 P.2d 878, 31 Cal. Rptr. 606 (1963).
LR: Jackson v. Pasadena City School Dist., 59 Cal. 2d 876, 382 P.2d 878, 31 Cal. Rptr. 606 (1963).

32 188 271 360 442 547   Cal. Rptr. Vol. # 32   Penal § 1382
The People, Plaintiff and Respondent, v. William R. Wilson, Defendant and Appellant (July 9, 1963)
M/B: People v. Wilson, 60 Cal. 2d 139, 383 P.2d 452, 32 Cal. Rptr. 44 (1963).

33 189 272 361 443 548   Cal. Rptr. Vol. # 33   Civ. Proc. § 681
Dorothy DiMarco, Plaintiff and Appellant, v. Frank DiMarco, Defendant and Resondent (September 19, 1963)
M/B: DiMarco v. DiMarco, 60 Cal. 2d 387, 385 P.2d 2, 33 Cal. Rptr. 610 (1963).

34 190 273 362 444 549   Cal. Rptr. Vol. # 34   Rev. & Tax. § 6204
Union Oil Company of California, Plaintiff and Appellant, v. State Board of Equalization, Defendant and Respondent (November 14, 1963)
M/B: Union Oil Co. v. State Board of Equalization, 60 Cal. 2d 441, 386 P.2d 496, 34 Cal. Rptr. 872 (1963).
LR: Union Oil Co. v. State Bd. of Equalization, 60 Cal. 2d 441, 386 P.2d 496, 34 Cal. Rptr. 872 (1963).

35 191 274 363 445 550   Cal. Rptr. Vol. # 35   Civ. § 3399
Horace F. French et al., Plaintiffs and Respondents, v. Edsel W. Brinkman et al., Defendants and Appellants (December 3, 1963)
M/B: French v. Brinkman, 60 Cal. 2d 547, 387 P.2d 1, 35 Cal. Rptr. 289 (1963).

36 192 275 364 446 551   Cal. Rptr. Vol. # 36   Civ. Proc. § 1845
The People, Plaintiff and Respondent, v. Clarence Spriggs, Defendant and Appellant (February 25, 1964)
M/B: People v. Spriggs, 60 Cal. 2d 868, 389 P.2d 377, 36 Cal. Rptr. 841 (1964).

37 193 276 365 447 552   Cal. Rptr. Vol. # 37   Rev. & Tax. § 17745
Robert P. McCulloch, Plaintiff and Appellant, v. Franchise Tax Board, Defendant and Respondent (March 24, 1964)
M/B: McCulloch v. Franchise Tax Board, 61 Cal. 2d 186, 390 P.2d 412, 37 Cal. Rptr. 636 (1964).
LR: McCulloch v. Franchise Tax Bd., 61 Cal. 2d 186, 390 P.2d 412, 37 Cal. Rptr. 636 (1964).

38 194 277 366 448 553   Cal. Rptr. Vol. # 38   Lab. § 3202
David D. Schreifer, Petitioner, v. Industrial Accident Commission, County of Los Angeles, et al., Respondents (May 5, 1964)
M/B: Schreifer v. Industrial Accident Commission, 61 Cal. 2d 289, 391 P.2d 832, 38 Cal. Rptr. 352 (1964).
LR: Schreifer v. Industrial Accident Comm'n, 61 Cal. 2d 289, 391 P.2d 832, 38 Cal. Rptr. 352 (1964).

39 195 278 367 449 554   Cal. Rptr. Vol. # 39   Veh. § 22850

EXERCISE 13. CALIFORNIA REPORTER   (CONTINUED)

The People, Plaintiff and Respondent, v. Roy Charles Burke, Defendant and Appellant (July 30, 1964)
M/B: People v. Burke, 61 Cal. 2d 575, 394 P.2d 67, 39 Cal. Rptr. 531 (1964).

40 196 279 368 450 555   Cal. Rptr. Vol. # 40   Civ. Proc. § 1190.1(h)
A-1 Door and Materials Company, Plaintiff, Cross-defendant and Respondent, v. Fresno Guarantee Savings & Loan Association, Defendant, Cross-complainant and Appellant (August 25, 1964)
M/B: A-1 Door & Materials Co. v. Fresno Guarantee Savings & Loan Association, 61 Cal. 2d 728, 394 P.2d 829, 40 Cal. Rptr. 85 (1964).
LR: A-1 Door & Materials Co. v. Fresno Guar. Sav. & Loan Ass'n, 61 Cal. 2d 728, 394 P.2d 829, 40 Cal. Rptr. 85 (1964).

41 197 280 369 451 556   Cal. Rptr. Vol. # 41   Penal § 1367
The People, Plaintiff and Respondent, v. Sideny Lincoln Westbrook, Defendant and Appellant (December 28, 1964)
M/B: People v. Westbrook, 62 Cal. 2d 197, 397 P.2d 545, 41 809 (1964).

42 198 281 370 452 557   Cal. Rptr. Vol. # 42   Penal § 1043
In re Albert Lessard on Habeas Corpus (February 18, 1965)
M/B: In re Lessard, 62 Cal. 2d 497, 399 P.2d 39, 42 Cal. Rptr. 583 (1965).
LR: In re Lessard, 62 Cal. 2d 497, 399 P.2d 39, 42 Cal. Rptr. 583 (1965).

43 199 282 371 453 558   Cal. Rptr. Vol. # 43   Civ. § 140.5
Leona Addison, Plaintiff and Appellant, v. Morton Cutler Addison, Defendant and Appellant (March 15, 1965)
M/B: Addison v. Addison, 62 Cal. 2d 588, 399 P.2d 897, 43 Cal. Rptr. 97 (1965).

44 200 283 372 454 559   Cal. Rptr. Vol. # 44   Penal § 203
The People, Plaintiff and Respondent, v. Earl Clarence Sears, Defendant and Appellant (May 21, 1965)
M/B: People v. Sears, 62 Cal. 2d 737, 401 P.2d 938, 44 Cal. Rptr. 330 (1965).

45 101 284 373 455 560   Cal. Rptr. Vol. # 45   Civ. § 1732
Daniel J. Seely, Plaintiff and Appellant, v. White Motor Company, Defendant and Appellant (June 23, 1965)
M/B: Seely v. White Motor Co., 63 Cal. 2d 9, 403 P.2d 145, 45 Cal. Rptr. 17 (1965).

46 102 285 374 456 561   Cal. Rptr. Vol. # 46   Penal § 203
The People, Plaintiff and Respondent, v. Robert Arthur Anderson, Defendant and Appellant (October 1, 1965)
M/B: People v. Anderson, 63 Cal. 2d 351, 406 P.2d 43, 46 Cal. Rptr. 763 (1965).

47 103 286 375 457 562   Cal. Rptr. Vol. # 47   Bus. & Prof. § 7071.5
E. W. Tracy, Plaintiff and Respondent, v. Contractors' State License Board, Defendant and Appellant (November 23, 1965)
M/B: Tracy v. Contractors' State License Board, 63 Cal. 2d 598, 407 P.2d 865, 47 Cal. Rptr. 561 (1965).
LR: Tracy v. Contractors' State License Bd., 63 Cal. 2d 598, 407 P.2d 865, 47 Cal. Rptr. 561 (1965).

48 104 287 376 458 563   Cal. Rptr. Vol. # 48   Lab. § 4600
Janet McCoy, Petitioner, v. Industrial Accident Commission, Longview Fiber Company et al., Respondents (February 3, 1966)
M/B: McCoy v. Industrial Accident Commission, 64 Cal. 2d 82, 410 P.2d 362, 48 Cal. Rptr. 858 (1966).
LR: McCoy v. Industrial Accident Comm'n, 64 Cal. 2d 82, 410 P.2d 362, 48 Cal. Rptr. 858 (1966).

49 105 288 377 459 564   Cal. Rptr. Vol. # 49   Penal § 1555.2
In re George F. Patterson on Habeas Corpus (March 17, 1966)
M/B: In re Patterson, 64 Cal. 2d 357, 411 P.2d 897, 49 Cal. Rptr. 801 (1966).
LR: In re Patterson, 64 Cal. 2d 357, 411 P.2d 897, 49 Cal. Rptr. 801 (1966).

EXERCISE 13.   CALIFORNIA REPORTER   (CONTINUED)

50 106 289 378 460 565   Cal. Rptr. Vol. # 50   Penal § 1555.1
In re James W. Satterfield on Habeas Corpus (April 12, 1966)
M/B: In re Satterfield, 64 Cal. 2d 419, 412 P.2d 540, 50 Cal. Rptr. 284 (1966).
LR: In re Satterfield, 64 Cal. 2d 419, 412 P.2d 540, 50 Cal. Rptr. 284 (1966).

51 107 290 379 461 566   Cal. Rptr. Vol. # 51   Penal §§ 4852.01-.17
Katsuki James Otsuka et al., Plaintiffs and Appellants, v. Benjamin S. Hite, as Registrar of Voters, etc., Defendants and Respondent (May 24, 1966)
M/B: Otsuka v. Hite, 64 Cal. 2d 596, 414 P.2d 412, 51 Cal. Rptr. 284 (1966).

52 108 291 380 462 567   Cal. Rptr. Vol. # 52   Civ. Proc. § 1870(15)
Charlotte Lee Taylor, Plaintiff and Appellant, v. Centennial Bowl, Inc., Defendant and Respondent (August 15, 1966)
M/B: Taylor v. Centennial Bowl, Inc., 65 Cal. 2d 114, 416 P.2d 793, 52 Cal. Rptr. 561 (1966).

53 109 292 381 463 568   Cal. Rptr. Vol. # 53   Welf. & Inst. § 5501
In re George Anthony Perez on Habeas Corpus (September 21, 1966)
M/B: In re Perez, 65 Cal. 2d 224, 418 P.2d 6, 53 Cal. Rptr. 414 (1966).
LR: In re Perez, 65 Cal. 2d 224, 418 P.2d 6, 53 Cal. Rptr. 414 (1966).

54 110 293 382 464 569   Cal. Rptr. Vol. # 54   Penal § 3047.5
In re Louis D. Ponce on Habeas Corpus (November 30, 1966)
M/B: In re Ponce, 65 Cal. 2d 341, 420 P.2d 224, 54 Cal. Rptr. 752 (1966).
LR: In re Ponce, 65 Cal. 2d 341, 420 P.2d 224, 54 Cal. Rptr. 752 (1966).

55 111 294 383 465 570   Cal. Rptr. Vol. # 55   Veh. § 23102
The People, Plaintiff and Resondent, v. Louis Eugene Sudduth, Defendant and Appellant (December 23, 1966)
M/B: People v. Sudduth, 65 Cal. 2d 543, 421 P.2d 401, 55 Cal. Rptr. 393 (1966).

56 112 295 384 466 571   Cal. Rptr. Vol. # 56   Penal § 816
The People, Plaintiff and Respondent, v. George L. Webb, Defendant and Appellant (March 8, 1967)
M/B: People v. Webb, 66 Cal. 2d 107, 424 P.2d 342, 56 Cal. Rptr. 902 (1967).

57 113 296 385 467 572   Cal. Rptr. Vol. # 57   Evid. § 623
R. D. Reeder Lathing Co., Inc., Plaintiff and Respondent, v. Francis E. Allen, Jr., Defendant and Appellant (April 18, 1967)
M/B: R.D. Reeder Lathing Co. v. Allen, 66 Cal. 2d 373, 425 P.2d 785, 57 Cal. Rptr. 841 (1967).

58 114 297 386 468 573   Cal. Rptr. Vol. # 58   Ins. § 700
The People, Plaintiff and Appellant, v. United National Life Insurance Co., Defendant and Respondent (May 4, 1967)
M/B: People v. United National Life Insurance Co., 66 Cal. 2d 577, 427 P.2d 199, 58 Cal. Rptr. 599 (1967).
LR: People v. United Nat'l Life Ins. Co., 66 Cal. 2d 577, 427 P.2d 199, 58 Cal. Rptr. 599 (1967).

59 115 298 387 469 574   Cal. Rptr. Vol. # 59   Civ. § 1710(4)
Green Trees Enterprises, Inc., Plaintiff and Appellant, v. Palm Springs Alpine Estates, Inc., Defendant and Appellant (May 29, 1967)
M/B: Green Trees Enterprises v. Palm Springs Alpine Estates, 66 Cal. 2d 782, 427 P.2d 805, 59 Cal. Rptr. 141 (1967).
LR: Green Trees Enters. v. Palm Springs Alpine Estates, 66 Cal. 2d 782, 427 P.2d 805, 59 Cal. Rptr. 141 (1967).

60 116 299 388 470 575   Cal. Rptr. Vol. # 60   Penal § 288
The People, Plaintiff and Respondent, v. Frank W. Cramer, Defendant and Appellant (July 27, 1967)
M/B: People v. Cramer, 67 Cal. 2d 127, 429 P.2d 582, 60 Cal. Rptr. 230 (1967).

EXERCISE 13. CALIFORNIA REPORTER   (CONTINUED)

61 117 300 389 471 576 Cal. Rptr. Vol. # 61   Evid. § 1105
Faye Driscoll et al., Plaintiffs and Appellants, v. City of Los Angeles et
al., Defendants and Appellants (September 13, 1967)
M/B: Driscoll v. City of Los Angeles, 67 Cal. 2d 297, 431 P.2d 245, 61 Cal.
Rptr. 661 (1967).

62 118 201 390 472 577 Cal. Rptr. Vol. # 62   Corp. § 9300
Thomas C. Lynch, as Attorney General, etc., Plaintiff and Appellant, v. Lyle
A. Spilman et al., Defendants and Appellants (September 12, 1967)
M/B: Lynch v. Spilman, 67 Cal. 2d 251, 431 P.2d 636, 62 Cal. Rptr. 12 (1967).

63 119 202 391 473 578 Cal. Rptr. Vol. # 63   Rev. & Tax. § 4151
Arthur L. Smith et al., Plaintiffs and Appellants, v. Jimmie Anderson, as Tax
Collector, etc., et al., Defendants and Respondents (Novmeber 9, 1967)
M/B: Smith v. Anderson, 67 Cal. 2d 635, 433 P.2d 183, 63 Cal. Rptr. 391
(1967).

64 120 203 392 474 579 Cal. Rptr. Vol. # 64   Welf. & Inst. § 707
In re Jack R. Harris on Habeas Corpus (December 13, 1967)
M/B: In re Harris, 67 Cal. 2d 876, 434 P.2d 615, 64 Cal. Rptr. 319 (1967).
LR: In re Harris, 67 Cal. 2d 876, 434 P.2d 615, 64 Cal. Rptr. 319 (1967).

65 121 204 393 475 580 Cal. Rptr. Vol. # 65   Streets & Highways § 102
The People ex rel. Department of Public Works, Petitioner, v. The Superior
Court of Merced County, Respondent (February 1, 1968)
M/B: People ex rel. Department of Public Works v. Superior Court, 68 Cal. 2d
206, 436 P.2d 342, 65 Cal. Rptr. 342 (1968).
LR: People ex rel. Dep't of Pub. Works v. Superior Court, 68 Cal. 2d 206, 436
342, 65 Cal. Rptr. 342 (1968).

66 122 205 394 476 581 Cal. Rptr. Vol. # 66   Rev. & Tax. § 987
State Board of Equalization, Petitioner, v. Philip E. Watson, as Assessor,
etc., Respondent (March 4, 1968)
M/B: State Board of Equalization v. Watson, 68 Cal. 2d 307, 437 P.2d 761, 66
Cal. Rptr. 377 (1968).
LR: State Bd. of Equalization v. Watson, 68 Cal. 2d 307, 437 P.2d 761, 66
Cal. Rptr. 377 (1968).

67 123 206 395 477 582 Cal. Rptr. Vol. # 67   Pub. Util. § 1757
Greyhound Lines, Inc., Petitioner, v. Public Utilities Commission, Respondent
(March 29, 1968)
M/B: Greyhound Lines v. Public Utilities Commission, 68 Cal. 2d 406, 438 P.2d
801, 67 Cal. Rptr. 97 (1968).
LR: Greyhound Lines v. Public Utils. Comm'n, 68 Cal. 2d 406, 438 P.2d 801, 67
Cal. Rptr. 97 (1968).
Note: "PUC" is probably a widely enough recognized abbreviation of "Public
Utilities Commission" to be acceptable and should be counted as correct.

68 124 207 396 478 583 Cal. Rptr. Vol. # 68   Civ. Proc. § 335
Donald Williams, a minor, etc., Plaintiff and Appellant, v. Los Angeles
Metropolitan Transit Authority, Defendant and Respondent (May 17, 1968)
M/B: Williams v. Los Angeles Metropolitan Transit Authority, 68 Cal. 2d 599,
440 P.2d 497, 68 Cal. Rptr. 297 (1968).
LR: Williams v. Los Angeles Metropolitan Transit Auth., 68 Cal. 2d 599, 440
P.2d 497, 68 Cal. Rptr. 297 (1968).

69 125 208 397 479 584 Cal. Rptr. Vol. # 69   Civ. Proc. § 170(4)
Ronald O. Reichert, Plaintiff and Appellant, v. General Insurance Company of
America et al., Defendants and Resondents (July 3, 1968)
M/B: Reichert v. General Insurance Co. of America, 68 Cal. 2d 822, 442 P.2d
377, 69 Cal. Rptr. 321 (1968).
LR: Reichert v. General Ins. Co. of Am., 68 Cal. 2d 822, 442 P.2d 377, 69
Cal. Rptr. 321 (1968).

70 126 209 398 480 585 Cal. Rptr. Vol. # 70   Penal § 285
The People, Plaintiff and Resondent, v. Thomas John Russel, Defendant and
Apellant (August 14, 1968)

EXERCISE 13.   CALIFORNIA REPORTER   (CONTINUED)

M/B: People v. Russel, 69 Cal. 2d 187, 443 P.2d 794, 70 Cal. Rptr. 210 (1968).

71 127 210 399 481 586 Cal. Rptr. Vol. # 71 Lab. § 6407
Erik H. Lundberg, Petitioner, v. Workmen's Compensation Appeals Board, F. S. Huyck Construction Co., et al., Respondents (October 4, 1968)
M/B: Lundberg v. Workmen's Compensation Appeals Board, 69 Cal. 2d 436, 445 P.2d 300, 71 Cal. Rptr. 684 (1968).
LR: Lundberg v. Workmen's Compensation Appeals Bd., 69 Cal. 2d 436, 445 P.2d 300, 71 Cal. Rptr. 684 (1968).

72 128 211 400 482 587 Cal. Rptr. Vol. # 72 Evid. § 621
Templeton Feed and Grain, Plaintiff and Appellant, v. Ralston Purina Company, Defendant and Appellant (October 25, 1968)
M/B: Templeton Feed & Grain v. Ralston Purina Co., 69 Cal. 2d 461, 446 P.2d 152, 72 Cal. Rptr. 344 (1968).

73 129 212 301 483 588 Cal. Rptr. Vol. # 73 Welf. & Inst. § 1176
Ina Mae Johnson, Plaintiff and Appellant, v. State of California, Defendant and Respondent (December 4, 1968)
M/B: Johnson v. State, 69 Cal. 2d 782, 447 P.2d 352, 73 Cal. Rptr. 240 (1968).

74 130 213 302 484 589 Cal. Rptr. Vol. # 74 Ins. § 10115
Beverly M. Slobojan, Plaintiff and Appellant, v. Western Travelers Life Insurance Company, Defendant and Appellant (February 20, 1969)
M/B: Slobojan v. Western Travelers Life Insurance Co., 70 Cal. 2d 432, 450 P.2d 271, 74 Cal. Rptr. 895 (1969).
LR: Slobojan v. Western Travelers Life Ins. Co., 70 Cal. 2d 432, 450 P.2d 271, 74 Cal. Rptr. 895 (1969).

75 131 214 303 485 590 Cal. Rptr. Vol. # 110 Civ. Proc. § 259a(4)
Peter Rooney et al., Plaintiffs and Respondents, v. Vermont Investment Corporation et al., Defendants and Appellants (November 2, 1973)
M/B: Rooney v. Vermont Investment Corp., 10 Cal. 3d 351, 515 P.2d 297, 110 Cal. Rptr. 353 (1973).
LR: Rooney v. Vermont Inv. Corp., 10 Cal. 3d 351, 515 P.2d 297, 110 Cal. Rptr. 353 (1973).

76 132 215 304 486 591 Cal. Rptr. Vol. # 76 Evid. § 1235
The People, Plaintiff and Respondent, v. Dennis Councie McGautha and William Rodney Wilkinson, Defendants and Appellants (April 14, 1969)
M/B: People v. McGautha, 70 Cal. 2d 770, 452 P.2d 650, 76 Cal. Rptr. 434 (1969).

77 133 216 305 487 592 Cal. Rptr. Vol. # 77 Agric. § 52256-52258
In re Johnny B. Dapper on Habeas Corpus (May 28, 1969)
M/B: In re Dapper, 71 Cal. 2d 184, 454 P.2d 905, 77 Cal. Rptr. 897 (1969).
LR: In re Dapper, 71 Cal. 2d 184, 454 P.2d 905, 77 Cal. Rptr. 897 (1969).

78 134 217 306 488 593 Cal. Rptr. Vol. # 78 Civ. Proc. § 544
Abe Boyle, Plaintiff and Resondent, v. Marilee Jo Hawkins, Defendant and Appellant (June 16, 1969)
M/B: Boyle v. Hawkins, 71 Cal. 2d 229, 455 P.2d 97, 78 Cal. Rptr. 161 (1969).

79 135 218 307 489 594 Cal. Rptr. Vol. # 79 Penal § 188
The People, Plaintiff and Respondent, v. Oliver Stanley Williams, Defendant and Appellant (July 7, 1969)
M/B: People v. Williams, 71 Cal. 2d 614, 456 P.2d 633, 79 Cal. Rptr. 65 (1969).

80 136 219 308 490 595 Cal. Rptr. Vol. # 80 Penal § 1086
The People, Plaintiff and Respondent, v. William Westwood McClellan, Defendant and Appellant (August 20, 1969)
M/B: People v. McClellan, 71 Cal. 2d 793, 457 P.2d 871, 80 Cal. Rptr. 31 (1969).

EXERCISE 13. CALIFORNIA REPORTER   (CONTINUED)

81 137 220 309 491 596   Cal. Rptr. Vol. # 81   Civ. Proc. § 631.8
Leon J. Pinsker, Plaintiff and Appellant, v. Pacific Coast Society of
Orthodontists et al., Defendants and Respondents (November 12, 1969)
M/B: Pinsker v. Pacific Coast Society of Orthodontists, 1 Cal. 3d 160, 460
P.2d 495, 81 Cal. Rptr. 623 (1969).
LR: Pinsker v. Pacific Coast Soc'y of Orthodontists, 1 Cal. 3d 160, 460 P.2d
495, 81 Cal. Rptr. 623 (1969).

82 138 221 310 492 597   Cal. Rptr. Vol. # 82   Evid. § 12(b)
The People, Plaintiff and Respondent, v. Kenneth Lloyd Brawley and Larry
Andrew Baker, Defendants and Appellants (November 21, 1969)
M/B: People v. Brawley, 1 Cal. 3d 277, 461 P.2d 361, 82 Cal. Rptr. 161
(1969).

83 139 222 311 493 598   Cal. Rptr. Vol. # 83   Penal § 1239(b)
The People, Plaintiff and Respondent, v. Barry Floyd and Johnny Milton,
Defendants and Appellants (January 27, 1970)
M/B: People v. Floyd, 1 Cal. 3d 694, 464 P.2d 64, 83 Cal. Rptr. 608 (1970).

84 140 223 312 494 599   Cal. Rptr. Vol. # 84   Penal § 1096
The People, Plaintiff and Respondent, v. Earl Clarence Sears, Defendant and
Appellant (March 13, 1970)
M/B: People v. Sears, 2 Cal. 3d 180, 465 P.2d 847, 84 Cal. Rptr. 711 (1970).

85 141 224 313 495 600   Cal. Rptr. Vol. # 85   Civ. Proc. § 1211
In re Silvio J. Marcario on Habeas Corpus (April 1, 1970)
M/B: In re Marcario, 2 Cal. 3d 329, 466 P.2d 679, 85 Cal. Rptr. 135 (1970).
LR: In re Marcario, 2 Cal. 3d 329, 466 P.2d 679, 85 Cal. Rptr. 135 (1970).

86 142 225 314 496 501   Cal. Rptr. Vol. # 86   Civ. Proc. § 1048
Brunzell Construction Co., Inc., of Nevada, Plaintiff and Appellant, v.
William C. Wagner et al., Defendants and Respondents (May 5, 1970)
M/B: Brunzell Construction Co. v. Wagner, 2 Cal. 3d 545, 468 P.2d 553, 86
Cal. Rptr. 297 (1970).
LR: Brunzell Constr. Co. v. Wagner, 2 Cal. 3d 545, 468 P.2d 553, 86 Cal.
Rptr. 297 (1970).

87 143 226 315 497 502   Cal. Rptr. Vol. # 87   Penal § 1474
In re Hulen T. Harrell on Habeas Corpus (June 18, 1970)
M/B: In re Harrell, 2 Cal. 3d 675, 470 P.2d 640, 87 Cal. Rptr. 504 (1970).
LR: In re Harrell, 2 Cal. 3d 675, 470 P.2d 640, 87 Cal. Rptr. 504 (1970).

88 144 227 316 498 503   Cal. Rptr. Vol. # 88   Penal § 187
In re James W. Saunders on Habeas Corpus (August 7, 1970)
M/B: In re Saunders, 2 Cal. 3d 1033, 472 P.2d 921, 88 Cal. Rptr. 633 (1970).
LR: In re Saunders, 2 Cal. 3d 1033, 472 P.2d 921, 88 Cal. Rptr. 633 (1970).

89 145 228 317 499 504   Cal. Rptr. Vol. # 89   Evid. § 1200
The People, Plaintiff and Respondent, v. Richard Randolph Nichols, Defendant
and Appellant (September 25, 1970)
M/B: People v. Nichols, 3 Cal. 3d 150, 474 P.2d 673, 89 Cal. Rptr. 721
(1970).

90 146 229 318 500 505   Cal. Rptr. Vol. # 90   Bus. & Prof. § 6083(c)
John E. Crooks, Petitioner, v. The State Bar of California, Respondent
(October 29, 1970)
M/B: Crooks v. State Bar, 3 Cal. 3d 346, 475 P.2d 872, 90 Cal. Rptr. 600
(1970).

91 147 230 319 401 506   Cal. Rptr. Vol. # 91   Health & Safety § 24101.4
Ethel Haft et al., Plaintiffs and Appellants, v. Lone Palm Hotel et al.,
Defendants and Respondents (December 29, 1970)
M/B: Haft v. Lone Palm Hotel, 3 Cal. 3d 756, 478 P.2d 465, 91 Cal. Rptr. 745
(1970).

92 148 231 320 402 507   Cal. Rptr. Vol. # 92   Educ. § 925

EXERCISE 13.   CALIFORNIA REPORTER   (CONTINUED)

San Francisco Unified School District et al., Petitioners, v. Donald Johnson, as Complex Planning Officer, etc., Respondent (January 26, 1971)
M/B: San Francisco Unified School District v. Johnson, 3 Cal. 3d 937, 479 P.2d 669, 92 Cal. Rptr. 309 (1971).
LR: San Francisco Unified School Dist. v. Johnson, 3 Cal. 3d 937, 479 P.2d 669, 92 Cal. Rptr. 309 (1971).

93 149 232 321 403 508   Cal. Rptr. Vol. # 93   Corp. § 25510
Fred H. Bixby, Plaintiff and Appellant v. Anthony R. Pierno, As Commissioner of Corporations, etc., Defendant and Resondent (February 23, 1971)
M/B: Bixby v. Pierno, 4 Cal. 3d 130, 481 P.2d 242, 93 Cal. Rptr. 234 (1971).

94 150 233 322 404 509   Cal. Rptr. Vol. # 94   Evid. § 351
The People, Plaintiff and Resondent v. Lawrence Earl Lavergne, Defendant and Appellant (May 5, 1971)
M/B: People v. Lavergne, 4 Cal. 3d 735, 484 P.2d 77, 94 Cal. Rptr. 405 (1971).

95 151 234 323 405 510   Cal. Rptr. Vol. # 95   Gov't §§ 17300-17302
Houston I. Flournoy, Controller of the State of California, Petitioner, v. Ivy Baker Priest, Treasurer of the State of California, Respondent (July 9, 1971)
M/B: Flournoy v. Priest, 5 Cal. 3d 350, 486 P.2d 689, 95 Cal. Rptr. 793 (1971).

96 152 235 324 406 511   Cal. Rptr. Vol. # 96   Evid. § 1103
In re William K. C. Ferguson on Habeas Corpus (August 24, 1971)
M/B: In re Ferguson, 5 Cal. 3d 525, 487 P.2d 1234, 96 Cal. Rptr. 594 (1971).
LR: In re Ferguson, 5 Cal. 3d 525, 487 P.2d 1234, 96 Cal. Rptr. 594 (1971).

97 153 236 325 407 512   Cal. Rptr. Vol. # 97   Bus. & Prof. § 6101
In re Edward R. Plotner on Disbarment (September 14, 1971)
M/B: In re Plotner, 5 Cal. 3d 714, 488 P.2d 385, 97 Cal. Rptr. 193 (1971).
LR: In re Plotner, 5 Cal. 3d 714, 488 P.2d 385, 97 Cal. Rptr. 193 (1971).

98 154 237 326 408 513   Cal. Rptr. Vol. # 98   Welf. & Inst. § 11450
Virginia Villa et al., Petitioners, v. James M. Hall, as Secretary, etc., et al., Respondents (December 6, 1971)
M/B: Villa v. Hall, 6 Cal. 3d 227, 490 P.2d 1148, 98 Cal. Rptr. 460 (1971).

99 155 238 327 409 514   Cal. Rptr. Vol. # 99   Gov't § 75070
Jean L. Waite, Plaintiff and Respondent, v. Russell S. Waite et al., Defendants and Appellants (January 14, 1972)
M/B: Waite v. Waite, 6 Cal. 3d 461, 492 P.2d 13, 99 Cal. Rptr. 325 (1972).

100 156 239 328 410 515   Cal. Rptr. Vol. # 100   Civ. Proc. § 284
George Fracasse, Plaintiff and Appellant, v. Ray Raka Brent, Defendant and Respondent (March 10, 1972)
M/B: Fracasse v. Brent, 6 Cal. 3d 784, 494 P.2d 9, 100 Cal. Rptr. 385 (1972).

LIBRARY EXERCISE 14. NEW YORK SUPPLEMENT.

INSTRUCTOR'S NOTE: For this exercise, students are required to find and cite a case in West's New York Supplement. They are to use the appropriate volume of Shepard's New York Supplement Citations when necessary to find parallel citations. If the relevant Shepard's volume is unavailable, they are to use the Table of Cases volumes accompanying West's New York Digest to find parallel citations. For purposes of this exercise, the students have been instructed not include the subsequent history of the case in their citation.

1 155 219 383 448 596   32 N.Y.S.2d 59
Barrett v. Matson et al. 177 Misc. 863 (Supreme Court, Tompkins County Jan. 8, 1942)
M/B: Barrett v. Matson, 177 Misc. 863, 32 N.Y.S.2d 59 (Sup. Ct. 1942).

2 156 220 384 449 597   33 N.Y.S.2d 673
Hanley et al. v. Boland et al., New York State Labor Relations Board 177 Misc. 973 (Supreme Court, Special Term, Albany County July 22, 1939)
M/B: Hanley v. Boland, 177 Misc. 973, 33 N.Y.S.2d 673 (Sup. Ct. 1939).

3 157 221 385 450 598   34 N.Y.S.2d 556
Goldberg v. Volkman 178 Misc. 375 (Supreme Court, Monroe County April 25, 1942)
M/B: Goldberg v. Volkman, 178 Misc. 375, 34 N.Y.S.2d 556 (Sup. Ct. 1942).

4 158 222 386 451 599   35 N.Y.S.2d 221
Geiger v. Louis Yasser, Inc., et. al 178 Misc. 526 (Supreme Court, Special Term, New York County May 6, 1942)
M/B: Geiger v. Louis Yasser, Inc., 178 Misc. 526, 35 N.Y.S.2d 221 (Sup. Ct. 1942).

5 159 223 387 452 600   36 N.Y.S.2d 786
People ex rel. Ryder v. Woodworth, City Assessor, et al. 178 Misc. 921 (Supreme Court , Monroe County April 29, 1942)
M/B: People ex rel. Ryder v. Woodworth, 178 Misc. 921, 36 N.Y.S.2d 786 (Sup. Ct. 1942).
LR: People ex rel. Ryder v. Woodworth, 178 Misc. 921, 36 N.Y.S.2d 786 (Sup. Ct. 1942).

6 160 224 388 453 501   37 N.Y.S.2d 511
Ostrow v. Joseph P. Day, Inc. 265 App. Div. 827 (Supreme Court, Appellate Division, Second Department Oct. 13, 1942)
M/B: Ostrow v. Joseph P. Day, Inc., 265 A.D. 827, 37 N.Y.S.2d 511 (1942).

7 161 225 389 454 502   38 N.Y.S.2d 619
Welles v. Danin 179 Misc. 268 (Supreme Court, Trial Term, New York County Dec. 9, 1942)
M/B: Welles v. Danin, 179 Misc. 268, 38 N.Y.S.2d 619 (Sup. Ct. 1942).

8 162 226 390 455 503   179 N.Y.S.2d 393
Constance Mills, Plaintiff, v. Everett R. Montana and Althea Montana, Defendants 14 Misc. 2d 414 (Supreme Court, Oneida County. Argued Sept. 9, 1958. Decided Sept. 11, 1958)
M/B: Mills v. Montana, 14 Misc. 2d 414, 179 N.Y.S.2d 393 (Sup. Ct. 1958).

9 163 227 391 456 504   180 N.Y.S.2d 287
Society of the New York Hospital, Respondent, v. John W. Johnson, as Superintendent of Public Works of the State of New York, Appellant 5 N.Y.2d 102 (Court of Appeals of New York Nov. 13, 1958)
M/B: Society of the New York Hospital v. Johnson, 5 N.Y.2d 102, 154 N.E.2d 550, 180 N.Y.S.2d 287 (1958).
LR: Society of the N.Y. Hosp. v. Johnson, 5 N.Y.2d 102, 154 N.E.2d 550, 180 N.Y.S.2d 287 (1958).
Note: "The" should be retained in the citation because it is not the first word of the party name. See Rule 10.2.1(d).

10 164 228 392 457 505   181 N.Y.S.2d 633
People of the State of New York ex rel. Amos Williams, Respondent v. Robert E. Murphy, as Warden of Auburn State Prison, Respondent, People of the State of

EXERCISE 14. NEW YORK SUPPLEMENT   (CONTINUED)

New York, Appellant 7 A.D.2d 893 (Supreme Court, Appellate Division Fourth
Department. Argued Sept. 16, 1958. Decided Jan. 15, 1959)
M/B: People ex rel. Williams v. Murphy, 7 A.D.2d 893, 181 N.Y.S.2d 633
(1959).
LR: People ex rel. Williams v. Murphy, 7 A.D.2d 893, 181 N.Y.S.2d 633 (1959).

11 165 229 393 458 506   183 N.Y.S.2d 605
5 East 73rd, Inc., Plaintiff, v. 11 East 73rd Street Corporation, Defendant 16
Misc. 2d 49 (Supreme Court, Special and Trial Term, New York County, Part
XXIII Feb. 17, 1959)
M/B: 5 East 73rd, Inc. v. 11 East 73rd Street Corp., 16 Misc. 2d 49, 183
N.Y.S.2d 605 (Sup. Ct. 1959).
LR: 5 E. 73rd, Inc. v. 11 E. 73rd St. Corp., 16 Misc. 2d 49, 183 N.Y.S.2d 605
(Sup. Ct. 1959).

12 166 230 394 459 507   182 N.Y.S.2d 411
Neco Distributors Corp., Plaintiff-Respondent, v. David L. Wilkoff,
Defendant-Appellant, and Albert deKoninck, Defendant 7 A.D.2d 903 (Supreme
Court, Appellate Division, First Department Feb. 17, 1959)
M/B: Neco Distributors Corp. v. Wilkoff, 7 A.D.2d 903, 182 N.Y.S.2d 411
(1959).
LR: Neco Distribs. Corp. v. Wilkoff, 7 A.D.2d 903, 182 N.Y.S.2d 411 (1959).

13 167 231 395 460 508   184 N.Y.S.2d 613
In the Matter of the Accounting of Adrian R. Allan, Jr., et al., as Executors
of Adrian R. Allan, Deceased, Respondents. Irving Trust Company, as Executor
of Helen H. Allan, Deceased, Appellant; Virginia A. Carter et al., Respondents
5 N.Y.2d 333 (Court of Appeals of New York March 5, 1959)
M/B: In re Allan, 5 N.Y.2d 333, 157 N.E.2d 607, 184 N.Y.S.2d 613 (1959).
LR: In re Allan, 5 N.Y.2d 333, 157 N.E.2d 607, 184 N.Y.S.2d 613 (1959).

14 168 232 396 461 509   185 N.Y.S.2d 538
Alice M. Kelley, Appellant, v. Paul Wasserman, Respondent 5 N.Y.2d 425 (Court
of Appeals of New York April 9, 1959)
M/B: Kelley v. Wasserman, 5 N.Y.2d 425, 158 N.E.2d 241, 185 N.Y.S.2d 538
(1959).

15 169 233 397 462 510   186 N.Y S.2d 73
Theodore Thibadeau v. Benjamin Lonschein 17 Misc. 2d 645 (Supreme Court,
Special Term, Queens County, Part I March 25, 1959)
M/B: Thibadeau v. Lonschein, 17 Misc. 2d 645, 186 N.Y S.2d 73 (Sup. Ct.
1959).

16 170 234 398 463 511   178 N.Y.S.2d 270
Martin Schoenbrun v. M.J.B. Holding Corp., a domestic corporation, Jack
Spolan, Evelyn Spolan and Rebecca Spolan 13 Misc. 2d 574 (Supreme Court,
Special Term, Queens County, Part I Aug. 8, 1958)
M/B: Schoenbrun v. M.J.B. Holding Corp., 13 Misc. 2d 574,178 N.Y.S.2d 270
(Sup. Ct. 1958).

17 171 235 399 464 512   194 N.Y.S.2d 695
Jack Schiff, Plaintiff, v. Jack Kirby, David Wood and Dick Wood, Defendants 22
Misc. 2d 786 (Supreme Court, Special Term, Westchester County, Part II Dec. 3,
1959)
M/B: Schiff v. Kirby, 22 Misc. 2d 786, 194 N.Y.S.2d 695 (Sup. Ct. 1959).

18 172 236 400 465 513   415 N.Y.S.2d 529
People of the State of New York, Respondent, v. John F. Keller, Appellant 67
A.D.2d 153 (Supreme Court, Appellate Division, Fourth Department April 6,
1979)
M/B: People v. Keller, 67 A.D.2d 153, 415 N.Y.S.2d 529 (1979).

19 173 237 301 466 514   187 N.Y.S.2d 737
Norman La Porte et al., Appellants, v. State of New York, Respondent (Claim
No. 33115) 6 N.Y.2d 1 (Court of Appeals of New York, May 15, 1959)
M/B: La Porte v. State, 6 N.Y.2d 1, 159 N.E.2d 540, 187 N.Y.S.2d 737 (1959).

EXERCISE 14. NEW YORK SUPPLEMENT   (CONTINUED)

20 174 238 302 467 515   188 N.Y.S.2d 295
Thor Eckert & Co., Inc., Plaintiff-Respondent-Appellant, v. John W. Routsis, Defendant-Appellant-Respondent 8 A.D.2d 793 (Supreme Court, Appellate Division, First Department June 18, 1959)
M/B: Thor Eckert & Co. v. Routsis, 8 A.D.2d 793, 188 N.Y.S.2d 295 (1959).

21 175 239 303 468 516   189 N.Y.S.2d 194
People of the State of New York, Respondent, v. Enrico Porcaro, Appellant 6 N.Y.2d 248 (Court of Appeals of New York July 8, 1959)
M/B: People v. Porcaro, 6 N.Y.2d 248, 160 N.E.2d 488, 189 N.Y.S.2d 194 (1959).

22 176 240 304 469 517   190 N.Y.S.2d 656
Claim of Harry Schechter, Appellant, v. State Insurance Fund, Respondent 6 N.Y.2d 506 (Court of Appeals of New York July 8, 1959)
M/B: Schechter v. State Insurance Fund, 6 N.Y.2d 506, 160 N.E.2d 901, 190 N.Y.S.2d 656 (1959).
LR: Schechter v. State Ins. Fund, 6 N.Y.2d 506, 160 N.E.2d 901, 190 N.Y.S.2d 656 (1959).

23 177 241 305 470 518   191 N.Y.S.2d 673
Sy Friedman, Plaintiff v. Maurey Garber, Defendant 20 Misc. 2d 360 (Supreme Court, Special Term, New York County, Part I Sept. 4, 1959)
M/B: Friedman v. Garber, 20 Misc. 2d 360, 191 N.Y.S.2d 673 (Sup. Ct. 1959).

24 178 242 306 471 519   192 N.Y.S.2d 797
Claire L. Brilliant, individually and as Executrix of the Estate of Morton Brilliant, Deceased, and as a Stockholder of Long Island Waste Co., Inc. and Siam Realty Corp., Plaintiff, v. Long Island Waste Co., Inc., Siam Realty Corp., Stanley Brilliant, Ira Brilliant, and Anna S. Brilliant, Defendants 23 Misc. 2d 780 (Supreme Court, Special Term, Kings County, Part I Oct. 5, 1959)
M/B: Brilliant v. Long Island Waste Co., 23 Misc. 2d 780, 192 N.Y.S.2d 797 (Sup. Ct. 1959).

25 179 243 307 472 520   193 N.Y.S.2d 166
Application of Henry Payson and 2 Sutton Place South Tenant's Corp., Pretitioners-Appellants, for an order under Article 78 of the Civil Practice Act, v. Joseph J. Caputa, State Rent Administrator, Respondent-Respondent, and Various Tenants of 2 Sutton Place South, Intervenors-Respondents-Respondents 9 A.D.2d 226 (Supreme Court, Appellate Division, First Department Nov. 17, 1959)
M/B: Payson v. Caputa, 9 A.D.2d 226, 193 N.Y.S.2d 166 (1959).

26 180 244 308 473 521   303 N.Y.S.2d 245
In the Matter of Joseph Figari et al., Appellants, v. New York Telephone Company, Respondent 32 A.D.2d 434 (Supreme Court, Appellate Division, Second Department July 25, 1969)
M/B: Figari v. New York Telephone Co., 32 A.D.2d 434, 303 N.Y.S.2d 245 (1969).
LR: Figari v. New York Tel. Co., 32 A.D.2d 434, 303 N.Y.S.2d 245 (1969).

27 181 245 309 474 522   304 N.Y.S.2d 810
Loretta M. Hart, Administratrix of the Estate of Bruce F. Hart, Deceased, Plaintiff, v. American Airlines, Inc., Defendant. All other American Airlines, Inc. cases subject to the Order of Joint Trial of the Appellate Division, First Department, Dated November 10, 1967). Suzanne Landano, as Administratrix of the Estate of Matthew Michael Landano, Deceased, Plaintiff, v. American Airlines, Inc., Defendant. Dorothy M. Kirchstein, as Administratrix of the Estate of John M. Kirchstein, Deceased, Plaintiff, v. American Airlines, Inc. and the Boeing Company, Defendants 61 Misc. 2d 41 (Supreme Court, Special Term, New York County, Part I Oct. 7, 1969)
M/B: Hart v. American Airlines, 61 Misc. 2d 41, 304 N.Y.S.2d 810 (Sup. Ct. 1969).

28 182 246 310 475 523   305 N.Y.S.2d 477
Caroline B. Kennard, as Administratrix of the Estate of Leonard E. Coker, Deceased, v. Welded Tank & Construction Co., Inc., defendant and Third-Party Plaintiff-Appellant. Colorado Fuel & Iron Co., Inc., Third-Party

EXERCISE 14. NEW YORK SUPPLEMENT   (CONTINUED)

Defendant-Respondent. (Action No. 1.) (And Three other Actions.) 25 N.Y.2d 324 (Court of Appeals of New York Oct. 29, 1969)
M/B: Kennard v. Welded Tank & Construction Co., 25 N.Y.2d 324, 253 N.E.2d 197, 305 N.Y.S.2d 477 (1969).
LR: Kennard v. Welded Tank & Constr. Co., 25 N.Y.2d 324, 253 N.E.2d 197, 305 N.Y.S.2d 477 (1969).

29 183 247 311 476 524   306 N.Y.S.2d 789
The People of the State of New York ex rel. Mark Fein, Relator, v. Harold W. Follette, Warden of Green Haven Prison, Stormville, New York, Respondent 61 Misc. 2d 826 (Supreme Court, Dutchess County Jan. 19, 1970)
M/B: People ex rel. Fein v. Follette, 61 Misc. 2d 826, 306 N.Y.S.2d 789 (Sup. Ct. 1970).
LR: People ex rel. Fein v. Follette, 61 Misc. 2d 826, 306 N.Y.S.2d 789 (Sup. Ct. 1970).

30 184 248 312 477 525   416 N.Y.S.2d 573
The People of the State of New York, Respondent, v. James Thomas, Appellant 389 N.E.2d 1094 (Court of Appeals of New York April 26, 1979)
M/B: People v. Thomas, 47 N.Y.2d 37, 389 N.E.2d 1094, 416 N.Y.S.2d 573 (1979).

31 185 249 313 478 526   308 N.Y.S.2d 385
People, etc., Respondent, v. Samuel Valentine, Appellant 26 N.Y.2d 654 (Court of Appeals of New York Jan. 8, 1970)
M/B: People v. Valentine, 26 N.Y.2d 654, 256 N.E.2d 540, 308 N.Y.S.2d 385 (1970).

32 186 250 314 479 527   309 N.Y.S.2d 145
The People of the State of New York, Respondent v. Marion G. Adams, Appellant 26 N.Y.2d 129 (Court of Appeals of New York Jan. 22, 1970)
M/B: People v. Adams, 26 N.Y.2d 129, 257 N.E.2d 610, 309 N.Y.S.2d 145 (1970).

33 187 251 315 480 528   310 N.Y.S.2d 500
Ashland Oil & Refining Company, Appellant, v. State of New York, Respondent (Claim No. 42843) 26 N.Y.2d 390 (Court of Appeals of New York April 23, 1970)
M/B: Ashland Oil & Refining Co. v. State, 26 N.Y.2d 390, 258 N.E.2d 915, 310 N.Y.S.2d 500 (1970).
LR: Ashland Oil & Ref. Co. v. State, 26 N.Y.2d 390, 258 N.E.2d 915, 310 N.Y.S.2d 500 (1970).

34 188 252 316 481 529   311 N.Y.S.2d 481
The People of the State of New York, Respondent v. Thomas Alfred Ruppert, Appellant 26 N.Y.2d 437 (Court of Appeals of New York May 13, 1970)
M/B: People v. Ruppert, 26 N.Y.2d 437, 259 N.E.2d 906, 311 N.Y.S.2d 481 (1970).

35 189 253 317 482 530   312 N.Y.S.2d 317
Hempstead Bank, Appellant, v. Andy's Car Rental System, Inc. et al., Defendants, and Auto Buyers, Inc., Respondent 35 A.D.2d 35 (Supreme Court, Appellate Division, Second Department July 6, 1970)
M/B: Hempstead Bank v. Andy's Car Rental System, 35 A.D.2d 35, 312 N.Y.S.2d 317 (1970).
LR: Hempstead Bank v. Andy's Car Rental Sys., 35 A.D.2d 35, 312 N.Y.S.2d 317 (1970).

36 190 254 318 483 531   313 N.Y.S.2d 97
In the Matter of Franklin E. Simonson as Foreman of the December Term, 1969, Grand Jury, Respondent, v. William Cahn, as District Attorney of the County of Nassau, et al., Appellants 27 N.Y.2d 1 (Court of Appeals of New York July 1, 1970)
M/B: Simonson v. Cahn, 27 N.Y.2d 1, 261 N.E.2d 246, 313 N.Y.S.2d 97 (1970).

37 191 255 319 484 532   314 N.Y.S.2d 638
Application of Marvin D. Christenfeld, Commissioner of Elections of Nassau County, Petitioner, v. William D. Meisser, Commissioner of Elections of Nassau

EXERCISE 14. NEW YORK SUPPLEMENT   (CONTINUED)

County, Respondent 64 Misc. 2d 296 (Supreme Court, Special Term, Nassau County, Part I Sept. 24, 1970)
M/B: Christenfeld v. Meisser, 64 Misc. 2d 296, 314 N.Y.S.2d 638 (Sup. Ct. 1970).

38 192 256 320 485 533   315 N.Y.S.2d 353
Douglas A. Miller, Plaintiff, v. The Metropolitan Life Insurance Company and the Reuben H. Donnelley Corporation, Defendants 64 Misc. 2d 658 (Supreme Court, Erie County Nov. 2, 1970)
M/B: Miller v. Metropolitan Life Insurance Co., 64 Misc. 2d 658, 315 N.Y.S.2d 353 (Sup. Ct. 1970).
LR: Miller v. Metropolitan Life Ins. Co., 64 Misc. 2d 658, 315 N.Y.S.2d 353 (Sup. Ct. 1970).

39 193 257 321 486 534   316 N.Y.S.2d 221
Minnie Green et al., Appellants, v. Hugh Downs et al., Respondents 27 N.Y.2d 205 (Court of Appeals of New York Nov. 12, 1970)
M/B: Green v. Downs, 27 N.Y.2d 205, 265 N.E.2d 68, 316 N.Y.S.2d 221 (1970).

40 194 258 322 487 535   317 N.Y.S.2d 73
Sadie Motyl, Respondent, v. John Motyl, Appellant 35 A.D.2d 1051 (Supreme Court, Appellate Division, Third Department Dec. 29, 1970)
M/B: Motyl v. Motyl, 35 A.D.2d 1051, 317 N.Y.S.2d 73 (1970).

41 195 259 323 488 536   318 N.Y.S.2d 467
Edwin S. Lowe, Appellant, v. Jayne D. Quinn, Respondent 27 N.Y.2d 397 (Court of Appeals of New York Jan. 14, 1971)
M/B: Lowe v. Quinn, 27 N.Y.2d 397, 267 N.E.2d 251, 318 N.Y.S.2d 467 (1971).

42 196 260 324 489 537   319 N.Y.S.2d 89
Phillip Sweedler, Plaintiff, v. Martin Oboler and Dorothy Oboler, individually and doing business as Hecht Printing Co., and the Merchants Bank of New York, Defendants 65 Misc. 2d 789 (Supreme Court, Special Term, New York County, Part I Jan. 20, 1971)
M/B: Sweedler v. Oboler, 65 Misc. 2d 789, 319 N.Y.S.2d 89 (Sup. Ct. 1971).

43 197 261 325 490 538   320 N.Y.S.2d 433
Joseph Jacobson, et al., Plaintiffs, v. Henry Moskowitz, et al., Defendants 66 Misc. 2d 218 (Supreme Court, Special Term, New York County, Part I April 6, 1970)
M/B: Jacobson v. Moskowitz, 66 Misc. 2d 218, 320 N.Y.S.2d 433 (Sup. Ct. 1970).

44 198 262 326 491 539   321 N.Y.S.2d 239
Hannah Cronin, etc., Respondent, v. Pierce & Stevens Chemical Corporation, Appellant, et al., Defendant 36 A.D.2d 764 (Supreme Court, Appellate Division, Second Department March 29, 1971)
M/B: Cronin v. Pierce & Stevens Chemical Corp., 36 A.D.2d 764, 321 N.Y.S.2d 239 (1971).
LR: Cronin v. Pierce & Stevens Chem. Corp., 36 A.D.2d 764, 321 N.Y.S.2d 239 (1971).

45 199 263 327 492 540   322 N.Y.S.2d 238
Phyllis Payne, Appellant, v. Leonard R. Payne, Individually and as a Partner Doing Business under the Assumed Name of Paynes Body and Fender Garage, Respondent, et al., Defendant 28 N.Y.2d 399 (Court of Appeals of New York May 26, 1971)
M/B: Payne v. Payne, 28 N.Y.2d 399, 271 N.E.2d 220, 322 N.Y.S.2d 238 (1971).

46 200 264 328 493 541   323 N.Y.S.2d 440
Jacqueline Houston et al., Respondents v. Empire Mutual Insurance Company, Respondent, Motor Vehicle Accident Indemnification Corporation, Appellant, et al., Defendants 37 A.D.2d 605 (Supreme Court, Appellate Division, Second Department June 21, 1971)
M/B: Houston v. Empire Mutual Insurance Co., 37 A.D.2d 605, 323 N.Y.S.2d 440 (1971).
LR: Houston v. Empire Mut. Ins. Co., 37 A.D.2d 605, 323 N.Y.S.2d 440 (1971).

EXERCISE 14. NEW YORK SUPPLEMENT   (CONTINUED)

47 101 265 329 494 542   330 N.Y.S.2d 336
In the Matter of Lake George Steamboat Co., Inc., et al., Appellants v. Robert M. Blais et al., as Trustees of the Village of Lake George, et al., Respondents 30 N.Y.2d 48 (Court of Appeals of New York. Decided February 10, 1972)
M/B: Lake George Steamboat Co. v. Blais, 30 N.Y.2d 48, 281 N.E.2d 147, 330 N.Y.S.2d 336 (1972).

48 102 266 330 495 543   331 N.Y.S.2d 377
Stanley Novak, Appellant, v. Greater New York Savings Bank, Respondent 30 N.Y.2d 136 (Court of Appeals of New York March 16, 1972)
M/B: Novak v. Greater New York Savings Bank, 30 N.Y.2d 136, 282 N.E.2d 285, 331 N.Y.S.2d 377 (1972).
LR: Novak v. Greater N.Y. Sav. Bank, 30 N.Y.2d 136, 282 N.E.2d 285, 331 N.Y.S.2d 377 (1972).

49 103 267 331 496 544   332 N.Y.S.2d 552
Edward D. Murray, Plaintiff, v. Rupp Rental Corp., Defendant. Rupp Rental Corp., Third-Party Plaintiff-Appellant, v. S. A. Lindstrom Co., Inc., Third-Party Defendant-Respondent 39 A.D.2d 637 (Supreme Court, Appellate Division, Fourth Department April 19, 1972)
M/B: Murray v. Rupp Rental Corp., 39 A.D.2d 637, 332 N.Y.S.2d 552 (1972).

50 104 268 332 497 545   333 N.Y.S.2d 410
Marie Boland, Appellant, v. State of New York, Respondent 30 N.Y.2d 337 (Court of Appeals of New York May 5, 1972)
M/B: Boland v. State, 30 N.Y.2d 337, 284 N.E.2d 569, 333 N.Y.S.2d 410 (1972).

51 105 269 333 498 546   206 N.Y.S. 391
In re Winder 210 App. Div. 627 (Supreme Court, Appellate Division, First Department November 14, 1924)
M/B: In re Winder, 210 A.D. 627, 206 N.Y.S. 391 (1924).
LR: In re Winder, 210 A.D. 627, 206 N.Y.S. 391 (1924).

52 106 270 334 499 547   207 N.Y.S. 721
In re Simpson's Will 211 App. Div. 408 (Supreme Court Appellate Division, Second Department January 26, 1925)
M/B: In re Simpson's Will, 211 A.D. 408, 207 N.Y.S. 721 (1925).
LR: In re Simpson's Will, 211 A.D. 408, 207 N.Y.S. 721 (1925).

53 107 271 335 500 548   209 N.Y.S. 759
People ex rel. Steiger v. Collins, Acting Mayor of New York, et al. 213 App. Div. 76 (Supreme Court, Appellate Division, First Department May 15, 1925)
M/B: People ex rel. Steiger v. Collins, 213 A.D. 76, 209 N.Y.S. 759 (1925).
LR: People ex rel. Steiger v. Collins, 213 A.D. 76, 209 N.Y.S. 759 (1925).

54 108 272 336 401 549   210 N.Y.S. 737
Van Dyk v. Dujardin 213 App. Div. 791 (Supreme Court, Appellate Division, First Department July 6, 1925)
M/B: Van Dyk v. Dujardin, 213 A.D. 791, 210 N.Y.S. 737 (1925).

55 109 273 337 402 550   211 N.Y.S. 858
Ohio Match Sales Co. v. Everhard 126 Misc. 23 (Supreme Court, Special Term, New York County September 29, 1925)
M/B: Ohio Match Sales Co. v. Everhard, 126 Misc. 23, 211 N.Y.S. 858 (Sup. Ct. 1925).

56 110 274 338 403 551   212 N.Y.S. 189
Rolnick v. Borden's Farm Products Co., Inc., et al. 214 App. Div. 259 (Supreme Court, Appellate Division, First Department October 30, 1925)
M/B: Rolnick v. Borden's Farm Products Co., 214 A.D. 259, 212 N.Y.S. 189 (1925).
LR: Rolnick v. Borden's Farm Prods. Co., 214 A.D. 259, 212 N.Y.S. 189 (1925).

57 111 275 339 404 552   300 N.Y.S. 932
Chapin v. Austin 165 Misc. 414 (Supreme Court, Nassau County Nov. 26, 1937)

EXERCISE 14. NEW YORK SUPPLEMENT (CONTINUED)

M/B: Chapin v. Austin, 165 Misc. 414, 300 N.Y.S. 932 (Sup. Ct. 1937).

58 112 276 340 405 553   299 N.Y.S. 593
In re Osborn [consolidated on appeal with In re Citizens Trust Co. of Patchologue, listed second] 252 App.Div. 438 (Supreme Court, Appellate Division, Second Department Nov. 12, 1937)
M/B: In re Osborn, 252 A.D. 438, 299 N.Y.S. 593 (1937).
LR: In re Osborn, 252 A.D. 438, 299 N.Y.S. 593 (1937).

59 113 277 341 406 554   298 N.Y.S. 433
Gerry et al. v. Volger, Commissioner of Jurors 252 App. Div. 217 (Supreme Court, Appellate Division, Fourth Department Sept. 1, 1937)
M/B: Gerry v. Volger, 252 A.D. 217, 298 N.Y.S. 433 (1937).

60 114 278 342 407 555   297 N.Y.S. 827
Van Schaick, Superintendent of Insurance v. Title Guarantee & Trust Co. 252 App. Div. 188 (Supreme Court, Appellate Division, Second Department July 8, 1937)
M/B: Van Schaick v. Title Guarantee & Trust Co., 252 A.D. 188, 297 N.Y.S. 827 (1937).
LR: Van Schaick v. Title Guar. & Trust Co., 252 A.D. 188, 297 N.Y.S. 827 (1937).

61 115 279 343 408 556   296 N.Y.S. 649
Brand v. Teachers' Retirement Board et al. 163 Misc. 217 (Supreme Court, Special Term, New York County May 25, 1937)
M/B: Brand v. Teachers' Retirement Board, 163 Misc. 217, 296 N.Y.S. 649 (Sup. Ct. 1937).
LR: Brand v. Teachers' Retirement Bd., 163 Misc. 217, 296 N.Y.S. 649 (Sup. Ct. 1937).

62 116 280 344 409 557   295 N.Y.S. 360
Wall v. Great Atlantic & Pacific Tea Co. 162 Misc. 635 (Supreme Court, Delaware County April 7, 1937)
M/B: Wall v. Great Atlantic & Pacific Tea Co., 162 Misc. 635, 295 N.Y.S. 360 (Sup. Ct. 1937).
LR: Wall v. Great Atl. & Pac. Tea Co., 162 Misc. 635, 295 N.Y.S. 360 (Sup. Ct. 1937).

63 117 281 345 410 558   294 N.Y.S. 381
In re Lawyers Title & Guaranty Co. 162 Misc. 188 (Supreme Court, Additional Special Term, New York County Feb. 2, 1937)
M/B: In re Lawyers Title & Guaranty Co., 162 Misc. 188, 294 N.Y.S. 381 (Sup. Ct. 1937).
LR: In re Lawyers Title & Guar. Co., 162 Misc. 188, 294 N.Y.S. 381 (Sup. Ct. 1937).

64 118 282 346 411 559   293 N.Y.S. 85
Donohue v. Yonkers Sash Weight Corporation et al. 249 App.Div. 473 (Supreme Court, Appellate Division, Third Department Jan. 21, 1937)
M/B: Donohue v. Yonkers Sash Weight Corp., 249 A.D. 473, 293 N.Y.S. 85 (1937).

65 119 283 347 412 560   292 N.Y.S. 502
In re Mix 249 App. Div. 442 (Supreme Court, Appellate Division, Fourth Department Jan. 15, 1937)
M/B: In re Mix, 249 A.D. 442, 292 N.Y.S. 502 (1937).
LR: In re Mix, 249 A.D. 442, 292 N.Y.S. 502 (1937).

66 120 284 348 413 561   291 N.Y.S. 314
Title Guarantee & Trust Co. v. Mortgage Commission 248 App. Div. 509 (Supreme Court, Appellate Division, First Department Oct. 30, 1936)
M/B: Title Guarantee & Trust Co. v. Mortgage Commission, 248 A.D. 509, 291 N.Y.S. 314 (1936).
LR: Title Guar. & Trust Co. v. Mortgage Comm'n, 248 A.D. 509, 291 N.Y.S. 314 (1936).

EXERCISE 14. NEW YORK SUPPLEMENT   (CONTINUED)

67 121 285 349 414 562   290 N.Y.S. 726
Ferguson v. Janosec 248 App. Div. 898 (Supreme Court, Appellate Division, Second Department Oct. 23, 1936)
M/B: Ferguson v. Janosec, 248 A.D. 898, 290 N.Y.S. 726 (1936).

68 122 286 350 415 563   289 N.Y.S. 687
Singer et al. v. Title Guarantee & Trust Co. et al. 160 Misc. 447 (Supreme Court, Special Term, Kings County June 20, 1936)
M/B: Singer v. Title Guarantee & Trust Co., 160 Misc. 447, 289 N.Y.S. 687 (Sup. Ct. 1936).
LR: Singer v. Title Guar. & Trust Co., 160 Misc. 447, 289 N.Y.S. 687 (Sup. Ct. 1936).

69 123 287 351 416 564   288 N.Y.S. 500
Ament v. H. C. Bohack Co., Inc., et al. 159 Misc. 584 (Supreme Court, Nassau County May 29, 1936)
M/B: Ament v. H.C. Bohack Co., 159 Misc. 584, 288 N.Y.S. 500 (Sup. Ct. 1936).

70 124 288 352 417 565   287 N.Y.S. 396
Mendoza Fur Dyeing Works, Inc. v. Taylor 247 App. Div. 368 (Supreme Court, Appellate Division, First Department May 1, 1936)
M/B: Mendoza Fur Dyeing Works v. Taylor, 247 A.D. 368, 287 N.Y.S. 396 (1936).

71 125 289 353 418 566   286 N.Y.S 208
In re Gavrin 246 App. Div. 397 (Supreme Court, appellate Division, First Department March 13, 1936)
M/B: In re Gavrin, 246 A.D. 397, 286 N.Y.S 208 (1936).
LR: In re Gavrin, 246 A.D. 397, 286 N.Y.S 208 (1936).

72 126 290 354 419 567   285 N.Y.S. 548
Grengard Corporation v. Kew Gardens Corporation et al. 247 App. Div. 744 (Supreme Court, Appellate Division, Second Department Feb. 21, 1936)
M/B: Grengard Corp. v. Kew Gardens Corp., 247 A.D. 744, 285 N.Y.S. 548 (1936).

73 127 291 355 420 568   284 N.Y.S. 409
Zimmermann et al. v. Roessler & Hasslacher Chemical Co. 246 App. Div. 306 (Supreme Court, Appellate Dvision, First Department Dec. 30, 1935)
M/B: Zimmermann v. Roessler & Hasslacher Chemical Co., 246 A.D. 306, 284 N.Y.S. 409 (1935).
LR: Zimmermann v. Roessler & Hasslacher Chem. Co., 246 A.D. 306, 284 N.Y.S. 409 (1935).

74 128 292 356 421 569   283 N.Y.S. 681
Gunder v. 164 East 72d Street Corporation 246 App. Div. 139 (Supreme Court, Appellate Division, First Department Nov. 29, 1935)
M/B: Gunder v. 164 East 72d Street Corp., 246 A.D. 139, 283 N.Y.S. 681 (1935).
LR: Gunder v. 164 E. 72d St. Corp., 246 A.D. 139, 283 N.Y.S. 681 (1935).

75 129 293 357 422 570   282 N.Y.S. 593
Phillips v. New York Trap Rock Co. et al. 245 App. Div. 353 (Supreme Court, Appellate Division, Third Department Sept. 27, 1935)
M/B: Phillips v. New York Trap Rock Co., 245 A.D. 353, 282 N.Y.S. 593 (1935).

76 130 294 358 423 571   106 N.Y.S. 330
People ex rel. Eggers v. Bingham, Police Com'r. 121 App. Div. 593 (Supreme Court, Appellate Division, Second Department October 23, 1907)
M/B: People ex rel. Eggers v. Bingham, 121 A.D. 593, 106 N.Y.S. 330 (1907).
LR: People ex rel. Eggers v. Bingham, 121 A.D. 593, 106 N.Y.S. 330 (1907).

77 131 295 359 424 572   75 N.Y.S. 209
People ex rel. Argus Co. v. Bresler, Clerk of Common Council, et al. 70 App. Div. 294 (Supreme Court, Appellate Division, Third Department, March 21, 1902)
M/B: People ex rel. Argus Co. v. Bresler, 70 A.D. 294, 75 N.Y.S. 209 (1902).
LR: People ex rel. Argus Co. v. Bresler, 70 A.D. 294, 75 N.Y.S. 209 (1902).

EXERCISE 14. NEW YORK SUPPLEMENT (CONTINUED)

78 132 296 360 425 573   76 N.Y.S. 293
People ex rel. Wilson v. Flynn, Warden 72 App. Div. 67 (Supreme Court, Appellate Division, First Department May 9, 1902)
M/B: People ex rel. Wilson v. Flynn, 72 A.D. 67, 76 N.Y.S. 293 (1902).
LR: People ex rel. Wilson v. Flynn, 72 A.D. 67, 76 N.Y.S. 293 (1902).

79 133 297 361 426 574   39 N.Y.S. 744
Covert v. City of Brooklyn 6 App. Div. 73 (Supreme Court, Appellate Division, Second Department June 2, 1896)
M/B: Covert v. City of Brooklyn, 6 A.D. 73, 39 N.Y.S. 744 (1896).

80 134 298 362 427 575   42 N.Y.S. 576
Carll v. Village of Northport 11 App. Div. 120 (Supreme Court, Appellate Division, Second Department December 30, 1896)
M/B: Carll v. Village of Northport, 11 A.D. 120, 42 N.Y.S. 576 (1896).

81 135 299 363 428 576   94 N.Y.S. 178
Shaw v. Youmans et al. 105 App. Div. 329 (Supreme Court, Appellate Division, Third Department May 23, 1905)
M/B: Shaw v. Youmans, 105 A.D. 329, 94 N.Y.S. 178 (1905).

82 136 300 364 429 577   93 N.Y.S. 283
In re Preston 46 Misc. Rep. 46 (Supreme Court, Special Term, Suffolk County December, 1904)
M/B: In re Preston, 46 Misc. 46, 93 N.Y.S. 283 (Sup. Ct. 1904).
LR: In re Preston, 46 Misc. 46, 93 N.Y.S. 283 (Sup. Ct. 1904).

83 137 201 365 430 578   92 N.Y.S. 163
Bell v. Clarke 45 Misc. Rep. 272 (Supreme Court, Special Term, New York County November, 1904)
M/B: Bell v. Clarke, 45 Misc. 272, 92 N.Y.S. 163 (Sup. Ct. 1904).

84 138 202 366 431 579   91 N.Y.S. 503
In re Long Beach Land Co. 101 App. Div. 159 (Supreme Court, Appellate Division, Second Department January 6, 1905)
M/B: In re Long Beach Land Co., 101 A.D. 159, 91 N.Y.S. 503 (1905).
LR: In re Long Beach Land Co., 101 A.D. 159, 91 N.Y.S. 503 (1905).

85 139 203 367 432 580   88 N.Y.S. 52
In re Ryer 94 App. Div. 449 (Supreme Court, Appellate Division, First Department May 13, 1904)
M/B: In re Ryer, 94 A.D. 449, 88 N.Y.S. 52 (1904).
LR: In re Ryer, 94 A.D. 449, 88 N.Y.S. 52 (1904).

86 140 204 368 433 581   126 N.Y.S. 880
Pernisi v. John Schmalz's Sons Inc. 142 App. Div. 53 (Supreme Court, Appellate Division, Second Department December 30 1910)
M/B: Pernisi v. John Schmalz's Sons, 142 A.D. 53, 126 N.Y.S. 880 (1910).

87 141 205 369 434 582   125 N.Y.S. 613
People ex rel. Lyon v. Wallin, Commissioner of Elections et al. 141 App. Div. 34 (Supreme Court, Appellate Division, Second Department November 4, 1910)
M/B: People ex rel. Lyon v. Wallin, 141 A.D. 34, 125 N.Y.S. 613 (1910).
LR: People ex rel. Lyon v. Wallin, 141 A.D. 34, 125 N.Y.S. 613 (1910).

88 142 206 370 435 583   124 N.Y.S. 406
In re Hammond 140 App. Div. 19 (Supreme Court, Appellate Division, Fourth Department July 12, 1910)
M/B: In re Hammond, 140 A.D. 19, 124 N.Y.S. 406 (1910).
LR: In re Hammond, 140 A.D. 19, 124 N.Y.S. 406 (1910).

89 143 207 371 436 584   123 N.Y.S. 301
Miller v. American Sugar Refining Co. 138 App. Div. 512 (Supreme Court, Appellate Division, Second Department May 26, 1910)
M/B: Miller v. American Sugar Refining Co., 138 A.D. 512, 123 N.Y.S. 301 (1910).
LR: Miller v. American Sugar Ref. Co., 138 A.D. 512, 123 N.Y.S. 301 (1910).

EXERCISE 14.   NEW YORK SUPPLEMENT   (CONTINUED)

90 144 208 372 437 585   122 N.Y.S. 793
People ex rel. Webb v. Milliken et al. 66 Misc. Rep. 192 (Supreme Court, Special Term, Queens County February 1910)
M/B: People ex rel. Webb v. Milliken, 66 Misc. 192, 122 N.Y.S. 793 (1910).
LR: People ex rel. Webb v. Milliken, 66 Misc. 192, 122 N.Y.S. 793 (1910).

91 145 209 373 438 586   121 N.Y.S. 11
Mersereau v. L. K. Hirsch Co. 136 App. Div. 271 (Supreme Court, Appellate Division, Fourth Department January 12, 1910)
M/B: Mersereau v. L.K. Hirsch Co., 136 A.D. 271, 121 N.Y.S. 11 (1910).

92 146 210 374 439 587   120 N.Y.S. 580
In re Commissioner of Elections of Onondaga County 64 Misc. Rep. 620 (Supreme Court, Special Term, Onondaga County October 1909)
M/B: In re Commissioner of Elections, 64 Misc. 620, 120 N.Y.S. 580 (Sup. Ct. 1909).
LR: In re Comm'r of Elections, 64 Misc. 620, 120 N.Y.S. 580 (Sup. Ct. 1909).

93 147 211 375 440 588   119 N.Y.S. 751
Hedges v. Keiser 135 App. Div. 12 (Supreme Court, Appellate Division, First Department December 3, 1909)
M/B: Hedges v. Keiser, 135 A.D. 12, 119 N.Y.S. 751 (1909).

94 148 212 376 441 589   118 N.Y.S. 591
Heim v. New York Stock Exchange 64 Misc. 529 (Supreme Court, Special Term, Kings County September 3, 1909)
M/B: Heim v. New York Stock Exchange, 64 Misc. 529, 118 N.Y.S. 591 (Sup. Ct. 1909).
LR: Heim v. New York Stock Exch., 64 Misc. 529, 118 N.Y.S. 591 (Sup. Ct. 1909).

95 149 213 377 442 590   141 N.Y.S. 868
Morah v. Steele 157 App. Div. 109 (Supreme Court, Appellate Division, Third Department May 22, 1913)
M/B: Morah v. Steele, 157 A.D. 109, 141 N.Y.S. 868 (1913).

96 150 214 378 443 591   140 N.Y.S. 916
National Cash Register Co. v. McCann 80 Misc. Rep. 165 (Supreme Court, Trial Term, Cattaraugus County March 1913)
M/B: National Cash Register Co. v. McCann, 80 Misc. 165, 140 N.Y.S. 916 (Sup. Ct. 1913).

97 151 215 379 444 592   139 N.Y.S. 6
Post et al. v. Thomas et al. 153 App. Div. 865 (Supreme Court, Appellate Division, First Department December 13, 1912)
M/B: Post v. Thomas, 153 A.D. 865, 139 N.Y.S. 6 (1912).

98 152 216 380 445 593   138 N.Y.S. 456
Jostlen v. Great Atlantic & Pacific Tea Co. 153 App. Div. 528 (Supreme Court, Appellate Division, Third Department November 13, 1912)
M/B: Jostlen v. Great Atlantic & Pacific Tea Co., 153 A.D. 528, 138 N.Y.S. 456 (1912).
LR: Jostlen v. Great Atl. & Pac. Tea Co., 153 A.D. 528, 138 N.Y.S. 456 (1912).

99 153 217 381 446 594   137 N.Y.S. 466
Turner v. Bryant 152 App. Div. 601 (Supreme Court, Appellate Division, Third Department September 27, 1912)
M/B: Turner v. Bryant, 152 A.D. 601, 137 N.Y.S. 466 (1912).

100 154 218 382 447 595   136 N.Y.S. 688
People ex rel. Werner v. Prendergast. City Comptroller, et al. 152 App. Div. 104 (Supreme Court, Appellate Division, First Department July 11, 1912)
M/B: People ex rel. Werner v. Prendergast, 152 A.D. 104, 136 N.Y.S. 688 (1912).
LR: People ex rel. Werner v. Prendergast, 152 A.D. 104, 136 N.Y.S. 688 (1912).

LIBRARY EXERCISE 15.   AMERICAN LAW REPORTS ANNOTATED.

INSTRUCTOR'S NOTE: (a) Students are to cite the A.L.R. annotation that is listed below in proper USOC form. See Rule USOC 16.1.4. (b) The students are then to cite the case accompanying (preceding) the annotation in proper USOC form. They have been instructed not to include a reference to the A.L.R. citation the case nor a notation of the subsequent history of the case (e.g., certiorari denied, rehearing denied) in their citation. They are to use Shepard's Citations to find any missing parallel citations. (c) The students are then to state in what section or sections of the annotation have cases dealing the topic listed with their problem number below? For their answer, they are to state the sections (e.g., §§ 3[b], 5, 6). No special form is required for this answer. The relevant entry precedes the answers in this answer sheet for your information; the students will not show that entry in their answers. (d) For this part, the students are to find the "Total Client-Service Library References" listing at the beginning of the annotation. This list provides references to several other related (and very useful) research sources. They are told to examine this list and determine what topic(s) and section(s) of American Jurisprudence (a legal encyclopedia) that they could look to find a textual discussion of the topic covered by the annotation (e.g., 63 Am. Jur. 2d Public Officers & Employees § 197). For purposes of this Exercise, they are to state the reference to American Jurisprudence in the manner that it is given in the "Total Client-Service Library References." USOC form need not be used. If the student's typewriter does not have section signs, they are to write them in with a pen or pencil.

The following two Quick-Reference Abbreviations are particularly relevant to this exercise:

ANNOTATION CITATION 1.   CITE AN ANNOTATION (ABBREVIATED "ANNOT.") BY A.L.R. VOLUME, PAGE, AND A.L.R. PUBLICATION DATE. DO NOT INCLUDE THE NAME OF THE AUTHOR OR THE TITLE. [ANNOT 1]
ANNOTATION CITATION 2.   DO NOT INCLUDE A PARALLEL REFERENCE TO THE A.L.R. SERIES EVEN THOUGH THE CASE IS REPORTED IN THAT SERIES. [ANNOT 2]

1 146 230 308 427 529 39 A.L.R.3d 719   Improper grading of bar examination
Application of Arthur H. Peterson for Admission to the Alaska Bar Association (Alaska) 459 P2d 703, 39 ALR3d 708 (Alaska Supreme Court September 17, 1969)
(a)   Annot., 39 A.L.R.3d 719 (1971).
(b)   M/B: In re Peterson, 459 P.2d 703 (Alaska 1969).
      LR: In re Peterson, 459 P.2d 703 (Alaska 1969).
(c)   Grading, improper, §§ 3, 4
(d)   7 Am Jur 2d, Attorneys at Law §§ 8-11

2 147 231 309 428 530 14 A.L.R. Fed. 806   A general discussion of the "Scope-of-the-Project" Test
United States of America v 327 Acres of Land, situated in Murray County, Georgia, and John Campbell Mabem, John Brindie and Tax Collector of Murray County 320 F Supp 844, 14 ALR Fed 799 (United States District Court, N. D. Georgia, Rome Division January 4, 1971)
(a)   Annot., 14 A.L.R. Fed. 806 (1973).
(b)   M/B: United States v. 327 Acres of Land, 320 F. Supp. 844 (N.D. Ga. 1971).
(c)   "Scope-of-the-project" test, generally, §§ 2[a], 3
(d)   27 Am Jur 2d, Eminent Domain § 284; 8 Am Jur Trials 57, Condemnation of Rural Property for Highway Purposes; 11 Am Jur Trials 189, Condemnation of Urban Property

3 148 232 310 429 531 13 A.L.R. Fed. 416 Use of school records to meet age requirement
James T. Blanks, Plaintiff-Appellant, v Elliot Richardson, Secretary of Health, Education & Welfare, Defendant-Appellee 439 F2d 1158, 13 ALR Fed 410 (United States Court of Appeals, Fifth Circuit - March 25, 1971)
(a)   Annot., 13 A.L.R. Fed. 416 (1972).
(b)   M/B: Blanks v. Richardson, 439 F.2d 1158 (5th Cir. 1971).
(c)   School records, § 9
(d)   Am Jur, Social Security, Unemployment Insurance, and Retirement Funds (1st ed §§ 46-50)

EXERCISE 15. AMERICAN LAW REPORTS ANNOTATED   (CONTINUED)

4 149 233 311 430 532   9 A.L.R. Fed. 533   Review of arbitrary decisions
Southern Pacific Company, Appt., v W. H. Wilson 378 F2d 533, 9 ALR Fed 525 (United States Court of Appeals, Fifth Circuit - May 11, 1967)
(a) Annot., 9 A.L.R. Fed. 533 (1971).
(b) M/B: Southern Pacific Co. v. Wilson, 378 F.2d 533 (5th Cir. 1967).
     LR: Southern Pac. Co. v. Wilson, 378 F.2d 533 (5th Cir. 1967).
(c) Arbitrary decisions, § 5
(d) 48 Am Jur 2d, Labor and Labor Relations § 1146

5 150 234 312 431 533   8 A.L.R. Fed. 180   Value of a coal interest for eminant domain purposes
United States v Helen Louise Corbin, Virginia May Wyllie, et al., Appts. 423 F2d 821, 8 ALR Fed 168 (United States Court of Appeals, Tenth Circuit - March 23, 1970)
(a) Annot., 8 A.L.R. Fed. 180 (1971).
(b) M/B: United States v. Corbin, 423 F.2d 821 (10th Cir. 1970).
(c) Coal interest, value of, §§ 8[c], 19
(d) 27 Am Jur 2d, Eminent Domain §§ 381, 408, 409, 413-415, 418, 446, 447

6 151 235 313 432 534   7 A.L.R. Fed. 876   Scope of review of decisions relying on an exemption of material by the Freedom of Information Act
Julius Epstein, Plff.-Appt., v Stanley Resor, Secretary of the Army; Department of the Army; Department of Defense, Defts. 421 F2d 930, 7 ALR Fed 870, cert den 398 US 965, 26 L Ed 2d 549, 90 S Ct 2176 (United States Court of Appeals, Ninth Circuit - February 6, 1970)
(a) Annot., 7 A.L.R. Fed. 876 (1971).
(b) M/B: Epstein v. Resor, 421 F.2d 930 (9th Cir. 1970).
(c) Exempted material, scope of review of, § 6
(d) 2 Am Jur 2d, Administrative Law §§ 560, 642, 645, 701

7 152 236 314 433 535   5 A.L.R. Fed. 566   The probative value of expert testimony about claims of mineral interests on public lands
Ford M. Converse, Appt., v Stewart L. Udall, Secretary of the Interior 399 F2d 616, 5 ALR Fed 553, cert den 393 US 1025, 21 L Ed 2d 569, 89 S Ct 635 (United States Court of Appeals, Ninth Circuit - August 19, 1968)
(a) Annot., 5 A.L.R. Fed. 566 (1970).
(b) M/B: Converse v. Udall, 399 F.2d 616 (9th Cir. 1968).
(c) Expert witnesses - probative value of testimony of, § 7[b]
(d) 2 Am Jur 2d, Administrative Law §§ 553 et seq.; Am Jur, Public Lands (1st ed § 63)

8 153 237 315 434 536   2 A.L.R. Fed. 691   Requirement of pleading substantial evidence in a "dispute clause" case
United States, Appt., v Pickett's Food Service 360 F2d 338, 2 ALR Fed 682 (United States Court of Appeals, Fifth Circuit - May 6, 1966)
(a) Annot., 2 A.L.R. Fed. 691 (1969).
(b) M/B: United States v. Pickett's Food Service, 360 F.2d 338 (5th Cir. 1966).
     LR: United States v. Pickett's Food Serv., 360 F.2d 338 (5th Cir. 1966).
Evidence - substantial evidence - pleading lack of, § 4
Am Jur, Public Works and Contracts (1st ed § 70.5)

9 154 238 316 435 537   11 A.L.R. Fed. 368   Improper composition of a draft board as a denial of due process
United States of America, Appellee, v Robert Edward Reeb, Appellant 433 F2d 381, 11 ALR Fed 361, cert den 402 US 912, 28 L Ed 2d 654, 91 S Ct 1391 (United States Court of Appeals, Ninth Circuit - October 27, 1970)
(a) Annot., 11 A.L.R. Fed. 368 (1972).
(b) M/B: United States v. Reeb, 433 F.2d 381 (9th Cir. 1970).
(c) Due process, denial of, §§ 5, 7, 8[e], 10
(d) 53 Am Jur 2d, Military and Civil Defense § 57

10 155 239 317 436 538   38 A.L.R.3d 452   Loss of driving privileges because of advance age
William Lee Ormond, Petr., v Joe W. Garrett, North Carolina Commissioner of Motor Vehicles, Respt. 8 NC App 662, 175 SE2d 371, 38 ALR3d 448 (North Carolina Court of Appeals - July 15, 1970)

EXERCISE 15. AMERICAN LAW REPORTS ANNOTATED   (CONTINUED)

(a)   Annot., 38 A.L.R.3d 452 (1971).
(b)   M/B: Ormond v. Garrett, 8 N.C. App. 662, 175 S.E.2d 371 (1970).
(c)   Advanced age, § 14
(d)   7 Am Jur 2d, Automobiles and Highway Traffic §§ 106, 109, 11

11 156 240 318 437 539   6 A.L.R. Fed. 988   Safety standards for car windows
Boating Industry Association and Holsclaw Brothers, Inc., Petrs., v Honorable
Alan S. Boyd, Secretary of Transportation, Lowell K. Bridwell et al., Respts.
409 F2d 408, 6 ALR Fed 981 (United States Court of Appeals, Seventh Circuit -
March 27, 1969)
(a)   Annot., 6 A.L.R. Fed. 988 (1971).
(b)   M/B: Boating Industry Association v. Boyd, 409 F.2d 408 (7th Cir. 1969).
      LR: Boating Indus. Ass'n v. Boyd, 409 F.2d 408 (7th Cir. 1969).
(c)   Windows, § 1[c]
(d)   7 Am Jur 2d, Automobiles and Highway Traffic §§ 21, 149 et seq.

12 157 241 319 438 540   98 A.L.R.3d 453   Effect of subsequent illegitimate
children on a divorce decree
Irene J. Fleming, Appellee, v Frank M. Fleming, Appellant 221 Kan 290, 559 P2d
329, 98 ALR3d 445 (Supreme Court of Kansas January 22, 1977)
(a)   Annot., 98 A.L.R.3d 453 (1980).
(b)   M/B: Fleming v. Fleming, 221 Kan. 290, 559 P.2d 329 (1977).
(c)   Illegitimate children, effect of, § 8
(d)   24 Am Jur 2d, Divorce and Separation §§ 685-88

13 158 242 320 439 541   27 A.L.R.3d 1254   Wearing dress of the opposite sex
in a bar
One Eleven Wines & Liquors, Inc., Appt., v Division of Alcoholic Beverage
Control et al., Respts. 50 NJ 329, 235 A2d 12, 27 ALR3d 1242 (New Jersey
Supreme Court - November 6, 1967)
(a)   Annot., 27 A.L.R.3d 1254 (1969).
(b)   M/B: One Eleven Wines & Liquors, Inc. v. Division of Alcoholic Beverage
      Control, 50 N.J. 329, 235 A.2d 12 (1967).
(c)   Dress of opposite sex, wearing of, §§ 5, 6[c]
(d)   Am Jur, Intoxicating Liquors (Rev ed §§ 174-176)

14 159 243 321 440 542   17 A.L.R.3d 1408   Entrapment of a pharmacist
Cecil Randle, Doing Business as McPike Drug Company et al., Appts., v
California State Board of Pharmacy, Respt. 240 Cal App 2d 254, 49 Cal Rptr
485, 17 ALR3d 1398 (California District Court of Appeal, First District,
Division 2 - February 18, 1966)
(a)   Annot., 17 A.L.R.3d 1408 (1968).
(b)   M/B: Randle v. California State Board of Pharmacy, 240 Cal. App. 2d 254,
      49 Cal. Rptr. 485 (1966).
      LR: Randle v. California State Bd. of Pharmacy, 240 Cal. App. 2d 254, 49
      Cal. Rptr. 485 (1966).
(c)   Entrapment, § 11
(d)   25 Am Jur 2d, Drugs, Narcotics, and Poisons § 14

15 160 244 322 441 543   22 A.L.R.3d 749   Effect on an alien's return after
an unintentional or involuntary departure from the United States
Toon-Ming Wong v Immigration & Naturalization Service, Respt. 363 F2d 234, 22
ALR3d 743 (United States Court of Appeals, Ninth Circuit - July 18, 1966)
(a)   Annot., 22 A.L.R.3d 749 (1968).
(b)   M/B: Toon-Ming Wong v. Immigration & Naturalization Service, 363 F.2d
      234 (9th Cir. 1966).
      LR: Toon-Ming Wong v. Immigration & Naturalization Serv., 363 F.2d 234
      (9th Cir. 1966).
Note: "INS" probably is a widely enough recognized abbreviation to be
acceptable in the above citations.
(c)   Unintentional or involuntary departure, returning after, § 3
(d)   3 Am Jur 2d, Aliens and Citizens § 57

16 161 245 323 442 544   47 A.L.R.3d 822   Best evidence objection to radar
devices
Henry Arthur Sweeny v Commonwealth of Virginia 211 Va 668, 179 SE2d 509, 47
ALR3d 817 (Virginia Supreme Court of Appeals - March 8, 1971)

EXERCISE 15. AMERICAN LAW REPORTS ANNOTATED   (CONTINUED)

(a)   Annot., 47 A.L.R.3d 822 (1973).
(b)   M/B: Sweeny v. Commonwealth, 211 Va. 668, 179 S.E.2d 509 (1971).
(c)   Best evidence objection, § 14
(d)   7 Am Jur 2d, Automobiles and Highway Traffic §§ 315, 326-328

17 162 246 324 443 545   28 A.L.R.3d 788   Acceptance of the work by the owner
R. B. Bell et al., Appts., v J. A. Carver, d.b.a. Carver Air Conditioning Co.
245 Ark 30, 431 SW2d 452, 28 ALR3d 781 (Arkansas Supreme Court - September 3,
1968)
(a)   Annot., 28 A.L.R.3d 788 (1969).
(b)   M/B: Bell v. Carver, 245 Ark. 30, 431 S.W.2d 452 (1968).
(c)   Acceptance of work - by owner, §§ 6, 7, 12
(d)   13 Am Jur 2d, Building and Construction Contracts §§ 44, 67-71; 17 Am Jur
2d, Contracts §§ 384, 404, 405, 411, 414

18 163 247 325 444 546   15 A.L.R.3d 847   Assessments for turnpikes
Southwest Delaware County Municipal Authority, Appt., v Township of Aston et
al. 413 Pa 526, 198 A2d 867, 15 ALR3d 836 (Pennsylvania Supreme Court - March
17, 1964)
(a)   Annot., 15 A.L.R.3d 847 (1967).
(b)   M/B: Southwest Delaware County Municipal Authority v. Township of Aston,
413 Pa. 526, 198 A.2d 867 (1964).
      LR: Southwest Del. County Mun. Auth. v. Township of Aston, 413 Pa. 526,
198 A.2d 867 (1964).
(c)   Turnpike, assessment for, § 3[a]
(d)   Am Jur, Special or Local Assessments (1st ed §§ 93-95)

19 164 248 326 445 547   33 A.L.R.3d 229   Assistance of counsel in labor
relations hearings
Bud Brown, Appt., v Air Pollution Control Board 37 Ill 2d 450, 227 NE2d 754,
33 ALR3d 222 (Illinois Supreme Court - June 22, 1967)
(a)   Annot., 33 A.L.R.3d 229 (1970).
(b)   M/B: Brown v. Air Pollution Control Board, 37 Ill. 2d 450, 227 N.E.2d
754 (1967).
      LR: Brown v. Air Pollution Control Bd., 37 Ill. 2d 450, 227 N.E.2d 754
(1967).
(c)   Labor relations, § 11
(d)   2 Am Jur 2d, Administrative law §, 273, 274

20 165 249 327 446 548   32 A.L.R.3d 1151   Effect of reciprocity between
states
Milton Costello, Appt., v Emil A. Schmidlin, Deft. and Third-Party Plff. 404
F2d 87, 32 ALR3d 1139 (United States Court of Appeals, Third Circuit -
November 1, 1968)
(a)   Annot., 32 A.L.R.3d 1151 (1970).
(b)   M/B: Costello v. Schmidlin, 404 F.2d 87 (3d Cir. 1968).
(c)   Reciprocity between states, § 2
(d)   5 Am Jur 2d, Architects § 4; Am Jur, Licenses (1st ed §§ 68 et seq.)

21 166 250 328 447 549   20 A.L.R.3d 599   Requirements as to written
contracts
Joseph H. Silverberg, Appt., v Industrial Commission, Respt. 24 Wis 2d 144,
128 NW2d 674, 20 ALR3d 588 (Wisconsin Supreme Court - June 2, 1964)
(a)   Annot., 20 A.L.R.3d 599 (1968).
(b)   M/B: Silverberg v. Industrial Commission, 24 Wis. 2d 144, 128 N.W.2d 674
(1964).
      LR: Silverberg v. Industrial Comm'n, 24 Wis. 2d 144, 128 N.W.2d 674
(1964).
(c)   Written contracts - requirements as to, § 32
(d)   27 Am Jur 2d, Employment Agencies §§ 1-15

22 167 251 329 448 550   1 A.L.R. Fed. 838 Gambling conducted on vessels
United States v George Barrow et al., Appts. 363 F2d 62, 1 ALR Fed 826 (United
States Court of Appeals, Third Circuit - July 18, 1966) (a)   Annot., 1 A.L.R.
Fed. 838 (1969).
(b)   M/B: United States v. Barrow, 363 F.2d 62 (3d Cir. 1966).
(c)   Vessel, gambling conducted on, §§ 6, 11, 16[a]

EXERCISE 15. AMERICAN LAW REPORTS ANNOTATED   (CONTINUED)

(d)   15 Am Jur 2d, Commerce §§ 8, 25, 64, 68

23 168 252 330 449 551   1 A.L.R.4th 411   Absence of a "kill switch"
Blanche C. Young, Executrix of the Estate of Novel Young, Respondent, v Tide Craft, Inc., Dan Bell, d/b/a/ Bell's Winter Park, and Henry H. Hegel, d/b/a/ Berkeley Marine Center, of which Tide Craft, Inc. is Appellant 270 SC 453, 242 SE2d 671, 1 ALR4th 394
(a)   Annot., 1 A.L.R.4th 411 (1980).
(b)   M/B: Young v. Tide Craft, Inc., 270 S.C. 453, 242 S.E.2d 671 (1978).
(c)   "Kill switch," absence of, §§ 3[b], 4[a]
(d)   12 Am Jur 2d, Boats and Boating § 85; 63 Am Jur 2d, Products Liability §§ 5, 9, 82, 89, 114, 143

24 169 253 331 450 552   8 A.L.R.3d 749   Impeachment of a witness based on intoxication in a conversion action
People of the State of California, Respt., v Dean T. Stanley, Appt. 206 Cal App 2d 795, 24 Cal Rptr 128, 8 ALR3d 745 (California District Court of Appeal, Second District, Division 2 - August 16, 1962)
(a)   Annot., 8 A.L.R.3d 749 (1966).
(b)   M/B: People v. Stanley, 206 Cal. App. 2d 795, 24 Cal. Rptr. 128 (1962).
(c)   Conversion action, impeachment of witness in, § 7
(d)   Am Jur, Witnesses (1st ed §§ 704, 723, 758-764)

25 170 254 332 451 553   3 A.L.R.3d 1082   Warranty of fitness for duty
Joe Dragich et al., Appts., v Nikola Strika 309 F2d 161, 3 ALR3d 1077 (United States Court of Appeals, Ninth Circuit - September 26, 1962)
(a)   Annot., 3 A.L.R.3d 1082 (1965).
(b)   M/B: Dragich v. Strika, 309 F.2d 161 (9th Cir. 1962).
(c)   Warranty of fitness for duty, § 4[e]
(d)   Am Jur, Shipping (1st ed §§ 167, 169, 170

26 171 255 333 452 554   1 A.L.R.3d 642   Death on the High Seas Act
Furness, Withy & Co., Ltd., etc., Appts., v William Carter 281 F2d 264, 1 ALR3d 636 (United States Court of Appeals, Ninth Circuit - July 11, 1960)
(a)   Annot., 1 A.L.R.3d 642 (1965).
(b)   M/B: Furness, Withy & Co. v. Carter, 281 F.2d 264 (1968).
(c)   Death on High Seas Act, § 4
(d)   Am Jur, Evidence (1st ed § 218); Negligence (1st ed §§ 295 et seq.); Shipping (1st ed §§ 179-187, §§ 364-368).

27 172 256 334 453 555   50 A.L.R. Fed. 420 Failure to publish an allowance in a tarriff schedule
Bud Antle, Inc., Plaintiff-Appellant, v United States of America, Interstate Commerce Commission, Robert W. Meserve, Paul W. Cherington and Charles W. Bartlett, Trustees of the property of Boston & Maine Corporation, a corporation, debtor, Delaware & Hudson Railway Company, a corporation, Thomas F. Patton and Ralph S. Tyler, Jr., trustees of the property of Erie Lackawanna Railway Company, a corporation, debtor George P. Baker, Richard C. Bond, Jervis Langdon, Jr., and Willard Wirtz, trustees of the property of Penn Central Transportation Company, a corporation, debtor, Southern Pacific Transportation Company, a corporation, and Atchison, Topeka & Santa Fe Railway Company, a corporation, Defendants-Appellees 593 F2d 865, 50 ALR Fed 402 (United States Court of Appeals, Ninth Circuit March 21, 1979)
(a)   Annot., 50 A.L.R. Fed. 420 (1980).
(b)   M/B: Bud Antle, Inc. v. United States, 593 F.2d 865 (9th Cir. 1979).
(c)   Tariff schedule, failure to publish allowance in, §§ 3, 13[a]
(d)   13 Am Jur 2d, Carriers §§ 144, 470

28 173 257 335 454 556   3 A.L.R. Fed. 203   Necessity of signals
Petition of Marina Mercante Nicaraguense, S.A., as owner of the Motor Vessel El Salvador, for exoneration from or limitation of liability, Petitioner-Appellant-Appellee 364 F2d 118, 3 ALR Fed 187 (United States Court of Appeals, Second Circuit - July 21, 1966)
(a)   Annot., 3 A.L.R. Fed. 203 (1970).
(b)   M/B: In re Marina Mercante Nicaraguense, S.A., 364 F.2d 118 (2d Cir. 1966).

EXERCISE 15. AMERICAN LAW REPORTS ANNOTATED   (CONTINUED)

    LR: In re Marina Mercante Nicaraguense, S.A., 364 F.2d 118 (2d Cir. 1966).
(c) Signals, necessity of, § 5[c], 6[c, d]
(d) 2 Am Jur 2d, Admiralty § 189; 12 Am Jur 2d, Boats and Boating § 64; Am Jur, Shipping (1st ed § 230)

29 174 258 336 455 557   9 A.L.R. Fed. 768   Contributory negilgence
Brown & Root Marine Operators, Inc., and Brown & Root, Inc., Successor to Brown & Root Marine Operators, Inc., Appts., v Zapata Off-Shore Company 377 F2d 724, 9 ALR Fed 759 (United Sttes Court of Appeals, Fifth Circuit - April 24, 1967)
(a) Annot., 9 A.L.R. Fed. 768 (1971).
(b) M/B: Brown & Root Marine Operators, Inc. v. Zapata Off-Shore Co., 377 F.2d 724 (5th Cir. 1967).
(c) Contributory negligence, §§ 7, 8
(d) Am Jur, Shipping (1st ed § 578)

30 175 259 337 456 558   35 A.L.R.3d 907   Election of remedies in unauthorized policy cases
H. Albert Crawford and Walter S. Buckingham d.b.a. Buckingham-Wheeler Agency and Fidelity-Phenix Insurance Corporation, Appts., v Charles R. DiMicco et al. (Fla App) 216 So 2d 769, 35 ALR3d 899 (Florida District Court of Appeal, Fourth District December 31, 1968)
(a) Annot., 35 A.L.R.3d 907 (1971).
(b) M/B: Crawford v. DiMicco, 216 So. 2d 769 (Fla. Dist. Ct. App. 1968).
(c) Election of a remedy, § 5
(d) 43 Am Jur 2d, Insurance §§ 169-172

31 176 260 338 457 559   6 A.L.R.3d 519   Waiver of the right to object
Lynn Warden et al., Plffs. in Err., v State of Tennessee 214 Tenn 398, 381 SW2d 247, 6 ALR3d 513 (Tennessee Supreme Court - July 15, 1964)
(a) Annot., 6 A.L.R.3d 519 (1966).
(b) M/B: Warden v. State, 214 Tenn. 398, 381 S.W.2d 247 (1964).
(c) Waiver of right to object, §§ 6, 9, 14
(d) Am Jur, Jury (Rev ed §§ 173, 176, 226, 227)

32 177 261 339 458 560   4 A.L.R.3d 224   Teller of a bank as a dual agent
Franz Farr, Respt., v George W. Newman and Elbert C. Hardy, Appt. 14 NY2d 183, 250 NYS2d 272, 199 NE2d 369, 4 ALR3d 215
(a) Annot., 4 A.L.R.3d 224 (1965).
(b) M/B: Farr v. Newman, 14 N.Y.2d 183, 199 N.E.2d 369, 250 N.Y.S.2d 272 (1964).
(c) Teller of bank as dual agent, § 6[b]
(d) 3 Am Jur 2d, Agency §§ 233-238, 282-286

33 178 262 340 459 561   42 A.L.R.3d 1099   Block-busting rule
Ray Ford, Appellant, v Wisconsin Real Estate Examining Board, Respondent 48 Wis 2d 91, 179 NW2d 786, 42 ALR3d 1085 (Wisconsin Supreme Court - October 9, 1970)
(a) Annot., 42 A.L.R.3d 1099 (1972).
(b) M/B: Ford v. Wisconsin Real Estate Examining Board, 48 Wis. 2d 91, 179 N.W.2d 786 (1970).
    LR: Ford v. Wisconsin Real Estate Examining Bd., 48 Wis. 2d 91, 179 N.W.2d 786 (1970).
(c) Block-busting rule, § 3[b]
(d) 12 Am Jur 2d, Brokers §§ 19-22

34 179 263 341 460 562   30 A.L.R.3d 1395   Privity of contract as a factor
Ellsworth Dobbs, Inc., a New Jersey Corporation, Plff.-Appt., v John R. Johnson and Adelaide P. Johnson, His Wife, Defts. and Third-Party Plffs.-Respts.
(a) Annot., 30 A.L.R.3d 1395 (1970).
(b) M/B: Ellsworth Dobbs, Inc. v. Johnson, 50 N.J. 528, 236 A.2d 843 (1967).
(c) Privity of contract between parties as factor, § 3[a]
(d) 7 Am Jur 2d, Auctions and Auctioneers § 61; 12 Am Jur 2d, Brokers § 164

EXERCISE 15. AMERICAN LAW REPORTS ANNOTATED   (CONTINUED)

35 180 264 342 461 563   45 A.L.R.3d 1181   Liability of attorneys for negligent drafting or execution of wills
Robert E. Donald, Plaintiff and Appellant, v Lee A. Garry, Defendant and Respondent 19 Cal App 3d 769, 97 Cal Rptr 191, 45 ALR3d 1177 (California Court of Appeal, Second District, Division One - August 31, 1971)
(a)   Annot., 45 A.L.R.3d 1181 (1972).
(b)   M/B: Donald v. Garry, 19 Cal. App. 3d 769, 97 Cal. Rptr. 191 (1971).
(c)   Will drafting or execution, § 5
(d)   7 Am Jur 2d, Attorneys at Law §§ 198, 199

36 181 265 343 462 564   40 A.L.R.3d 1158   Effect of residency on the power to confess judgments
General Electric Credit Corporation, Plaintiff-Appellee, v Harold Tidenberg and Ben Hatcher, Defendants-Appellants 78 NM 59, 428 P2d 33, 40 ALR3d 1151 (New Mexico Supreme Court - May 29, 1967)
(a)   Annot., 40 A.L.R.3d 1158 (1971).
(b)   M/B: General Electric Credit Corp. v. Tidenberg, 78 N.M. 59, 428 P.2d 33 (1967).
      LR: General Elec. Credit Corp. v. Tidenberg, 78 N.M. 59, 428 P.2d 33 (1967).
(c)   Residency, effect of, § 4
(d)   47 Am Jur 2d, Judgments §§ 1107-1109

37 182 266 344 463 565   31 A.L.R.3d 953   Disqualification in quo warranto proceedings
Robert K. Corbin, County Attorney, County of Maricopa, the State of Arizona, Appt., v Ira Broadman, Wade Church, Arthur Daniels, Irving Fogel, and James Mack, Individually and/or Severally 6 Ariz App 436, 433 P2d 289, 31 ALR3d 943 (Arizona Court of Appeals - November 10, 1967)
(a)   Annot., 31 A.L.R.3d 953 (1970).
(b)   M/B: Corbin v. Broadman, 6 Ariz. App. 436, 433 P.2d 289 (1967).
(c)   Quo warranto proceeding, § 6
(d)   7 Am Jur 2d, Attorneys at Law § 158; 41 Am Jur 2d, Indictments and Informations §§ 249, 251; Am Jur, Prosecuting Attorneys (1st ed § 10)

38 183 267 345 464 566   57 A.L.R. Fed. 661 Validity of "Bad Boy" clauses
David C. Hepple, Appellant, v Roberts & Dybdahl, Inc., Restated Employee Profit-Sharing Plan, Appellee 622 F2d 962, 57 ALR Fed 653 (United States Court of Appeals, Eighth Circuit June 3, 1980)
(a)   Annot., 50 A.L.R. Fed. 661 (1980).
(b)   M/B: Hepple v. Roberts & Dybdahl, Inc., 622 F.2d 962 (1980).
(c)   "Bad boy" clauses, validity of, § 5
(d)   Am Jur 2d, New Topic Service; Pension Reform act §§ 92 et seq.

39 184 268 346 465 567   21 A.L.R.3d 483   The English common-law rule and exception to taking a client's oath
Storz Brewing Company, a Corporation, v R. N. Kuester, Appt. 178 Neb 135, 132 NW2d 341, 21 ALR3d 476 (Nebraska Supreme Court - January 8, 1965)
(a)   Annot., 21 A.L.R.3d 483 (1968).
(b)   M/B: Storz Brewing Co. v. Kuester, 178 Neb. 135, 132 N.W.2d 341 (1965).
(c)   English common law rule and exception, § 2
(d)   1 Am Jur 2d, Acknowledgments § 18; 3 Am Jur 2d, Affidavits § 9

40 185 269 347 466 568   97 A.L.R.3d 989   Resentment of wife working as a ground for divorce
Anna Lee Lillis, Appellee, v James F. Lillis, Appellant 1 Kan App 2d 164, 563 P2d 492, 97 ALR3d 981 (Court of Appeals of Kansas April 8, 1977)
(a)   Annot., 97 A.L.R.3d 989 (1980).
(b)   M/B: Lillis v. Lillis, 1 Kan. App. 2d 164, 563 P.2d 492 (1977).
(c)   Working wife, resentment as to, § 7
(d)   24 Am Jur 2d, Divorce and Separation § 166

41 186 270 348 467 569   17 A.L.R.3d 743   Validity of minimum area restrictions
Maurice M. Filister et al., Appts., v City of Minneapolis et al., Respts. 270 Minn 53, 133 NW2d 500, 17 ALR3d 733 (Minnesota Supreme Court - December 31, 1964)

EXERCISE 15. AMERICAN LAW REPORTS ANNOTATED   (CONTINUED)

(a)   Annot., 17 A.L.R.3d 743 (1968).
(b)   M/B: Filister, v. City of Minneapolis, 270 Minn. 53, 133 N.W.2d 500 (1964).
(c)   Minimum area restrictions, attacking validity of, § 3[b]
(d)   Am Jur, Municipal Corporations (1st ed § 170); Zoning (1st ed §§ 14, 209)

42 187 271 349 468 570   2 A.L.R.4th 859   Sales and use taxes on leased roadside advertising signs
Great Lakes Dredge and Dock Company v John H. Norberg, Tax Administrator 117 RI 600, 369 A2d 1101, 2 ALR4th 847 (Supreme Court of Rhode Island February 23 1977)
(a)   Annot., 2 A.L.R.4th 859 (1980).
(b)   M/B: Great Lakes Dredge & Dock Co. v. Norberg, 117 R.I. 600, 369 A.2d 1101 (1977).
(c)   Roadside advertising sign, § 9[b]
(d)   68 Am Jur 2d, Sales and Use Taxes §§ 53, 54, 68, 88, 113, 125, 210, 211

43 188 272 350 469 571   12 A.L.R. Fed. 638 Traditional authority of military commanders to exclude civilians from military installations
United States of America, Appellee, v Scott Bradley, Appellant 418 F2d 688, 12 ALR Fed 630 (United States Court of Appeals, Fourth Circuit - November 28, 1969)
(a)   Annot., 12 A.L.R. Fed. 638 (1972).
(b)   M/B: United States v. Bradley, 418 F.2d 688 (4th Cir. 1969).
(c)   Traditional authority of military commander to exclude civilians, § 3
(d)   Am Jur, Trespass (1st ed § 85)

44 189 273 351 470 572   60 A.L.R.3d 550   Fixed liquidated damage sums in sign or billboard contracts
Young Electric Sign Company, a corporation, Plaintiff-Respondent and Cross-Appellant, v O. M. Capps and Ralph E. Faught, Defendants-Appellants and Cross-Respondents 94 Idaho 518, 492 P2d 57, 60 ALR3d 541 (Supreme Court of Idaho - December 23, 1971)
(a)   Annot., 60 A.L.R.3d 550 (1974).
(b)   M/B: Young Electric Sign Co. v. Capps, 94 Idaho 518, 492 P.2d 57 (1971).
      LR: Young Elec. Sign Co. v. Capps, 94 Idaho 518, 492 P.2d 57 (1971).
(c)   Fixed sum, § 5
(d)   22 Am Jur 2d, Damages §§ 212 et seq.

45 190 274 352 471 573   43 A.L.R.3d 971   Mental condition of the depositor as a factor
Harold L. Rutchick, Executor of Estate of Jacob Salute, Respondent, v Nathan M. Salute, Appellant 288 Minn 258, 179 NW2d 607, 43 ALR3d 963 (Minnesota Supreme Court - August 28, 1970)
(a)   Annot., 43 A.L.R.3d 971 (1972).
(b)   M/B: Rutchick v. Salute, 288 Minn. 258, 179 N.W.2d 607 (1970).
(c)   Mental condition of depositor as factor, § 21
(d)   10 Am Jur 2d, Banks §§ 378-383; 38 Am Jur 2d, Gifts § 70

46 191 275 353 472 574   96 A.L.R.3d 22   Defective toys
Ray P. Barker, Plaintiff and Appellant, v Lull Engineering Company, Inc., et al., Defendants and Respondents; Employers Insurance of Wausau, Intervener and Respondent 20 Cal 3d 413, 143 Cal Rptr 225, 573 P2d 443, 96 ALR3d 1 (California Supreme Court January 16, 1978)
(a)   Annot., 96 A.L.R.3d 22 (1980).
(b)   M/B: Barker v. Lull Engineering Co., 20 Cal. 3d 413, 573 P.2d 443, 143 Cal. Rptr. 225 (1978).
      LR: Barker v. Lull Eng'g Co., 20 Cal. 3d 413, 573 P.2d 443, 143 Cal. Rptr. 225 (1978).
(c)   Toys, defectiveness of, § 33
(d)   8 Am Jur 2d, Automobiles and Highway Traffic §§ 646-657; 662-666; 63 Am Jur 2d, Products Liability §§ 62, 63, 65-68, 71-74; Am Jur 2d New Topic Service, Consumer Product Safety Acts §§ 1 et seq.

47 192 276 354 473 575   24 A.L.R.3d 1193   Unjust enrichment theory of recovery

EXERCISE 15. AMERICAN LAW REPORTS ANNOTATED   (CONTINUED)

Robert B. Sympson, as Assignee of Alfred H. Osborne, Appt., v Clay C. Rogers et al., Respts. (Mo) 406 SW2d 26, 24 ALR3d 1183 (Missouri Supreme Court, Division 2 - September 12, 1966
 (a) Annot., 24 A.L.R.3d 1193 (1969).
 (b) M/B: Sympson v. Rogers, 406 S.W.2d 26 (Mo. 1966).
 (c) Unjust enrichment, §§ 4, 5
 (d) 7 Am Jur 2d, Attorneys at Law § 225

48 193 277 355 474 576 11 A.L.R.3d 918   Prejudicial effect of a jury's unauthorized visit to the scene of the accident or premises in question
Joseph E. McBroom, Respt., v Cecil R. Orner et al., Appts. 64 Wash 2d 887, 395 P2d 95, 11 ALR3d 914 (Washington Supreme Court, Department 1 - September 3, 1964)
 (a) Annot., 11 A.L.R.3d 918 (1967).
 (b) M/B: McBroom v. Orner, 64 Wash. 2d 887, 395 P.2d 95 (1964).
 (c) Prejudicial effect of visit, §§ 3-6, 11, 12, 20
 (d) 5 Am Jur 2d, Appeal and Error §§ 888-890; Am Jur, New Trial (1st ed § 78); Am Jur, Trial (1st ed §§ 897, 1111)

49 194 278 356 475 577 50 A.L.R.3d 1164   Mind-altering drugs
The People of the State of Illinois, Appellee, v Thomas McCabe, Appellant 49 Ill 2d 338, 275 NE2d 407, 50 ALR3d 1149 (Supreme Court of Illinois - October 15, 1971)
 (a) Annot., 50 A.L.R.3d 1164 (1973).
 (b) M/B: People v. McCabe, 49 Ill. 2d 338, 275 N.E.2d 407 (1971).
 (c) Mind-altering drugs, § 3[b]
 (d) 25 Am Jur 2d, Drugs, Narcotics, and Poisons §§ 2, 17-22, 34-36

50 195 279 357 476 578 23 A.L.R.3d 683   Pick-up service as a branch bank
First National Bank of Logan, Appt., v Walker Bank and Trust Company, Respt. 19 Utah 2d 18, 425 P2d 414, 23 ALR3d 673 (Utah Supreme Court - March 20, 1967)
 (a) Annot., 23 A.L.R.3d 683 (1969).
 (b) M/B: First National Bank v. Walker Bank & Trust Co., 19 Utah 2d 18, 423 P.2d 414 (1967).
     LR: First Nat'l Bank v. Walker Bank & Trust Co., 19 Utah 2d 18, 423 P.2d 414 (1967).
 (c) Pickup service as branch bank, § 7
 (d) 10 Am Jur 2d, Banks §§ 324-329

51 196 280 358 477 579 41 A.L.R.3d 904   Child injured by unreasonable punishment
Sharon Streenz, a Minor, by Her Guardian ad Litem, William J. Francy, Appellant, v James T. Streenz and Ramona Streenz, Husband and Wife, Appellees 106 Ariz 86, 471 P2d 282, 41 ALR3d 891 (Arizona Supreme Court - June 11, 1970)
 (a) Annot., 41 A.L.R.3d 904 (1972).
 (b) M/B: Streenz v. Streenz, 106 Ariz. 86, 471 P.2d 282 (1970).
 (c) Unreasonable punishment, § 2[a]
 (d) Am Jur, Parent and Child (1st ed §§ 46, 90)

52 197 281 359 478 580 10 A.L.R. Fed. 940 Actions for violation of the Trust Indenture Act of 1939
Bruns, Nordeman & Co., a Limited Partnership, Plaintiff-Appellant, v American National Bank & Trust Company, Defendant-Appellee, and The Exchange Corp., Maurice Benjamin and Edward H. Levitt, Defendants 394 F2d 300, 10 ALR Fed 932, cert den 393 US 855, 21 L Ed 2d 125, 89 S Ct 97 (United States Court of Appeals, Second Circuit - April 19, 1968)
 (a) Annot., 10 A.L.R. Fed. 940 (1972).
 (b) M/B: Bruns, Nordeman & Co. v. American National Bank & Trust Co., 394 F.2d 300 (2d Cir. 1968).
     LR: Bruns, Nordeman & Co. v. American Nat'l Bank & Trust Co., 394 F.2d 300 (2d Cir. 1968).
 (c) Trust Indenture Act of 1939, action for violations of, § 4[a]
 (d) 10 Am Jur 2d, Banks § 836

53 198 282 360 479 581 7 A.L.R.3d 908   Right to set off with regard to deposits made in the name of a legatee

EXERCISE 15.   AMERICAN LAW REPORTS ANNOTATED   (CONTINUED)

Ames Trust and Savings Bank, an Iowa Corporation, v Herma E. Reichardt, Admrx., etc., of Charles R. Reichardt, Appt. 254 Iowa 1272, 121 NW2d 200, 7 ALR3d 900 (Iowa Supreme Court - April 9, 1963)
(a)   Annot., 7 A.L.R.3d 908 (1966).
(b)   M/B: <u>Ames Trust & Savings Bank v. Reichardt</u>, 254 Iowa 1272, 121 N.W.2d 200 (1963).
      LR: Ames Trust & Sav. Bank v. Reichardt, 254 Iowa 1272, 121 N.W.2d 200 (1963).
(c)   Legatee, deposit in name of, § 6[d]
(d)   10 Am Jur 2d, Banks § 671

54 199 283 361 480 582   44 A.L.R.3d 1283   Relation to a direct civil action
The Trustees of Tufts College v Volpe Construction Company, Inc. (Mass) 264 NE2d 676, 44 ALR3d 1272 (Massachusetts Supreme Judicial Court - December 8, 1970)
(a)   Annot., 44 A.L.R.3d 1283 (1972).
(b)   M/B: <u>Trustees of Tufts College v. Volpe Construction Co.</u>, 358 Mass. 331, 264 N.E.2d 676 (1970).
      LR: Trustees of Tufts College v. Volpe Constr. Co., 358 Mass. 331, 264 N.E.2d 676 (1970).
(c)   Direct civil rights action, relation to, § 4
(d)   15 Am Jur 2d, Civil Rights §§ 56-62

55 200 284 362 481 583   46 A.L.R.3d 369   Unwholesome influence of women employed in bars
Sail'er Inn, Inc., et al., Petitioners, v Edward J. Kirby, as Director, etc., et al., Respondents 5 Cal 3d 1, 95 Cal Rptr 329, 485 P2d 529, 46 ALR3d 351 (California Supreme Court - May 27, 1971)
(a)   Annot., 46 A.L.R.3d 369 (1972).
(b)   M/B: <u>Sail'er Inn v. Kirby</u>, 5 Cal. 3d 1, 485 P.2d 529, 95 Cal. Rptr. 329 (1971).
(c)   "Unwholesome influence," § 3[b]
(d)   16 Am Jur 2d, Constitutional Law § 514; 45 Am Jur 2d, Intoxicating Liquors §§ 151, 286

56 101 285 363 482 584   50 A.L.R.3d 1089   Discriminatory bussing plans
Citizens Against Mandatory Bussing, a Washington Corporation, et al., Respondents v Edward P. Palmason et al., Appellants 80 Wash 2d 445, 495 P2d 657, 50 ALR3d 1076 (Supreme Court of Washington, En Banc - April 6, 1972)
(a)   Annot., 50 A.L.R.3d 1089 (1973).
(b)   M/B: <u>Citizens Against Mandatory Bussing v. Palmason</u>, 80 Wash. 2d 445, 495 P.2d 657 (1972).
(c)   Discriminatory plan, § 3
(d)   15 Am Jur 2d Civil Rights § 40.5; Am Jur, Schools (1st ed § 162)

57 102 286 364 483 585   37 A.L.R.3d 645   Necessity of a hearing
Maynard V. Foster and Lebaron A. Foster, Appts., v Mobile County Hospital Board et al. (CA5 Ala) 398 F2d 227, 37 ALR3d 637 (United States Court of Appeals, Fifth Circuit - June 24, 1968)
(a)   Annot., 37 A.L.R.3d 645 (1971).
(b)   M/B: <u>Foster v. Mobile County Hospital Board</u>, 398 F.2d 227 (5th Cir. 1968).
      LR: Foster v. Mobile County Hosp. Bd., 398 F.2d 227 (5th Cir. 1968).
(c)   Hearing, necessity of, § 2[b]
(d)   40 Am Jur 2d, Hospitals and Asylums §§ 8-11

58 103 287 365 484 586   19 A.L.R.3d 1297   Indorsement on allonge
John Lopez et al., Appts., v Milo v. Puzina et al., Respts. 239 Cal App 2d 708, 49 Cal Rptr 122, 19 ALR3d 1291 (California District Court of Appeal, First District, Division 1 - January 28, 1966)
(a)   Annot., 19 A.L.R.3d 1297 (1968).
(b)   M/B: <u>Lopez v. Puzina</u>, 239 Cal. App. 2d 708, 49 Cal. Rptr. 122 (1966).
(c)   Allonge, indorsement on, §§ 4, 5, 6[a]
(d)   11 Am Jur 2d, Bills and Notes § 353

59 104 288 366 485 587   43 A.L.R.3d 824   Actions on rent notes

EXERCISE 15. AMERICAN LAW REPORTS ANNOTATED   (CONTINUED)

Walker McCune, Appellant, v Dynamics Research, Inc., an Arizona Corporation, and Pioneer Bank of Arizona, an Arizona Banking Institution, Appellees 8 Ariz App 13, 442 P2d 550, 43 ALR3d 813 (Arizona Court of Appeals - June 12, 1968)
(a)   Annot., 43 A.L.R.3d 824 (1972).
(b)   M/B: <u>McCune v. Dynamics Research, Inc.</u>, 8 Ariz. App. 13, 442 P.2d 550 (1968).
(c)   Rent note, action on, §§ 5, 9[b]
(d)   12 Am Jur 2d, Bills and Notes § 1088; 15 Am Jur 2d, Commercial Code; Am Jur 2d, Secured Transactions (1st ed, Pledge and Collateral Security § 71)

60 105 289 367 486 588   48 A.L.R.3d 240   Surviving spouse's right to custody of a dead body
Joseph V. Papieves and Margaret Papieves, his wife, Appellants, v Owen Norman Lawrence and Joseph J. Kelly 437 Pa 373, 263 A2d 118, 48 ALR3d 233 (Supreme Court of Pennsylvania - March 20, 1970)
(a)   Annot., 48 A.L.R.3d 240 (1973).
(b)   M/B: <u>Papieves v. Lawrence</u>, 437 Pa. 373, 263 A.2d 118 (1970).
(c)   Surviving spouse's right to custody of dead body, § 3
(d)   22 Am Jur 2d, Damages §§ 195, 196; 22 Am Jur 2d, Dead Bodies §§ 4, 14, 17, 34, 36, 40-43; 38 Am Jur 2d, Fright, Shock, and Mental Disturbance §§ 4-7

61 106 290 368 487 589   25 A.L.R.3d 1367   Whether the right to cancel depends on the noninterference with the intervening rights of other parties
Plantations Bank of Rhode Island et al. v Lawrence G. Desormier, d/b/a/ L. G. Desormier Roofing Co. (RI) 232 A2d 371, 25 ALR3d 1362 (Rhode Island Supreme Court - July 25, 1967)
(a)   Annot., 25 A.L.R.3d 1367 (1969).
(b)   M/B: <u>Plantations Bank v. Desormier</u>, 102 R.I. 565, 232 A.2d 371 (1967).
(c)   Intervening rights of other parties, right of cancellation as dependent upon noninterference with, § 3
(d)   10 Am Jur 2d, Banks §§ 592, 593

62 107 291 369 488 590   49 A.L.R. Fed. 511 Seizure of a tape recorder
United States of America, Plaintiff-Appellee, v Carl Will Sumlin, Defendant-Appellant 567 F2d 684, 49 ALR Fed 503, cert den 435 US 932, 55 L Ed 2d 529, 98 S Ct 1507 (United States Court of Appeals, Sixth Circuit December 14, 1977)
(a)   Annot., 49 A.L.R. Fed. 511 (1980).
(b)   M/B: <u>United States v. Sumlin</u>, 567 F.2d 684 (6th Cir. 1977).
(c)   Tape recorder, seizure of, § 5[a]
(d)   68 Am Jur 2d, Searches and Seizures §§ 49-53

63 108 292 370 489 591   62 A.L.R. Fed. 733 Conduct in excess of simple negligence
Mayview Corp., an Illinois Corporation, Plaintiff-Appellant, v Harvey B. Rodstein, an Individual and Rodac Pneumatic Tools, Inc., a California Corporation, and Rodac International Corporation, a California Corporation, Defendants-Appellees 620 F2d 1347, 62 ALR Fed 713 (United States Court of Appeals, Ninth Circuit February 4, 1980)
(a)   Annot., 62 A.L.R. Fed. 733 (1983).
(b)   M/B: <u>Mayview v. Rodstein</u>, 620 F.2d 1347 (9th Cir. 1980).
(c)   Simple negligence, conduct in excess of, § 4
(d)   60 Am Jur 2d, Patents §§ 487, 488

64 109 293 371 490 592   19 A.L.R.4th 861   "Sudden hate" in a prosecution for manslaughter
State of North Carolina v Jimmy Darrell Ray 299 NC 151, 261 SE2d 789, 19 ALR4th 841 (Supreme Court of North Carolina February 1, 1980)
(a)   Annot., 19 A.L.R.4th 861 (1983).
(b)   M/B: <u>State v. Ray</u>, 299 N.C. 151, 261 S.E.2d 789 (1980).
(c)   "Sudden hate", § 7
(d)   21 Am Jur 2d, Criminal Law § 226; 40 Am Jur 2d, Homicide §§ 216, 533, 534, 543, 544; 41 Am Jur 2d, Indictment and Information § 313; 75 Am Jur 2d, Trial §§ 422, 878-881

65 110 294 372 491 593   20 A.L.R.4th 637   Intoxication as a bar to unemployment compensation

EXERCISE 15. AMERICAN LAW REPORTS ANNOTATED   (CONTINUED)

Leonard M. Parker, Claimant-Respondent, v St. Maries Plywood, Employer, Defendant-Appellant, and Department of Employment, Defendant-Respondent. 101 Idaho 415, 614 P2d 955, 20 ALR4th 629 (Supreme Court of Idaho. July 3, 1980)
(a)   Annot., 20 A.L.R.4th 637 (1983).
(b)   M/B: Parker v. St. Maries Plywood, 101 Idaho 415, 614 P.2d 955 (1980).
(c)   Intoxication, § 5[a]
(d)   76 Am Jur 2d, Unemployment Compensation §§ 52, 53, 55, 57

66 111 295 373 492 594 22 A.L.R.4th 321   Termination of an employee's group insurance coverage as a result of the employer's mistake
Elbery Hendrix, Appellant, v Republic National Life Insurance Co., Appellee 270 Ark 955, 606 SW2d 601, 22 ALR4th 315 (Court of Appeals of Arkansas October 29, 1980)
(a)   Annot., 22 A.L.R.4th 321 (1983).
(b)   M/B: Hendrix v. Republic National Life Insurance Co., 270 Ark. 955, 606 S.W.2d 601 (1980).
      LR: Hendrix v. Republic Nat'l Life Ins. Co., 270 Ark. 955, 606 S.W.2d 601 (1980).
(c)   Mistake of employer, §§ 5, 7, 12
(d)   44 Am Jur 2d, Insurance § 1867

67 112 296 374 493 595 63 A.L.R. Fed. 446 Projects affecting marshlands
Save the Bay, Inc., Plaintiff-Appellant, v The United States Corps of Engineers, United States Army, Colonel Drake Wilson, and E.I. Du Pont De Nemours and Company, Defendants-Appellees 610 F2d 322, 63 ALR Fed 437, cert den 449 US 900, 66 L Ed 2d 130, 101 S Ct 269 (United States Court of Appeals, Fifth Circuit January 24, 1980)
(a)   Annot., 63 A.L.R. Fed. 446 (1983).
(b)   M/B: Save the Bay, Inc. v. United States Corps of Engineers, 610 F.2d 322 (1980).
(c)   Marshland, projects affecting, §§ 3[a], 4
(d)   2 Am Jur 2d, Administrative Law § 576; 59 Am Jur 2d, Parties §§ 20-44, 129-160, 61A Am Jur 2d, Pollution Control § 35

68 113 297 375 494 596   64 A.L.R. Fed. 552 Sufficiency of the notice
United States of America and Monroe Hollander, Special Agent, Internal Revenue Service, Petitioners-Appellees, v New York Telephone Company and K. Haupt, Business Office Supervisor, Respondents-Appellants, and Patsy Tuccio, Intervenor-Appellant 644 F2d 953, 81-1 USTC ¶ 9306, 64 ALR Fed 539 (United States Court of Appeals, Second Circuit March 27, 1981)
(a)   Annot., 64 A.L.R. Fed. 552 (1983).
(b)   M/B: United States v. New York Telephone Co., 644 F.2d 953 (2d Cir. 1981).
      LR: United States v. New York Tel. Co., 644 F.2d 953 (2d Cir. 1981).
(c)   Sufficiency of notice, § 5
(d)   34 Am Jur 2d, Federal Taxation §§ 9021-9023; 35 Am Jur 2d, Federal Tax Enforcement § 55.5

69 114 298 376 495 597 24 A.L.R.4th 870   Waiver by a guardian
Eldon Rufus Wakefield v Raymond Stevens 249 Ga 254, 290 SE2d 58, 24 ALR4th 865, on remand 163 Ga App 40, 292 SE2d 516 (Supreme Court of Georgia April 7, 1982)
(a)   Annot., 24 A.L.R.4th 870 (1983).
(b)   M/B: Wakefield v. Stevens, 249 Ga. 254, 290 S.E.2d 58 (1982).
(c)   Guardian, §§ 15[a], 16[b], 24
(d)   5 Am Jur 2d, Appeal and Error § 614; 46 Am Jur 2d, Judges §§ 224-229; 47 Am Jur 2d, Justices of the Peace § 8; 52 Am Jur 2d, Mandamus §§ 322, 323; 63 Am Jur 2d, Prohibition § 27; 77 Am Jur 2d, Venue §§ 61, 62

70 115 299 377 496 598 25 A.L.R.4th 787 Aiding and abetting suicide of victim
In the Matter of the Estate of Helen v. Safran Martin B. Gedlen, Edward F. Gedlen and Roman Safran, Appellants and Cross-Respondents, v Unborn Children of Bernard V. Safran, Jr., by their guardian ad litem, Louis D. Kaiser, Respondents, Bernard Safran, Jr., Respondent and Cross-Appellant 102 Wis 2d 79, 306 NW2d 27, 25 ALR4th 766 (Supreme Court of Wisconsin June 2, 1981)
(a)   Annot., 25 A.L.R.4th 787 (1983).

EXERCISE 15. AMERICAN LAW REPORTS ANNOTATED   (CONTINUED)

(b) M/B: Estate of Helen v. Gedlen, 102 Wis. 2d 79, 306 N.W.2d 27 (1981).
(c) Suicide of victim, aiding and abetting, § 16[a]
(d) 23 Am Jur 2d, Descent and Distribution §§ 94-101; 79 Am Jur 2d, Wills § 170

71 116 300 378 497 599   26 A.L.R.4th 396   Actions against landlords
Youvonna Stull, as Administratrix of the Estate of Windy Kay Stull, Deceased, and Individually, Appellant and Cross-Appellee, v James M. Ragsdale, Appellee and Cross-Appellant 273 Ark 277, 620 SW2d 264, 26 ALR4th 385 (Supreme Court of Arkansas July 6, 1981)
(a) Annot., 26 A.L.R.4th 396 (1983).
(b) M/B: Stull v. Ragsdale, 273 Ark. 277, 620 S.W.2d 264 (1981).
(c) Landlord, action against, § 10[b]
(d) 22 Am Jur 2d, Death §§ 112, 113; 59 Am Jur 2d, Parent and Child § 125

72 117 201 379 498 600   27 A.L.R.4th 864   Effect of summer employment
Gary M. Petersen, Appellant, v Linda J. Petersen, Appellee. 208 Neb 1, 301 NW2d 592, 27 ALR4th 858 (Supreme Court of Nebraska. February 6, 1981)
(a) Annot., 27 A.L.R.4th (1984).
(b) M/B: Petersen v. Petersen, 208 Neb. 1, 301 N.W.2d 592 (1981).
(c) Summer employment, §§ 13[b], 20[d]
(d) 24 Am Jur 2d, Divorce and Separation §§ 839-841

73 118 202 380 499 501   28 A.L.R.4th 227   Bail in treason cases
In re Thomas Hercules Pipinos on Habeas Corpus 33 Cal 3d 189, 187 Cal Rptr 730, 654 P2d 1257, 28 ALR4th 205 (California Supreme Court, En Banc December 10, 1982)
(a) Annot., 28 A.L.R.4th 227 (1984).
(b) M/B: In re Pipinos, 33 Cal. 3d 189, 654 P.2d 1257, 187 Cal. Rptr. 730 (1982).
    LR: In re Pipinos, 33 Cal. 3d 189, 654 P.2d 1257, 187 Cal. Rptr. 730 (1982).
(c) Treason, §§ 3, 4[b], 5[b], 10, 11
(d) 8 Am Jur 2d, Bail and Recognizance §§ 15, 36, 38, 41, 48, 49 74 119 203 381 500 502   29 A.L.R.4th 104   Identification by pickpocket victim
Robert Bedford, Jr. v State of Maryland 293 Md 172, 443 A2d 78, 29 ALR4th 91 (Court of Appeals of Maryland March 24, 1982)
(a) Annot., 29 A.L.R.4th 104 (1984).
(b) M/B: Bedford v. State, 293 Md. 172, 443 A.2d 78 (1982).
(c) Pickpocket victim, §7
(d) 29 Am Jur 2d, Evidence §§ 371-373, 828; 81 Am Jur 2d, Witnesses §§ 492, 632, 655

75 120 204 382 401 503   48 A.L.R. Fed. 131 Wife's consent to a warrantless search and seizure
United States of America, Appellee, v Lloyd Wright, Appellant 564 F2d 785, 48 ALR Fed 119 (United States Court of Appeals, Eighth Circuit October 14, 1977)
(a) Annot., 48 A.L.R. Fed. 131 (1980).
(b) M/B: United States v. Wright, 564 F.2d 785 (8th Cir. 1977).
(c) Wife consent to warrantless search and seizure by, §§ 3, 5-9[a], 11[b]
(d) 68 Am Jur 2d, Searches and Seizures §§ 49-53

76 121 205 383 402 504   18 A.L.R.4th 360   Use of tape-recorded conversations
Bobby Joe Maxwell, Petitioner, v The Superior Court of Los Angeles County, Respondent The People, Real Party in Interest 30 Cal 3d 606, 180 Cal Rptr 177, 639 P2d 248, 18 ALR4th 333 (California Supreme Court January 28, 1982)
(a) Annot., 18 A.L.R.4th 360 (1982).
(b) M/B: Maxwell v. Superior Court, 30 Cal. 3d 606, 639 P.2d 248, 180 Cal. Rptr. 177 (1982).
(c) Tape-recorded conversation, use of, § 24[b]
(d) 7 Am Jur 2d, Attorneys at Law §§ 184-189; 18 Am Jur 2d, Coram Nobis and Allied Statutory Remedies § 18; 21 Am Jur 2d, Criminal Law §§ 315, 315.5, 321, 323; 39 Am Jur 2d, Habeas Corpus § 53; 58 Am Jur 2d, New Trial § 161

77 122 206 384 403 505   30 A.L.R.4th 414   Memory losses
Clifton Edward Gibbons v The State 248 Ga 858, 286 SE2d 717, 30 ALR4th 404 (Supreme Court of Georgia February 3, 1982)

EXERCISE 15.   AMERICAN LAW REPORTS ANNOTATED   (CONTINUED)

(a)   Annot., 30 A.L.R.4th 414 (1984).
(b)   M/B: <u>Gibbon v. State</u>, 248 Ga. 858, 286 S.E.2d 717 (1982).
(c)   Memory loss, § 5[a]
(d)   29 Am Jur 2d, Evidence § 500; 81 Am Jur 2d, Witnesses §§ 599, 631

78 123 207 385 404 506   31 A.L.R.4th 851   Use of expert witnesses
Mack E. Vincent, Plaintiff-Appellant, v John Raglin, James Goodman, Salome Williams, Melvin Timmons, James Bradfield, Drucilla Bradfield, William O. Martin and North End Patrol Service, Inc., a Michigan Corporation, a/k/a North End Patrol Security Service, Defendants-Appellees, and Theodore Ritter, William Moore, Fred McGee, Allen Johnson, James Patterson, Lee Scott, George Keller, Rafe Evans, Bronson Shuler, Harold Steward and Greater St. John Baptist Church, Inc., Defendants-Appellees 114 Mich App 242, 318 NW2d 629, 31 ALR4th 842 (Court of Appeals of Michigan March 17, 1982)
(a)   Annot., 31 A.L.R.4th 851 (1984).
(b)   M/B: <u>Vincent v. Raglin</u>, 114 Mich. App. 242, 318 N.W.2d 629 (1982).
(c)   Expert witness, § 5[b]
(d)   66 Am Jur 2d, Religious Societies §§ 28, 29, 35

79 124 208 386 405 507   47 A.L.R. Fed. 490 Claims for cargo losses
Helena Marine Service, Inc., as owner of the Barge HMS-6, Appellee, v Sioux City and New Orleans Barge Lines, Inc., Appellant 564 F2d 15, 47 ALR Fed 483 (United States Court of Appeals, Eight Circuit October 17, 1977)
(a)   Annot., 47 A.L.R. Fed. 490 (1980).
(b)   M/B: <u>Helena Marine Service v. Sioux City & New Orleans Barge Lines</u>, 564 F.2d 15 (8th Cir. 1977).
      LR: <u>Helena Marine Serv. v. Sioux City & New Orleans Barge Lines</u>, 564 F.2d 15 (8th Cir. 1977).
(c)   Cargo losses, claims for, § 6[a]
(d)   70 Am Jur 2d, Shipping §§ 332, 333, 335, 336, 340, 346

80 125 209 387 406 508   32 A.L.R.4th 504   Failure of the judge to hold court because of illness
State of North Carolina v John Bangle Corl, Defendant, and Rutherford Leroy Corl and Elizabeth Flynn Corl, Sureties 58 NC App 107, 293 SE2d 264, 32 ALR4th 499 (Court of Appeals of North Carolina July 6, 1982)
(a)   Annot., 32 A.L.R.4th 504 (1984).
(b)   M/B: <u>State v. Corl</u>, 58 N.C. App. 107, 293 S.E.2d 264 (1982).
(c)   Illness of judge, failure to hold court, § 28
(d)   8 Am Jur 2d, Bail and Recognizance §§ 104-115

81 126 210 388 407 509   33 A.L.R.4th 663   Detention in a foreign country
State of New Mexico, Plaintiff-Appellee, v John Amador and Cotton Belt Insurance Company, Defendants-Appellants, and Finn Lee Patton, Defendant 98 NM 270, 648 P2d 309, 33 ALR4th 656 (Supreme Court of New Mexico July 13, 1982)
(a)   Annot., 33 A.L.R.4th 663 (1984).
(b)   M/B: <u>State v. Amador</u>, 98 N.M. 270, 648 P.2d 309 (1982).
(c)   Foreign country, detention in, §§ 7, 8
(d)   8 Am Jur 2d, Bail and Recognizance §§ 190-200

82 127 211 389 408 510   34 A.L.R.4th 609   Disciplinary actions against physicians for fee spliting
Sherwin H. Raymond v Board of Registration in Medicine 387 Mass 708, 443 NE2d 391, 34 ALR4th 600 (Supreme Judicial Court of Massachusetts, Suffolk December 8, 1982)
(a)   Annot., 34 A.L.R.4th 609 (1984).
(b)   M/B: <u>Raymond v. Board of Registration in Medicine</u>, 387 Mass. 708, 443 N.E.2d 391 (1982).
(c)   Fee splitting, § 6
(d)   61 Am Jur 2d, Physicians, Surgeons, and Other Healers §§ 80-101

83 128 212 390 409 511   35 A.L.R.4th 538   Punitive damages in oil pollution cases
St. Regis Paper Company, Appellant/Cross Appellee v J. B. Watson, Sr., Appellee/Cross Appellant 409 So 2d 75, 35 ALR4th 532 (District Court of Appeal of Florida January 14, 1982)
(a)   Annot., 35 A.L.R.4th 538 (1985).

EXERCISE 15.   AMERICAN LAW REPORTS ANNOTATED   (CONTINUED)

(b) M/B: St. Regis Paper Co. v. Watson, 409 So. 2d 75 (Fla. Dist. Ct. App. 1982).
(c) Oil pollution, § 10[a, b]
(d) 22 Am Jur 2d, Damages §§ 263-266

84 129 213 391 410 512   36 A.L.R.4th 544   Timeliness of substitution of conforming tender
T. W. Oil, Inc., Formerly Known as Joc Oil USA, Inc., Respondent v Consolidated Edison Company of New York, Inc., Appellant 57 NY2d 574, 457 NYS2d 458, 443 NE2d 932, 35 UCCRS 12, 36 ALR4th 533 (Court of Appeals of New York December 15, 1982)
(a) Annot., 36 A.L.R.4th 544 (1985).
(b) M/B: T.W. Oil, Inc. v. Consolidated Edison Co., 57 N.Y.2d 574, 443 N.E.2d 932, 457 N.Y.S.2d 458 (1982).
(c) Timeliness of substitution of conforming tender, § 7
(d) 67 Am Jur 2d, Sales § 361

85 130 214 392 411 513   37 A.L.R.4th 10   Use of a walking test
Commonwealth v Harvey McGeoghegan (and fourteen companion cases) 389 Mass 137, 449 NE2d 349, 37 ALR4th 1 (Supreme Judicial Court of Massachussets, Suffolk May 11, 1983)
(a) Annot., 37 A.L.R.4th 10 (1985).
(b) M/B: Commonwealth v. McGeoghegan, 389 Mass. 137, 449 N.E.2d 349 (1983).
(c) Walking test, § 4
(d) 7A Am Jur 2d, Automobiles and Highway Traffic § 101; 62 Am Jur 2d, Privacy § 17; 68 Am Jur 2d, Searches and Seizures §§ 16, 34-40

86 131 215 393 412 514   38 A.L.R.4th 648   Riots at sporting events
Ronald E. Campbell v The City of Birmingham 405 So 2d 65, 38 ALR4th 638 (Court of Criminal Appeals of Alabama October 6, 1981)
(a) Annot., 38 A.L.R.4th 648 (1985).
(b) M/B: Campbell v. City of Birmingham, 405 So. 2d 65 (Ala. Crim. App. 1981).
(c) Sports event, §§ 17[b], 28[a]
(d) 54 Am Jur 2d, Mobs and Riots § 17

87 132 216 394 413 515   39 A.L.R.4th 633   Use of a writ of attachment
In the Matter of the Estate of Nina Savage, Deceased Mona Joy Love, Claimant-Respondent v Joe Pogue, Personal Representative, Defendant-Appellant 650 SW2d 346, 39 ALR4th 625 (Missouri Court of Appeals, Southern District, Division Two April 14, 1983)
(a) Annot., 39 A.L.R.4th 633 (1985).
(b) M/B: Estate of Savage v. Pogue, 650 S.W.2d 346 (Mo. Ct. App. 1983).
(c) Writ of attachment, § 4
(d) 21 Am Jur 2d, Creditors' Bills §§ 34, 39, 40; 80 Am Jur 2d, Wills §§ 1597, 1598, 1616, 1635; Am Jur 2d, New Topic Service, Uniform Probate Code § 25

88 133 217 395 414 516   65 A.L.R. Fed. 835 Notes taken by juror as evidence
Raul Lara Martinez, et al., Plaintiffs-Appellees, v Food City, Inc., d/b/a Foodland, Defendant-Appellant 658 F2d 369, 65 ALR Fed 823 (United States Court of Appeals, Fifth Circuit October 7, 1981)
(a) Annot., 65 A.L.R. Fed. 835 (1983).
(b) M/B: Martinez v. Food City, Inc., 658 F.2d 369 (5th Cir. 1981).
(c) Note-taking by juror, § 6
(d) 32B Am Jur 2d, Federal Rules of Evidence §§ 327-330

89 134 218 396 415 517   66 A.L.R. Fed. 119 Search of the anal cavity
United States of America, Plaintiff-Appellee, v Mary Mae Harvey, Defendant-Appellant. 701 F2d 800, 66 ALR Fed 107, reh den (CA9 Ariz) 711 F2d 144 (United States Court of Appeals, Ninth Circuit. March 15, 1983)
(a) Annot., 66 A.L.R. Fed. 119 (1984).
(b) M/B: United States v. Harvey, 701 F.2d 800 (9th Cir. 1983).
(c) Anal cavity search, § 8
(d) 21 Am Jur 2d, Criminal Law § 364, Customs Duties and Import Regulations § 113.7; 60 Am Jur 2d, Penal and Correctional Institutions § 52.5; 68 Am Jur 2d, Searches and Seizures §§ 29, 47, 105

EXERCISE 15.   AMERICAN LAW REPORTS ANNOTATED   (CONTINUED)

90 135 219 397 416 518   6 A.L.R.3d 973   Absence of a warranty clause in the deed
Harvest Queen Mill & Elevator Company, a Corporation, et al., v John E. Sanders et al. 189 Kan 536, 370 P2d 419, 6 ALR3d 962 (Kansas Supreme Court - April 7, 1962)
(a)   Annot., 6 A.L.R.3d 973 (1966).
(b)   M/B: Harvest Queen Mill & Elevator Co. v. Sanders, 189 Kan. 536, 370 P.2d 419 (1962).
(c)   Warranty clause - absence of, § 6[b]
(d)   Am Jur, Railroads (1st ed §§ 100-104)

91 136 220 398 417 519   67 A.L.R. Fed. 282 Tolling of the statute
Arthur Haynes, for himself and all others similarly situated, Plaintiff-Appellant, v Singer Company, Inc., a New Jersey corporation licensed to do business in the State of Florida, Third Party Defendant-Appellee 696 F2d 884, 67 ALR Fed 275 (United States Court of Appeals, Eleventh Circuit January 24, 1983)
(a)   Annot., 67 A.L.R. Fed. 282 (1984).
(b)   M/B: Haynes v. Singer Co., 696 F.2d 884 (11th Cir. 1983).
(c)   Tolling of statute, §§ 4, 7
(d)   48A Am Jur 2d, Labor & Labor Relations §§ 2467-2475

92 137 221 399 418 520   68 A.L.R. Fed. 861 Seizure of articles in plain view
N. W. Whitley, Plaintiff-Appellee, Cross-Appellant, v George W. Seibel, individually and as a police officer of the Chicago Police Department, Defendant-Appellant, Cross-Appellee 676 F2d 245, 68 ALR Fed 848, cert den (US) 74 L Ed 2d 198, 103 S Ct 254 (United States Court of Appeals, Seventh Circuit March 24, 1982)
(a)   Annot., 68 A.L.R. Fed. 861 (1984).
(b)   M/B: Whitley v. Seibel, 676 F.2d 245 (7th Cir. 1982).
(c)   Plain view, seizure of articles in, § 6[b]
(d)   15 Am Jur 2d, Civil Rights §§ 16-27, 279-287.5; 46 Am Jur 2d, Judgments §§ 394-429

93 138 222 400 419 521   46 A.L.R. Fed. 657 Fees charged by utility companies
Herby Berryhill and Lucille Berryhill, Plaintiffs-Appellees, v Rich Plan of Pensacola, a corporation et al., Defendants-Appellants 578 F2d 1092, 46 ALR Fed 642 (United States Court of Appeals, Fifth Circuit August 24, 1978)
(a)   Annot., 46 A.L.R. Fed. 657 (1980).
(b)   M/B: Berryhill v. Rich Plan, 578 F.2d 1092 (5th Cir. 1978).
(c)   Utility company, fees charged by, §§ 4[b], 12
(d)   Am Jur 2d, New Topic Service, Consumer Credit Protection §§ 21-25

94 139 223 301 420 522   58 A.L.R.3d 188   Accured payments
Ruth Lacy Carpenter, as Administratrix of the Estate of Donn Michael Carpenter, Deceased, Appellant, v Mildred M. Sylvester, Appellee (Fla App) 267 So 2d 370, 58 ALR3d 183 (District Court of Appeal of Florida, Third District October 17, 1972)
(a)   Annot., 58 A.L.R.3d 188 (1974).
(b)   M/B: Carpenter v. Sylvester, 267 So. 2d 370 (Fla. Dist. Ct. App. 1972).
(c)   Accrued payments, §§ 3, 5
(d)   1 Am Jur 2d, Abatement, Survival, and Revival § 47; 10 Am Jur 2d, Bastards §§ 68, 97

95 140 224 302 421 523   69 A.L.R. Fed. 130 Reliance on novel theories
Emil F. Goldhaber, Martin Katz d/b/a Atlas Reporting Service, and Helen Mattis v William E. Foley, Edward Garabedian, Donald Seay, Paul R. Tuell, and Rhoda Abovitz and Sally Nitchie d/b/a Abovitz & Nitchie, Appellees 698 F2d 193, 69 ALR Fed 120 (United States Court of Appeals, Third Circuit January 17, 1983)
(a)   Annot., 69 A.L.R. Fed. 130 (1984).
(b)   M/B: Goldhaber v. Foley, 698 F.2d 193 (3d Cir. 1983).
(c)   Novel theories, reliance on, § 6
(d)   35 Am Jur 2d, Federal Tort Claims Act § 142; 77 Am Jur 2d, United States §§ 122-124

96 141 225 303 422 524   70 A.L.R. Fed. 427 Accidents related to work

EXERCISE 15. AMERICAN LAW REPORTS ANNOTATED   (CONTINUED)

Roger E. Dorman, Plaintiff-Appellant, v Patricia R. Harris, Secretary of
Health and Human Services, Defendant-Appellee 633 F2d 1035, 70 ALR Fed 418
(United States Court of Appeals, Second Circuit October 15, 1980)
(a)   Annot., 70 A.L.R. Fed. 427 (1984).
(b)   M/B: <u>Dorman v. Harris</u>, 633 F.2d 1035 (2d Cir. 1980).
(c)   Work-related accident, §§ 6[a], 8[b]
(d)   70 Am Jur 2d, Social Security and Medicare §§ 44, 46

97 142 226 304 423 525   21 A.L.R.3d 1383   Disability of preachers
Avemco Life Insurance Company, Appt., v Albert H. Luebker 240 Ark 349, 399
SW2d 265, 21 ALR3d 1378 (Arkansas Supreme Court - February 21, 1966)
(a)   Annot., 21 A.L.R.3d 1383 (1968).
(b)   M/B: <u>Avemco Life Insurance Co. v. Luebker</u>, 240 Ark. 349, 399 S.W.2d 265
      (1966).
      LR: Avemco Life Ins. Co. v. Luebker, 240 Ark. 349, 399 S.W.2d 265
      (1966).
(c)   Preacher, §§ 10, 26[b]
(d)   Am Jur, Insurance (Rev ed §§ 1515-1521)

98 143 227 305 424 526   71 A.L.R. Fed. 875 Applicability of state law
Lam Quy, et al., v Air America, Inc., Appellant 215 App DC 181, 667 F2d 1059,
32 FR Serv 2d 1346, 71 ALR Fed 859 (United States Court of Appeals, District
of Columbia Circuit October 20, 1981)
(a)   Annot., 71 A.L.R. Fed. 875 (1985).
(b)   M/B: <u>Quy v. Air America, Inc.</u>, 667 F.2d 1059 (D.C. Cir. 1981).
      LR: Quy v. Air Am., Inc., 667 F.2d 1059 (D.C. Cir. 1981).
(c)   State law, applicability, § 9
(d)   20 Am Jur 2d, Costs § 65

99 144 228 306 425 527   72 A.L.R. Fed. 191 Termination of gas service
Richard Boudreaux, Plaintiff-Appellant, v Pat Puckett, d/b/a Pat Puckett Auto
Sales et al., Defendants, Western Surety Co., Defendant-Appellee 611 F2d 1028,
72 ALR Fed 183 (United States Court of Appeals, Fifth Circuit February 14
1980)
(a)   Annot., 72 A.L.R. Fed. 191 (1985).
(b)   M/B: <u>Boudreauz v. Puckett</u>, 611 F.2d 1028 (5th Cir. 1980).
(c)   Gas utility service, termination, § 8[d]
(d)   32A Am Jur 2d, Federal Practice and Procedure §§ 1246-1248, 1250

100 145 229 307 426 528   73 A.L.R. Fed. 112 Disclosure in a television report
United States of America, Plaintiff-Appellant v Lance E. Eisenberg and T.
Lamar Chester, Defendants-Appellees 711 F2d 959, 73 ALR Fed 101 (United States
Court of Appeals, Eleventh Circuit July 26, 1983)
(a)   Annot., 73 A.L.R. Fed. 112 (1985).
(b)   M/B: <u>United States v. Eisenberg</u>, 711 F.2d 959 (11th Cir. 1983).
(c)   Television reports, § 5[a]
(d)   21A Am Jur 2d, Criminal Law § 775; 38 Am Jur 2d, Grand Jury §§ 18, 39, 40

LIBRARY EXERCISE 16. ANNOTATIONS IN U.S. SUPREME COURT REPORTS, LAWYER'S EDITION.

INSTRUCTOR'S NOTE: (a) Students are required to answer the question given for their problem number. (b) They then are required to cite the reported Supreme Court case that accompanies the annotation in the <u>United States Reports</u>. In L. Ed. 2d, that case is in the main part of the volume. They are specifically instructed to cite the case to <u>United States Reports</u> without parallel citations.

1 109 290 319 408 581
District of Columbia, Petitioner, v. Georgiana Thompson 281 U.S. 25-33 (1930)
(a)   Yes.
(b)   M/B: <u>District of Columbia v. Thompson</u>, 21 U.S. 25 (1930).

2 110 291 320 409 582
Chicago, Milwaukee, & St. Paul Railway Company, Plff. in Err., v. Patrick L. Solan 169 U.S. 133 (January 17, 1898)
(a)   No.
(b)   M/B: <u>Chicago, Milwaukee. & St. Paul Railway</u>, 169 U.S. 133 (1898).
      LR: Chicago, M. & St. P. Ry., 169 U.S. 133 (1898) OR Chicago, M. & S.P. Ry., 169 U.S. 133 (1898).

3 111 292 321 410 583
Thomas E. Pollard, Petitioner, v United States of America 352 US 354 (February 25, 1957)
(a)   Yes.
(b)   M/B: <u>Pollard v. United States</u>, 352 U.S. 354 (1957).

4 112 293 322 411 584
American Banan Company, Plff. in Err., v. United Fruit Company 213 U.S. 347 (April 26, 1909)
(a)   Yes.
(b)   M/B: <u>American Banana Co. v. United Fruit Co.</u>, 213 U.S. 347 (1909).

5 113 294 323 412 585
United States, Petitioner, v. Binghamton Construction Company, Inc. 347 US 171 (March 8, 1954)
(a)   Davis-Bacon Act
(b)   M/B: <u>United States v. Binghamton Construction Co.</u>, 347 U.S. 171 (1954).
      LR: United States v. Binghamton Constr. Co., 347 U.S. 171 (1954).

6 114 295 324 413 585
James C. Woodard, Secretary of Corrections of North Carolina, et al. v James W. Hutchins 464 U.S. 377 (January 13, 1984)
(a)   Yes.
(b)   M/B: <u>Woodard v. Hutchins</u>, 464 U.S. 377 (1984).

7 115 296 325 414 587
United States of America, Petitioner, v. Edward A. Rumely 345 US 41 (March 9, 1953)
(a)   No.
(b)   M/B: <u>United States v. Rumely</u>, 345 U.S. 41 (1953).

8 116 297 326 415 588
United States of America, Petitioner, v. Alexander Lawrence Alpers 338 US 680-688 (February 6, 1950)
(a)   Ejusdem generis
(b)   M/B: <u>United States v. Alpers</u>, 338 U.S. 680 (1950).

9 117 298 327 416 589
Frederick W. Wade, Petitioner, v. Walter A. Hunter, Warden, United States Penitentiary, Leavenworth, Kansas 336 US 684-694 (April 25, 1949)
(a)   Two
(b)   M/B: <u>Wade v. Hunter</u>, 336 U.S. 684 (1949).

10 118 299 328 417 590
California Reduction Company et al., Petitioners, v. Sanitary Reduction Works of San Francisco 199 U.S. 306 (November 27, 1905)

EXERCISE 16. ANNOTATIONS IN U.S. SUPREME COURT REPORTS, L. ED. (CONTINUED)

(a) Yes.
(b) M/B: California Reduction Co. v. Sanitary Reduction Works, 199 U.S. 306 (1905).

11 119 300 329 418 591
Stephen A. Ralli et al., Appts., v. Howard D. Troop et al. 157 U.S. 386 (April 1, 1895)
(a) General average
(b) M/B: Ralli v. Troop, 157 U.S. 386 (1895).

12 120 201 330 419 592
John Miles, Plff. in Err., v. United States. 103 U.S. (April 4, 1881)
(a) No.
(b) M/B: Miles v. United States, 103 U.S. 304 (1881).

13 121 202 331 420 593
Louis Loeb, Plff. in Err., v. Trustees of Columbia Township, Hamilton County, Ohio 179 U.S. 472 (December 10, 1900)
(a) No.
(b) M/B: Loeb v. Trustees of Columbia Township, 179 U.S. 472 (1900).

14 122 203 332 421 594
Fred Y. Oyama and Kajiro Oyama, Individually and as Guardian of Fred Y. Oyama, Petitioners, v. State of California 332 US 633-689 (January 19, 1948)
(a) Alien land laws.
(b) M/B: Oyama v. California, 332 U.S. 633 (1948).

15 123 204 333 422 595
Clifford Vaughan, Petitioner, v N. J. Atkinson, etc., et al. 369 US 527 (May 14, 1962)
(a) Yes.
(b) M/B: Vaughan v. Atkinson, 369 U.S. 527 (1962).

16 124 205 334 423 596
National Labor Relations Board, Petitioner, v C & C Plywood Corp. 385 US 421 (January 9, 1967)
(a) Yes.
(b) M/B: NLRB v. C & C Plywood Corp., 385 U.S. 421 (1967).

17 125 206 335 424 597
George Henry Warren et al., Appts., v. William King, Ohio and Mississippi Railway Company, Allan Campbell, Farmers' Loan and Trust Company et al. 108 U.S. (May 7, 1883)
(a) Yes.
(b) M/B: Warren v. King, 108 U.S. 389 (1883).

18 126 207 335 425 598
Christian F. Braen, Petitioner, v Pfeifer Oil Transportation Company, Inc. 361 US 129 (December 14, 1959)
(a) Yes.
(b) M/B: Braen v. Pfeifer Oil Transportation Co., 361 U.S. 129 (1959).
    LR: Braen v. Pfeifer Oil Transp. Co., 361 U.S. 129 (1959).

19 127 208 337 426 599
Paul Scharrenberg, Petitioner, v. Dollar Steamship Company et al. _____ (November 5, 1917)
(a) Aliens imported into the United States under contract to perform labor or service.
(b) M/B: Scharrenberg v. Dollar Steamship Co., 245 U.S. 122 (1917).
    LR: Scharrenberg v. Dollar S.S. Co., 245 U.S. 122 (1917).

20 128 209 338 427 600
Jay Burns Baking Company et al., Plffs. in Err., v. Charles W. Bryan, as Governor of the State of Nebraska, et al. 264 U.S. (April 14, 1924)
(a) No.
(b) M/B: Jay Burns Baking Co. v. Bryan, 264 U.S. 504 (1924).

EXERCISE 16.   ANNOTATIONS IN U.S. SUPREME COURT REPORTS, L. ED.   (CONTINUED)

21 129 210 339 428 501
New Orleans Insurance Company, Plff. in Err., v. The E. D. Albro Company 112 U.S. 506-510 (Dec. 8, 1884)
(a)   Yes.
(b)   M/B: New Orleans Insurance Co. v. E.D. Albro Co., 112 U.S. 506 (1884).
      LR: New Orleans Ins. Co. v. E.D. Albro Co., 112 U.S. 506 (1884).

22 130 211 340 429 502
United States, Petitioner, v. Robert Morss Lovett. (No. 809.) 328 US 303-330 (June 3, 1946)
(a)   Bill of attainder.
(b)   M/B: United States v. Lovett, 328 U.S. 303 (1946).

23 131 212 341 430 503
Carl Schnell et al., Petitioners, v Peter Eckrich & Sons, Inc., et al. 365 US 260 (February 20, 1961)
(a)   No.
(b)   M/B: Schnell v. Peter Eckrich & Sons, 365 U.S. 260 (1961).

24 132 213 342 431 504
The Hot Springs Railroad Company, Plff. in Err., v. Frannie G. Williamson 136 U.S. 121-130 (May 19, 1890)
(a)   Yes.
(b)   M/B: Hot Springs Railroad v. Williamson, 136 U.S. 121 (1890).
      LR: Hot Springs R.R. v. Williamson, 136 U.S. 121 (1890).

25 133 214 343 432 505
Hartsville Oil Mill, Appt., v. United States 271 U.S. 43-50 (April 12, 1926)
(a)   No.
(b)   M/B: Hartsville Oil Mill v. United States, 271 U.S. 43 (1926).

26 134 215 344 433 506
Touche Ross & Co., Petitioner, v Edward S. Redington, Etc., et al. 442 US 560 (June 18, 1979)
(a)   (1) whether the plaintiff is one of the class for whose especial benefit the statute was created; (2) whether there is any indication of legislative intent, explicit or implicit, either to create or to deny such a remedy; (3) whether it is consistent with the underlying purposes of the legislative scheme to imply such a remedy for the plaintiff; and (4) whether the cause of action is on traditionally relegated to state law, in an area basically the concern of the states, so that it would be inappropriate to infer a cause of action based solely on federal law.
(b)   M/B: Touche Ross & Co. v. Redington, 442 U.S. 560 (1979).

27 135 216 345 434 507
United States, Petitioner, v 564.54 Acres of Land, More or Less, Situated in Monroe and Pike Counties, Pennsylvania, et al. 441 US 506 (May 14, 1979) (a) Yes.
(b)   M/B: United States v. 564.54 Acres of Land, 441 U.S. 506 (1979).

28 136 217 346 435 508
United States, Petitioner, v Alfredo L. Caceres 440 US 741 (April 2, 1979)
(a)   No.
(b)   M/B: United States v. Caceres, 440 U.S. 741 (1979).

29 137 218 347 436 509
Joseph A. Califano, Jr., Secretary of Health, Education, and Welfare, Appellant, v Grace Aznavorian, Etc. (No. 77-991) 439 US 170 (December 11, 1978)
(a)   No.
(b)   M/B: Califano v. Aznavorian, 439 U.S. 170 (1978).

30 138 219 348 437 510
Allied Structural Steel Company, Appellant, v Warren Spannaus et al. 438 US 234 (June 28, 1978)
(a)   To inquire into the severity of the enactment's impact on the contract.

EXERCISE 16.   ANNOTATIONS IN U.S. SUPREME COURT REPORTS, L. ED.   (CONTINUED)

(b)   M/B: <u>Allied Structural Steel Co. v. Spannaus</u>, 438 U.S. 234 (1978).

31 139 220 349 438 511
Arthur F. Quern, etc., et al., Petitioners, v Venus Mandley et al. (No. 76-1159) 436 US 725 (June 6, 1978)
(a)   No.
(b)   M/B: <u>Quern v. Mandley</u>, 436 U.S. 725 (1978).

32 140 221 350 439 512
National Society of Professional Engineers, Petitioner, v United States 435 US 679 (April 25, 1978)
(a)   Yes.
(b)   M/B: <u>National Society of Professional Engineers v. United States</u>, 435 U.S. 679 (1978).
      LR: <u>National Soc'y of Professional Eng'rs v. United States</u>, 435 U.S. 679 (1978).

33 141 222 351 440 513
Gary David Smith, Petitioner, v James F. Digmon, Warden, et al. 434 US 332 (January 16, 1978)
(a)   No.
(b)   M/B: <u>Smith v. Digmon</u>, 434 U.S. 332 (1978).

34 142 223 352 441 514
Richard M. Nixon, Appellant, v Administrator of General Services et al. 433 US 425 June 28, 1977)
(a)   No.
(b)   M/B: <u>Nixon v. Administrator of General Services</u>, 433 U.S. 425 (1977).
      LR: <u>Nixon v. Administrator of Gen. Servs.</u>, 433 U.S. 425 (1977).

35 143 224 353 442 515
James E. Douglas, Jr., Commissioner, Virginia Marine Resources Commission, Appellant, v Seacoast Products, Inc., et al. 41 US 265 (May 23, 1977)
(a)   The state was the "owner" of the fish and wildlife within its jurisdiction.
(b)   M/B: <u>Douglas v. Seacoast Products, Inc.</u>, 431 U.S. 265 (1977).
      LR: <u>Douglas v. Seacoast Prods., Inc.</u>, 431 U.S. 265 (1977).

36 144 225 354 443 516
United States Steel Corporation, et al., Petitioners, v Fortner Enterprises, Inc. 429 US 610 (February 22, 1977)
(a)   Yes.
(b)   M/B: <u>United States Steel Corp. v. Fortner Enterprises</u>, 429 U.S. 610 (1977).
      LR: <u>United States Steel Corp. v. Fortner Enters.</u>, 429 U.S. 610 (1977).

37 145 226 355 444 517
Curtis Craig et al., Appellants, v David Boren, Governor of Oklahoma, et al. 429 US 190 (December 20, 1976)
(a)   Yes.
(b)   M/B: <u>Craig v. Boren</u>, 429 U.S. 190 (1976).

38 146 227 356 445 518
Dave Pernell, Petitioner, v Southall Realty 416 US 363 (April 24, 1974)
(a)   No.
(b)   M/B: <u>Pernell v. Southall Realty</u>, 416 U.S. 363 (1974).

39 147 228 357 446 519
Joseph Anthony Davis, Petitioner, v United States 417 US 333 (June 10, 1974)
(a)   No.
(b)   M/B: <u>Davis v. United States</u>, 417 U.S. 333 (1974).

40 148 229 358 447 520
Allenberg Cotton Company, Inc., Appellant, v Ben E. Pittman 419 US 20 (November 19, 1974)
(a)   No.
(b)   M/B: <u>Allenberg Cotton Co. v. Pittman</u>, 419 U.S. 20 (1974).

EXERCISE 16.   ANNOTATIONS IN U.S. SUPREME COURT REPORTS, L. ED.   (CONTINUED)

41 149 230 359 448 521
John P. Wood et al., Petitioners, v Peggy Strickland, A Minor, by Mr. and Mrs. Virgil Justice, Her Parents and Next Friends, et al. 420 US 308 (February 25, 1975)
(a)   Yes.
(b)   M/B: Wood v. Strickland, 420 U.S. 308 (1975).

42 150 231 360 449 522
Lewis H. Goldfarb et ux., Petitioners, v Virginia State Bar et al. 421 US 773 (June 16, 1975)
(a)   Yes.
(b)   M/B: Goldfarb v. Virginia State Bar, 421 U.S. 773 (1975).

43 151 232 361 450 523
Michelin Tire Corporation, Petitioner, v W. L. Wages, Tax Commissioner et al. 423 US 276 (January 14, 1976)
(a)   Yes.
(b)   M/B: Michelin Tire Corp. v. Wages, 423 U.S. 276 (1976).

44 152 233 362 451 524
Eugene R. Kelley, Commissioner of the Suffolk County Police Department, Petitioner, v Edward Johnson, Etc. 425 US 238 (April 5, 1976)
(a)   Yes.
(b)   M/B: Kelley v. Johnson, 425 U.S. 238 (1976).

45 153 234 363 452 525
Edward H. Hynes et al., Appellants, v The Mayor and Council of the Borough of Oradell et al. 425 US 610 (May 19, 1976)
(a)   No.
(b)   M/B: Hynes v. Mayor of Oradell, 425 U.S. 610 (1976).

46 154 235 364 453 526   49 L. Ed. 2d 1296   Are corporations created by a federal statute "persons" protected by the equal protection clause?
Harry R. Hughes, Etc., et al., Appellants, v Alexandria Scrap Corporation 426 US 794 (June 24, 1976)
(a)   Yes
(b)   M/B: Hughes v. Alexandria Scrap Corp., 426 U.S. 794 (1976).

47 155 236 365 454 527   30 L. Ed. 2d 952   Does a Circuit Justice have the power to grant an application for bail when the applicant's appeal from a state trial court's conviction is still pending in a state appellate court?
Robert E. Lopez, Appellee, v United States 404 US 1213 (August 23, 1971)
(a)   No
(b)   M/B: Lopez v. United States, 404 U.S. 1213 (1971).

48 156 237 366 455 528   31 L. Ed. 2d 1006   After the Erie decision, does federal common law or state law apply to interstate water pollution issues?
State of Illinois, Plaintiff, v City of Milwaukee, Wisconsin, et al. 406 US 91 (April 24, 1972)
(a)   Federal common law.
(b)   M/B: Illinois v. City of Milwaukee, 406 U.S. 91 (1972).

49 157 238 367 456 529   32 L. Ed. 2d 942   Can the police in a "frisk" permissibly look for items other than concealed weapons unrelated to the protection of the officer?
Frederick E. Adams, Warden, Petitioner, v Robert Williams 407 US 143 (June 12, 1972)
(a)   No.
(b)   M/B: Adams v. Williams, 407, U.S. 143 (1972).

50 158 239 368 457 530   33 L. Ed. 2d 865   Does the constitutional right of association include the right to associate for the assertion of mutual economic interests?
Catherine J. Healy et al., Petitioners, v F. Don James et al. 408 US 169 (June 26, 1972)
(a)   Yes.
(b)   M/B: Healy v. James, 408 U.S. 169 (1972).

EXERCISE 16. ANNOTATIONS IN U.S. SUPREME COURT REPORTS, L. ED.   (CONTINUED)

51 159 240 369 458 531   34 L. Ed. 2d 839   On what basis is the due process issue to be decided when the manner of conducting a police lineup is alleged to be unnecessarily suggestive?
William S. Neil, Warden, v Archie Nathaniel Biggers 409 US 188 (December 6, 1972)
(a)   Based on the totality of the circumstances.
(b)   M/B: Neil v. Biggers, 409 U.S. 188 (1972).

52 160 241 370 459 532   36 L. Ed. 2d 1077   Must prior notice be given to an alleged parole violator of when and where his final revocation hearing will be held and which conditions of his parole agreement he or she is alleged to have violated?
John R. Gagnon, Warden, Petitioner, v Gerald H. Scarpelli 411 US 778 (May 14, 1973)
(a)   Yes.
(b)   M/B: Gagnon v. Scarpelli, 411 U.S. 778 (1973).

53 161 242 371 460 533   38 L. Ed. 2d 835   In a prosecution under what act was the "clear and present danger" rule first announced by Mr. Justice Holmes?
Communist Party of Indiana et al., Appellants, v Edgar D. Whitcomb, Etc., et al. 414 US 441 (January 9, 1974)
(a)   Espionage Act of 1917
(b)   M/B: Communist Party v. Whitcomb, 414 U.S. 441 (1974).

54 162 243 372 461 534   37 L. Ed. 2d 1147   Do the First Amendment's religion clauses allow parents to withhold medical treatment from their children based upon the parents' religious beliefs?
Dolores Norwood et al., Appellants, v D.L. Harrison, Sr., et al. 413 US 455 (June 25, 1973)
(a)   No.
(b)   M/B: Norwood v. Harrison, 413 U.S. 455 (1973).

55 163 244 373 462 535   39 L. Ed. 2d 942   Has the "deference rule" ever been applied in the construction of the Passport Act by the Department of State?
Rogers C. B. Morton, Secretary of the Interior, Petitioner, v Ramon Ruiz et ux. 415 US 199 (February 20, 1974)
(a)   Yes.
(b)   M/B: Morton v. Ruiz, 415 U.S. 199 (1974).

56 164 245 374 463 536   25 L. Ed. 2d 1025   In order for a guilty plea to be valid, must the accused understand the consequences of that plea?
Robert M. Brady, Petitioner, v United States 397 US 742 (May 4, 1970)
(a)   Yes.
(b)   M/B: Brady v. United States, 397 U.S. 742 (1970).

57 165 246 375 464 537
Robert Baldwin, Appellant. v State of New York 399 US 66 (June 22, 1970)
(a)   The severity of the maximum penalty authorized for the
      commission of that offense.
(b)   M/B: Baldwin v. New York, 399 U.S. 66 (1970).

58 166 247 376 465 538
Ida Phillips, Petitioner, v Martin Marietta Corporation 400 US 542 (January 25, 1971)
(a)   Whether they were eligible for jury service under the law
      of the state where the federal court sat.
(b)   M/B: Phillips v. Martin Marietta Corp., 400 U.S. 542 (1971).

59 167 248 377 466 539
Harold Whiteley, Petitiorer, v Warden of Wyoming State Penitentiary 402 US 560 (March 29, 1971)
(a)   No.
(b)   M/B: Whiteley v. Warden of Wyoming State Penitentiary, 401 U.S. 560 (1971).
      LR: Whiteley v. Warden of Wyo. State Penitentiary, 401 U.S. 560 (1971).

EXERCISE 16.   ANNOTATIONS IN U.S. SUPREME COURT REPORTS, L. ED.   (CONTINUED)

60 168 249 378 467 540
Edward H. Coolidge, Jr., Petitioner, v New Hampshire 403 US 443 (June 21, 1971)
(a) Yes.
(b) M/B: Coolidge v. New Hampshire, 403 U.S. 443 (1971).

61 169 250 379 468 541
Commissioner of Internal Revenue, Petitioner, v Estate of Herman J. Bosch, Deceased 387 US 456 (June 5, 1967)
(a) No.
(b) M/B: Commissioner v. Estate of Bosch, 387 U.S. 456 (1967).

62 170 251 380 469 542
Lester J. Albrecht, Petitioner, v The Herald Company, etc. 390 US 145 (March 4, 1968)
(a) Yes.
(b) M/B: Albrecht v. Herald Co., 390 U.S. 145 (1968).

63 171 252 381 470 543
Kaiser Steel Corporation, Petitioner, v W. S. Ranch Company 391 US 593 (June 3, 1968)
(a) Abstention doctrine.
(b) M/B: Kaiser Steel Corp. v. W.S. Ranch Co., 391 U.S. 593 (1968).

64 172 253 382 471 544
Richard M. Smith, Petitioner, v Fred M. Hooey, Judge, Criminal District Court of Harris County, Texas 393 US 374 (January 20, 1969)
(a) Yes.
(b) M/B: Smith v. Hooey, 393 U.S. 374 (1969).

65 173 254 383 472 545
Samuel Desist et al., Petitioners, v United States 394 US 244 (March 24, 1969)
(a) (1) The purpose to be served by the particular new rule; (2) the extent of reliance which had been placed upon the old rule; and (3) the effect on the administration of justice of a retroactive application of the new rule.
(b) M/B: Desist v. United States, 394 U.S. 244 (1969).

66 174 255 384 473 546
Adam Clayton Powell, Jr., et al., Petitioners, v John W. McCormack et al. 395 US 486 (June 16, 1969)
(a) No.
(b) M/B: Powell v. McCormack, 395 U.S. 486 (1969).

67 175 256 385 474 547
E. S. Evans et al., Petitioners, v Guyton G. Abney et al. 396 US 435 (January 26, 1970)
(a) Yes.
(b) M/B: Evans v. Abney, 396 U.S. 435 (1970).

68 176 257 386 475 548
Federal Trade Commission, Petitioner, v Sun Oil Company 731 US 505 (January 14, 1963)
(a) Yes.
(b) M/B: FTC v. Sun Oil Co., 371 U.S. 505 (1963).

69 177 258 387 476 549
George K. Rosenberg, District Director, Immigration and Naturalization Service, Petitioner, v George Fleuti 374 US 449 (June 17, 1963)
(a) Yes.
(b) M/B: Rosenberg v. Fleuti, 374 U.S. 449 (1963).

70 178 259 388 477 550
New York Times Company, Petitioner, v L. B. Sullivan 376 US 254 (March 9, 1964)
(a) No.
(b) M/B: New York Times Co. v. Sullivan, 376 U.S. 254 (1964).

EXERCISE 16.   ANNOTATIONS IN U.S. SUPREME COURT REPORTS, L. ED.   (CONTINUED)

71 179 260 389 478 551
B. A. Reynolds, etc., et al., Appellants, v M. O. Sims et al. 377 US 533 (June 15, 1964)
(a)   No.
(b)   M/B: Reynolds v. Sims, 377 U.S. 533 (1964).

72 180 261 390 479 552
Howard Farmer, Petitioner, v Arabian American Oil Company 379 US 227 (December 14, 1964)
(a)   No.
(b)   M/B: Farmer v. Arabian American Oil Co., 379 U.S. 227 (1964).
      LR: Farmer v. Arabian Am. Oil Co., 379 U.S. 227 (1964).

73 181 262 391 480 553
Federal Trade Commission, Petitioner, v Consolidated Foods Corporation 380 US 592 (April 28, 1965)
(a)   Yes.
(b)   M/B: FTC v. Consolidated Foods Corp., 380 U.S. 592 (1965).

74 182 263 392 481 554
Armando Schmerber, Petitioner, v State of California 384 US 757 (June 20, 1966)
(a)   No.
(b)   M/B: Schmerber v. California, 384 U.S. 757 (1966).

75 183 264 393 482 555
Koehring Company, Petitioner, v Hyde Construction Company, Inc., et al. 382 US 362 (January 17, 1966)
(a)   No.
(b)   M/B: Koehring Co. v. Hyde Construction Co., 382 U.S. 362 (1966).
      LR: Koehring Co. v. Hyde Constr. Co., 382 U.S. 362 (1966).

76 184 265 394 483 556
Nashville Milk Company, Petitioner, v Carnation Company 355 US 373 (January 20, 1958)
(a)   No.
(b)   M/B: Nashville Milk Co. v. Carnation Co., 355 U.S. 373 (1958).

77 185 266 395 484 557
James P. Mitchell, Secretary of Labor, United States Department of Labor, Petitioner, v Kentucky Finance Company, Inc., and Kentucky Discount, Inc. 359 US 290 (April 20, 1959)
(a)   Yes.
(b)   M/B: Mitchell v. Kentucky Finance Co., 359 U.S. 290 (1959).
      LR: Mitchell v. Kentucky Fin. Co., 359 U.S. 290 (1959).

78 186 267 396 485 558
Dante Edward Gori, Petitioner, v United States 367 US 364 (June 12, 1961)
(a)   Yes.
(b)   M/B: Gori v. United States, 367 U.S. 364 (1961).

79 187 268 397 486 559
Charles Dowd Box Co., Inc., Petitioner, v John F. Courtney et al., etc 368 US 502 (February 19, 1962)
(a)   No.
(b)   M/B: Charles Dowd Box Co. v. Courtney, 368 U.S. 502 (1962).

80 188 269 398 487 560
Alton Railroad Company, Atchison, Topeka & Santa Fe Railway Company, Charles M. Thomson, Trustee of Chicago & Eastern Illinois Railway Company, et al., Appellants, v. United States of America, Interstate Commerce Commission, and John P. Fleming, an an Individual Doing Business as John P. Fleming Driveaway Service. 315 US 15-25 (January 2, 1942)
(a)   Yes.
(b)   M/B: Alton Railroad v. United States, 315 U.S. 15 (1942).
      LR: Alton R.R. v. United States, 315 U.S. 15 (1942).

EXERCISE 16. ANNOTATIONS IN U.S. SUPREME COURT REPORTS, L. ED.   (CONTINUED)

81 189 270 399 488 561
United States of America, Appellant, v. Midstate Horticultural Company, Inc., and Arpaxat Setrakian 306 U.S. 161-167 (January 30, 1939)
(a) In the district in which the conspiracy was entered into or in district in which an overt act was done to effectuate the object of such conspiracy.
(b) M/B: United States v. Midstate Horticultural Co., 306 U.S. 161 (1939).

82 190 271 400 489 562
Huron Holding Corporation and National Surety Corporation, Petitioners, v. Lincoln Mine Operating Company 312 US 183-194 (1941)
(a) No.
(b) M/B: Huron Holding Corp. v. Lincoln Mine Operating Co., 312 U.S. 183 (1941).

83 191 272 301 490 563
United States of America, Petitioner, v. Socony-Vacuum Oil Company, Inc., et al. 310 US 150-267 (May 6, 1940)
(a) Yes.
(b) M/B: United States v. Socony-Vacuum Oil Co., 310 U.S. 150 (1940).

84 192 273 302 491 564
Fred Steffler, Petitioner, v. United States 319 US 38-41 (1943)
(a) Yes.
(b) M/B: Steffler v. United States, 319 U.S. 38 (1943).

85 193 274 303 492 565
Arkansas Electric Cooperative Corporation, Appellant v. Arkansas Public Service Commission 461 US 375 (May 16, 1983)
(a) Yes.
(b) M/B: Arkansas Electric Cooperative Corp. v. Arkansas Public Service Commission, 461 U.S. 375 (1983).
     LR: Arkansas Elec. Coop. Corp. v. Arkansas Pub. Serv. Comm'n, 461 U.S. 375 (1983).

86 194 275 304 493 566
Jim Skidmore et al., Petitioners, v. Swift & Company 323 US 134-140 (December 4, 1944)
(a) No.
(b) M/B: Skidmore v. Swift & Co., 323 U.S. 134 (1944).

87 195 276 305 494 567
Unemployment Compensation Commission of the Territory of Alaska et al., Petitioners v. Frank L. Aragon and Other Applicants, Members of Alaska Cannery Workers Union Local No. 5 et al., Respondents 329 US 143-156 (Dec. 9, 1946)
(a) A lockout.
(b) M/B: Unemployment Compensation Commission v. Aragon, 329 U.S. 143 (1946).
     LR: Unemployment Compensation Comm'n v. Aragon, 329 U.S. 143 (1946).

88 196 277 306 495 568
Anna Desper, Admrx. of the Estate of Thomas J. Desper, Jr., Deceased, Petitioner, v. Starved Rock Ferry Company, a Corporation 342 US 187 (1952)
(a) Yes.
(b) M/B: Desper v. Starved Rock Ferry Co., 342 U.S. 187 (1952).

89 197 278 307 496 569
National City Bank of New York, Petitioner, v. Republic of China et al. 348 US 356 (March 7, 1955)
(a) Yes.
(b) M/B: National City Bank v. Republic of China, 348 U.S. 356 (1955).

90 198 279 308 497 570
Earl P. Greenwood, Petitioner, v United States of America 350 US 366 (March 5, 1956)
(a) No.
(b) M/B: Greenwood v. United States, 350 U.S. 366 (1956).

EXERCISE 16.   ANNOTATIONS IN U.S. SUPREME COURT REPORTS, L. ED.   (CONTINUED)

91 199 280 309 498 571
Asa H. Whitfield, Petitioner, v. State of Ohio 297 U. S. 431-441 (1936)
(a)   No.
(b)   M/B: Whitfield v. Ohio, 297 U.S. 431 (1936).

92 200 281 310 499 572
Concordia Insurance Company of Milwaukee, Petitioner, v. School District No. 98 of Payne County, State of Oklahoma 282 U. S. 545-555 (1931)
(a)   No.
(b)   M/B: Concordia Insurance Co. v. School District No. 98, 282 U.S. 545 (1931).
       LR: Concordia Ins. Co. v. School Dist. No. 98, 282 U.S. 545 (1931).

93 101 282 311 500 573
United States, Appt., v. George Otis Smith 286 U.S. 6-49 (May 2, 1932)
(a)   No.
(b)   M/B: United States v. Smith, 286 U.S. 6 (1932).

94 102 283 312 401 574
City of Harrisonville, Missouri, Petitioner, v. W. S. Dickey Clay Manufacturing Company 289 U. S. 334-341 (May 8, 1933)
(a)   Yes.
(b)   M/B: City of Harrisonville v. W.S. Dickey Clay Manufacturing Co., 289 U.S. 334 (1933).
       LR: City of Harrisonville v. W.S. Dickey Clay Mfg. Co., 289 U.S. 334 (1933).

95 103 284 313 402 575
Continental Illinois National Bank & Trust Company of Chicago, Petitioner, v. Chicago, Rock Island, & Pacific Railway Company et al. 294 U.S. 648-685 (1935)
(a)   Yes.
(b)   M/B: Continental Illinois National Bank & Trust Co. v. Chicago, Rhode Island, & Pacific Railway, 294 U.S. 648 (1935).
       LR: Continental Ill. Nat'l Bank & Trust Co. v. Chicago, R.I., & Pac. Ry., 294 U.S. 648 (1935)   OR   Continental Ill. Nat'l Bank & Trust Co. v. Chicago, R.I. & P. Ry, 294 U.S. 648 (1935).

96 104 285 314 403 576
B. C. Lee, Petitioner, v. Central of Georgia Railway Company et al. 252 U.S. (March 1, 1920)
(a)   Yes.
(b)   M/B: Lee v. Central Railway, 252 U.S. 109 (1920).
       LR: Lee v. Central Ry., 252 U.S. 109 (1920).

97 105 286 315 404 577
Evelyn P. Ferry, Appt., v. Spokane, Portland, & Seattle Railway Company and Central Trust Company of New York. 258 U.S. 314-321 (April 10, 1922)
(a)   No.
(b)   M/B: Ferry v. Spokane, Portland, & Seatle Railway, 258 U.S. 314 (1922).
       LR: Ferry v. Spokane, P., & S. Ry., 258 U.S. 314 (1922).

98 106 287 316 405 578
T. M. Duche & Sons, Ltd., Petitioner, v. American Schooner John Twohy, Her Tackle, etc., Albert D. Cummins and Howard Compton, Claimants 255 U.S. 77 (February 28, 1921)
(a)   Yes.
(b)   M/B: T.M. Duche & Sons v. American Schooner John Twohy, 255 U.S. 77 (1921).

99 107 288 317 406 579
People of the State of New York on the Relation of Emeline F. Clyde, Plff. in Err., v. John F. Gilchrist, President, et al., as Members of the State Tax Commission of the State of New York 262 U.S. 94-99 (April 30, 1923)
(a)   Yes.
(b)   M/B: New York ex rel. Clyde v. Gilchrist, 262 U.S. 94 (1923).
       LR: New York ex rel. Clyde v. Gilchrist, 262 U.S. 94 (1923).

EXERCISE 16.   ANNOTATIONS IN U.S. SUPREME COURT REPORTS, L. ED.   (CONTINUED)

100 108 289 318 407 580
Ex Parte Jesse W. Uppercu, Petitioner. 239 U.S. 435-441 (December 20, 1915)
(a)   Yes.
(b)   M/B: Ex parte Uppercu, 239 U.S. 435 (1915).
      LR: Ex parte Uppercu, 239 U.S. 435 (1915).

EXERCISE 17. ENGLISH REPORTS, FULL REPRINT.

INSTRUCTOR'S NOTE: This exercise is designed to familiarize students with English Reports, Full Reprint. For part (a), the students are required to find and cite a designated case in that series. For part (b), they are to list the original volume number, the reporter, and the page of the original report on which the relevant case began. No special form is required for part (b). Thus, the manner in which the reporter is cited in part (b) may vary from that listed below. If the page number used in the student's citation varies from the one noted in part (b) below, however, it is most likely that the student has not correctly used the star paging.

The following two Quick-Reference Abbreviations are particularly relevant to this exercise:

CASE NAME 19. OMIT "THE" WHEN IT IS THE FIRST WORD OF A PARTY'S NAME EXCEPT WHEN CITING A POPULAR NAME, THE NAME OF THE OBJECT OF AN IN REM ACTION, OR "THE KING" OR "THE QUEEN." [CN 19]

ENGLISH COURT CITATION 2. INCLUDE A PARENTHETICAL ABBREVIATION OF THE COURT OF DECISION IN THE CITATION. USE THE YEAR OF THE TERM OF THE COURT IF THE EXACT DATE OF DECISION IS NOT LISTED. [ENG 2]

1 111 251 361 471 581
John Turner,--Appellant; William Smith, and Others--Respondents [31st March 1715] VI Brown. 7
(a) M/B: Turner v. Smith, 3 Eng. Rep. 5 (H.L. 1715).
(b) VII Brown. 7

2 112 252 362 472 582
Joshua Rowe,--Plaintiff in Error; Isaac Young,--Defendant in Error [17th July, 1820] II Bligh. 391
(a) M/B: Rowe v. Young, 4 Eng. Rep. 372 (H.L. 1820).
(b) II Bligh. 391

3 113 253 363 473 583
John Harcourt Powell,--Appellant; Anna Grigby,--Respondent [1835] III Clark & Finnelly. 103
(a) M/B: Powell v. Grigby, 6 Eng. Rep. 1376 (H.L. 1835).
(b) III Clark & Finnelly 103

4 114 254 364 474 584
Thomas Maunsell Wilson,--Plaintiff in error; John Loveland, Lessee of the Rev. J. W. Forster,--Defendant in error [July 10, 13, 1846] XII Clark & Finnelly 677
(a) M/B: Wilson v. Loveland, 8 Eng. Rep. 1576 (H.L. 1846).
(b) XII Clark & Finnelly 677

5 115 255 365 475 585
Church against Edwards [15th May 1787] 2 Bro. C. C. 180
(a) M/B: Church v. Edwards, 29 Eng. Rep. 103 (Ch. 1787).
(b) 2 Bro. C.C. 180

6 116 256 366 476 586
Mary Wordsworth and George Wordsworth, infants, by William Gillett, their next friend,--Appellants; Frederick Wood and Others,--Respondents [May 17, 18, and 20, 1847] I H.L.C. 129
(a) M/B: Woodsworth v. Wood, 9 Eng. Rep. 702 (H.L. 1847).
(b) I H.L.C. 129

7 117 257 367 477 587
Marcus Synnot and Others,--Appellants; The Rev. John Edward Henry Simpson and Others,--Respondents [May 16, 18, 19, 30, 1854] V H.L.C. 121
(a) M/B: Synnot v. Simpson, 10 Eng. Rep. 844 (H.L. 1854).
(b) V H.L.C. 121

8 118 258 368 478 588
Church v. The Inclosure Commissioners. Re Old Oak Common. [Jan. 31st, 1862] 11 C. B. (N. S.) 664
(a) M/B: Church v. Inclosure Commissioners, 142 Eng. Rep. 956 (C.P. 1862).

EXERCISE 17. ENGLISH REPORTS, FULL REPRINT   (CONTINUED)

LR: Church v. Inclosure Comm'rs, 142 Eng. Rep. 956 (C.P. 1862).
(b) 11 C.B.N.S. 664

9 119 259 369 479 589
Edmund Backhouse,--Plaintiff in Error; Ignatius Bonomi and Wife,--Defendants in Error [June 28, 1861]   IX H.L.C. 503
(a) M/B: Backhouse v. Bonomi, 11 Eng. Rep. 825 (H.L. 1861).
(b) IX H.L.C. 503

10 120 260 370 480 590
Church v. Kemble [Nov. 20, 23, 1832]   5 Sim. 525
(a) M/B: Church v. Kemble, 58 Eng. Rep. 435 (V.C. 1832).
(b) 5 Sim. 525

11 121 261 371 481 591
Church v. King [Nov. 21, 1836]   2 My. & Cr. 220
(a) M/B: Church v. King, 40 Eng. Rep. 624 (Ch. 1836).
(b) 2 My. & Cr. 220

12 122 262 372 482 592
Fuge v. Cockram [Tuesday, May 2, 1815]   1 Price. 317
(a) M/B: Fuge v. Cockram, 145 Eng. Rep. 1415 (Ex. 1815).
(b) 1 Pri. 317

13 123 263 373 483 593
Church v. Legeyt [17th December 1815]   2 Price. 45
(a) M/B: Church v. Legeyt, 106 Eng. Rep. 16 (Ex. 1815).
(b) 2 Pri. 45

14 124 264 374 484 594
Church v. Marsh [July 21, Nov. 18, 20, 24, 1843]   2 Hare. 652
(a) M/B: Church v. Marsh, 67 Eng. Rep. 269 (V.C. 1843).
(b) 2 Hare 652

15 125 265 375 485 595
John Dunmore Lang,--Appellant; William Purves and Others,--Respondents [Feb. 17, 18, 24, 25, 1862]   XV Moore 389
(a) M/B: Lang v. Purves, 15 Eng. Rep. 541 (P.C. 1862).
(b) XV Moore 389

16 126 266 376 486 596
Church v. Wright [Jan. 29th, 1864]   15 C. B. (N.S.) 750
(a) M/B: Church v. Wright, 143 Eng. Rep. 979 (C.P. 1864).
(b) 15 C.B.N.S. 750

17 127 267 377 487 597
Thomas Henry Cooper, Appellant, Arthur Ashfield, Respondent [Nov. 16th, 1858] 5 C. B. (N.S.) 16
(a) M/B: Cooper v. Ashfield, 141 Eng. Rep. 6 (C.P. 1858).
(b) 5 C.B.N.S. 16

18 128 268 378 488 598
Pennell v. Roy.   Before the Lords Justices. [March 5, 9, 1853]   3 De G. M. & G. 126
(a) M/B: Pennell v. Roy, 43 Eng. Rep. 50 (Ch. 1853).
(b) 3 De G.M. & G. 126

19 129 269 379 489 599
Green against Miller [1831]   3 B. & AD. 781
(a) M/B: Green v. Miller, 109 Eng. Rep. 1335 (K.B. 1831).
(b) 2 B. & Ad. 781

20 130 270 380 490 600
In re Winans' Patent [Jan. 11, 1872]   VIII Moore N.S. 306
(a) M/B: In re Winans' Patent, 17 Eng. Rep. 327 (P.C. 1872).
LR: In re Winans' Patent, 17 Eng. Rep. 327 (P.C. 1872).
(b) VIII Moore N.S. 306

EXERCISE 17. ENGLISH REPORTS, FULL REPRINT   (CONTINUED)

21 131 271 381 491 501
Hide against Pettit [October 25, 1667] 1 Chan. Cas. 91
(a) M/B: Hide v. Pettit, 22 Eng. Rep. 709 (Ch. 1667).
(b) 1 Ch. Cas. 91

22 132 272 382 492 502
Watkins v. Weston. Before the Lords Justices. [March 4, 1863] 3 De G. J. & S. 434
(a) M/B: Watkins v. Weston, 46 Eng. Rep. 703 (Ch. 1863).
(b) 3 De G.J. & S. 434

23 133 273 383 493 503
The King against Marsh [Monday, January 23d, 1837] 6 AD. & E. 236
(a) M/B: The King v. Marsh, 112 Eng. Rep. 89 (K.B. 1837).
(b) 6 Ad. & E. 236

24 134 274 384 494 504
Carter and Others v. Sanderson [June 19, 1828] 5 Bing. 79
(a) M/B: Carter v. Sanderson, 130 Eng. Rep. 990 (C.P. 1828).
(b) 5 Bing. 79

25 135 275 385 495 505
Warner and Others, Executors of Edward Hankin, deceased, Plaintiffs; Watkins and Villiers, Assignees of Ezekiel Woolley, a Bankrupt, Defendants [1737] 2 Atk. 4
(a) M/B: Warner v. Watkins, 26 Eng. Rep. 400 (Ch. 1737).
(b) 2 Atk. 4

26 136 276 386 496 506
Crop and Norton [Novemb. 8, 1740] Barn. C. 179
(a) M/B: Crop v. Norton, 27 Eng. Rep. 603 (Ch. 1740).
(b) Barn. C. 179

27 137 277 387 497 507
Churchill v. Evans [May 1, 1809] 1 Taunt. 529
(a) M/B: Churchill v. Evans, 127 Eng. Rep. 939 (C.P. 1809).
(b) 1 Taunt. 529

28 138 278 388 498 508
Peppin against Solomons [Monday, Feb. 3d, 1794] 5 T. R. 496
(a) M/B: Peppin v. Solomons, 101 Eng. Rep. 279 (K.B. 1794).
(b) 5 T.R. 496

29 139 279 389 499 509
Elizabeth Webster and Others,--Appellants; Herbert Power, George Henry Davenport, and Robert Burke,--Respondents [March 13, 1868] V Moore N.S. 92
(a) M/B: Webster v. Power, 16 Eng. Rep. 450 (P.C. 1868).
(b) V Moore N.S. 92

30 140 280 390 500 510
Bradbury v. Hunter [July 7th, 1796] 3 Ves. Jun. 187
(a) M/B: Bradbury v. Hunter, 30 Eng. Rep. 961 (Ch. 1796).
(b) 3 Ves. Jun. 187

31 141 281 391 401 511
Brander v. Brander [July 22d, 1799] 4 Ves. Jun. 800
(a) M/B: Brander v. Brander, 31 Eng. Rep. 414 (Ch. 1799).
(b) 4 Ves. Jun. 800

32 142 282 392 402 512
Churchill v. Marks [Nov. 9, 18, 1844] 1 Coll. 441
(a) M/B: Churchill v. Marks, 63 Eng. Rep. 491 (V.C. 1844).
(b) 1 Coll. 441

33 143 283 393 403 513
Churchill v. Shepherd [July 18, 1863] 33 Beav. 107
(a) M/B: Churchill v. Shepherd, 55 Eng. Rep. 307 (M.R. 1863).

EXERCISE 17. ENGLISH REPORTS, FULL REPRINT   (CONTINUED)

(b) 33 Beav. 107

34 144 284 394 404 514
Davies v. Cottle [Monday, Nov. 9th, 1789] 3 T. R. 405
(a) M/B: Davies v. Cottle, 100 Eng. Rep. 645 (K.B. 1789).
(b) 3 T.R. 405

35 145 285 395 405 515
Carter versus Carter [31 Octobris 1684] 1 Vern. 259
(a) M/B: Carter v. Carter, 23 Eng. Rep. 454 (Ch. 1684).
(b) 1 Vern. 259

36 146 286 396 406 516
Churchill against Wilkins [Friday, Nov. 17th, 1786] 1 T. E. 447
(a) M/B: Churchill v. Wilkins, 99 Eng. Rep. 1191 (K.B. 1786).
(b) 1 T.R. 447

37 147 287 397 407 517
Churchman v. Ireland (1) [Dec. 13, 14, 20, 1831] 1 Russ. & M. 250
(a) M/B: Chuchman v. Ireland, 39 Eng. Rep. 96 (Ch. 1831).
(b) 1 Russ. & M. 250

38 148 288 398 408 518
Charles Tottie,--Appellant; Edmund Heathcote and Francis Hart Dyke, Her
Majesty's Procurator-General,--Respondents [August 1, 1855] X Moore 70
(a) M/B: Tottie v. Heathcote, 14 Eng. Rep. 415 (P.C. 1855).
(b) X Moore, 70

39 149 289 399 409 519
Fruer v. Bouquet [June 23, 26, 1855] 21 Beav. 33
(a) M/B: Fruer v. Bouquet, 52 Eng. Rep. 770 (Rolls 1855).
(b) 21 Beav. 33

40 150 290 400 410 520
Churchward against Studdy [Friday, June 21st, 1811] 14 East. 249
(a) M/B: Churchward v. Studdy, 104 Eng. Rep. 594 (K.B. 1811).
(b) 14 East. 249

41 151 291 301 411 521
Leigh v. Leigh [Feb. 1st, May 9th, 1808] 15 Ves. Jun. 92
(a) M/B: Leigh v. Leigh, 33 Eng. Rep. 690 (Ch. 1808).
(b) 15 Ves. Jun. 92

42 152 292 302 412 522
Staines v. Morris [Nov. 11, 16, 1812] 1 V. & B. 8
(a) M/B: Staines v. Morris, 35 Eng. Rep. 4 (Ch. 1812).
(b) 1 V. & B. 8

43 153 293 303 413 523
Andrew Caird Churton, George Bankart and Michael Stocks Hirst, Plaintiffs; and
John Douglas, Defendant [March 16, 17, 1859] Johns. 174
(a) M/B: Churton v. Douglas, 70 Eng. Rep. 385 (V.C. 1859).
(b) Johns. 174

44 154 294 304 414 524
Churton v. Frewen [March 1, 2, 1865] 2 Dr. & SM. 390
(a) M/B: Churton v. Frewen, 62 Eng. Rep. 669 (V.C. 1865).
(b) 2 Dr. & Sm. 390

45 155 295 305 415 525
William Henry Walker, Appellant, Julian Payne, Respondent [Nov. 17, 1845] 2
C.B. 12
(a) M/B: Walker v. Payne, 135 Eng. Rep. 844 (C.P. 1845).
(b) 2 C.B. 12

46 156 296 306 416 526
Smith v. Thompson [June 8, 1849] 8 C. B. 44

EXERCISE 17. ENGLISH REPORTS, FULL REPRINT   (CONTINUED)

(a) M/B: Smith v. Thompson, 137 Eng. Rep. 424 (C.P. 1849).
(b) 8 C.B. 44

47 157 297 307 417 527
Wheeler against Horne. T. 13 & 14 G. 2 [Thursday, June 19th, 1740]   Willes 208
(a) M/B: Wheeler v. Horne, 125 Eng. Rep. 1135 (C.P. 1740).
(b) Willes 208

48 158 298 308 418 528
Bishop against Hatch, Clerk. Chuter against The Same. [Tuesday, April 29th, 1834] 1 AD. & E. 171
(a) M/B: Bishop v. Hatch, 110 Eng. Rep. 1172 (K.B. 1834).
(b) 1 Ad. & E. 171

49 159 299 309 419 529
Rowe v. Wood [April 20, 22, 25, 29, May 9, 1820] 1 Jac. & W. 315
(a) M/B: Rowe v. Wood, 37 Eng. Rep. 396 (Ch. 1820).
(b) 1 Jac. & W. 315

50 160 300 310 420 530
Caldecott v. Harrison [July 11, 1840] 9 Sim. 457
(a) M/B: Caldecott v. Harrison, 59 Eng. Rep. 435 (V.C. 1840).
(b) 9 Sim. 457

51 161 201 311 421 531
Long verus Dennis [Tuesday 19th May 1767] 4 Burr. 2052
(a) M/B: Long v. Dennis, 98 Eng. Rep. 69 (K.B. 1767).
(b) 4 Burr. 2052

52 162 202 312 422 532
Sutton v. Clarke [Feb. 1, 1815] 6 Taunt. 29
(a) M/B: Sutton v. Clarke, 128 Eng. Rep. 943 (C.P. 1815).
(b) 6 Taunt. 29

53 163 203 313 423 533
Circuitt v. Perry [Nov. 11, 1856] 23 Beav. 275
(a) M/B: Circuitt v. Perry, 53 Eng. Rep. 108 (M.R. 1856).
(b) 23 Beav. 275

54 164 204 314 424 534
In re Spence [May 7, 1847] 2 Ph. 247
(a) M/B: In re Spence, 41 Eng. Rep. 937 (Ch. 1847).
LR: In re Spence, 41 Eng. Rep. 937 (Ch. 1847).
(b) 2 Ph. 247

55 165 205 315 425 535
Tulk v. Moxhay [Dec. 21, 22, 1848] 1 H. & TW. 105
(a) M/B: Tulk v. Moxhay, 47 Eng. Rep. 1345 (Ch. 1848).
(b) 1 H. & TW. 105

56 166 206 316 426 536
Thomas Johnson v. Simcock and Jackson [July 6, 1860] 6 H. & N. 6
(a) M/B: Johnson v. Simcock, 158 Eng. Rep. 3 (Ex. 1860).
(b) 6 H. & N. 6

57 167 207 317 427 537
Forrest v. The Manchester, Sheffield and Lincolnshire Railway Company. Before the Lord Chancellor Lord Westbury. [July 3, 1861] 4 De G. F. & J. 126
(a) M/B: Forrest v. Manchester, Sheffield & Lincolnshire Railway, 45 Eng. Rep. 1131 (Ch. 1861).
LR: Forrest v. Manchester, S. & L. Ry., 45 Eng. Rep. 1131 (Ch. 1861).
(b) 4 De G.F. & J. 126

58 168 208 318 428 538
Cook against Cox [Monday, June 27th, 1814] 3 M. & S. 110
(a) M/B: Cook v. Cox, 105 Eng. Rep. 552 (K.B. 1814).
(b) 3 M. & S. 110

EXERCISE 17. ENGLISH REPORTS, FULL REPRINT   (CONTINUED)

59 169 209 319 429 539
Rogers v. Thomas [March 18, 1837]   2 Keen. 8
(a) M/B: Rogers v. Thomas, 48 Eng. Rep. 531 (Rolls 1837).
(b) 2 Keen 8

60 170 210 320 430 540
Clack v. Sainsbury [Nov. 20, 1851]   11 C. B. 695
(a) M/B: Clack v. Sainsbury, 138 Eng. Rep. 648 (C.P. 1851).
(b) 11 C.B. 695

61 171 211 321 431 541
John Cary,--Appellant; John White and others,--Respondents [28th March 1710]
V Brown. 325
(a) M/B: Cary v. White, 2 Eng. Rep. 708 (H.L. 1710).
(b) V Brown. 325

62 172 212 322 432 542
Sperling v. Rochfort [Feb. 19th, 21st, 24th, 1803]   8 Ves. Jun. 164
(a) M/B: Sperling v. Rochfort, 32 Eng. Rep. 316 (Ch. 1803).
(b) 8 Ves. Jun. 164

63 173 213 323 433 543
Brown v. Gordon [May 6, 25, Nov. 3, 1852]   16 Beav. 302
(a) M/B: Brown v. Gordon, 51 Eng. Rep. 795 (M.R. 1852).
(b) 16 Beav. 302

64 174 214 324 434 544
Clancy against Piggott [Friday, January 16th, 1835]   2 AD. & E. 473
(a) M/B: Clancy v. Piggott, 111 Eng. Rep. 183 (K.B. 1835).
(b) 2 Ad. & E. 473

65 175 215 325 435 545
Ramsden v. Smith [May 2, 9, 1854]   2 Drewry. 298
(a) M/B: Ramsden v. Smith, 61 Eng. Rep. 734 (V.C. 1854).
(b) 2 Drewry 298

66 176 216 326 436 546
Green v. Barrett [Nov. 2, 7, 1826]   1 Sim. 45
(a) M/B: Green v. Barrett, 57 Eng. Rep. 495 (V.C. 1826).
(b) 1 Sim. 45

67 177 217 327 437 547
Barwick against Reade [Monday, May 16th, 1791]   1 H. Bl. 627
(a) M/B: Barwick v. Reade, 126 Eng. Rep. 357 (C.P. 1791).
(b) 1 H. Bl. 627

68 178 218 328 438 548
Lucas v. James [Feb. 27, March 1, 2, April 18, 1849]   7 Hare. 410
(a) M/B: Lucas v. James, 68 Eng. Rep. 170 (V.C. 1849).
(b) 7 Hare 410

69 179 219 329 439 549
George Horner, Thomas Beare, Esqrs., and others, Trustees of Warwick
Bampfield, Esq. deceased, for Payment of his Debts and Legacies, and of the
Debts and Legacies of Henry Rogers, Esq. deceased, and Sir Coppleston Warwick
Bampfield, Bart. and John Bampfield, both Infants,--Petitioners; Alexander
Popham, Esq.--Respondent [18th January 1697] Colles 1
(a) M/B: Horner v. Popham, 1 Eng. Rep. 150 (H.L. 1697).
(b) Colles 1

70 180 220 330 440 550
Clapham v. Shillito [Jan. 24, Feb. 1, 16, 1844]   7 Beav. 146
(a) M/B: Clapham v. Shillito, 49 Eng. Rep. 1019 (M.R. 1844).
(b) 7 Beav. 146

71 181 221 331 441 551
Stringer against New [1741]   9 Mod. 363

EXERCISE 17. ENGLISH REPORTS, FULL REPRINT   (CONTINUED)

(a) M/B: Stringer v. New, 88 Eng. Rep. 509 (Ch. 1741).
(b) 9 Mod. 363

72 182 222 332 442 552
Davis v. Blackwell, Executor [May 29, 1832] 9 Bing. 5
(a) M/B: Davis v. Blackwell, 131 Eng. Rep. 516 (C.P. 1832).
(b) 9 Bing. 5

73 183 223 333 443 553
Smythe v. Smythe [May 28, 1818] 2 Swans. 251
(a) M/B: Smythe v. Smythe, 36 Eng. Rep. 611 (Ch. 1818).
(b) 2 Swans. 251

74 184 224 334 444 554
Clapperton and Wife v. Catherine Monteith [Jan. 12, 1844] 6 Man. & G. 909
(a) M/B: Clapperton v. Monteith, 134 Eng. Rep. 1160 (C.P. 1844).
(b) 6 Man. & G. 909

75 185 225 335 445 555
Price v. Anderson [Jan. 18, 1847] 15 Sim. 473
(a) M/B: Price v. Anderson, 60 Eng. Rep. 703 (V.C. 1847).
(b) 15 Sim. 473

76 186 226 336 446 556
Yates v. Yates [July 9, 10, 1860] 28 Beav. 637
(a) M/B: Yates v. Yates, 54 Eng. Rep. 511 (M.R. 1860).
(b) 28 Beav. 637

77 187 227 337 447 557
Kemble v. Mills [June 17, 1840] 1 Man. & G. 565
(a) M/B: Kemble v. Mills, 133 Eng. Rep. 456 (C.P. 1840).
(b) 1 Man. & G. 565

78 188 228 338 448 558
Henry Gibbs, administrator of his wife Elizabeth Gibbs, late Elizabeth Davis, deceased, Plaintiff; Henry Davis, surviving executor of Dame Margaret Boreman, deceased, and brother and heir of his late sister, the said Elizabeth Gibbs, Defendant [Saturday, February the 7th 1730] Mosely 269
(a) M/B: Gibbs v. Davis, 25 Eng. Rep. 389 (Ch. 1730).
(b) Mos. 269

79 189 229 339 449 559
Clarke v. Cooke [Jan. 25, 1838] 4 Bing. (N. C.) 269
(a) M/B: Clare v. Cooke, 132 Eng. Rep. 792 (C.P. 1838).
(b) 4 Bing. N.C. 269

80 190 230 340 450 560
Robert Bridgewater, Appellant; Benjamin Chandler Durant, Respondent [Nov. 11th, 1861] 11 C. B. (N. S.) 7
(a) M/B: Bridgewater v. Durant, 142 Eng. Rep. 695 (C.P. 1861).
(b) 11 C.B.N.S. 7

81 191 231 341 451 561
Merry v. Ryves [14th & 15th July 1757] 1 Eden 1
(a) M/B: Merry v. Ryves, 28 Eng. Rep. 584 (Ch. 1757).
(b) 1 Eden 1

82 192 232 342 452 562
Steff v. Andrews and Ux [August 22, 1816] 2 Madd. 6
(a) M/B: Steff v. Andrews, 56 Eng. Rep. 237 (V.C. 1816).
(b) 2 Madd. 6

83 193 233 343 453 563
Clare v. Wood [Feb. 18, 19, 1842] 1 Hare. 314
(a) M/B: Clare v. Wood, 66 Eng. Rep. 1052 (V.C. 1842).
(b) 1 Hare 314

EXERCISE 17. ENGLISH REPORTS, FULL REPRINT   (CONTINUED)

84 194 234 344 454 564
Parry v. Wright [May 5, 1828] 5 Russ. 142
(a) M/B: Parry v. Wright, 38 Eng. Rep. 981 (Ch. 1828).
(b) 5 Russ. 142

85 195 235 345 455 565
McIntyre v. Miller [Jan. 24, 25, 1845] 13 M. & W. 725
(a) M/B: M'Intyre v. Miller, 153 Eng. Rep. 304 (Ex. 1845).
(b) 13 M. & W. 725

86 196 236 346 456 566
Scorell v. Boxall and Another. Exch. of Pleas. [Saturday, May 26th, 1827] 1 Y. & J. 396
(a) M/B: Scorell v. Boxall, 148 Eng. Rep. 724 (Ex. 1827).
(b) 1 Y. & J. 396

87 197 237 347 457 567
In Re Claridge's Patent [May 15, 1851] VII Moore 394
(a) M/B: In re Claridge's Patent, 13 Eng. Rep. 932 (P.C. 1851).
LR: In re Claridge's Patent, 13 Eng. Rep. 932 (P.C. 1851).
(b) VII Moore 394

88 198 238 348 458 568
Toft v. Stephenson. Before the Lords Justices. [Nov. 7, 8, 25, 1851] 1 De G. M. & G. 28
(a) M/B: Toft v. Stephenson, 42 Eng. Rep. 461 (Ch. 1851).
(b) 1 De G.M. & G. 28

89 199 239 349 459 569
Wing v. Murrells and Others [1823] 11 Price 723
(a) M/B: Wing v. Murrells, 147 Eng. Rep. 616 (Ex. 1823).
(b) 11 Price 723

90 200 240 350 460 570
Ann Mortimer, Widow and Executrix of George Mortimer,--Appellant; Peter Trezevant, and Others,--Respondents [May 8, 9, 23; June 12 1837] IV Clark & Finnelly 657
(a) M/B: Mortimer v. Trezevant, 7 Eng. Rep. 250 (H.L. 1837).
(b) IV Clark & Finnelly 657

91 101 241 351 461 571
Clarke v. Allatt [May 4, 1847] 4 C.B. 335
(a) M/B: Clarke v. Allatt, 136 Eng. Rep. 536 (C.P. 1847).
(b) 4 C.B. 335

92 102 242 352 462 572
Clark against Askew [Thursday, Nov. 13th, 1806] 8 East. 28
(a) M/B: Clark v. Askew, 103 Eng. Rep. 255 (K.B. 1806).
(b) 8 East. 28

93 103 243 353 463 573
Clark v. Bates [Feb. 19, 1848] 2 Deg. & SM. 203
(a) M/B: Clark v. Bates, 64 Eng. Rep. 90 (V.C. 1848).
(b) 2 De G. & Sm. 203

94 104 244 354 464 574
Sidaway against Hay [1824] 3 B. & C. 12
(a) M/B: Sidaway v. Hay, 107 Eng. Rep. 639 (K.B. 1824).
(b) 3 B. & C. 12

95 105 245 355 465 575
Clark v. Browne [July 25, 1854] 2 SM. & Giff. 524
(a) M/B: Clarke v. Browne, 65 Eng. Rep. 510 (V.C. 1854).
(b) 2 Sm. & Giff. 524

96 106 246 356 466 576
Beeman v. Duck. Exch. of Pleas. [Feb. 25, 1843] 11 M. & W. 251

211

EXERCISE 17. ENGLISH REPORTS, FULL REPRINT   (CONTINUED)

(a) M/B: Beeman v. Duck, 152 Eng. Rep. 796 (Ex. 1843).
(b) 11 M. & W. 251

97 107 247 357 467 577
Clark v. Burgh [July 9, 1845] 2 Holt, Eq. 317
(a) M/B: Clark v. Burgh, 71 Eng. Rep. 891 (V.C. 1845).
(b) 2 Holt, Eq. 317

98 108 248 358 468 578
John Stephenson Robson, Appellant, Lawrence Lawson Brown, Respondent [Nov. 14, 1856] 1 C. B. (N.S.) 34
(a) M/B: Robson v. Brown, 140 Eng. Rep. 14 (C.P. 1856).
(b) 1 C.B.N.S. 34

99 109 249 359 469 579
Clark and Another v. Clavert [Feb. 11, 1819] 8 Taunt. 742
(a) M/B: Clark v. Calvert, 129 Eng. Rep. 573 (C.P. 1819).
(b) 8 Taunt. 742

100 110 250 360 470 580
Fenwick v. Greenwell [July 8, 9, 12, 24, 1847] 10 Beav. 412
(a) M/B: Fenwick v. Greenwell, 50 Eng. Rep. 640 (M.R. 1847).
(b) 10 Beav. 412

EXERCISE 18.   LAW REPORTS

INSTRUCTOR'S NOTE: This exercise is designed to familiarize students with the semi-official English Law Reports series. To complete this exercise, students must find a designated case and cite it in proper form. The following two Quick-Reference Abbreviations are particularly relevant to this exercise:

ENGLISH COURT CITATION 4.   USE BRACKETS TO ENCLOSE THE YEAR OF A LAW REPORTS CITATION WHEN SEPARATELY NUMBERED VOLUMES WERE PUBLISHED IN THAT YEAR. OTHERWISE, DO NOT USE BRACKETS.   PLACE THE YEAR OF DECISION, IF IT DIFFERS FROM THE VOLUME YEAR, IN A PARENTHETICAL AT THE END OF THE CITATION.   [ENG 4]
ENGLISH COURT CITATION 5.   INDICATE THE COURT OF DECISION IN CITATIONS OF K.B., Q.B., CH., P., OR FAM. LAW REPORTS ONLY IF IT IS THE COURT OF APPEAL (C.A.).   FOR A.C. LAW REPORTS, INDICATE THE COURT OF DECISION ONLY IF IT IS THE PRIVY COUNCIL.   [ENG. 5]

1 122 227 321 425 506
Curtis v. French. [1929] 1 Ch. 253   1928
M/B: Curtis v. French, [1929] 1 Ch. 253 (1928).

2 123 228 322 426 507
Clark v. Barnes. [1929] 2 Ch. 368   1929
M/B: Clark v. Barnes, [1929] 2 Ch. 368.

3 124 229 323 427 508
Vanderpant v. Mayfair Hotel Company, Limited. [1930] 1 Ch. 138   1929
M/B: Vanderpant v. Mayfair Hotel Co., [1930] 1 Ch. 138 (1929).

4 125 230 324 428 509
Fuel Economy Company, Limited v. Murray. [1930] 2 Ch. 93   C.A.   1930
M/B: Fuel Economy Co. v. Murray, [1930] 2 Ch. 93 (C.A.).

5 126 231 325 429 510
In re Harris. [1931] 1 Ch. 138   1930
M/B: In re Harris, [1931] 1 Ch. 138 (1930).
LR: In re Harris, [1931] 1 Ch. 138 (1930).

6 127 232 326 430 511
Spyer v. Phillipson. [1931] 2 Ch. 183   C.A.   1930
M/B: Spyer v. Phillipson, [1931] 2 Ch. 183 (C.A. 1930).

7 128 233 327 431 512
Wilson v. Tyneside Window Cleaning Co. [1958] 2 Q.B. 110   C.A.   1958
M/B: Wilson v. Tyneside Window Cleaning Co., [1958] 2 Q.B. 110 (C.A.).

8 129 234 328 432 513
Baker v. Sims. [1959] 1 Q.B. 114   C.A.   1959
M/B: Baker v. Sims, [1959] 1 Q.B. 114 (C.A. 1958).

9 130 235 329 433 514
Pender v. Smith. [1959] 2 Q.B. 84   1959
M/B: Pender v. Smith, [1959] 2 Q.B. 84.

10 131 236 330 434 515
In re Vernazza. [1960] 1 Q.B. 197   C.A.   1959
M/B: In re Vernazza, [1960] 1 Q.B. 197 (C.A. 1959).
LR: In re Vernazza, [1960] 1 Q.B. 197 (C.A. 1959).

11 132 237 331 435 516
Gladstone v. Bower. [1960] 2 Q.B. 384   C.A.   1960
M/B: Gladstone v. Bower, [1960] 2 Q.B. 384 (C.A.).

12 133 238 332 436 517
In re Merrall. Greener v. Merrall. [1924] 1 Ch. 45   1923
M/B: In re Merrall, [1924] 1 Ch. 45 (1923).
LR: In re Merrall, [1924] 1 Ch. 45 (1923).

13 134 239 333 437 518
In re Letters Patent N. 139, 207. In re Carbonit Aktiengesellschaft. [1924]

EXERCISE 18. LAW REPORTS   (CONTINUED)

2 Ch. 53 C.A. 1924
M/B: In re Letters Patent No. 139,207, [1924] 2 Ch. 53 (C.A.).
LR: In re Letters Patent No. 139,207, [1924] 2 Ch. 53 (C.A.).

14 135 240 334 438 519
Iveagh v. Martin and Another. [1961] 1 Q.B. 232 1960
M/B: Iveagh v. Martin, [1961] 1 Q.B. 232 (1960).

15 136 241 335 439 520
Garnett v. Pratt. [1926] 1 Ch. 897 1926
M/B: Garnett v. Pratt, [1926] 1 Ch. 897.

16 137 242 336 440 521
Hortons' Estate, Limited v. James Beattie, Limited. [1927] 1 Ch. 75 1926
M/B: Hortons' Estate, Ltd. v. James Beattie, Ltd., [1927] 1 Ch. 75 (1926).

17 138 243 337 441 522
Horlick v. Scully. [1927] 2 Ch. 150 1927
M/B: Horlick v. Scully, [1927] 2 Ch. 150.

18 139 244 338 442 523
Alder v. Moore. [1961] 2 Q.B. 57 C.A. 1960
M/B: Alder v. Moore, [1961] 2 Q.B. 57 (C.A. 1960).

19 140 245 339 443 524
Slattery v. Mance. [1962] 1 Q.B. 676 1962
M/B: Slattery v. Mance, [1962] 1 Q.B. 676.

20 141 246 340 444 525
Evans and Others v. Thomas and Another. [1962] 2 Q.B. 350 1962
M/B: Evans v. Thomas, [1962] 2 Q.B. 350.

21 142 247 341 445 526
Marrinan v. Vibart and Another. [1963] 1 Q.B. 528 C.A. 1962
M/B: Marrinan v. Vibart, [1963] 1 Q.B. 528 (C.A. 1962).

22 143 248 342 446 527
Lipmans Wallpaper Ltd. v. Mason & Hodghton Ltd. and Another. [1969] 1 Ch. 20 1967
M/B: Lipmans Wallpaper Ltd. v. Mason & Hodghton Ltd., [1969] 1 Ch. 20 (1967).

23 144 249 343 447 528
Muspratt v. Johnston. [1963] 2 Q.B. 383 1962
M/B: Muspratt v. Johnston, [1963] 2 Q.B. 383 (C.A.).

24 145 250 344 448 529
Hewer v. Bryant. [1970] 1 Q.B. 357 1969 [Court of Appeal]
M/B: Hewer v. Bryant, [1970] 1 Q.B. 357 (C.A. 1969).

25 146 251 345 449 530
Burns v. Edman. [1970] 2 Q.B. 541 1969
M/B: Burns v. Edman, [1970] 2 Q.B. 541 (1969).

26 147 252 346 450 531
Keys and Another v. Boulter and Others. [1971] 1 Q.B. 300 1970 [Court of Appeal]
M/B: Keys v. Boulter, [1971] 1 Q.B. 300 (C.A. 1970).

27 148 253 347 451 532
Nettleship v. Weston. [1971] 2 Q.B. 691 1971 [Court of Appeal]
M/B: Nettleship v. Weston, [1971] 2 Q.B. 691 (C.A.).

28 149 254 348 452 533
Barrington v. Lee. [1972] 1 Q.B. 326 1971 [Court of Appeal]
M/B: Barrington v. Lee, [1972] 1 Q.B. 326 (C.A. 1971).

29 150 255 349 453 534

EXERCISE 18. LAW REPORTS   (CONTINUED)

In re Ponder. Ponder v. Ponder. [1921] 2 Ch. 59 1920
M/B: In re Ponder, [1921] 2 Ch. 59.
LR: In re Ponder, [1921] 2 Ch. 59.

30 151 256 350 454 535
In re Astor.   Astor v. Astor. [1922] 1 Ch. 364 C.A. 1921
M/B: In re Astor, [1922] 1 Ch. 364 (C.A. 1921).
LR: In re Astor, [1922] 1 Ch. 364 (C.A. 1921).

31 152 257 351 455 536
Upjohn v. Macfarlane. [1922] 2 Ch. 256 C.A. 1922
M/B: Upjohn v. Macfarlane, [1922] 2 Ch. 256 (C.A.).

32 153 258 352 456 537
In re Berchtold. Berchtold v. Capron. [1923] 1 Ch. 192 1922
M/B: In re Berchtold, [1923] 1 Ch. 192 (1922).
LR: In re Berchtold, [1923] 1 Ch. 192 (1922).

33 154 259 353 457 538
Price v. Rhondda Urban District Council. [1923] 2 Ch. 372 1923
M/B: Price v. Rhondda Urban District Council, [1923] 2 Ch. 372.
LR: Price v. Rhondda Urban Dist. Council, [1923] 2 Ch. 372.

34 155 260 354 458 539
Tradax S.A. v. Volkswagenwerk A.G. [1969] 2 Q.B. 599 1969
M/B: Tradax S.A. v. Volkswagenwerk A.G., [1969] 2 Q.B. 599.

35 156 261 355 459 540
Askinex Ltd. v. Green and Others. [1969] 1 Q.B. 272 C.A. 1966
M/B: Askinex Ltd. v. Green, [1969] 1 Q.B. 272 (C.A. 1966).

36 157 262 356 460 541
Millard v. Turvey. [1968] 2 Q.B. 390 1968
M/B: Millard v. Turvey, [1968] 2 Q.B. 390.

37 158 263 357 461 542
Plymouth Corporation v. Hurrell. [1968] 1 Q.B. 455 C.A. 1967
M/B: Plymouth Corp. v. Hurrell, [1968] 1 Q.B. 455 (C.A. 1967).

38 159 264 358 462 543
Regina v. Cleghorn. [1967] 2 Q.B. 584 C.A. 1967
M/B: Regina v. Cleghorn, [1967] 2 Q.B. 584 (C.A.).

39 160 265 359 463 544
Kearney v. Eric Waller Ltd. and Another. [1967] 1 Q.B. 29 1965
M/B: Kearney v. Erick Waller Ltd., [1967] 1 Q.B. 29 (1965).

40 161 266 360 464 545
Moore v. Minister of Housing and Local Government and Another. [1966] 2 Q.B. 602 1965
M/B: Moore v. Minister of Housing & Local Government, [1966] 2 Q.B. 602 (1965).
LR: Moore v. Minister of Hous. & Local Gov't, [1966] 2 Q.B. 602 (1965).

41 162 267 361 465 546
Ward v. James. [1966] 1 Q.B. 273 C.A. 273
M/B: Ward v. James, [1966] 1 Q.B. 273 (C.A. 1964).

42 163 268 362 466 547
Kirby v. Leather. [1965] 2 Q.B. 367 C.A. 1965
M/B: Kirby v. Leather, [1965] 2 Q.B. 367 (C.A.).

43 164 269 363 467 548
Keefe v. Amor. [1965] 1 Q.B. 334 C.A. 1964
M/B: Keefe v. Amor, [1965] 1 Q.B. 334 (C.A. 1964).

44 165 270 364 468 549

EXERCISE 18. LAW REPORTS   (CONTINUED)

Meah v. Mouskos. [1964] 2 Q.B. 23 C.A. 1963
M/B: Meah v. Mouskos, [1964] 2 Q.B. 23 (C.A. 1963).

45 166 271 365 469 550
Pieper v. Harvey. [1958] 1 Q.B. 439 C.A. 1958
M/B: Piper v. Harvey, [1958] 1 Q.B. 439 (C.A.).

46 167 272 366 470 551
Triefus & Co. Ltd. v. Post Office. [1957] 2 Q.B. 352 C.A. 1957
M/B: Triefus & Co. v. Post Office, [1957] 2 Q.B. 352 (C.A.).

47 168 273 367 471 552
Paddington Borough Council v. War Damage Commission. Associated London Properties Ltd. v. Paddington Borough Council. [1957] 1 Q.B. 294 C.A. 1956
M/B: Paddington Borough Council v. War Damage Commission, [1957] 1 Q.B. 294 (C.A. 1956).
LR: Paddington Borough Council v. War Damage Comm'n, [1957] 1 Q.B. 294 (C.A. 1956).

48 169 274 368 472 553
Owen v. Gadd and Others. [1956] 2 Q.B. 99 C.A. 1956
M/B: Owen v. Gadd, [1956] 2 Q.B. 99 (C.A.).

49 170 275 369 473 554
Vine v. National Dock Labour Board [1956] 1 Q.B. 658 C.A. 1955
M/B: Vine v. National Dock Labour Board, [1956] 1 Q.B. 658 (C.A. 1955).
LR: Vine v. National Dock Labour Bd., [1956] 1 Q.B. 658 (C.A. 1955).

50 171 276 370 474 555
McCombe v. Read and Another. [1955] 2 Q.B. 429 1955
M/B: McCombe v. Read, [1955] 2 Q.B. 429.

51 172 277 371 475 556
Rands v. McNeil. [1955] 1 Q.B. 253 C.A. 1954
M/B: Rands v. McNeil, [1955] 1 Q.B. 253 (C.A. 1954).

52 173 278 372 476 557
Lockwood v. Lowe. [1952] 2 Q.B. 267 C.A. 1953
M/B: Lockwood v. Lowe, [1954] 2 Q.B. 267 (C.A. 1953).

53 174 279 373 477 558
Gough v. National Coal Board. [1954] 1 Q.B. 191 1953
M/B: Gough v. National Coal Board, [1954] 1 Q.B. 191 (C.A. 1953).
LR: Gough v. National Coal Bd., [1954] 1 Q.B. 191 (C.A. 1953).

54 175 280 374 478 559
Dickson v. Flack. [1953] 2 Q.B. 464 C.A. 1953
M/B: Dickson v. Flack, [1953] 2 Q.B. 464 (C.A.).

55 176 281 375 479 560
Cooden Engineering Co. Ld. v. Stanford. [1953] 1 Q.B. 86 C.A. 1952
M/B: Cooden Engineering Co. v. Stanford, [1953] 1 Q.B. 86 (C.A. 1952).
LR: Cooden Eng'g Co. v. Stanford, [1953] 1 Q.B. 86 (C.A. 1952).

56 177 282 376 480 561
Jaglom v. Excess Insurance Co. Ltd. and Another. [1972] Q.B. 250 1971
M/B: Jaglom v. Excess Insurance Co., [1972] 2 Q.B. 250 (1971).
LR: Jaglom v. Excess Ins. Co., [1972] 2 Q.B. 250 (1971).

57 178 283 377 481 562
Stumbles v. Whitley. [1930] 1 K.B. 393 C.A. 1929
M/B: Stumbles v. Whitley, [1930] 1 K.B. 393 (C.A. 1929).

58 179 284 378 482 563
Fisher v. Oldham Corporation. [1930] 2 K.B. 364 1930
M/B: Fisher v. Oldham Corp., [1930] 2 K.B. 364.

EXERCISE 18.   LAW REPORTS   (CONTINUED)

59 180 285 379 483 564
Daniels and Others v. Pinks. [1931] 1 K.B. 1930
M/B: Daniels v. Pinks, [1931] 1 K.B. 374 (1930).

60 181 286 380 484 565
Slingsby and Others v. Westminster Bank, Limited. [1931] 2 K.B. 583 1930
M/B: Slingsby v. Westminster Bank, Ltd., [1931] 2 K.B. 583 (1930).

61 182 287 381 485 566
Bottomley and Another v. Bannister and Another. [1932] 1 K.B. 458 C.A. 1931
M/B: Bottomley v. Bannister, [1932] 1 K.B. 458 (C.A. 1931).

62 183 288 382 486 567
Fanton v. Dennville. [1932] 2 K.B. 309 C.A. 1932
M/B: Fanton v. Denville, [1932] 2 K.B. 309 (C.A.)

63 184 289 383 487 568
Cunard and Wife v. Antifyre, Limited. [1933] 1 K.B. 551 1932
M/B: Cunard v. Antifyre, Ltd., [1933] 1 K.B. 551 (1932).

64 185 290 384 488 569
Karflex, Limited v. Poole. [1933] 2 K.B. 251 1933
M/B: Karflex, Ltd. v. Poole, [1933] 2 K.B. 251.

65 186 291 385 489 570
Rossi v. Blunden. [1934] 1 K.B. 357 1933
M/B: Rossi v. Blunden, [1934] 1 K.B. 357 (1933).

66 187 292 386 490 571
Phillips v. Parnaby. [1934] 2 K.B. 299 1934
M/B: Phillips v. Parnaby, [1934] 2 K.B. 299.

67 188 293 387 491 572
Waldock v. Winfield. [1901] 2 K.B. 596 C.A. 1901
M/B: Waldock v. Winfield, [1901] 2 K.B. 596 (C.A.).

68 189 294 388 492 573
Haynes v. Harwood. [1935] 1 K.B 146 C.A. 1934
M/B: Haynes v. Harwood, [1935] 1 K.B. 146 (C.A. 1934).

69 190 295 389 493 574
Brooks, Appellant; Mason, Respondent. [1902] 2 K.B. 743 1902
M/B: Brooks v. Mason, [1902] 2 K.B. 743.

70 191 296 390 494 575
Atkinson v. Lumb. [1903] 1 K.B. 861 C.A. 1903
M/B: Atkinson v. Lumb, [1903] 1 K.B. 861 (C.A.).

71 192 297 391 495 576
Greennock Steamship Company v. Maritime Insurance Company, Limited. [1903]
2 K.B. 657 C.A. 1903
M/B: Greenock Steamship Co. v. Maritime Insurance Co., [1903] 2 K.B. 657
(C.A.).
LR: Greenock S.S. Co. v. Maritime Ins. Co., [1903] 2 K.B. 657 (C.A.).

72 193 298 392 496 577
Dover, Appellant; Prosser, Respondent. [1904] 1 K.B. 84 1903
M/B: Dover v. Prosser, [1904] 1 K.B. 84 (1903).

73 194 299 393 497 578
Bolland v. Young. [1904] 2 K.B. 824 C.A. 1904
M/B: Bolland v. Young, [1904] 2 K.B. 824 (C.A.).

74 195 300 394 498 579
Castle Spinning Company, Limited v. Atkinson. [1905] 1 K.B. 336 C.A. 1905
M/B: Castle Spinning Co. v. Atkinson, [1905] 1 K.B. 336 (C.A.).

EXERCISE 18. LAW REPORTS   (CONTINUED)

75 196 201 395 499 580
Symons, Appellant v. Baker, Respondent. [1905] 2 K.B. 723 1905
M/B: Symons v. Baker, [1905] 2 K.B. 723.

76 197 202 396 500 581
Deen v. Davies. [1935] 2 K.B. 282 C.A. 1935
M/B: Deen v. Davies, [1935] 2 K.B. 282 (C.A.).

77 198 203 397 401 582
Bruce v. Odhams Press, Limited. [1936] 1 K.B. 697 C.A. 1936
M/B: Bruce v. Odhams Press, Ltd., [1936] 1 K.B. 697 (C.A.).

78 199 204 398 402 583
Phillips v. Barnett. [1921] 2 K.B. 799 1921
M/B: Phillips v. Barnett, [1921] 2 K.B. 799.

79 200 205 399 403 584
In re Oxted Motor Company, Limited. [1921] 3 K.B. 32 1921
M/B: In re Oxted Motor Co., [1921] 3 K.B. 32.
LR: In re Oxted Motor Co., [1921] 3 K.B. 32.

80 101 206 400 404 585
Dennis v. Hutchinson. Trafford v. The Same. [1922] 1 K.B. 693 1922
M/B: Dennis v. Hutchinson, [1922] 1 K.B. 693.

81 102 207 301 405 586
Harrison v. Wythemoor Colliery Company, Limited. 2 K.B. [1922] 674 C.A. 1922
M/B: Harrison v. Wythemoor Colliery Co., [1922] 2 K.B. 674 (C.A.).

82 103 208 302 406 587
Iossifoglu v. Coumantaros. [1941] 1 K.B. 396 C.A. 1940
M/B: Iossifoglu v. Coumantaros, [1941] 1 K.B. 396 (C.A. 1940).

83 104 209 303 407 588
Pope v. Beaumont. [1941] 2 K.B. 321 1941
M/B: Pope v. Beaumont, [1941] 2 K.B. 321.

84 105 210 304 408 589
Kiddle v. City Business Properties, Limited. [1942] 1 K.B. 269 1941
M/B: Kiddle v. City Business Properties, Ltd., [1942] 1 K.B. 269 (1941).

85 106 211 305 409 590
Blunt v. Park Lane Hotel, Limited, and Another. [1942] 2 K.B. 253 C.A. 1942
M/B: Blunt v. Park Lane Hotel, [1942] 2 K.B. 253 (C.A.).

86 107 212 306 410 591
Jenkins v. Jenkins. [1928] 2 K.B. 501 1928
M/B: Jenkins v. Jenkins, [1928] 2 K.B. 501.

87 108 213 307 411 592
Grinham and Another v. Davies. [1929] 2 K.B. 249 1928
M/B: Grinham v. Davies, [1929] 2 K.B. 249 (1928).

88 109 214 308 412 593
Glaskie v. Watkins and Another. [1927] 2 K.B. 181 C.A. 1927
M/B: Glaskie v. Watkins, [1927] 2 K.B. 181 (C.A.).

89 110 215 309 413 594
Hambrook v. Stokes Brothers. [1925] 1 K.B. 141 C.A. 1924
M/B: Hambrook v. Stokes Brothers, [1925] 1 K.B. 141 (C.A. 1924).
LR: Hambrook v. Stokes Bros., [1925] 1 K.B. 141 (C.A. 1924).

90 111 216 310 414 595
Buerger v. Cunard Steamship Company. [1925] 2 K.B. 646 C.A. 1925
M/B: Buerger v. Cunard Steamship Co., [1925] 2 K.B. 646 (C.A.).
LR: Buerger v. Cunard S.S. Co., [1925] 2 K.B. 646 (C.A.).

EXERCISE 18.   LAW REPORTS   (CONTINUED)

91 112 217 311 415 596
Wheeler v. Evans. [1948] 1 K.B. 459 C.A. 1947
M/B: Wheeler v. Evans, [1948] 1 K.B. 459 (C.A. 1947).

92 113 218 312 416 597
Clift v. Taylor. [1948] 2 K.B. 394 C.A. 1948
M/B: Clift v. Taylor, [1948] 2 K.B. 394 (C.A.).

93 114 219 313 417 598
Beck v. Binks. [1949] 1 K.B. 250 1948
M/B: Beck v. Binks, [1949] 1 K.B. 250 (1948).

94 115 220 314 418 599
Rose v. Hurst. [1949] 2 K.B. 372 C.A. 1949
M/B: Rose v. Hurst, [1949] 2 K.B. 372 (C.A.).

95 116 221 315 419 600
Welch v. Nagy. [1950] 1 K.B. 455 C.A. 1949
M/B: Welch v. Nagy, [1950] 1 K.B. 455 (C.A. 1949).

96 117 222 316 420 501
Turburville and Another v. West Ham Corporation. [1950] 2 K.B. 208 C.A. 1950
M/B: Turburville v. West Ham Corp., [1950] 2 K.B. 208 (C.A.).

97 118 223 317 421 502
Cook v. Shoesmith. [1951] 1 K.B. 752 C.A. 1950
M/B: Cook v. Shoesmith, [1951] 1 K.B. 752 (C.A. 1950).

98 119 224 318 422 503
Perry v. Dembowski. [1951] 2 K.B. 420 C.A. 1951
M/B: Perry v. Dembowski, [1951] 2 K.B. 420 (C.A.).

99 120 225 319 423 504
Boots v. E. Christopher & Co. [1952] 1 K.B. 89 C.A. 1951
M/B: Boots v. E. Christopher & Co., [1952] 1 K.B. 89 (C.A. 1951).

100 121 226 320 424 505
Rowell v. Pratt. [1936] 2 K.B. 226 C.A. 1936
M/B: Rowell v. Pratt, [1936] 2 K.B. 226 (C.A.).

LIBRARY EXERCISE 19. WEST'S DIGESTS: KEY NUMBER DIGESTS IN WEST'S REPORTER VOLUMES. The students are required to find the volume of the reporter shown below. In that volume, they are to turn to the "Key Number Digest" section [usually] located at the end of the volume. The instructions explain that this section is an index to the digest topics and key numbers contained in the volume. Students must find the digest topic, "Appeal and Error," in the digest section and locate the <u>first</u> key number given under this topic. They then must find the <u>first</u> case digested under this key number in the main part of the volume. For their answer, they are to cite the case. They are to use <u>Shepard's Citations</u> to find parallel citations when necessary. Since some volumes are occasionally bound without including the "Key Digest" section, the students are to check for the section in a duplicate copy of the reporter or have a different problem assigned if they have difficulty locating the section.

1 121 241 331 421 521   11 S.E.2d
Summerell v. Chilean Nitrate Sales Corporation et al. 218 N.C. 451 (Supreme Court of North Carolina Nov. 7, 1940)
M/B: <u>Summerell v. Chilean Nitrate Sales Corp.</u>, 218 N.C. 451, 11 S.E.2d 304 (1940).

2 122 242 332 422 522   10 S.E.2d
Utilities Commission v. Carolina Scenic Coach Co. 218 N.C. 233 (Supreme Court of North Carolina October 9, 1940)
M/B: <u>Utilities Commission v. Carolina Scenic Coach Co.</u>, 218 N.C. 233, 10 S.E.2d 824 (1940).
LR: Utilities Comm'n v. Carolina Scenic Coach Co., 218 N.C. 233, 10 S.E.2d 824 (1940).

3 123 342 333 423 523   7 S.E.2d
Senn v. Spartanburg County et al. 192 S.C. 489 (Supreme Court of South Carolina February 6, 1940)
M/B: <u>Senn v. Spartanburg County</u>, 192 S.C. 489, 7 S.E.2d 454 (1940).

4 124 244 334 424 524   99 A.2d
Sorokach v. Trusewich et al. 12 N.J. 363 (Supreme Court of New Jersey October 13, 1953)
M/B: <u>Sorokach v. Trusewich</u>, 12 N.J. 363, 99 A.2d 790 (1953).

5 125 245 335 425 525   146 S.E.2d
William J. Cody v. Virginia Cody (now Mitchell) 221 Ga 677 (Supreme Court of Georgia January 18, 1966)
M/B: <u>Cody v. Cody</u>, 221 Ga. 677, 146 S.E.2d 778 (1966).

6 126 246 336 426 526   148 S.E.2d
E.M. Jenkins, Sr. v. Joe W. Winecoff, trading as Joe W. Winecoff Agency, Realtors. 267 N.C. 639 (Supreme Court of North Carolina June 16, 1966)
M/B: <u>Jenkins v. Winecoff</u>, 267 N.C. 639, 148 S.E.2d 577 (1966).

7 127 247 337 427 527   188 S.W.2d
Mercer v. Federal Land Bank of Louisville. 300 Ky 311 (Court of Appeals of Kentucky June 22, 1945)
M/B: <u>Mercer v. Federal Land Bank</u>, 300 Ky. 311, 188 S.E.2d 489 (1945).

8 128 248 338 428 528   100 A.2d
Jeffers v. State 203 Md. 227 (Court of Appeals of Maryland November 12, 1953)
M/B: <u>Jeffers v. State</u>, 203 Md. 227, 100 A.2d 10 (1953).

9 129 249 339 429 529   190 S.W.2d
Anson v. Tietze et al. 354 Mo. 552 (Supreme Court of Missouri November 5, 1945)
M/B: <u>Anson v. Tietze</u>, 354 Mo. 552, 190 S.W.2d 193 (1945).

10 130 250 340 430 530   697 S.W.2d
Midland Bank, Plaintiff/Appellant, v. St. Paul Fire and Marine Insurance Company, Comercial Union Insurance Companies, and the Travelers Indemnity Company, Defendnats/Respondents (Missouri Court of Appeals, Western District June 25, 1985)

EXERCISE 19. WEST'S DIGESTS: KEY NUMBER DIGESTS IN WEST'S REPORTER VOLUMES

M/B: Midland Bank v. St. Paul Fire & Marine Insurance Co., 697 S.W.2d 203 (Mo. Ct. App. 1985).
LR: Midland Bank v. St. Paul Fire & Marine Ins. Co., 697 S.W.2d 203 (Mo. Ct. App. 1985).

11 131 251 341 431 531   255 S.W.2d
Yount et al. v. City of Frankfort (Court of Appeals of Kentucky February 27, 1953)
M/B: Yount v. City of Frankfort, 255 S.W.2d 632 (Ky. 1953).

12 132 252 342 432 532   254 S.W.2d
Phillips Pipe Line Co. v. Brandstetter et ux. (Supreme Court of Missouri Division No. 2 February 9, 1953)
M/B: Phillips Pipe Line Co. v. Brandstetter, 363 Mo. 904. 254 S.W.2d 636 (1953).

13 133 253 343 433 533   376 N.W.2d
K. Bruce Doland and Cynda K. Doland, Appellants, v. Boone County, Iowa, Appellee (Supreme Court of Iowa Nov. 13, 1985)
M/B: Doland v. Boone County, 376 N.W.2d 870 (Iowa 1985).

14 134 254 344 434 534   167 N.W.2d
Simon Mitzel, Plaintiff and Respondent, v. Kasper Schatz, Defendant and Appellant (Supreme Court of North Dakota December 10, 1968)
M/B: Mitzel v. Schatz, 167 N.W.2d 519 (N.D. 1968).

15 135 255 345 435 535   188 N.W.2d
Thos. F. Burns, Appellant, v. LaRue Y. Stewart (Donna Rae Johnson, as admrx. c. t. a. of the estate of Harriet LaRue Y. Stewart, substituted for LaRue Y. Stewart), Respondent (Supreme Court of Minnesota May 28, 1971)
M/B: Burns v. Stewart, 290 Minn. 289, 188 N.W.2d 760 (1971).

16 136 256 346 436 536   602 P.2d
In the Matter of the Estate of Clarence W. Corson, Deceased, Appellee v. Mary Lou Erickson, Appellant 226 Kan. 673 (Supreme Court of Kansas December 1, 1979)
M/B: Estate of Corson v. Erickson, 226 Kan. 673, 602 P.2d 1320 (1979).

17 137 257 347 437 537   387 P.2d
Lawrence Materi, Appellant v. Stanley Spurrier and C. L. Bruce, Appellees (Supreme Court of Kansas December 7, 1963)
M/B: Materi v. Spurrier, 192 Kan. 291, 387 P.2d 221 (1963).

18 138 258 348 438 538   603 P.2d
In the Matter of the Estate of Erie L. Kempkes, Deceased 4 Kan. App. 154 (Court of Appeals of Kansas December 7, 1979)
M/B: In re Estate of Kempkes, 4 Kan. App. 154, 603 P.2d 642 (1979).
LR: In re Estate of Kempkes, 4 Kan. App. 154, 603 P.2d 642 (1979).

19 139 259 349 439 539   98 A.2d
Judkins v. Buckland (Supreme Judicial Court of Maine July 8, 1953)
M/B: Judkins v. Buckland, 149 Me. 59, 98 A.2d 538 (1953).

20 140 260 350 440 540   384 P.2d
International Association of Fire Fighters, Local No. 1319, AFL-CIO et al., Plaintiffs and Respondents, v. City of Palo Alto et al., Defendants and Appellants (Supreme Court of California In Bank August 13, 1963)
M/B: International Association of Fire Fighters, Local No. 1319 v. City of Palo Alto, 60 Cal. 2d 295, 384 P.2d 170, 32 Cal. Rptr. 842 (1963).
LR: International Ass'n of Fire Fighters, Local No. 1319 v. City of Palo Alto, 60 Cal. 2d 295, 384 P.2d 170, 32 Cal. Rptr. 842 (1963).

21 141 261 351 441 541   91 N.E.2d
City of Quincy v. Brooks-Skinner, Inc. (Two cases). (Supreme Judicial Court of Massachusetts Norfolk March 3, 1950)
M/B: City of Quincy v. Brooks-Skinner, Inc., 325 Mass. 406, 91 N.E.2d 206 (1950).

EXERCISE 19. WEST'S DIGESTS: KEY NUMBER DIGESTS IN WEST'S REPORTER VOLUMES

22 142 262 352 442 542   93 N.E.2d
Fino v. Municipal Court of City of Boston (Supreme Judicial Court of
Massachusetts Suffolk July 10, 1950)
M/B: Fino v. Municipal Court, 326 Mass. 277, 93 N.E.2d 558 (1950).

23 143 263 353 443 543   90 N.E.2d
Tims et al. v. Holland Furnace Co. et al. 152 Ohio St. 469 (Supreme Court of
Ohio January 11, 1950)
M/B: Tims v. Holland Furnace Co., 152 Ohio St. 469, 90 N.E.2d 376 (1950).

24 144 264 354 444 544   109 N.E.2d
Chapman v. Chapman (Supreme Court of Indiana January 13, 1953)
M/B: Chapman v. Chapman, 231 Ind. 556, 109 N.E.2d 724 (1953).

25 145 265 355 445 545   95 N.E.2d
Frerichs v. Foreman et al. 407 Ill. 507 (Supreme Court of Illinois November
27, 1950)
M/B: Frerichs v. Foreman, 407 Ill. 507, 95 N.E.2d 452 (1950).

26 146 266 356 446 546   190 So. 2d
Jerry G. Marsh v. J.L. Wittmeier (Supreme Court of Alabama October 13, 1966)
M/B: Marsh v. Wittmeier, 280 Ala. 172, 190 So. 2d 920 (1966).
Note: "280 Ala. 715" is the parallel citation for a different case on page 920
and is incorrect.

27 147 267 357 447 547   179 So. 2d
Gulf States Utilities Company v. Dixie Electric Membership Corporation 248 La.
458 (Supreme Court of Louisiana November 8, 1965)
M/B: Gulf States Utilities Co. v. Dixie Electric Membership Corp., 248 La.
458, 179 So. 2d 637 (1965).
LR: Gulf States Utils. Co. v. Dixie Elec. Membership Corp., 248 La. 458, 179
So. 2d 637 (1965).

28 148 268 358 448 548   44 So. 2d
Succession of Tullier 216 La. 821 (Supreme Court of Louisiana February 13,
1950)
M/B: Succession of Tullier, 216 La. 821, 44 So. 2d 880 (1950).

29 149 269 359 449 549   43 So. 2d
Ex parte Shade (Supreme Court of Alabama December 8, 1949)
M/B: Ex parte Shade, 253 Ala. 139, 43 So. 2d 319 (1949).
LR: Ex parte Shade, 253 Ala. 139, 43 So. 2d 319 (1949).

30 150 270 360 450 550   30 N.W.2d
In re Brand (consolidated with Brand v. Milwaukee County et al.) (listed
second) (Supreme Court of Wisconsin December 23, 1947)
M/B: In re Brand, 251 Wis. 531, 30 N.W.2d 238 (1947).
LR: In re Brand, 251 Wis. 531, 30 N.W.2d 238 (1947).

31 151 271 361 451 551   29 N.W.2d
Curran v. Nash et al. (Supreme Court of Minnesota October 31, 1947)
M/B: Curran v. Nash, 224 Minn. 571, 29 N.W.2d 436 (1947).

32 152 272 362 452 552   28 N.W.2d
In re Swanson's Estate (consolidated with Wallingford v. Eastman) (listed
second) (Supreme Court of South Dakota August 29, 1947)
M/B: In re Swanson's Estate, 71 S.D. 622, 28 N.W.2d 663 (1947).
LR: In re Swanson's Estate, 71 S.D. 622, 28 N.W.2d 663 (1947).

33 153 273 363 453 553   31 N.W.2d
H. Christiansen & Sons, Inc. v. City of Duluth (Supreme Court of Minnesota
February 20, 1948)
M/B: H. Christiansen & Sons v. City of Duluth, 225 Minn. 486, 31 N.W.2d 277
(1948).

34 154 274 364 454 554   63 P.2d

EXERCISE 19. WEST'S DIGESTS: KEY NUMBER DIGESTS IN WEST'S REPORTER VOLUMES

Wasatch Oil Refining Co. v. Wade, Judge, et al. (Supreme Court of Utah December 30, 1936)
M/B: Wasatch Oil Refining Co. v. Wade, 92 Utah 50, 63 P.2d 1070 (1936).
LR: Wasatch Oil Ref. Co. v. Wade, 92 Utah 50, 63 P.2d 1070 (1936).

35 155 275 365 455 555   62 P.2d
In re Benson (Supreme Court of Oklahoma November 10, 1936)
M/B: In re Benson, 178 Okla. 299, 62 P.2d 962 (1936).
LR: In re Benson, 178 Okla. 299, 62 P.2d 962 (1936).

36 156 276 366 456 556   61 P.2d
Moltzner v. Cutler et al. (Supreme Court of Oregon October 6, 1936)
M/B: Moltzner v. Cutler, 154 Or. 573, 61 P.2d 93 (1936).

37 157 277 367 457 557   59 P.2d
Arcade Hotel, Inc., v. Peterson (Supreme Court of Oregon July 14, 1936)
M/B: Arcade Hotel v. Peterson, 154 Or. 679, 59 P.2d 384 (1936).
Note: "154 Or. 369" is the parallel citation of a different case on page 384 and is incorrect.

38 158 278 368 458 558   131 P.
Grover Irrigation & Land Co. v. Lovella Ditch, Reservoir & Irrigation Co. (Supreme Court of Wyoming April 7, 1913)
M/B: Grover Irrigation & Land Co. v. Lovella Ditch, Reservoir & Irrigation Co., 21 Wyo. 204, 131 P.2d 43 (1913).

39 159 279 369 459 559   590 P.2d
Bernard M. Lloyd, Respondent, v. Alfred Zollman, Appellant 285 Or. 161 (Supreme Court of Oregon February 7, 1979)
M/B: Lloyd v. Zollman, 285 Or. 161, 590 P.2d 222 (1979).

40 160 280 370 460 560   133 P.
Bateman et al. v. Gitts et al. (Supreme Court of New Mexico April 10, 1913)
M/B: Bateman v. Gitts, 17 N.M. 619, 133 P. 969 (1913).

41 161 281 371 461 561   134 P.
Columbia City Land Co. v. Ruhl (Supreme Court of Oregon September 9, 1913)
M/B: Columbia City Land Co. v. Ruhl, 70 Or. 246, 134 P. 1035 (1913).

42 162 282 372 462 562   45 N.E.2d
Watts v. Watts (Supreme Judicial Court of Massachusetts December 1, 1942)
M/B: Watts v. Watts, 312 Mass. 442, 45 N.E.2d 273 (1942).

43 163 283 373 463 563   42 N.E.2d
Orth et al. v. Paramount Pictures, Inc., et al. (Supreme Judicial Court of Massachusetts May 28, 1942)
M/B: Orth v. Paramount Pictures, Inc., 311 Mass. 580, 42 N.E.2d 524 (1942).

44 164 284 374 464 564   39 N.E.2d
Peoples Store of Roseland et al. v. McKibbin, Director of Finance, et al. 379 Ill. 148 (Supreme Court of Illinois January 20, 1942)
M/B: Peoples Store v. McKibbin, 379 Ill. 148, 39 N.E.2d 995 (1942).

45 165 285 375 465 565   33 N.E.2d
Durkin, Director of Labor, v. Hey et al. 376 Ill. 292 (Supreme Court of Illinois April 10, 1941)
M/B: Durkin v. Hey, 376 Ill. 292, 33 N.E.2d 463 (1941).

46 166 286 376 466 566   36 N.E.2d
Krinsky v. Stevens Coal Sales Co., (Supreme Judicial Court of Massachusetts September 9, 1941)
M/B: Krinsky v. Stevens Coal Sales Co., 309 Mass. 528, 36 N.E.2d 411 (1941).

47 167 287 377 467 567   236 A.2d
Steven M. Castle et al. v. Planning and Zoning Commission of the Town of Stonington et al. (Supreme Court of Connecticut December 7, 1967)

EXERCISE 19. WEST'S DIGESTS: KEY NUMBER DIGESTS IN WEST'S REPORTER VOLUMES

M/B: Castle v. Planning & Zoning Commission, 155 Conn. 617, 236 A.2d 460 (1967).
LR: Castle v. Planning & Zoning Comm'n, 155 Conn. 617, 236 A.2d 460 (1967).

48 168 288 378 468 568   234 A.2d
Marjorie J. Elliott, Plaintiff, v. George M. Elliott, Defendant 97 N.J. Super. 10 (Superior Court of New Jersey Appellate Division September 12, 1967)
M/B: Elliott v. Elliott, 97 N.J. Super. 10, 234 A.2d 101 (App. Div. 1967).

49 169 289 379 469 569   233 A.2d
David G. Middleberg v. William T. Middleberg et ux. et al., Appellants 427 Pa. 114 (Supreme Court of Pennsylvania September 26, 1967)
M/B: Middleberg v. Middleberg, 427 Pa. 114, 233 A.2d 889 (1967).

50 170 290 380 470 570   231 A.2d
Ivy Young Kelley v. Hopkinton Village Precinct (Supreme Court of New Hampshire June 30, 1967)
M/B: Kelley v. Hopkinton Village Precinct, 108 N.H. 206, 231 A.2d 269 (1967).

51 171 291 381 471 571   237 A.2d
James C. Peters and Anthony Palumbo Plaintiff-Respondents, v. Nezzie Kelly, Defendant-Appellant 98 N.J. Super. 441 (Superior Court of New Jersey Appellate Division January 12, 1968)
M/B: Peters v. Kelly, 98 N.J. Super. 441, 237 A.2d 635 (App. Div. 1968).

52 172 292 382 472 572   239 A.2d
Commonwealth of Pennsylvania ex rel. Ransom Township v. Peter Mascheska, Appellant 429 Pa. 168 (Supreme Court of Pennsylvania March 15, 1968)
M/B: Commonwealth ex rel. Ransom Township v. Mascheska, 429 Pa. 168, 239 A.2d 386 (1968).
LR: Commonwealth ex rel. Ransom Township v. Mascheska, 429 Pa. 168, 239 A.2d 386 (1968).

53 173 293 383 473 573   240 A.2d
City of Philadelphia, Appellant v. Chase and Walker Corporation, Regent Management Corporation, Central Corporation, Samuel Elgart, Trustee, and Samuel Elgart (Supreme Court of Pennsylvania March 15, 1968)
M/B: City of Philadelphia v. Chase & Walker Corp., 429 Pa. 161, 240 A.2d 65 (1968).

54 174 294 384 474 574   91 A.2d
Dolloff v. Gardiner (Supreme Judicial Court of Maine September 9, 1952)
M/B: Dolloff v. Gardiner, 148 Me. 176, 91 A.2d 320 (1952).

55 175 295 385 475 575   92 A.2d
Clapperton v. United States Fidelity & Guaranty Co. et al. (Supreme Judicial Court of Maine November 3, 1952)
M/B: Clapperton v. United States Fidelity & Guaranty Co., 148 Me. 257, 92 A.2d 336 (1952).
LR: Clapperton v. United States Fidelity & Guar. Co., 148 Me. 257, 92 A.2d 336 (1952).

56 176 296 386 476 576   93 A.2d
Black v. Fiandaca et al. (Supreme Court of New Hampshire Rockingham January 6, 1953)
M/B: Black v. Fiandaca, 98 N.H. 33, 93 A.2d 663 (1953).

57 177 297 387 477 577   94 A.2d
Panther Valley Television Co., Inc. v. Borough of Summit Hill 372 Pa. 524 (Supreme Court of Pennsylvania February 13, 1953)
M/B: Panther Valley Television Co. v. Borough of Summit Hill, 372 Pa. 524, 94 A.2d 735 (1953).

58 178 298 388 478 578   95 A.2d
Haefele et al. v. Davis, President et al. 373 Pa. 34 (Supreme Court of Pennsylvania February 13, 1953)
M/B: Haefele v. Davis, 373 Pa. 34, 95 A.2d 195 (1953).

EXERCISE 19. WEST'S DIGESTS: KEY NUMBER DIGESTS IN WEST'S REPORTER VOLUMES

59 179 299 389 479 579   588 F.2d
Billy J. McKinzie and wife, Judy McKinzie, Individually and as Next Friend of
Stuart McKinzie, a Minor, Plaintiffs-Appellants, v. Michael Wayne Fleming and
Star Tool Company, Defendant-Appellees (United States Court of Appeals Fifth
Circuit January 18, 1979)
M/B: McKinzie v. Fleming, 588 F.2d 165 (5th Cir. 1979).

60 180 300 390 480 580   566 F.2d
Paul G. Rabalais, Plaintiff-Appellant v. Dresser Industries, Inc.
Defendant-Appellee (United States Court of Appeals Fifth Circuit January 19,
1978)
M/B: Rabalais v. Dresser Industries, 566 F.2d 518 (5th Cir. 1978).
LR: Rabalais v. Dresser Indus., 566 F.2d 518 (5th Cir. 1978).

61 181 201 391 481 581   530 F.2d
The Rath Packing Company, a Corporation, Plaintiff, Counter-Defendant and
Appellant v. M.H. Becker, as Director of the County of Los Angeles Department
of Weights and Measures, Defendant, Appellee and Cross-Appellant C.B.
Christensen, as Director of Agriculture of the State of California,
Intervenor, Appellee and Cross-Appellant (United States Court of Appeals,
Ninth Circuit October 29, 1975)
M/B: Rath Packing Co. v. Becker, 530 F.2d 1295 (9th Cir. 1975).

62 182 202 392 482 582   529 F.2d
Otis Williams, et al. Plaintiffs-Appellants v. United Distributive Workers,
Council 30 AFL-CIO (Silvercup Bakeries), et al., Defendants-Appellees (United
States Court of Appeals, Sixth Circuit February 3, 1976)
M/B: Williams v. United Distributive Workers, Council 30, 529 F.2d 509 (6th
Cir. 1976).

63 183 203 393 483 583   528 F.2d
Universe Tankships, Inc., as Owner of the SS Ore Chief, Appellant, v. United
States Court of America, (United States Court of Appeals, Third Circuit
September 11, 1975)
M/B: Universe Tankships, Inc. v. United States, 528 F.2d 73 (3d Cir. 1975).

64 184 204 394 484 584   527 F.2d
Michael-Regan Co., Inc., a California Corporation, Plaintiff-Appellant, v.
Martin Lindell, a sole proprietor doing business under the firm name of
Lindell Enterprises, Defendant and Third-Party Plaintiff-Appellee (United
States Court of Appeals Ninth Circuit August 6, 1975)
M/B: Michael-Regan Co. v. Lindell, 527 F.2d 653 (9th Cir. 1975).

65 185 205 395 485 585   526 F.2d
Jamison Company, Inc. Plaintiff-Appellee, v. Westvaco Corporation, formerly
West Virginia Pulp and Paper Company, Defendant-Appellant (United States Court
of Appeals, Fifth Circuit February 6, 1976)
M/B: Jamison Co. v. Westvaco Corp., 526 F.2d 922 (5th Cir. 1976).

66 186 206 396 486 586   525 F.2d
Marie Pierre et al., Petitioners-Appellants v. United States of America,
Respondent-Appellee (United States Court of Appeals, Fifth Circuit January 8,
1976)
M/B: Pierre v. United States, 525 F.2d 933 (5th Cir. 1976).

67 187 207 397 487 587   524 F.2d
United States of America Appellant, v. The Valley National Bank, Executor of
the Estate of Maurice H. Berkson, Deceased, et al., Appellees (United States
Court of Appeals, Ninth Circuit August 22, 1975)
M/B: United States v. Valley National Bank, 524 F.2d 199 (9th Cir. 1975).
LR: United States v. Valley Nat'l Bank, 524 F.2d 199 (9th Cir. 1975).

68 188 208 398 488 588   523 F.2d
Robert C. Vaughn v. Bernard Rosen, Executive Director, U.S. Civil Service
Commission, et al., Appellants (United States Court of Appeals District of
Columbia Circuit November 21, 1975)

EXERCISE 19. WEST'S DIGESTS: KEY NUMBER DIGESTS IN WEST'S REPORTER VOLUMES

M/B: Vaughn v. Rosen, 523 F.2d 1136 (D.C. Cir. 1975).

69 189 209 399 489 589   479 F.2d
Vance D. Krause, as Administrator of Estate of Mary R. Krause, Appellant v.
Sacramento Inn et al., Appellees (United States Court of Appeals, Ninth
Circuit May 10, 1973)
M/B: Krause v. Sacramento Inn, 479 F.2d 988 (9th Cir. 1973).

70 190 210 400 490 590   478 F.2d
O.W. Donald, Plaintiff-Appellant v. Uarco Business Forms Defendant-Appellee
(United States Court of Appeals Eighth Circuit January 30, 1973)
M/B: Donald v. Uarco Business Forms, 478 F.2d 764 (8th Cir. 1973).

71 191 211 301 491 591   477 F.2d
J. William Wolf et al., Plaintiffs Appellants-Cross Appellees, v. Robert R.
Frank et al., Defendants Appellees-Cross Appellants (United States Court of
Appeals Fifth Circuit April 24, 1973)
M/B: Wolf v. Frank, 477 F.2d 467 (5th Cir. 1973).

72 192 212 302 492 592   510 F.2d
Don Rothman, as receiver of Highlander, Inc., a corporation dba Highlander
Sanitarium, Debtor in Proceedings under Chapter XI, Plaintiff-Appellants, v.
Hospital Service of Southern California dba Blue Cross of Southern Californa
and Secretary of Health, Education and Welfare, Defendants-Appellees (United
States Court of Appeals Ninth Circuit February 3, 1975)
M/B: Rothman v. Hospital Service, 510 F.2d 956 (9th Cir. 1975).
LR: Rothman v. Hospital Serv., 510 F.2d 956 (9th Cir. 1975).

73 193 213 303 493 593   475 F.2d
George C. Stafford, Plaintiff, Appellee, v. Perini Corporation, Defendant,
Appellant (United States Court of Appeals First Circuit December 7, 1972)
M/B: Stafford v. Perini Corp., 475 F.2d 507 (1st Cir. 1972).

74 194 214 304 494 594   487 F.2d
Frank Geraci, Jr., Individually and on behalf of all other persons similarly
situated, Plaintiff-Appellant, v. James Treuchtlinger, Commissioner of
Corrections for the County of Nassau, and Walter Flood, Warden of the Nassau
County Jail, Individually and in their official capacities,
Defendants-Respondents (United States Court of Appeals Second Circuit October
9, 1973)
M/B: Geraci v. Treuchtlinger, 487 F.2d 590 (2d Cir. 1973).

75 195 215 305 495 595   485 F.2d
Charles F. Zimmer, Plaintiff Stewart Marshall, Intervenor-Appellant, v. John
J. McKeithen et al., Defendants-Appellees (United States Court of Appeals
Fifth Circuit (September 12, 1973)
M/B: Zimmer v. McKeithen, 485 F.2d 1297 (5th Cir. 1973).

76 196 216 306 496 596   775 F.2d
Hutchinson Utilities Commission of the City of Hutchinson, Hutchinson,
Minnesota, Appellee/Cross-Appellant, v. Curtis-Wright Corporation, a Delaware
corporation, Appellant/Cross-Appellee (United States Court of Appeals, Eighth
Circuit Oct. 11, 1985)
M/B: Hutchinson Utilities Commission v. Curtis-Wright Corp., 775 F.2d 231
(8th Cir. 1985).
LR: Hutchinson Utils. Comm'n v. Curtis-Wright Corp., 775 F.2d 231 (8th Cir.
1985).

77 197 217 307 497 597   483 F.2d
Claxton L. Burns, on behalf of himself and others similarly situated,
Plaintiff-Appellant, v. Thiokol Chemical Corporation, Defendant-Appellee
(United States Court of Appeals Fifth Circuit July 19, 1973)
M/B: Burns v. Thiokol Chemical Corp., 483 F.2d 300 (5th Cir. 1973).
LR: Burns v. Thiokol Chem. Corp., 483 F.2d 300 (5th Cir. 1973).

78 198 218 308 498 598   482 F.2d

EXERCISE 19. WEST'S DIGESTS: KEY NUMBER DIGESTS IN WEST'S REPORTER VOLUMES

Francisco Enterprises, Inc., a Corporation, Plaintiff-Appellant, v. Edward J. Kirby, et al., Defendants-Appellees (United States Court of Appeals Ninth Circuit July 19, 1973)
M/B: Francisco Enterprises, v. Kirby, 482 F.2d 481 (9th Cir. 1973).
LR: Francisco Enters., v. Kirby, 482 F.2d 481 (9th Cir. 1973).

79 199 219 309 499 599   481 F.2d
Jean T. Terkildsen, formerly doing business under the firm name and style of Singer and Carlberg. Plaintiff-Appellant-Appellee, v. Eric H. Waters et al., Defendants Appellees-Appellants (United States Court of Appeals Second Circuit May 29 1973)
M/B: Terkildsen v. Waters, 481 F.2d 201 (2d Cir. 1973).

80 200 220 310 500 600   305 F.2d
Joseph Pettus, Plaintiff-Appellee, v. Grace Line, Inc., Defendant and Third Party Plaintiff-Appellee (United States Court of Appeals, Second Circuit January 10, 1962)
M/B: Pettus v. Grace Line, 305 F.2d 151 (2d Cir. 1962).

81 101 221 311 401 501   307 F.2d
Pacific Queen Fisheries et al., Appellants v. L. Symes et al., Appellees. (United States Court of Appeals Ninth Circuit August 3, 1962)
M/B: Pacific Queen Fisheries v. Symes, 307 F.2d 700 (9th Cir. 1962).

82 102 222 312 402 502   309 F.2d
Betty Kuc, Plaintiff-Appellee, v. Mill Owners Mutual Insurance Company, Defendant-Appellant (United States Court of Appeal Seventh Circuit November 14, 1962)
M/B: Kuc v. Mill Owners Mutual Insurance Co., 309 F.2d 728 (7th Cir. 1962).
LR: Kuc v. Mill Owners Mut. Ins. Co., 309 F.2d 728 (7th Cir. 1962).

83 103 223 313 403 503   310 F.2d
Brotherhood of Locomotive Engineers et al., Plaintiffs-Appellants v. The Baltimore & Ohio Railroad Company, a corporation, et al., Defendants-Appellees (United States Court of Appeals Seventh Circuit November 28, 1962)
M/B: Brotherhood of Locomotive Engineers v. Baltimore & Ohio Railroad, 310 F.2d 503 (7th Cir. 1962).
LR: Brotherhood of Locomotive Eng'rs v. Baltimore & O.R.R., 310 F.2d 503 (7th Cir. 1962).

84 104 224 314 404 504   311 F.2d
Hap Corporation, Defendant Appellant, v. Heyman Manufacturing Company NY, Plaintiff, Appellee. (United States Court of Appeals First Circuit October 2, 1962)
M/B: Hap Corp. v. Heyman Manufacturing Co., 311 F.2d 839 (1st Cir. 1962).
LR: Hap Corp. v. Heyman Mfg. Co., 311 F.2d 839 (1st Cir. 1962).

85 105 225 315 405 505   312 F.2d
Franklin Life Insurance Company, Plaintiff-Appellant v. Mary E. Bieniek and Sewickley Savings & Loan Association, Defendant Appellees (United States Court of Appeals Third Circuit October 5, 1962)
M/B: Franklin Life Insurance Co. v. Bieniek, 312 F.2d 365 (3d Cir. 1962).
LR: Franklin Life Ins. Co. v. Bieniek, 312 F.2d 365 (3d Cir. 1962).

86 106 226 316 406 506   322 F.2d
Annie Mae Petty, Plaintiff-Appellant v. Harry Porter, Defendant-Appellee (United States Court of Appeals Sixth Circuit September 10, 1963)
M/B: Petty v. Porter, 322 F.2d 308 (6th Cir. 1963).

87 107 227 317 407 507   318 F.2d
J. Polk Smartt and Isabel Smartt, Plaintiffs-Appellants v. Coca-Cola Bottling Corporation (Sued as Cincinnati Coca-Cola Bottling Co.) Defendant-Appellee (United Sstates Court of Appeals Sixth Circuit June 18, 1963)
M/B: Smartt v. Coca-Cola Bottling Corp., 318 F.2d 447 (6th Cir. 1963).

88 108 228 318 408 508   316 F.2d

EXERCISE 19. WEST'S DIGESTS: KEY NUMBER DIGESTS IN WEST'S REPORTER VOLUMES

John E. Calhoun et al., d/b/a Rosen Dahl Guernsey Farms, et al., Appellants, v. Orville Freeman, Secretary, United States Department of Agribulture Appellee (United States Court of Appeals District of Columbia Circuit October 29, 1962)
M/B: Calhoun v. Freeman, 316 F.2d 386 (D.C. Cir. 1962).

89 109 229 319 409 509   315 F.2d
Premier Roof Co., a corporation American Casualty Company of Reading, Pennsylvania, Appellants, v. United States of America for the Use and Benefit of Alpaca Electric Corporation, Appellee (United States Court of Appeals Ninth Circuit March 26, 1963)
M/B: Premier Roof Co. v. United States ex rel. Alpaca Electric Corp., 315 F.2d 18 (9th Cir. 1963).
LR: Premier Roof Co. v. United States ex rel. Alpaca Elec. Corp., 315 F.2d 18 (9th Cir. 1963).

90 110 230 320 410 510   314 F.2d
Pacific Coast Cheese, Inc., and Evert L. Hagan, Appellants, v. W. Willard Wirtz, Secretary of Labor, United States Department of Labor, Appellee (United States Court of Appeals Ninth Circuit February 11, 1963)
M/B: Pacific Coast Cheese, Inc. v. Wirtz, 314 F.2d 145 (9th Cir. 1963).

91 111 231 321 411 511   365 F.2d
John Marshall, Appellant, v. Grant Sawyer, as Governor of the State of Nevada, et al., Appellees (United States Court of Appeals Ninth Circuit August 10, 1966)
M/B: Marshall v. Sawyer, 365 F.2d 105 (9th Cir. 1966).

92 112 232 322 412 512   767 F.2d
Wesly Rhea, Plaintiff-Appellee, v. Massey-Ferguson, Inc., Defendant-Appellant (United States Court of Appeals, Sixth Circuit July 3, 1985)
M/B: Rhea v. Massey-Ferguson, Inc., 767 F.2d 266 (6th Cir. 1985).

93 113 233 323 413 513   367 F.2d
Lester J. Albrecht, Appellant, v. The Herald Company, a corporation, d/b/a Globe-Democrat Publishing Company, Appellee (United States Court of Appeals Eighth Circuit October 20, 1966)
M/B: Albrecht v. Herald Co., 367 F.2d 517 (8th Cir. 1966).

94 114 234 324 414 514   368 F.2d
United States of America, Appellee, v. T.W. Ferguson and Edith R. Ferguson, his wife, Appellants (United States Court of Appeals Fourth Circuit June 1, 1966)
M/B: United States v. Ferguson, 368 F.2d 324 (4th Cir. 1966).

95 115 235 325 415 515   375 F.2d
Harold N. Skogen, David Skogen, a Minor, by Harold N. Skogen, His Father and Natural Guradian, and Douglas Skogen, a Minor, by Harold N. Skogen, His Father and Natural Guardian, Appellants v. The Dow Chemical Company, a Corporation and Ralston Purina Company, a Corporation Jointly and Severally (United States Court of Appeals Eighth Circuit March 30, 1967)
M/B: Skogen v. Dow Chemical Co., 375 F.2d 692 (8th Cir. 1967).
LR: Skogen v. Dow Chem. Co., 375 F.2d 692 (8th Cir. 1967).

96 116 236 326 416 516   376 F.2d
United States of America Appellant, v. Charles C. Gates, Jr. June S. Gates Brown W. Cannon and Charia Gates Cannon, Appelees (United States Court of Appeals Tenth Circuit March 10, 1967)
M/B: United States v. Gates, 376 F.2d 65 (10th Cir. 1967).

97 117 237 327 417 517   378 F.2d
Ralph R. Poston, Marin P. Bessell, and Willard J. Wylie, as Association Trustees of the Miami Iron Workers Pension Fund, Local No. 272, Appellants, v. Charles C. Caraker et al., etc. Appellees (Uinted States Court of Appeals Fifth Circuit June 8, 1967)
M/B: Poston v. Caraker, 378 F.2d 439 (5th Cir. 1967).

EXERCISE 19. WEST'S DIGESTS: KEY NUMBER DIGESTS IN WEST'S REPORTER VOLUMES

98 118 238 328 418 518   379 F.2d
Bobby Jean McKissick, Appellant, v. United States of America Appellee (United
States Court of Appeals Fifth Circuit June 30, 1967)
M/B: McKissick v. United States, 379 F.2d 754 (5th Cir. 1967).

99 119 239 329 419 519   370 F.2d
The Hidden Splendor Mining Company, Appellant, v. General Insurance Company of
America, Appellee (United States Court of Appeals Tenth Circuit December 23,
1966)
M/B: Hidden Splendor Mining Co. v. General Insurance Co. of America, 370 F.2d
515 (10th Cir. 1966).
LR: Hidden Splendor Mining Co. v. General Ins. Co. of Am., 370 F.2d 515 (10th
Cir. 1966).

100 120 240 330 420 520   574 F.2d
Miriam Winters, Plaintiff-Appellant, v. Abe Lavine, Individually and as
Commissioner of the New York State Department of Social Services, and James R.
Dumpson, Individually and as Commissioner of the New York City Department of
Social Services Defendents-Appellees (United States Court of Appeals Second
Circuit Jan. 16, 1978)
M/B: Winters v. Lavine, 574 F.2d 46 (2d Cir. 1978).

LIBRARY EXERCISE 20. WEST'S DIGESTS: FINDING CASES USING KNOWN TOPICS AND KEY NUMBERS.

INSTRUCTOR'S NOTE: For this exercise, students are to assume that they have located a reference to the topic and key number [listed below] which appears to bear directly on a point of law that they are researching. Using West's Southern Digest, they are to find a case decided in the year listed and arising in the state listed that is abstracted under that topic and key number. They then are to find the case in the relevant volume of West's Southern Reporter and cite the case. Students are directed not to include the subsequent history of the case in their citation. The WESTLAW topic heading number given in the exercise is used to complete a later exercise.

1 143 231 380 477 526   Appeal & Error 1133   1912   Ala.
Drummond v. Lamar (Supreme Court of Alabama April 4, 1912)
M/B: Drummond v. Lamar, 177 Ala. 530, 58 So. 194 (1912).

2 144 232 381 478 527   Appeal & Error 1006(3)   1937   Miss.
Universal Truck Loading Co. v. Taylor et al. (Supreme Court of Mississippi March 1, 1937)
M/B: Universal Truck Loading Co. v. Taylor, 178 Miss. 143, 172 So. 746 (1937).

3 145 233 382 479 528   Appeal & Error 880(2)   1965   Ala.
City of Montgomery v. Nellie Jones (Supreme Court of Alabama March 18, 1965)
M/B: City of Montgomery v. Jones, 277 Ala. 617, 173 So. 2d 781 (1965).

4 146 234 383 480 529   Appeal & Error 655(1)   1893   Miss.
Young et al. v. Walker (Supreme Court of Mississippi May 8, 1893)
M/B: Young v. Walker, 70 Miss. 813, 12 So. 901 (1893).

5 147 235 384 481 530   Appeal & Error 262(2)   1908   Fla.
Loeffler v. City of West Tampa (Supreme Court of Florida January 22, 1908)
M/B: Loeffler v. City of West Tampa, 55 Fla. 276, 46 So. 426 (1908).
LR: Loeffler v. City of W. Tampa, 55 Fla. 276, 46 So. 426 (1908).

6 148 236 385 482 531   Appeal & Error 197(5)   1909   Miss.
Mississippi Cotton Oil Co. v. Smith et al. (Supreme Court of Mississippi March 15, 1909)
M/B: Mississippi Cotton Oil Co. v. Smith, 95 Miss. 528, 48 So. 735 (1909).

7 149 237 386 483 532   Bills & Notes 519   1930   Ala.
Culwell v. Edmondson (Supreme Court of Alabama April 10, 1930)
M/B: Culwell v. Edmondson, 221 Ala. 424, 129 So. 276 (1930).

8 150 238 387 484 533   Banks & Banking 270(10)   1924   Ala.
Jones v. Moore (Supreme Court of Alabama Nov. 6, 1924)
M/B: Jones v. Moore, 212 Ala. 248, 102 So. 200 (1924).

9 151 239 388 485 534   Automobiles 357   1931   La.
State v. Stelljes (Supreme Court of Louisiana March 30, 1931)
M/B: State v. Stelljes, 172 La. 401, 134 So. 373 (1931).

10 152 240 389 486 535   Automobiles 79   1949   Ala.
Alabama Public Service Commission et al v. Nunis (Supreme Court of Alabama March 17, 1949)
M/B: Alabama Public Service Commission v. Nunis, 252 Ala. 30, 39 So. 2d 409 (1949).
LR: Alabama Pub. Serv. Comm'n v. Nunis, 252 Ala. 30, 39 So. 2d 409 (1949).

11 153 241 390 487 536   Attorney & Client 39   1931   Miss.
In re Marshall (Supreme Court of Mississippi)
M/B: In re Marshall, 162 Miss. 364, 138 So. 298 (1931).
LR: In re Marshall, 162 Miss. 364, 138 So. 298 (1931).

12 154 242 391 488 537   Adverse Possession 112   1902   Miss.
Cohn v. Pearl River Lumber Co. et al. (Supreme Court of Mississippi June 9, 1902)
M/B: Cohn v. Pearl River Lumber Co., 80 Miss. 649, 32 So. 292 (1902).

EXERCISE 20.   WEST'S DIGESTS: FINDING CASES USING KNOWN TOPICS AND KEY NUMBERS

13 155 243 392 489 538   Account Stated 5   1969   Fla.
Solar Research Corp. v. Julius F. Parker, Jr. (Supreme Court of Florida April 2, 1969)
M/B: Solar Research Corp. v. Parker, 221 So. 2d 138 (Fla. 1969).

14 156 244 393 490 539   Carriers 320(27)   1943   Fla.
Tampa Electric Co. v. Fleischaker (Supreme Court of Florida April 6, 1943)
M/B: Tampa Electric Co. v. Fleischaker, 152 Fla. 701, 12 So. 2d 901 (1943).
LR: Tampa Elec. Co. v. Fleischaker, 152 Fla. 701, 12 So. 2d 901 (1943).

15 157 245 394 491 540   Constitutional Law 296(2)   1950   La.
Ransome et al. v. Police Jury of Parish of Jefferson (Supreme Court of Louisiana Feb. 13, 1950)
M/B: Ransome v. Police Jury, 216 La. 994, 45 So. 2d 601 (1950).

16 158 246 395 492 541   Certiorari 47   1947   Fla.
State Beverage Department v. Willis (Supreme Court of Florida Nov. 21, 1947)
M/B: State Beverage Department v. Willis, 159 Fla. 698, 32 So. 2d 580 (1947).
LR: State Beverage Dep't v. Willis, 159 Fla. 698, 32 So. 2d 580 (1947).

17 159 247 396 493 542   Contracts 155   1956   Miss.
Globe Music Corporation v. Sherman Johnson et al. (Supreme Court of Mississippi Jan. 9, 1956)
M/B: Globe Music Corp. v. Johnson, 226 Miss. 329, 84 So. 2d 509 (1956).

18 160 248 397 494 543   Corporations 523   1926   Miss.
Gulf Refining Co. et al. v. Cleveland Trust Co. et al. (Supreme Court of Mississippi April 12, 1926)
M/B: Gulf Refining Co. v. Cleveland Trust Co., 166 Miss. 759, 108 So. 158 (1926).
LR: Gulf Ref. Co. v. Cleveland Trust Co., 166 Miss. 759, 108 So. 158 (1926).

19 161 249 398 495 544   Courts 204   1938   Ala.
Ex parte Burch; Burch v. Burch (Supreme Court of Alabama November 25, 1938)
M/B: Ex parte Burch, 236 Ala. 662, 184 So. 694 (1938).
LR: Ex parte Burch, 236 Ala. 662, 184 So. 694 (1938).

20 162 250 399 496 545   Criminal Law 241   1910   Miss.
Wray v. Kelly (Supreme Court of Mississippi November 21, 1910)
M/B: Wray v. Kelly, 98 Miss. 172, 53 So. 492 (1910).

21 163 251 400 497 546   Criminal Law 351(7)   1904   Miss.
Harper v. State (Supreme Court of Mississippi January 11, 1904)
M/B: Harper v. State, 83 Miss. 402, 35 So. 572 (1904).

22 164 252 301 498 547   Criminal Law 518(2)   1924   Fla.
Phillips v. State (Supreme Court of Florida July 2, 1924)
M/B: Phillips v. State, 88 Fla. 117, 101 So. 204 (1924).

23 165 253 302 499 548   Counties 199   1930   Miss.
People's Bank of Weir v. Attala County (Supreme Court of Mississippi February 17, 1930)
M/B: People's Bank v. Attala County, 156 Miss. 560, 126 So. 192 (1930).

24 166 254 303 500 549   Powers 32   1922   Miss.
Hammett et al. v. Markham (Supreme Court of Mississippi February 27, 1922)
M/B: Hammett v. Markham, 128 Miss. 39, 99 So. 848 (1922).

25 167 255 304 401 550   Divorce 206   1953   Fla.
Landy v. Landy (Supreme Court of Florida January 20, 1953)
M/B: Landy v. Landy, 62 So. 2d 707 (Fla. 1953).

26 168 256 305 402 551   Depositions 38   1945   Ala.
Ex parte Cross (Supreme Court of Alabama April 12, 1945)
M/B: Ex parte Cross, 247 Ala. 85, 22 So. 2d 378 (1945).
LR: Ex parte Cross, 247 Ala. 85, 22 So. 2d 378 (1945).

EXERCISE 20. WEST'S DIGESTS: FINDING CASES USING KNOWN TOPICS AND KEY NUMBERS

27 169 257 306 403 552   Deeds 114(1)   1890   Fla.
Andreu et al. v. Watkins (Supreme Court of Florida August 4, 1890)
M/B: Andreu v. Watkins, 26 Fla. 390, 7 So. 876 (1890).

28 170 258 307 404 553   Damages 131(4)   1901   La.
Joseph v. Edison Electric Co. et al (Supreme Court of Louisiana January 7, 1901)
M/B: Joseph v. Edison Electric Co., 104 La. 634, 29 So. 223 (1901).
LR: Joseph v. Edison Elec. Co., 104 La. 634, 29 So. 223 (1901).

29 171 259 308 405 554   Dead Bodies 9   1941   Fla.
Dunahoo v. Bess (Supreme Court of Florida Feb. 18, 1941)
M/B: Dunahoo v. Bess, 146 Fla. 182, 200 So. 541 (1941).

30 172 260 309 406 555   Damages 198   1929   Fla.
Douglass et al. v. Oemler (Supreme Court of Florida September 27, 1929)
M/B: Douglass v. Oemler, 98 Fla. 497, 124 So. 19 (1929).

31 173 261 310 407 556   Criminal Law 799   1934   Miss.
Stewart v. State (Supreme Court of Mississippi June 11, 1934)
M/B: Stewart v. State, 170 Miss. 540, 155 So. 347 (9134).

32 174 262 311 408 557   Evidence 147   1914   Ala.
Planters' Chemical & Oil Co. v. Stearnes et al. (Supreme Court of Alabama Nov. 7, (1914)
M/B: Planters' Chemical & Oil Co. v. Stearnes, 189 Ala. 503, 66 So. 699 (1914).
LR: Planters' Chem. & Oil Co. v. Stearnes, 189 Ala. 503, 66 So. 699 (1914).

33 175 263 312 409 558   Equity 245   1908   Ala.
McCrory v. Guyton (Supreme Court of Alabama February 5, 1908)
M/B: McCrory v. Guyton, 154 Ala. 355, 45 So. 658 (1908).

34 176 264 313 410 559   Embezzlement 39   1904   Fla.
Eatman v. State (Supreme Court of Florida November 30, 1904)
M/B: Eatman v. State, 48 Fla. 21, 37 So. 576 (1904).

35 177 265 314 411 560   Factors 1   1933   Miss.
D.S. Pate Lumber Co. v. Weathers (Supreme Court of Mississippi March 6, 1933)
M/B: D.S. Pate Lumber Co. v. Weathers, 167 Miss. 228, 146 So. 433 (1933).

36 178 266 315 412 561   Executors & Admin. 206(2)   1904   Ala.
Meyers v. Meyers (Supreme Court of Alabama July 21, 1904)
M/B: Meyers v. Meyers, 141 Ala. 343, 37 So. 451 (1904).

37 179 267 316 413 562   Evidence 543(4)   1921   Ala.
Sykes v. Wood (Supreme Court of Alabama Oct. 20, 1921)
M/B: Sykes v. Wood, 206 Ala. 534, 91 So. 320 (1921).

38 180 268 317 414 563   Fraudulent Conveyances 299(10) 1924   La.
In re Morgan & Co., Inc. (consolidated with Lumberman's Bank & Trust Co. v. De Ridder Light & Power Co.; Same v. Morgan & Co. et al.) (listed second) (Supreme Court of Louisiana October 29, 1923)
M/B: In re Morgan & Co., 155 La. 915, 99 So. 696 (1924).
LR: In re Morgan & Co., 155 La. 915, 99 So. 696 (1924).

39 181 269 318 415 564   Highways 153   1927   Fla.
Couture et al. v. Dade County et al. (Supreme Court of Florida Feb. 26, 1927)
M/B: Couture v. Dade County, 93 Fla. 342, 112 So. 75 (1927).

40 182 270 319 416 565   Homicide 181   1910   Ala.
Phillips v. State (Supreme Court of Alabama December 22, 1910)
M/B: Phillips v. State, 170 Ala. 5, 54 So. 111 (1910).

41 183 271 320 417 566   Husband & Wife 129(3)   1917   Miss.
Wilkinson v. Posey (Supreme Court of Mississippi February 19, 1917)

EXERCISE 20. WEST'S DIGESTS: FINDING CASES USING KNOWN TOPICS AND KEY NUMBERS

M/B: Wilkinson v. Posey, 113 Miss. 274, 74 So. 125 (1917).

42 184 272 321 418 567   Infants 10   1909   Ala.
Hays v. Bowden et al. (Supreme Court of Alabama February 18, 1909)
M/B: Hays v. Bowden, 115 Ala. 600, 49 So. 122 (1909).

43 185 273 322 419 568   Insurance 104(1)   1979   Ala.
William D. Guilford, etc. v. Spartan Food Systems, Inc., a corporation, et al.
(Supreme Court of Alabama June 15, 1979)
M/B: Guilford v. Spartan Food Systems, 372 So. 2d 7 (Ala. 1979).
LR: Guilford v. Spartan Food Sys., 372 So. 2d 7 (Ala. 1979).

44 186 274 323 420 569   Insurance 730.1   1926   Ala.
Royal Neighbors of America v. Fortenberry (Supreme Court of Alabama Jan. 14,
1926)
M/B: Royal Neighbors of America v. Fortenberry, 214 Ala. 387, 107 So. 846
(1926).
LR: Royal Neighbors of Am. v. Fortenberry, 214 Ala. 387, 107 So. 846 (1926).

45 187 275 324 421 570   Interest 46(1)   1902   Fla.
Ross et al v. Walker et al. (Supreme Court of Florida September 30, 1902)
M/B: Ross v. Walker, 44 Fla. 704, 32 So. 934 (1902).

46 188 276 325 422 571   Judgment 107   1932   Fla.
Johnson et al. v. City of Sebring (Supreme Court of Florida March 29, 1932)
M/B: Johnson v. City of Sebring, 104 Fla. 584, 140 So. 672 (1932).

47 189 277 326 423 572   Jury 42   1914   Ala.
Spicer v. State (Supreme Court of Alabama June 11, 1914)
M/B: Spicer v. State, 188 Ala. 9, 65 So. 972 (1914).

48 190 278 327 424 573   Labor Relations 924   1954   La.
Douglas Public Service Corp. et al. v. Gaspard et al. (Supreme Court of
Louisiana July 2, 1954)
M/B: Douglas Public Service Corp. v. Gaspard, 225 La. 972, 74 So. 2d 182
(1954).
LR: Douglas Pub. Serv. Corp. v. Gaspard, 225 La. 972, 74 So. 2d 182 (1954).

49 191 279 328 425 574   Licenses 8(1)   1943   Fla.
Hillsborough County et al. v. Knight & Wall Co. (Supreme Court of Florida July
30, 1943)
M/B: Hillsborough County v. Knight & Wall Co., 153 Fla. 346, 14 So. 2d 703
(1943).

50 192 280 329 426 575   Municipal Corp. 725   1937   Fla.
Lewis v City of Miami (Supreme Court of Florida March 4, 1937)
M/B: Lewis v. City of Miami, 127 Fla. 426, 173 So. 150 (1937).

51 193 281 330 427 576   Municipal Corp. 284(4)   1950   Ala.
Hillard v. City of Mobile et al (Supreme Court of Alabama June 15, 1950)
M/B: Hillard v. City of Mobile, 253 Ala. 676, 47 So. 2d 162 (1950).

52 194 282 331 428 577   Mortgages 307   1898   Ala.
Gravlee v. Lamkin (Supreme Court of Alabama October 29, 1898)
M/B: Gravlee v. Lamkin, 120 Ala. 210, 24 So. 756 (1898).

53 195 283 332 429 578   Mental Health 55   1961   Miss.
Mrs. Lawrence Lyle and Miss Doris J. Nordlie, v. Oscar R. Johnson et al.
(Supreme Court of Mississippi January 23, 1961)
M/B: Lyle v. Johnson, 240 Miss. 154, 126 So. 2d 266 (1961).

54 196 284 333 430 579   Master & Servant 240(2)   1916   La.
Langston v. Tremont Lumber Co. (Supreme Court of Louisiana April 24, 1916)
M/B: Langston v. Tremont Lumber Co., 139 La. 473, 71 So. 771 (1916).

55 197 285 334 431 580   Mandamus 73(1)   1943   Fla.

EXERCISE 20. WEST'S DIGESTS: FINDING CASES USING KNOWN TOPICS AND KEY NUMBERS

State ex rel. Watson, Attorney General, v. Gray, Secretary of State (Supreme Court of Florida July 30, 1943)
M/B: State ex rel. Watson v. Gray, 153 Fla. 462, 14 So. 2d 721 (1943).
LR: State ex rel. Watson v. Gray, 153 Fla. 462, 14 So. 2d 721 (1943).

56 198 286 335 432 581   Rape 59 (16)   1925   Miss.
Lee v. State (Supreme Court of Mississippi April 13, 1925)
M/B: Lee v. State, 138 Miss. 868, 103 So. 793 (1925).

57 199 287 336 433 582   Pleading 280   1925   Ala.
Life & Casualty Co. of Tennessee v. Street (Supreme Court of Alabama June 30, 1925)
M/B: Life & Casualty Co. v. Street, 213 Ala. 588, 105 So. 672 (1925).

58 200 288 337 434 583   Process 79   1917   Miss.
Hendricks v. Kellogg et al. (Supreme Court of Mississippi November 26, 1917)
M/B: Hendricks v. Kellogg, 116 Miss. 22, 76 So. 672 (1917).

59 101 289 338 435 584   Pleading 36(3)   1944   Fla.
Clark v. Groves et al. (Supreme Court of Florida January 18, 1944)
M/B: Clark v. Groves, 154 Fla. 13, 16 So. 2d 340 (1944).

60 102 290 339 436 585   Partnership 242(7)   1929   La.
Perez v. Leake et al. (Supreme Court of Louisiana July 8, 1929)
M/B: Perez v. Leake, 169 La. 29, 124 So. 135 (1929).

61 103 291 340 437 586   Officers 83   1927   La.
Blanchard v. Norman et al. (Supreme Court of Louisiana July 11, 1927)
M/B: Blanchard v. Norman, 164 La. 433, 114 So. 87 (1927).

62 104 292 341 438 587   Names 18   1910   Ala.
Reid v. State (Supreme Court of Alabama July 6, 1910)
M/B: Reid v. State, 168 Ala. 118, 53 So. 254 (1910).

63 105 293 342 439 588   Sunday 4   1920   Miss.
Jones v. Brantley (Supreme Court of Mississippi March 8, 1920)
M/B: Jones v. Brantley, 121 Miss. 721, 83 So. 802 (1920).

64 106 294 343 440 589   Statutes 130   1927   Fla.
In re De Woody (Supreme Court of Florida July 5, 1927)
M/B: In re De Woody, 94 Fla. 96, 113 So. 677 (1927).
LR: In re De Woody, 94 Fla. 96, 113 So. 677 (1927).

65 107 295 344 441 590   Shipping 29   1956   La.
William N. Rojas v. Vincent Robin III and Eustis Engineering Co. et al. (Supreme Court of Louisiana June 29, 1956)
M/B: Rojas v. Robin, 230 La. 1096, 90 So. 2d 58 (1956).

66 108 296 345 442 591   Salvage 39   1921   Miss.
Mengel Box Co. et al. v. Joest (Supreme Court of Mississippi December 19, 1921)
M/B: Mengel Box Co. v. Joest, 127 Miss. 461, 90 So. 161 (1921).

67 109 297 346 443 592   Sales 54   1919   Miss.
International Harvester Co. of America v. Merrimac Veneer Co. (Supreme Court of Mississippi April 14, 1919)
M/B: International Harvester Co. of America v. Merrimac Veneer Co., 120 Miss. 550, 81 So. 277 (1919).

68 110 298 347 444 493   Seamen 29(1)   1937   Miss.
Orleans Dredging Co. v. Frazie (Supreme Court of Mississippi March 22, 1937)
M/B: Orleans Dredging Co. v. Frazie, 179 Miss. 188, 173 So. 431 (1937).

69 111 299 348 445 594   Warehousemen 15(2)   1938   Fla.
Mutual Bankers Co. v. Terrell (Supreme Court of Florida January 8, 1938)
M/B: Mutual Bankers Co. v. Terrell, 130 Fla. 583, 178 So. 399 (1938).

EXERCISE 20. WEST'S DIGESTS: FINDING CASES USING KNOWN TOPICS AND KEY NUMBERS

70 112 300 349 446 595   Trusts 203   1928   Fla.
Standard Oil Company v. Mehrtens et al. (Supreme Court of Florida October 9, 1928)
M/B: Standard Oil Co. v. Mehrtens, 96 Fla. 455, 118 So. 216 (1928).

71 113 201 350 447 596   Trial 133(5)   1953   Miss.
Overing v. Skrmetta et al. (Supreme Court of Mississippi November 9, 1953)
M/B: Overing v. Skrmetta, 218 Miss. 648, 67 So. 2d 606 (1953).

72 114 202 351 448 597   Towns 59   1947   Fla.
Town of Lake Hamilton et al. v. Hughes et al. (Supreme Court of Florida July 18, 1947)
M/B: Town of Lake Hamilton v. Hughes, 159 Fla. 600, 32 So. 2d 283 (1947).

73 115 203 352 449 598   Telecommunications 89   1954   Fla.
Alabama Operating Co. v. City of Winter Park (Supreme Court of Florida 1953)
M/B: Alabama Operating Co. v. City of Winter Park, 68 So. 2d 601 (Fla. 1954).

74 116 203 353 450 599   Zoning 613   1959   Fla.
Theresa Schauer et al., Petitioners v. City of Miami Beach, a municipal corporation, et al., Respondents (Supreme Court of Florida May 8, 1959)
M/B: Schauer v. City of Miami Beach, 112 So. 2d 838 (Fla. 1959).

75 117 205 354 451 600   Workmen's Compensation 1545   1949   Fla.
Morris v. American Machinery Corporation et al. (Supreme Court of Florida June 3, 1949)
M/B: Morris v. American Machinery Corp., 40 So. 2d 839 (Fla. 1949).
LR: Morris v. American Mach. Corp., 40 So. 2d 839 (Fla. 1949).

76 118 206 355 452 501   Workmen's Comepnsation 712   1930   Ala.
Sloss-Sheffield Steel & Iron Co. v. Thomas (Supreme Court of Alabama January 16, 1930)
M/B: Sloss-Sheffield Steel & Iron Co. v. Thomas, 220 Ala. 686, 127 So. 165 (1930).

77 119 207 356 453 502   Witnesses 302   1966   La.
State of Louisiana v. Prien Ceaser (Supreme Court of Louisiana June 6, 1966)
M/B: State v. Ceaser, 249 La. 435, 187 So. 2d 432 (1966).

78 120 208 357 454 503   Wills 618   1925   Fla.
Cole v. Cole (Supreme Court of Florida November 29, 1924)
M/B: Cole v. Cole, 88 Fla. 347, 103 So. 78 (1966).

79 121 209 358 455 504   Wills 67   1955   Fla.
Elizabeth S. Tod, Individually and as Executrix under the Last Will and Testament of Andrew Kinnaird Tod, deceased Appellant, v. Constance Peabody Fuller, Appellee (Supreme Court of Florida February 9, 1955)
M/B: Tod v. Fuller, 78 So. 2d 713 (Fla. 1955).

80 122 210 359 456 505   Waste 9   1956   Ala.
Hoyt Wilder et al. v. Velma Ayres Scott et al. (Supreme Court of Alabama September 13, 1956)
M/B: Wilder v. Scott, 265 Ala. 106, 89 So. 2d 682 (1956).

81 123 211 360 457 506   Wills 754   1942   Fla.
In re McDougald's Estate (Supreme Court of Florida February 10, 1942)
M/B: In re McDougald's Estate, 149 Fla. 468, 6 So. 2d 274 (1942).
LR: In re McDougald's Estate, 149 Fla. 468, 6 So. 2d 274 (1942).

82 124 212 361 458 507   Work & Labor 22   1930   Fla.
Waters Realty Co. v. Miami Tripure Water Co. (Supreme Court of Florida July 22, 1930)
M/B: Waters Realty Co. v. Miami Tripure Water Co., 100 Fla. 221, 129 So. 763 (1930).

83 125 213 362 459 508   Workmen's Compensation 799   1956   Miss.

EXERCISE 20. WEST'S DIGESTS: FINDING CASES USING KNOWN TOPICS AND KEY NUMBERS

Prentiss Truck and Tractor Company and Federated Mutual Implement and Hardware Insurance Company v. Mrs. Mattle Spencer and Shirley Ann Spencer (Supreme Court of Mississippi May 7, 1956)
M/B: Prentiss Truck & Tractor Co. v. Spencer, 228 Miss. 66, 87 So. 2d 272 (1956).

84 126 214 363 460 509   Workmen's Compensation 1552   1946   Ala.
Consolidated Coal Co. v. Dill (Supreme Court of Alabama May 9, 1946)
M/B: Consolidated Coal Co. v. Dill, 248 Ala. 5, 26 So. 2d 88 (1946).

85 127 215 364 461 510   Workmen's Compensation 1966   1940   Fla.
Firestone Auto Supply & Service Stores et al. v. Bullard (Supreme Court of Florida January 5, 1940)
M/B: Firestone Auto Supply & Service Stores v. Bullard, 141 Fla. 282, 192 So. 865 (1940).
LR: Firestone Auto Supply & Serv. Stores v. Bullard, 141 Fla. 282, 192 So. 865 (1940).

86 128 216 365 462 511   Municipal Corporations 5   1956   Fla.
State of Florida, Appellant, v. Daytona Beach Racing and Recreational Facilities District (Supreme Court of Florida August 1, 1956)
M/B: State v. Daytona Beach Racing & Recreational Facilities District, 89 So. 2d 34 (Fla. 1956).
LR: State v. Daytona Beach Racing & Recreational Facilities Dist., 89 So. 2d 34 (Fla. 1956).

87 129 217 366 463 512   Mortgages 2   1929   Miss.
Fitzgerald v. McKee et al (Supreme Court of Mississippi January 14, 1929)
M/B: Fitzgerald v. McKee, 153 Miss. 198, 121 So. 127 (1929).

88 130 218 367 464 513   Money Paid 4   1932   Fla.
Carter v. First Trust & Savings Bank (Supreme Court of Florida December 5, 1932)
M/B: Carter v. First Trust & Savings Bank, 107 Fla. 360, 144 So. 885 (1932).
LR: Carter v. First Trust & Sav. Bank, 107 Fla. 360, 144 So. 885 (1932).

89 131 219 368 465 514   Master & Servant 256 (3)   1905   Ala.
Pierson Lumber Co. v. Hart (Supreme Court of Alabama November 29, 1905)
M/B: Pierson Lumber Co. v. Hart, 144 Ala. 239, 39 So. 566 (1905).

90 132 220 369 466 515   Lotteries 6   1938   Ala.
Try-Me Bottling Co. et al. v. State (Supreme Court of Alabama January 13, 1938)
M/B: Try-Me Bottling Co. v. State, 235 Ala. 207, 178 So. 231 (1938).

91 133 221 370 467 516   Admiralty 4   1938   Miss.
Frazie v. Orleans Dredging Co. (Supreme Court of Mississippi May 2, 1938)
M/B: Frazie v. Orleans Dredging Co., 182 Miss. 193, 180 So. 816 (1938).

92 134 222 371 468 517   Corporations 507(5)   1931   Miss.
Natchez Coca-Cola Bottling Co. v. Watson (Supreme Court of Mississippi April 13, 1931)
M/B: Natchez Coca-Cola Bottling Co. v. Watson, 160 Miss. 173, 133 So. 677 (1931).

93 135 223 372 469 518   Contracts 345   1905   Ala.
Gates v. O'Gara (Supreme Court of Alabama December 21, 1905)
M/B: Gates v. O'Gara, 145 Ala. 665, 39 So. 729 (1905).

94 136 224 373 470 519   Animals 50(1)   1894   Ala.
Spigener v. Rives (Supreme Court of Alabama August 9, 1894)
M/B: Spigener v. Rives, 104 Ala. 437, 16 So. 74 (1894).

95 137 225 374 471 520   Cemeteries 21   1895   Ala.
Bonham v. Loeb (Supreme Court of Alabama July 31, 1895)
M/B: Bonham v. Loeb, 107 Ala. 604, 18 So. 300 (1895).

EXERCISE 20.   WEST'S DIGESTS: FINDING CASES USING KNOWN TOPICS AND KEY NUMBERS

96 138 226 375 472 521   Bastards 78   1939   Fla.
Bishop v. State ex rel. Garnette (Supreme Court of Florida February 3, 1939)
M/B: Bishop v. State ex rel. Garnette, 136 Fla. 268, 186 So. 413 (1939).
LR: Bishop v. State ex rel. Garnette, 136 Fla. 268, 186 So. 413 (1939).

97 139 227 376 473 522   Brokers 74   1912   Ala.
Handley et al. v. Shaffer (Supreme Court of Alabama May 30, 1912)
M/B: Handley v. Shaffer, 177 Ala. 636, 59 So. 286 (1912).

98 140 228 377 474 523   Automobiles 238(2)   1914   Ala.
Barfield v. Evans (Supreme Court of Alabama May 14, 1914)
M/B: Barfield v. Evans, 187 Ala. 579, 65 So. 928 (1914).

99 141 229 378 475 524   Continuance 48   1964   Ala.
City of Prichard v. George L. Moulton (Supreme Court of Alabama November 5, 1964)
M/B: City of Prichard v. Moulton, 277 Ala. 231, 168 So. 2d 602 (1964).

100 142 230 379 476 525   Burglary 46(4)   1890   Fla.
Clifton v. State (Supreme Court of Florida July 28, 1890)
M/B: Clifton v. State, 26 Fla. 523, 7 So. 863 (1890).

LIBRARY EXERCISE 21. WEST'S DIGESTS: DESCRIPTIVE WORD INDEXES.

INSTRUCTOR'S NOTE: Using the designated digest's Descriptive Word Index, the students are to (a) answer the question based upon the most relevant digest paragraph found in that digest (if appropriate); (b) list the topic and key number under which the digest paragraph was abstracted; (c) cite the case from which the digest paragraph was abstracted; (d) list the entry in the Descriptive Word Index from which they were directed to their answer. Note that the entry listed in part (d) below is not necessarily the only entry in the Descriptive Word Index that would lead a researcher to the proper digest entry. The students are to use <u>Shepard's Citations</u> to find missing parallel citations and are specifically directed to not include the subsequent history of the cited case in their answer. They are to find missing information by consulting the case in the reporter. If some other case is cited, you should check to see whether it satisfies the requirements of the problem.

1 118 227 318 415 523
(a)   Yes
(b)   Specific Performance 32(3)
(c)   M/B: <u>Dorsey v. Packwood</u>, 53 U.S. (12 How.) 126 (1851).
(d)   Specific Performance/Mutuality of Obligation

2 119 228 319 416 524
(a)   Yes
(b)   Cemeteries 20
(c)   M/B: <u>Bushers v. Graceland Cemetery Association</u>, 171 F. Supp. 205 (E.D. Ill. 1958).
      LR: Bushers v. Graceland Cemetery Ass'n, 171 F. Supp. 205 (E.D. Ill. 1958).
Note: "Ass'n" is abbreviated in the digest but not in the reporter.
(d)   Cemeteries/Damages/Mental Suffering/Disturbing Grave

3 120 229 320 417 525
(a)   No
(b)   Admirality 2
(c)   M/B: <u>Frankel v. Bethlehem-Fairfield Shipyard</u>, 46 F. Supp. 242 (D. Md. 1942).
(d)   Admiralty/Workmen's Compensation

4 121 230 321 418 526
(a)   ----
(b)   Copyrights 4
(c)   M/B: <u>Boucher v. Du Boyes, Inc.</u>, 253 F.2d 948 (2d Cir. 1958).
(d)   Copyright/Jewelry

5 122 231 322 419 527
(a)   No
(b)   Common Law 11 OR 12, OR Statutes 222
(c)   M/B: <u>Saala v. McFarland</u>, 63 Cal. 2d 124, 403 P.2d 400, 45 Cal. Rptr. 144 (1965) OR <u>Morris v. Oney</u>, 217 Cal. App. 2d 864, 32 Cal. Rptr. 88 (1963) OR <u>Lowman v. Stafford</u>, 226 Cal. App. 2d 31, 37 Cal. Rptr. 681 (1964).
(d)   Presumption/Statutes

6 123 232 323 420 528
(a)   Only when the owner of a tract of land or building places on the premises movable things also owned by him.
(b)   Fixtures 1
(c)   M/B: <u>Hilltop Bowl, Inc. v. United States Fidelity & Guaranty Co.</u>, 248 F. Supp. 572 (W.D. La. 1966).
      LR: Hilltop Bowl, Inc. v. United States Fidelity & Guar. Co., 248 F. Supp. 572 (W.D. La. 1966).
(d)   Fixtures/Immobilization

7 124 333 324 421 529
(a)   ----
(b)   Seamen 5
(c)   M/B: <u>Isthmian Lines v. Haire</u>, 334 F.2d 521 (5th Cir. 1964).
(d)   Shipping Commissioners/Seamen

EXERCISE 21. WEST'S DIGESTS: DESCRIPTIVE WORD INDEXES   (CONTINUED)

8 125 234 325 422 530
(a) No
(b) Estoppel 29(1)
(c) M/B: Gulf Oil Corp. v. Oliver, 412 F.2d 938 (5th Cir. 1969).
(d) Estoppel/Grantees, estoppel by deed

9 126 235 326 423 531
(a) ----
(b) Workmen's Compensation 1302
(c) M/B: Trzoniec v. General Controls Co., 100 R.I. 448, 216 A.2d 886 (1966).
(d) Workmen's Compensation/Limitations/Waiver/ Employer's right to assert

10 127 236 327 424 532
(a) No
(b) Social Security and Public Welfare 140.5
(c) M/B: King v. Celebrezze, 240 F.Supp. 177 (E.D. Tenn. 1965).
(d) Social Security/Disability benefits/Factors considered

11 128 237 328 425 533
(a) The measure of damages upon a breach of the covenant of right to convey is, as a general rule, the purchase money and interest.
(b) Covenants 126 or 126[a]
(c) M/B: Overhiser v. McCollister, 10 Ind. 41 (1858).
(d) Covenants/Breach/Damages

12 129 238 329 426 534
(a) Yes
(b) Party Walls 4(4)
(c) M/B: Carley v. Lawrence, 170 F.2d 381 (7th Cir. (1948).
(d) Party Walls/Prescriptive right

13 130 239 330 427 535
(a) ----
(b) Mandamus 76
(c) M/B: McClendon v. Blount, 452 F.2d 381 (7th Cir. 1971).
(d) Mandamus/Employees/Removed

14 131 240 331 428 536
(a) No
(b) Grand Jury 39
(c) M/B: Cereghino v. Superior Court, 177 Cal. App. 2d 328, 2 Cal. Rptr. 159 (1960).
(d) Grand Jury/Presence or participation of unauthorized persons

15 132 241 332 429 537
(a) Yes
(b) Seduction 39 or 42
(c) M/B: Catron v. Commonwealth, 268 Ky. 536, 105 S.W.2d 618 (1937) OR Byrley v. Commonwealth, 264 Ky. 403, 94 S.W.2d 1008 (1936).
(d) Seduction/Evidence/Criminal prosecution/Character of female

16 133 242 333 430 538
(a) Yes
(b) Marriage 7
(c) M/B: Keuhmstead v. Turnwall, 103 Fla. 1180, 138 So. 775 (1932).
(d) Mental condition or capacity/Marriage/Capacity to marry

17 134 243 334 431 539
(a) No
(b) Release 13(6)
(c) M/B: Sears, Sucsy & Co. v. Insurance Co. of North America, 396 F. Supp. 820 (N.D. Ill. 1975).
    LR: Sears, Sucsy & Co. v. Insurance Co. of N. Am., 396 F. Supp. 820 (N.D. Ill. 1975).
(d) Release/Failure of consideration

EXERCISE 21. WEST'S DIGESTS: DESCRIPTIVE WORD INDEXES   (CONTINUED)

18 135 244 335 432 540
(a) No.
(b) Lewdness 1
(c) M/B: West v. State, 27 Okla. Crim. 125, 225 P. 556 (1924).
(d) Lewdness/Elements of the offense

19 136 245 336 433 541
(a) Yes
(b) Assignments 24(3)
(c) M/B: Stroman v. Atlas Refining Corp., 112 Neb. 187, 199 N.W.26 (1924).
    LR: Stroman v. Atlas Ref. Corp., 112 Neb. 187, 199 N.W.26 (1924).
(d) Fraud/Assignment/Right of action for fraud

20 137 246 337 434 542
(a) Yes
(b) Wills 109 or 302(3)
(c) M/B: In re Bose's Estate, 136 Neb. 156, 285 N.W. 319 (1939) OR In re Goist's Estate, 146 Neb. 1, 18 N.W.2d 513 (1945).
    LR: In re Bose's Estate, 136 Neb. 156, 285 N.W. 319 (1939) OR In re Goist's Estate, 146 Neb. 1, 18 N.W.2d 513 (1945).
(d) Notice/Wills/Contents by testator

21 138 247 338 435 543
(a) Yes
(b) Pilots 14
(c) M/B: Gulf Oil Corp. v. United States, 295 F.Supp. 696 (D.R.I. 1969).
(d) Pilots/Authority or functions

22 139 248 339 436 544
(a) Yes
(b) Mines and Minerals 24
(c) M/B: Hartman Gold Mining Co. v. Warning, 40 Ariz. 267, 11 P.2d 854 (1932).
(d) Abandonment/Mines and Minerals/Location or claim

23 140 249 440 437 545
(a) Yes
(b) Highways 153
(c) M/B: Harbuck v. Richland Box Co., 204 Ga. 352, 49 S.E.2d 883 (1948); Hardy v. Thomas, 208 Ga. 752, 69 S.E.2d 609 (1952).
(d) Nuisances/Obstruction or encroachment/Highway

24 141 250 341 438 546
(a) Yes
(b) Theaters & Shows 6(19)
(c) M/B: Leopold v. Okemo Mountain, Inc., 420 F. Supp. 781 (D. Vt. 1976).
(d) Assumption of risks/Skier, collision with chair lift tower

25 142 251 342 439 547
(a) ----
(b) Certiorari 17
(c) M/B: Enfinger v. Baxley, 96 So. 2d 538 (Fla. 1957).
(d) Certiorari/Venue/Review

26 143 252 343 440 548
(a) No
(b) Copyright 40
(c) M/B: Rohaver v. Killiam Shows, 379 F.Supp. 723 (S.D.N.Y. 1974).
Note: "Inc." may be added to the above citation.
(d) Abandonments/Copyright

27 144 253 344 441 549
(a) Yes
(b) Kidnapping 2
(c) M/B: Hattaway v. United States, 339 F.2d 431 (5th Cir. 1968).
(d) Kidnapping/Defenses

EXERCISE 21. WEST'S DIGESTS: DESCRIPTIVE WORD INDEXES   (CONTINUED)

28 145 254 345 442 550
(a) Yes
(b) Wills 470(2)
(c) M/B: Moore v. Bean, 82 N.M. 189, 477 P.2d 823 (1970).
(d) Wills/Construction/Four corners of will

29 146 255 346 443 551
(a) No
(b) Embezzlement 23
(c) M/B: Jurgensen v. State, 135 Neb. 537, 283 N.W. 228 (1939).
(d) Embezzlement/Defenses

30 147 256 347 444 552
(a) ----
(b) Indians 5
(c) M/B: United States v. Vulles, 283 F. Supp. 829 (D. Mont. 1968).
(d) Indians/Lands/Rights-of-way

31 148 257 348 445 553
(a) Yes
(b) Adoption 21
(c) M/B: Brock v. Dorman, 339 Mo. 611, 98 S.W.2d 672 (1937).
(d) Adoption/Inheritance/By adopted child

32 149 258 349 446 554
(a) No
(b) Sheriffs & Constables 98(4)
(c) M/B: Andrews v. Wilcox, 277 Mich. 697, 270 N.W. 191 (1937).
(d) Supersedeas/Sheriff/As protected by writ of supersedeas valid on its face

33 150 259 350 447 555
(a) Yes
(b) Fraud 13(3)
(c) M/B: White v. United States, 20 F. Supp. 623 (W.D. Ky. 1937).
(d) Fraud/Recklessly made statements

34 151 260 351 448 556
(a) Yes
(b) Charities 13
(c) M/B: Biscoe v. Thweatt, 74 Ark. 545, 86 S.W. 432 (1905).
(d) Charities/Religion

35 152 261 352 449 557
(a) Yes
(b) Money Received 8
(c) M/B: Central Bank & Trust Co. v. General Finance Corp., 297 F.2d 126 (5th Cir. 1961).
LR: Central Bank & Trust Co. v. General Fin. Corp., 297 F.2d 126 (5th Cir. 1961).
(d) Money Received/Wrongfully obtained money

36 153 262 353 450 558
(a) No
(b) Tenancy in Common 55(9)
(c) M/B: In re Victor, 218 F. Supp. 218 (S.D. Ill. 1963).
     LR: In re Victor, 218 F. Supp. 218 (S.D. Ill. 1963).
(d) Tenancy in common/Execution--actions between cotenants and third parties OR Tenancy in common/Judgment--actions between cotenants and third parties

37 154 263 354 451 559
(a) No
(b) Aliens 13
(c) M/B: Carneal v. Banks, 23 U.S. (10 Wheat.) 181 (1825).
(d) Aliens/Treaties/Right to hold real property or Treaties/Alien's right to hold property thereby

38 155 264 355 452 560

EXERCISE 21. WEST'S DIGESTS: DESCRIPTIVE WORD INDEXES   (CONTINUED)

(a) ----
(b) Weapons 17(4)
(c) M/B: Courtney v. State, 424 S.W.2d 440 (Tex. Crim. App. 1968).
(d) Weapons/Automobiles/Carrying in glove compartment

39 156 265 356 453 561
(a) Yes
(b) Charities 8
(c) M/B: Russell v. Allen, 107 U.S. 163 (1882).
(d) Charities/Beneficiaries/number

40 157 266 357 454 562
(a) ----
(b) Treason 3
(c) M/B: Cramer v. United States, 325 U.S. 1 (1945).
(d) Treason/Intent

41 158 267 358 455 563
(a) No
(b) Innkeeper 11(11)
(c) M/B: Stoll v. Almon C. Judd Co., 106 Conn. 551, 138 A. 479 (1927).
(d) Innkeeper/Loss of property/of guest

42 159 268 359 456 564
(a) No
(b) Labor Relations 1609
(c) M/B: Roberg v. Phipps Estate, 156 F.2d 958 (2d Cir. 1946).
(d) Wages and Hours Regulations/Injunctions/Persons entitled to sue

43 160 269 360 457 565
(a) Yes
(b) Bailment 5
(c) M/B: Wells v. West, 212 N.C. 656, 194 S.E. 313 (1938).
(d) Bailment/Acceptances of property by bailee or Bailment/Delivery/Property to bailee in general or Acceptance/Bailment

44 161 270 361 458 566
(a) No
(b) Easements 25
(c) M/B: Eveleth v. Best, 322 Mich. 637, 34 N.W.2d 504 (1948).
(d) Reciprocal negative easements/Commencement

45 162 271 362 459 567
(a) Yes
(b) Embezzlement 17
(c) M/B: Commonwealth v. Barton, 20 Pa. Super. 447 (1902).
(d) Attorney and Client/Embezzlement or Embezzlement/Attorneys

46 163 272 363 460 568
(a) Yes
(b) Brokers 11
(c) M/B: Allison v. Fuller-Smith & Co., 20 Ala. App. 216, 101 So. 626 (1924).
(d) Brokers/Breach of contract of employment by principal

47 164 364 461 569
(a) No
(b) Mechanics Liens 8 OR Mechanics Liens 114(3)
(c) M/B: Eureka Stone Co. v. First Christian Church, 86 Ark. 212, 110 S.W. 1042 (1908) OR Roland v. Lindsay, 104 Ark. 49, 146 S.W. 115 (1912).
(d) Mechanics Liens/Persons/Entitled to/Lien OR Mechanics Liens/Principal and surety/Transfer of contract to contractor's sureties as affecting rights of subcontractors and contractor's workmen and materialmen

48 165 274 365 462 570
(a) Question of law
(b) Estoppel 119

EXERCISE 21. WEST'S DIGESTS: DESCRIPTIVE WORD INDEXES   (CONTINUED)

(c) M/B: Holt v. New England Telephone & Telegraph Co., 110 Me. 10, 85 A. 159 (1912).
     LR: Holt v. New Eng. Tel. & Tel. Co., 110 Me. 10, 85 A. 159 (1912).
Note: "New England" should also be considered correct in the Law Review citation.
(d) Estoppel/Questions for jury, on issue of estoppel

49 166 275 366 463 571   (a) ----
(b) Copyrights 9
(c) M/B: Cleland v. Thayer, 121 F. 71 (8th Cir. 1903).
(d) Copyrights/Photographs

50 167 276 367 464 572
(a) ----
(b) Trusts 88
(c) M/B: Babcock v. Wyman, 60 U.S. (19 How.) 289 (1856).
(d) Resulting Trusts/Evidence to establish trust/Parol evidence OR Parol or Extrinsic Evidence/Resulting trust/evidence to establish

51 168 277 368 465 573
(a) ----
(b) Public Service Commission 6
(c) M/B: Ex parte Golik, 23 Cal. App. 2d 743, 72 P.2d 169 (1937).
     LR: Ex parte Golik, 23 Cal. App. 2d 743, 72 P.2d 169 (1937).
(d) Habeas Corpus/Railroad Commission's order, habeas corpus to procure releases for violating

52 169 278 369 466 574
(a) Capacity of the parties and mutual consent.
(b) Marriage 12.
(c) M/B: United States v. Layton, 68 F. Supp. 247 (S.D. Fla. 1946).
(d) Common Law/Marriage/Essentials

53 170 279 370 467 575
(a) No.
(b) Negligence 74.
(c) M/B: Jones v. Mackay Telegraph Cable Co., 137 La. 121, 68 So. 379 (1915).
     LR: Jones v. Mackay Tel. Cable Co., 137 La. 121, 68 So. 379 (1915).
(d) Emergencies/Negligence in general/Contributory negligence/Danger incurred to save life

54 171 280 371 468 576
(a) No
(b) False Pretenses 9
(c) M/B: Pioneer Valley Savings Bank v. Indemnity Insurance Co. of North America, 225 F. Supp. 404 (N.D. Iowa 1964).
     LR: Pioneer Valley Sav, Bank v. Indemnity Ins. Co. of N. Am., 225 F. Supp. 404 (N.D. Iowa 1964).
Note: Several of the words in the case title are abbreviated in the digest but are not abbreviated in the reporter.
(d) False Pretenses/Reliance on pretence

55 172 372 469 577
(a) Only such force as is necessary to protect himself and prevent infliction of bodily injury upon him.
(b) Assault and battery 67.
(c) M/B: State v. Mox Mox, 28 Idaho 176, 152 P. 802 (1915).
(d) Arrest/Assault in making or resisting arrest/Criminal responsibility

56 173 273 470 578
(a) A single act.
(b) Vagrancy 3.
(c) M/B: Ex parte Lund, 137 Cal. App. 616, 31 P. 2d 221 (1934).
     LR: Ex parte Lund, 137 Cal. App. 616, 31 P. 2d 221 (1934).
(d) Vagrancy/Evidence

EXERCISE 21.   WEST'S DIGESTS: DESCRIPTIVE WORD INDEXES   (CONTINUED)

57 174 283 374 471 579
(a) He is liable for compensatory damages only.
(b) Insane Persons 80
(c) M/B: Bryant v. Carrier, 214 N.C. 191, 198 S.E. 619 (1938).
(d) Insane Persons/Torts

58 175 284 375 472 580
(a) No.
(b) Attorney and Client 17.
(c) M/B: United States Fidelity & Guaranty Co. v. Sabath, 286 Ill. App. 320, 3 N.E.2d 330 (1936).
     LR: United States Fidelity & Guar. Co. v. Sabath, 286 Ill. App. 320, 3 N.E.2d 330 (1936).
(d) Attorney & Client/Principal and Surety/Attorney as surety

59 176 285 376 473 581
(a) "One who strolls from place to place; one who has no settled habitation; an idle wanderer; a sturdy beggar; an incorrigible rouge; a vagabound."
(b) Vagrancy 1.
(c) M/B: Ex parte Branch, 234 Mo. 446, 137 S.W. 886 (1911).
     LR: Ex parte Branch, 234 Mo. 446, 137 S.W. 886 (1911).
(d) Vagrancy/Elements of the offense

60 177 286 377 474 582
(a) No.
(b) Escrows 14(1).
(c) M/B: Harris v. Geneva Mill Co., 209 Ala. 538, 96 So. 622 (1923).
(d) Escrow/Delivery/By Depository/Unauthorized or wrongful delivery OR Escrow/Depositories/Delivery by/Authority

61 178 287 378 475 583
(a) Yes
(b) Torts 22
(c) M/B: Brown v. City of Webster City, 115 Iowa 511, 88 N.W. 1070 (1902).
     LR: Brown v. City of Webster City, 115 Iowa 511, 88 N.W. 1070 (1902).
Note: "City of Webster" is also correct.
(d) Torts/Joint and several liability

62 179 288 379 476 584
(a) The state.
(b) Fish 17.
(c) M/B: State v. Cramer, 167 Wash. 159, 8 P.2d 1004 (1932).
(d) Fish/Property/Rights of property in fish illegally taken

63 180 289 380 477 585
(a) Yes.
(b) Frauds, Statute of 78
(c) M/B: Remington v. Linthicum, 39 U.S. (14 Pet.) 84 (1840).
(d) Frauds, Statute of/Judicial sales, real property and estates and interest therein

64 181 290 381 478 586
(a) No
(b) Cemeteries 22
(c) M/B: State v. Glass, 27 Ohio Op. 2d 214, 273 N.E.2d 893 (1971).
(d) Cemeteries/Grave robbing

65 182 291 382 479 587
(a) ----
(b) Workmen's Compensation 1530
(c) M/B: Aleutians Homes v. Fischer, 418 P.2d 769 (Alaska 1976).
(d) Thermofax paper/sensitivity, occupational disease OR Thermofax paper/ Workmen's Compensation, extreme sensitivity

66 183 292 383 480 588
(a) Yes
(b) Arson 11

EXERCISE 21. WEST'S DIGESTS: DESCRIPTIVE WORD INDEXES   (CONTINUED)

(c) M/B: United States v. Carter, 522 F.2d 666 (D.C. Cir. 1975).
(d) Arson/Burning or setting fire/Element of offense

67 184 293 384 481 589
(a) Yes
(b) Evidence 417(18)
(c) M/B: Gardner v. Collector of Customs, 73 U.S. (6 Wall.) 499 (1867).
(d) Parol or extrinsic evidence/Date--/Establish date of instrument

68 185 294 385 482 590
(a) Yes
(b) Turnpike 17
(c) M/B: Arnovits v. Commonwealth, 341 Pa. 149, 19 A.2d 287 (1941).
    LR: Arnovits v. Commonwealth, 341 Pa. 149, 19 A.2d 287 (1941).
(d) Turnpikes and Toll Roads/Construction OR Charters/Turnpikes

69 186 295 386 483 591
(a) Yes
(b) Arrest 16
(c) M/B: New England Acceptance Corp. v. Nicholas, 110 Vt. 478, 8 A.2d 665 (1939).
    LR: New Eng. Acceptance Corp. v. Nicholas, 110 Vt. 478, 8 A.2d 665 (1939).
Note: "New England" should also be considered correct in the Law Review citation.
(d) Arrest/Fraudulent removal or disposition of property OR Arrest/Grounds for Arrest or Fraudulent conveyances/Arrest on ground of fraudulent removal or disposition of property OR Fraud/Arrest/Removal or disposition of property

70 187 296 387 484 592
(a) Yes
(b) Embezzlement 11(1)
(c) M/B: Stegall v. Commonwealth, 208 Va. 719, 160 S.E.2d 566 (1968).
(d) Embezzlement/Failure to return rental automobile

71 188 297 388 485 593
(a) Yes
(b) Aliens 7
(c) M/B: De Tenorio v. McGowan, 364 F. Supp. 1051 (S.D. Miss. 1973).
(d) Wills/Aliens--/Capacity to take by will

72 189 298 389 486 594
(a) Yes
(b) Fish (8)
(c) M/B: The Volant, 59 U.S. (18 How.) 71 (1855).
(d) Fish & Game/Power to regulate

73 190 299 390 487 595
(a) No
(b) Stipulations 3
(c) M/B: Rusan's Inc. v. State, 78 Wash. 2d 601, 478 P.2d 724 (1970).
(d) Stipulations/Law, stipulations as to, invalidity OR Law/Stipulations as to law, invalidity

74 191 300 391 488 596
(a) No
(b) Piracy 3
(c) M/B: United States v. Palmer, 16 U.S. (3 Wheat.) 610 (1818).
(d) Piracy/Nature and elements of offense

75 192 201 392 489 597
(a) Yes.
(b) Champerty & Maintenance 1.
(c) M/B: Boettcher v. Criscione, 180 Kan. 39, 299 P.2d 806 (1956).
(d) Barratry/Champtery and maintenance

76 193 202 393 490 598

EXERCISE 21. WEST'S DIGESTS: DESCRIPTIVE WORD INDEXES   (CONTINUED)

(a) No
(b) Assault and Battery 29
(c) M/B: Rennie v. Skellett Co., 151 Minn. 63, 186 N.W. 130 (1922).
(d) Assault and Battery/Evidence/Civil Actions OR Assault and Battery/Character of parties/evidence of OR Character/Accused

77 194 203 394 491 599
(a) Yes, the principal as well as interest
(b) Usuary 145 OR 146
(c) M/B: Pellerin Laundry Machinery Sales Co., 300 F.2d 305 (8th Cir. 1962).
    LR: Pellerin Laundry Mach. Sales Co., 300 F.2d 305 (8th Cir. 1962).
(d) Forfeitures/Usury/Principal of indebtedness OR Forfeitures/Usury/Interest

78 195 204 395 492 600
(a) Yes
(b) Adverse Possession 10
(c) M/B: Harpending v. Reformed Dutch Church, 41 U.S. (16 Pet.) 455 (1842).
(d) Adverse Possession/Persons entitled to claim by prescription

79 196 205 396 493 501
(a) Yes
(b) Partnership 362.
(c) M/B: Bank of Commerce & Trust Co. v. North, 11 Tenn. App. 519 (1929).
(d) Limited Partnership/Statutory provisions OR Limited Partnership/Term/Continuance on renewal

80 197 206 397 494 502
(a) Yes
(b) Patents 46 OR Patents 47
(c) M/B: Union Sulphur Co. v. Freeport Texas Co., 251 F. 634 (D. Del. 1918).
(d) Patents/Utility/Nature OR Patents/Utility/Capacity to produce results OR Patents/Utility/Necessity

81 198 207 398 495 503
(a) One who gambles for his livlihood or who maintains a gambling establishment
(b) Gaming 78
(c) M/B: United States ex rel. Yates v. Rundle, 326 F. Supp. 344 (_.D. Pa. 1971).
    LR: United States ex rel. Yates v. Rundle, 326 F. Supp. 344 (_.D. Pa. 1971).
(d) Common Gamblers/Criminal Responsibility OR Gaming/Common gambers, criminal responsibility

82 199 208 399 496 504
(a) Yes.
(b) Replevin 4.
(c) M/B: Eaton v. Blood, 201 Iowa 834, 208 N.W. 508 (1926).
(d) Replevin/Property subject to or Bank book/Replevin of savings account represented by book

83 200 209 400 497 505
(a) ----
(b) Adverse Possession 22
(c) M/B: Shepard v. Mahannah, 220 F.2d 737 (5th Cir. 1955).
(d) Fences/Grazing Land, adverse possession; necessity of fencing OR Adverse possession/Grazing Land, necessity of fencing

84 101 210 301 498 506
(a) A trust not created by any words, either expressly or impliedly, evidencing a direct intention to create a trust, but by construction of equity in order to satisfy demands of justice.
(b) Trusts 91.
(c) M/B: Long v. Reiss, 290 Ky. 198, 160 S.W.2d 668 (1942).
(d) Constructive trust/Nature of constructive trust

85 102 211 302 499 507

EXERCISE 21. WEST'S DIGESTS: DESCRIPTIVE WORD INDEXES   (CONTINUED)

(a) Not an absolute defense; only evidence of intent
(b) Perjury 15
(c) M/B: United States v. Geller, 154 F. Supp. 727 (S.D.N.Y. 1947).
(d) Perjury/Recantation, defense or Recantation/Perjury, defense

86 103 212 303 500 508
(a) No
(b) Prohibition 3(1)
(c) M/B: State ex rel. Adamson v. District Court, 128 Mont. 538, 279 P.2d 691 (1955).
     LR: State ex rel. Adamson v. District Court, 128 Mont. 538, 279 P.2d 691 (1955).
(d) Prohibition/Adequacy of remedy of law

87 104 213 304 401 509
(a) Yes
(b) Seamen 34
(c) M/B: Tucker v. Alexandroff, 183 U.S. 242 (1902).
(d) Seamen/Penalties

88 105 214 305 402 510
(a) ----
(b) Specific Performance 88.
(c) M/B: Durretts v. Hook, 8 Mo. 374 (1844).
(d) Specific Performance/Good Faith of plaintiff

89 106 215 306 403 511
(a) Yes
(b) Trover & Conversion 9(1)
(c) M/B: Russell-Vaugh Ford, Inc. v. Rouse, 281 Ala. 567, 206 So. 2d 371 (1968).
(d) Trover & Conversion/Automobile Keys

90 107 216 307 404 512
(a) No
(b) Trial 404(1)
(c) M/B: Huntoon v. Hurley, 136 Cal. App. 2d 332, 288 P.2d 529 (1955).
(d) Negative pregnant/Trial courts finding of fact

91 108 217 308 405 513
(a) Yes
(b) Livery Stable Keepers 8(2)
(c) M/B: Susi v. Belle Acton Stables, 261 F. Supp. 219 (S.D.N.Y. 1966).
(d) Livery Stable Keepers/Lien

92 109 218 309 406 514
(a) No
(b) Partnership 225
(c) M/B: Gelder Medical Group v. Webber, 53 A.D.2d 994, 385 N.Y.S.2d 867 (1976).
(d) Parntership/Expulsion, contract permitting, bad faith

93 110 219 310 407 515
(a) Only a profit a pendre
(b) Logs & Logging 3(7) OR Logs & Logging 4
(c) M/B: M. & I. Timber Co. v. Hope Silver-Lead Mines, 91 Idaho 638, 428 P.2d 955 (1967).
(d) Logs/Profit a pendre

94 111 220 311 408 516
(a) Forcible abduction or stealing or carrying away of person from his own country to another. (It embraces all elements of false imprisonment and secrecy is not an element.)
(b) Kidnapping 1
(c) M/B: State v. Evans, 72 Idaho 458, 243 P.2d 975 (1952).
(d) Kidnapping/Elements

EXERCISE 21. WEST'S DIGESTS: DESCRIPTIVE WORD INDEXES   (CONTINUED)

95 112 221 312 409 517
(a)   ----
(b)   Domicile 8
(c)   M/B: Janzen v. Goos, 302 F.2d 421 (8th Cir. 1962).
(d)   Domicile or Residence/Presumption

96 113 222 313 410 518
(a)   No
(b)   War & National Defense 20
(c)   M/B: The Peterhoff, 72 U.S. (5 Wall.) 28 (1866).
(d)   War/Visit and search of neutral vessels

97 114 223 314 411 519
(a)   ----
(b)   Indemnity 15(1)
(c)   M/B: Beetler v. Zotos, 388 F.2d 243 (7th Cir. 1967).
(d)   Indemnity/Form of remedy to recover indemnity

98 115 224 315 412 520
(a)   Yes
(b)   Homicide 9
(c)   M/B: State v. Hizel, 179 Neb. 661, 139 N.W.2d 832 (1966).
(d)   Intent/Homicide/Conviction of murder without proof of actual intent to kill or Intent/Homicide/Murder in second degree

99 116 225 316 412 521
(a)   No
(b)   Counterfeiting 2
(c)   M/B: United States v. Gardner, 35 U.S. (10 Pet.) 618 (1836).
(d)   Counterfeiting/Subject imitated or altered

100 117 226 317 413 522
(a)   Yes
(b)   Remainders 14
(c)   M/B: In re Camden, 217 F. Supp. 634 (W.D. Va. 1963).
      LR: In re Camden, 217 F. Supp. 634 (W.D. Va. 1963).
(d)   Remainders/Deeds

LIBRARY EXERCISE 22.   LAWYERS CO-OPERATIVE'S DIGESTS.

INSTRUCTOR'S NOTE: Students are to find the digest entry listed below in the <u>U.S. Supreme Court Digest, Lawyers' Edition</u>. They are required to cite the Supreme Court case that <u>distinguished</u> the digested case noted below. They are then to find the distinguishing case in <u>United States Reports</u> to determine additional information (e.g., case name, date, volume number, page number) needed for their citation. Note that the Digest often cites the page of treatment, not the beginning page of the case that the studentsu will be citing. For this exercise, students are specifically instructeddo not give parallel citations to the <u>Supreme Court Reporter</u> or <u>Lawyers' Edition</u>.

1 103 217 320 423 555   Abatement & Revival § 16   Watson   205 U.S.
Hunt v. New York Cotton Exchange (April 8, 1907)
M/B: <u>Hunt v. New York Cotton Exchange</u>, 205 U.S. 322 (1907).

2 104 218 321 424 556   Administrative Law § 238   Silberschien   311 U.S.
Wilson & Co., Inc. v. United States (November 18, 1940)
M/B: <u>Wilson & Co. v. United States</u>, 311 U.S. 104 (1940).

3 105 219 322 425 557   Admiralty § 65   Post   172 U.S.
The Elfrida (December 12, 1898)
M/B: <u>The Elfrida</u>, 172 U.S. 186 (1898).

4 106 220 323 426 558   Alteration of Instruments § 7   Wood   112 U.S.
Mersman v. Werges (November 3, 1884)
M/B: <u>Mersman v. Werges</u>, 112 U.S. 139 (1884).

5 107 221 324 427 559   Appeal & Error § 80.5   Osborne   166 U.S.
Forsyth v. Hammond (April 19, 1897)
M/B: <u>Forsyth v. Hammond</u>, 166 U.S. 506 (1897).

6 108 222 325 428 560   Appeal & Error § 383   Rogers   214 U.S.
Smithsonian Institution v. St. John, Executor of Wallace C. Andrews, Deceased (May 17, 1909)
M/B: <u>Smithsonian Institution v. St. John</u>, 214 U.S. 19 (1909).
LR: <u>Smithsonian Inst. v. St. John</u>, 214 U.S. 19 (1909).

7 109 223 326 429 561   Appeal & Error § 544   Mitchell   188 U.S.
Tarrance v. Florida (February 23, 1903)
M/B: <u>Tarrance v. Florida</u>, 188 U.S. 519 (1903).

8 110 224 327 430 562   Appeal & Error § 707   Field   203 U.S.
Mississippi Railroad Commission v. Illinois Central Railroad Company (December 3, 1906)
M/B: <u>Mississippi Railroad Commission v. Illinois Central Railroad</u>, 203 U.S. 335 (1906).
LR: <u>Mississippi R.R. Comm'n v. Illinois Cent. R.R.</u>, 203 U.S. 335 (1906) OR <u>Mississippi R.R. Comm'n v. Illinois C.R.R.</u>, 203 U.S. 335 (1906).

9 111 225 328 431 563   Appeal & Error § 822   Marshall   21 Wall.
Moore v. Mississippi (October Term 1874)
M/B: <u>Moore v. Mississippi</u>, 88 U.S. (21 Wall.) 636 (1874).

10 112 226 329 432 564   Appeal & Error § 917   Knox County   219 U.S.
Merrimack River Savings Bank v. City of Clay Center (February 20, 1911)
M/B: <u>Merrimack River Savings Bank v. City of Clay Center</u>, 219 U.S. 527 (1911).
LR: <u>Merrimack River Sav. Bank v. City of Clay Center</u>, 219 U.S. 527 (1911).

11 113 227 330 433 565   Appeal & Error § 1071   Davis   143 U.S.
Michigan Insurance Bank v. Eldred (February 29, 1892)
M/B: <u>Michigan Insurance Bank v. Eldred</u>, 143 U.S. 293 (1892).
LR: <u>Michigan Ins. Bank v. Eldred</u>, 143 U.S. 293 (1892).

12 114 228 331 434 566   Appeal & Error § 1170   Johnson   322 U.S.
United States v. Ballard et al. (April 24, 1944)
M/B: <u>United States v. Ballard</u>, 322 U.S. 78 (1944).

EXERCISE 22. LAWYERS CO-OPERATIVE'S DIGESTS   (CONTINUED)

13 115 229 332 435 567 Appeal & Error § 1296   Roy   180 U.S.
Throckmorton v. Holt (March 25, 1901)
M/B: Throckmorton v. Holt, 180 U.S. 552 (1901).

14 116 230 333 436 568 Appeal & Error § 1553   Baldwin   124 U.S.
Hopkins v. Orr (February 6, 1888)
M/B: Hopkins v. Orr, 124 U.S. 510 (1888).

15 117 231 334 437 569 Appeal & Error § 1656   St. Pierre 329 U.S.
Fiswick et al. v. United States (December 9, 1946)
M/B: Fiswick v. United States, 329 U.S. 211 (1946).

16 118 232 335 438 570 Bailment § 2   Prescott   15 Wall.
United States v. Thomas (December Term 1872)
M/B: United States v. Thomas, 82 U.S. (15 Wall.) 337 (1872).

17 119 233 336 439 571 Banks § 94   Armstrong   176 U.S.
Alrich v. Chemical National Bank (March 5, 1900)
M/B: Alrich v. Chemical National Bank, 176 U.S. 618 (1900).
LR: Alrich v. Chemical Nat'l Bank, 176 U.S. 618 (1900).

18 120 234 337 440 572 Bonds § 14   Pauly   183 U.S.
Guarantee Company of North America v. Mechanics' Savings Bank and Trust
Company (January 6, 1902)
M/B: Guarantee Co. of North America v. Mechanics' Savings Bank & Trust Co.,
183 U.S. 402 (1902).
LR: Guarantee Co. of N. Am. v. Mechanics' Sav. Bank & Trust Co., 183 U.S. 402
(1902).

19 121 235 338 441 573 Carriers § 122   Piper   360 U.S.
Southwestern Sugar & Molasses Co., Inc., v. River Terminals Corp. (June 22,
1959)
M/B: Southwestern Sugar & Molasses Co. v. River Terminals Corp., 360 U.S. 411
(1959).

20 122 236 339 442 574 Citizenship § 11   Campbell   204 U.S.
Zartarian v. Billings, Commissioner of Immigration (January 7, 1907)
M/B: Zartarian v. Billings, 204 U.S. 170 (1907).

21 123 237 340 443 575 Claims § 2   Smith   273 U.S.
United States v. Burton Coal Company (February 21, 1927)
M/B: United States v. Burton Coal Co., 273 U.S. 337 (1927).

22 124 238 341 444 576 Commerce § 45   Erie R.R.   298 U.S.
Pennsylvania Railroad Co. et al. v. Public Utilities Commission of Ohio et al.
(April 27, 1936)
M/B: Pennsylvania Railroad v. Public Utilities Commission, 298 U.S. 170
(1936).
LR: Pennsylvania R.R. v. Public Utils. Comm'n, 298 U.S. 170 (1936).
Note: "PUC" is probably a widely enough recognized abbreviation of "Public
Utilities Commission" to be acceptable.

23 125 239 342 445 577 Commerce § 97   Fry   426 U.S.
National League of Cities et al. v. Usery, Secretary of Labor (June 24, 1976)
M/B: National League of Cities v. Usery, 426 U.S. 833 (1976).

24 126 240 343 446 578 Commerce § 299   Morf   300 U.S.
Ingels, Director of the Motor Vehicle Department, et al. v. Morf et al. (March
1, 1937)
M/B: Ingels v. Morf, 300 U.S. 290 (1937).

25 127 241 344 447 579 Constitutional Law § 78   Duncan   170 U.S.
Thompson v. Utah (April 25, 1898)
M/B: Thompson v. Utah, 170 U.S. 343 (1898).

26 128 242 345 448 580 Constitutional Law § 174   Yard   173 U.S.
Citizens' Savings Bank of Owensboro v. Owensboro (April 3, 1899)

EXERCISE 22. LAWYERS CO-OPERATIVE'S DIGESTS   (CONTINUED)

M/B: Citizens' Savings Bank v. Owensboro, 173 U.S. 636 (1899).
LR: Citizens' Sav. Bank v. Owensboro, 173 U.S. 636 (1899).

27 129 243 346 449 581 Constitutional Law § 299   Gantly   290 U.S.
Home Building & Loan Association v. Blaisdell et al. (January 8, 1934)
M/B: Home Building & Loan Association v. Blaisdell, 290 U.S. 398 (1934).
LR: Home Bldg. & Loan Ass'n v. Blaisdell, 290 U.S. 398 (1934).

28 130 244 347 450 582 Constitutional Law § 805   Turner   263 U.S.
McGregor v. Hogan, Sheriff of Warren County, Georgia, et al. (November 12, 1923)
M/B: McGregor v. Hogan, 263 U.S. 234 (1923).

29 131 245 348 451 583 Constitutional Law § 484   Louisville   184 U.S.
Louisville & Nashville Railroad Company v. Eubank (January 27, 1902)
M/B: Louisville & Nashville Railroad Company v. Eubank, 184 U.S. 27 (1902).
LR: Louisville & N.R.R. v. Eubank, 184 U.S. 27 (1902).

30 132 246 349 452 584 Constitutional Law § 731   Sands   147 U.S.
Harman v. Chicago (January 23, 1893)
M/B: Harman v. Chicago, 147 U.S. 396 (1893).

31 133 247 350 453 585 Contracts § 107   McMullen   184 U.S.
Connolly v. Union Sewer Pipe Company (March 10, 1902)
M/B: Connolly v. Union Sewer Pipe Co., 184 U.S. 540 (1901).

32 134 248 351 454 586 Contracts § 153   Gavinzel   105 U.S.
Rives v. Duke (October Term 1881)
M/B: Rives v. Duke, 105 U.S. 132 (1881).

33 135 249 352 455 587 Corporations § 16   James   268 U.S.
The Baltimore and Ohio Railroad v. The City of Parkersburg (April 13, 1925)
M/B: Baltimore & Ohio Railroad v. City of Parkersburg, 268 U.S. 35 (1925).
LR: Baltimore & O.R.R. v. City of Parkersburg, 268 U.S. 35 (1925).

34 136 250 353 456 588 Corporations § 164   Webster   165 U.S.
Pauly v. State Loan and Trust Company (March 1, 1897)
M/B: Pauly v. State Loan & Trust Co., 165 U.S. 606 (1897).

35 137 251 354 457 589 Courts § 115   Erie R.R.   236 U.S.
Coppage v. State of Kansas (January 25, 1915)
M/B: Coppage v. Kansas, 236 U.S. 1 (1915).

36 138 252 355 458 590 Courts § 381   Ambler   235 U.S.
Brown, and Schermerhorn, Trustee Under Will of Cunningham, v. Fletcher, Trustee of Braker (January 5, 1915)
M/B: Brown v. Fletcher, 235 U.S. 589 (1915).

37 139 253 356 459 591 Courts § 848   Moore-Mansfield 281 U.S.
Brinkerhoff-Faris Trust & Savings Company v. Hill, Treaurer and Ex-Officio Collecotr of Henry County, Missouri (June 2, 1930)
M/B: Brinkerhoff-Faris Trust & Savings Co. v. Hill, 281 U.S. 673 (1930).
LR: Brinkerhoff-Faris Trust & Sav. Co. v. Hill, 281 U.S. 673 (1930).

38 140 254 357 460 592 Criminal Law § 29   Ball   199 U.S.
Trono v. Unites States (December 4, 1905)
M/B: Trono v. Unites States, 199 U.S. 521 (1905).

39 141 255 358 461 593 Criminal Law § 49   Diaz   291 U.S.
Snyder v. Massachusetts (January 8, 1934)
M/B: Snyder v. Massachusetts, 291 U.S. 97 (1934).

40 142 256 359 462 594 Damages § 117   Benson Min.   237 U.S.
Guffey v. James A. Smith (April 5, 1915)
M/B: Guffey v. Smith, 237 U.S. 101 (1915).

41 143 257 360 463 595 Descent & Distribution § 8 Blythe   239 U.S.

EXERCISE 22. LAWYERS CO-OPERATIVE'S DIGESTS   (CONTINUED)

Truax and the Attorney General of the State of Arizona v. Raich (November 1, 1915)
M/B: Truax v. Raich, 239 U.S. 33 (1915).

42 144 258 361 464 596 Discovery & Inspection § 16   Botsford   177 U.S.
Camden and Suburban Railway Company v. Stetson (April 9, 1900)
M/B: Camden & Suburban Railway v. Stetson, 177 U.S. 172 (1900).
LR: Camden & Suburban Ry. v. Stetson, 177 U.S. 172 (1900) OR Camden & S. Ry. v. Stetson, 177 U.S. 172 (1900) OR Camden & Sub. Ry. v. Stetson, 177 U.S. 172 (1900).

43 145 259 362 465 597 Domicil § 2   Penfield   147 U.S.
Bauserman v. Blunt (March 6, 1893)
M/B: Bauserman v. Blunt, 147 U.S. 647 (1893).

44 146 260 363 466 598 Ejectment § 16   Christy   124 U.S.
Sabariego v. Maverick (January 23, 1888)
M/B: Sabariego v. Maverick, 124 U.S. 261 (1888).

45 147 261 364 467 599 Eminent Domain § 7   Shoemaker   261 U.S.
Albert Hanson Lumber Company, Ltd. v. United States (April 9, 1923)
M/B: Albert Hanson Lumber Co. v. United States, 261 U.S. 581 (1923).

46 148 262 365 468 600 Eminent Domain § 106   Sweet   200 U.S.
Chicago, Burlington and Quincy Railway Company v. People of the State of Illinois ex rel. Drainage Commissioners (March 5, 1906)
M/B: Chicago, Burlington & Quincy Railway v. Illinois ex rel. Drainage Commissioners, 200 U.S. 561 (1906).
LR: Chicago, B. & Q. Ry. v. Illinois ex rel. Drainage Comm'rs, 200 U.S. 561 (1906).

47 149 263 366 469 501 Estoppel & Waiver § 11   Swann   111 U.S.
Williams & Another v. Morgan & Another, Trustees (May 5th 1884)
M/B: Williams v. Morgan, 111 U.S. 684 (1884).

48 150 264 367 470 502 Evidence § 272   Jennings   107 U.S.
Cushing v. Laird (October Term 1882)
M/B: Cushing v. Laird, 107 U.S. 69 (1882).

49 151 265 368 471 503 Evidence § 683   Pierce   168 U.S.
Bram v. United States (December 13, 1897)
M/B: Bram v. United States, 168 U.S. 532 (1897).

50 152 266 369 472 504 Extradition § 4   Ker   148 U.S.
Lascelles v. Georgia (April 3, 1893)
M/B: Lascelles v. Georgia, 148 U.S. 537 (1893).

51 153 267 370 473 505 Food & Drugs § 5   Blockburger   357 U.S.
Gore v. United States (June 30, 1958)
M/B: Gore v. United States, 357 U.S. 386 (1958).

52 154 268 371 474 506 Gift & Taxes § 4   Smith   318 U.S.
Robinette v. Helvering, Commissioner of Internal Revenue (February 15, 1943)
M/B: Robinette v. Helvering, 318 U.S. 184 (1943).

53 155 269 372 475 507 Habeas Corpus § 62   Lange   218 U.S.
Harlan v. McGourin, Marshal.; Gallagher v. the Same (November 28, 1910)
M/B: Harlan v. McGourin, 218 U.S. 442 (1910).

54 156 270 373 476 508 Highways & Streets § 17   St. Louis   172 U.S.
Wall Walla City v. Walla Walla Water Company (November 14, 1898)
M/B: Wall Walla City v. Walla Walla Water Co., 172 U.S. 1 (1898).

55 157 271 374 477 509 Insolvency § 19   Union Bank   133 U.S.
Geilinger v. Philippi (February 3, 1890)
M/B: Geilinger v. Philippi, 133 U.S. 246 (1890).

EXERCISE 22.   LAWYERS CO-OPERATIVE'S DIGESTS   (CONTINUED)

56 158 272 375 478 510   Insurance § 78   Warnock   222 U.S.
Grisby v. Russell (December 4, 1911)
M/B: Grisby v. Russell, 222 U.S. 149 (1911).

57 159 273 376 479 511   Interest § 35   No. Carolina   229 U.S.
National Home for Disabled Volunteer Soldiers v. Parrish (June 9, 1913)
M/B: National Home for Disabled Volunteer Soldiers v. Parrish, 229 U.S. 494 (1913).

58 160 274 377 480 512   International Law § 14   The Exchange   183 U.S.
Tucker v. Alexandroff (January 6, 1902)
M/B: Tucker v. Alexandroff, 183 U.S. 424 (1902).

59 161 275 378 481 513   Interstate Commerce   Merchants' &   295 U.S.
                         Commission § 82   Mfgrs.' Traffic Ass'n
Youngstown Sheet & Tube Co. et al. v. United States et al. (May 20, 1935)
M/B: Youngstown Sheet & Tube Co. v. United States, 295 U.S. 476 (1935).

60 162 276 379 482 514   Limitation of Actions § 61 Prevost   2 Wall.
Badger v. Badger (December Term 1864)
M/B: Badger v. Badger, 69 U.S. (2 Wall.) 87 (1864).

61 163 277 380 483 515   Labor § 129   Virginian R.   312 U.S.
National Labor Relations Board v. Express Publishing Co. (March 3, 1941)
M/B: NLRB v. Express Publishing Co., 312 U.S. 426 (1941).

62 164 278 381 484 516   Levy & Seizure § 3   Stevens   105 U.S.
Ager v. Murray (October Term 1881)
M/B: Ager v. Murray, 105 U.S. 126 (1881).

63 165 279 382 485 517   Limitation of Actions § 17 Southern P. Co. 270 U.S.
Barnette v. Wells Fargo Nevada National Bank et al. (March 15, 1926)
M/B: Barnette v. Wells Fargo Nevada National Bank, 270 U.S. 438 (1926).
LR: Barnette v. Wells Fargo Nev. Nat'l Bank, 270 U.S. 438 (1926).

64 166 280 383 486 518   Limitation of Actions § 201 Greene   145 U.S.
Sessions v. Romadka (April 25, 1892)
M/B: Sessions v. Romadka, 145 U.S. 29 (1892).

65 167 281 384 487 519   Master & Servant § 5   Standard Oil   284 U.S.
Denton v. Yazoo & Mississippi Valley Railroad Co. et al. (January 4, 1932)
M/B: Denton v. Yazoo & Mississippi Valley Railroad, 284 U.S. 305 (1932).
LR: Denton v. Yazoo & Miss. V. R.R., 284 U.S. 305 (1932) OR Denton v. Yazoo & M.V.R.R., 284 U.S. 305 (1932).

66 168 282 385 488 520   Master & Servant § 61   Raymond   349 U.S.
Mitchell, Secretary of Labor, v. C. W. Vollmer & Co. (June 6, 1955)
M/B: Mitchell v. C.W. Vollmer & Co., 349 U.S. 427 (1955).

67 169 283 386 489 521   Mines § 29   Deffeback   221 U.S.
United States v. Hammers (May 15, 1911)
M/B: United States v. Hammers, 221 U.S. 220 (1911).

68 170 284 387 490 522   Mortgage § 148   Miltenberger   197 U.S.
Gregg v. Metropolitan Trust Company (March 6, 1905)
M/B: Gregg v. Metropolitan Trust Co., 197 U.S. 183 (1905).

69 171 285 388 491 523   Parties § 3   Perkins   330 U.S.
Oklahoma v. United States Civil Service Commission (February 10, 1947)
M/B: Oklahoma v. United States Civil Service Commission, 330 U.S. 127 (1947).
LR: Oklahoma v. United States Civil Serv. Comm'n, 330 U.S. 127 (1947).

70 172 286 389 492 524   Patents § 27   Hoyt   155 U.S.
Deering v. Winona Harvester Works (December 3, 1894)
M/B: Deering v. Winona Harvester Works, 155 U.S. 286 (1894).

71 173 287 390 493 525   Patents § 240   Bauer   247 U.S.

EXERCISE 22. LAWYERS CO-OPERATIVE'S DIGESTS   (CONTINUED)

United States v. United Shoe Machinery Company of New Jersey et al. (May 20, 1918)
M/B: <u>United States v. United Shoe Machinery Co.</u>, 247 U.S. 32 (1918).
LR: United States v. United Shoe Mach. Co., 247 U.S. 32 (1918).

72 174 288 391 494 526 Pleading § 274   Southern P. Co. 151 U.S.
Central Trust Company v. McGeorge (January 3, 1894)
M/B: <u>Central Trust Co. v. McGeorge</u>, 151 U.S. 129 (1894).

73 175 289 392 495 527 Principal & Surety § 9   Smith   112 U.S.
Mersman v. Werges (November 3, 1884)
M/B: <u>Mersman v. Werges</u>, 112 U.S. 139 (1884).

74 176 290 393 496 528 Private Land Claims § 87   Hornsby   97 U.S.
McMicken v. United States (October Term 1877)
M/B: <u>McMicken v. United States</u>, 97 U.S. 204 (1877).

75 177 291 394 497 529 Public Lands § 56   Leavenworth   127 U.S.
United States v. McLaughlin (May 14, 1888)
M/B: <u>United States v. McLaughlin</u>, 127 U.S. 428 (1888).

76 178 292 395 498 530 Public Lands § 83   Kissell   9 Wall.
Public Schools v. Walker (December Term 1869)
M/B: <u>Public Schools v. Walker</u>, 76 U.S. (9 Wall.) 282 (1869).

77 179 293 396 499 531 Public Lands § 239   Davis   154 U.S.
Barden v. Northern Pacific Railroad Company (May 26, 1894)
M/B: <u>Barden v. Northern Pacific Railroad</u>, 154 U.S. 288 (1894).
LR: Barden v. Northern Pac. R.R., 154 U.S. 288 (1894) OR Barden v. Northern P.R.R., 154 U.S. 288 (1894).

78 180 294 397 500 532 Public Utilities § 16   So. Iowa Elec. 268 U.S.
Southern Utilities Company v. City of Palatka (May 11, 1925)
M/B: <u>Southern Utilities Co. v. City of Palatka</u>, 268 U.S. 232 (1925).
LR: Southern Utils. Co. v. City of Palatka, 268 U.S. 232 (1925).

79 181 295 398 401 533 Receivers § 59   St. Louis R.R. 136 U.S.
Kneeland v. American Loan and Trust Company (May 19, 1890)
M/B: <u>Kneeland v. American Loan & Trust Co.</u>, 136 U.S. 89 (1890).

80 182 296 399 402 534 Salvage § 11   Cope   191 U.S.
The Robert W. Parsons (October 26, 1903)
M/B: <u>The Robert W. Parsons</u>, 191 U.S. 17 (1903).

81 183 297 400 403 535 Seamen § 15   O'Donnell   328 U.S.
Swanson v. Marra Brothers, Inc. (April 22, 1946)
M/B: <u>Swanson v. Marra Brothers</u>, 328 U.S. 1 (1946).
LR: Swanson v. Marra Bros., 328 U.S. 1 (1946).

82 184 298 301 404 536 Shipping § 74   The Freeman   24 How.
Henry T. Bulkley, Claimant of the Barque Edwin, Appellant, v. The Naumkeag Steam Cotton Company (December Term 1860)
M/B: <u>Bulkley v. Naumkeag Steam Cotton Co.</u>, 65 U.S. (24 How.) 386 (1860).

83 185 299 302 405 537 Specific Performance § 10 Marshall   138 U.S.
Joy v. St. Louis (January 19, 1891)
M/B: <u>Joy v. St. Louis</u>, 138 U.S. 1 (1891).

84 186 300 303 406 538 States § 45   Clark   366 U.S.
Kolovrat v. Oregon (May 1, 1961)
M/B: <u>Kolovrat v. Oregon</u>, 366 U.S. 187 (1961).

85 187 201 304 407 539 Statutes § 39   Pollock   220 U.S.
Flint v. Stone Tracy Co. (March 13, 1911)
M/B: <u>Flint v. Stone Tracy Co.</u>, 220 U.S. 107 (1911).

86 188 202 305 408 540 Statutes § 132   Brewster   141 U.S.

EXERCISE 22. LAWYERS CO-OPERATIVE'S DIGESTS   (CONTINUED)

United States v. Missouri, Kansas & Texas Railway Company (October 19, 1891)
M/B: United States v. Missouri, Kansas & Texas Railway, 141 U.S. 358 (1891).
LR: United States v. Missouri, Kan. & Tex. Ry., 141 U.S. 358 (1891) OR United
     States v. Missouri, K. & T. Ry., 141 U.S. 358 (1891).

87 189 203 306 409 541 Statutes § 246   King   113 U.S.
Ayers & Another v. Watson (March 2, 1885)
M/B: Ayers v. Watson, 113 U.S. 594 (1885).

88 190 204 307 410 542 Succession & Estate Taxes §6 Keeney   253 U.S.
F.S. Royster Guano Company v. Commonwealth of Virginia (June 7, 1920)
M/B: F.S. Royster Guano Co. v. Virginia, 253 U.S. 412 (1920).

89 191 205 308 411 543 Taxes § 45   Baltic Min. Co.   245 U.S.
Crew Levick Company v. Commonwealth of Pennsylvania (December 10, 1917)
M/B: Crew Levick Co. v. Pennsylvania, 245 U.S. 292 (1917).

90 192 206 309 412 544 Taxes § 177   State Assessors   206 U.S.
Buck v. Beach, Treasurer of Tippecanoe County, Indiana (May 27, 1907)
M/B: Buck v. Beach, 206 U.S. 392 (1907).

91 193 207 310 413 545 Territories, Dependencies, Miners' Bank   186 U.S.
                        Possessions § 17
Murphy v. Utter (May 19, 1902)
M/B: Murphy v. Utter, 186 U.S. 95 (1902).

92 194 208 311 414 546 Trial § 324   Winston   225 U.S.
Johnson v. United States (June 7, 1912)
M/B: Johnson v. United States, 225 U.S. 405 (1912).

93 195 209 312 415 547 Trusts § 41   Magruder   318 U.S.
Securities and Exchange Commission v. Chenery Corporation et al. (February 1,
1943)
M/B: SEC v. Chenery Corp., 318 U.S. 80 (1943).

94 196 210 313 416 548 War § 10   Hiatt   271 U.S.
Sutherland, Alien Property Custodian v. Mayer et al. (May 24, 1926)
M/B: Sutherland v. Mayer, 271 U.S. 272 (1926).

95 197 211 314 417 549 War § 17   Hamilton   197 U.S.
Lincoln v. United States (April 3, 1905)
M/B: Lincoln v. United States, 197 U.S. 419 (1905).

96 198 212 315 418 550 Waters § 16   Wisconsin   180 U.S.
Missouri v. Illinois and the Sanitary District of Chicago (January 28, 1901)
M/B: Missouri v. Illinois, 180 U.S. 208 (1901).

97 199 213 316 419 551 Witnesses § 84   Counselman   161 U.S.
Brown v. Walker (March 23, 1896)
M/B: Brown v. Walker, 161 U.S. 591 (1896).

98 200 214 317 420 552 Writ & Process § 27   Davis   218 U.S.
Hunter v. Mutual Reserve Life Insurance Company (December 12, 1910)
M/B: Hunter v. Mutual Reserve Life Insurance Co., 218 U.S. 573 (1910).
LR: Hunter v. Mutual Reserve Life Ins. Co., 218 U.S. 573 (1910).

99 101 215 318 421 553 Banks § 16   Bramwell   288 U.S.
Spicer v. Smith, Sepcial Deputy Banking Commissioner (March 13, 1933)
M/B: Spicer v. Smith, 288 U.S. 430 (1933).

100 102 216 319 422 554 Bills & Notes § 76   Hortsman   252 U.S.
United States v. Chase National Bank (April 19, 1920)
M/B: United States v. Chase National Bank, 252 U.S. 485 (1920).
LR: United States v. Chase Nat'l Bank, 252 U.S. 485 (1920).

LIBRARY EXERCISE 23. SHEPARD'S CASE CITATIONS: SUBSEQUENT HISTORY.

INSTRUCTOR'S NOTE: The students are required to find the subsequent judicial history (certiorari denied, reversed, vacated, modified, certiorari dismissed, affirmed, affirmed per curiam, reversed per curiam, etc.) of the case listed below in the appropriate volume of Shepard's Citations. For their answer, they are to cite the case showing its subsequent history; however, they are not show the history on remand or a denial of a rehearing in the citation. If there is no subsequent history, they are instructed to answer "none." If they do so, they are incorrect because all of the problems assigned will have a subsequent history. The students are also instructed to use Shepard's Citations to find any missing parallel citations. For Supreme Court actions, they are told to cite only United States Reports. The students may include the phrase "per curiam" in describing the subsequent history, but use of that phrase is not required. See Rule 10.7.1.

The following Quick-Reference Abbreviations are particularly relevant to this exercise:

CASE HISTORY 3. USE ITALICIZED EXPLANATORY PHRASES TO APPEND THE PRIOR OR SUBSEQUENT HISTORY TO THE PRIMARY CITATION. [CH 3]
CASE HISTORY 4. THE YEAR OF DECISION SHOULD BE INCLUDED ONLY WITH THE LAST CITED DECISON WHEN SEVERAL DECISIONS WITHIN THE SAME YEAR ARE CITED. IF THE EXACT DATE IS REQUIRED, HOWEVER, BOTH DATES SHOULD BE INCLUDED. [CH 4]
CASE HISTORY 5. WHEN THE NAME OF THE CASE DIFFERS IN PRIOR OR SUBSEQUENT HISTORY, USE BOTH NAMES IN THE CITATION UNLESS THE SECOND NAME MERELY REVERSES THE PARTIES' NAMES OR THE DIFFERENCE IN NAMES OCCURS IN A CITATION TO A DENIAL OF A WRIT OF CERTIORARI OR A REHEARING. [CH 5]

1 190 270 350 430 520   269 A.2d 737
Entry Indicated by Shepard's: US cert den in 402 US 946
Commonwealth of Pennsylvania v. John McBride, Appellant, 440 Pa. 81 (Supreme Court of Pennsylvania Oct. 9, 1970)
Subsequent History: 402 U.S. 946 No. 6427. McBride v. Pennsylvania. Sup. Ct. Pa. Certiorari denied. May 3. 1971.
M/B: Commonwealth v. McBride, 440 Pa. 81, 269 A.2d 737 (1970), cert. denied, 402 U.S. 946 (1971).

2 191 271 351 431 521   276 A.2d 18
Entry Indicated by Shepard's: US cert den in 404 US 965
State of Vermont v. Maurice W. Oakes. (Supreme Court of Vermont, Windsor Feb. 18, 1971)
Subsequent History: 404 U.S. 965 No. 71-5054. Oakes v. Vermont. Sup. Ct. Vt. Certiorari denied. November 22, 1971.
M/B: State v. Oakes, 129 Vt. 241, 276 A.2d 18, cert. denied, 404 U.S. 965 (1971).

3 192 272 352 432 522   329 A.2d 376
Entry Indicated by Shepard's: US cert den in 421 US 919
The State of New Hampshire v. Frances Booton. (Supreme Court of New Hampshire, Rockingham Nov. 29, 1974)
Subsequent History: 421 U.S. 919 No. 74-6085. Booton v. New Hampshire. Sup Ct. N. H. Certiorari denied. April 14, 1975.
M/B: State v. Booton, 114 N.H. 750, 329 A.2d 376 (1974), cert. denied, 421 U.S. 919 (1975).

4 193 273 353 433 523   239 A.2d 409
Entry Indicated by Shepard's: US cert den in 383 US 882
Commonwealth of Pennsylvania v. Samuel Moody, Appellant, 429 Pa. 39 (Supreme Court of Pennsylvania March 15, 1968)
Subsequent History: 393 U.S. 882 No. 267, Misc. Moody v. Pennsylvania. Sup. Ct. Pa. Certiorari denied. October 14, 1968.
M/B: Commonwealth v. Moody, 429 Pa. 39, 239 A.2d 409, cert. denied, 393 U.S. 882 (1968).

5 194 274 354 434 524   315 A.2d 501
Entry Indicated by Shepard's: US cert den in 417 US 950
State of Vermont v. Frank J. Berard, Jr. (Supreme Court of Vermont, Windsor Feb. 5, 1974)

EXERCISE 23.   SHEPARD'S CASE CITATIONS: SUBSEQUENT HISTORY   (CONTINUED)

Subsequent History: 417 U.S. 950 No. 73-6582. Berard v. Vermont. Sup. Ct. Vt. Certiorari denied. June 10, 1974.
M/B: State v. Berard, 132 Vt. 138, 315 A.2d 501, cert. denied, 417 U.S. 950 (1974).

6 195 275 355 435 525   284 A.2d 700
Entry Indicated by Shepard's: US cert den in 406 US 910
Commonwealth of Pennsylvania v. Paul D. Ware, Appellant. (Supreme Court of Pennyslvania Dec. 20, 1971)
Subsequent History: 406 U.S. 910 No. 71-964. Pennsylvania v. Ware. Sup. Ct. Pa. The order of this Court dated March 20, 1972 [405 U.S. 987], insofar as it granted the petition for writ of certiorari, is vacated. Certiorari denied, it appearing that the judgment below rests upon an adequate state ground. April 24, 1972.
M/B: Commonwealth v. Ware, 446 Pa. 52, 284 A.2d 700 (1971), cert. denied, 406 U.S. 910 (1972).

7 196 276 356 436 526   352 A.2d 4
Entry Indicated by Shepard's: US cert den in 429 US 867
Commonwealth of Pennsylvania ex rel. George Walton, Appellee, v. Louis Aytch, Superintendent, Philadelphia County Prisons, Appellant (two cases). (Supreme Court of Pennsylvania Jan. 29, 1976)
Subsequent History: 429 U.S. 867 No. 75-1764. Aytch, Prisons Superintendent v. Walton. Sup. Ct. Pa. Motion of respondent for leave to proceed in forma pauperis granted. October 4, 1976.
M/B: Commonwealth ex rel. Walton v. Aytch, 466 Pa. 172, 352 A.2d 4, cert. denied, 429 U.S. 867 (1976).
LR: Commonwealth ex rel. Walton v. Aytch, 466 Pa. 172, 352 A.2d 4, cert. denied, 429 U.S. 867 (1976).

8 197 277 357 437 527   356 A.2d 897
Entry Indicated by Shepard's: US cert den in 423 US 829
State of Connecticut v. Thomas P. Lally, 167 Conn. 601 (Supreme Court of Connecticut Feb. 11, 1975)
Subsequent History: 423 U.S. 829 No. 74-1417. Lally v. Connecticut. Sup. Ct. Conn. Certiorari denied. October 6, 1975.
M/B: State v. Lally, 167 Conn. 601, 356 A.2d 897, cert. denied, 423 U.S. 829 (1975).

9 198 278 358 438 528   288 A.2d 863
Entry Indicated by Shepard's: m304 A2d 197
Josephine Tramultola and Fred N. Tramutola, her husband, Plaintiffs-Respondents and Cross-Appellants, v. Frank Bortone, M.D., Defendant-Appellant and Cross-Respondent, 118 N.J. Super. 503 (Superior Court of New Jersey, Appellate Division March 20, 1972)
Subsequent History: Modified same name 63 N.J. 9, 304 A.2d 197 (Supreme Court of New Jersey May 7, 1973)
M/B: Tramutola v. Bortone, 118 N.J. Super. 503, 288 A.2d 863 (App. Div. 1972), modified, 63 N.J. 9, 304 A.2d 197 (1973).

10 199 279 359 439 529   273 A.2d 361
Entry Indicated by Shepard's: r294 A2d 1
State of New Jersey, Plaintiff-Respondent, v. William B. Ebron, Defendant-Appellant, 113 N.J. Super. 152 (Superior Court of New Jersey, Appellate Division Jan. 21, 1971)
Subsequent History: Reversed same name 61 N.J. 207, 294 A.2d 1 (Supreme Court of New Jersey July 21, 1972)
M/B: State v. Ebron, 113 N.J. Super. 152, 273 A.2d 361 (App. Div. 1971), rev'd, 61 N.J. 207, 294 A.2d 1 (1972).

11 200 280 360 440 530   420 P.2d 693
Entry Indicated by Shepard's: US cert den in 386 US 997
The State of Washington, Respondent, v. Richard E. Loux, Appellant (Supreme Court of Washington, Department 1 Dec. 1, 1966)
Subsequent History: 386 U.S. 997 No. 1291, Misc. Loux v. Washington. Sup. Ct. Wash. Certiorari denied. Petitioner pro se. James E. Kennedy for respondent. April 10, 1967.

EXERCISE 23. SHEPARD'S CASE CITATIONS: SUBSEQUENT HISTORY   (CONTINUED)

M/B: State v. Loux, 69 Wash. 2d 855, 420 P.2d 693 (1966), cert. denied, 386 U.S. 997 (1967).

12 101 281 361 441 531   450 P.2d 364
Entry Indicated by Shepard's: US cert den in 396 US 868
The State of Arizona, Appellee, v. Ernest A. Miranda, Appellant, 104 Ariz. 174 (Supreme Court of Arizona. In Banc. Feb. 6, 1969)
Subsequent History: 396 U.S. 868 No. 314, Misc. Miranda v. Arizona. Sup. Ct. Ariz. Certiorari denied. Mr. Justice Marshall took no part in the consideration or decision of this petition. John P. Frank and John J. Flynn for petitioner. Gary K. Nelson, Attorney General of Arizona, and Carl Waag, Assistant Attorney General, for respondent. October 13, 1969.
M/B: State v. Miranda, 104 Ariz. 174, 450 P.2d 364, cert. denied, 396 U.S. 868 (1969).

13 102 282 362 442 532   455 P.2d 34
Entry Indicated by Shepard's: m408 US 935
Joseph Miles Walker, Appellant, v. The State of Nevada, Respondent (Supreme Court of Nevada May 28, 1969)
Subsequent History: 408 U.S. 935 No. 69-5011. Walker v. Nevada. Sup. Ct. Nev. June 29, 1972.
M/B: Walker v. State, 85 Nev. 337, 455 P.2d 34 (1969), modified, 408 U.S. 935 (1972).

14 103 283 263 443 533   455 P.2d 395
Entry Indicated by Shepard's: US cert den in 406 US 972
The People, Plaintiff and Respondent, v. Robert Lee Nye, Defendant and Appellant, 78 Cal. Rptr. 467 (Supreme Court of California, In Bank June 19, 1969)
Subsequent History: 406 U.S. 972 No. 69-5022. Nye v. California. Sup. Ct. Cal. Certiorari denied. Aikens v. California, ante, p. 813. June 7, 1972.
M/B: People v. Nye, 71 Cal. 2d 356, 455 P.2d 395, 78 Cal. Rptr. 467 (1969), cert. denied, 406 U.S. 972 (1972).

15 104 284 364 444 534   524 P.2d 97
Entry Indicated by Shepard's: US cert den in 419 US 1022
Laura Cooper et al., Plaintiffs and Appellants, v. David B. Swoap, as Director, etc., Defendant and Respondent, 115 Cal. Rptr. 1 (Supreme Court of California, In Bank July 2, 1974)
Subsequent History: 419 U.S. 1022 No. 74-311. Swoap, Director, Department of Social Welfare, et al. v. Cooper et al. Sup. Ct. Cal. Certiorari denied. November 18, 1974.
M/B: Cooper v. Swoap, 11 Cal. 3d 856, 524 P.2d 97, 115 Cal. Rptr. 1, cert. denied, 419 U.S. 1022 (1974).

16 105 285 365 445 535   503 P.2d 1322
Entry Indicated by Shepard's: US cert den in 411 US 968
The People, Plaintiff and Respondent, v. Robert Nelson, Defendant and Appellant, 105 Cal. Rptr. 314 (Supreme Court of California, In Bank Dec. 14, 1972)
Subsequent History: 411 U.S. 968 No. 72-6162. Nelson v. California. Sup. Ct. Cal. Certiorari denied. May 7, 1973.
M/B: People v. Nelson, 8 Cal. 3d 463, 503 P.2d 1322, 105 Cal. Rptr. 314 (1972), cert. denied, 411 U.S. 968 (1973).

17 106 286 366 446 536   408 P.2d 116
Entry Indicated by Shepard's: US cert den in 389 US 1006
The People, Plaintiff and Respondent, v. Ivy Dell Cockrell et al., Defendants and Appellants, 47 Cal. Rptr. 788 (Supreme Court of California, In Bank December 9, 1965)
Subsequent History: 389 U.S. 1006 No. 387, Misc. Cockrell et al. v. California. Sup. Ct. Cal. Certiorari denied. Burton Marks for petitioners. Thomas C. Lynch, Attorney General of California, William E. James, Assistant Attorney General, and Rose-Marie Gruenwald, Deputy Attorney General, for respondent. December 11, 1967.
M/B: People v. Crockrell, 63 Cal. 2d 659, 408 P.2d 116, 47 Cal. Rptr. 788 (1965), cert. denied, 389 U.S. 1006 (1967).

EXERCISE 23. SHEPARD'S CASE CITATIONS: SUBSEQUENT HISTORY   (CONTINUED)

18 107 287 367 447 537   466 P.2d 961
Entry Indicated by Shepard's: US cert dis in 406 US 912
The People, Plaintiff and Respondent, v. Harold Roger Terry and Juanelda
Allen, Defendants and Appellants, 85 Cal. Rptr. 409 (Supreme Court of
California, In Bank April 2, 1970)
Subsequent History: 406 U.S. 912 No. 70-5005. Terry v. California. Sup. Ct.
Cal. Petition for writ of certiorari dismissed pursuant to Rule 60 of the
Rules of this Court. May 8, 1972.
M/B: People v. Terry, 2 Cal. 3d 362, 466 P.2d 961, 85 Cal. Rptr. 409 (1970),
cert. dismissed, 406 U.S. 912 (1972).

19 108 288 368 448 538   435 P.2d 692
Entry Indicated by Shepard's: US cert den in 393 US 872
The City of Seattle, Respondent, v. Wayne J. Hill, Appellant (Supreme Court of
Washington, En Banc December 21, 1967)
Subsequent History: 393 U.S. 872 No. 131, Misc. Hill v. City of Seattle.
Sup. Ct. Wash. Certiorari denied. Michael H. Rosen for petitioner. A. L.
Newbould for respondent. October 14, 1968.
M/B: City of Seattle v. Hill, 72 Wash. 2d 786, 435 P.2d 692 (1967), cert.
denied, 393 U.S. 872 (1968).

20 109 289 369 449 539   213 N.E.2d 438
Entry Indicated by Shepard's: US cert den in 386 US 1008
The People of the State of New York, Respondent, v. Stanley White, Appellant,
16 N.Y.2d 270 (Court of Appeals of New York Dec. 30, 1965)
Subsequent History: 386 U.S. 1008 No. 245, Misc. White v. New York. Ct. App.
N.Y. Gretchen White Oberman for petitioner. Frank S. Hogan for respondent.
April 17, 1967.
M/B: People v. White, 16 N.Y.2d 270, 213 N.E. 2d 438, 266 N.Y.S.2d 100
(1965), cert. denied, 386 U.S. 1008 (1967).

21 110 290 370 450 540   218 N.E.2d 428
Entry Indicated by Shepard's: US cert den in 386 US 957
The State ex rel. Sibarco Corp. et al., Appellees, v. City of Berea et al.,
Appellants, 7 Ohio St.2d 85 (Supreme Court of Ohio July 6, 1966)
Subsequent History: 386 U.S. 957 No. 899. Ohio ex rel. Sibarco Corp. et al.
v. City of Berea et al. Sup. Ct. Ohio. Certiorari denied. Sanford W. Likover
for petitioners. George I. Meisel for respondents. March 13, 1967.
M/B: State ex rel. Sibarco Corp. v. City of Berea, 7 Ohio St. 2d 85, 218
N.E.2d 428 (1966), cert. denied, 386 U.S. 957 (1967).
LR: State ex rel. Sibarco Corp. v. City of Berea, 7 Ohio St. 2d 85, 218
N.E.2d 428 (1966), cert. denied, 386 U.S. 957 (1967).

22 111 291 371 451 541   219 N.E.2d 194
Entry Indicated by Shepard's: US cert den in 385 US 973
In the Matter of William R. Klein, an Attorney, Appellant, v. Solomon A.
Klein, Respondent, 18 NY2d 598 (Court of Appeals of New York July 7, 1966)
Subsequent History: 385 U.S. 973 No. 665. Klein v. Klein. Ct. App. N. Y.
Certiorari denied. Petitioner pro se. Solomon A. Klein, respondent, pro se.
December 5, 1966.
M/B: Klein v. Klein, 18 N.Y.2d 598, 219 N.E.2d 194, 272 N.Y.S.2d 372, cert.
denied, 385 U.S. 973 (1966).

23 112 292 372 452 542   241 N.E.2d 419
Entry Indicated by Shepard's: US cert den in 394 US 965
The People of the State of Illinois, Appellee, v. Sam Tassone, Appellant, 41
Ill.2d 7 (Supreme Court of Illinois Sept. 24, 1968)
Subsequent History: 394 U.S. 965 No. 1544, Misc. Tassone v. Illinois. Sup.
Ct. Ill. Certiorari denied. Albert I. Zemel for petitioner. April 7, 1969.
M/B: People v. Tassone, 41 Ill. 2d 7, 241 N.E.2d 419 (1968), cert. denied,
394 U.S. 965 (1969).

24 113 293 373 453 543   244 N.E.2d 89
Entry Indicated by Shepard's: US cert den in 396 US 821
S.W. Asher, Appellant, v. State of Indiana, Appellee (Supreme Court of Indiana
Feb. 3, 1969)

EXERCISE 23.   SHEPARD'S CASE CITATIONS: SUBSEQUENT HISTORY   (CONTINUED)

Subsequent History: 396 U.S. 821 No. 130. Asher v. Indiana. Sup. Ct. Ind. Certiorari denied. William C. Erbecker and James Manahan for petitioner. Theodore L. Sendak, Attorney General of Indiana, and William F. Thompson, Deputy Attorney General, for respondent. October 13, 1969.
M/B: Asher v. State, 253 Ind. 25, 244 N.E.2d 89, cert. denied, 396 U.S. 821 (1969).

25 114 294 374 454 544   245 N.E.2d 771
Entry Indicated by Shepard's: US cert den in 396 US 1016
The People of the State of Illinois, Appellee, v. Charles Earnest Nicholls, Appellant, 42 Ill.2d 91 (Supreme Court of Illinois Jan. 29, 1969)
Subsequent History: 396 U.S. 1016 No. 515, Misc. Nicholls v. Illinois. Sup. Ct. Ill. Certiorari denied. Walter D. Williams for petitioner. William J. Scott, Attorney General of Illinois, and Joel M. Flaum, Thomas J. Immel, and Roger C. Nauert, Assistant Attorneys general, for respondent. January 12, 1970.
M/B: People v. Nicholls, 42 Ill. 2d 91, 245 N.E.2d 771 (1969), cert. denied, 396 U.S. 1016 (1970).

26 115 295 375 455 545   193 N.E.2d 449
Entry Indicated by Shepard's: US cert den in 377 US 955
The People of the State of Illinois, Defendant In Error, v. George Wilson, Plaintiff In Error, 29 Ill.2d 82 (Supreme Court of Illinois Sept. 27, 1963)
Subsequent History: 377 U.S. 955 No. 1059, Misc. Wilson v. Illinois. Supreme Court of Illinois. Certiorari denied. Petitioner pro se. Daniel P. Ward and Elmer C. Kissane for respondent. June 1, 1964.
M/B: People v. Wilson, 29 Ill. 2d 82, 193 N.E.2d 449 (1963), cert. denied, 377 U.S. 955 (1964).

27 116 296 376 456 546   190 N.E.2d 719
Entry Indicated by Shepard's: US cert den in 375 US 865
The People of the State of Illinois, Defendant In Error, v. Memphis Bridges, Plaintiff In Error (Supreme Court of Illinois May 27, 1963)
Subsequent History: 375 U.S. 865 No. 380, Misc. Bridges v. Illinois. Supreme Court of Illinois. Certiorari denied. October 14, 1963.
M/B: People v. Bridges, 28 Ill. 2d 165, 190 N.E.2d 719, cert. denied, 375 U.S. 865 (1963).

28 117 297 377 457 547   134 N.E.2d 914
Entry Indicated by Shepard's: US cert den in 352 US 895
Bay State Cafe, Inc. v. Louis R. Cohen (Supreme Judicial Court of Massachusetts, Hampden June 6, 1956)
Subsequent History: 352 U.S. 895 No. 356. Bay State Cafe, Inc., et al. v. Cohen. Supreme Judicial Court, and Superior Court, of Massachusetts. Certiorari denied. Angus M. MacNeil for petitioners. Respondent pro se. November 5, 1956.
M/B: Bay State Cafe v. Cohen, 334 Mass. 705, 134 N.E.2d 914, cert. denied, 352 U.S. 895 (1956).

29 118 298 378 458 548   256 So. 2d 98
Entry Indicated by Shepard's: US cert den in 407 US 911
State of Louisiana v. Philip J. Anselmo, Jr. and Terrance C. Lee, 260 La. 306 (Supreme Court of Louisiana Dec. 13, 1971)
Subsequent History: 407 U.S. 911 No. 71-1335. Anselmo et al. v. Louisiana. Sup. Ct. La. Certiorari denied. June 12, 1972.
M/B: State v. Anselmo, 260 La. 306, 256 So. 2d 98 (1971), cert. denied, 407 U.S. 911 (1972).

30 119 299 379 459 549   241 So. 2d 390
Entry Indicated by Shepard's: m408 US 938
Alvin Eugene Anderson, Appellant, v. State of Florida, Appellee (Supreme Court of Florida Nov. 12, 1970)
Subsequent History: 408 U.S. 938 No. 70-5070. Anderson v. Florida. Sup. Ct. Fla. June 29, 1972.
M/B: Anderson v. State, 241 So. 2d 390 (Fla. 1970), modified, 408 U.S. 938 (1972).

EXERCISE 23. SHEPARD'S CASE CITATIONS: SUBSEQUENT HISTORY   (CONTINUED)

31 120 300 380 460 550   197 So. 2d 241
Entry Indicated by Shepard's: US cert den in 389 US 1050
Billy Preston Phillips v. State of Mississippi (Supreme Court of Mississippi April 3, 1967)
Subsequent History: 389 U.S. 1050 No. 215, Misc. Phillips v. Mississippi. Sup. Ct. Miss. Certiorari denied. Joe T. Patterson, Attorney General of Mississippi, and Guy N. Rogers, Assistant Attorney General, for respondent. January 15, 1968.
M/B: Phillips v. State, 197 So. 2d 241 (Miss. 1967), cert. denied, 389 U.S. 1050 (1968).

32 121 201 381 461 551   123 F. 817
Entry Indicated by Shepard's: r127F320
Snyder v. Bonbright. Schoettler v. Same. (Circuit Court, E. D. Pennsylvania June 27, 1903)
Subsequent History: Reversed Bonbright v. Schoettler, 127 F. 320 (3d Cir. 1933).
M/B: Snyder v. Bonbright, 123 F. 817 (E.D. Pa.), rev'd sub nom. Bonbright v. Schoettler, 127 F. 320 (1903).

33 122 202 382 462 552   128 F. 527
Entry Indicated by Shepard's: r133 F 912 r13 AB341 s198 US 583
In re Janes et al. (District Court, W. D. New York March 7, 1904)
Subsequent History: Reversed same name 133 F. 912 (Second Cir. Dec. 6, 1904)
M/B: In re Janes, 128 F. 527 (W.D.N.Y.), rev'd, 133 F. 912 (2d Cir. 1904).
LR: In re Janes, 128 F. 527 (W.D.N.Y.), rev'd, 133 F. 912 (2d Cir. 1904).

34 123 203 383 463 553   374 F. Supp. 301
Entry Indicated by Shepard's: r514 F2d 561
Thelma H. Lauritzen, Plaintiff, v. Caspar Weinberger, Secretary of Health, Education and Welfare, Defendant (United States District Court, E. D. Missouri, E. D. March 29, 1974)
Subsequent History: Reversed same name 514 F.2d 561 (Eighth Circuit April 11, 1975)
M/B: Lauritzen v. Weinberger, 374 F. Supp. 301 (E.D. Mo. 1974), rev'd, 514 F.2d 561 (8th Cir. 1975).

35 124 204 384 464 554   239 F.2d 97
Entry Indicated by Shepard's: r353 US 944
Sunray Mid-Continent Oil Company (formerly Sunray Oil Corporation), Petitioner, v. Federal Power Commission, Respondent (United States Court of Appeals Tenth Circuit Oct. 29, 1956)
Subsequent History: 353 U.S. 944 No. 814. Sunray Mid-Continent Oil Co. v. Federal Power Commission. Reversed per curiam: April 29, 1957.
M/B: Sunray Mid-Continent Oil Co. v. FPC, 239 F.2d 97 (10th Cir. 1956), rev'd per curiam, 353 U.S. 944 (1957).

36 125 205 385 465 555   262 F.2d 501
Entry Indicated by Shepard's: r367 US 290
United States of America, Appellee, v. John Francis Noto, Appellant, No. 381, Docket 25156 (United States Court of Appeals Second Circuit Dec. 31, 1958)
Subsequent History: Reversed Noto v. United States 367 U.S. 290 (June 5, 1961)
M/B: United States v. Noto, 262 F.2d 501 (2d Cir. 1958), rev'd, 367 U.S. 290 (1961).

37 126 206 386 466 556   281 F.2d 59
Entry Indicated by Shepard's: r369 US 749
Alden Whitman, Appellant, v. United States of America, Appellee (United States Court of Appeals District of Columbia Circuit July 7, 1960)
Subsequent History: Reversed sub nom. Russell v. United States, 369 U.S. 749 (May 21, 1962)
M/B: Whitman v. United States, 281 F.2d 59 (D.C. Cir. 1960), rev'd sub nom. Russell v. United States, 369 U.S. 749 (1962).

38 127 207 387 467 557   240 N.W.2d 729
Entry Indicated by Shepard's: US cert den in 429 US 951

EXERCISE 23. SHEPARD'S CASE CITATIONS: SUBSEQUENT HISTORY   (CONTINUED)

The People of the State of Michigan, Plaintiff-Appellee, v. Alvin Johnson, Defendant-Appellant, 396 Mich. 424 (Supreme Court of Michigan April 21, 1976) Subsequent History: 429 U.S. 951 No. 76-372. Michigan v. Johnson. Sup. Ct. Mich. Motion of respondent for leave to proceed in forma pauperis granted. Certiorari denied, it appearing that judgment below rests on adequate state grounds. November 8, 1976.
M/B: People v. Johnson, 396 Mich. 424, 240 N.W.2d 729, cert. denied, 429 U.S. 951 (1976).

39 128 208 388 468 558   221 N.W.2d 357
Entry Indicated by Shepard's: US cert den in 420 US 912
People of the State of Michigan, Plaintiff-Appellee, v. James White, Defendant-Appellant, 392 Mich. 404 (Supreme Court of Michigan Sept. 6, 1974) Subsequent History: 420 U.S. 912 No. 74-704. Michigan v. White. Sup. Ct. Mich. Motion of respondent for leave to proceed in forma pauperis granted. Certiorari denied. January 27, 1975.
M/B: People v. White, 392 Mich. 404, 221 N.W.2d 357 (1974), cert. denied, 420 U.S. 912 (1975).

40 129 209 389 469 559   219 N.W.2d 920
Entry Indicated by Shepard's: US cert den in 419 US 1023
Minnesota State Bar Association, Respondent, v. Divorce Education Associates, et al., Defendants, Charles Thibodeau and Donna Thibodeau, et al., Petitioners (Supreme Court of Minnesota June 28, 1974)
Subsequent History: 419 U.S. 1023 No. 74-359. Thibodeau et al. v. Minnesota State Bar Assn. Sup. Ct. Minn. Certiorari denied. November 18, 1974.
M/B: Minnesota State Bar Association v. Divorce Educuation Associates, 300 Minn. 323, 219 N.W.2d 920, cert. denied, 419 U.S. 1023 (1974).
LR: Minnesota State Bar Ass'n v. Divorce Educ. Assocs., 300 Minn. 323, 219 N.W.2d 920, cert. denied, 419 U.S. 1023 (1974).

41 130 210 390 470 560   377 F. Supp. 1065
Entry Indicated by Shepard's: a506 F2d 1375
Michael J. Daley v. Capitol Bank and Trust Company, Civ. A. No. 71-2398-C. (United States District Court, D. Massachusetts June 20, 1974)
Subsequent History: Affirmed same name 506 F.2d 1375 (First Circuit Nov. 29, 1974)
M/B: Daley v. Capitol Bank & Trust Co., 377 F. Supp. 1065 (D. Mass.), aff'd, 506 F.2d 1375 (1st Cir. 1974).

42 131 211 391 471 561   211 N.W.2d 642
Entry Indicated by Shepard's: US cert den in 416 US 906
Eugene H. Skaar et al., Respondents, v. Wisconsin Department of Revenue, Appellant, 61 Wis.2d 93 (Supreme Court of Wisconsin Nov. 12, 1973)
Subsequent History: 416 U.S. 906 No. 73-1268. Skaar et ux. v. Wisconsin Department of Revenue. Sup. Ct. Wis. Certiorari denied. April 1, 1974.
M/B: Skaar v. Wisconsin Department of Revenue, 61 Wis. 2d 93, 211 N.W.2d 642 (1973), cert. denied, 416 U.S. 906 (1974).
LR: Skaar v. Wisconsin Dep't of Revenue, 61 Wis. 2d 93, 211 N.W.2d 642 (1973), cert. denied, 416 U.S. 906 (1974).

43 132 212 392 472 562   199 N.W.2d 480
Entry Indicated by Shepard's: US cert den in 430 US 947
State of Nebraska, Appellee, v. David L. Rice, Appellant, 188 Neb. 728 (Supreme Court of Nebraska July 14, 1972)
Subsequent History: 430 U.S. 947 No. 76-5862. Rice v. Nebraska. Sup. Ct. Neb. Certiorari denied. March 28, 1977.
M/B: State v. Rice, 188 Neb. 728, 199 N.W.2d 480 (1972), cert. denied, 430 U.S. 947 (1977).

44 133 213 393 473 563   182 N.W.2d 887
Entry Indicated by Shepard's:US cert den in 404 US 886
Douglas M. Head, Attorney General, State of Minnesota, Respondent, Keith W. Davidson, et al., Respondents, v. Special School District No. 1, etc., et al., Appellants (Supreme Court of Minnesota Dec. 9, 1970)
Subsequent History: 404 U.S. 886 No. 70-152. Minneapolis Federation of Teachers, Local No. 59 v. Spannaus, Attorney General of Minnesota, et al. Sup.

EXERCISE 23.   SHEPARD'S CASE CITATIONS: SUBSEQUENT HISTORY   (CONTINUED)

Ct. Minn. Certiorari denied. Mr. Justice Douglas is of the opinion that certiorari should be granted and case set for oral argument. October 29, 1971.
M/B: Head v. Special School District No. 1, 288 Minn. 496, 182 N.W.2d 887 (1970), cert. denied, 404 U.S. 886 (1971).
LR: Head v. Special School Dist. No. 1, 288 Minn. 496, 182 N.W.2d 887 (1970), cert. denied, 404 U.S. 886 (1971).

45 134 214 394 474 564   174 N.W.2d 504
Entry Indicated by Shepard's: US cert den in 400 US 917
State of Wisconsin, Respondent, v. Keith Ritchie, Appellant, v. Keith Ritchie, Appellant (Supreme Court of Wisconsin March 3, 1970)
Subsequent History: 400 U.S. 917 No. 5246. Ritchie v. Wisconsin. Sup. Ct. Wis. Certiorari denied. November 16, 1970.
M/B: State v. Ritchie, 46 Wis. 2d 47, 174 N.W.2d 504, cert. denied, 400 U.S. 917 (1970).

46 135 215 395 475 565   149 N.W.2d 557
Entry Indicated by Shepard's: US cert den in 390 US 959
Thomas James Whitty, Plaintiff in Error, v. State of Wisconsin, Defendant In Error (two cases), 34 Wis.2d 278 (Supreme Court of Wisconsin April 11, 1967)
Subsequent History: 390 U.S. 959 No. 420, Misc. Whitty v. Wisconsin. Sup. Ct. Wis. Certiorari denied. March 4, 1968.
M/B: Whitty v. State, 34 Wis. 2d 278, 149 N.W.2d 557 (1967), cert. denied, 390 U.S. 959 (1968).

47 136 216 396 476 566   163 S.E.2d 589
Entry Indicated by Shepard's: US cert den in 394 US 991
Charles D. Carter v. Commonwealth of Virginia, 209 Va. 317 (Supreme Court of Appeals of Virginia Oct. 14, 1968)
Subsequent History: 394 U.S. 991 No. 1477, Misc. Carter v. Virginia. Sup. Ct. App. Va. Certiorari denied. April 21, 1969.
M/B: Carter v. Commonwealth, 209 Va. 317, 163 S.E.2d 589 (1968), cert. denied, 394 U.S. 991 (1969).

48 137 217 397 477 567   197 S.E.2d 502
Entry Indicated by Shepard's: US cert den in 414 US 1000
John R. Fowler et al. v. The State, 128 Ga. App. 501 (Court of Appeals of Georgia, Division No. 1 Feb. 21, 1973)
Subsequent History: 414 U.S. 1000 No. 73-172. Fowler et al. v. Georgia. Ct. App. Ga. Certiorari denied. November 5, 1973.
M/B: Fowler v. State, 128 Ga. App. 501, 197 S.E.2d 502, cert. denied, 414 U.S. 1000 (1973).

49 138 218 398 478 568   176 S.E.2d 818
Entry Indicated by Shepard's: US cert den in 401 US 959
George Delano Woodson v. Commonwealth of Virginia (Supreme Court of Appeals of Virginia Oct. 12, 1970)
Subsequent History: 401 U.S. 959 No. 6422. Woodson v. Virginia. Sup. Ct. App. Va. Certiorari denied. March 8, 1971.
M/B: Woodson v. Commonwealth, 211 Va. 285, 176 S.E.2d 818 (1970), cert. denied, 401 U.S. 959 (1971).

50 139 219 399 479 569   199 S.E.2d 183
Entry Indicated by Shepard's: r418 US 153
Billy Jenkins v. The State, 230 Ga. 726 (Supreme Court of Georgia July 2, 1973)
Subsequent History: Reversed Jenkins v. Georgia 418 U.S. 153 (June 24, 1974)
M/B: Jenkins v. State, 230 Ga. 726, 199 S.E.2d 183 (1973), rev'd, 418 U.S. 153 (1974).

51 140 220 400 480 570   188 S.E.2d 296
Entry Indicated by Shepard's: US cert den in 409 US 1047
State of North Carolina v. Elizabeth Cradle, 281 N.C. 198 (Supreme Court of North Carolina May 10, 1972)

EXERCISE 23. SHEPARD'S CASE CITATIONS: SUBSEQUENT HISTORY   (CONTINUED)

Subsequent History: 409 U.S. 1047 No. 72-5203. Cradle v. North Carolina. Sup. Ct. N. C. Certiorari denied. Mr. Justice Douglas would grant certiorari.
M/B: State v. Cradle, 281 N.C. 198, 188 S.E.2d 296, cert. denied, 409 U.S. 1047 (1972).

52 141 221 301 481 571   236 S.E.2d 353
Entry Indicated by Shepard's: US cert den in 434 US 975
Jack Carlton House v. LeRoy Stynchcombe, Sheriff, et al., 239 Ga. 222 (Supreme Court of Georgia June 7, 1977)
Subsequent History: 434 U.S. 975 No. 77-5439. House v. Stynchcombe, Sheriff, et al. Sup. Ct. Ga. Certiorari denied. November 28, 1977.
M/B: House v. Stynchcombe, 239 Ga. 222, 236 S.E.2d 353, cert. denied, 434 U.S. 975 (1977).

53 142 222 302 482 572   216 S.E.2d 608
Entry Indicated by Shepard's: US cert den in 424 US 914
W. H. Ingram v. The State, 134 Ga. App. 935 (Court of Appeals of Georgia, Division No. 1 May 12, 1975)
Subsequent History: 424 U.S. 914 No. 75-862. Ingram v. Georgia. Ct. App. Ga. Certiorari denied. February 23, 1976.
M/B: Ingram v. State, 134 Ga. App. 935, 216 S.E.2d 608 (1975), cert. denied, 424 U.S. 914 (1976).

54 143 223 303 483 573   215 S.E.2d 540
Entry Indicated by Shepard's: m428 US 903
State of North Carolina v. Thomas Lee King and Joseph Lee King (Supreme Court of North Carolina June 26, 1975)
Subsequent History: 428 U.S. 903 No. 75-5792. King et al. v. North Carolina. Sup.
M/B: State v. King, 287 N.C. 645, 215 S.E.2d 540 (1975), modified, 428 U.S. 903 (1976).

55 144 224 304 484 574   214 S.E.2d 742
Entry Indicated by Shepard's: m428 US 908
State of North Carolina v. Charles D. Thompson, 287 N.C. 303 (Supreme court of North Carolina June 6, 1975)
Subsequent History: 428 U.S. 908 No. 75-5983. Thompson v. North Carolina. Sup. Ct. N. C. Petitioner in this csae was sentenced to death. Imposition and carrying out of the death penalty in this case constitute cruel and unusual punishment in violation of Eighth and Fourteenth Amendments. Woodson v. North Carolina, ante, p. 280. Motion for leave to proceed in forma pauperis and certiorari granted. Judgment vacated insofar as it leaves undisturbed the death penalty imposed, and case remanded for further proceedings. Mr. Justice Brennan and Mr. Justice Marhsall would grant certiorari and set case for oral argument. July 6, 1976.
M/B: State v. Thompson, 287 N.C. 303, 214 S.E.2d 742 (1975), modified, 428 U.S. 908 (1976).

56 145 225 305 485 575   307 S.W.2d 385
Entry Indicated by Shepard's: r356 US 41
Fred Ferguson, Plaintiff-Appellant, v. St. Louis-San Francisco Railway Company, a Corporation, Defendant-Respondent (Supreme Court of Missouri, En Banc Nov. 12, 1957)
Subsequent History: 356 U.S. 41 Per Curiam reversed
M/B: Ferguson v. St. Louis-San Francisco Ry., 307 S.W.2d 385 (Mo. 1957), rev'd per curiam, 356 U.S. 41 (1958).
LR: Ferguson v. St. Louis-S.F. Ry., 307 S.W.2d 385 (Mo. 1957), rev'd per curiam, 356 U.S. 41 (1958).

57 146 226 306 486 576   389 S.W.2d 774
Entry Indicated by Shepard's: US cert den in 382 US 939
James E. Chance, Appellant, v. Atchison, Topeka and Sante Fe Railway Company, a corporation, Respondent (Supreme Court of Missouri, Division No. 2 April 12, 1965)
Subsequent History: 382 U.S. 939 No. 546. Chance v. Atchison, Topeka & Santa Fe Railway Co. Sup. Ct. Mo. Certiorari denied. December 6, 1965.

EXERCISE 23. SHEPARD'S CASE CITATIONS: SUBSEQUENT HISTORY   (CONTINUED)

M/B: Chance v. Atchison, Topeka & Santa Fe Railway, 389 S.W.2d 774 (Mo.), cert. denied, 382 U.S. 939 (1965).
LR: Chance v. Atchison, T. & S.F. Ry., 389 S.W.2d 774 (Mo.), cert. denied, 382 U.S. 939 (1965).

58 147 227 307 487 577   481 S.W.2d 473
Entry Indicated by Shepard's: US cert den in 409 US 1028
Joseph Barnett Dominey, Jr., Appellant, v. Louise Ellen Dominey, Appellee (Court of Civil Appeals of Texas, El Paso April 19, 1972)
Subsequent History: 409 U.S. 1028 No. 72-406. Dominey v. Dominey. Ct. Civ. App. Tex., 8th Sup. Jud. Dist. Certiorari denied. Mr. Justice Douglas would grant certiorari. November 20, 1972.
M/B: Dominey v. Dominey, 481 S.W.2d 473 (Tex. Civ. App.), cert. denied, 409 U.S. 1028 (1972).

59 148 228 308 488 578   277 S.W.2d 125
Entry Indicated by Shepard's: r289 SW 228
L. O. Gleason, d/b/a Alice Pipe and Supply Co., Appellant, v. Wesley Davis, d/b/a Davis Well Service, Appellee (Court of Civil Appeals of Texas. San Antonio Feb. 16, 1955)
Subsequent History: Reversed same name 289 S.W.2d 228 (Supreme Court of Texas March 21, 1956)
M/B: Gleason v. Davis, 277 S.W.2d 125 (Tex. Civ. App. 1955), rev'd, 155 Tex. 467, 289 S.W.2d 228 (1956).

60 149 229 309 489 579   278 S.W.2d 398
Entry Indicated by Shepard's: r284 SW 898
Edith Marie McCain, Appellant, v. Neva Yost, Temporary Administratrix of the Estate of Lillard Russell McCain, Deceased, Appellee (Court of Civil Appeals of Texas. Fort Worth March 18, 1955)
Subsequent History: Reversed same name 284 S.W.2d 898 (Supreme Court of Texas Dec. 14, 1955)
M/B: McCain v. Yost, 278 S.W.2d 398 (Tex. Civ. App.), rev'd, 155 Tex. 174, 284 S.W.2d 898 (1955).

61 150 230 310 490 580   418 S.W.2d 708
Entry Indicated by Shepard's: r422 SW 722
Geneva Fields, d/b/a Fields Funeral Home, Appellant, v. Universal Life and Accident Insurance Company, Appellee (Court of Civil Appeals of Texas. Houston (1st Dist.) August 31, 1967)
Subsequent History: Reversed Universal Life and Accident Insurance Co. v. Fields 422 S.W.2d 722 (Supreme Court of Texas Dec. 6, 1967)
M/B: Fields v. Universal Life & Accident Insurance Co., 418 S.W.2d 708 (Tex. Civ. App.), rev'd per curiam, 422 S.W.2d 722 (Tex. 1967).
LR: Fields v. Universal Life & Accident Ins. Co., 418 S.W.2d 708 (Tex. Civ. App.), rev'd per curiam, 422 S.W.2d 722 (Tex. 1967).

62 151 231 311 491 581   362 S.W.2d 695
Entry Indicated by Shepard's: US cert den in 373 US 922
Paul Burke, Appellant, v. State of Arkansas, Appellee (Supreme Court of Arkansas Dec. 10, 1962)
Subsequent History: 373 U.S. 922 No. 972. Burke v. Arkansas. Supreme Court of Arkansas. Certiorari denied. John W. Goodson for petitioner. May 20, 1963.
M/B: Burke v. State, 235 Ark. 882, 362 S.W.2d 695 (1962), cert. denied, 373 U.S. 922 (1963).

63 152 232 312 492 582   518 S.W.2d 207
Entry Indicated by Shepard's: US cert den in 421 US 966
State of Missouri, Plaintiff-Respondent, v. Ernest Turley, Defendant-Appellant (Missouri Court of Appeals, St. Louis District, Division One Nov. 6, 1974)
Subsequent History: 421 U.S. 966 No. 74-5955. Turley v. Missouri. ct. App. Mo., St. Louis District. Certiorari denied. May 12, 1975.
M/B: State v. Turley, 518 S.W.2d 207 (Mo. Ct. App. 1974), cert. denied, 421 U.S. 966 (1975).

64 153 233 313 493 583   520 S.W.2d 424

EXERCISE 23. SHEPARD'S CASE CITATIONS: SUBSEQUENT HISTORY   (CONTINUED)

Entry Indicated by Shepard's: US cert den in 429 US 907
In the Interest of K, a child (Court of Civil Appeals of Texas, Corpus Christi Feb. 27, 1975)
Subsequent History: 429 U.S. 907 No. 76-5114. In Re K, a Minor, by Atchley. Sup. Ct. Tex. Certiorari denied. Mr. Justice Stewart and Mr. Justice White would grant certiorari. October 18, 1976.
M/B: In re K, 520 S.W.2d 424 (Tex. Civ. App. 1975), aff'd, 535 S.W.2d 168 (Tex.), cert. denied, 429 U.S. 907 (1976).
LR: In re K, 520 S.W.2d 424 (Tex. Civ. App. 1975), aff'd, 535 S.W.2d 168 (Tex.), cert. denied, 429 U.S. 907 (1976).

65 154 234 314 494 584   337 F.2d 891
Entry Indicated by Shepard's: US cert den in 380 US 988
Nathaniel Vincent, Appellant, v. United States of America, Appellee (United States Court of Appeals Eighth Circuit Nov. 4, 1964)
Subsequent History: 380 U.S. 988 No. 1027, Misc. Vincent v. United States. C. A. 8th Cir. Certiorari denied. April 26, 1965.
M/B: Vincent v. United States, 337 F.2d 891 (8th Cir. 1964), cert. denied, 380 U.S. 988 (1965).

66 155 235 315 495 585   335 F.2d 1021
Entry Indicated by Shepard's: US cert den in 379 US 979
John Thomas Fitts, Appellant v. United States of America, Appellee (United States Court of Appeals Tenth Circuit Aug. 12, 1964)
Subsequent History: 379 U.S. 979 No. 559, Misc. Fitts v. United States. C. A. 10th Cir. Certiorari denied. January 18, 1965.
M/B: Fitts v. United States, 335 F.2d 1021 (10th Cir. 1964), cert. denied, 379 U.S. 979 (1965).

67 156 236 316 496 586   431 F.2d 1282
Entry Indicated by Shepard's: s401 US 936 a405 US 251
State of Hawaii, Plaintiff-Appellee, v. Standard Oil Company of California, Union Oil Company of California, Shell Oil Company and Dhevron Asphalt Company, Defendants-Appellants (United States Court of Appeals, Ninth Circuit Sept. 25, 1970)
Subsequent History: Affirmed Hawaii v. Standard Oil Co. of California et al. 405 U.S. 251 (March 1, 1972)
M/B: Hawaii v. Standard Oil Co., 431 F.2d 1282 (9th Cir. 1970), aff'd, 405 U.S. 251 (1972).

68 157 237 317 497 587   500 F.2d 144
Entry Indicated by Shepard's: US cert den in 420 US 907
Jane Doe et al., Plaintiffs, Appellees, v. Hale Hospital et al., Defendants, Appellants (United States Court of Appeals, First Circuit July 12, 1974)
Subsequent History: 420 U.S. 907 No. 74-289. Hale Hospital et al. v. Doe et al. C. A. 1st Cir. Certiorari denied. January 27, 1975.
M/B: Doe v. Hale Hospital, 500 F.2d 144 (1st Cir. 1974), cert. denied, 420 U.S. 907 (1975).
LR: Doe v. Hale Hosp., 500 F.2d 144 (1st Cir. 1974), cert. denied, 420 U.S. 907 (1975).

69 158 238 318 498 588   505 F.2d 426
Entry Indicated by Shepard's: s420 US 924 r423US122
United States of America v. Thomas W. Moore, Jr., Appellant (United States Court of Appeals, District of Columbia Circuit Oct. 18, 1974)
Subsequent History: Reversed same name 423 U.S. 122 (Dec. 9, 1975)
M/B: United States v. Moore, 505 F.2d 426 (D.C. Cir. 1974), rev'd, 423 U.S. 122 (1975).

70 159 239 319 499 589   320 F.2d 285
Entry Indicated by Shepard's: US reh den in 379 US 872 a378US123
Viking Theatre Corporation, Appellant, v. Paramount Film Distributing Corporation et al., Appellees (United States court of Appeals Third Circuit June 21, 1963)
Subsequent History: Judgment affirmed per curiam by an equally divided court June 15, 1964

EXERCISE 23. SHEPARD'S CASE CITATIONS: SUBSEQUENT HISTORY   (CONTINUED)

M/B: Viking Theatre Corp. v. Paramount Film Distributing Corp., 320 F.2d 285 (3d Cir. 1963), aff'd per curiam, 378 U.S. 123 (1964).
Note: "aff'd per curiam by an equally divided Court" is also correct.

71 160 240 320 500 590   317 F.2d 838
Entry Indicated by Shepard's: a377 US 426
Carl H. Borak, for and on behalf of himself and all of the other common stockholders of J. I. Case Company who are similarly situated to him, Plaitniff-Appellant, v. J. I. Case Company, a Wisconsin corporation et al., Defendants-Appellees (United States Court of Appeals Seventh Circuit May 29, 1963)
Subsequent History: Affirmed J. I. Case et al. v. Borak 377 U.S. 426 (June 8, 1964)
M/B: Borak v. J.I. Case Co., 317 F.2d 838 (7th Cir. 1963), aff'd, 377 U.S. 426 (1964).

72 161 241 321 401 591   251 F.2d 69
Entry Indicated by Shepard's: r358 US 415
Lurton Lewis Heflin, Jr., Appellant, v. United States of America, Appellee (United States Court of Appeals Fifth Circuit Jan. 24, 1958)
Subsequent History: Reversed same name 358 U.S. 415 (Febr. 24, 1959)
M/B: Heflin v. United States, 251 F.2d 69 (5th Cir. 1958), rev'd, 358 U.S. 415 (1959).

73 162 242 323 403 593   236 F.2d 708
Entry Indicated by Shepard's: r355 US 184
Everett D. Green, Appellant, v. United States of America, Appellee (United States Court of Appeals District of Columbia Court June 28, 1956)
Subsequent History: Reversed same name 355 U.S. 184 (Dec. 16, 1957)
M/B: Green v. United States, 236 F.2d 708 (D.C. Cir. 1956), rev'd, 355 U.S. 184 (1957).

74 163 243 323 403 593   65 F. Supp. 130
Entry Indicated by Shepard's: r160 F2d 1
Bowles v. Maule et al. (District court, S. D. Florida, Miami Division March 20, 1946)
Subsequent History: Porter v. Maule et al. Maule v. Porter 160 F.2d 1 (Feb. 24, 1947)
M/B: Bowles v. Maule, 65 F. Supp. 130 (S.D. Fla. 1946), rev'd sub nom. Porter v. Maule, 160 F.2d 1 (5th Cir. 1947).

75 164 244 324 404 594   76 F. Supp. 604
Entry Indicated by Shepard's: a175 F2d 698
Power Service Corporation v. Joslin (District Court, N. D. California, S.D. March 30, 1948)
Subsequent History: Affirmed same name 175 F.2d 698 (June 21, 1949)
M/B: Power Service Corp. v. Joslin, 76 F. Supp. 604 (N.D. Cal. 1948), aff'd, 175 F.2d 698 (9th Cir. 1949).
LR: Power Serv. Corp. v. Joslin, 76 F. Supp. 604 (N.D. Cal. 1948), aff'd, 175 F.2d 698 (9th Cir. 1949).

76 165 245 325 405 595   99 F. Supp. 81
Entry Indicated by Shepard's: a197 F2d 331
John Bremond Co. v. Scofield, Collector of Internal Revenue (District Court of United States, W.D. Texas, Austin D. June 1, 1951)
Subsequent History: Affirmed Scofield v. John Bremond Co. 197 F.2d 331 (Fifth Cir. 1952)
M/B: John Bremond Co. v. Scofield, 99 F. Supp. 81 (W.D. Tex. 1951), aff'd, 197 F.2d 331 (5th Cir. 1952).

77 166 246 326 406 596   100 F. Supp. 198
Entry Indicated by Shepard's: r201 F2d 521
Skinner et al. v. Rogers et al. (United States District Court N.D. Texas, Dallas Division October 2, 1951)
Subsequent History: Reversed Rogers v. Skinner 201 F.2d 521 (Fifth Circuit Jan. 29, 1953)

EXERCISE 23. SHEPARD'S CASE CITATIONS: SUBSEQUENT HISTORY   (CONTINUED)

M/B: Skinner v. Rogers, 100 F. Supp. 198 (N.D. Tex. 1951), aff'd, 201 F.2d 521 (5th Cir. 1953).

78 167 247 327 407 597   88 F. Supp. 64
Entry Indicated by Shepard's: r191 F2d 831
H. S. D. Co. v. Kavanagh, Collector of Internal Revenue (United States District Court E. D. Michigan, S. D. Sept. 30, 1949)
Subsequent History: Reversed same name 191 F.2d 831 (Sixth Circuit June 19, 1951)
M/B: H.S.D. Co. v. Kavanagh, 88 F. Supp. 64 (E.D. Mich. 1950), rev'd, 191 F.2d 831 (6th Cir. 1951).

79 168 248 328 408 598   98 F. Supp. 455
Entry Indicated by Shepard's: a202 F2d 850
C. J. Dick Towing Co. v. The Leo et al. (United States District Court, S. D. Texas, Houston Division March 12, 1951)
Subsequent History: affirmed same name 202 F.2d 850 (Fifth Circuit March 12, 1953)
M/B: C.J. Dick Towing Co. v. The Leo, 98 F. Supp. 455 (S.D. Tex. 1951), aff'd, 202 F.2d 850 (5th Cir. 1953).

80 169 249 329 409 599   111 F. Supp. 912
Entry Indicated by Shepard's: a236 F2d 744
Irwin v. United States et al. (United States District Court E. D. New York April 29, 1953)
Subsequent History: affirmed same name 236 F.2d 774 (Second Circuit Sept. 7, 1956)
M/B: Irwin v. United States, 111 F. Supp. 912 (E.D.N.Y. 1953), aff'd, 236 F.2d 774 (2d Cir. 1956).

81 170 250 330 410 600   116 F. Supp. 15
Entry Indicated by Shepard's: r216 F2d 223
United States ex rel. and for use of Tennessee Valley Authority v. Lacy (United States District Court N. D. Alabama, M. D. Oct. 21, 1953)
Subsequent History: Reversed Lacy v. United States etc. (Fifth Circuit Nov. 4, 1954)
M/B: United States ex rel. TVA v. Lacy, 116 F. Supp. 15 (N.D. Ala. 1953), rev'd, 216 F.2d 223 (5th Cir. 1954).
LR: United States ex rel. TVA v. Lacy, 116 F. Supp. 15 (N.D. Ala. 1953), rev'd, 216 F.2d 223 (5th Cir. 1954).
Note: "Tennessee Valley Authority" in the M/B citation and "Tennessee Valley Auth." in the LR citation are also correct.

82 171 251 331 411 501   119 F. Supp. 295
Entry Indicated by Shepard's: a214 F2d 187
Holt v. Middlebrook et al. (United States District Court, E. D. Virginia, Richmond Division Feb. 19, 1954)
Subsequent History: affirmed same name 214 F.2d 187 (Fourth Circuit July 13, 1954)
M/B: Holt v. Middlebrook, 119 F. Supp. 295 (E.D. Va.), aff'd, 214 F.2d 187 (4th Cir. 1954).

83 172 252 332 412 502   100 Cal. Rptr. 618
Entry Indicated by Shepard's: US cert den in 409 US 1061
The People, Plaintiff and Respondent, v. James McInnis, Defendant and Appellant (Supreme Court of California, In Bank March 23, 1972)
Subsequent History: 409 U.S. 1061 No. 72-5095. McInnis v. California. Sup. Ct. Cal. Certiorari denied. December 11, 1972.
M/B: People v. McInnis, 6 Cal. 3d 821, 494 P.2d 690, 100 Cal. Rptr. 618, cert. denied, 409 U.S. 1061 (1972).

84 173 253 333 413 503   549 F.2d 89
Entry Indicated by Shepard's: US cert den in 432 US 906
Jack D. Ringwalt, Appellant, v. United States of America, Appellee (United States Court of Appeals, Eighth Circuit Feb. 16, 1977)
Subsequent History: 432 U.S. 906 No. 76-1393. Ringwalt et al. v. United States. C.A. 8th Cir. Certiorari denied. June 20, 1977.

EXERCISE 23. SHEPARD'S CASE CITATIONS: SUBSEQUENT HISTORY   (CONTINUED)

M/B: Ringwalt v. United States, 549 F.2d 89 (8th Cir.), cert. denied, 432 U.S. 906 (1977).

85 174 254 334 414 504   125 Cal. Rptr. 265
Entry Indicated by Shepard's: v134 CaR 774
Paramount Convalescent Center, Inc., Plaintiff and Respondent, v. Department of Health Care SErvices et al., Defendants and Appellants; Department of Finance, Real Party In Interest, Appellant, 15 Cal.3d 489 (Supreme Court of California, In Bank Nov. 12, 1975)
Subsequent History: 425 U.S. 992 No. 75-1333. Paramount Convalescent Center, Inc. v. Department of Health Care Services et al. Sup. Ct. Cal. May 24, 1976.
M/B: Paramount Convalescent Center v. Department of Health Care Services, 15 Cal. 3d 489, 542 P.2d 1, 125 Cal. Rptr. 265 (1975), cert. denied, 425 U.S. 992 (1976).
LR: Paramount Convalescent Center v. Department of Health Care Servs., 15 Cal. 3d 489, 542 P.2d 1, 125 Cal. Rptr. 265 (1975), cert. denied, 425 U.S. 992 (1976).

86 175 255 335 415 505   384 F. Supp. 1231
Entry Indicated by Shepard's: r528 F2d 745
John B. King, Jr., etc., et al. v. Harris-Joyner Co., et al. (United States District Court, E. D. Virginia, Richmond Division Oct. 31, 1974)
Subsequent History: Reversed sub nom. John A. Richards, Appellee, v. Blake Builders Supply Inc., and William C. Blake, Appellants 528 F.2d 745 (Fourth Circuit Nov. 19, 1975)
M/B: King v. Harris-Joyner Co., 384 F. Supp. 1231 (E.D. Va. 1974), rev'd sub nom. Richards v. Blake Builders Supply, Inc., 528 F.2d 745 (4th Cir. 1975).

87 176 256 336 416 506   442 F. Supp. 1000
Entry Indicated by Shepard's: r586 F2d 925
Estate of Arthur K. Watson, Ann Hemingway Watson, Helen W. Buckner, Ann C. H. Watson and Jane W. Watson, as Executrices of the Will of Arthur K. Watson, Deceased, Plaintiffs, v. William E. Simon, as Secretary of the Treasury, and Hubert J. Hintgen, as Commissioner of the Bureau of Public Debt, Defendants (United States District Court, S. D. New York Oct. 28, 1977)
Subsequent History: Reversed sub nom. Estate of Arthur K. Watson etc. v. W. Michael Blumenthal, as Secretary of the Treasury, etc. 586 F.2d 925 (Second Circuit Oct. 30, 1978)
M/B: Estate of Watson v. Simon, 442 F.2d 1000 (S.D.N.Y. 1977), rev'd sub nom., Estate of Watson v. Blumenthal, 586 F.2d 925 (2d Cir. 1978).

88 177 257 337 417 507   82 Cal. Rptr. 473
Entry Indicated by Shepard's: US cert den in 398 US 909
The People, Plaintiff and Appellant, v. Kenneth T. McGrew, Defendant and Respondent, 1 Cal.3d 404, 462 P.2d 1 (Supreme Court of California, In Bank Dec. 17, 1969)
Subsequent History: 398 U.S. 909 No. 1331. California v. McGrew. Sup. Ct. Cal. Motion of respondent for leave to proceed in forma pauperis granted. Certiorari denied. May 18, 1970.
M/B: People v. McGrew, 1 Cal. 3d 404, 462 P.2d 1, 82 Cal. Rptr. 473 (1969), cert. denied, 398 U.S. 909 (1970).

89 178 258 338 418 508   67 Cal. Rptr. 409
Entry Indicated by Shepard's: US cert den in 393 US 1080
The People, Plaintiff and Respondent, v. Gerald Sesslin, Defendant and Appellant, 439 P.2d 321 (Supreme Court of California, In Bank April 10, 1968)
Subsequent History: 393 U.S. 1080 No. 372. California v. Sesslin. Sup. Ct. Cal. Certiorari denied. Thomas C. Lynch, Attorney General of California, Doris H. Maier, Assistant Attorney General, and Daniel J. Kremer, Deputy Attorney General, for petitioner. February 24, 1969.
M/B: People v. Sesslin, 68 Cal. 2d 418, 439 P.2d 321, 67 Cal. Rptr. 409 (1968), cert. denied, 393 U.S. 1080 (1969).

90 179 259 339 419 509   90 Cal. Rptr. 15
Entry Indicated by Shepard's: US cert den in 403 US 931
In re Clennon Washington King on Habeas Corpus, 474 P.2d 983, 3 Cal.3d 226 (Supreme Court of California, In Bank Oct. 2, 1970)

EXERCISE 23. SHEPARD'S CASE CITATIONS: SUBSEQUENT HISTORY   (CONTINUED)

Subsequent History: 403 U.S. 931 No. 1509. California v. King. Sup. Ct. Cal. Certiorari denied. June 21, 1971.
M/B: In re King, 3 Cal. 3d 226, 474 P.2d 983, 90 Cal. Rptr. 15 (1970), cert. denied, 403 U.S. 931 (1971).
LR: In re King, 3 Cal. 3d 226, 474 P.2d 983, 90 Cal. Rptr. 15 (1970), cert. denied, 403 U.S. 931 (1971).

91 180 260 340 420 510   42 Cal. Rptr. 169
Entry Indicated by Shepard's: US cert den in 381 US 937
The People, Plaintiff and Respondent, v. Robert B. Dorado, Defendant and Appellant, 398 P.2d 361 (Supreme Court of California, In Bank Jan. 29, 1965)
Subsequent History: 381 U.S. 946 No. 1264, Misc. Dorado v. California. Sup. Ct. Cal. Certiorari denied. William Klein for petitioner. June 1, 1965.
M/B: People v. Dorado, 62 Cal. 2d 338, 398 P.2d 361, 42 Cal. Rptr. 169, cert. denied, 381 U.S. 946 (1965).

92 181 261 341 421 511   258 N.Y.S.2d 109
Entry Indicated by Shepard's: US cert den in 382 US 947
The People, etc., Respondent, v. Moran Tyson, Appellant, 15 N.Y.2d 866 (Court of Appeals of New York March 11, 1965)
Subsequent History: 382 U.S. 947 No. 647, Misc. Tyson v. New York. Ct. App. N.Y. Certiorari denied. Robert M. Hitchcock for petitioner. Michael F. Dillon for respondent. December 6, 1965.
M/B: People v. Tyson, 15 N.Y.2d 866, 206 N.E.2d 196, 258 N.Y.S.2d 109, cert. denied, 382 U.S. 947 (1965).

93 182 262 342 422 512   175 N.Y.S.2d 794
Entry Indicated by Shepard's: r189 S2d 911
International Firearms Co. Ltd., Plaintiff-Appellant, v. Kingston Trust Company, Defendant-Respondent, 6 A.D.2d 171 (Supreme Court, Appellate Division, Third Department July 3, 1958)
Subsequent History: Affirmed same name 6 N.Y.2d 406 (Court of Appeals of New York July 8, 1959)
M/B: International Firearms Co. v. Kingston Trust Co., 6 A.D.2d 171, 175 N.Y.S.2d 794 (1958), rev'd, 6 N.Y.2d 406, 160 N.E.2d 656, 189 N.Y.S.2d 911 (1959).

94 183 263 343 423 513   264 N.Y.S.2d 557
Entry Indicated by Shepard's: US cet den in 383 US 952
The People, etc., Respondent, v. Carlo Tornetto, Appellant, 16 N.Y.2d 902 (Court of Appeals of New York Oct. 21, 1965)
Subsequent History: 383 U.S. 952 No. 1172, Misc. Tornetto v. New York. Ct. App. N.Y. Certiorari denied. March 21, 1966.
M/B: People v. Tornetto, 16 N.Y.2d 902, 212 N.E.2d 63, 264 N.Y.S.2d 557 (1965), cert. denied, 383 U.S. 952 (1966).

95 184 264 344 424 514   265 N.Y.S.2d 899
Entry Indicated by Shepard's: US cert den in 383 US 945
In the Matter of Louis Fried, Appellant, v. Brooklyn Bar Association, Respondent, 16 N.Y.2d 1014 (Court of Appeals of New York Nov. 24, 1965)
Subsequent History: 383 U.S. 945 No. 986. Fried v. Brooklyn Bar Association. Ct. App. N.Y. Certiorari denied. Petitioner pro se. Benjamin R. Raphael for respondent. March 21, 1966.
M/B: Fried v. Brooklyn Bar Association, 16 N.Y.2d 1014, 213 N.E.2d 310, 265 N.Y.S.2d 899 (1965), cert. denied, 383 U.S. 945 (1966).
LR: Fried v. Brooklyn Bar Ass'n, 16 N.Y.2d 1014, 213 N.E.2d 310, 265 N.Y.S.2d 899 (1965), cert. denied, 383 U.S. 945 (1966).

96 185 265 345 425 515   386 N.Y.S.2d 691
Entry Indicated by Shepard's: US cert den in 430 US 948
The People of the State of New York, Respondent, v. Melvin Murray, Appellant, 353 N.E.2d 605, 40 N.Y.2d 327 (Court of Appeals of New York July 13, 1976)
Subsequent History: 430 U.S. 948 No. 76-6010. Murray v. New York. Ct. App. N. Y. Certiorari denied. March 28, 1977.
M/B: People v. Murray, 40 N.Y.2d 327, 353 N.E.2d 605, 386 N.Y.S.2d 691 (1976), cert. denied, 430 U.S. 948 (1977).

EXERCISE 23. SHEPARD'S CASE CITATIONS: SUBSEQUENT HISTORY   (CONTINUED)

97 186 266 346 426 516   383 N.Y.S.2d 573
Entry Indicated by Shepard's: a432 US 197
The People of the State of New York, Respondent, v. Gordon G. Patterson, Appellant, 347 N.E.2d 898, 39 N.Y.2d 288 (Court of Appeals of New York April 1, 1976)
Subsequent History: Affirmed Patterson v. New York 432 U.S. 197 (June 17, 1977)
M/B: People v. Patterson, 39 N.Y.2d 288, 347 N.E.2d 898, 383 N.Y.S.2d 573 (1976), aff'd, 432 U.S. 197 (1977).

98 187 267 347 427 517   255 N.Y.S.2d 833
Entry Indicated by Shepard's: US cert den in 380 US 936
The People of the State of New York, Respondent, v. Burton N. Pugach, Appellant, 15 N.Y.2d 65 (Court of Appeals of New York Dec. 3, 1964)
Subsequent History: 380 U.S. 936 No. 811, Misc. Pugach v. New York. Ct. App. N.Y. Certiorari denied. March 8, 1965.
M/B: People v. Pugach, 15 N.Y.2d 65, 204 N.E.2d 176, 255 N.Y.S.2d 833 (1964), cert. denied, 380 U.S. 936 (1965).

99 188 268 348 428 518   228 N.Y.S.2d 641
Entry Indicated by Shepard's: a236 S2d 33
John William Vander, Appellant, v. John E. Casperson and Ray J. Boorman, Respondent, 16 A.D.2d 881 (Supreme Court, Appellate Division, Fourth Department May 18, 1962)
Subsequent History: Affirmed same name 12 N.Y.2d 33 (Court of Appeals of New York Dec. 6, 1962)
M/B: Vander v. Casperson, 16 A.D.2d 881, 228 N.Y.S.2d 641, aff'd, 12 N.Y.2d 56, 187 N.E.2d 109, 236 N.Y.S.2d 33 (1962).

100 189 269 349 429 519   282 N.Y.S.2d 491
Entry Indicated by Shepard's: r394 US 576
The People of the State of New York, Respondent, v. Sidney Street, Appellant, 20 N.Y.2d 231 (Court of Appeals of New York July 7, 1967)
Subsequent History: Reversed Street v. New York 394 U.S. 576 (April 21, 1969)
M/B: People v. Street, 20 N.Y.2d 231, 299 N.E.2d 187, 282 N.Y.S.2d 491 (1967), rev'd, 394 U.S. 576 (1969).

LIBRARY EXERCISE 24. SHEPARD'S CASE CITATIONS: SUBSEQUENT TREATMENT.

INSTRUCTOR'S NOTE: (a) Using the appropriate Shepard's Citations volume[s], students are required to find and cite the first case listed in Shepard's Citations that has treated the case identified below in the manner noted. Students are warned to be sure to begin their search with the volume of Shepard's Citations in which the case first appeared. Students are informed that they may have to check later Shepard's volumes or paper-bound supplements in order to find the required entry. They are also informed that Shepard's cites the page of treatment, not the beginning page of the case that you will be citing. If there is no entry in Shepard's treating the case in the manner noted, students are instructed to answer "none." If they do so, they are incorrect because each of the problem involves a situation in which subsequent treatment has occurred.

(b) The students are required to state headnote number to which the cited treatment in part (a) refers? If no headnote is specifically treated, they are instructed to answer "none."

1 190 270 350 430 520   91 A.2d 428   Followed
Subsequent Treatment Indicated by Shepard's: f137A2d^{1}433
State of New Jersey, Plaintiff-Respondent, v. Harry W. Craig, Defendant-Appellant 48 N.J. Super. 276 Superior Court of New Jersey, Appellate Division (Jan. 10, 1958)
(a) M/B: State v. Craig, 48 N.J. Super. 276, 137 A.2d 430 (App. Div. 1958).
(b) Headnote 1

2 191 271 351 431 521   588 F.2d 319   Distinguished
Subsequent Treatment Indicated by Shepard's: d470FS^{3}1014
James Peck, Plaintiff, v. The United States of America, Thomas J. Jenkins, Associate Director of the Federal Bureau of Investigation, Barrett G. Kemp, and Four Unknown Agent of the Federal Bureau of Investigation, Defendants. United States District Court, S.D. New York. (April 25, 1979)
(a) M/B: Peck v. United States, 470 F. Supp. 1003 (S.D.N.Y. 1979).
(b) Headnote 3

3 192 272 352 432 522   47 A. 579   Distinguished
Subsequent Treatment Indicated by Shepard's:d170FS^{3}279
Audrey Chittick, Subrogee of Charles Williams, Plaintiff v. State Farm Mutual Automobile Insurance Company, a Corporation of the State of Illinois, Defendant United States District Court D. Delaware (December 19, 1958)
(a) M/B: Chittick v. State Farm Mutual Automobile Insurance Co., 170 F. Supp. 276 (D. Del. 1958).
     LR: Chittick v. State Farm Mut. Auto. Ins. Co., 170 F. Supp. 276 (D. Del. 1958).
(b) Headnote 3

4 193 273 353 433 523   74 A. 1051   Distinguished
Subsequent Treatment Indicated by Shepard's: d157FS^{3}263
Roy J. Martin v. Continental Casualty Company, an Illinois Corporation. United States District Court S.D. Mississippi Jackson Div. (December 10, 1957)
(a) M/B: Martin v. Continental Casualty Co., 157 F. Supp. 259 (S.D. Miss. 1957).
(b) Headnote 3

5 194 274 354 434 524   51 A.2d 19   Distinguished
Subsequent Treatment Indicated by Shepard's: d172A2d^{7}24
Peter N. Paull, Julius Kaunacki and William Troutman, Plaintiffs v. Alfred R. Pierce, Director of the Department of Public Safety of the City of Camden, Joseph Hooven, Howard Clayton, Vincent Conley, Samuel Saunders, Roland Comerford, William Kelly, Edward Watson, William H. Neale, John W. Watkins, William Yeager, Stanley Zuchowiez, and George Weber, Defendants Superior Court of New Jersey Law Div. (June 30, 1961)
(a) M/B: Paull v. Pierce, 68 N.J. Super. 521, 172 A.2d 721 (Law Div. 1961).
(b) None

6 195 275 355 435 525   90 A. 677   Distinguished
Subsequent Treatment Indicated by Shepard's: d316f2d^{1}41

EXERCISE 24. SHEPARD'S CASE CITATIONS: SUBSEQUENT TREATMENT   (CONTINUED)

Clifford Barney (Plaintiff), Appellant in No. 14,043 v. The Staten Island
Rapid Transit Railway Company, a Corporation (Defendant). United States Court
of Appeals Third Circuit April 8, 1963
(a)   M/B: Barney v. Staten Island Rapid Transit Railway, 316 F.2d 38 (3d Cir.
1963).
      LR: Barney v. Staten Island Rapid Transit Ry., 316 F.2d 38 (3d Cir.
1963).
(b)   Headnote 1

7 196 276 356 436 526   103 A. 511   Explained
Subsequent Treatment Indicated by Shepard's: e387F^{1}1559 Agnes Haldeman v. The
Bell Telephone Company of Pennsylvania and W. Herbert Fry v. Mary K.
Wilkinson, Appellant United States Court of Appeals Third Circuit (December 7,
1967)
(a)   M/B: Haldeman v. Bell Telephone Co., 387 F.2d 557 (3d Cir. 1967).
      LR: Haldeman v. Bell Tel. Co., 387 F.2d 557 (3d Cir. 1967).
(b)   Headnote 1

8 197 277 357 437 527   126 A. 224   Explained
Subsequent Treatment Indicated by Shepard's: e151FS^{6}99
United States of America and the Western National Bank of Baltimore and Arthur
H. Doll, Trustee, and George Norrish and Louise Browning, Intervenors v.
Eastern Woodworks, Inc. (United States District Court D. Maryland (May 7,
1957)
(a)   M/B: United States v. Eastern Woodworks, 151 F. Supp. 95 (D. Md. 1957).
(b)   Headnote 6

9 198 278 358 438 528   162 A. 441   Questioned
Subsequent Treatment Indicated by Shepard's: q246FS^{5}1019
Charles W. Patton, Jr. v. Fiedelity-Philadelphia Trust Co. United States
District Court E.D. Pennsylvania (October 27, 1965)
(a)   M/B: Patton v. Fidelity-Philadelphia Trust Co., 246 F. Supp. 1015 (E.D.
Pa. 1965).
(b)   Headnote 5

10 199 279 359 439 529   267 A.2d 481   Distinguished
Subsequent Treatment Indicated by Shepard's: d278Ad^{2}01
Gerald P. Darrow and herma Darrow, Plaintiff-Appellants, v. Hanover Township,
a municipal corporation, Defendant-Respondent, and The County of Morris,
Defendant. Supreme Court of NEw Jersey (June 7, 1971)
(a)   M/B: Darrow v. Hanover Township, 58 N.J. 410, 278 A.2d 200 (1971).
(b)   Headnote 2

11 200 280 360 440 530   454 P.2d 993   Distinguished
Subsequent Treatment Indicated by Shepard's: dd533P2d^{4}670
The State of Arizona, Appellee v. Manuel Robert Ramirez, Appellant Supreme
Court of Arizona (March 31, 1975)
(a)   M/B: State v. Ramirez, 111 Ariz. 498, 533 P.2d 665 (1975).
(b)   Headnote 4

12 101 281 361 441 531   460 P.2d 578   Followed
Subsequent Treatment Indicated by Shepard's: f450F2d^{4}259
Misco Leasing, Inc., Plaintiff Appellant, v. James H. Vaughn et al.,
Defendants Appellee United States Court of Appeals (October 26, 1971)
(a)   M/B: Misco Leasing, Inc. v. Vaughn, 450 F.2d 257 (10th Cir. 1971).
(b)   Headnote 4

13 102 282 362 442 532   454 P.2d 987   Distinguished
Subsequent Treatment Indicated by Shepard's: d492P2d^{1}37
The State of Arizona, Appellee, v. William Greer, Appellant Court of Appeals
of Arizona (December 30, 1971)
(a)   M/B: State v. Greer, 16 Ariz. App. 156, 492 P.2d 36 (1971).
(b)   Headnote 1

14 103 283 363 443 533   244 P. 343   Distinguished
Subsequent Treatment Indicated by Shepard's: d486F2d^{6}411

EXERCISE 24. SHEPARD'S CASE CITATIONS: SUBSEQUENT TREATMENT   (CONTINUED)

John J. Donnelly, Petitioner, v. Honorable Barrington D. Parker et al., Respondents United States Court of Appeals District of Columbia Circuit (August 21, 1973)
(a)   M/B: Donnelly v. Parker, 486 F.2d 402 (D.C. Cir. 1973).
(b)   Headnote 6

15 104 284 364 444 534   206 P. 178   Questioned
Subsequent Treatment Indicated by Shepard's: q195FS^{9}172
W. Lynn Roberts, doing business as Roberts aircraft Company, Plaintiff, v. Underwriters at Lloyds London, an unincorporated association of individuals, and Haidinger-Hayes, Inc., a corporation, Defendants United States District Court D. Idaho, S.D. (June 12, 1961)
(a)   M/B: Roberts v. Underwriters at Lloyds London, 195 F. Supp. 168 (D. Idaho 1961).
(b)   Headnote 9

16 105 285 365 445 535   199 P. 396   Distinguished
Subsequent Treatment Indicated by Shepard's: d352F2d^{4}136
Grand River Dam Authority, a body corporate, Appellant, v. National Gypsum Company, a corporation, Appellee United States Court of Appeals (October 6, 1965)
(a)   M/B: Grand River Dam Authority v. National Gypsum Co., 352 F.2d 130 (10th Cir. 1965).
      LR: Grand River Dam Auth. v. National Gypsum Co., 352 F.2d 130 (10th Cir. 1965).
(b)   Headnote 4

17 106 286 366 446 536   117 P.2d 707   Distinguished
Subsequent Treatment Indicated by Shepard's: d129CaR^{6}386
Chad Hazelwood, a minor, v. Earl B. Hazelwood et al., Plaintiffs and Appellants, v. George W. White et al., Defendants. Court of Appeal, First District Div. 4 (June 24, 1976)
(a)   M/B: Hazelwood v. Hazelwood, 57 Cal. App. 3d 693, 129 Cal. Rptr. 384 (1976).
(b)   Headnote 6

18 107 287 367 447 537   52 P. 944   Distinguished
Subsequent Treatment Indicated by Shepard's: d438F2d^{3}1102
Eugene C. Mullendore, Linda V. Mullendore, Special Administratrix of the Estate of E.C. Mullendore, III, and Kathleen B. Mullendore, Appellants, v. Sohio Petroleum Company, a corporation Joseph E. Seagram & Sons, Inc., and Layton Oil Company, Inc., Appellees United States Court of Appeals (March 2, 1971)
(a)   M/B: Mullendore v. Sohio Petroleum Co., 438 F.2d 1099 (10th Cir. 1971).
(b)   Headnote 3

19 108 288 368 448 538   47 P. 521   Distinguished
Subsequent Treatment Indicated by Shepard's: d85FS^{1}184
La Prelle v. Cessna Aircraft Co. United States District Court D. Kansas, Second Div. (August 1, 1949)
(a)   M/B: La Prelle v. Cessna Aircraft Co., 85 F. Supp. 182 (D. Kan. 1949).
(b)   Headnote 1

20 109 289 369 449 539   29 N.E. 517   Criticized
Subsequent Treatment Indicated by Shepard's: c385US^{1}409
Garrity v. New Jersey Appeal from the Supreme Court of New Jersey (January 16, 1967)
(a)   M/B: Garrity v. New Jersey, 385 U.S. 493 (1967).
(b)   Headnote 1

21 110 290 370 450 540   64 N.E. 442   Criticized
Subsequent Treatment Indicated by Shepard's: c126FS^{1}148
Albert Ettore, Plaintiff, v. Philco Television Broadcasting Corporation and Chesebrough Manufacturing Company, Consolidated, Defendants United States District Court E.D. Pennsylvania (November 23, 1954)
(a)   M/B: Ettore v. Philco Television Broadcasting Corp., 126 F. Supp. 143 (E.D. Pa. 1954).

EXERCISE 24. SHEPARD'S CASE CITATIONS: SUBSEQUENT TREATMENT   (CONTINUED)

(b)   Headnote 1

22 111 291 371 451 541   33 N.E. 746   Distinguished
Subsequent Treatment Indicated by Shepard's: d60N^{2}2460
Leonard et al. v. Autocar Sales & Service Co. Appellate Court of Illinois.
First District Third Div. (March 21, 1945)
(a)   M/B: Leonard v. Autocar Sales & Service Co., 325 Ill. App. 375, 60
N.E.2d 457 (1945).
      LR: Leonard v. Autocar Sales & Serv. Co., 325 Ill. App. 375, 60 N.E.2d
457 (1945).
(b)   Headnote 2

23 112 292 372 452 542   33 N.E. 1054   Explained
Subsequent Treatment Indicated by Shepard's: e387FS^{2}1147
George P. Baker et al., Trustees of the Property of Penn Central
Transportation Company, Plaintiffs, v. National City Bank of Cleveland,
Defendant United States District Court, N.D. Ohio, E.D. (June 12, 1974)
(a)   M/B: Baker v. National City Bank, 387 F. Supp. 1137 (N.D. Ohio 1974).
(b)   Headnote 2

24 113 293 373 453 543   63 N.E. 110   Criticized
Subsequent Treatment Indicated by Shepard's: c176FS88
Hartford Accident and Indemnity Company, a Corporation, Plaintiff, v. Village
of Milan, a Municipal Corporation, Defendant United States District Court S.D.
Illinois, N.D. (August 6, 1959)
(a)   M/B: Hartford Accident & Indemnity Co. v. Village of Milan, 176 F. Supp.
84 (S.D. Ill. 1959).
      LR: Hartford Accident & Indem. Co. v. Village of Milan, 176 F. Supp. 84
(S.D. Ill. 1959).
(b)   None

25 114 294 374 454 544   153 N.E.2d 563   Explained
Subsequent Treatment Indicated by Shepard's: e341NE2d^{9}411
The people of the State of Illinois, Plaintiff-Appellee, v. David Lynn Giles,
Defendant-Appellant Appellate Court of Illinois (January 29, 1976)
(a)   M/B: People v. Giles, 35 Ill. App. 3d 514, 341 N.E.2d 410 (1976).
(b)   Headnote 9

26 115 295 375 455 545   204 N.E.2d 842   Questioned
Subsequent Treatment Indicated by Shepard's: q363S2d792
The People of the State of New York v. Frank Cassidy Supreme Court, Criminal
Term, Kings County (January 30, 1975)
(a)   M/B: People v. Cassidy, 80 Misc. 2d 713, 363 N.Y.S.2d 788 (Sup. Ct.
1975).
(b)   None

27 116 296 376 456 546   212 N.E.2d 279   Questioned
Subsequent Treatment Indicated by Shepard's: q342NE2d^{1}471
Emily M. Dezort, Administratrix of the Estate of Frank J. Dezort, Jr.,
Deceased, Plaintiff-Appellant v. Village of Hinsdale, a Municipal Corporation,
et al, Defendantis-Appellees Appellate Court of Illinois Second District,
First Div. (February 6, 1976)
(a)   M/B: Dezort v. Village of Hinsdale, 35 Ill. App. 3d 703, 342 N.E.2d 468
(1976).
(b)   Headnote 1

28 117 297 377 457 547   273 N.E.2d 592   Explained
Subsequent Treatment Indicated by Shepard's: e310NE2d^{2}846
Lincoln National Bank et al., Plaintiff-Appellants v. P.J. Cullerton et al.,
Defendants Appellees Appellate Court of Illinois First District, First Div.
(April 1, 1974)
(a)   M/B: Lincoln National Bank v. Cullerton, 18 Ill. App. 3d 953, 310 N.E.2d
845 (1974).
      LR: Lincoln Nat'l Bank v. Cullerton, 18 Ill. App. 3d 953, 310 N.E.2d 845
(1974).
(b)   Headnote 2

EXERCISE 24. SHEPARD'S CASE CITATIONS: SUBSEQUENT TREATMENT   (CONTINUED)

29 118 298 378 458 548   99 So. 716   Explained
Subsequent Treatment Indicated by Shepard's: e133FS^{1}167
Harmon Whittington, Charles F. Reed and W. Paul Edman, dM/B:bM/B:a Mid-Century
Oil & Gas Company and A.B. Dow v. Garvis I. Bazemore, C.T. Ruffin and Goodwyn
H. Harris, Jr. United States District Court W.D. Louisiana, Shreveport
Division (July 11, 1955)
(a) M/B: Whittington v. Bazemore, 133 F. Supp. 163 (W.D. La. 1955).
(b) Headnote 1

30 119 299 379 459 549   99 So. 27   Followed
Subsequent Treatment Indicated by Shepard's: f173So^{1}135
Mitcham et al. v. Mitcham et al. Supreme Court of Louisiana. (March 1, 1937)
(a) M/B: Mitcham v. Mitcham, 186 La. 641, 173 So. 132 (1937).
(b) Headnote 1

31 120 300 380 460 550   11 So. 2d 225   Limited
Subsequent Treatment Indicated by Shepard's: L19So2d^{1}348
Lunkin v. Triangle Farms, Inc. Court of Appeal of Louisiana (October 3, 1944)
(a) M/B: Lunkin v. Triangle Farms, 19 So. 2d 345 (La. Ct. App. 1944).
(b) Headnote 1

32 121 201 381 461 551   104 F.2d 837   Harmonized
Subsequent Treatment Indicated by Shepard's: h127F2d^{2}770
In re Imperial Brewing Co. (First case listed, consolidated with) Hamburger v.
International Harvester Co. Circuit Court of Appeals, Fourth Circuit (April
22, 1942)
(a) M/B: In re Imperial Brewing Co., 127 F.2d 766 (4th Cir. 1942).
     LR: In re Imperial Brewing Co., 127 F.2d 766 (4th Cir. 1942).
(b) Headnote 2

33 122 202 382 462 552   161 F.2d 636   Questioned
Subsequent Treatment Indicated by Shepard's: q239F2d^{4}434
The California Oregon Power Company, a Corporation Petitioner v. Federal Power
Commission Respondent United States Court of Appeals District of Columbia
(October 25, 1956)
(a) M/B: California Oregon Power Co. v. FPC, 239 F.2d 426 (D.C. Cir. 1956).
     LR: California Or. Power Co. v. FPC, 239 F.2d 426 (D.C. Cir. 1956).
(b) Headnote 4

34 123 203 383 463 553   516 F.2d 411   Explained
Subsequent Treatment Indicated by Shepard's: e423FS^{1}396
Wiley L. Bolden et al., Plaintiffs, v. City of Mobile, Alabama, et al.,
Defendats United States District Court S.D. Alabama, S. D. (October 28,1976)
(a) M/B: Bolden v. City of Mobile, 423 F. Supp. 384 (S.D. Ala. 1976).
(b) Headnote 1

35 124 204 384 464 554   512 F.2d 527   Questioned
Subsequent Treatment Indicated by Shepard's: q539F2d174
Arthur C. Kappelmann et al., Appellants v. Delta Air Lines, Inc., a
corporation, et al United States Court of Appeals, District of Columbia
Circuit (April 16, 1976)
(a) M/B: Kappelmann v. Delta Air Lines, 539 F.2d 165 (D.C. Cir. 1976).
(b) None

36 125 205 385 465 555   495 F.2d 1026   Criticized
Subsequent Treatment Indicated by Shepard's: c512F2d^{11}1353
Natural Resources Defense Council, Inc., et al., Petitioners, v. Environmental
Protection Agency, Respondent Unites States Court of Appeals District of
Columbia (June 24, 1975)
(a) M/B: Natural Resources Defense Council, Inc. v. EPA, 512 F.2d 1351 (D.C.
Cir. 1975).
Note: "Inc." may be omitted after "Council."
(b) Headnote 11

37 126 206 386 466 556   281 F. 744   Followed
Subsequent Treatment Indicated by Shepard's: f562F2d^{2}760

EXERCISE 24. SHEPARD'S CASE CITATIONS: SUBSEQUENT TREATMENT   (CONTINUED)

Warner-Lambert Company, Petitioner, v. Federal Trade Commission, Respondent
United States Court of Appeals, District of Columbia Circuit Aug. 2, 1977
(a)   M/B: Warner-Lambert Co. v. F.T.C., 562 F.2d 760 (D.C. Cir. 1977).
(b)   Headnote 2

38 127 207 387 467 557   112 N.W. 748   Distinguished
Subsequent Treatment Indicated by Shepard's: d129NW2d442
John C. Ernst, Petitioner, v. Martin Flynn and May Flynn, his wife,
Respondents in the matter of the Custody of Gerri Ernest, a Minor Supreme
Court of Michigan (July 9, 1964)
(a)   M/B: Ernst v. Flynn, 373 Mich. 337, 129 N.W.2d 430 (1964).
(b)   None

39 128 208 388 468 558   99 N.W. 395   Distinguished
Subsequent Treatment Indicated by Shepard's: d259FS^{1}615
National Acceptance Company of America, a Delaware corporation, Plaintiff and
Cross Defendant, v. Henry C. Mardigian, Barbara J. Mardigian, Stephen Domebek
and Annie Dombek , Defendants and Cross Defendants United States District
Court E.D. Michigan, S.D. (September 30, 1966)
(a)   M/B: National Acceptance Co. of America v. Mardigian, 259 F. Supp. 612
(E.D. Mich. 1966).
      LR: National Acceptance Co. of Am. v. Mardigian, 259 F. Supp. 612 (E.D.
Mich. 1966).
(b)   Headnote 1

40 129 209 389 469 559   103 N.W. 137   Questioned
Subsequent Treatment Indicated by Shepard's: q414F2d54
Gale H. Johnson, Appellant, v. John E. Bennett, Warden, Iowa State
Penitentiary, Appellee United States Court of Appeals (July 17, 1969)
(a)   M/B: Johnson v. Bennett, 414 F.2d 50 (8th Cir. 1969).
(b)   None

41 130 210 390 470 560   165 N.W. 297   Questioned
Subsequent Treatment Indicated by Shepard's: q64NW2d^{1}831
Dane County v. Bloomfield, Supreme Court of Wisconsin (June 8, 1954)
(a)   M/B: Dane County v. Bloomfield, 267 Wis. 193, 64 N.W.2d 829 (1954).
(b)   Headnote 1

42 131 211 391 471 561   109 N.W. 744   Explained
Subsequent Treatment Indicated by Shepard's: e433FS63
United States v. Roy Tibbals Wilson et al. United States District Court, N.D.
Iowa, W.D. (May 4, 1977)
(a)   M/B: United States v. Wilson, 433 F. Supp. 57 (N.D. Iowa 1977).
(b)   None

43 132 212 392 472 562   181 N.W. 135   Explained
Subsequent Treatment Indicated by Shepard's: e192F2d^{2}884
Ford et al. v. Luria Steel & Trading Corp United States Court of Appeals
(December 3, 1951)
(a)   M/B: Ford v. Luria Steel & Trading Corp., 192 F.2d 880 (8th Cir. 1951).
(b)   Headnote 2

44 133 213 393 473 563   113 N.W. 858   Questioned
Subsequent Treatment Indicated by Shepard's: q186FS^{7}359
United States of America, Plaintiff, v. Ben Tholen and Annie N. Tholen,
Defendants United States District Court N.D. Iowa (August 24, 1960)
(a)   M/B: United States v. Tholen, 186 F. Supp. 346 (N.D. Iowa 1960).
(b)   Headnote 7

45 134 214 394 474 564   235 N.W. 185   Overruled
Subsequent Treatment Indicated by Shepard's: o212NW2d^{5}193
People of the State of Michigan, Plaintiff-Appellee, v. Ned Ladd Bobo,
Defendant-Appellant Supreme Court of Michigan (November 21, 1973)
(a)   M/B: People v. Bobo, 390 Mich. 355, 212 N.W.2d 190 (1973).
(b)   Headnote 5

46 135 215 395 475 565   252 N.W. 650   Distinguished

EXERCISE 24. SHEPARD'S CASE CITATIONS: SUBSEQUENT TREATMENT   (CONTINUED)

Subsequent Treatment Indicated by Shepard's: d153FS^{10}648
Seaboard Surety ompany, a corporation, Plaintiff, v. (1) H & R Construction Corporation, a Minnesota corporation: (2) H.H. Rohr; (3) H.C. Nelson and Sidney A. Nelson, doing business as H.C. Nelson Investment Co.; (4) H & R Construction Corporation, a Minneosta corporation, and H.C. Nelson Investment Co., co-partners doing business under the firm name and style of H & E. Construction Corporation; (5) State of Minnesota, acting by and through M.J. Hoffman, its Commissioner of Highways; (6) Fred E. Trippl (7) The First National Bank of Saint Paul, Minnesota; (8) The Lummus Company, a Delaware corporation; (9) Woodrich Construction Co,. a Minnesota corporation; (10) Rosholt Equipment Co., a Minnesota corporation; (11) The George T. Ryan Company, a Minnesota corporation; (12) Wm. H. Ziegler Co., Inc., A Minnesota corporation; (13) Rocket Transfer, Inc., A minneosota corporation and John Doe, Richard Roe, Jane Doe, and all other persons, firms and corporations, bureaus, agencies, authorities or other agencies who have or claim to have any right or claim under the within mentioned payment bonds, or any of them, or against plaintiff by reason thereof, or against the within mentioned unpaid contract balances, or any of them, Defendants.
(a)   M/B: Seaboard Surety Co. v. H & R Construction Corp., 153 F. Supp. 641 (D. Minn. 1957).
         LR: Seaboard Sur. Co. v. H & R Constr. Corp., 153 F. Supp. 641 (D. Minn. 1957).
(b)   Headnote 10

47 136 216 396 476 566   86 S.E. 552   Distinguished
Subsequent Treatment Indicated by Shepard's: d118SE2d^{3}90
O. Violas Mitchell, Ex'r v. State Highway Department of Georgia , Supreme Court of Georgia (January 5, 1961)
(a)   M/B: Mitchell v. State Highway Department, 216 Ga. 517, 118 S.E.2d 88 (1961).
         LR: Mitchell v. State Highway Dep't, 216 Ga. 517, 118 S.E.2d 88 (1961).
(b)   Headnote 3

48 137 217 397 477 567   86 S.E. 340   Questioned
Subsequent Treatment Indicated by Shepard's: q86SE2d^{1}418
P.M. Reid v. W.A. Bristol and Mabel L. Bristol Supreme Court of North Carolina (March 23, 1955)
(a)   M/B: Reid v. Bristol, 241 N.C. 699, 86 S.E.2d 417 (1955).
(b)   Headnote 1

49 138 218 398 478 568   79 S.E. 806   Distinguished
Subsequent Treatment Indicated by Shepard's: d254FS^{2}1021
Kathryn S. Wright v. Pilot Life Insurance Company, Inc. United States District Court (September 14, 1966)
(a)   M/B: Wright v. Pilot Life Insurance Co., 254 F. Supp. 1018 (W.D. Va. 1966).
         LR: Wright v. Pilot Life Ins. Co., 254 F. Supp. 1018 (W.D. Va. 1966).
(b)   Headnote 2

50 139 219 399 479 569   23 S.E. 784   Questioned
Subsequent Treatment Indicated by Shepard's: q94SE2d^{1}247
Raymond Thomas Council v. Commonwealth of Virginia Supreme Court of Appeal of Virginia (September 4, 1956)
(a)   M/B: Council v. Commonwealth, 198 Va. 288, 94 S.E.2d 245 (1956).
(b)   Headnote 1

51 140 220 400 480 570   17 S.E. 812   Criticized
Subsequent Treatment Indicated by Shepard's: c296F2d^{12}159
United States of America, Appellee, v. Clarence Samuel Beach, Appellant United States Court of Appeals (November 10, 1961)
(a)   M/B: United States v. Beach, 296 F.2d 153 (4th Cir. 1961).
(b)   Headnote 12

52 141 221 301 481 571   81 S.E. 418   Distinguished
Subsequent Treatment Indicated by Shepard's: d250F2d^{3}761
Saint Paul Mercury Indemnity Company, Appellant, v. Wright Contracting Company, Appellee United States Court of Appeals (January 6, 1958)

EXERCISE 24. SHEPARD'S CASE CITATIONS: SUBSEQUENT TREATMENT   (CONTINUED)

(a) M/B: Saint Paul Mercury Indemnity Co. v. Wright Contracting Co., 250 F.2d 758 (4th Cir. 1958).
   LR: Saint Paul Mercury Indem. Co. v. Wright Contracting Co., 250 F.2d 758 (4th Cir. 1958).
(b) Headnote 3

53 142 222 302 482 572   399 F. Supp. 208   Followed
Subsequent Treatment Indicated by Shepard's: 415FS^{7}146
Mont Vernon Preservation Society v. John A. Clements, as New Hampshire Highway Commissioner, et al United States District Court, D. New Hampshire (May 17, 1976)
(a) M/B: Mont Vernon Preservation Society v. Clements, 415 F. Supp. 141 (D.N.H. 1976).
   LR: Mont Vernon Preservation Soc'y v. Clements, 415 F. Supp. 141 (D.N.H. 1976).
(b) Headnote 7

54 143 223 303 483 573   122 S.E. 327   Harmonized
Subsequent Treatment Indicated by Shepard's: h121SE2d^{8}310
Setzers Super Stores of Georgia, Inc. v. Mrs. Winnie Higgins Court Appeals of Georgia (June 9, 1961)
(a) M/B: Setzers Super Stores v. Higgins, 104 Ga. App. 116, 121 S.E.2d 305 (1961).
(b) Headnote 8

55 144 224 304 484 574   84 S.E. 69   Explained
Subsequent Treatment Indicated by Shepard's: e378F2d^{6}711
Har-Pen Truck Lines, Inc. et al., Appellants, v. Frederick Allen Mills, III, et al Appellees United States Court of Appeals (July 6, 1967)
(a) M/B: Har-Pen Truck Lines v. Mills, 378 F.2d 705 (5th Cir. 1967).
(b) Headnote 6

56 145 225 305 485 575   180 S.W. 663   Questioned
Subsequent Treatment Indicated by Shepard's: q370FS^{1}1234
Akron Canton & Youngstown Railroad Company, et al. Plaintiffs, and Freight Forwarders Tariff Bureau, Inc. et al., Intervening Plaintiffs v. United States of America United States District Court D. Maryland (January 14, 1974)
(a) M/B: Akron, Canton & Youngstown Railroad v. United States, 370 F. Supp. 1231 (D. Md. 1974).
   LR: Akron, C. & Y.R.R. v. United States, 370 F. Supp. 1231 (D. Md. 1974).
(b) Headnote 1

57 146 226 306 486 576   180 S.W. 839   Explained
Subsequent Treatment Indicated by Shepard's: e138FS^{1}815
United States of America v. Martin Solow, Defendant United States District Court S. D. New York (February 17, 1956)
(a) M/B: United States v. Solow, 138 F. Supp. 812 (S.D.N.Y. 1956).
(b) Headnote 1

58 147 227 307 487 577   63 S.W. 624   Questioned
Subsequent Treatment Indicated by Shepard's: q304SW2d^{2}177
Nell D. Cox, Appellant, v. Wilma C. Cox, Appellee Court of Civil Appeals of Texas (May 23, 1957)
(a) M/B: Cox v. Cox, 203 S.W.2d 175 (Tex. Civ. App. 1957).
(b) Headnote 2

59 148 228 308 488 578   80 S.W. 516   Overruled
Subsequent Treatment Indicated by Shepard's: o376SW2d^{2}695
Board of Education of ashland School District et al., Appellants, v. Charles E. Chattin, Appellee Court of Appeals of Kentucky (March 13, 1964)
(a) M/B: Board of Education v. Chattin, 376 S.W.2d 693 (Ky. 1964).
   LR: Board of Educ. v. Chattin, 376 S.W.2d 693 (Ky. 1964).
(b) Headnote 2

60 149 229 309 489 579   83 S.W. 680   Harmonized
Subsequent Treatment Indicated by Shepard's: h394SW2d678

EXERCISE 24. SHEPARD'S CASE CITATIONS: SUBSEQUENT TREATMENT   (CONTINUED)

C.T. Schneider et al., Appellants v. Delwood Center, Inc., Appellee Court of
Civil Appeals of Texas (October 6, 1965)
(a) M/B: Schneider v. Delwood Center, 394 S.W.2d 671 (Tex. Civ. App. 1965).
(b) None

61 150 230 310 490 580   107 S.W. 496   Questioned
Subsequent Treatment Indicated by Shepard's: q356SW2d^{4}84
Orion J. Litzinger, Appellant, v. Pulitzer Publishing Company Respondent
Supreme Court of Missouri (April 9, 1962)
(a) M/B: Litzinger v. Pulitzer Publishing Co., 356 S.W.2d 81 (Mo. 1962).
(b) Headnote 4

62 151 231 311 491 581   262 S.W. 387   Distinguished
Subsequent Treatment Indicated by Shepard's: d288US^{4}197
Dickson et al. v. Uhlmann Grain Co. Certiorari to the Circuit Court of Appeals
for the Eighth Circuit (February 6, 1933)
(a) M/B: Dickson v. Uhlmann Grain Co., 288 U.S. 188 (1933).
(b) Headnote 4

63 152 232 312 492 582   145 S.W. 582   Distinguished
Subsequent Treatment Indicated by Shepard's: d293SW2d^{7}614
George Cowden et al., Appellants v. W.H. Bell, Appelle Court of Civil Appeals
of Texas San Antonio (July 25, 1956)
(a) M/B: Cowden v. Bell, 293 S.W.2d 611 (Tex. Civ. App. 1956).
(b) Headnote 7

64 153 233 313 493 583   91 S.W. 834   Distinguished
Subsequent Treatment Indicated by Shepard's: d152FS^{2}679
Roy J. Underwood v. William E. Maloney, individually and as representative of
the International Union of Operating Engineers, United States District Court
E.D. Pennsylvania (May 23, 1957)
(a) M/B: Underwood v. Maloney, 152 F. Supp. 648 (E.D. Pa. 1957).
(b) Headnote 2

65 154 234 314 494 584   190 U.S. 197   Limited
Subsequent Treatment Indicated by Shepard's: L354US^{2}14
Curtis Reid, Superintendent of the District of Columbia Jail, Appellant, v.
Clarice B. Covert (June 10, 1957)
(a) M/B: Reid v. Covert, 354 U.S. 1 (1957).
(b) Headnote 2

66 155 235 315 495 585   191 U.S. 78   Harmonized
Subsequent Treatment Indicated by Shepard's: h168FS^{1}800
Albert Browne and Frank S. Ryskiewicz d/b/a Park Bowling Alley, Plaintiffs, v.
Hartford Fire Insurance Company, a Corporation, Springfield Fire & Marine
Insurance Company, a Corporation, Defendants United States District Court N.D.
Illinois, E. D. (January 7, 1959
(a) M/B: Browne v. Hartford Fire Insurance Co., 168 F. Supp. 796 (N.D. Ill.
1959).
     LR: Browne v. Hartford Fire Ins. Co., 168 F. Supp. 796 (N.D. Ill. 1959).
(b) Headnote 1

67 156 236 316 496 586   196 U.S. 217   Distinguished
Subsequent Treatment Indicated by Shepard's: d102FS^{2}123
Lundberg v. Prudential Steamship Corp. et al. United sstates District Court
S.D.
New York (March 31, 1951)
(a) M/B: Lundberg v. Prudential Steamship Corp., 102 F. Supp. 115 (S.D.N.Y.
1951).
     LR: Lundberg v. Prudential S.S. Corp., 102 F. Supp. 115 (S.D.N.Y. 1951).
(b) Headnote 2

68 157 237 317 497 587   205 U.S. 322   Questioned
Subsequent Treatment Indicated by Shepard's: q45FS^{2}955
Dixie Greyhound Lines, Inc., v. Elliott District Court, W.D. Kentucky, Paducah
(August 18, 1942)
(a) M/B: Dixie Greyhound Lines v. Elliott, 45 F. Supp. 953 (W.D. Ky. 1942).

EXERCISE 24. SHEPARD'S CASE CITATIONS: SUBSEQUENT TREATMENT   (CONTINUED)

(b) Headnote 2

69 158 238 318 498 588   234 U.S. 52   Explained
Subsequent Treatment Indicated by Shepard's: e192FS^{1}868
Mary McGuire, Libellant, v. City of New York, Respondent (S.D. New York March
30, 1961)
   (a) M/B: McGuire v. City of New York, 192 F. Supp. 866 (S.D.N.Y. 1961).
   (b) Headnote 1

70 159 239 319 499 589   328 U.S. 781   Harmonized
Subsequent Treatment Indicated by Shepard's: h461F2d^{5}518
Lamb Enterprises, Inc., Delaware Corporation, Wonderland Ventures, Inc., A
Michigan Corporation, Plaintiff-Appellants, v. The Toledo Blade Company et
al., Defendants-Appellee United states Court of Appeals (May 31, 1972)
   (a) M/B: Lamb Enterprises v. Toledo Blade Co., 461 F.2d 506 (6th Cir. 1972).
        LR: Lamb Enters. v. Toledo Blade Co., 461 F.2d 506 (6th Cir. 1972).
   (b) Headnote 5

71 160 240 320 500 590   335 U.S. 464   Criticized
Subsequent Treatment Indicated by Shepard's: c317FS^{1}606
Faith A. Seidenberg and Karen DeCrow, Plaintiffs, v. McSorleys' Old Ale House,
Inc., Defendant United States District Court S. D. New York (June 25, 1970)
   (a) M/B: Seidenberg v. McSorleys' Old Ale House, Inc., 317 F. Supp. 593
(S.D.N.Y. 1970).
Note: "Inc." may properly be omitted from the citation.
   (b) Headnote 1

72 161 241 321 401 591   348 U.S. 176   Questioned
Subsequent Treatment Indicated by Shepard's: q280F2d^{1}333
Glen Oaks Utilities, Inc. and Greenfield Utilities Corporation, Appellants, v.
City of Houston, Appellee United States Court of Appeals (June 30, 1960)
   (a) M/B: Glen Oaks Utilities v. City of Houston, 280 F.2d 330 (5th Cir.
1960).
        LR: Glen Oaks Utils. v. City of Houston, 280 F.2d 330 (5th Cir. 1960).
   (b) Headnote 1

73 162 242 322 402 592   389 U.S. 429   Distinguished
Subsequent Treatment Indicated by Shepard's: d406US^{1}765
First National City Bank v. Banco Nacional de Cuba, Certiorari to the United
States Court of Appeals for the Second Circuit (June 7, 1972)
   (a) M/B: First National City Bank v. Banco Nacional de Cuba, 406 U.S. 759
(1972).
        LR: First Nat'l City Bank v. Banco Nacional de Cuba, 406 U.S. 759
(1972).
   (b) Headnote 1

74 163 243 323 403 593   102 F. Supp. 399   Followed
Subsequent Treatment Indicated by Shepard's: f338FS^{1}1343
Vasser Bishop, as Executrix of the Estate of David H. Bishop, Deceased
Plaintiff v. United States of America Defendant United States District Court
N.D. Mississippi, W.D. (June 19, 1970)
   (a) M/B: Bishop v. United States, 338 F. Supp. 1336 (N.D. Miss. 1970).
   (b) Headnote 1

75 164 244 324 404 594   36 F.R.D. 37   Distinguished
Subsequent Treatment Indicated by Shepard's: d305FS^{4}393
E.F. Hutton & Company, Inc. Plaintiff, v. John D. Brown, Defendant, United
States District Court S.D. Texas Houston Division (September 18, 1969)
   (a) M/B: E.F. Hutton & Co. v. Brown, 305 F. Supp. 371 (S.D. Tex. 1969).
   (b) Headnote 4

76 165 245 325 405 595   226 F. Supp. 56   Distinguished
Subsequent Treatment Indicated by Shepard's: d322FS^{3}980
Lucy Gillien Miles v. United States of America, United States District Court
M.D. Tennessee, Nashville Div. (November 20, 1970)
   (a) M/B: Miles v. United States, 322 F. Supp. 979 (M.D. Tenn. 1970).
   (b) Headnote 3

EXERCISE 24. SHEPARD'S CASE CITATIONS: SUBSEQUENT TREATMENT   (CONTINUED)

77 166 246 326 406 596   235 F. Supp. 984   Explained
Subsequent Treatment Indicated by Shepard's: e 424F2d^{3}1356
The B.F. Goodrich Company v. Northwest Industries, Inc., and Interstate
Commerce Commission, the B.F. Goodrich Company, a corporation of the State of
New York, Appellant, United States Court of Appeals (April 14, 1970)
(a)   B.F. Goodrich Co. v. Northwest Industries, 424 F.2d 1349 (3d Cir. 1970).
      LR: B.F. Goodrich Co. v. Northwest Indus., 424 F.2d 1349 (3d Cir. 1970).
(b)   Headnote 3

78 167 247 327 407 597   249 F. Supp. 681   Distinguished
Subsequent Treatment Indicated by Shepard's: d405F2d^{5}1137
Dominick Vaccaro, Plaintiff-Appellee, v. Alcoa Steamship Company, Inc.,
Defendant and Third-Party Plaintiff Appellant, American Stevedores, Inc., and
Anderson-Linton Lumber Co., Inc., Third-Party Defendants-Appellees, United
States Court of Appeals (December 27, 1968)
(a)   M/B: Vaccaro v. Alcoa Steamship Co., 405 F.2d 1133 (2d Cir. 1968).
      LR: Vaccaro v. Alcoa S.S. Co., 405 F.2d 1133 (2d Cir. 1968).
(b)   Headnote 5

79 168 248 328 408 598   264 F. Supp. 146   Distinguished
Subsequent Treatment Indicated by Shepard's: d390US^{11}573
United States v. Jackson et al. Appeal from the United States District Court
for the District of Connecticut (April 8, 1968)
(a)   M/B: United States v. Jackson, 390 U.S. 570 (1968).
(b)   Headnote 11

80 169 249 329 409 599   195 F. Supp. 795   Criticized
Subsequent Treatment Indicated by Shepard's: c439F2d^{4}359
United States of America, Plaintiff-Appellee, v. Fred G. Amick et al.,
Defendants-Appellants, United States Court of Appeals (January 22, 1971)
(a)   M/B: United States v. Amick, 439 F.2d 351 (7th Cir. 1971).
(b)   Headnote 4

81 170 250 330 410 600   192 F. Supp. 373   Distinguished
Subsequent Treatment Indicated by Shepard's: d428F2d^{1}1008
Betty Jean Blankenship, Administratix of the Estate of Jack Blankenship,
Deceased, Plaintiff-Appellant, v. General Motors Corporation,
Defendant-Appellee, United States Court of Appeals, (June 26, 1970)
(a)   M/B: Blankenship v. General Motors Corp., 428 F.2d 1006 (6th Cir. 1970).
(b)   Headnote 1

82 171 251 331 411 501   149 F. Supp. 272   Distinguished
Subsequent Treatment Indicated by Shepard's: d416F2d^{3}182
United States of America Appellee, v. Benjamin Spock, Defendant, Appellant,
United States Court of Appeals (July 11, 1969)
(a)   M/B: United States v. Spock, 416 F.2d 165 (1st Cir. 1969).
(b)   Headnote 3

83 172 252 332 412 502   43 Cal. Rptr. 14   Overruled
Subsequent Treatment Indicated by Shepard's: o401P2d938
The People, Plaintiff and Respondent, v. Matias Romero Perez et al.,
Defendants and Appellants, Supreme Court of California (May 21, 1965)
(a)   M/B: People v. Perez, 62 Cal. 2d 769, 401 P.2d 934, 44 Cal. Rptr. 326
(1965).
(b)   None

84 173 253 333 413 503   55 Cal. Rptr. 1   Criticized
Subsequent Treatment Indicated by Shepard's: c158CaR893
Fayette L. Earhart, Plaintiff and Appellant, v. William Low Company et al.,
Defendants and Respondents, Supreme Court of California
(a)   M/B: Earhart v. William Low Co., 25 Cal. 3d 503, 600 P.2d 1344, 158 Cal.
Rptr. 887 (1979).
(b)   None

85 174 254 334 414 504   63 Cal. Rptr. 13   Followed
Subsequent Treatment Indicated by Shepard's: f125CaR^{1}813

EXERCISE 24. SHEPARD'S CASE CITATIONS: SUBSEQUENT TREATMENT   (CONTINUED)

Opal M. Hansford, Plaintiff, Cross Defendant and Appellant, v. Ben Lassar, Defendant, Cross-Complainant and Respondent, Court of Appeal, Second District (January 28, 1976)
(a) M/B: <u>Hansford v. Lassar</u>, 53 Cal. App. 3d 364, 125 Cal. Rptr. 804 (1975).
(b) Headnote 1

86 175 255 335 415 505   101 Cal. Rptr. 4   Explained
Subsequent Treatment Indicated by <u>Shepard's</u>: e527F2d^{22}657
Michael-Regan Co., Inc., a California Corporation, Plaintiff-Appellant, v. Martin Lindell, a sole proprietor doing business under the firm name of Lindell Enterprises, Defendant and Third-Party Plaintiff-Appellee, United States Court of Appeals (December 24, 1975)
(a) M/B: <u>Michael-Regan Co. v. Lindell</u>, 527 F.2d 653 (9th Cir. 1975).
(b) Headnote 22

87 176 256 336 416 506   82 Cal. Rptr. 489   Explained
Subsequent Treatment Indicated by <u>Shepard's</u>: e132CaR^{4}538
Florence M. Zastrow, Plaintiff adn Appellant, v. Herbert H. Zastrow, Defendant and Respondent, Court of Appeal, Third District, (September 3, 1976)
(a) M/B: <u>Zastrow v. Zastrow</u>, 61 Cal. App. 3d 710, 132 Cal. Rptr. 536 (1976).
(b) Headnote 4

88 177 257 337 417 507   102 Cal. Rptr. 36   Distinguished
Subsequent Treatment Indicated by <u>Shepard's</u>: d434FS^{3}1155
United States of America, Plaintiff-Appellee, v. Walter T. Best, Defendant-Appellant, United States District Court E.D. California (July 29, 1977)
(a) M/B: <u>United States v. Best</u>, 434 F. Supp. 1153 (E.D. Cal. 1977).
(b) Headnote 3

89 178 258 338 418 508   105 Cal. Rptr. 318   Distinguished
Subsequent Treatment Indicated by <u>Shepard's</u>: d535F2d^{2}545
Paul R. Bailleaux, Appellant, v. Hoyt C. Cupp, Superintendent, Oregon State Penitentiary, et al., Appellees, United States Court of Appeals (May 19, 1976)
(a) M/B: <u>Bailleaux v. Cupp</u>, 535 F.2d 543 (9th Cir. 1976).
(b) Headnote 2

90 179 259 339 419 509   102 Cal. Rptr. 547   Followed
Subsequent Treatment Indicated by <u>Shepard's</u>: d151CaR^{14}790
Vernon V. Vale, etc. et al., Plaintiffs, Cross-Defendants, Respondents and Appellants, v. Union Bank, etc., Defendant, Cross-Complainant, Appellant, and Respondent (Court of Appeal, First District Jan. 16, 1979)
(a) M/B: <u>Vale v. Union Bank</u>, 88 Cal. App. 3d 330, 151 Cal. Rptr. 790 (1979).
(b) Headnote 14 (<u>or</u> 14, 15, and 18)

91 180 260 340 420 510   105 Cal. Rptr. 568   Explained
Subsequent Treatment Indicated by <u>Shepard's</u>: e133CaR^{7}884
Estate of Mary Anderson Conroy, also known as Mary A. Conroy, Mary Conroy, M.A. Conroy, and Mrs. Thomas F. Conroy, Deceased (listed first and consolidated with) Kenneth Cory, Petitioner and Appellant, v. Thomas Francis Conroy, Executor Objector and Respondent, Court of Appeal, First District (November 10, 1976)
(a) M/B: <u>Estate of Conroy</u>, 63 Cal. App. 3d 516, 133 Cal. Rptr. 881 (1976).
(b) Headnote 7 (<u>or</u> Headnotes 7 and 4).

92 181 261 341 421 511   82 N.Y.S. 773   Questioned
Subsequent Treatment Indicated by <u>Shepard's</u>: q204F^{1}770
In re Morris, (Circuit Court of Appeals, Second Circuit) (April 14, 1913)
(a) M/B: <u>In re Morris</u>, 204 F. 770 (2d Cir. 1913).
     LR: <u>In re Morris</u>, 204 F. 770 (2d Cir. 1913).
(b) Headnote 1

93 182 262 342 422 512   172 N.Y.S. 673   Followed
Subsequent Treatment Indicated by <u>Shepard's</u>: f71FS^{2}232
Utterback v. Utterback, District Court of the United States for the District of Columbia, (April 16, 1947)
(a) M/B: <u>Utterback v. Utterback</u>, 71 F. Supp. 231 (D.D.C. 1947).

EXERCISE 24.   SHEPARD'S CASE CITATIONS: SUBSEQUENT TREATMENT   (CONTINUED)

(b)   Headnote 2

94 183 263 343 423 513   247 N.Y.S.2d 21   Distinguished
Subsequent Treatment Indicated by Shepard's: d417FS^{11}77
United States of America, Plaintiff, v. James J. Hage et al., Defendants,
United States District Court, N.D. New York (May 14, 1976)
(a)   M/B: United States v. Hage, 417 F. Supp. 74 (N.D.N.Y. 1976).
(b)   Headnote 11

95 184 264 344 424 514   247 N.Y.S.2d 269   Questioned
Subsequent Treatment Indicated by Shepard's: q360S2d^{1}991
Seymour R. Thaler, Claimant, v. The State of New York Defendant, Court of
Claims of New York (November 15, 1974)
(a)   M/B: Thaler v. State, 79 Misc. 2d 621, 360 N.Y.S.2d 986 (Ct. Cl. 1974).
(b)   Headnote 1

96 185 265 345 425 515   117 N.Y.S. 45   Distinguished
Subsequent Treatment Indicated by Shepard's: d21FS320
In re Prudence Co., Inc. District Court, E.D. New York (November 6, 1937)
(a)   M/B: In re Prudence Co., 21 F. Supp. 316 (E.D.N.Y. 1937).
      LR: In re Prudence Co., 21 F. Supp. 316 (E.D.N.Y. 1937).
(b)   None

97 186 266 346 426 516   101 N.Y.S. 1031   Distinguished
Subsequent Treatment Indicated by Shepard's: d296F^{1}46
Johnson v. Emerson Phonograph Co., Inc. Yellin v. Scholer et al. (Circuit
Court of Appeals Second) (January 7, 1924)
(a)   M/B: Johnson v. Emerson Phonograph Co., 296 F. 42 (2d Cir. 1924).
(b)   Headnote 1

98 187 267 347 427 517   99 N.Y.S. 721   Explained
Subsequent Treatment Indicated by Shepard's: 440FS^{1}879
Kahn v. Cecelia Co., District Court, S.D. New York (June 27, 1941)
(a)   M/B: Kahn v. Cecelia Co., 40 F. Supp. 878 (S.D.N.Y. 1941).
(b)   Headnote 1

99 188 268 348 428 518   396 N.Y.S.2d 883   Questioned
Subsequent Treatment Indicated by Shepard's: q77FRD423
Michelle George, Ronda Allen, Guillermina Lopez-Mendez, Mary Oates and
Hortense Williams, on behalf of themselves and all others similarly situated,
Plaintiffs, v. Henry Parry, Individually and in his capaicty as Commissioner
of the Orange County Department of Social Services, David Ritter, Individually
and in his capacity as Orange County District Attorney, Anne Molloy, Beverly
Connell, Madeline Smith and Robert Remer, Defendants, United States District
Court, S.D. New York (January 5, 1978)
(a)   M/B: George v. Parry, 77 F.R.D. 421 (S.D.N.Y. 1978).
(b)   None

100 189 269 349 429 519   225 N.Y.S.2d 193   Questioned
Subsequent Treatment Indicated by Shepard's: q361S2d^{1}457
People of the State of New York, Respondent, v. Richard Sylvester Anderson,
Jr., Appellant, Supreme Court, Appellate Division, Fourth Department (December
5, 1974)
(a)   M/B: People v. Anderson, 46 A.D.2d 150, 361 N.Y.S.2d 454 (1974).
(b)   Headnote 1

LIBRARY EXERCISE 25. WEST'S WORDS AND PHRASES.

INSTRUCTOR'S NOTE: In this exercise, students are required to locate the listed word or phrase in West's Words and Phrases. They are then to find the case squib indicated for their problem which defines that word or phrase. If they cannot locate the squib in the bound part of the volume, they should check the pocket supplement. For their answer, they are to give the citation to the case including the page on which that definition can be found, e.g., Variable Expenses [Waukeska] Ans. M/B: Waukeska Motor Co. v. United States, 322 F. Supp. 752, 756 (E.D. Wis. 1971). Note that the case begins on page 752 and the definition is on page 756. The students are told to consult the case to find any missing information and not to rely on the form used in the squib for their citation. The students are to use Shepard's Citations to find any missing parallel citations. Do not indicate the subsequent history of the case. Note also that the page on which the definition appears in each parallel source should be indicated, e.g., M/B: Kearney Elec. Co. v. Laughlin, 45 Neb. 390, 404, 63 N.W. 941, 946 (1895). If the exact page on which the definition is given in a parallel source is not noted in West's Words and Phrases, the missing page should be indicated in the following manner for the purposes of this exercise: M/B: Kearney Elec. Co. v. Laughlin, 45 Neb. 390, ___, 63 N.W. 941, 946 (1895). The students are also instructed to cite Supreme Court actions only to United States Reports.

1 130 252 356 435 508
Relevant Entry in West's Words and Phrases: A-B-C TEST Emplyment Sec. Commission v. Wilson, Alaska, 461 P.2d 425, 427.
Employment Security Commission (Alaska Department of Labor), Appellant, v. Harry H. Wilson, d/b/a Wilson's Auto Rebuild, Appellee (Supreme Court of Alaska Nov. 24, 1969)
M/B: Employment Security Commission v. Wilson, 461 P.2d 425, 427 (Alaska 1969).
LR: Employment Sec. Comm'n v. Wilson, 461 P.2d 425, 427 (Alaska 1969).

2 131 253 357 436 509
Relevant Entry in West's Words and Phrases: ACCIDENT POLICY In re Noel's Estate, C.A.N.J., 332 F.2d 950, 952.
In re Estate of Marshal L. Noel, Deceased. William H. Grantz and Ruth M. Noel, Executors, Petitioners, v. Commissioner of Internal Revenue, Respondent, (United States Court of Appeals Third Circuit June 17, 1964)
M/B: In re Estate of Noel, 332 F.2d 950, 952 (3d Cir. 1963).
LR: In re Estate of Noel, 332 F.2d 950, 952 (3d Cir. 1963)
Note: "In re Noel's Estate" is also correct (arguably as the popular name of the case).

3 132 254 358 437 510
Relevant Entry in West's Words and Phrases: ACCOUNT CURRENT BASIS Holbrook v. Institutional Ins. Co. of America, C.A.Ill., 369 F.2d 236, 238.
Garland A. Holbrook and Truck Acceptance Corporation, Plaintiffs-Appellees, v. Institutional Insurance Company of America, Defendant-Appellant. (United States Court of Appeals Seventh Circuit November 15, 1966)
M/B: Holbrook v. Institutional Insurance Co. of America, 369 F.2d 236, 238 (7th Cir. 1966).
LR: Holbrook v. Institutional Ins. Co. of Am., 369 F.2d 236, 238 (7th Cir. 1966).

4 133 255 359 438 511
Relevant Entry in West's Words and Phrases: ACT OF WAR Thomas v. Metropolitan Life Ins. Co., 131 A.2d 600, 605, 388 Pa. 499.
Francis R. Thomas, Sr., Appellant, v. Metropolitan Life Insurance Company. (Supreme Court of Pennsylvania March 25, 1957)
M/B: Thomas v. Metropolitan Life Insurance Co., 388 Pa. 499, ___, 131 A.2d 600, 605 (1957).
LR: Thomas v. Metropolitan Life Ins. Co., 388 Pa. 499, ___, 131 A.2d 600, 605 (1957).

5 134 256 360 439 512
Relevant Entry in West's Words and Phrases: AFTER-ACQUIRED TITLE Texas Sand Co. v. Shield, Tex.Civ.App., 367 S.W.2d 88, 95.

EXERCISE 25. WEST'S WORDS AND PHRASES   (CONTINUED)

Texas Sand Company et al., Appellants, v. Donald L. Shield et al., Appellees. (Court of Civil Appeals of Texas April 5, 1963)
M/B: Texas Sand Co. v. Shield, 367 S.W.2d 88, 95 (Tex. Civ. App. 1963).

6 135 257 361 440 513
Relevant Entry in West's Words and Phrases: ALEATORY PROMISE   Tyree v. Stone, 384 P.2d 626, 62 Wash.2d 694.
Gordon T. Tyree and Charles R. Cloud, dba a copartnership under the firm name and title of Richland Bakery, Plaintiffs, Appellants, v. Roy L. Stone et al., Defendants, Respondents, v. F.G. Campbell et al., Third-Party and Cross-Defendants. (Supreme Court of Washington, Department 2 August 8, 1963)
M/B: Tyree v. Stone, 62 Wash. 2d 694, ___, 384 P.2d 626, 629 (1963).

7 136 258 362 441 514
Relevant Entry in West's Words and Phrases: ALIBI   Massen v. State, 163 N.W.2d 616, 622, 41 Wis.2d 245.
Donald Richard Massen, Plaintiff in Error, v. State of Wisconsin, Defendant in Error (Supreme Court of Wisconsin January 7, 1969)
M/B: Massen v. State, 41 Wis. 2d 245, ___, 163 N.W.2d 616, 622 (1969).

8 137 259 363 442 515
Relevant Entry in West's Words and Phrases: APPARENT USE   Stuart v. Lake Washington Realty Corp., 92 S.E.2d 891, 899, 141 W.Va. 627.
Lola L. Stuart et al. v. Lake Washington Realty Corporation et al. (Supreme Court of Appeals of West Virginia March 14, 1956)
M/B: Stuart v. Lake Washington Realty Corp., 141 W. Va. 627, ___, 92 S.E.2d 891, 899 (1956).
LR: Stuart v. Lake Wash. Realty Corp., 141 W. Va. 627, ___, 92 S.E.2d 891, 899 (1956).
Note: In the LR citation, "Lake Washington" also is correct.

9 138 260 364 443 516
Relevant Entry in West's Words and Phrases: CLOSING OF THE CLASS   In re Liddle's Estate, 328 P.2d 35, 41, 162 C.A.2d 7.
In the Matter of the Estate of Anne McNally Liddle, Deceased. James W. Harvey, as Administrator of the Estate of Kathleen Ann Coffey, Deceased, Appellant, and Elizabeth K. MacPherson, Helen Keating, Mary Stella Keating, and Estate of Robert P. Keating, Deceased, Appellants, v. John F.P. Byrne, George J. O'Sullivan, Regina O'Sullivan, George J. (Jack) O'Sullivan, Margaret O'Sullivan McMorrow, Edward P. Coffey, Herbert L. V. Coffey and Cameron C. Coffey, Respondents. (District Court of Appeal, Second District, Division 2, California July 7, 1958)
M/B: In re Estate of Liddle, 162 Cal. App. 2d 7, ___, 328 P.2d 35, 41 (1958).
LR: In re Estate of Liddle, 162 Cal. App. 2d 7, ___, 328 P.2d 35, 41 (1958).
Note: "In re Liddle's Estate" is also correct (arguably as the popular name of the case).

10 139 261 365 444 517
Relevant Entry in West's Words and Phrases: CLEARED LAND   Marvel v. Regienus, 108 N.E.2d 545, 547, 329 Mass. 414.
Marvel v. Regienus (Supreme Judicial Court of Massachussetts September 23, 1952)
M/B: Marvel v. Regienus, 329 Mass. 414, ___, 108 N.E.2d 545, 547 (1952).

11 140 262 366 445 518
Relevant Entry in West's Words and Phrases: CONDITIONAL VENDEE   King v. Mack Intern. Motor Truck Corp., 60 N.W.2d 792, 794, 245 Iowa 48.
King et al. v. Mack International Motor Truck Corp. (Supreme Court of Iowa November 17, 1953)
M/B: King v. Mack International Motor Truck Corp., 245 Iowa 48, ___, 60 N.W.2d 792, 794 (1953).
LR: King v. Mack Int'l Motor Truck Corp., 245 Iowa 48, ___, 60 N.W.2d 792, 794 (1953).

12 141 263 367 446 519 Houston v. Harberger, 377 S.W.2d 673, 678 (Tex. Ct. App. 1967).

EXERCISE 25. WEST'S WORDS AND PHRASES   (CONTINUED)

Relevant Entry in West's Words and Phrases: CONTINGENT ESTATE Houston v. Harberger, Tex.Civ.App., 377 S.W.2d 673, 678.
Ramon Houston, Administrator, et al., Appellants, v. Billy Roy Harberger et al., Appellees (Court of Civil Appeals of Texas February 21, 1964)
M/B: Houston v. Harberger, 377 S.W.2d 673, 678 (Tex. Civ. App. 1964).

13 142 264 368 447 520
Relevant Entry in West's Words and Phrases: CONFESSION AND AVOIDANCE Sievers v. Brown, 63 So.2d 217, 219 216 Miss. 801.
Sievers v. Brown, (Supreme Court of Mississippi March 9, 1953)
M/B: Sievers v. Brown, 216 Miss. 801, ___, 63 So. 2d 217, 219 (1953).

14 143 265 369 448 521
Relevant Entry in West's Words and Phrases: ATTESTATION CLAUSE Succession of Peterson, La.App., 240 So.2d 39, 41.
Succession of William Fleet Peterson (Court of Appeal of Louisiana, Second Circuit September 15, 1970)
M/B: Succession of Peterson, 240 So. 2d 39, 41 (La. Ct. App. 1970).

15 144 266 370 449 522
Relevant Entry in West's Words and Phrases: ARTICULO MORTIS Beard v. State, Tenn.Cr.App., 485 S.W.2d 882, 884.
William Eugene Beard, Plaintiff in Error, v. State of Tennessee, Defendant in Error (Court of Criminal Appeals of Tennessee June 22, 1972)
M/B: Beard v. State, 485 S.W.2d 882, 884 (Tenn. Crim. App. 1972).

16 145 267 371 450 523
Relevant Entry in West's Words and Phrases: ASSAULT WITH WHIP OR COWHIDE Brenneman v. State, Tex.Cr.App., 458 S.W.2d 677, 678.
John Walter Brenneman, Appellant, v. The State of Texas, Appellee (Court of Criminal Appeals of Texas January 14, 1970)
M/B: Brenneman v. State, 458 S.W.2d 677, 678 (Tex. Crim. App. 1970).

17 146 268 372 451 524
Relevant Entry in West's Words and Phrases: COUNTER WILLS Wright v. Wright, 285 S.W. 188, 189, 215 Ky. 394.
Wright et al. v. Wright (Court of Appeals of Kentucky June 25, 1926)
M/B: Wright v. Wright, 215 Ky. 394, ___, 285 S.W.188, 189 (1926).

18 147 269 373 452 525
Relevant Entry in West's Words and Phrases: CONVERSION RULE American Fidelity Co. v. North British & Mercantile Ins. Co., 204 A.2d 110, 112, 124 Vt. 271.
American Fidelity Company v. North British & Mercantile Insurance Co., Ltd., et al. (Supreme Court of Vermont October 6, 19864)
M/B: American Fidelity Co. v. North British & Mercantile Insurance Co., 124 Vt. 271, ___, 204 A.2d 110, 112 (1964).
LR: American Fidelity Co. v. North British & Mercantile Ins. Co., 124 Vt. 271, ___, 204 A.2d 110, 112 (1964).

19 148 270 374 453 526
Relevant Entry in West's Words and Phrases: C & F Madeirense Do Brasil S/A v. Stulman-Emerick Lumber Co. C.C.A.N.Y., 147 F.2d 399, 402
Madeirense Do Brasil S/A v. Stulman-Emrick Lumber Co. (Circuit Court of Appeals, Second Circuit January 9, 1945)
M/B: Madeirense Do Brasil S/A v. Stulman-Emrick Lumber Co., 147 F.2d 399, 402 (2d Cir. 1945).

20 149 271 375 454 527
Relevant Entry in West's Words and Phrases: BURFORD DOCTRINE Clutchette v. Procunier, D.C.Cal., 328 F.Supp. 767, 772.
John Wesley Clutchette et al., Plaintiffs, v. Raymond J. Procunier et al., Defendants. (United States District Court, N. D. California June 21, 1971)
M/B: Clutchette v. Procunier, 328 F. Supp. 767, 772 (N.D. Cal. 1971).

21 150 272 376 455 528
Relevant Entry in West's Words and Phrases: BILL PAYABLE Guaranty Bond State Bank v. Tucker, Tex.Civ.App., 462 S.W.2d 398, 401.

EXERCISE 25. WEST'S WORDS AND PHRASES   (CONTINUED)

Guaranty Bond State Bank, Appellant, v. Charles Tucker, Appellee (Court of Civil Appeals of Texas December 24, 1970)
M/B: Guaranty Bond State Bank v. Tucker, 462 S.W.2d 398, 401 (Tex. Civ. App. 1970).

22 151 273 377 456 529
Relevant Entry in West's Words and Phrases: DETACHABLE WARRANT   Miller v. General Outdoor Advertising Co., D.C.N.Y., 223 F.Supp. 790, 794
Irving Miller, Plaintiff, v. General Outdoor Advertising Co., Inc., Gamble-Skogmo, Inc. and Alleghany Corporation, Defendants (United States District Court S. D. New York December 2, 1963)
M/B: Miller v. General Outdoor Advertising Co., 223 F. Supp. 790, 794 (S.D.N.Y. 1963).

23 152 274 378 457 530
Relevant Entry in West's Words and Phrases: DECEPTION DOCTRINE   Chapman v. Claxton, 497 P.2d 192, 195, 6 Wash.App. 852.
Marvin A. Chapman, Individually, and Manetta M. DeBois, Individually, Respondents, v. Kerry D. Claxton and Jane Doe Claxton, husband and wife, and their marital community, Appellants. (Court of Appeals of Washington May 3, 1972)
M/B: Chapman v. Claxton, 6 Wash. App. 852, ___, 497 P.2d 192, 195 (1972).

24 153 275 379 458 531
Relevant Entry in West's Words and Phrases: EMPTY CHAIR   Carraturo v. Lawrence, 268 A.2d 277, 280, 107 R.I. 463.
Carmine Carraturo, Adm'r v. Joseph Lawrence (Supreme Court of Rhode Island July 29, 1970)
M/B: Carraturo v. Lawrence, 107 R.I. 463, ___, 268 A.2d 277, 280 (1970).

25 154 276 380 459 532
Relevant Entry in West's Words and Phrases: EMBEZZLEMENT BY AGENT   Groves v. U.S., C.A.Mo., 343 F.2d 850, 854.
Robert Harry Groves, Appellant, v. United States of America, Appellee (United States Court of Appeals Eighth Circuit April 15, 1965)
M/B: Groves v. United States, 343 F.2d 850, 854 (8th Cir. 1965).

26 155 277 381 460 533
Relevant Entry in West's Words and Phrases: DYING WITH ISSUE   In re Turner's Will, 101 N.E. 905, 807, 208 N.Y. 261, Ann.Cas. 1914D, 245.
In re Turner's Will (Court of Appeals of New York April 22, 1913)
M/B: In re Turner's Will, 208 N.Y. 261, ___, 101 N.E. 905, 907 (1913).
LR: In re Turner's Will, 208 N.Y. 261, ___, 101 N.E. 905, 907 (1913).

27 156 278 382 461 534
Relevant Entry in West's Words and Phrases: DRAGNET CLAUSE   Kenneally v. Standard Electronics Corp., C.A. Minn., 364 F.2d 642, 647.
Edward R. Kenneally, Trustee in Bankruptcy of General Magnetics, Inc., a Corporation, Bankrupt, Appellant, v. Standard Electronics Corporation and First National Bank of Minneapolis, Appellees (United States Court of Appeals Eighth Circuit August 17, 1966)
M/B: Kenneally v. Standard Electronics Corp., 364 F.2d 642, 647 (8th Cir. 1966).
LR: Kenneally v. Standard Elecs. Corp., 364 F.2d 642, 647 (8th Cir. 1966).

28 157 279 383 462 535
Relevant Entry in West's Words and Phrases: DISABILITY INSURANCE BENEFITS   Banks v. Celebrezze, C.A.Ky., 341 F.2d 801, 803.
Lee Roy Banks, Plaintiff-Appellee, v. Anthony J. Celebrezze, Secretary of Health, Education and Welfare, Defendant-Appellant (United States Court of Appeals Sixth Circuit February 20, 1965)
M/B: Banks v. Celebrezze, 341 F.2d 801, 803 (6th Cir. 1965).

29 158 280 384 463 536
Relevant Entry in West's Words and Phrases: FUSE PLUG LEVESS   U.S. v. Sponenbarger, Ark. 60 S.Ct. 225, 227, 308 U.S. 256, 84 L.Ed. 230.

EXERCISE 25. WEST'S WORDS AND PHRASES   (CONTINUED)

United States v. Sponenbarger et al. (Certiorari to the Circuit Court of Appeals for the Eighth Circuit November 7, 8, 1939)
M/B: United States v. Sponenbarger, 308 U.S. 256, ___ (1939).
LR: United States v. Sponenbarger, 308 U.S. 256, ___ (1939).

30 159 281 385 464 537
Relevant Entry in West's Words and Phrases: F.O.B. Garrett v. Tubular Products, Inc., D.C.Va., 176 F.Supp. 101, 104.
Henry Lee Garrett v. Tubular Products, Incorporated and Frank Jett (United States District Court E. D. Virginia July 30, 1959)
M/B: Garrett v. Tubular Products, Inc., 176 F. Supp. 101, 104 (E.D. Va. 1959).
LR: Garrett v. Tubular Prods., Inc., 176 F. Supp. 101, 104 (E.D. Va. 1959).

31 160 282 386 465 538
Relevant Entry in West's Words and Phrases: FILLED MILK Milnot Co. v. Richardson, D.C.Ill., 350 F.Supp. 221, 223.
Milnot Company, a Michigan corporation, Plaintiff, v. Elliot Richardson, Secretary of Health, Education and Welfare, Defendant (United States District Court, S. D. Illinois, S. D. November 9, 1972)
M/B: Milnot Co. v. Richardson, 350 F. Supp. 221, 223 (S.D. Ill. 1972).

32 161 283 387 466 539
Relevant Entry in West's Words and Phrases: FATHOMETER U. S. v. Soriano, C.A. Wash., 366 F.2d 699, 704.
United States of America, Appellant, v. Dewey Soriano, Appellee (United States Court of Appeals Ninth Circuit September 27, 1966)
M/B: United States v. Soriano, 366 F.2d 699, 704 (9th Cir. 1966).

33 162 284 388 467 540
Relevant Entry in West's Words and Phrases: EXCESS OUTAGE Hunter-Wilson Distilling Co. v. Foust Distilling Co., C.A.Pa., 181 F.2d 543, 544.
Hunter-Wilson Distilling Co., Inc. v. Foust Distilling Co. (United States Court of Appeals Third Circuit January 19, 1950)
M/B: Hunter-Wilson Distilling Co. v. Foust Distilling Co., 181 F.2d 543, 544 (3d Cir. 1950).

34 163 285 389 468 541
Relevant Entry in West's Words and Phrases: ESTATE BY INHERITANCE Larrabee v. Tracy, 104 P.2d 61, 66, 39 Cal.App.2d 593.
Larrabee v. Tracy et al. (District Court of Appeals, Second Circuit June 21, 1940)
M/B: Larrabee v. Tracy, 39 Cal. App. 2d 593, ___, 104 P.2d 61, 66 (1940).

35 164 286 390 469 542
Relevant Entry in West's Words and Phrases: INTENT TO MAIM State v. Richardson, Mo., 460 S.W.2d 537, 539.
State of Missouri, Respondent, v. Robert Eugene Richardson, Appellant (Supreme Court of Missouri December 14, 1970)
M/B: State v. Richardson, 460 S.W.2d 537, 539 (Mo. 1970).

36 165 287 391 470 543
Relevant Entry in West's Words and Phrases: IRRESISTIBLE FORCE State v. Palacio, 559 P.2d 804, 806, 221 Kan. 394.
State of Kansas, Appellant, v. Antonio H. Palacio, Appellee (Supreme Court of Kansas Jan. 22, 1977)
M/B: State v. Palacio, 221 Kan. 394, ___, 559 P.2d 804, 806 (1977).

37 166 288 392 471 544
Relevant Entry in West's Words and Phrases: HIGH-WATER MARK State v. Bonelli Cattle Co., 495 P.2d 1312, 1314, 108 Ariz. 258.
The State of Arizona et al., Appellants, v. Bonelli Cattle Company, a California corporation, Appellee (Supreme Court of Arizona April 13, 1972)
M/B: State v. Bonelli Cattle Co., 108 Ariz. 258, ___, 495 P.2d 1312, 1314 (1972).

38 167 289 393 472 545

EXERCISE 25. WEST'S WORDS AND PHRASES   (CONTINUED)

Relevant Entry in West's Words and Phrases: HEAVING LINE   Marincovich v. Oriana, Inc., 91 Cal.Rptr. 417, 419, 13 C.A.3d 146.
Andrew J. Marincovich, Plaintiff and Respondent, v. Oriana, Inc., a corporation, and Marine Terminals Corp., of Los Angeles, a corporation, Defendants and Appellants (Court of Appeal, Second District November 30, 1970)
M/B: Marincovich v. Oriana, Inc., 13 Cal. App. 3d 146, ___, 91 Cal. Rptr. 417, 419 (1970).

39 168 290 394 473 546
Relevant Entry in West's Words and Phrases: GREAT WRIT   Harvey v. State of S. C., D.C.S.C., 310 F.Supp. 83, 84.
DeWitt Harvey, Petitioner, v. The State of South Carolina, Mr. W.D. Leeke, Director, South Carolina Department of Corrections, Columbia, S. C., et al., Respondents (United States District Court, D. South Carolina, Columbia Division March 12, 1970)
M/B: Harvey v. South Carolina, 310 F. Supp. 83, 84 (D.S.C. 1970).

40 169 291 395 474 547
Relevant Entry in West's Words and Phrases: GENERAL REVENUE CASES   Florida Citrus Commission v. U.S., D.C.Fla., 144 F.Supp. 517, 521.
Florida Citrus Commission, et al., Plaintiffs, and Ezra Taft Benson, Secretary of Agriculture, et al., Intervening Plaintiffs, v. United States of America, Interstate Commerce Commission, et al., Defendants, and Atchison, Topeka and Santa Fe Railway Company, Armour and Company, et al., Intervening Defendants (United States District Court N.D. Florida, Tallahassee Division September 7, 1956)
M/B: Florida Citrus Commission v. United States, 144 F. Supp. 517, 521 (N.D. Fla. 1956).
LR: Florida Citrus Comm'n v. United States, 144 F. Supp. 517, 521 (N.D. Fla. 1956).

41 170 292 396 475 548
Relevant Entry in West's Words and Phrases: KINETIC ENERGY   Friedman v. U. S., Cust.Ct., 296 F.Supp. 346, 348.
Morris Friedman v. United States (United States Customs Court, Second Division March 13, 1969)
M/B: Friedman v. United States, 296 F. Supp. 346, 348 (Cust. Ct. 1969).

42 171 293 397 476 549
Relevant Entry in West's Words and Phrases: JOINT WILL   Ellexson v. Ellexson, Tex.Civ.App., 467 S.W.2d 515, 519.
Milan F. Ellexson, Individually and as Independent Executor of the Estate of Ivy D. Williams, Deceased, et al., Appellants, v. Adrian Ellexson et al., Appellees (Court of Civil Appeals of Texas May 3, 1971)
M/B: Elexson v. Ellexson, 467 S.W.2d 515, 519 (Tex. Civ. App. 1971).

43 172 294 398 477 550
Relevant Entry in West's Words and Phrases: ILLUMINATING ARTICLES   New York Merchandise Co. v. U. S., Cust.Ct. 271 F.Supp. 308, 311.
New York Merchandise Co. et al. v. United States (United States Customs Court, Second Division August 10, 1967)
M/B: New York Merchandise Co. v. United States, 271 F. Supp. 308, 311 (Cust. Ct. 1967).

44 173 295 399 478 551
Relevant Entry in West's Words and Phrases: INCLINATION AND OPPORTUNITY RULE   Levitz v. Levitz, 185 A.2d 620, 622, 199 Pa.Super. 327.
Leon Levitz, Appellee, v. Ruth Levitz, Appellant (Superior Court of Pennsylvania November 15, 1962)
M/B: Levitz v. Levitz, 199 Pa. Super. 327, ___, 185 A.2d 620, 622 (1962).

45 174 296 400 479 552
Relevant Entry in West's Words and Phrases: INTEGRATED GAS COMPANY   Arkansas Louisiana Gas Co. v. U. S., 291 F.2d 936, 937, 154 Ct.Cl. 654.
Arkansas Louisiana Gas Company v. United States (United States Court of Claims July 19, 1961)

EXERCISE 25. WEST'S WORDS AND PHRASES   (CONTINUED)

M/B: <u>Arkansas Louisiana Gas Co. v. United States</u>, 291 F.2d 936, 937 (Ct. Cl. 1961).
LR: Arkansas La. Gas Co. v. United States, 291 F.2d 936, 937 (Ct. Cl. 1961).

46 175 297 301 480 553
Relevant Entry in West's Words and Phrases: LAND WAREHOUSING   Connor v. Great Western Sav. & Loan Ass'n, 73 Cal.Rptr. 369, 373, 447 P.2d 609, 39 A.L.R.3d 224.
Raymond E. Connor et al., Plaintiffs, Cross-Defendants and Appellants, v. Great Western Savings and Loan Association, Defendant, Cross-Defendant and Respondent; Meyer Pritkin et al., Defendants, Cross-Complainants and Appellants. (Supreme Court of California December 12, 1968)
M/B: <u>Connor v. Great Western Savings & Loan Association</u>, 69 Cal. 2d 850, ___, 447 P.2d 609, ___, 73 Cal. Rptr. 369, 373 (1968).
LR: Connor v. Great W. Sav. & Loan Ass'n, 69 Cal. 2d 850, ___, 447 P.2d 609, ___, 73 Cal. Rptr. 369, 373 (1968).

47 176 298 302 481 554
Relevant Entry in West's Words and Phrases: LAPPING   State v. Randecker, 464 P.2d 447, 449, 1 Wash.App. 834.
State of Washington, Appellant, v. Dorothy Mae Randecker, Respondent (Court of Appeals of Washington January 26, 1970)
M/B: <u>State v. Randecker</u>, 1 Wash. App. 834, ___, 464 P.2d 447, 449 (1970).

48 177 299 303 482 555
Relevant Entry in West's Words and Phrases: MACH SPEED INDICATOR   Bell Intercontinental Corp. v. U. S., 381 F.2d 1004, 1016, 180 Ct.Cl. 1071.
Bell Intercontinental Corporation v. The United States (United States Court of Claims July 20, 1967)
M/B: <u>Bell Intercontinental Corp. v. United States</u>, 381 F.2d 1004, 1016 (Ct. Cl. 1967).

49 178 300 304 483 556
Relevant Entry in West's Words and Phrases: MCNAGHTEN RULE   State v. White, 142 A.2d 65, 68, 69, 87 N.J. 158.
The State of New Jersey, Plaintiff-Respondent, v. LeRoy White, Defendant-Appellant (Supreme Court of New Jersey March 17, 1958)
M/B: <u>State v. White</u>, 87 N.J. 158, ___, 142 A.2d 65, 68 (1958).

50 179 201 305 484 557
Relevant Entry in West's Words and Phrases: LOCUS PENITENTIAE   Morris v. Johnson, 132 S.E.2d 45, 51, 219 Ga. 81.
Mrs. J. L. Morris v. Estelle Johnson (Supreme Court of Georgia June 11, 1963)
M/B: <u>Morris v. Johnson</u>, 219 Ga. 81, ___, 132 S.E.2d 45, 51 (1963).

51 180 202 306 485 558
Relevant Entry in West's Words and Phrases: LIMITED CAPACITY WELLS   Zimmerman v. Texaco, Inc., Tex.Civ.App., 409 S.W.2d 607, 615.
Cora Zimmerman, Appellant, v. Texaco, Inc., et al., Appellees (Court of Civil Appeals of Texas November 23, 1966)
M/B: <u>Zimmerman v. Texaco, Inc.</u>, 409 S.W.2d 607, 615 (Tex. Civ. App. 1966).

52 181 203 307 486 559
Relevant Entry in West's Words and Phrases: LETTER STOCK   Kaufman v. Diversified Industries, Inc., C.A.N.Y., 460 F.2d 1331, 1335.
Aubrey Kaufman, Plaintiff-Appellee, v. Diversified Industries, Inc., Defendant-Appellant (United States Court of Appeals, Second Circuit May 3, 1972)
M/B: <u>Kaufman v. Diversified Industries</u>, 460 F.2d 1331, 1335 (2d Cir. 1972).
LR: Kaufman v. Diversified Indus., 460 F.2d 1331, 1335 (2d Cir. 1972).

53 182 204 308 487 560
Relevant Entry in West's Words and Phrases: ORGANOLEPTIC TEST   U.S. v. Commercial Creamery Co., D.C.Wash., 43 F.Supp. 714, 718.
United States v. Commercial Creamery Co. (District Court, E.D. Washington, N.D. March 12, 1942)

EXERCISE 25. WEST'S WORDS AND PHRASES   (CONTINUED)

M/B: United States v. Commercial Creamery Co., 43 F. Supp. 714, 718 (E.D. Wash. 1942).

54 183 205 309 488 561
Relevant Entry in West's Words and Phrases: OIL PAYMENT Alamo Nat. Bank of San Antonio v. Hurd, Tex.Civ.App., 485 S.W.2d 335, 340.
Alamo National Bank of San Antonio, Texas, et al., Appellants, v. Harry H. Hurd et al., Appellees (Court of Civil Appeals of Texas, San Antonio September 13, 1972)
M/B: Alamo National Bank v. Hurd, 485 S.W.2d 335, 340 (Tex. Civ. App. 1972).
LR: Alamo Nat'l Bank v. Hurd, 485 S.W.2d 335, 340 (Tex. Civ. App. 1972).

55 184 206 310 489 562
Relevant Entry in West's Words and Phrases: OATH OR AFFIRMATION People v. Sullivan, 437 N.E.2d 1130, 1132, 56 N.Y.2d 378, 452 N.Y.S.2d 373, 375.
The People of the State of New York, Respondent, v. James F. Sullivan, Jane R. Liebman and Mark L. Guido, Appellants (Court of Appeals of New York June 23, 1982)
M/B: People v. Sullivan, 56 N.Y.2d 378, ___, 437 N.E.2d 1130, 1132, 452 N.Y.S.2d 373, 375 (1982).

56 185 207 311 490 563
Relevant Entry in West's Words and Phrases: NET WORTH THEORY U.S. v. O'Connor, C.A. N.Y., 273 F.2d 358, 361.
United States of America, Plaintiff-Appellee, v. Raymond A. O'Connor, Defendant-Appellant (United States Court of Appeals Second Circuit October 14, 1959)
M/B: United States v. O'Connor, 273 F.2d 358, 361 (2d Cir. 1959).

57 186 208 312 491 565
Relevant Entry in West's Words and Phrases: NEUROMA Skidmore v. Drumon Fine Foods, Inc., La.App., 110 So.2d 770, 771.
Percy Skidmore v. Drumon Fine Foods, Inc., and Hardware Mutual Casualty Co. (Court of Appeal of Louisiana April 13, 1959)
M/B: Skidmore v. Drumon Fine Foods, Inc., 110 So. 2d 770, 771 (La. Ct. App. 1959).

58 187 209 313 492 565
Relevant Entry in West's Words and Phrases: NATURAL GAS ROYALTY J. M. Huber Corp. v. Denman, C.A.Tex., 367 F.2d 104, 115.
J. M. Huber Corporation, Appellant, v. William Harvey Denman and Jay Pumphrey, Trustees of the Estate of S. B. Burnett, Deceased, et al., Appellees (United States Court of Appeals Fifth Circuit September 20, 1966)
M/B: J.M. Huber Corp. v. Denman, 367 F.2d 104, 115 (5th Cir. 1966).

59 188 210 314 493 566
Relevant Entry in West's Words and Phrases: MONITION Hunt v. Paco Tankers, Inc., D.C.Tex., 226 F.Supp. 279, 280.
James G. Hunt, Libelant, v. Paco Tankers, Inc., Respondent (United States District Court January 31, 1964)
M/B: Hunt v. Paco Tankers, Inc., 226 F. Supp. 279, 280 (S.D. Tex. 1964).

60 189 211 315 494 567
Relevant Entry in West's Words and Phrases: PETTIFOGGERY Kraft v. U.S., C.A.Minn., 238 F.2d 794, 800.
Edwin Arnold Kraft, Appellant, v. United States of America, Appellee (United States Court of Appeals Eighth Circuit December 17, 1956)
M/B: Kraft v. United States, 238 F.2d 794, 800 (8th Cir. 1956).

61 190 212 316 495 568
Relevant Entry in West's Words and Phrases: PER MY ET PER TOUT In re Gerling's Estate, Mo., 303 S.W.2d 915, 917.
In the Matter of the Estate of Rose M. Gerling, Deceased (Supreme Court of Missouri July 8, 1957)
M/B: In re Estate of Gerling, 303 S.W.2d 915, 917 (Mo. 1957).
LR: In re Estate of Gerling, 303 S.W.2d 915, 917 (Mo. 1957).

EXERCISE 25.   WEST'S WORDS AND PHRASES   (CONTINUED)

Note: "In re Gerling's Estate" is also correct (arguably as the popular name of the case).

62 191 213 317 496 569
Relevant Entry in West's Words and Phrases: PEDIS POSSESSIO Ranchers Exploration & Development Co. v. Anaconda Co., D.C.Utah, 248 F.Supp. 708, 720.
Ranchers Exploration and Development Co., a New Mexico corporation, Plaintiff, v. The Anaconda Company, a Montana corporation, Topaz Beryllium Company, a Utah corporation, W.T. Hudson, Lenard Rockwell and M. G. White, Defendants (United States District Court December 22, 1965)
M/B: Ranchers Exploration & Development Co. v. Anaconda Co., 248 F. Supp. 708, 720 (C.D. Utah 1965).
LR: Ranchers Exploration & Dev. Co. v. Anaconda Co., 248 F. Supp. 708, 720 (C.D. Utah 1965).

63 192 214 318 497 570
Relevant Entry in West's Words and Phrases: PARENS PATRIAE Wilson v. Wilson, 474 P.2d 789, 791, 172 Colo. 566.
Juanita Phyllis Wilson, Plaintiff in Error, v. LeRay Cameron Wilson, a/k/a Larry Wilson, Defendant in Error (Supreme Court of Colorado September 28, 1970)
M/B: Wilson v. Wilson, 172 Colo. 566, ___. 474 P.2d 789, 791 (1970).

64 193 215 319 498 571
Relevant Entry in West's Words and Phrases: READY-TO-SERVE CHARGES Authority v. Finnigan, 195 A.2d 821, 822, 202 Pa.Super. 335.
East Taylor Municipal Authority, Appellant, v. James H. Finnigan and Rose Mary Finnigan (Superior Court of Pennsylvania December 12, 1963)
M/B: East Taylor Municipal Authority v. Finnigan, 202 Pa. Super. 335, ___, 195 A.2d 821, 822 (1963).
LR: East Taylor Mun. Auth. v. Finnigan, 202 Pa. Super. 335, ___, 195 A.2d 821, 822 (1963).

65 194 216 320 499 572
Relevant Entry in West's Words and Phrases: PUG MILL Schultz & Lindsay Const. Co. v. State, 494 P.2d 612, 616, 83 N.M. 534.
Schultz & Lindsay Construction Co., a North Dakota Corporation, licensed and doing business in the State of New Mexico, Plaintiff-Appellant, v. State of New Mexico and New Mexico State Highway Commission, Defendants-Appellees (Supreme Court of New Mexico March 3, 1972)
M/B: Schultz & Lindsay Construction Co. v. State, 83 N.M. 534, ___, 494 P.2d 612, 616 (1972).
LR: Schultz & Lindsay Constr. Co. v. State, 83 N.M. 534, ___, 494 P.2d 612, 616 (1972).

66 195 217 321 500 573
Relevant Entry in West's Words and Phrases: PULMONARY FIBROSIS Koshorek v. Pennsylvania R.Co., C.A.Pa., 318 F.2d 364, 365.
Alexander F. Koshorek, Appellant, v. The Pennsylvania Railroad Company (United States Court of Appeals Third Circuit April 2, 1962)
M/B: Brockett v. Abbe, 3 Conn. Cir. 12, ___, 206 A.2d 447, 448 (1964).

67 196 218 322 401 574
Relevant Entry in West's Words and Phrases: PRUNO State v. Herr, 423 P.2d 631, 632, 70 Wash.2d 446.
The State of Washington, Respondent, v. Edward L. Herr, Appellant (Supreme Court of Washington February 9, 1967)
M/B: State v. Herr, 70 Wash. 2d 446, ___, 423 P.2d 631, 632 (1967).

68 197 219 323 402 575
Relevant Entry in West's Words and Phrases: PROPERTY RATIONE SOLI Alford v. Finch, Fla., 155 So.2d 790, 792.
Julian Alford, as Chairman, T. Payne Kelly, Jr., Charles L. Hoffman, Thomas W. McBroom and Don Southwell, as Members of and constituting the Game and Fresh Water Fish Commission of the State of Florida; A.D. Aldrich, as Director of said Commission; Mack Hodges and Joe Shephard, Appellants, v. K. O. Finch, Howard P. Rives, Charles A. Johnson, Jr., R-J Farms, Inc., a Florida

EXERCISE 25.   WEST'S WORDS AND PHRASES   (CONTINUED)

corporation, Levy Land Co., Inc., a Florida corporation, Appellees (Supreme Court of Florida June 28, 1963)
M/B: Alford v. Finch, 155 So. 2d 790, 792 (Fla. 1963).

69 198 220 324 403 576
Relevant Entry in West's Words and Phrases: PREJUDICIAL SURPRISE   State v. HOffman, 190 S.E.2d 842, 848, 281 N.C. 727.
State of North Carolina v. James Ray Hoffman (Supreme Court of North Carolina August 31, 1972)
M/B: State v. Hoffman, 281 N.C. 727, ___, 190 S.E.2d 842, 848 (1972).

70 199 221 325 404 577
Relevant Entry in West's Words and Phrases: STOWERS DOCTRINE   Lacy v. Mid-Continent Cas. Co., D.C.Tex., 247 F.Supp. 667, 668.
Archie Lacy, Plaintiff, v. Mid-Continent Casualty Co., Defendant (United States District Court November 17, 1965)
M/B: Lacy v. Mid-Continent Casualty Co., 247 F. Supp. 667, 668 (S.D. Tex. 1965).

71 200 222 326 405 478
Relevant Entry in West's Words and Phrases: STRAIGHT LINE METHOD OF DEPRECIATION   Chadwick v. Cross, Abbott Co., 205 A.2d 416, 419, 124 Vt. 325.
Nelson W. Chadwick v. Cross, Abbott Company (Supreme Court of Vermont December 1, 1964)
M/B: Chadwick v. Cross, Abott Co., 124 Vt. 325, ___, 205 A.2d 416, 419 (1964).

72 101 223 327 406 579
Relevant Entry in West's Words and Phrases: SPITE FENCE   Welsh v. Todd, 133 S.E.2d 171, 173, 260 N.C. 527.
Landis H. Welsh and wife, Margaret W. Welsh, v. Leon M. Todd and wife, Mittie J. Todd (Supreme Court of North Carolina November 20, 1963)
M/B: Welsh v. Todd, 260 N.C. 527, ___, 133 S.E.2d 171, 173 (1963).

73 102 224 328 407 580
Relevant Entry in West's Words and Phrases: SIC UTERE TUO UT ALIENUM NON LAEDUS   Chapman v. Barnett, 169 N.E.2d 212, 214, 131 Ind.App. 30.
Raymond L. Chapman, Appellant, v. Noah Barnett and Ida Barnett, Appellees (Appellate Court of Indiana September 15, 1960)
M/B: Chapman v. Barnett, 131 Ind. App. 30, ___, 169 N.E.2d 212, 214 (1968).

74 103 225 329 408 581
Relevant Entry in West's Words and Phrases: SERVICE MARK   National Trailways Bus System v. Trailway Van Lines, Inc., D.C. N.Y., 269 F.Supp. 352, 356.
National Trailways Bus System, etc., Plaintiff, v. Trailway Van Lines, Inc., etc., Defendant   (United States District Court March 25, 1965)
M/B: National Trailways Bus System v. National Van Lines, 269 F. Supp. 352, 356 (E.D.N.Y. 1965).
LR: National Trailways Bus Sys. v. National Van Lines, 269 F. Supp. 352, 356 (E.D.N.Y. 1965).

75 104 226 330 409 582
Relevant Entry in West's Words and Phrases: SCULLING   Young v. U.S., D.C.S.C., 272 F.Supp. 738, 740.
Alice E. Young, as Administratrix of the Estate of Henry E. Young, Deceased, Plaintiff, v. United States of America, Defendant and Third-Party Plaintiff (United States District Court September 6, 1967)
M/B: Young v. United States, 272 F. Supp. 738, 740 (D.S.C. 1967).

76 105 227 331 410 583
Relevant Entry in West's Words and Phrases: REST. RESIDUE AND REMAINDER   Sinnott v. Gidney, 322 S.W.2d 507, 511, 159 Tex. 366, 74 A.L.R.2d 544.
Elizabeth K. Sinnott, Petitioner, v. Margaret K. Gidney et al., Respondents (Supreme Court of Texas March 4, 1959)
M/B: Sinnott v. Gidney, 159 Tex. 366, ___, 322 S.W.2d 507, 511 (1959).

77 106 228 332 411 584

EXERCISE 25.   WEST'S WORDS AND PHRASES   (CONTINUED)

Relevant Entry in West's Words and Phrases: RES INTEGRA   Reynolds v. Reynolds, 123 S.E.2d 115, 126, 217 Ga. 234.
Muriel M. Reynolds v. Richard J. Reynolds (Supreme Court of Georgia September 8, 1961)
M/B: Reynolds v. Reynolds, 217 Ga. 234, ___, 123 S.E.2d 115, 126 (1961).

78 107 229 333 412 585
Relevant Entry in West's Words and Phrases: RES INTER ALIOS ACTA   Roosth & Genecov Production Co. v. White, Tex.Civ.App., 281 S.W.2d 333, 339.
Roosth & Genecov Production Company, Inc., Appellant, v. Loren Lee White et al., Appellees (Court of Civil Appeals of Texas June 16, 1955)
M/B: Roosth & Genecov Production Co. v. White, 281 S.W.2d 333, 339 (Tex. Civ. App. 1955).
LR: Roosth & Genecov Prod. Co. v. White, 281 S.W.2d 333, 339 (Tex. Civ. App. 1955).

79 108 230 334 413 586
Relevant Entry in West's Words and Phrases: RED-BLUE-YELLOW   Advance Business Systems & Supply Co. v. SCM Corp., D.C.Md., 287 F.Supp. 143, 163.
Advance Business Systems & Supply Company, a body corporate of the State of Maryland, v. SCM Corporation, a body corporate of the State of New York (United States District Court June 20, 1968)
M/B: Advance Business Systems & Supply Co. v. SCM Corp., 287 F. Supp. 143, 163 (D. Md. 1968).
LR: Advance Business Sys. & Supply Co.v. SCM Corp., 287 F. Supp. 143, 163 (D. Md. 1968).

80 109 231 335 414 587
Relevant Entry in West's Words and Phrases: ULLAGE   The E.H. Blum, D.C.Pa., 74 F.Supp. 516, 521.
The E. H. Blum. Atlantic Refining Co. v. United States (District Court, E.D. Pennsylvania November 21, 1947)
M/B: The E.H. Blum, 74 F. Supp. 516, 521 (E.D. Pa. 1947).

81 110 232 336 415 588
Relevant Entry in West's Words and Phrases: TREASURY BILL   U.S. v. Manufacturers Hanover Trust Co., D.C.N.Y., 240 F.Supp. 867, 897.
United States of America, Plaintiff, v. Manufacturers Hanover Trust Company, Defendant (United States District Court March 10, 1965)
M/B: United States v. Manufacturers Hanover Trust Co., 240 F. Supp. 867, 897 (S.D.N.Y. 1965).

82 111 233 337 416 589
Relevant Entry in West's Words and Phrases: TREASURY STOCK   Fuller v. Krogh, 113 N.W.2d 25, 31, 15 Wis.2d 412.
Harold E. Fuller, Appellant, v. John T. Krogh, Respondent (Supreme Court of Wisconsin January 15, 1962)
M/B: Fuller v. Krogh, 15 Wis. 2d 412, 113 N.W.2d 25, 31 (1962).

83 112 234 338 417 590
Relevant Entry in West's Words and Phrases: TOUTING   People v. Owens, 23 Cal. Rptr. 449, 452, 205 C.A.2d 775.
The People of the State of California, Plaintiff and Respondent, v. John Owens, Defendant and Appellant (District Court of Appeal, Second Circuit July 23, 1962)
M/B: People v. Ownes, 205 Cal. App. 2d 775, ___, 23 Cal. Rptr. 449, 452 (1962).

84 113 235 339 418 591
Relevant Entry in West's Words and Phrases: TRADE ACCEPTANCE   Gilliland & Echols Farm Supply & Hatchery v. Credit Equipment Corp., 112 So.2d 331, 332, 269 Ala. 190.
Gilliland & Echols Farm Supply & Hatchery v. Credit Equipment Corporation (Supreme Court of Alabama May 21, 1959)
M/B: Gilliland & Echols Farm Supply & Hatchery v. Credit Equipment Corp., 269 Ala. 190, ___, 112 So. 2d 331 332 (1959).

EXERCISE 25. <u>WEST'S WORDS AND PHRASES</u> (CONTINUED)

LR: Gilliland & Echols Farm Supply & Hatchery v. Credit Equip. Corp., 269 Ala. 190, ___, 112 So. 2d 331 332 (1959).

85 114 236 340 419 592
Relevant Entry in West's Words and Phrases: TESTAMENTARY CLASS GIFT Lux v. Lux, R.I., 288 A.2d 701, 705.
Anthony J. Lux, Jr., as Executor uM/B:w Philomena Lux v. Donna M. Lux et al. (Supreme Court of Rhode Island March 21, 1972)
M/B: <u>Lux v. Lux</u>, 109 R.I. 592, ___, 288 A.2d 701, 705 (1972).

86 115 237 341 420 593
Relevant Entry in West's Words and Phrases: TACHYCARDIA Bertrand v. Coal Operators Cas. Co., La.App., 204 So.2d 620, 621.
Milton Bertrand, Plaintiff and Appellee, v. Coal Operators Casualty Company, Defendant and Appellant (Court of Appeal of Louisiana Third Circuit November 29, 1967)
M/B: <u>Bertrand v. Coal Operators Casualty Co.</u>, 204 So. 2d 620, 621 (La. Ct. App. 1967).

87 116 238 342 421 594
Relevant Entry in West's Words and Phrases: TACKING Cheatham v. Vanderwey, 499 P.2d 986, 988, 18 Ariz.App. 35.
Earnest C. Cheatham and Adele Cheatham, his wife, G. W. Cheatham and Edna Cheatham, his wife, Armon D. Cheatham and Ruth Cheatham, his wife, and L. F. Cheatham and Rita E. Cheatham, his wife, Appellants and Cross-Appellees, v. John A. Vandervey aka Johannes Auke Van Der Weij and Angellna R. Vanderwey, his wife, Appellees and Cross-Appellants (Court of Appeals of Arizona August 1, 1972)
M/B: <u>Cheatham v. Vanderwey</u>, 18 Ariz. App. 35, ___, 499 P.2d 986, 988 (1972).

88 117 239 343 422 595
Relevant Entry in West's Words and Phrases: WINDSTORM Napanoch Realty Corp. v. Public Service Mut. Ins. Co., 336 N.Y.S.2d 489, 490, 39 A.D.2d 438.
Napanoch Realty Corp., Appellant, v. Public Service Mutual Insurance Company, Respondent (Supreme Court, Appellate Division, Third Department October 19, 1972)
M/B: <u>Napanoch Realty Corp. v. Public Service Mutual Insurance Co.</u>, 39 A.D.2d 438, ___, 336 N.Y.S.2d 489, 490 (1972).
LR: Napanoch Realty Corp. v. Public Serv. Mut. Ins. Co., 39 A.D.2d 438, ___, 336 N.Y.S.2d 489, 490 (1972).

89 118 240 344 423 596
Relevant Entry in West's Words and Phrases: WOOD BUTCHER Rapisardi v. United Fruit Co., C.A.N.Y., 441 F.2d 1308, 1310.
Salvatore Rapisardi, Plaintiff-Appellee, v. United Fruit Company, Defendant and Third-Party Plaintiff-Appellant (United States Court of Appeals, Second Circuit January 12, 1971)
M/B: <u>Rapisardi v. United Fruit Co.</u>, 441 F.2d 1308, 1310, (2d Cir. 1971).

90 119 241 345 424 597
Relevant Entry in West's Words and Phrases: WHARFAGE Howmet Corp. v. Tokyo Shipping Co., D.C.Del., 320 F.Supp. 975, 978.
Howmet Corporation, Plaintiff, v. Tokyo Shipping Co., Ltd., etc. (United States District Court January 8, 1971)
M/B: <u>Howmet Corp. v. Tokyo Shipping Co.</u>, 320 F. Supp. 975, 978 (D. Del. 1971).

91 120 242 346 425 598
Relevant Entry in West's Words and Phrases: WITH HER CONSENT Torres v. State, Alaska, 521 P.2d 386, 388.
Rudolph Valle Torres, Appellant, v. State of Alaska (Supreme Court of Alaska April 19, 1974)
M/B: <u>Torres v. State</u>, 521 P.2d 386, 388 (Alaska 1974).

92 121 243 347 426 599
Relevant Entry in West's Words and Phrases: VALUED POLICY Houston Fire & Cas. Ins. Co. v. Nichols, Tex., 435 S.W.2d 140, 142.

EXERCISE 25. WEST'S WORDS AND PHRASES   (CONTINUED)

Houston Fire and Casualty Insurance Company, Petitioner, v. Benny Nichols, Respondent (Supreme Court of Texas December 11, 1968)
M/B: Houston Fire & Casualty Insurance Co. v. Nichols, 435 S.W.2d 140, 142 (Tex. 1968).
LR: Houston Fire & Casualty Ins. Co. v. Nichols, 435 S.W.2d 140, 142 (Tex. 1968).

93 122 244 348 427 600
Relevant Entry in West's Words and Phrases: UNLIMITED ARBITRATION CLAUSE
International Service Ins. Co. v. Ross, 457 P.2d 917, 923, 169 Colo. 451.
International Service Insurance Company, Plaintiff in Error, v. Earl G. Ross, Defendant in Error (Supreme Court of Colorado August 5, 1969)
M/B: International Service Insurance Co. v. Ross, 169 Colo. 451, ___, 457 P.2d 917, 923 (1969).
LR: International Serv. Ins. Co. v. Ross, 169 Colo. 451, ___, 457 P.2d 917, 923 (1969).

94 123 245 349 428 501
Relevant Entry in West's Words and Phrases: UTTERING OF FORGED INSTRUMENT
State v. Reyers, 458 P.2d 960, 961, 105 Ariz. 26.
The State of Arizona, Appellee, v. Eluterio Flores Reyes, Jr., Appellant (Supreme Court of Arizona September 25, 1969)
M/B: State v. Reyes, 105 Ariz. 26, ___, 458 P.2d 960, 961 (1969).

95 124 246 350 429 502
Relevant Entry in West's Words and Phrases: VAPOR LOCK ACF Industries, Inc. v. Airtex Products, Inc., D.C.Ill., 241 F.Supp. 916, 919.
ACF Industries, Incorporated, Plaintiff, v. Airtex Products, Incorporated (United States District Court May 20, 1965)
M/B: ACF Industries v. Airtex Products, Inc., 241 F. Supp. 916, 919 (E.D. Ill. 1965).
LR: ACF Indus. v. Airtex Prods., Inc., 241 F. Supp. 916, 919 (E.D. Ill. 1965).

96 125 247 351 430 503
Relevant Entry in West's Words and Phrases: WARRANTY OF SEAWORTHINESS Young v. Clear Lake Yacht Basin, Inc., D.C.Tex., 337 F.Supp. 1305, 1315.
Robert B. Young, Plaintiff, v. Clear Lake Yacht Basin, Inc., et al., Defendants (United States District Court January 19, 1972)
M/B: Young v. Clear Lake Yacht Basin, Inc., 337 F. Supp. 1305, 1315 (S.D. Tex. 1972).

97 126 248 352 431 504
Relevant Entry in West's Words and Phrases: WASHOUT Westinghouse Elec. Supply Co. v. Reagan, Fla., 159 So.2d 222, 225.
Westinghouse Electric Supply Co. v. Ruth W. Reagan and Florida Industrial Commission, Respondents (Supreme Court of Florida December 18, 1963)
M/B: Westinghouse Electric Supply Co. v. Reagan, 159 So. 2d 222, 225 (Fla. 1963).
LR: Westinghouse Elec. Supply Co. v. Reagan, 159 So. 2d 222, 225 (Fla. 1963).

98 127 249 353 432 505
Relevant Entry in West's Words and Phrases: WILLFULLY NEGLIGENT Hannon v. J. L. Brandeis & Sons, Inc., 181 N.W.2d 253, 256, 186 Neb. 122.
Sylvia R. Hannon, Widow of Thomas E. Hannon, Deceased, Appellee, v. J. L. Brandeis & Sons, Inc., Appellant (Supreme Court of Nebraska November 20, 1970)
M/B: Hannon v. J.L. Brandeis & Sons, 186 Neb. 122, ___, 181 N.W.2d 253, 256 (1970).

99 128 250 354 433 506
Relevant Entry in West's Words and Phrases: WORK STOPPAGE City of Grandview v. Moore, Mo.App., 481 S.W.2d 555, 557.
City of Grandview, Missouri, Respondent, v. Larry L. Moore et al., Appellants (Missouri Court of Appeals April 3, 1972)
M/B: City of Grandview v. Moore, 481 S.W.2d 555, 557 (Mo. Ct. App. 1972).

100 129 251 355 434 507

EXERCISE 25.   WEST'S WORDS AND PHRASES   (CONTINUED)

Relevant Entry in West's Words and Phrases: XYLEM Rico Import Co. v. U.S., Cust. & Pat.App., 469 F.2d 699, 701.
Rico Import Company, Appellant, v. The United States, Appellee (United States Court of Customs and Patent Appeals November 30, 1972)
M/B: Rico Import Co. v. United States, 469 F.2d 699, 701 (C.C.P.A. 1972).

LIBRARY EXERCISE 26. TABLES OF CASES AND POPULAR NAME TABLES.

INSTRUCTOR'S NOTE: Using the information provided below, students are asked to find the relevant entry in the designated Table of Cases, Defendant/Plaintiff Table, or Popular Name Table and to cite the case. They are specifically instructed not show the case's subsequent history in your citation and to cite Supreme Court cases only to <u>United States Reports</u>. The following abbreviations are used below: P = Plaintiff; D = Defendant; T/C = Table of Cases; D/P = Defendant/Plaintiff Table; PNT = Popular Name Table; Dec. = Decennial; Dig. = Digest; Shep. PNT = <u>Shepard's Acts and Cases By Popular Names--Federal and State</u>; S. Ct. = U.S. Supreme Court. Note that the listing of popular names of cases is located at the end of the <u>Shepard's</u> volume. Students are specifically instructed not to rely on the form used in the table for their citations.

1 104 233 344 452 579
Relevant Entry in the Table: Schumaat v. Mellies 231 Mich 277, 203 NW 990
Schmaat et al. v. Mellies et al. (Supreme Court of Michigan June 3, 1925)
M/B: <u>Schumaat v. Mellies</u>, 231 Mich. 277, 203 N.W. 990 (1925).

2 105 234 345 453 580
Relevant Entry in the Table: Spreading Fire Case 121 Colo 227, 214 P2d 793
Boynton et al. v. Fox Denver Theaters, Inc. (Supreme Court of Colorado, in Department January 30, 1950)
M/B: <u>Boynton v. Fox Denver Theaters</u>, 121 Colo. 227, 214 P.2d 793 (1950).

3 106 235 346 454 581
Relevant Entry in the Table: Electric Theater Co. v. Darby 123 Kan. 225, 254 P. 1035
Electric Theater Co. et al. v. Darby et al. (Supreme court of Kansas April 9, 1927)
M/B: <u>Electric Theater Co. v. Darby</u>, 123 Kan. 225, 254 P. 1035 (1927).

4 107 236 347 455 582
Relevant Entry in the Table: Densen's Estate, Re 163 Misc 232, 296 N.Y.S. 567
In re Densen's Estate (Surrogate's Court, Kings County June 1, 1937)
M/B: <u>In re Densen's Estate</u>, 163 Misc. 232, 296 N.Y.S. 567 (Sur. Ct. 1937).
LR: <u>In re Densen's Estate</u>, 163 Misc. 232, 296 N.Y.S. 567 (Sur. Ct. 1937).

5 108 237 348 456 583
Relevant Entry in the Table: Hodson-Smallwood 101 USAppDC 354, 249 F2d 110
Grahame Thomas Smallwood, Jr., et al., Appellants, v. Viola A. Hodson et al., Appellees (United States Court of Appeals District of Columbia Circuit May 29, 1957)
M/B: <u>Smallwood v. Hodson</u>, 249 F.2d 110 (D.C. Cir. 1957).

6 109 238 349 457 584
Relevant Entry in the Table: World's Fair Mining Co. v. Powers 224 U.S. 173
World's Fair Mining Co. v. Powers (Error to the Supreme Court of the Territory of Arizona April 1, 1912)
M/B: <u>World's Fair Mining Co. v. Powers</u>, 224 U.S. 173 (1912).

7 110 239 350 458 585
Relevant Entry in the Table: Hlavaty v. Muffitt, 190 F. Supp. 541
Albert Hlavaty, Plaintiff,
M/B: <u>Hlavaty v. Muffitt</u>, 190 F. Supp. 541 (W.D. Va. 1960).

8 111 240 351 459 586
Relevant Entry in the Table: Landa Cotton Oil Co Refining Co. Tex. 23 SCt 754, 190 US 540, 47
Globe Refining Company v. Landa Cotton Oil Company (Error to the Circuit Court of the United States for the Western District of Texas June 1, 1903)
M/B: <u>Globe Refining Co. v. Landa Cotton Oil Co.</u>, 190 U.S. 540 (1903).
LR: Globe Ref. Co. v. Landa Cotton Oil Co., 190 U.S. 540 (1903).

9 112 241 352 460 587
Relevant Entry in the Table: Rouselle - State of La, CALa, 418, F2d 873
State of Louisiana, Appellee, v. Lawrence J. Rouselle, Jr., Appellant (United States Court of Appeals November 5, 1969)

EXERCISE 26. TABLES OF CASES AND POPULAR NAME TABLES   (CONTINUED)

M/B: United States v. Rouselle, 534 F.2d 584 (5th Cir. 1976).

10 113 242 353 461 588
Relevant Entry in the Table: Vandike v. Brown, LaApp, 139 So2d 803 - Admin Law 788; Social So 388, 392, 584, 671
Alex Vandike, Plaintiff-Appellant, v. Richard E. Brown, Jr., Administrator, Defendant-Appellee (Court of Appeal of Louisiana April 9, 1962)
M/B: Vandike v. Brown, 139 So. 2d 803 (La. Ct. App. 1962).

11 114 243 354 462 589
Relevant Entry in the Table: Heckman v. United States, 224 US 413, 32 S Ct 424, 56 L Ed 820
Heckman v. United States (Appeal from the Circuit Court of Appeals for the April 1, 1912)
M/B: Heckman v. United States, 224 U.S. 413 (1912).

12 115 244 355 463 590
Relevant Entry in the Table: American Quasar Petroleum Co. of N M-Continental Oil Co DCWyo, 438 FSupp 909
Continental Oil Company, a corporation, and Gulf Oil Corporation, corporation, Plaintiffs, v. American Quasar Petroleum Co. of New Mexico, a corporation, Defendant (United States District Court, D. Wyoming October 21, 1977)
M/B: Continental Oil Co. v. American Quasar Petroleum Co., 438 F. Supp. 909 (D. Wyo. 1977).

13 116 245 356 464 591
Relevant Entry in the Table: Hindle v. National Bulk Carriers, DC NY. 18 FRD 198-Fed Civ Proc 1556,1599
Herbert C. Hindle, Plaintiff, v. National Bulk Carriers, Inc., (United States District Court S.D. New York August 9, 1955)
M/B: Hindle v. National Bulk Carriers, 18 F.R.D. 198 (S.D.N.Y. 1955).

14 117 246 357 465 592
Relevant Entry in the Table: West's Will, In re 246 Wis 199, 16 NW2d 806
In re West's Will; Darwin v. West (Supreme COurt of Wisconsin December 19, 1944)
M/B: In re West's Will, 246 Wis. 199, 16 N.W.2d 806 (1944).
LR: In re West's Will, 246 Wis. 199, 16 N.W.2d 806 (1944).

15 118 247 358 466 593
Relevant Entry in the Table: Nelse Mortensen & Co v. Treadwell, CA Wash, 217 F2d 325 - Chat Mtg 16; Courts 406.3(8); Fed Civ Proc 1900; Fixt 4, 18(1), 19, 27(1), 29, 35(2); Mtg 624(1)
Nelse Mortensen & Co., Inc., Appellant, v. Kenneth S. Treadwell, Trustee of Puget Sound Products Co.,
M/B: Nelse Mortenson & Co. v. Treadwell, 217 F.2d 325 (9th Cir. 1954).

16 119 248 359 467 594
Relevant Entry in the Table: Hartline v. Clary, DCSC, 141 FSupp 151 - Dist & Pros Attys 10; Evid 44; Fed Civ Proc 1832; Int Rev 1230; Judges 36; Offic 114, 116
P.F. Hartline, Plaintiff, v. H.P. Clary and Edward Carswell, Defendants (United States District Court E.D. South Carolina, Charleston Division May 5, 1956)
M/B: Hartline v. Clary, 141 F. Supp. 151 (E.D.S.C. 1956).

17 120 249 360 468 595
Relevant Entry in the Table: The Cow Place, Ltd., a Washington Corporation, and the Dolsen Company, a Washington Corporation, Plaintiffs v. Associated Milk Producers, Inc., a corporation, Defendant (United States District Court, D.Colorado February 10, 1975)
M/B: Cow Palace, Ltd. v. Associated Milk Producers, Inc., 390 F. Supp. 696 (D. Colo. 1975).

18 121 250 361 469 596
Relevant Entry in the Table: Lebosky v. Saxbe, CAGa, 508 F2d 1047 - Courts 495; Crim Law 273.1 (2); Mand 173; States 4.16

EXERCISE 26. <u>TABLES OF CASES AND POPULAR NAME TABLES</u>   (CONTINUED)

George M. Lebosky, aka Michael G. Lacey, Petitioner-Appellant, v. William B. Saxbe, Attorney General of the United States, et al., Respondents-Appellees (United States Court of Appeals February 13, 1975)
M/B: <u>Lebosky v. Saxbe</u>, 508 F.2d 1047 (5th Cir. 1975).

19 122 251 362 470 597
Relevant Entry in the Table: Yellowwolf v. Morris, CAWash, 536 F2d 813 - Courts 100(1); Crim Law 1166(3)
Lester Yellowwolf, Jr., Petitioner-Appellant, v. Charles Morris, Secretary, Department of Social and Health Services, Respondent-Appellee
M/B: <u>Yellowwolf v. Morris</u>, 536 F.2d 813 (9th Cir. 1976).

20 123 252 363 471 598
Relevant Entry in the Table: Taylor v. Leesnitzer 220 US 90, 31 S Ct 371, 55 L Ed 382
Taylor v. Leesnitzer (March 20, 1911)
M/B: <u>Taylor v. Leesnitzer</u>, 220 U.S. 90 (1911).

21 124 253 364 472 599
Relevant Entry in the Table: Cappis v. Wiedemann 86Minn, 156 90N.W. 368; D App & E 302(1) 8 D Evid §408(2)
Cappis v. Wiedemann (Supreme Court of Minnesota May 9, 1902)
M/B: <u>Cappis v. Wiedemann</u>, 86 Minn. 156, 90 N.W. 368 (1902).

22 125 254 365 473 600
Relevant Entry in the Table: Leonidas, The, Fed Cas No 8262, Olc12; 1 C Adm §267, 279, 282, 327, 684; 43 C Seamen §2, 86, 131; 44 C Ship §312 437, 612
Leonard v. The Volunteer (District Court S.D¶ New York October 1843)
M/B: <u>The Leonidas</u>, 15 F. Cas. 348 (S.D.N.Y. 1843) (No. 8262).

23 126 255 366 474 501
Relevant Entry in the Table: Sehy v. Salt Lake City 41Utah 535, 126 P691 42LRA (NS) 915; Mun. Corp. 723, 747(3), 834
Sehy v. Salt Lake City (Supreme Court of Utah July 22, 1912)
M/B: <u>Sehy v. Salt Lake City</u>, 41 Utah 535, 126 P. 691 (1912).

24 127 256 367 475 502
Relevant Entry in the Table: Rutland Provision Co. v. Hall 71 Vt.208, 44A94; 3 D Bills & N. §371
Ruthland Provision Co. v. Hall (Supreme Court of Vermont Windsor January 26, 1899)
M/B: <u>Rutland Provision Co. v. Hall</u>, 71 Vt. 208, 44 A. 94 (1899).

25 128 257 368 476 503

Relevant Entry in the Table: Yamataya v. Fisher, 189 US 86, 23 S Ct 611, 47 L Ed 721
U.S Reports: The Japanese Immigrant Case (April 6, 1903) (Popular name)
S. Ct. Rptr: Kaoru Yamataya, Appt., v. Thomas M. Fisher, Immigrant and Chinese Inspector (April 6, 1903)
M/B: <u>Yamataya v. Fisher</u>, 189 U.S. 86 (1903) OR <u>The Japanese Immigrant Case</u>, 189 U.S. 86 (1903).

26 129 258 369 477 504
Relevant Entry in the Table: Roschen v. Ward, 279 US 337, 49 S Ct 336, 73 L Ed 722
Roschen v. Ward, Attorney General of New York, et al. S.S. Krege Company v. Same (April 22, 1929)
M/B: <u>Roschen v. Ward</u>, 279 U.S. 337 (1929).

27 130 259 370 478 505
Relevant Entry in the Table: First Nat Bank of Bellevue v. Bank of Bellevue, DCNeb, 341 FSupp 960 - Rem of C 21, 82
First National Bank of Bellevue, a National Banking Association, Plaintiff, v. Bank of Bellevue, a Nebraska Corporation, et al., Defendants (United States District Court, D. Nebraska April 6, 1972)

EXERCISE 26. TABLES OF CASES AND POPULAR NAME TABLES   (CONTINUED)

M/B: First National Bank v. Bank of Bellevue, 341 F. Supp. 960 (D. Neb. 1972).
LR: First Nat'l Bank v. Bank of Bellevue, 341 F. Supp. 960 (D. Neb. 1972).

28 131 260 371 479 506
Relevant Entry in the Table: Wiskie v. Montello Granite Co. 111 Wis 443. 87N. W.461 87Am St. Rep 885; 13 D Mast & S §190(6), 217(29)
Wiskie v. Montello Granite Co. (Supreme Court of Wisconsin October 15, 1901)
M/B: Wiskie v. Montello Granite Co., 111 Wis. 443, 87 N.W. 461 (1901).

29 132 261 372 480 507
Relevant Entry in the Table: Hamberger v. Wolfe-Smith Co. 205 AppDiv 739, 200 NYS 803 - Insurance 229(2); Mast & S 397
Hamberger v. Wolfe-Smith Co. et al. (Supreme Court Appellate Div. Third Department June 19, 1923)
M/B: Hamberger v. Wolfe-Smith Co., 205 A.D. 739, 200 N.Y.S. 803 (1923).

30 133 262 373 481 508
Relevant Entry in the Table: Sabbatino Case 376 US 398, 11 LE2d 804, 84 SC 923
Banco Nacional de Cuba v. Sabbatino, Receiver, et al (Certiorari to the United States Court of Appeals March 23, 1964)
M/B: Banco Nacional de Cuba v. Sabbatino, 376 U.S. 398 (1964).

31 134 263 374 482 509
Relevant Entry in the Table: Tenore v. McKinley 119 PaSuper 368, 181 A 325 - App & E 930(1); Autos 245(14); Evid 588
Tenore v. McKinley (Superior Court of Pennsylvania November 13, 1935)
M/B: Tenore v. McKinley, 119 Pa. Super. 368, 181 A. 325 (1935).

32 135 264 375 483 510
Relevant Entry in the Table: Burkley v. City of Philadelphia 339 Pa 426. 15 A2d 201 - Mun Corp. 957(3, 4), 980(3); Schools 106.37; Statut 95(1); Tax 44; Trial 388(1)
Burkley v. City of Philadelphia et al. (Supreme Court of Pennsylvania September 10, 1940)
M/B: Burkley v. City of Philadelphia, 339 Pa. 426, 15 A.2d 201 (1940).

33 136 265 376 484 511
Relevant Entry in the Table: Dri Mark Products, Inc - Speedry Products, Inc. CANY, 271 F2d 646
Speedry Products, Inc., Plaintiff Appellant, v. Dri Mark Products, Inc., Suburban Dyers & Finishers, Inc., Milton Dinowitz d/b/a Commodore Stationers, Lanart Associates, Inc., Milton Landin and Arthur S. Romm, Defendants-Appellees (United states Court of Appeals November 6, 1959)
M/B: Speedry Products, Inc. v. Dri Mark Products, Inc., 271 F.2d 646 (2d Cir. 1959).
LR: Speedry Prods., Inc. v. Dri Mark Prods., Inc., 271 F.2d 646 (2d Cir. 1959).

34 137 266 377 485 512
Relevant Entry in the Table: Federal Reserve Bank of Richmond v. Malloy NC, 44 SCt 296, 264 US 160, 68 LEd 617, 31 ALR 1261 - Banks 161(3), 171(1) 288 1M/B:2; Cust & U 6, 8; Evid 65; Princ & A 105 (9)
Federal Reserve Bank of Richmond v. Malloy et al., Trading as Malloy Brothers (Error to the Circuit Court of Appeals for the Fourth Circuit February 18,1924)
M/B: Federal Reserve Bank v. Malloy, 264 U.S. 160 (1924).

35 138 267 378 486 513
Relevant Entry in the Table: Cech v. Moore-McCormack Lines, Inc, CANY, 294 F2d 584 - Fed Civ Proc 1706
Peter A. Cech, Plaintiff-Appellant, v. Moore-McCormack Lines, Inc., Defendant-Appellee (United States Court of Appeals September 28, 1961)
M/B: Cech v. Moore-McCormack Lines, 294 F.2d 584 (2d Cir. 1961).

36 139 268 379 487 514

EXERCISE 26. TABLES OF CASES AND POPULAR NAME TABLES   (CONTINUED)

Relevant Entry in the Table: Van Dolsen - Abendroth, NY, 9 S Ct 619, 131 US 66, 33 LEd 57
Abendroth v. Van Dolsen (Error to the City Court of New York May 13, 1889)
M/B: <u>Abendroth v. Van Dolsen</u>, 131 U.S. 66 (1889).

37 140 269 380 488 515
Relevant Entry in the Table: REDUS - US, CACal, 469 F2d 185
United States of America, Plaintiff-Appellant, v. Bennie Sherman Redus Defendant Appellee (United States Court of Appeals October 12, 1972)
M/B: <u>United States v. Redus</u>, 469 F.2d 185 (9th Cir. 1972).

38 141 270 381 489 516
Relevant Entry in the Table: Riggs Optical Co. v. Riggs 270 NW 667, 132 Neb 26 - TRade Reg 466, 492
Riggs Optical Co. v. Riggs (Supreme Court of Nebraska January 5, 1937)
M/B: <u>Riggs Optical Co. v. Riggs</u>, 132 Neb. 26, 270 N.W. 667 (1937).

39 142 271 382 490 517
Relevant Entry in the Table: Burdell v. Denig, 92 US 716 23 L Ed 764 - contr§58h; damg §§138a, 142a, g, o, 144a, 850g; pat §210h; tr §§231b, 233b
Burdell et al. v. Denig et al., 1966)
M/B: <u>Burdell v. Denig</u>, 92 U.S. 716 (1875).

40 143 272 383 491 518
Relevant Entry in the Table: Carrell - U S, DCDC, 231 FSupp 724
United States of America Plaintiff, v. Reginald Carrell, Defendant (United States District Court June 12, 1964)
M/B: <u>United States v. Carrell</u>, 231 F. Supp. 724 (D.D.C. 1964).

41 144 273 384 492 519
Relevant Entry in the Table: Farin v. Sercarz 179 Misc 490, 39 NYS 2d 482 - Labor 433
Farin v. Sercarz et al (Supreme Court, Sepcial Term, New York County December 11, 1942)
M/B: <u>Farin v. Sercarz</u>, 179 Misc. 490, 39 N.Y.S.2d 482 (Sup. Ct. 1942).

42 145 274 385 493 520
Relevant Entry in the Table: Smith v. Frinkel 130 Conn 354, 34 A2d 209 - App & E 440, 656(3), 1008(1); Auto 148, 201(5); Plead 406(7)
Smith et al. v. Finkel et al. (Supreme Court of Errors of Connecticut July 22, 1943)
M/B: <u>Smith v. Finkel</u>, 130 Conn. 354, 34 A.2d 209 (1943).

43 146 275 386 494 521
Relevant Entry in the Table: Bottle-Stopper Case Putnam v. Tinkham 4 F 411
Putnam v. Tinkham (Circuit Court, D. Connecticut October 23, 1880)
M/B: <u>Putnam v. Tinkham</u>, 4 F. 411 (2d Cir. 1880).

44 147 276 387 495 522
Relevant Entry in the Table: Cradic v. Eastman Kodak Co, DC Tenn, 202 FSupp 590 - Work Comp 2161
Roy Cradic, Plaintiff, v. Eastman Kodak Company and Tennessee Eastman Company Defendants (United States District Court E. D. Tennessee March 5, 1962)
M/B: <u>Cradic v. Eastman Kodak Co.</u>, 202 F. Supp. 590 (E.D. Tenn. 1962).

45 148 277 388 496 523
Relevant Entry in the Table: C-Line, Inc. v. U S, DCRI, 376 FSUPP 1043 - Admin Law 502, 760, 763, 791; Commerce 85.6, 85.25, 99, 108, 120, 161, 174, 176; Statut 179, 189, 217.4
C-Line, Inc. and American Institute for Shippers' Association, Inc. Plaintiffs, v. United States of America and Interstate Commerce Commission Defendants (United States District Court, D. Rhode ISland May 22, 1974)
M/B: <u>C-Line, Inc. v. United States</u>, 376 F. Supp. 1043 (D.R.I. 1974).

46 149 278 389 497 524
Relevant Entry in the Table: Kenier v. Canal Nat Bank, CAMe 489 F2d 482 - Atty & C 109; Corp 128, 130, 133, 134; U S 78(8)

EXERCISE 26.   TABLES OF CASES AND POPULAR NAME TABLES   (CONTINUED)

Myron L. Kenler and Regina O. Kenler, Plaintiffs, Appellants, v. Canal National Bank, Defendant, Appellee (United States Court of Appeals October 18, 1973)
M/B: Kenler v. Canal National Bank, 489 F.2d 482 (1st Cir. 1973).
LR: Kenler v. Canal Nat'l Bank, 489 F.2d 482 (1st Cir. 1973).

47 150 279 390 498 525
Relevant Entry in the Table: Troglione v. McIntyre Aviation Inc, DCPa, 60 FRD 511 Fed Civ Proc 1603
Vincent R. Troglione, Plaintiff, v. McIntyre Aviation, Inc., et al., Defendants (United States District Court W.D. Pennsylvania September 13, 1973)
M/B: Troglione v. McIntyre Aviation, Inc., 60 F.R.D. 511 (W.D. Pa. 1973).

48 151 280 391 499 526
Relevant Entry in the Table: Blair v. Bemis 43 Tex. Civ. App. 134, 94S.W¶ 116; 8D Evid §271(19); 16D Princ & A §134; 17 D Sales §38(9), 114, 121, 233(1); 19D Trial §198
Blair v. Bemis (District Court, D. Connecticut 1863)
M/B: Blair v. Bemis, 3 F. Cas. 577 (D. Conn. 1863) (No. 1484).

49 152 281 392 500 527
Relevant Entry in the Table: Danielly v. Cheeves 94 Ga. 263, 21 S.E. 524
Danielly v. Cheeves (Supreme Court of Georgia August 14, 1894)
M/B: Danielly v. Cheeves, 94 Ga. 263, 21 S.E. 524 (1894).

50 153 282 393 401 528
Relevant Entry in the Table: Indianapolis Brewing Co. v. Claypool, 149 Ind. 193, 48 N.E. 228
Indianapolis Brewing Co. v. Claypool et al. (Supreme Court of Indiana November 5, 1897)
M/B: Indianapolis Brewing Co. v. Claypool, 149 Ind. 193, 48 N.E. 228 (1897).

51 154 283 394 402 529
Relevant Entry in the Table: Clay Lumber Co. v. Hart's Branch Coal Co. 174Mich613, 140NW912; Contracts 187(3); Frds.,St of 33(1); Garn 13; Nova. 5
Clay Lumber Co. v. Hart's Branch Coal Co. (Steffens et al., Garnishees). (Supreme Court of Michigan April 8, 1913)
M/B: Clay Lumber Co. v. Hart's Branch Coal Co., 174 Mich. 613, 140 N.W. 912 (1913).

52 155 284 395 403 530
Relevant Entry in the Table: Morico v United States, 399 US 526, 70 S Ct 2230, 26 L Ed 2d 776
Morico v. United States (June 29, 1970)
M/B: Morico v. United States, 399 U.S. 526 (1970).

53 156 285 396 404 531
Relevant Entry in the Table: U.S. v. Rembrandt Electronics, Inc, Cust & Pat App, 542 F2d 1154 Courts 89; Cust Dut 26(2, 3) Statut 188.
The United States, Appellant, v. Rembrandt Electronics, Inc., Appellee (United States Court of Customs and Patent Appeals October 21, 1976)
M/B: United States v. Rembrandt Electronics, Inc., 542 F.2d 1154 (C.C.P.A. 1976).
LR: United States v. Rembrandt Elecs., Inc., 542 F.2d 1154 (C.C.P.A. 1976).

54 157 286 397 405 532
Relevant Entry in the Table: Loughrey v. Landon, DCPa, 381 F Supp 884 Consp 8; Fed civ Proc 1126, 1135; Libel 76; Lim of Act 30, 55(1); Torts 12
Rose Loughrey v. George Landon et al. (United States District Court E.D. Pennsylvania September 20, 1974)
M/B: Loughrey v. Landon, 381 F. Supp. 884 (E.D. Pa. 1974).

55 158 287 398 406 533
Relevant Entry in the Table: Laue v. Nelson, DCCal, 279 FSupp 265-Hab Corp 48.
Richard Laue, Petitioner, v. Louis S. Nelson, Warden, California State Prison, San Quentin, California Respondent, (United Stated District Court N.D. California February 8, 1968)

EXERCISE 26. TABLES OF CASES AND POPULAR NAME TABLES   (CONTINUED)

M/B: Laue v. Nelson, 279 F. Supp. 265 (N.D. Cal. 1968).

56 159 288 399 407 534
Relevant Entry in the Table: Sage v. Halversen, 72 Minn. 294, 75 N.W. 229
Sage v. Halversen (Supreme Court of Minnesota May 19, 1898)
M/B: Sage v. Halversen, 72 Minn. 294, 75 N.W. 229 (1898).

57 160 289 400 408 535
Relevant Entry in the Table: Board of Trade Livery Co. v. Georgia Casualty co.
160 Minn 490, 200 NW 633, 40 ALR 678 - Insurance 435
Board of Trade Livery Co. v. Georgia Casualty Co. (Supreme Court of Minnesota
November 9, 1924)
M/B: Board of Trade Livery Co. v. Georgia Casualty Co., 160 Minn. 490, 200
N.W. 633 (1924).

58 161 290 301 409 536
Relevant Entry in the Table: Parked Auto Injury Case 312 Ky 536, 228 SW2d 432
Lewis v. Wolk, Court of Appeals of Kentucky March 3, 1950)
M/B: Lewis v. Wolk, 312 Ky. 536, 228 S.W.2d 432 (1950).

59 162 291 302 410 537
Relevant Entry in the Table: National Raditor Case 290 US 504, 78 LE 465, 54
SC 298
First National Bank of Cincinnati etal. v. Flershem et al. (certiorari to the
Circuit Court of Appeals for the Third Circuit January 8, 1934)
M/B: First National Bank v. Flershem, 290 U.S. 504 (1934).
LR: First Nat'l Bank v. Flershem, 290 U.S. 504 (1934).

60 163 292 303 411 538
Relevant Entry in the Table: Ginder v. Gluffrida 61 AppDC 338, 62 F2d 877 -
App & E 1078(1) Judgm 784, 795(2)
Ginder v. Giuffrida (Court of appeals of the District of Columbia December 29,
1932)
M/B: Delaware v. Irving Trust Co., 296 U.S. 652 (1935).
LR: Delaware v. Irving Trust Co., 296 U.S. 652 (1935).

61 164 293 304 412 539
Relevant Entry in the Table: Hutchings v. Low; Cal., 82 U.S. 77, 15 Wall 77,
21 L.Ed. 82
Hutchings v. Low
M/B: Hutchings v. Low, 82 U.S. (15 Wall.) 77 (1872).
LR: Hutchings v. Low, 82 U.S. (15 Wall.) 77 (1872).
Note: "Yosemite Valley Case" for the case name is also correct as the popular
name of the case.

62 165 294 305 413 540
Relevant Entry in the Table: General Shaver Corp - Schick Dry Shaver. DCConn,
26 FSupp 190
Schick Dry Shaver, Inc., et al. v. General Shaver Coporation et al. (District
Court, D. Connecticut December 30, 1938)
M/B: Schick Dry Shaver, Inc. v. General Shaver Corp., 26 F. Supp. 190 (D.
Conn. 1938).

63 166 295 306 414 541
Relevant Entry in the Table: Terhune - Welch, CCAMass, 126 F 2d 695
Welch, Collector of Internal Revenue, v. Terhune et al. (Circuit Court of
Appeals, First Circuit March 23, 1942)
M/B: Welch v. Terhune, 126 F.2d 695 (1st Cir. 1942).

64 167 296 307 415 542
Relevant Entry in the Table: Frank F Fasi Supply Co v. Wigwam Inv. Co.
DCHawaii, 308 FSupp 59 - Attach 1, 4, 7, 8; Garn 1, 4.
Frank F. Fasi Supply Company, a Hawaiian Limited Partnership, Plaintiff, v.
The Wigwam Investment Company, a Washington corporation, et al., Defendants,
and American Security Bank et al., Garnishees (United States District Court D.
Hawaii November 3, 1969)

EXERCISE 26. TABLES OF CASES AND POPULAR NAME TABLES   (CONTINUED)

M/B: Frank F. Fasi Supply Co. v. Wigwam Investment Co., 308 F. Supp. 59 (D. Hawaii 1969).
LR: Frank F. Fasi Supply Co. v. Wigwam Inv. Co., 308 F. Supp. 59 (D. Hawaii 1969).

65 168 297 308 416 543
Relevant Entry in the Table: Gormley v Bunyan, 138 US 623, 11 S Ct 453, 34 L Ed 1086
Gormley v. Bunyan (March 2, 1891)
M/B: Gormley v. Bunyan, 138 U.S. 623 (1891).

66 169 298 309 417 544
Relevant Entry in the Table: Metzger v. Know 77 Misc 271, 136 NYS 681 - Trade Reg 475
Metzger v. Knox et al. (Supreme Court, Special Term, Kings County. June 15, 1912)
M/B: Metzger v. Knox, 77 Misc. 271, 136 N.Y.S. 681 (Sup. Ct. 1912).

67 170 299 310 418 545
Relevant Entry in the Table: Sewall v. Haymaker, 127 US 719, 8 S Ct 1348, 32 L Ed 299 - ack §§7d 9i
Sewall v. Haymaker, (Error to the Circuit Court of the United States for the Southern District of Ohio May 14, 1888)
M/B: Sewall v. Haymaker, 127 U.S. 719 (1888).

68 171 300 311 419 546
Relevant Entry in the Table: Gallinghouse - Davis, DCLa, 246 FSupp 208
Reverend A. L. Davis, Earline Nealey and Caleb Hadley, and all Negroes Similarly Situated, Plaintiffs, v. A.P. Gallinghouse, Registrar of Voters of the Parish of Orleans, State of Louisiana, Honorable John J. McKeithen, Governor of Louisiana, and the Board of Registration of the State of Louisiana, Comprised of Honorable John J. McKeithen, Governor of Louisiana, Vail M. Delony, Speaker of the Louisiana House of Representatives, and C. C. "Taddy" Aycock, Lieutenant Governor of the State of Louisiana, Defendants, (United States District Court E.D. Louisiana, New Oreleans Div. September 30, 1965)
M/B: Davis v. Gallinghouse, 246 F. Supp. 208 (E.D. La. 1965).

69 172 201 312 420 547
Relevant Entry in the Table: Brockelsby v. W U Tel Co. 148 Iowa 273, 126 NW 1105 - Tel 218, 224
Brockelsby v. Western Union Telegraph Co. (Supreme Court of Iowa. July 9, 1910)
M/B: Brockelsby v. Western Union Telegraph Co., 148 Iowa 273, 126 N.W. 1105 (1910).
LR: Brockelsby v. Western Union Tel. Co., 148 Iowa 273, 126 N.W. 1105 (1910).

70 173 202 313 421 548
Relevant Entry in the Table: Rimnik Corp. v. Wallace 61 RI 282, 200 A 765 - Land & Ten 114 (3), 115 (3), 116 (5), 118 (4), 119 (2)
Rimnik Corp. v. Wallace (Supreme Court of Rhode Island July 12, 1938)
M/B: Rimnik Corp. v. Wallace, 61 R.I. 282, 200 A. 765 (1938).

71 174 203 314 422 549
Relevant Entry in the Table: Kuehner v Irving Trust Co. 299 US 445, 57 S Ct 298, 81 L Ed 340
Kuehner et al., Trustees, v. Irving Trust Co., Trustee in Bankruptcy, et al. (June 4, 1937)
M/B: Kuehner v. Irving Trust Co., 299 U.S. 445 (1937).

72 175 204 315 423 550
Relevant Entry in the Table: Phillips v. Lust, DCDC, 82 FSupp 63 - Abate & R 54
Phillips v. Lust (United States District Court District of Columbia January 31, 1949)
M/B: Phillips v. Lust, 82 F. Supp. 63 (D.D.C. 1949).

EXERCISE 26.   TABLES OF CASES AND POPULAR NAME TABLES   (CONTINUED)

73 176 205 316 424 551
Relevant Entry in the Table: Allen v. McCarthy 37 Minn. 349, 34 NW 416 - Trade Reg 544
Allen and others v. McCarthy (Supreme Court of Minnesota October 10, 1887)
M/B: Allen v. McCarthy, 37 Minn. 349, 34 N.W. 416 (1887).

74 177 206 317 425 552
Relevant Entry in the Table: Beasley-Gilbert's, Inc, In re, DCOhfo, 285 FSupp 359 - Bankr 11 (1), 145 (1), 226, 228 (13), 278, 288 (6, 8, 16), 308, 326; Guar 100; Jury 13 (5), 31 (3); Princ & S 174;
In re Beasley - Gilbert's, Inc., Bankrupt (United States District Court May 7, 1968)
M/B: In re Beasley-Gilbert's, Inc., 285 F. Supp. 359 (S.D. Ohio 1968).
LR: In re Beasley-Gilbert's, Inc., 285 F. Supp. 359 (S.D. Ohio 1968).

75 178 207 318 426 553
Relevant Entry in the Table: Highway Products, Inc. v. U S, CtCl, 530 F2d 911 - Fed Cts 1113; Ref of Inst 1, 16, 17 (1), 19 (2), 31, 45 of Inst 1, 16, 17 (1), 19 (2), 31, 45 (2); U S 64, 70 (4, 26), 73 (14), 74 (6);
Highway Products, Inc. v. The United States (United States Court of Claims January 28, 1976)
M/B: Highway Products, Inc. v. United States, 530 F.2d 911 (Ct. Cl. 1976).
LR: Highway Prods., Inc. v. United States, 530 F.2d 911 (Ct. Cl. 1976).

76 179 208 319 427 554
Relevant Entry in the Table: Lay v. Lay, 248 US 24, 39 S Ct 13, 63 L Ed 103
Lay et al. v. Lay et al. (Per curiam Nov. 18, 1918)
M/B: Lay v. Lay, 248 U.S. 24 (1918).

77 180 209 320 428 555
Relevant Entry in the Table: Bryden's Estate, In Re, 211Pa, 633, 61A.250; 10 D Ins.Per. §30, 33 (1)
In re Bryden's Estate (Supreme Court of Pennsylvania May 1, 1905)
M/B: In re Bryden's Estate, 211 Pa. 633, 61 A. 250 (1905).
LR: In re Bryden's Estate, 211 Pa. 633, 61 A. 250 (1905).

78 181 210 321 429 556
Relevant Entry in the Table: Stefanich v. American Motors Corp, DCWis 70 FRD 62 - Fed Civ Proc 1793
Emil Stefanich, Plaintiff, v. American Motors Corp., a Foreign Corpation, and United Automobile Workers Union, Local 75, Defendants (United States District Court E.D. Wisconsin December 22, 1975)
M/B: Stefanich v. American Motors Corp., 70 F.R.D. 62 (E.D. Wis. 1975).

79 182 211 322 430 557
Relevant Entry in the Table: Farnsworth v. Farnsworth, 58Vt. 555, 5A. 401; 17 C Divorce §95
Farnsworth v. Farnsworth (Supreme Court of Vermont August 9, 1886)
M/B: Farnsworth v. Farnsworth, 58 Vt. 555, 5 A. 401 (1886).

80 183 212 323 431 558
Relevant Entry in the Table: Hoon 126 Iowa 391, 102 N.W. 105; 16 D Plead §8 (15); 19 D Trusts §17 (4), 86
Hoon v. Hoon (Supreme Court of Iowa January 14, 1905)
M/B: Hoon v. Hoon, 126 Iowa 391, 102 N.W. 105 (1905).

81 184 213 324 432 559
Relevant Entry in the Table: Huls v. Janeway 42 Okl 33, 140p419; Frds., St. of 23 (4); J.P. 152
Huls v. Janeway (Supreme Court of Oklahoma April 17, 1914)
M/B: Huls v. Janeway, 42 Okla. 33, 140 P. 419 (1914).

82 185 214 325 433 560
Relevant Entry in the Table: Chamoy v. Schlesinger, DCHawaii, 371 FSUPP 685 - Armed S 3, 11.
Lewis Chamoy Petitioner, v. James R. Schlesinger, Secretary of Defense, et al., Respondents (United States District Court D. Hawaii February 11, 1974)

EXERCISE 26. TABLES OF CASES AND POPULAR NAME TABLES   (CONTINUED)

M/B: Chamoy v. Schlesinger, 371 F. Supp. 685 (D. Hawaii 1974).

83 186 215 326 434 561
Relevant Entry in the Table: Massi v. Lavine 139 Mich. 140, 102 N.W. 665; 9 D Fraud. Conv. §174 (3)
Massi v. Lavine et al (Supreme Court of Mighigan February 27, 1905)
M/B: Massi v. Lavine, 139 Mich. 140, 102 N.W. 665 (1905).

84 187 218 327 435 562
Relevant Entry in the Table: Holstine v. Connecticut General Life Ins. Co. DCTex, 338 FSupp 817 - Insurance 454 467.1 (1, 3)
Louise L. Holstine, Plaintiff v. Connecticut General Life Insurance Company, Defendant (United States Districe Court E.D. Texas Beaumont Division February 22, 1972)
M/B: Holstine v. Connecticut General Life Insurance Co., 338 F. Supp. 817 (E.D. Tex. 1972).
LR: Holstine v. Connecticut Gen. Life Ins. Co., 338 F. Supp. 817 (E.D. Tex. 1972).

85 188 219 328 436 563
Relevant Entry in the Table: U S v. Carbo, CACal, 474 F2d 698 - Crim. Law 997.11.
United States of America Plaintiff-Appellee v. Paul John Carbo, Defendant Appellant (United States Court of Appeals Ninth Ciruit February 23, 1973)
M/B: United States v. Carbo, 474 F.2d 698 (9th Cir. 1973).

86 189 220 329 437 564
Relevant Entry in the Table: McFadden 84 Iowa 262, 50 N.W. 1070; 18C Elections §214; 36 C Mun. Corp. §739, 2042, 2070
Taylor v. McFadden (Supreme Court of Iowa January 23, 1892)
M/B: Taylor v. McFadden, 84 Iowa 262, 50 N.W. 1070 (1892).

87 190 221 330 438 565
Relevant Entry in the Table: Sage v. Halversen 72 Minn, 294, 75N.W. 229; 12 D Land & Ten §62 (30.
Sage v. Halversen (Supreme Court of Minnesota May 19, 1898)
M/B: Sage v. Halversen, 72 Minn. 294, 75 N.W. 229 (1898).

88 191 222 331 439 566
Relevant Entry in the Table: Del Pilar v. Eastern Air Lines, Inc. DCNY, 172 FSupp 158 - Carr 318 (1).
Jose Del Pilar, Plaintiff v. Eastern Air Lines, Incorporated, Defendant (United States District Court S.D. New York April 10, 1959)
M/B: Del Pilar v. Eastern Air Lines, 172 F. Supp. 158 (S.D.N.Y. 1959).

89 192 223 332 440 567
Relevant Entry in the Table: King v. McGinnis, DCNY, 289 FSupp 466 - Civil R 2, 13; Const Law 84; Mental H 436
William C. King by (The Rev.) Paul Frampton King, Attorney-In-Fact Plaintiff, v. Paul D. McGinnis, Commissioner, New York State Department of Correction Jack Pulliam and the State of New York, Defendant (United States District Court S. D. New York August 8, 1968)
M/B: King v. McGinnis, 289 F. Supp. 466 (S.D.N.Y. 1968).

90 193 224 333 441 568
Relevant Entry in the Table: Beauttas v. US 324 US 768, 65 S Ct 1000, 89 L Ed 1354 - US §§ 198d, 200h
United States v. Bettas et al., Trading as B-W Construction Co. (Certiorari to the court of Claims April 23, 1945)
M/B: United States v. Beuttas, 324 U.S. 768 (1945).

91 194 225 334 442 569
Relevant Entry in the Table: Hale v. Bimco Trading, Inc., 306 US 375, 59 S Ct 526 83L Ed 771 - com §§230b, 243c; cts §§6911 699e; judg §388.5b
Hale Chairman, et al v. Bimco Trading Inc. et al. Appeal from the District Court of the United State for the Northern District of Florida February 27, 1939)

EXERCISE 26. <u>TABLES OF CASES AND POPULAR NAME TABLES</u>   (CONTINUED)

M/B: <u>Hale v. Bimco Trading, Inc.</u>, 306 U.S. 375 (1939).

92 195 226 335 443 570
Relevant Entry in the Table: Huford Case 317 Ill 203, 148 NE 69
Village of Glencoe v. Hurford (Supreme Court of Illinois April 24, 1925)
M/B: <u>Village of Glencoe v. Hurford</u>, 317 Ill. 203, 148 N.E. 69 (1925).

93 196 227 336 444 571
Relevant Entry in the Table: Corker v Jones 110 US 317, 4 S Ct 19, 28 L Ed 161
Corker v. Jones, Executor, & Another (February 4, 1884)
M/B: <u>Corker v. Jones</u>, 110 U.S. 317 (1884).

94 197 228 337 445 572
Relevant Entry in the Table: Dotson v. Milliken 209 US 237, 28 S Ct 489, 52 L Ed 768
Dotson v. Millikin (March 23, 1908)
M/B: <u>Dotson v. Millikin</u>, 209 U.S. 237 (1908).

95 198 229 338 446 573
Relevant Entry in the Table: FAAS - Hutchens, CACAL, 249 F2d 465
Ralph O. Hutchens, Appellants, v. Louis D. Faas, Bernice H. Faas, Leonard A. Faas, Genevieve E. Faas, Copartners doing business as King O'Lawn Manufacturing Co., Walter Faas, Rudolph Faas, M.W. Engleman, Assignee for Benefit of Creditors for King O'Lawn Manufacturing Co., King O'Lawn, Inc., a California Corporation, Appellees (United States Court of Appeals Ninth Circuit July 1, 1957)
M/B: <u>Hutchens v. Faas</u>, 249 F.2d 465 (9th Cir. 1957).

96 199 230 339 447 574
Relevant Entry in the Table: Sheff - U S, CACal, 194 F2d 596.
United States v. Sheff et al (United States Court of Appeals Ninth Circuit February 29, 1952)
M/B: <u>United States v. Sheff</u>, 194 F.2d 596 (9th Cir. 1952).

97 200 231 340 448 575
Relevant Entry in the Table: Brucker - Gibbs & Sterrett Mfg Co, Mo, 41 SCt 572, 111 US 597, 28 L Ed 534
Gibbs & Sterrett Manufacturing Company v. Brucker (In error to the Circuit Court of the United States for the Eastern District of Wisconsin May 5, 1884)
M/B: <u>Gibbs & Sterrett Manufacturing Co. v. Brucker</u>, 111 U.S. 597 (1884).
LR: <u>Gibbs & Sterrett Mfg. Co. v. Brucker</u>, 111 U.S. 597 (1884).

98 101 232 341 449 576
Relevant Entry in the Table: Royal Spy Case (Ky) 380 SW2d 233
William Bobinchuck et al., Appellants v. James Levitch, Appellee (Court of Appeals of Kentucky June 19, 1964)
M/B: <u>Bobinchuck v. Levitch</u>, 380 S.W.2d 233 (Ky. 1964).

99 102 233 342 450 577
Relevant Entry in the Table: Southern Ice Co - Gladiola Biscuit Co. CATex, 267 F2d 138
Gladiola Biscuit Company, Appellant v. Southern Ice Company, Appellee (United States Court of Appeals Fifth Circuit May 27, 1959)
M/B: <u>Gladiola Biscuit Co. v. Southern Ice Co.</u>, 267 F.2d 138 (5th Cir. 1959).

100 103 234 343 451 578
Relevant Entry in the Table: Hader - Jackson DCMo, 271 FSupp 990
George Washington Jackson, Plaintiff, v. H. Townsend Hader, Defendant (United States District Court W.D. Missouri, C.D. August 30, 1967)
M/B: <u>Jackson v. Hader</u>, 271 F. Supp. 990 (W.D. Mo. 1967).

LIBRARY EXERCISE 27.   AMERICAN JURISPRUDENCE SECOND.

INSTRUCTOR'S NOTE: For this exercise, students are required to locate a title and section in <u>American Jurisprudence Second</u>. For their answers, they are required to cite the section, and they are instructed to abbreviate "and" to "&" when it appears in an <u>Am. Jur. 2d</u> title. If a student uses a later than the date listed or uses a slightly different volume designation (17A instead of 17, etc.) in the citation, the student's answer most likely reflects a reissuance of the <u>Am. Jur. 2d</u> volume after these answers below were prepared. Such an answer should be counted correct.

    The following Quick-Reference Abbreviations are particularly relevant to this (and the next) exercise:

    LEGAL ENCYCLOPEDIA CITATION 1.   CITE <u>AMERICAN JURISPRUDENCE SECOND</u> AND <u>CORPUS JURIS SECUNDUM</u> BY VOLUME, ABBREVIATED TITLE (Am. Jur. 2d OR C.J.S), TOPIC, SECTION, AND DATE OF THE PUBLICATION OF THE VOLUME (OR SUPPLEMENT). [ENCY 1]
    LEGAL ENCYCLOPEDIA CITATION 2.   IN CITING A SECTION OF A LEGAL ENCYCLOPEDIA, ADD A REFERENCE TO THE PAGE NUMBER ONLY WHEN IT IS NECESSARY FOR FURTHER IDENTIFICATION.   [ENCY 2]
    LEGAL ENCYCLOPEDIA CITATION 3.   IN MEMORANDA AND BRIEFS, UNDERSCORE (ITALICIZE) THE TOPIC CITED.   IN LAW REVIEW FOOTNOTES, ITALICIZE THE TOPIC CITED AND GIVE THE TITLE OF THE ENCYCLOPEDIA IN LARGE AND SMALL CAPITAL LETTERS.   [ENCY 3]

1 155 206 322 421 533   Abandoned, Lost, & Unclaimed Property § 27
M/B: 1 Am. Jur. 2d <u>Abandoned, Lost, & Unclaimed Property</u> § 27 (1962).

2 156 207 323 422 534   Homestead § 179
M/B: 40 Am. Jur. 2d <u>Homestead</u> § 179 (1968).

3 157 208 324 423 535   Laundries, Dyers, & Dry Cleaners § 12
M/B: 50 Am. Jur. 2d <u>Laudries, Dyers, & Drycleaners</u> § 12 (1970).

4 158 209 325 424 536   Public Lands § 89
M/B: 63 Am. Jur. 2d <u>Public Lands</u> § 89 (1972).

5 159 210 326 425 537   Restitution & Implied Contracts § 79
M/B: 66 Am. Jur. 2d <u>Restitution & Implied Contracts</u> § 79 (1973).

6 160 211 327 426 538   Landlord & Tenant § 619
M/B: 49 Am. Jur. 2d <u>Landlord & Tenant</u> § 619 (1970).

7 161 212 328 427 539   Death § 304
M/B: 22 Am. Jur. 2d <u>Death</u> § 304 (1965).

8 162 213 329 428 540   Abstracts of Title § 12
M/B: 1 Am. Jur. 2d <u>Abstracts of Title</u> § 12 (1962).

9 163 214 330 429 541   Abuse of Process § 16
M/B: 1 Am. Jur. 2d <u>Abuse of Process</u> § 16 (1962).

10 164 215 331 430 542   Mortgages § 371
M/B: 55 Am. Jur. 2d <u>Mortages</u> § (1971).

11 165 216 332 431 543   Highways, Streets, & Bridges § 178
M/B: 39 Am. Jur. 2d <u>Highways, Streets, & Bridges</u> § 178 (1968).

12 166 217 333 432 544 Evidence § 217
M/B: 29 Am. Jur. 2d <u>Evidence</u> § 217 (1967).

13 167 218 334 433 545   Carriers § 871
M/B: 14 Am. Jur. 2d <u>Carriers</u> § 871 (1964).

14 168 219 335 434 546   Landlord & Tenant § 878
M/B: 19 Am. Jur. 2d <u>Landlord & Tenant</u> § 878 (1970).

15 169 220 336 435 547   Fraud & Deceit § 403

EXERCISE 27. AMERICAN JURISPRUDENCE SECOND   (CONTINUED)

M/B: 37 Am. Jur. 2d Fraud & Deceit § 403 (1968).

16 170 221 337 436 548   Acknowledgments § 117
M/B: 1 Am. Jur. 2d Acknowledgments § 117 (1962).

17 171 222 338 437 549   Boundaries § 85
M/B: 12 Am. Jur. 2d Boundaires § 85 (1964).

18 172 223 339 438 550   Carriers § 521
M/B: 14 Am. Jur. 2d Carriers § 521 (1964).

19 173 224 340 439 551   International Law § 83
M/B: 45 Am. Jur. 2d International Law § 83 (1969).

20 174 225 341 440 552   Adverse Possession § 9
M/B: 3 Am. Jur. 2d Adverse Possession § 9 (1962).

21 175 226 342 441 553   Labor & Labor Relations § 1757
M/B: 48 Am. Jur. 2d Labor & Labor Relations § 1757 (1979).

22 176 227 343 442 554   Incompetent Persons § 137
M/B: 41 Am. Jur. 2d Incompetent Persons § 137 (1968).

23 177 228 344 443 555   Insolvency § 19
M/B: 42 Am. Jur. 2d Insolvency § (1969).

24 178 229 345 444 556   Federal Tort Claims Act § 54
M/B: 35 Am. Jur. 2d Federal Tort Claims Act § 54 (1967).

25 179 230 346 445 557   Admiralty § 130
M/B: 2 Am. Jur. 2d Admiralty § 130 (1962).

26 180 231 347 446 558   Parent & Child § 101
M/B: 59 Am. Jur. 2d Parent & Child § 101 (1971).

27 181 232 348 447 559   Adultery & Fornication § 13
M/B: 2 Am. Jur. 2d Adultery & Fornication § 13 (1962).

28 182 233 349 448 560   Deeds § 294
M/B: 23 Am. Jur. 2d Deeds § 294 (1965).

29 183 234 350 449 561   Negligence § 223
M/B: 57 Am. Jur. 2d Negligence § 223 (1971).

30 184 235 351 450 562   Husband & Wife § 487
M/B: 41 Am. Jur. 2d Husband & Wife § 487 (1968).

31 185 236 352 451 563   Banks § 772
M/B: 10 Am. Jur. 2d Banks § 772 (1963).

32 186 237 353 452 564   Costs § 52
M/B: 20 Am. Jur. 2d Costs § 52 (1965).

33 187 238 354 453 565
M/B: 56 Am. Jur. 2d Municipal Corporations, Counties, & Other Political Subdivisions § 55 (1971).

34 188 239 355 454 566
M/B: 51 Am. Jur. 2d Life Tenants & Remaindermen § 56 (1970).

35 189 240 356 455 567   Sales § 519
M/B: 67 Am. Jur. 2d Sales § 519 (1973).

36 190 241 357 456 568   Appeal & Error § 345
M/B: 4 Am. Jur. 2d Appeal & Error § 345 (1962).

37 191 242 358 457 569   Pardon & Parole § 43

EXERCISE 27. <u>AMERICAN JURISPRUDENCE SECOND</u>   (CONTINUED)

M/B: 59 Am. Jur. 2d <u>Pardon & Parole</u> § 43 (1971).

38 192 243 359 458 570   Fixtures § 91
M/B: 35 Am. Jur. 2d <u>Fixtures</u> § 91 (1967).

39 193 244 360 459 571   Railroads § 201
M/B: 65 Am. Jur. 2d <u>Railroads</u> § 201 (1972).

40 194 245 361 460 572   Mobs & Riots § 5
M/B: 54 Am. Jur. 2d <u>Mobs & Riots</u> § 5 (1971).

41 195 246 362 461 573   Patents § 330
M/B: 60 Am. Jur. 2d <u>Patents</u> § 330 (1972).

42 196 247 363 462 574   Electricity, Gas, & Steam § 136
M/B: 26 Am. Jur. 2d <u>Electricity, Gas, & Steam</u> § 136 (1966).

43 197 248 364 463 575   Champerty & Maintenance § 4
M/B: 14 Am. Jur. 2d <u>Champerty & Maintenance</u> § 4 (1964).

44 198 249 365 464 576   Judgments § 724
M/B: 46 Am. Jur. 2d <u>Judgments</u> § 724 (1969).

45 199 250 366 465 577   Damages § 30
M/B: 22 Am. Jur. 2d <u>Damages</u> § 30 (1965).

46 200 251 367 466 578   Infants § 84
M/B: 42 Am. Jur. 2d <u>Infants</u> § 84 (1969).

47 101 252 368 467 579   Ne Exeat § 18
M/B: 57 Am. Jur. 2d <u>Ne Exeat</u> § 18 (1971).

48 102 253 369 468 580   Bankruptcy § 772
M/B: 9 Am. Jur. 2d <u>Bankruptcy</u> § 772 (1980).

49 103 254 370 469 581
M/B: 54 Am. Jur. 2d <u>Monopolies, Restraints of Trade, & Unfair Trade Practices</u> § 206 (1971).

50 104 255 371 470 582   Banks § 428
M/B: 10 Am. Jur. 2d <u>Banks</u> § 428 (1963).

51 105 256 372 471 583   Bigamy § 16
M/B: 10 Am. Jur. 2d <u>Bigamy</u> § 16 (1963).

52 106 257 373 472 584   Labor & Labor Relations § 37
M/B: 48 Am. Jur. 2d <u>Labor & Labor Relations</u> § 37 (1979).

53 107 258 374 473 585   Federal Employers' Liability & Compensation Acts § 38
M/B: 32 Am. Jur. 2d <u>Federal Employer's Liability & Compensation Acts</u> § 38 (1967).

54 108 259 375 474 586   Extradition § 30
M/B: 31 Am. Jur. 2d <u>Extradition</u> § 30 (1967).

55 109 260 376 475 587   Drugs, Narcotics, & Poisons § 28
M/B: 25 Am. Jur. 2d <u>Drugs, Narcotics, & Poisons</u> § 28 (1966).

56 110 261 377 476 588   Domicil § 87
M/B: 25 Am. Jur. 2d <u>Domicil</u> § 87 (1966).

57 111 262 378 477 589   Gifts § 92
M/B: 38 Am. Jur. 2d <u>Gifts</u> § 92 (1968).

58 112 263 379 478 590   Malicious Prosecution § 128
M/B: 52 Am. Jur. 2d <u>Malicious Prosecution</u> § 128 (1970).

EXERCISE 27. AMERICAN JURISPRUDENCE SECOND   (CONTINUED)

59 113 264 380 479 591   Death § 219
M/B: 22 Am. Jur. 2d Death § 219 (1965).

60 114 265 381 480 592   Insurance § 1386
M/B: 44 Am. Jur. 2d Insurance § 1386 (1969).

61 115 266 382 481 593   Mobs & Riots § 14
M/B: 50 Am. Jur. 2d Mobs & Riots § 14 (1971).

62 116 267 383 482 594   Irrigation § 97
M/B: 45 Am. Jur. 2d Irrigation § 97 (1969).

63 117 268 384 483 595   Jury § 213
M/B: 47 Am. Jur. 2d Jury § 213 (1969).

64 118 269 385 484 596   Cemeteries § 39
M/B: 14 Am. Jur. 2d Cemeteries § 39 (1964).

65 119 270 386 485 597   Certiorari § 39
M/B: 14 Am. Jur. 2d Certiorari § 39 (1964).

66 120 271 387 486 598   Libel & Slander § 60
M/B: 50 Am. Jur. 2d Libel & Slander § 60 (1970).

67 121 272 388 487 599   Rape § 82
M/B: 65 Am. Jur. 2d Rape § 82 (1972).

68 122 273 389 488 600   Public Works & Contracts § 70
M/B: 64 Am. Jur. 2d Public Works & Contracts § 70 (1972).

69 123 274 390 489 501   Civil Service § 20
M/B: 15A Am. Jur. 2d Civil Service § 20 (1976).

70 124 275 391 490 502   Public Officers & Employees § 15
M/B: 63 Am. Jur. 2d Public Officers & Employees § 15 (1972).

71 125 276 392 491 503   Money § 14
M/B: 54 Am. Jur. 2d Money § 14 (1971).

72 126 277 393 492 504   Interest & Usury § 194
M/B: 45 Am. Jur. 2d Interest & Usury § 194 (1969).

73 127 278 394 493 505   Customs Duties & Import Regulations § 101
M/B: 21 Am. Jur. 2d Customs Duties & Import Regulations § 101 (1965).

74 128 279 395 494 506   Collection & Credit Agencies § 22
M/B: 15A Am. Jur. 2d Collection & Credit Agencies § 22 (1976).

75 129 280 396 495 507   Improvements § 12
M/B: 41 Am. Jur. 2d Improvements § 12 (1968).

76 130 281 397 496 508   Extradition § 13
M/B: 31 Am. Jur. 2d Extradition § 13 (1967).

77 131 282 398 497 509   Copyright & Literary Property § 6
M/B: 18 Am. Jur. 2d Copyright & Literary Property § 6 (1965).

78 132 283 399 498 510   Community Property § 92
M/B: 15A Am. Jur. 2d Community Property § 92 (1976).

79 133 284 400 499 511   Gambling § 172
M/B: 38 Am. Jur. 2d Gambling § 172 (1968).

80 132 285 301 500 512   Public Utilities § 189
M/B: 64 Am. Jur. 2d Public Utilities § 189 (1972).

81 135 286 302 401 513   Conspiracy § 7

EXERCISE 27. AMERICAN JURISPRUDENCE SECOND   (CONTINUED)

M/B: 16 Am. Jur. 2d Conspiracy § 7 (1979).

82 136 287 303 402 514   Records & Recording Laws § 102
M/B: 66 Am. Jur. 2d Records & Recording Laws § 102 (1973).

83 137 288 304 403 515   Inheritance, Estate, & Gift Taxes § 82
M/B: 42 Am. Jur. 2d Inheritance, Estate, & Gift Taxes § 82 (1969).

84 138 289 305 404 516   Contempt § 115
M/B: 17 Am. Jur. 2d Contempt § 115 (1964).

85 139 290 306 405 517   Gas & Oil § 259
M/B: 38 Am. Jur. 2d Gas & Oil § 259 (1968).

86 140 291 307 406 518   Contracts § 324
M/B: 17 Am. Jur. 2d Contracts § 324 (1968).

87 141 292 308 407 519   Lobbying § 7
M/B: 51 Am. Jur. 2d Lobbying § 7 (1970).

88 142 293 309 408 520   Markets & Marketing § 42
M/B: 52 Am. Jur. 2d Markets & Marketing § 42 (1970).

89 143 294 310 409 521   Mines & Minerals § 165
M/B: 54 Am. Jur. 2d Mines & Minerals § 165 (1971).

90 144 295 311 410 522   Fires § 30
M/B: 35 Am. Jur. 2d Fires § 30 (1967).

91 145 296 312 411 523   Cotenancy & Joint Ownership § 9
M/B: 20 Am. Jur. 2d Cotenancy & Joint Ownership § 9 (1965).

92 146 297 313 412 524   Lost & Destroyed Instruments § 40
M/B: 52 Am. Jur. 2d Lost & Destroyed Instruments § 40 (1970).

93 147 298 314 413 525   Libel & Slander § 454
M/B: 50 Am. Jur. 2d Libel & Slander § 454 (1970).

94 148 299 315 414 526   New Trial § 148
M/B: 58 Am. Jur. 2d New Trial § 148 (1971).

95 149 300 316 415 527   Prenatal Injuries § 22
M/B: 62 Am. Jur. 2d Prenatal Injuries § 22 (1972).

96 150 201 317 416 528   Logs & Timber § 125
M/B: 52 Am. Jur. 2d Logs & Timber § 125 (1970).

97 151 202 318 417 529   Names § 24
M/B: 57 Am. Jur. 2d Names § 24 (1971).

98 152 203 319 418 530   Dead Bodies § 42
M/B: 22 Am. Jur. 2d Dead Bodies § 42 (1965).

99 153 204 320 419 531   Occupations, Trades, & Professions § 61
M/B: 58 Am. Jur. 2d Occupations, Trades, & Professions § 61 (1971).

100 154 205 321 420 532   Private Franchise Contracts § 15
M/B: 62 Am. Jur. 2d Private Franchise Contracts § 15 (1972).

LIBRARY EXERCISE 28.   CORPUS JURIS SECUNDUM.

INSTRUCTOR'S NOTE: For this exercise, the students are required to locate the listed title and section in Corpus Juris Secundum (C.J.S.). The student is required to cite the section. Note that many of the C.J.S. volumes used in this exercise are also used to complete Exercise 29. If a student uses a date later than the one given in the citation below or a slightly different volume designation, the student's answer most likely reflects a reissuance of the C.J.S. volume after these answers were prepared. Such an answer should be counted as correct.

1 170 236 344 485 592
M/B: 86 C.J.S. Territories § 1 (1954).

2 171 237 345 486 593
M/B: 73 C.J.S. Property § 15 (1951).

3 172 238 346 487 594
M/B: 81A C.J.S. States § 195 (1977).

4 173 239 347 488 595
M/B: 98 C.J.S. Witnesses § 527 (1957).

5 174 240 348 489 596
M/B: 97 C.J.S. Wills § 1308 (1957).

6 175 241 349 490 597
M/B: 96 C.J.S. Wills § 1066 (1957).

7 176 242 350 491 598
M/B: 95 C.J.S. Wills § 514 (1957).

8 177 243 351 492 599
M/B: 94 C.J.S. Waters § 308 (1956).

9 178 244 352 493 600
M/B: 93 C.J.S. Waste § 19 (1956).

10 179 245 353 494 501
M/B: 92 C.J.S. Venue § 86 (1955).

11 180 246 354 495 502
M/B: 91 C.J.S. Usury § 79 (1955).

12 181 247 355 496 503
M/B: 90 C.J.S. Trusts § 288 (1955).

13 182 248 356 497 504
M/B: 89 C.J.S. Trial § 631 (1955).

14 183 249 357 498 505
M/B: 88 C.J.S. Trial § 242 (1955).

15 184 250 358 499 506
M/B: 87 C.J.S. Trespass § 44 (1954).

16 185 251 359 500 507
M/B: 86 C.J.S. Territories § 38 (1954).

17 186 252 360 401 508
M/B: 85 C.J.S. Taxation § 1093 (1954).

18 187 253 361 402 509
M/B: 84 C.J.S. Taxation § 349 (1954).

19 188 254 362 403 510
M/B: 83 C.J.S. Subrogation § 57 (1953).

20 189 255 363 404 511

Territories § 1

Property § 15

States § 195

Witnesses § 527

Wills § 1308

Wills § 1066

Wills § 514

Waters § 308

Waste § 19

Venue § 86

Usury § 79

Trusts § 288

Trial § 631

Trial § 242

Trespass § 44

Territories § 38

Taxation § 1093

Taxation § 349

Subrogation § 57

Statutes § 357

EXERCISE 28. CORPUS JURIS SECUNDUM   (CONTINUED)

M/B: 82 C.J.S. Statutes § 357 (1953).

21 190 256 364 405 512   States § 82
M/B: 81A C.J.S. States § 82 (1977).

22 191 257 365 406 513   Sodomy § 15
M/B: 81 C.J.S. Sodomy § 15 (1977).

23 192 258 366 407 514   Shipping § 11
M/B: 80 C.J.S. Shipping § 11 (1953).

24 193 259 367 408 515   Sequestration § 9
M/B: 79 C.J.S. Sequestration § 9 (1952).

25 194 260 368 409 516   Salvage § 1
M/B: 78 C.J.S. Salvage § 1 (1952).

26 195 261 369 410 517   Replevin § 171
M/B: 77 C.J.S. Replevin § 171 (1952).

27 196 262 370 411 518   Religious Societies § 29
M/B: 76 C.J.S. Religious Societies § 29 (1952).

28 197 263 371 412 519   Rape § 58
M/B: 75 C.J.S. Rape § 58 (1952).

29 198 264 372 413 520   Quo Warranto § 28
M/B: 74 C.J.S. Quo Warranto § 28 (1951).

30 199 265 373 414 521   Public Lands § 282
M/B: 73 C.J.S. Public Lands § 282 (1951).

31 200 266 374 415 522   Post Office § 47
M/B: 72 C.J.S. Post Office § 47 (1951).

32 101 267 375 416 523   Pleading § 269
M/B: 71 C.J.S. Pleading § 269 (1951).

33 102 268 376 417 524   Perjury § 77
M/B: 70 C.J.S. Perjury § 77 (1951).

34 103 269 377 418 525   Patents § 269
M/B: 69 C.J.S. Patents § 269 (1951).

35 104 270 378 419 526   Partnership § 427
M/B: 68 C.J.S. Partnership § 427 (1950).

36 105 271 379 420 527   Officers § 143
M/B: 67 C.J.S. Officers § 143 (1978).

37 106 272 380 421 528   New Trial § 77
M/B: 66 C.J.S. New Trial § 77 (1950).

38 107 273 381 422 529   Negligence § 220.7
M/B: 65A C.J.S. Negligence § 220.7 (1966).

39 108 274 382 423 530   Negligence § 63(9).
M/B: 65 C.J.S. Negligence § 63(9). (1966).

40 109 275 383 424 531   Municipal Corporations § 2058
M/B: 64 C.J.S. Municipal Corporations § 2058 (1950).

41 110 276 384 425 532   Municipal Corporations § 931
M/B: 63 C.J.S. Municipal Corporations § 931 (1950).

42 111 277 385 426 533   Municipal Corporations § 93
M/B: 62 C.J.S. Municipal Corporations § 93 (1949).

EXERCISE 28.   CORPUS JURIS SECUNDUM   (CONTINUED)

43 112 278 386 427 534   Motor Vehicles § 632(1).
M/B: 61A C.J.S. Motor Vehicles § 632(1). (1970).

44 113 279 387 428 535   Motor Vehicles § 518(14).
M/B: 61 C.J.S. Motor Vehicles § 518(14). (1970).

45 114 280 388 429 536   Motor Vehicles § 270
M/B: 60A C.J.S. Motor Vehicles § 270 (1969).

46 115 281 389 430 537   Motor Vehicles § 5
M/B: 60 C.J.S. Motor Vehicles § 5 (1969).

47 116 282 390 431 538   Mortgages § 313
M/B: 59 C.J.S. Mortgages § 313 (1949).

48 117 283 391 432 539   Monopolies § 81
M/B: 58 C.J.S. Monopolies § 81 (1948).

49 118 284 392 433 540   Mechanics' Liens § 171
M/B: 57 C.J.S. Mechanics' Liens § 171 (1948).

50 119 285 393 434 541   Marriage § 16
M/B: 55 C.J.S. Marriage § 16 (1948).

51 120 286 394 435 542   Mandamus § 228
M/B: 55 C.J.S. Mandamus § 228 (1948).

52 121 287 395 436 543   Lis Pendens § 43
M/B: 54 C.J.S. Lis Pendens § 43 (1948).

53 122 288 396 437 544   Licenses § 30
M/B: 53 C.J.S. Licenses § 30 (1948).

54 123 289 397 438 545   Homesteads § 187
M/B: 40 C.J.S. Homesteads § 187 (1944).

55 124 290 398 439 546   Fraud § 13
M/B: 37 C.J.S. Fraud § 13 (1943).

56 125 291 399 440 547   Garnishment § 251
M/B: 38 C.J.S. Garnishments § 251 (1943).

57 126 292 400 441 548   Larceny § 143
M/B: 52A C.J.S. Larceny § 143 (1968).

58 127 293 301 442 549   Associations § 13
M/B: 7 C.J.S. Associations § 13 (1980).

59 128 294 302 443 550   Justices of the Peace § 22(1).
M/B: 51 C.J.S. Justices of the Peace § 22(1). (1967).

60 129 295 303 444 551   Juries § 111
M/B: 50 C.J.S. Juries § 111 (1947).

61 130 296 304 445 552   Bail § 44
M/B: 8 C.J.S. Bail § 44 (1962).

62 131 297 305 446 553   Attachment § 49
M/B: 7 C.J.S. Attachment § 49 (1980).

63 132 298 306 447 554   Assignments § 39
M/B: 6A C.J.S. Assignments § 39 (1975).

64 133 299 307 448 555   Embezzlement § 35
M/B: 29A C.J.S. Embezzlement § 35 (1965).

65 134 300 308 449 556   Arrest § 15

EXERCISE 28. CORPUS JURIS SECUNDUM   (CONTINUED)

M/B: 6A C.J.S. Arrest § 15 (1975).

66 135 201 309 450 557   Appearances § 51
M/B: 6 C.J.S. Appearances § 51 (1975).

67 136 202 310 451 558   Contracts § 548
M/B: 17A C.J.S. Contracts § 548 (1963).

68 137 203 311 452 559   Continuances § 94(1)
M/B: 17 C.J.S. Continuances § 94(1). (1963).

69 138 204 312 453 560   Contracts § 397
M/B: 17A C.J.S. Contracts § 397 (1963).

70 139 205 313 454 561   Railroads § 439
M/B: 74 C.J.S. Railroads § 439 (1951).

71 140 206 314 455 562   Certiorari § 144
M/B: 14 C.J.S. Certiorari § 144 (1939).

72 141 207 315 456 563   Carriers § 334
M/B: 13 C.J.S. Carriers § 334 (1939).

73 142 208 316 457 564   Brokers § 95
M/B: 12 C.J.S. Brokers § 95 (1980).

74 143 209 317 458 565   Boundaries § 34
M/B: 11 C.J.S. Boundaries § 34 (1938).

75 144 210 318 459 566   Brokers § 22
M/B: 12 C.J.S. Brokers § 22 (1980).

76 145 211 319 460 567   Animals § 51
M/B: 3A C.J.S. Animals § 51 (1973).

77 146 212 320 461 568   Criminal Law § 1959
M/B: 24B C.J.S. Criminal Law § 1959 (1962).

78 147 213 321 462 569   Damages § 41
M/B: 25 C.J.S. Damages § 41 (1966).

79 148 214 322 463 570   Dead Bodies § 8(4)
M/B: 25A C.J.S. Dead Bodies § 8(4). (1966).

80 149 215 323 464 571   Deeds § 32
M/B: 26 C.J.S. Deeds § 32 (1956).

81 150 216 324 465 572   Agency § 548
M/B: 3 C.J.S. Agency § 548 (1973).

82 151 217 325 466 573   Death § 107
M/B: 25A C.J.S. Death § 107 (1966).

83 152 218 326 467 574   Admiralty § 127
M/B: 2 C.J.S. Admirality § 127 (1972).

84 153 219 327 468 575   Embezzlement § 27
M/B: 29A C.J.S. Embezzlement § 27 (1965).

85 154 220 328 469 576   Eminent Domain § 419
M/B: 30 C.J.S. Eminent Domain § 419 (1965).

86 155 221 329 470 577   Equity § 454
M/B: 30A C.J.S. Equity § 454 (1965).

87 156 222 330 471 578   Estoppel § 43
M/B: 31 C.J.S. Estoppel § 43 (1964).

EXERCISE 28.   CORPUS JURIS SECUNDUM   (CONTINUED)

88 157 223 331 472 579   Executions § 383
M/B: 33 C.J.S. Executions § 383 (1942).

89 158 224 332 473 580   Evidence § 1022
M/B: 32A C.J.S. Evidence § 1022 (1964).

90 159 225 333 474 581   Evidence § 638
M/B: 32 C.J.S. Evidence § 638 (1964).

91 160 226 334 475 582   Evidence § 58
M/B: 31A C.J.S. Evidence § 58 (1964).

92 161 227 335 476 583   Depositaries § 2
M/B: 26A C.J.S. Depositaries § 2 (1956).

93 162 228 336 477 584   Disorderly Houses § 11
M/B: 27 C.J.S. Disorderly Houses § 11 (1959).

94 163 229 337 478 585   Divorce § 137
M/B: 27A C.J.S. Divorce § 137 (1959).

95 164 230 338 479 586   Electricity § 41
M/B: 29 C.J.S. Electricity § 41 (1965).

96 165 231 339 480 587   Drains § 12
M/B: 28 C.J.S. Drains § 12 (1941).

97 166 232 340 481 588   Divorce § 312
M/B: 27B C.J.S. Divorce § 312 (1959).

98 167 233 341 482 589   Homesteads § 78
M/B: 40 C.J.S. Homesteads § 78 (1944).

99 168 234 342 483 590   Fraud § 95
M/B: 37 C.J.S. Fraud § 95 (1943).

100 169 235 343 484 591   False Imprisonment § 9
M/B: 35 C.J.S. False Imprionment § 9 (1960).

LIBRARY EXERCISE 29.   TOPIC METHOD OF SEARCH IN LEGAL ENCYCLOPEDIAS.

INSTRUCTOR'S NOTE: Using the "Analysis" and "Sub-Analysis" at the beginning of the topic in Corpus Juris Secundum listed below, students are required to find the section of Corpus Juris Secundum that most directly treats the question given with their problem number. (a) They are to answer the question based upon the material discussed in the section. (b) They are to list the "Analysis" and "Sub-Analysis" entries (including the section entry) that directed them to the relevant section. A student may cite a substantially different section in part (b) of this exercise if the material presented in the topic has been reorganized as a result of reissuance of the C.J.S. volume after the preparation of this exercise.

1 170 236 344 485 592   Theaters and Shows   May a theater owner make an admission ticket nontransferable by printing that condition on it?
(a)   Yes.
(b)   IV. Admission and Accommodation; Tickets
            § 37. Transfer or resale of tickets.

2 171 237 345 486 593   Public Utilities   Is inability to comply with an order a defense to proceedings for contempt of a public utility commission?
(a)   Yes.
(b)   V. Public Utility Commissions
           § 62. --- Contempt Proceedings.

3 172 238 346 487 594   States   Are state warrants generally considered to be negotiable instruments?
(a)   No.
(b)   VII. Fiscal Management, Public Debt, and Securities
       D.   Warrants, Scrip, and Certificates of Indebtedness
             § 246. Negotiability and transfer.

4 173 239 347 488 595   Work and Labor   When services are rendered in contemplation of marriage, without expectation of pecuniary compensation, may the person performing the services recover compensation when the recipient dies before the marriage?
(a)   No.
(b)   II. Effect of Relation or Status of Parties
            § 26. Persons contemplating marriage.

5 174 240 348 489 596   Witnesses   Under the common law, are witnesses entitled to compensation for testifying?
(a)   No.
(b)   II. Attendance, Production of Documents, and Compensation
            C. Compensation
                § 35. Right in general.

6 175 241 349 490 597   Wills   Does an advancement bear interest during the lifetime of the testator?
(a)   No. (unless the payment of interest is provided for in the will).
(b)   XII. Rights and Liabilities of Devisees and Legatees
             F. Advancements
                 § 1194. Interest on advancement.

7 176 242 350 491 598   Wills   May a testator properly delegate to a third party the power to execute a revocation of a will at his option after the death of the testator?
(a)   No.
(b)   VII. Revocation
              B. By Act of Testator
                  § 265. Delegation of power to revoke.

8 177 243 351 492 599   Wills   According to the weight of authority, may a person dispose of his own dead body by will?
(a)   Yes.
(b)   III. What May Pass by Will
             § 90. Testator's dead body.

EXERCISE 29. TOPIC METHOD OF SEARCH IN LEGAL ENCYLOPEDIAS   (CONTINUED)

9 178 244 352 493 600   Warehousemen and Safe Depositaries   In general, does a public warehouseman have a duty to receive goods delivered to him, provided the goods are within the class he is authorized to receive and store?
(a)   Yes.
(b)   II.   Powers, Duties, Rights, and Liabilities
            A.   In General
                § 11. ---Duty to receive and keep goods for storage.

10 179 245 353 494 501   Venue   In most jurisdictions, where does an action to foreclose a lien on personal property have to be brought?
(a)   In the county where the property is located at the time of suit.
(b)   II.   Nature or Subject of Action As Fixing Venue
            E.   Actions Relating to Personal Property
                § 50. Foreclosure of liens or charges.

11 180 246 354 495 502   United States   Are Senators privileged from arrest in civil cases when they are returning from a session of Congress?
(a)   Yes.
(b)   II.   Government
            B.   Congress
                § 18. Privileges and immunities of members.

12 181 247 355 496 503   Trusts   Can a person be a "de facto" trustee when there is no de jure trusteeship?
(a)   No.
(b)   IV.   Appointment, Qualification, and Tenure of Trustee; Survivorship.
            F.   Executors and Administrators as Trustees, De Facto Trustees, and Trustee de Son Tort
                § 245. De facto trustees, and trustees de son tort.

13 182 248 356 497 504   Trusts   May an express trust be declared by means of several instruments rather than one trust document?
(a)   Yes.
(b)   II.   Creation, Existence, and Validity
            A.   Express Trusts
                3.   Declaration of Trust
                    § 48. Use of several instruments.

14 183 249 357 498 505   Trial   May a demurrer to the evidence be made before all the plaintiff's proof is heard?
(a)   No.
(b)   VI.   Taking Case or Question From Jury
            B.   Demurrer to Evidence
                § 227. Time for demurrer.

15 184 250 358 499 506   Towns   Are anticipation warrants considered to be demand warrants?
(a)   No.
(b)   V.   Fiscal Management, Public Debt, Securities, and Taxation
            C.   Warrants, Orders, and Certificates of Indebtedness
                § 133. Anticipation warrants.

16 185 251 359 500 507   Tenancy in Common   Are statutes that authorize treble damages for waste committed by tenants in common strictly construed?
(a)   Yes.
(b)   IV.   Mutual Rights, Duties, and Liabilities of Cotenants
            D.   Waste
                § 57. Treble damages for waste.

17 186 252 360 401 508   Taxation   If a specific form of a tax deed is not prescribed by statute, will a common-law conveyance be sufficient if it is in such a form as to transfer the title of the former owner and vest the estate in the purchaser?
(a)   Yes.

EXERCISE 29. TOPIC METHOD OF SEARCH IN LEGAL ENCYLOPEDIAS   (CONTINUED)

(b)   XIV. Tax Titles
           B. Tax Deeds
              2. Form and Contents
                 § 928. In general.

18 187 253 361 402 509   Taxation   Does taxation of trust property to both the trustee and the cestui que trust constitute improper double taxation?
(a)   Yes.
(b)   II. Taxing Power, Limitations, and Constitutional Restrictions
           C. Double Taxation
              § 46. Trust property.
Note: "§ 100 Property Held in Trust" is not specifically responsive to the question asked and should not be considered correct.

19 188 254 362 403 510   Subrogation   Will an indemnitor of a surety be subrogated to the surety's rights when the indemnitor is compelled to satisfy the surety's liability?
(a)   Yes.
(b)   III. Particular Applications of Doctrine
           B. Sureties or Guarantors
              § 62. Indemnitors of sureties.

20 189 255 363 404 511   Statutes   When the proper construction of a statute is in doubt, must the court refer to the statute's preamble in order to ascertain the legislature's intent?
(a)   Yes.
(b)   IX. Construction and Operation
           A. Rules of Construction
              4. Statute as a Whole and Intrinsic Aids to Construction
                 § 349. Preamble and recitals.

21 190 256 364 405 512   States   Must a state use its property only for public purposes?
(a)   Yes.
(b)   IV. Property and Public Improvements
           § 146. Use of property.

22 191 257 365 406 513   Social Security and Public Welfare   Has the federal Social Security Act been extended to cover self-employed persons (who otherwise meet the statutory requirements)?
(a)   Yes.
(b)   II. Coverage of Social Security Statutes in General
           § 30. Self-employed persons.

23 192 258 366 407 514   Shipping   After a wrecked vessel has been abandoned by its owners, may a person be prosecuted for destroying the wrecked vessel?
(a)   No.
(b)   XIII. Wreck
           § 262. Offenses.

24 193 259 367 408 515   Seamen   In cases of an aggravated character, may a seaman be punished by forfeiture of his clothing and effects on board ship?
(a)   Yes.
(b)   XIV. Loss of Clothing and Effects
           § 217. Forfeiture as disciplinary measure.

25 194 260 368 409 516   Salvage   Is the pendency of a suit for salvage a bar to a subsequent action by other salvors against the same property to recover salvage for other services performed during the same voyage?
(a)   No.
(b)   X. Suits for Salvage
           § 147. Defenses.

26 195 261 369 410 517   Replevin   Will replevin lie for the recovery of a corpse?
(a)   No.
(b)   II. Property Recoverable

EXERCISE 29. TOPIC METHOD OF SEARCH IN LEGAL ENCYLOPEDIAS (CONTINUED)

    A. In General
     § 18. Dead Bodies.

27 196 262 370 411 518 Religious Societies As a general rule, is the property of a religious society divided among its members upon dissolution of the society?
(a) No.
(b) XII. Dissolution and Reogranization
    § 100. --Disposition of property.

28 197 263 371 412 519 Rape Can a railroad company be held civilly liable for a rape when the rape was committed by one of its employees on one of its passengers?
(a) Yes.
(b) III. Civil Liability
    § 90. Persons liable.

29 198 264 372 413 520 Quieting Title Is there a split of authority under quieting title statutes whether a holder of an easement has the right to bring an action to quiet title?
(a) Yes.
(b) I. Right of Action and Defenses
    D. Title or Interest of Plaintiff
     § 25. --Easements.

30 199 265 373 414 521 Public Utilities Is good will normally considered in setting the value of a public utility for the purposes of rate making?
(a) No.
(b) IV. Rates and Rate Making
    § 20. ---Good will.

31 200 266 374 415 522 Process Is a person confined in jail ordinarily exempt from service of civil process?
(a) No.
(b) II. Service of process
    F. Privileges and Exemptions
     § 82. Persons charged with crime or confined in prison.

32 101 267 375 416 523 Pleading Do some jurisdictions permit the use of a demurrer to attack the failure to attach necessary exhibits to a pleading when such attaching is required by statute?
(a) Yes.
(b) V. Demurrer or Exception
    § 229. ---Failure to attach exhibits.

33 102 268 376 417 524 Physicians and Surgeons May practice of a profession under a trade name be prohibited by statute?
(a) Yes.
(b) III. Regulation of Professional Conduct
    § 33. Practice under forbidden name.

34 103 269 377 418 525 Patents What rights are transferred when an expired patent is assigned?
(a) The right to sue for past infringements is transferred.
(b) X. Ownership, Transfers, Assignments, Licenses, and Contracts
    B. Assignments and Other Transfers
     § 234. Assignment after expiration of patent.

35 104 270 378 419 526 Partnership May a partner engage in business of the same nature as that of the partnership without the consent of his copartners (unless otherwise provided by the partnership agreement)?
(a) No.
(b) IV. Mutual Rights, Duties, and Liabilities of Partners
    B. Individual Transactions
     § 106. Engaging in Other Business.

EXERCISE 29.   TOPIC METHOD OF SEARCH IN LEGAL ENCYLOPEDIAS   (CONTINUED)

36 105 271 379 420 527   Officers   In general, are de facto officers entitled to the emoluments of an office where there is a de jure officer also claiming the office?
(a)   No.
(b)   X.   De Facto Officers
            § 275.---Right to compensation or other emolument.

37 106 272 380 421 528   Nuisances   May a structure which heats the property of another so as to make it untenantable be a nuisance?
(a)   Yes.
(b)   III.   Particular Annoyances
             § 24. Heat.

38 107 273 381 422 529   Negligence   In determining whether a child is capable of exercising any care for his own safety for purposes of the law of contributory negligence, must consideration be given to all factors bearing on his capacity, not just his age?
(a)   Yes.
(b)   VII.   Contributory Negligence
         B.   Persons under Disability
              § 145. ---Age at which contributory negligence is chargeable.

39 108 274 382 423 530   Navigable Waters   May an individual obtain an absolute exclusive right to possession of an island in the sea by virtue of discovering it?
(a)   No.
(b)   VII.   Islands
             § 118. Possession and other rights in general.

40 109 275 383 424 531   Municipal Corporations   In absence of a statute or ordinance controlling the matter, may claims against a municipal corporation be assigned?
(a)   Yes.
(b)   XX.   Claims Against Municipality
            § 2183. Assignment.

41 110 276 384 425 532   Municipal Corporations   In general, is a municipal corporation liable in tort for injuries resulting from defects in a street not yet opened for public use?
(a)   No.
(b)   XIII.   Torts
         E.   Defects or Obstructions in Streets or Other Public Ways
              § 787.---Unopened or unimproved streets or ways.

42 111 277 385 426 533   Municipal Corporations   In general, may proceedings for annexation of territory to a municipal corporation be attacked collaterally on the ground that they are absolutely void for want of jurisdiction?
(a)   Yes.
(b)   II.   Creation, Alteration, Incidents, Existence, and Dissolution
         B.   Boundaries; Change or Subdivision of Territory
              2.   Alteration
                   c.   Prevention of or attack on, and cure of defects
                        § 66. Collateral attack.

43 112 278 386 427 534   Motor Vehicles   Is a spectator's right to recover for injuries because of a speed contest along a public way affected by the fact the spectator was a trespasser on land adjacent to the highway?
(a)   No.
(b)   X.   Races and Speed Trials
         A.   Races or Tests upon Highways or Streets
              § 574. Trespass by spectator.

44 113 279 387 428 535   Securities Regulation   Does a plaintiff have the privilege of nationwide service of process in a civil action based upon a violation of the federal securities laws (the Securities Act of 1933 and the Securities Exchange Act of 1934)?

EXERCISE 29. TOPIC METHOD OF SEARCH IN LEGAL ENCYLOPEDIAS   (CONTINUED)

(a)   Yes.
(b)   II.   Federal Regulation
             F. Civil Effects of Violations
                 2. Remedies in General
                     § 136. Process.

45 114 280 388 429 536   Products Liability   May a manufacturer limit by contract his strict liability for injuries resulting from product defects?
(a)   No.
(b)   III. Persons Entitled to Sue; Persons Liable; Defenses
             § 48. Limitation of liability.

46 115 281 389 430 537   Motor Vehicles   What is an auto stage?
(a)   It is a motor vehicle used for carrying passengers, freight, baggage on a regular schedule of time and rates.
(b)   I.   Definitions and Distinctions
             § 3. Auto stage.

47 116 282 390 431 538   Mortgages   May a creditor (not a judgment creditor), who is not a party to a mortgage, question or impeach the consideration supporting a mortgage?
(a)   Yes.
(b)   VI.   Consideration
             § 97. Who may impeach consideration.

48 117 283 391 432 539   Monopolies   Under the federal antitrust laws, are reasonable attorney's fees expressly granted to a successful plaintiff in an action for damages?
(a)   Yes.
(b)   VII. Actions for Injuries to Third Persons Resulting from
             Unlawful Contracts or Combinations
             § 104. Costs and attorney's fees.

49 118 284 392 433 540   Mechanics' Liens   Is scire facias used as a proceeding to enforce a mechanic's lien in some jurisdictions?
(a)   Yes.
(b)   VIII. Enforcement
             A. In General
                 § 288. Scire facias

50 119 285 393 434 541   Marriage   At common law, what was the age of legal consent to marriage for a female?
(a)   Twelve.
(b)   II.   Essentials
             § 11. Age.

51 120 286 394 435 542   Marriage   What is jactitation of marriage?
(a)   It is where one person, not married to another, pretends to be married to that other person and proclaims their marriage to others.
(b)   V. Jactitation of Marriage
             § 70. Nature, grounds for relief, defenses and remedy.

52 121 287 395 436 543   Master and Servant   does the insanity of an employee which prevents the performance of his contract terminate his employment contract unless the parties have agreed otherwise?
(a)   Yes.
(b)   I.   The Relation
             D. Termination of Relation
                 § 38. Death or disability of servant.

53 122 288 396 437 544   Licenses   Is a license in respect of real property ordinarily assignable by the licensee without the consent of the licensor?
(a)   No.
(b)   II.   In Respect of Real Property
             § 86. Assignability.

EXERCISE 29.   TOPIC METHOD OF SEARCH IN LEGAL ENCYLOPEDIAS   (CONTINUED)

54 123 289 397 438 545   Homesteads   Are there ordinarily moral qualification requiremetns that must be met in order to obtain a homestead exemption?
(a)   No.
(b)   I.   Nature, Acquisition, and Extent
      B.   Persons Entitled to Homestead
        § 21. Moral character of claimant.

55 124 290 398 439 546   Fraud   Where an injury sufficient to sustain an action for fraud has been established, is the plaintiff entitled to at lesat nominal damages?
(a)   Yes.
(b)   V.   Actions
      G.   Damages
        § 139. Nominal damages.

56 125 291 399 440 547   Garnishment   does securing a garnishment on the basis of false allegations of fact ordinarily render the garnishment "wrongful"?
(a)   Yes.
(b)   XV.   Wrongful Garnishment
      § 310. What constitutes.

57 126 292 400 441 548   Larceny   May lost property be the subject of larceny?
(a)   Yes.
(b)   I.   Offenses and Responsibility Therefore
      B.   Particular Elements
        § 18. ---Lost property.

58 127 293 301 442 549   Attachment   May vested interests under contracts be attached?
(a)   Yes.
(b)   IV.   Property Subject to Attachment
      § 56. Interest under contract.

59 128 294 302 443 550   Justices of the Peace   In a civil case, as a general rule does a judgment of a jsutice of the peace prior to execution create a lien on property in absence of a statute regulating the matter?
(a)   No.
(b)   IV.   Procedure in Civil Cases
      § 118. ---Lien.

60 129 295 303 444 551   Juries   In absence of a statute regulating the matter, is it necessary for the court to issue a formal written summons for talesmen?
(a)   No.
(b)   VII.   Jury Panel
      C.   Talesmen
        § 188. Order for summons.

61 130 296 304 445 552   Bail   Has it been held that a recital of the defendant's arrest in a bail bond in a civil action is not essential to the validity of the bail bond?
(a)   Yes.
(b)   II.   In Civil Actions
      C.   Bond, Undertaking, or Recognizance
        § 14. Recitals.

62 131 297 305 446 553   Attachment   Is a voidable writ of attachment amendable?
(a)   Yes.
(b)   VI.   Writ, Warrant, or Order
      § 168. Amendments.

63 132 298 306 447 554   Assignments   Is an action for injury to reputation assignable in absence of a statute regulating the matter?
(a)   No.

EXERCISE 29. TOPIC METHOD OF SEARCH IN LEGAL ENCYLOPEDIAS   (CONTINUED)

(b) II. Property, Estates, and Rights Assignable
      E. Rights of Action
          § 38. ---Injury to person or reputation.

64 133 299 307 448 555   Eminent Domain   Is the establishment of a public ferry considered to be a public use for which private property may be condemned?
(a) Yes.
(b) IV. Public Use.
      B. Particular Uses
         § 52. Ferries.

65 134 300 308 449 556   Assignments   Is an action for tortious injury to a person's property generally assignable in absence of a statute regulating the matter?
(a) Yes.
(b) II. Property, Estates, and Rights Assignable
      E. Rights of Action
         § 39. ---Injury to property.

66 135 201 309 450 557   Arbitration   Is a party competent to act as an arbitrator in his own dispute?
(a) No.
(b) III. Arbitral Forum; Arbitrators and Umpires
      § 63. Competency.

67 136 202 310 451 558   Contracts   Must a contract generally be rescinded in toto or can any contract be rescinded in part and affirmed in part?
(a) In general, rescission must be in toto; indivisible contracts may not be rescinded in part and affirmed in part.
(b) XIII. Termination or Discharge and Rescission
      B. Rescission for Invalidity of Contract or for Wrong or Default of Adverse Party.
        1. In General
          § 416. Pattial rescission.

68 137 203 311 452 559   Continuances   Is the loss of papers in the case a good ground for a continuance when the applicant for the continuance is not at fault and the papers cannot readily be replaced?
(a) Yes.
(b) II. Grounds for Continuance
      § 19. Loss or absence of papers.

69 138 204 312 453 560   Civil Rights   Is racial discrimination in the use of public facilities unlawful?
(a) Yes.
(b) II. Rights Protected and Discrimination Prohibited
      B. Public Accomodations and Facilities
         § 31. Public Facilities.

70 139 205 313 454 561   Railroads   After two railroads have been consolidated, are actions on a cause arising prior to consolidation generally maintainable against the consolidated company?
(a) Yes.
(b) VIII. Sales, Leases, Traffic Contracts, and Consolidation
      E. Consolidation
         § 242. Actions brought after consolidation.

71 140 206 314 455 562   Charities   Is a gift for the care of a public burial ground a gift for a charitable use?
(a) Yes.
(b) III. Charitable Purposes
      § 14. Care, maintenance or improvement of burial grounds and monuments.

EXERCISE 29.   TOPIC METHOD OF SEARCH IN LEGAL ENCYLOPEDIAS   (CONTINUED)

72 141 207 315 456 563   Carriers   According to the usually accepted view, does a carrier have a right to a common law lien for demurrage charges in absence of usage, statute, or contract providing such a right?
(a)   No.
(b)   II.   Carriers of Goods and Live Stock
    S.   Charges, Liens, and Demurrage
     3.   Dumurrage
      § 346. Lien.

73 142 208 316 457 564   Brokers   Under what power does a state have the authority to regulate the business or occupation of a broker?
(a)   Police power.
(b)   II.   Regulation and Conduct of Business
    A.   In General
     § 6. Power to regulate.

74 143 209 317 458 565   Boundaries   Does a conveyance of land bounded by a wall carry title to the center of the wall unless a contrary intention appears?
(a)   Yes.
(b)   II.   Description, Elements, and Construction
    § 46. ---Walls.

75 144 210 318 459 566   Burglary   Under the common law, is the breaking and entering of a railroad car with the intent to steal burglary?
(a)   No.
(b)   III.   Character, Location, and Occupancy of Structure or
    Place Involved.
    § 37.   Vehicles, railroad cars, and vessels.

76 145 211 319 460 567   Animals   In general, what is the difference between a rescue and a pound breach?
(a)   A rescue is an unlawful setting at liberty of distrained
  animals before they are confined in the legal pound; a
  pound breach as a setting at liberty and driving away animals
  from a legal pound.
(b)   XVII. Pounds and Poundkeepers.
    C.   Rescue and Pound Breach
     § 343. In General.

77 146 212 320 461 568   Criminal Law   May the age of the accused be considered in fixing the accused's punishment?
(a)   Yes.
(b)   XX.   Punishment of Crime
    B.   Extent of Punishment
     § 1989. Age as affecting punishment.

78 147 213 321 462 569   Customs Duties   In order to recover excessive duties paid, is it necessary that they were paid under some form of protest?
(a)   Yes.
(b)   VII. Recovery of Duties Paid.
    § 231. ---Protest.

79 148 214 322 463 570   Death   Where it is shown that a person was alive at a certain time, will it be presumed that this person was alive at a subsequent time, unless the contrary is shown by proof or a different presumption arises?
(a)   Yes.
(b)   II.   Evidence of Death and Survivorship
    § 5. Presumption of continuance of life.

80 149 215 323 464 571   Deeds   Is the affixing of a revenue stamp to a deed, in absence of an intent to evade the revenue law, essential to the validity of the deed?
(a)   No.
(b)   III.   Requisites and Validity
    C.   Execution
     § 36. Revenue stamps.

EXERCISE 29. TOPIC METHOD OF SEARCH IN LEGAL ENCYLOPEDIAS   (CONTINUED)

81 150 216 324 465 572   Agency   Does an agent have a specific lien upon the principal's property in his possession for his expenses during the course of the agency with respect to that property?
(a)   Yes.
(b)   XI.   Duties and Liabilities of Principal to Agent
              C.   Agent's Lien
                   § 357. In General.

82 151 217 325 466 573   Death   Is justifiable homicide recognized as a defense to a wrongful death action?
(a)   Yes.
(b)   III. Actions for Causing Death
              E.   Defenses
                   § 44. Justifiable homicide.

83 152 218 326 467 574   Admiralty   Is a charter party a contract within admiralty jurisdiction so as to be enforceable in admiralty?
(a)   Yes.
(b)   II.   Jurisdiction
              E.   Subject Matter of Jurisdiction
                   1.   Contracts
                        § 39. Charter party.

84 153 219 327 468 575   Eminent Domain   May the powers of eminent domain be conferred on a territory by implication?
(a)   Yes.
(b)   III. Who May Exercise Power
              § 20. Territories.

85 154 220 328 469 576   Eminent Domain   Is a market, public in character, a public use for which private property may be condemned?
(a)   Yes.
(b)   IV.   Public Use
              B.   Particular Uses
                   § 60. Markets.

86 155 221 329 470 577   Equity   Does a court have the power to render and enter a decree nunc pro tunc, assuming it has exercised proper discretion?
(a)   Yes.
(b)   XXII. Decrees
              B.   Rendition; Pronouncement and Settlement; Entry
                   and Enrollment
                   § 593. Nunc pro tunc.

87 156 222 330 471 578   Estoppel   Must estoppel ordinarily be specially pleaded?
(a)   Yes.
(b)   VIII. Procedure
              A.   Pleading
                   § 153(1). Necessity for pleading.

88 157 223 331 472 579   Executions   Is a franchise subject to execution under the common law?
(a)   No.
(b)   II.   Property Subject to Execution
              § 22. Franchises.

89 158 224 332 473 580   Evidence   Under the best evidence rule, is parol evidence ordinarily admissible to prove the contents of a newspaper?
(a)   No (although there is some authority to the contrary).
(b)   XIX. Best and Secondary Evidence
              B.   Parol Evidence Secondary to Written Evidence
                   2.   Application of Rule
                        § 805. ---Newspapers.

90 159 225 333 474 581   Evidence   Will a nonexpert witness be permitted to state his opinion as to the cause of a sound?

EXERCISE 29.   TOPIC METHOD OF SEARCH IN LEGAL ENCYLOPEDIAS   (CONTINUED)

(a)   Yes.
(b)   XII. Opinion
            D. Subjects of Testimony of Ordinary Observer
                § 546(50). Sound.

91 160 226 334 475 582   Evidence   May an application for a continuance that contains admissions be introduced in evidence as a judicial admission?
(a)   Yes.
(b)   VIII. Admissions
            C. Judicial Admissions
                § 313. Applications for continuances.

92 161 227 335 476 583   Descent and Distribution   May community property be the subject of an advancement?
(a)   Yes.
(b)   III. Rights and Liabilities of Heirs and Distributees
            B. Advancements
                § 96. Property subject of advancements.

93 162 228 336 477 584   Dismissal and Nonsuit   What is a retraxit?
(a)   A retraxit is an open and voluntary renunciation of a
       claim in court.
(b)   I. Definitions
            § 5. Retraxit.

94 163 229 337 478 585   Divorce   Is adultery a generally recognized ground for divorce in most jurisdictions?
(a)   Yes.
(b)   II. Grounds
            C. Postnuptial Grounds
                § 21. Adultery.

95 164 230 338 479 586   Electricity   Is there a duty, independent of statute, imposed on an electric company to serve without discrimination all similarity situated members of the public it professes to serve, provided they have complied with all proper conditions precedent for service?
(a)   Yes.
(b)   IV. Supply to Consumers in General
            § 25. Duty to furnish service.

96 165 231 339 480 587   Drains   Does a drainage assessment constitute a lien on lands within the district in absence of a statute so providing?
(a)   No.
(b)   II. Assessments and Special Taxes
            § 77. Lien.

97 166 232 340 481 588   Divorce   Does the full faith and credit provision of the federal Constitution apply to a decree rendered in a foreign country?
(a)   No.
(b)   VIII. Foreign Divorce
            A. Recognition of Foreign Divorces
                1. In General
                    § 328. ---Full faith and credit.

98 167 233 341 482 589   Drugs and Narcotics   May the ownership of a pharmacy be restricted to persons who are licensed or registered pharmacists?
(a)   Yes.
(b)   II. Drugs, Druggists, and Manufacturers in General
            B. Regulation of Drug Stores and Pharmacists
                § 36. Ownership of pharmacy or drug store.

99 168 234 342 483 590   Attorney and Client   Is an attorney's possessory lien assignable?
(a)   No.
(b)   X. Lien of Attorney
            A. In General
                § 362. Assignment of lien.

EXERCISE 29.   TOPIC METHOD OF SEARCH IN LEGAL ENCYLOPEDIAS   (CONTINUED)

100 169 235 343 484 591   <u>False Imprisonment</u>   Is there a right to at least nominal damages as a result of an illegal restraint amounting to false imprisonment?
(a)   Yes.
(b)   VI.   Damages and Penalties
              § 63. Nominal damages.

LIBRARY EXERCISE 30. LEGAL PERIODICALS.

INSTRUCTOR'S NOTE: The students are required to find and cite the article, comment, note, case comment, or case note that begins on the page of the volume of the designated law review listed below. All of the references are to articles. The following Quick-Reference Abbreviations are particularly relevant to this exercise:

PERIODICAL CITATION 1. CITE LEAD ARTICLES BY THE LAST NAME OF THE AUTHOR, TITLE, VOLUME, ABBREVIATED NAME OF THE PERIODICAL, PAGE, AND DATE. [PERIOD 1]
PERIODICAL CITATION 5. USE THE USOC ABBREVIATION OF THE PERIODICAL TITLE IN THE CITATION. FOLLOW THE GENERAL SPACING RULES IN USOC RULE 6.1(A). [PERIOD 5]
PERIODICAL CITATION 8. IN MEMORANDA AND BRIEFS, UNDERSCORE (ITALICIZE) THE TITLE OF THE ARTICLE. IN LAW REVIEW FOOTNOTES, ITALICIZE THE TITLE OF THE ARTICLE, AND CITE THE NAME OF THE PERIODICAL IN LARGE AND SMALL CAPITALS. [PERIOD 8]

1 119 209 375 470 584   61 Mich. L. Rev. 425
M/B: Libin & Haydon, *Embezzled Funds as Taxable Income: A Study in Judicial Footwork*, 61 Mich. L. Rev. 425 (1963).

2 120 210 376 471 585   57 Mich. L. Rev. 945
M/B: Ross, *Commitment of the Mentally Ill: Problems of Law and Policy*, 57 Mich. L. Rev. 945 (1959).

3 121 211 377 472 586   39 Mich. L. Rev. 561
M/B: Lindsay, *Council and Court: The Handbill Ordinances, 1889-1939*, 39 Mich. L. Rev. 561 (1941).

4 122 212 378 473 587   37 Mich. L. Rev. 841
M/B: Gellhorn & Linfield, *Administrative Adjudication of Contract Disputes: The Walsh-Healey Act*, 37 Mich. L. Rev. 841 (1939).

5 123 213 379 474 588   44 Mich. L. Rev. 955
M/B: Lobinger, *Precedent in Past and Present Legal Systems*, 44 Mich. L. Rev. 955 (1946)

6 124 214 380 475 589   63 Calif. L. Rev. 926
M/B: Travis, *Primary Jurisdiction: A General Theory and Its Application to the Securities Exchange Act*, 63 Calif. L. Rev. 926 (1975).

7 125 215 381 476 590   64 Calif. L. Rev. 678
M/B: Grodin, *Political Aspects of Public Sector Interest Arbitration*, 64 Calif. L. Rev. 678 (1976).

8 126 216 382 477 591   42 Mich. L. Rev. 383
M/B: Lourie, *"Enemy" Under the Trading with the Enemy Act and Some Problems of International Law*, 42 Mich. L. Rev. 383 (1943).

9 127 217 383 478 592   36 Mich. L. Rev. 56
M/B: Linville, *Purchaser's Remedies for Absence of Marketable Title*, 36 Mich. L. Rev. 56 (1937).

10 128 218 384 479 593   50 Mich. L. Rev. 1291
M/B: Luce, *Trends in Modern Corporation Legislation*, 50 Mich. L. Rev. 1291 (1952).

11 129 219 385 480 594   49 Mich. L. Rev. 1103
M/B: Lunsford, *Woe Unto You Trade-Mark Owners*, 49 Mich. L. Rev. 1103 (1951).

12 130 220 386 481 595   77 Mich. L. Rev. 63
M/B: Langbein, *Living Probate: The Conservatorship Model*, 77 Mich. L. Rev. 63 (1978).

13 131 221 387 482 596   48 Mich. L. Rev. 745
M/B: Marshall, *Mr. Justice Murphy and Civil Rights*, 48 Mich. L. Rev. 745 (1950).

EXERCISE 30. LEGAL PERIODICALS   (CONTINUED)

14 132 222 388 483 597   47 Mich. L. Rev. 775
M/B: Meader, Limitations on Congressional Investigation, 47 Mich. L. Rev. 775
(1949).

15 133 223 389 484 598   65 Calif. L. Rev. 546
M/B: Simmons, The Problem of "Issue" in the Administration of the Fairness
Doctrine, 65 Calif. L. Rev. 546 (1977).

16 134 224 390 485 599   66 Calif. L. Rev. 935
M/B: Westen, Order of Proof: An Accused's Right to Control the Timing and
Sequence of Evidence in His Defense, 66 Calif. L. Rev. 935 (1978).

17 135 225 391 486 600   54 Mich. L. Rev. 71
M/B: Mittenthal, Partial Strikes and National Labor Policy, 54 Mich. L. Rev.
71 (1955).

18 136 226 392 487 501   59 Mich. L. Rev. 1017
M/B: Mittenthal, Past Practice and the Administration of Collective
Bargaining Agreements, 59 Mich. L. Rev. 1017 (1961).

19 137 227 393 488 502   56 Mich. L. Rev. 33
M/B: Nadelmann, Full Faith and Credit to Judgments and Public Acts: A
Historical-Analystical Reappraisal, 56 Mich. L. Rev. 33 (1957).

20 138 228 394 489 503   41 Mich. L. Rev. 815
M/B: Nemmers, Key Problems in the Apportionment of Increase Between
Successive Interests in Personality, 41 Mich. L. Rev. 815 (1943).

21 139 229 395 490 504   60 Mich. L. Rev. 169
M/B: Newman, Federal Agency Investigations: Procedural Rights of the
Subpoenaed Witness, 60 Mich. L. Rev. 169 (1961).

22 140 230 396 491 505   23 Stanford L. Rev. 1
M/B: Friedenthal, Joinder of Claims, Counterclaims, and Cross-Complaints:
Suggested Revision of the California Provisions, 23 Stanford L. Rev. 1 (1970).

23 141 231 397 492 506   52 Mich. L. Rev. 479
M/B: Norris, The Seaman as Ward of the Admiralty, 52 Mich. L. Rev. 479
(1954).

24 142 232 398 493 507   24 Stanford L. Rev. 439
M/B: Franklin, Tort Liability for Hepatitis: An Analysis and a Proposal, 24
Stanford L. Rev. 439 (1972).

25 143 233 399 494 508   58 Mich. L. Rev. 55
M/B: Oberer, Voluntary Impartial Review of Labor: Some Reflections, 58 Mich.
L. Rev. 55 (1959).

26 144 234 400 495 509   74 Mich. L. Rev. 1258
M/B: Owen, Punitive Damages in Products Liability Litigation, 74 Mich. L.
Rev. 1258 (1976).

27 145 235 301 496 510   25 Minn. L. Rev. 730
M/B: Dwan & Smith, Judicial Self-Limitation in Administrative Law: Examples
in Tariff Administration, 25 Minn. L. Rev. 730 (1941).

28 146 236 302 497 511   20 Minn. L. Rev. 1
M/B: Eagleton, The New Minnesota Probate Code, 20 Minn. L. Rev. 1 (1935).

29 147 237 303 498 512   30 Minn. L. Rev. 435
M/B: East, Physical Factors and Criminal Behaviour, 30 Minn. L. Rev. 435
(1946).

30 148 238 304 499 513   125 U. Pa. L. Rev. 947
M/B: Nimmer, Termination of Transfers Under the Copyright Act of 1976, 125 U.
Pa. L. Rev. 947 (1977).

EXERCISE 30. LEGAL PERIODICALS   (CONTINUED)

31 149 239 305 500 514   23 Minn. L. Rev. 879
M/B: Ebenstein, The Law of Public Housing, 23 Minn. L. Rev. 879 (1939).

32 150 240 306 401 515   36 Minn. L. Rev. 1
M/B: Ehrenzweig, The Place of Acting in Intentional Multistate Torts: Law and Reason Versus the Restatement, 36 Minn. L. Rev. 1 (1951).

33 151 241 307 402 516   5 Minn. L. Rev. 493
M/B: Rice & Harno, Shares With No Par Value, 5 Minn. L. Rev. 493 (1921).

34 152 242 308 403 517   127 U. Pa. L. Rev. 581
M/B: White, Police Trickery in Inducing Confessions, 127 U. Pa. L. Rev. 581 (1979).

35 153 243 309 404 518   33 Minn. L. Rev. 331
M/B: Hale, Agreements Among Competitors: Incidental and Reasonable Restraints of Trade, 33 Minn. L. Rev. 331 (1949).

36 154 244 310 405 519   24 Minn. L. Rev. 607
M/B: Evans, Legal Immunity for Defamation, 24 Minn. L. Rev. 607 (1940).

37 155 245 311 406 520   12 Minn. L. Rev. 129
M/B: Feezer, Acceptance of Bills of Exchange by Conduct, 12 Minn. L. Rev. 129 (1928).

38 156 246 312 407 521   14 Minn. L. Rev. 124
M/B: Feezer, Death of a Drawer of a Check, 14 Minn. L. Rev. 124 (1930).

39 157 247 313 408 522   9 Minn. L. Rev. 101
M/B: Feezer, May the Payee of a Negotiable Instrument Be a Holder in Due Course?, 9 Minn. L. Rev. 101 (1925).

40 158 248 314 409 523   11 Minn. L. Rev. 313
M/B: Feezer, Social Justice in the Field of Torts, 11 Minn. L. Rev. 313 (1927).

41 159 249 315 410 524   10 Minn. L. Rev. 1
M/B: Feezer, Tort Liability of Manufacturers and Vendors, 10 Minn. L. Rev. 1 (1925).

42 160 250 316 411 525   128 U. Pa. L. Rev. 361
M/B: Arnold, Accident, Mistake, and Rules of Liability in the Fourteenth-Century Law of Torts, 128 U. Pa. L. Rev. 361 (1979).

43 161 251 317 412 526   17 Minn. L. Rev. 689
M/B: Hoshour, The Minnesota Business Corporation Act, 17 Minn. L. Rev. 689 (1933).

44 162 252 318 413 527   18 Minn. L. Rev. 269
M/B: Hoshour, The Minnesota Business Corporation Act, 17 Minn. L. Rev. 689 (1933).

45 163 253 319 414 528   22 Minn. L. Rev. 1008
M/B: Field, The Constitutional Theory of the National Industrial Recovery Act, 18 Minn. L. Rev. 269 (1934).

46 164 254 320 415 529   13 Minn. L. Rev. 439
M/B: Field, The Effect of an Unconstitutional Statute in the Law of Public Officers: Effect on Official Status, 13 Minn. L. Rev. 439 (1929).

47 165 255 321 416 530   59 Calif. L. Rev. 1091
M/B: Binder, Sex Discrimination in the Airline Industry: Title VII Flying High, 59 Calif. L. Rev. 1091 (1971).

48 166 256 322 417 531   15 Minn. L. Rev. 261

EXERCISE 30. LEGAL PERIODICALS   (CONTINUED)

M/B: Fordham, Preferences of Prereceivership Claims in Equity Receiverships, 15 Minn. L. Rev. 261 (1931).

49 167 257 323 418 532   31 Minn. L. Rev. 301
M/B: Fraenkel, The Federal Civil Rights Laws, 31 Minn. L. Rev. 301 (1947).

50 168 258 324 419 533   35 Minn. L. Rev. 262
M/B: Hagan, Wire Communications Utilities and Bookmaking, 35 Minn. L. Rev. 262 (1951).

51 169 259 325 420 534   44 Yale L.J. 782
M/B: Eno, Price Movement and Unstated Objections to the Defective Performance of Sales Contracts, 44 Yale L.J. 782 (1935).

52 170 260 326 421 535   45 Yale L.J. 1201
M/B: Corstvet, Inadequate Bookkeeping as a Factor in Business Failure, 45 Yale L.J. 1201 (1936).

53 171 261 327 422 536   46 Yale L.J. 52
M/B: Fuller and Perdue, The Reliance Interest in Contract Damages, 46 Yale L.J. 52 (1936).

54 172 262 328 423 537   47 Yale L.J. 724
M/B: Herring, The Politics of Fiscal Policy, 47 Yale L.J. 724 (1938).

55 173 263 329 424 538   48 Yale L.J. 195
M/B: Witmer, Collective Labor Agreements in the Courts, 48 Yale L.J. 195 (1938).

56 174 264 330 425 539   49 Yale L.J. 18
M/B: Alpert, The Alien and Public Charge Clauses, 49 Yale L.J. 18 (1939).

57 175 265 331 426 540   50 Yale L.J. 1376
M/B: Meck & Bogue, Federal Regulation of Motor Carrier Unification, 50 Yale L.J. 1376 (1941).

58 176 266 332 427 541   51 Yale L.J. 213
M/B: Pavenstedt, The Broadened Scope of Section 22(a): The Evolution of the Clifford Doctrine, 51 Yale L.J. 213 (1941).

59 177 267 333 428 542   86 Yale L.J. 809
M/B: Berger & Bernstein, An Analytical Framework for Antitrust Standing, 86 Yale L.J. 809 (1977).

60 178 268 334 429 543   88 Yale L.J. 1623
M/B: Dellinger, The Recurring Question of the "Limited" Constitutional Convention, 88 Yale L.J. 1623 (1979).

61 179 269 335 430 544   54 Yale L.J. 809
M/B: Becker, Some Problems of Legal Analysis, 54 Yale L.J. 809 (1945).

62 180 270 336 431 545   55 Yale L.J. 76
M/B: Asia, Employment Relation: Common-Law Concept and Legislative Definition, 55 Yale L.J. 76 (1945).

63 181 271 337 432 546   56 Yale L.J. 605
M/B: Frank, Disqualification of Judges, 56 Yale L.J. 605 (1947).

64 182 272 338 433 547   57 Yale L.J. 1207
M/B: Jacobs, Unit Operation of Oil and Gas Fields, 57 Yale L.J. 1207 (1948).

65 183 273 339 434 548   58 Yale L.J. 213
M/B: Ball, Shaping the Law of Weather Control, 58 Yale L.J. 213 (1949).

66 184 274 340 435 549   29 U. Fla. L. Rev. 789
M/B: Pelham, Regulating Developments of Regional Impact: Florida and the Model Code, 29 U. Fla. L. Rev. 789 (1977).

EXERCISE 30. LEGAL PERIODICALS   (CONTINUED)

67 185 275 341 436 550   28 U. Fla. L. Rev. 1
M/B: Kulzer, Law and the Housewife: Property, Divorce, and Death, 28 U. Fla. L. Rev. 1 (1975).

68 186 276 342 437 551   26 U. Fla. L. Rev. 191
M/B: Levinson & Mills, Impoundment: A Search for Legal Principles, 26 U. Fla. L. Rev. 191 (1974).

69 187 277 343 438 552   44 U. Chi. L. Rev. 271
M/B: Dam, The American Fiscal Constitution, 44 U. Chi. L. Rev. 271 (1977).

70 188 278 344 439 553   43 U. Chi. L. Rev. 667
M/B: Frase, The Speedy Trial Act of 1974, 43 U. Chi. L. Rev. 667 (1976).

71 189 279 345 440 554   46 U. Chi. L. Rev. 3
M/B: Langbein, Torture and Plea Bargaining, 46 U. Chi. L. Rev. 3 (1978).

72 190 280 346 441 555   47 U. Chi. L. Rev. 1
M/B: Eisenberg, Donative Promises, 47 U. Chi. L. Rev. 1 (1979).

73 191 281 347 442 556   79 Colum. L. Rev. 1227
M/B: Linzer, The Meaning of Certiorari Denials, 79 Colum. L. Rev. 1227 (1979).

74 192 282 348 443 557   76 Colum. L. Rev. 48
M/B: Robertson, Organ Donations by Incompetents and the Substituted Judgment Doctrine, 76 Colum. L. Rev. 48 (1976).

75 193 283 349 444 558   77 Colum. L. Rev. 511
M/B: Gobert, Victim Precipitation, 77 Colum. L. rev. 511 (1977).

76 194 284 350 445 559   75 Colum. L. Rev. 771
M/B: Gellhorn & Robinson, Perspectives on Administrative Law, 75 Colum. L. Rev. 771 (1975).

77 195 285 351 446 560   74 Colum. L. Rev. 40
M/B: Hill, Breach of Contract as a Tort, 74 Colum. L. Rev. 40 (1974).

78 196 286 352 447 561   62 Harv. L. Rev. 987
M/B: Bunn, The National Law of Unfair Competition, 62 Harv. L. Rev. 987 (1949).

79 197 287 353 448 562   63 Harv. L. Rev. 27
M/B: Adelman, Integration and Antitrust Policy, 63 Harv. L. Rev. 27 (1949).

80 198 288 354 449 563   64 Harv. L. Rev. 417
M/B: Baker, Debt Discount and Expense, 64 Harv. L. Rev. 417 (1951).

81 199 289 355 450 564   89 Harv. L. Rev. 1685
M/B: Kennedy, Form and Substance in Private Law Adjudication, 89 Harv. L. Rev. 1685 (1976).

82 200 290 356 451 565   86 Harv. L. Rev. 1380
M/B: Gellhorn, Adverse Publicity by Administrative Agencies, 86 Harv. L. Rev. 1380 (1973).

83 101 291 357 452 566   85 Harv. L. Rev. 537
M/B: Fletcher, Fairness and Utility in Tort Theory, 85 Harv. L. Rev. 537 (1972).

84 102 292 358 453 567   68 Harv. L. Rev. 257
M/B: Austin, Surrey, Warren, & Winokur, The Internal Revenue Code of 1954: Tax Accounting, 68 Harv. L. Rev. 257 (1954).

85 103 293 359 454 568   69 Harv. L. Rev. 1

EXERCISE 30. LEGAL PERIODICALS (CONTINUED)

M/B: Bickel, The Original Understanding and the Segregation Decision, 69 Harv. L. Rev. 1 (1955).

86 104 294 360 455 569   70 Harv. L. Rev. 1183
M/B: Darrell, The Use of Reorganization Techniques in Corporate Acquisitions, 70 Harv. L. Rev. 1183 (1957).

87 105 295 361 456 570   71 Harv. L. Rev. 1401
M/B: Cox, The Duty to Bargain in Good Faith, 71 Harv. L. Rev. 1401 (1958).

88 106 296 362 457 571   72 Harv. L. Rev. 609
M/B: Cox, The Role of Law in Preserving Union Democracy, 72 Harv. L. Rev. 609 (1959).

89 107 297 363 458 572   73 Harv. L. Rev. 625
M/B: Blake, Employee Agreements Not to Compete, 73 Harv. L. rev. 625 (1960).

90 108 298 364 459 573   74 Harv. L. Rev. 473
M/B: Fleischer & Cary, The Taxation of Covertible Bonds and Stock, 74 Harv. L. Rev. 473 (1961).

91 109 299 365 460 574   75 Harv. L. Rev. 1532
M/B: Aaron, Reflections on the Legal Nature and Enforceability of Seniority Rights, 75 Harv. L. Rev. 1532 (1962).

92 110 300 366 461 575   76 Harv. L. Rev. 303
M/B: Carrington, The Modern Utility of Quasi In Rem Jurisdiction, 76 Harv. L. Rev. 303 (1962).

93 111 201 367 462 576   77 Harv. L. Rev. 1037
M/B: Jaffe, Primary Jurisdiction, 77 Harv. L. Rev. 1037 (1964).

94 112 202 368 463 577   78 Harv. L. Rev. 1578
M/B: Stone, Roscoe Pound and Sociological Jurisprudence, 78 Harv. L. Rev. 1578 (1965).

95 113 203 369 464 578   79 Harv. L. Rev. 733
M/B: Eldredge, The Spurious Rule of Libel Per Quod, 79 Harv. L. Rev. 733 (1966).

96 114 204 370 465 579   80 Harv. L. Rev. 1432
M/B: Doerfer, The Limits on Trade Secret Law Imposed By Federal Patent and Antitrust Supremacy, 80 Harv. L. Rev. 1432 (1967).

97 115 205 371 466 580   81 Harv. L. Rev. 1439
M/B: Van Alstyne, The Demise of the Right-Privilege Distinction in Constitutional Law, 81 Harv. L. Rev. 1439 (1968).

98 116 206 372 467 581   82 Harv. L. Rev. 42
M/B: Driver, Confessions and the Social Psychology of Coercion, 82 Harv. L. Rev. 42 (1968).

99 117 207 373 468 582   83 Harv. L. Rev. 1362
M/B: Davis, Hearsay in Nonjury Cases, 83 Harv. L. Rev. 1362 (1970).

100 118 208 374 469 583   84 Harv. L. Rev. 281
M/B: Breyer, The Uneasy Case for Copyright: A Study of Copyright in Books, Photocopies, and Computer Programs, 84 Harv. L. Rev. 281 (1970).

LIBRARY EXERCISE 31.   INDEX TO LEGAL PERIODICALS: ARTICLES.

INSTRUCTOR'S NOTE: Students are required to find the article listed below in the Index to Legal Periodicals and cite the article in proper form based upon the information given in the Index. Note that the volume of the Index to Legal Periodicals used to complete this Exercise is also used in many instances to complete Library Exercise 32. The student is asked to cite the article based upon the information given in the Index to Legal Periodicals. The title of the article given may vary slightly from the actual title in the periodical. The answers listed below are based on the Index entries, not the title of the article as it actually appeared in the legal periodical. Slight variations should be permitted.

The following Quick-Reference Abbreviations are particularly relevant to this exercise:

PERIODICAL CITATION 1. CITE LEAD ARTICLES BY THE LAST NAME OF THE AUTHOR, TITLE, VOLUME, ABBREVIATED NAME OF THE PERIODICAL, PAGE, AND DATE. [PERIOD 1]
PERIODICAL CITATION 5. USE THE USOC ABBREVIATION OF THE PERIODICAL TITLE IN THE CITATION. FOLLOW THE GENERAL SPACING RULES IN USOC RULE 6.1(A). [PERIOD 5]
PERIODICAL CITATION 6. IF A PERIODICAL DOES NOT HAVE A VOLUME NUMBER BUT IS PAGINATED CONSECUTIVELY THROUGHOUT THE ENTIRE VOLUME, USE THE YEAR OF PUBLICATION AS THE VOLUME NUMBER. OMIT THE YEAR DESIGNATION AT THE END OF THE CITATION. [PERIOD 6]
PERIODICAL CITATION 7. IF EACH ISSUE OF A PERIODICAL IS PAGINATED SEPARATELY, CITE THE PERIODICAL BY THE DATE OR PERIOD OF PUBLICATION. OMIT THE YEAR DESIGNATION AT THE END OF THE CITATION. [PERIOD 7]
PERIODICAL CITATION 8. IN MEMORANDA AND BRIEFS, UNDERSCORE (ITALICIZE) THE TITLE OF THE ARTICLE. IN LAW REVIEW FOOTNOTES, ITALICIZE THE TITLE OF THE ARTICLE, AND CITE THE NAME OF THE PERIODICAL IN LARGE AND SMALL CAPITALS. [PERIOD 8]

1 172 289 355 428 534   E.H. Levi, "The sovereignty of the courts" (1983).
M/B: Levi, The Sovereignty of the Courts, 50 U. Chi. L. Rev. 679 (1983).

2 173 290 356 429 535   R.E. Epstein, "Blackmail, Inc." (1983).
M/B: Epstein, Blackmail, Inc., 50 U. Chi. L. Rev. 553 (1983).

3 174 291 357 430 536   M. Gibson, "The case of the Burnside Foundry" (1984).
M/B: Gibson, The Case of the Burnside Foundry, 8 Nova L.J. 547 (1984).

4 175 292 358 431 537   E. Warren, "Formal and operative rules under common law and code" (1983).
M/B: Warren, Formal and Operative Rules under Common Law and Code, 30 UCLA L. Rev. 898 (1983).

5 176 293 359 432 538   J. Reno, Dealing with child abuse and neglect: a prosecutor's viewpoint" (1984).
M/B: Reno, Dealing with Child Abuse and Neglect: a Prosecutor's Viewpoint, 8 Nova L.J. 271 (1984).

6 177 294 360 433 539   R.H. Coase, "Lighthouse in economics" (1974).
M/B: Coase, Lighthouse in Economics, 17 J.L. & Econ. 357 (1974).

7 178 295 361 434 540   E.D. Eshelman, "Proposed joint tenancy statute" (1971).
M/B: Eshelman, Proposed Joint Tenancy Statute, 32 Ala. Law. 45 (1971).

8 179 296 362 435 541   R.H. Neuman, "Oil on troubled waters: the international control of marine pollution" (1971).
M/B: Neuman, Oil on Troubled Waters: The International Control of Marine Pollution, 2 J. Mar. L. 349 (1971).

9 180 297 363 436 542   M.H. Redish, "Campaign spending laws and the first amendment" (1971).
M/B: Redish, Campaign Spending Laws and the First Amendment, 46 N.Y.U. L. Rev. 900 (1971).

EXERCISE 31. INDEX TO LEGAL PERIODICALS: ARTICLES   (CONTINUED)

10 181 298 364 437 543   R. Nimmer, "Public drunk: formalizing the police role as a social help agency" (1970).
M/B: Nimmer, <u>Public Drunk: Formalizing the Police Role as a Social Help Agency</u>, 58 Geo. L.J. 1089 (1970).

11 182 299 365 438 544   C.P. Paquin, "Valuation of wrongful death actions in Georgia" (1973).
M/B: Paquin, <u>Valuation of Wrongful Death Actions in Georgia</u>, 9 Ga. St. B.J. 293 (1973).

12 183 300 366 439 545   W.G. Rothenberg, "Stockholder loans to insolvent corporations" (1971).
M/B: Rothenberg, <u>Stockholder Loans to Insolvent Corporations</u>, 38 Brooklyn L. Rev. 95 (1971).

13 184 201 367 440 546   D.R. Packard, "Fair procedure in welfare hearings" (1969).
M/B: Packard, <u>Fair Procedure in Welfare Hearings</u>, 42 S. Cal. L. Rev. 600 (1969).

14 185 202 368 441 547   H.H. Hackley, "Our discriminatory banking structure" (1969).
M/B: Hackley, <u>Our Discriminatory Banking Structure</u>, 55 Va. L. Rev. 1421 (1969).

15 186 203 369 442 548   E.G. West, "Agency shops and the public sector: an economic analysis" (1979).
M/B: West, <u>Agency Shops and the Public Sector: An Economic Analysis</u>, 33 U. Miami L. Rev. 645 (1979).

16 187 204 370 443 549   E.Y. Semerjian, "Right of confrontation" (1969).
M/B: Semerjian, <u>Right of Confrontation</u>, 55 A.B.A.J. 152 (1969).

17 188 205 371 444 550   L.V. Kaplan, "Civil commitment 'as you like it'" (1969).
M/B: Kaplan, <u>Civil Commitment "As You Like It"</u>, 49 B.U. L. Rev. 4 (1969).

18 189 206 372 445 551   J.K. Weeks, "Broker-dealer disclosure of corporate inside information" (1969).
M/B: Weeks, <u>Broker-Dealer Disclosure of Corporate Inside Information</u>, 18 Clev. St. L. Rev. 549 (1969).

19 190 207 373 446 552   D.F. Clifford, "Colorado's 'short arm' jurisdiction" (1965).
M/B: Clifford, <u>Colorado's "Short-Arm" Jurisdiction</u>, 37 U. Colo. L. Rev. 309 (1965).

20 191 208 374 447 553   L.D. Lowenfels, "Rule 10b-5 and the stockholder's derivative action" (1965).
M/B: Lowenfels, <u>Rule 10b-5 and the Stockholder's Derivative Action</u>, 18 Vand. L. Rev. 893 (1965).

21 192 209 375 448 554   M.W. Macey, "Bring your fixtures up to date" (1965).
M/B: Macey, <u>Bring Your Fixtures Up to Date</u>, 16 Mercer L. Rev. 404 (1965).

22 193 210 376 449 555   W.E. Knepper, "Alimony for accident victims?" (1966). M/B: Knepper, <u>Alimony for Accident Victims?</u>, 15 Def. L.J. 513 (1966).
Note: The comma after the question mark may be omitted.

23 194 211 377 450 556   M. Domke, "American arbitral awards: enforcement in foreign countries" (1965).
M/B: Domke, <u>American Arbitral Awards: Enforcement in Foreign Countries</u>, 1965 U. Ill. L.F. 399.

24 195 212 378 451 557   R.F. Shryock, "Survey evidence in contested trademark cases" (1967).

EXERCISE 31. INDEX TO LEGAL PERIODICALS: ARTICLES (CONTINUED)

M/B: Shryock, <u>Survey Evidence in Contested Trademark Cases</u>, 57 Trademark Rep. 377 (1967).

25 196 213 379 452 558   D.S. Cohan, "Pennsylvania tentative trusts: problems and problem areas" (1962).
M/B: Cohan, <u>Pennsylvania Tentative Trusts: Problems and Problem Areas</u>, 110 U. Pa. L. Rev. 972 (1962).

26 197 214 380 453 559   A. Lenhoff, "New procedural code in New York" (1963). M/B: Lenhoff, <u>New Procedural Code in New York</u>, 13 Buffalo L. Rev. 119 (1963).

27 198 215 381 454 560   L.B. Orfield, "Consolidation in federal criminal procedure" (1961).
M/B: Orfield, <u>Consolidation in Federal Criminal Procedure</u>, 40 Or. L. Rev. 318 (1961).

28 199 216 382 455 561   G.J. Weiser, "Antitrust aspects of the joint venture in the European economic community" (1963).
M/B: Weiser, <u>Antitrust Aspects of the Joint Venture in the European Economic Community</u>, 111 U. Pa. L. Rev. 421 (1963).

29 200 217 383 456 562   H.B. Stover, Jr., "Longshoremen-shipowner-stevedore: the circle of liability" (1963).
M/B: Stover, <u>Longshoreman-Shipowner-Stevedore: the Circle of Liability</u>, 61 Mich. L. Rev. 539 (1963).

30 101 218 384 457 563   J.K. Weeks, "Comparative law of privacy" (1963).
M/B: Weeks, <u>Comparative Law of Privacy</u>, 12 Clev.-Mar. L. Rev. 484 (1963).

31 102 219 385 458 564   H. Griese, "Marine insurance contracts in the conflict of laws: a comparative study of the case law" (1959).
M/B: Griese, <u>Marine Insurance Contracts in the Conflict of Laws: A Comparative Study of the Case Law</u>, 6 U.C.L.A. L. Rev. 55 (1959).

32 103 220 386 459 565   H.W. Felton, "Federal tax liens, their priority and enforcement" (1960).
M/B: Felton, <u>Federal Tax Liens, Their Priority and Enforcement</u>, 10 Drake L. Rev. 3 (1960).

33 104 221 387 460 566   G.M. Fenner and J.L. Koley, "Rights of the press and the closed court criminal proceeding" (1978).
M/B: Fenner & Koley, <u>Rights of the Press and the Closed Court Criminal Proceeding</u>, 57 Neb. L. Rev. 442 (1978).

34 105 222 388 461 567   R.E. Keeton, "Conditional fault in the law of torts" (1959).
M/B: Keeton, <u>Conditional Fault in the Law of Torts</u>, 72 Harv. L. Rev. 401 (1959).

35 106 223 389 462 568   R.C. Bernhard, "English law and American law on monopolies and restraints of trade" (1960).
M/B: Bernhard, <u>English Law and American Law on Monopolies and Restraints of Trade</u>, 3 J.L. & Econ. 136 (1960).

36 107 224 390 463 569   F.M. Covey, Jr., "French law of eminent domain" (1959).
M/B: Covey, <u>French Law of Eminent Domain</u>, 35 N.D. L. Rev. 209 (1959).

37 108 225 391 464 570   I.R. Kaufman, "Masters in the federal courts: rule 53" (1958).
M/B: Kaufman, <u>Masters in the Federal Courts: Rule 53</u>, 58 Colum. L. Rev. 452 (1958).

38 109 226 392 465 571   C.W. Ehrhardt, "Using convictions to impeach under the Florida Evidence Code" (1982).

EXERCISE 31. INDEX TO LEGAL PERIODICALS: ARTICLES (CONTINUED)

M/B: Ehrhardt, Using Convictions to Impeach under the Florida Evidence Code, 10 Fla. St. U.L. Rev. 235 (1982).

39 110 227 393 466 572   T. Scribner, "Professional goodwill in dissolution proceedings: the personification of property" (1982).
M/B: Scribner, Professional Goodwill in Dissolution Proceedings: the Personification of Property, 17 Gonz. L. Rev. 303 (1982).

40 111 228 394 467 573   C. Hancock, "State court activism and searches incident to arrest" (1982).
M/B: Hancock, State Court Activism and Searches Incident to Arrest, 68 Va. L. Rev. 1085 (1982).

41 112 229 395 468 574   B. Tarlow, "RICO revisited" (1983).
M/B: Tarlow, RICO Revisited, 17 Ga. L. Rev. 291 (1983).

42 113 230 396 469 575   R.W. Peterson, "Few things you should know about paternity test (but were afraid to ask)" (1982).
M/B: Peterson, Few Things You Should Know about Paternity Tests (But Were Afraid to Ask), 22 Santa Clara L. Rev. 667 (1982).

43 114 231 397 470 576   G.W. Goble, "Alternative to the strike" (1955).
M/B: Goble, Alternative to the Strike, 6 Lab. L.J. 83 (1955).

44 115 232 398 471 577   J.W. Castles, III, "Personal contract doctrine: an anomaly in American maritime law" (1953).
M/B: Castles, Personal Contract Doctrine: An Anomaly in American Maritime Law, 62 Yale L.J. 1031 (1953).

45 116 233 399 472 578   C.L. Newman, "Should trial by jury be modernized?" (1953).
M/B: Newman, Should Trial by Jury Be Modernized?, 29 N.D. L. Rev. 365 (1953).
Note: The comma after the question mark may be omitted.

46 117 234 400 473 579   R.M. Perkins, "Self-defense re-examined" (1954).
M/B: Perkins, Self-defense Re-examined, 1 U.C.L.A. L. Rev. 133 (1954).

47 118 235 301 474 580   R. Pound, "Chinese Civil Code in action" (1955).
M/B: Pound, Chinese Civil Code in Action, 29 Tul. L. Rev. 277 (1955).

48 119 236 302 475 581   G. Gilmore, "Commercial doctrine of good faith purchase" (1954).
M/B: Gilmore, Commercial Doctrine of Good Faith Purchase, 63 Yale L.J. 1057 (1954).

49 120 237 303 476 582   T.W. Samuels, "Drafting a partnership agreement" (1950).
M/B: Samuels, Drafting a Partnership Agreement, 39 Ill. B.J. 86 (1950).

50 121 238 304 477 583   R.P. Hoff, "Implications for farm ownership of the tax preferred status of pension trust investment in real estate" (1981).
M/B: Hoff, Implications for Farm Ownership of the Tax Preferred Status of Pension Trust Investment in Real Estate, 23 Ariz. L. Rev. 179 (1981).

51 122 239 305 478 584   K.S. Abraham, "Judge-made law and judge-made insurance: honoring the reasonable expectations of the insured" (1981).
M/B: Abraham, Judge-Made Law and Judge-Made Insurance: Honoring the Reasonable Expectations of the Insured, 67 Va. L. Rev. 1151 (1981).

52 123 240 306 479 585   R.F. Pannier, "Nature of the judicial process and judicial discretion" (1981).
M/B: Pannier, Nature of the Judicial Process and Judicial Discretion, Wm. Mitchell L. Rev. 573 (1981).

53 124 241 307 480 586   D.H. Haynes, "Language and logic of law: a case study" (1981).

EXERCISE 31. INDEX TO LEGAL PERIODICALS: ARTICLES   (CONTINUED)

M/B: Haynes, Language and Logic of Law: a Case Study, 35 U. Miami L. Rev. 183 (1981).

54 125 242 308 481 587   J.N. Hazard, "Soviet socialism and embezzlement" (1951).
M/B: Hazard, Soviet Socialism and Embezzlement, 26 Wash. L. Rev. 301 (1951).

55 126 243 309 482 588   H.A. Kooman, "Judicial supervision of trusts" (1948). M/B: Kooman, Judicial Supervision of Trusts, 1 U. Fla. L. Rev. 242 (1948).

56 127 244 310 483 589   A.T. Spence, "Parental liability" (1948).
M/B: Spence, Parental Liability, 1948 Ins. L.J. 787.

57 128 245 311 484 590   M.H. Merrill, "Basic doctrine of Oklahoma public law" (1948).
M/B: Merrill, Basic Doctrine of Oklahoma Public Law, 1 Okla. L. Rev. 262 (1948).

58 129 246 312 485 591   B. Reich, "Entertainment industry and the Federal Antitrust Laws" (1946).
M/B: Reich, Entertainment Industry and the Federal Antitrust Laws, 20 S. Cal. L. Rev. 1 (1946).

59 130 247 313 486 592   J.T. Ganoe, "The Yamashita case and the Constitution" (1946).
M/B: Ganoe, The Yamashita Case and the Constitution, 25 Or. L. Rev. 143 (1946).

60 131 248 314 487 593   L. Garment, "Real evidence: use and abuse" (1948).
M/B: Garment, Real Evidence: Use and Abuse, 14 Brooklyn L. Rev. 261 (1948).

61 132 249 315 488 594   C.B. Nutting, "Policy making by the Supreme Court" (1947).
M/B: Nutting, Policy Making by the Supreme Court, 9 U. Pitt. L. Rev. 59 (1947).

62 133 250 316 489 595   F.F. Stone, "Modern problems in ancient dress" (1980).
M/B: Stone, Modern Problems in Ancient Dress, 54 Tul. L. Rev. 812 (1980).

63 134 251 317 490 596   W.B. Stoebuck, "Police power, takings, and due process" (1980).
M/B: Stoebuck, Police Power, Takings, and Due Process, 37 Wash. & Lee L. Rev. 1057 (1980).

64 135 252 318 491 597   J. Dolan, "Good faith purchase study: true owners and the warehouse lien" (1981).
M/B: Dolan, Good Faith Purchase Study: True Owners and the Warehouse Lien, 18 Hous. L. Rev. 267 (1981).

65 136 253 319 492 598   R.M. Twiss, "Impact of RICO upon labor unions" (1980).
M/B: Twiss, Impact of RICO upon Labor Unions, 14 Akron L. Rev. 49 (1980).

66 137 254 320 493 599   R.N. Jackson, "Right to bail and suspensive appeal in the Louisiana juvenile courts" (1946).
M/B: Jackson, Right to Bail and Suspensive Appeal in the Louisiana Juvenile Courts, 20 Tul. L. Rev. 363 (1946).

67 138 255 321 494 600   D. Williams, "Care and custody of children in Mississippi" (1944).
M/B: Williams, Care and Custody of Children in Mississippi, 16 Miss. L.J. 278 (1944).

68 139 256 322 495 501   D. Dowling, "Parents' usufruct of child's estate during marriage" (1945).

EXERCISE 31. INDEX TO LEGAL PERIODICALS: ARTICLES   (CONTINUED)

M/B: Dowling, <u>Parents' Usufruct of Child's Estate During Marriage</u>, 20 Tul. L. Rev. 163 (1945).

69 140 257 323 496 502   D.J. Snyder, Jr., "Computing municipal indebtedness under Pennsylvania constitutional limitations" (1941).
M/B: Snyder, <u>Computing Municipal Indebtedness Under Pennsylvania Constitutional Limitations</u>, 7 U. Pitt. L. Rev. 198 (1941).

70 141 258 324 497 503   E.B. Cass, "The blackout and its relation to civil liabilities" (1942).
M/B: Cass, <u>The Blackout and Its Relation to Civil Liabilities</u>, 22 B.U. L. Rev. 287 (1942).

71 142 259 325 498 504   J.H. Ottman, "Partition in Missouri" (1941).
M/B: Ottman, <u>Partition in Missouri</u>, 6 Mo. L. Rev. 87 (1941).

72 143 260 326 499 505   S.O. Bates, "Holographic Wills" (1942).
M/B: Bates, <u>Holographic Wills</u>, 17 Tenn. L. Rev. 440 (1942).

73 144 261 327 500 506   P. Shirley, "Special issue submission in workmen's compensation cases" (1940).
M/B: Shirley, <u>Special Issue Submission in Workmen's Compensation Cases</u>, 18 Tex. L. Rev. 365 (1940).

74 145 262 328 401 507   R. Magill, "Relief from excess profits tax" (1941).
M/B: Magill, <u>Relief from Excess Profits Tax</u>, 89 U. Pa. L. Rev. 843 (1941).

75 146 263 329 402 508   P. Schiff, "Married women's suretyship contracts in the United States" (1939).
M/B: Schiff, <u>Married Women's Suretyship Contracts in the United States</u>, 28 Ky. L.J. 74 (1939).

76 147 264 330 403 509   M.S. Isseks, "The executive and his use of the militia" (1937).
M/B: Isseks, <u>The Executive and His Use of the Militia</u>, 16 Or. L. Rev. 301 (1937).

77 148 265 331 404 510   F.B. McCall, "Destructibility of contingent remainders in North Carolina" (1938).
M/B: McCall, <u>Distructibility of Contingent Remainders in North Carolina</u>, 16 N.C. L. Rev. 87 (1938).

78 149 266 332 405 511   M.M. Harrison, "Remission in the Civil Law" (1940). M/B: Harrison, <u>Remission in the Civil Law</u>, 2 La. L. Rev. 365 (1940).

79 150 267 333 406 512   W.C. Johnstone, "New commercial treaty with Siam" (1938).
M/B: Johnstone, <u>New Commercial Treaty with Siam</u>, 32 Am. J. Int'l L. 796 (1938).

80 151 268 334 407 513   S.P. Sandrock, "Tort liability of a non-manufacturing franchisor for acts of its franchisee" (1979).
M/B: Sandrock, <u>Tort Liability of a Non-Manufacturing Franchisor for Acts of its Franchisee</u>, 48 U. Cin. L. Rev. 699 (1979).

81 152 269 335 408 514   M. Siegel, "Implication doctrine and the foreign corrupt practices act" (1979).
M/B: Siegel, <u>Implication Doctrine and the Foreign Corrupt Practices Act</u>, 79 Colum. L. Rev. 1085 (1979).

82 153 270 336 409 515   R.H. Coase, "Payola in radio and television broadcasting" (1979).
M/B: Coase, <u>Payola in Radio and Television Broadcasting</u>, 22 J.L. & Econ. 269 (1979).

83 154 271 337 410 516   H.W. Brill, "Protection for the hard of hearing: state and federal regulation of hearing aid dealers" (1977).

EXERCISE 31. INDEX TO LEGAL PERIODICALS: ARTICLES   (CONTINUED)

M/B: Brill, <u>Protection for the Hard of Hearing: State and Federal Regulation of Hearing Aid Dealers</u>, 27 De Paul L. Rev. 45 (1977).

84 155 272 338 411 517   J.M. Hughes, "'Notice of Claim' as a Condition Precedent to Suit: Is the Proprietary-Governmental Distinction Important?"
M/B: Hughes, "Notice of Claim" as a Condition Precedent to Suit: Is the <u>Proprietary-Governmental Distinction Important?</u>, 31 Baylor L. Rev. 427 (1979).
<u>Note</u>: The comma after the question mark may be omitted.

85 156 273 339 412 518   L.S. May, "Scientific methods of criminal investigation" (1935).
M/B: May, <u>Scientific Methods of Criminal Investigation</u>, 14 Or. L. Rev. 385 (1935).

86 157 274 340 413 519   R.H. Schnell, "Co-tenancy of personal property in New York" (1936).
M/B: Schnell, <u>Co-tenancy of Personal Property in New York</u>, 6 Brooklyn L. Rev. 54 (1936).

87 158 275 341 414 520   B. Eskin, "Legality of 'peaceful coercion' in labor disputes" (1937).
M/B: Eskin, <u>Legality of "Peaceful Coercion" in Labor Disputes</u>, 85 U. Pa. L. Rev. 456 (1937).

88 159 276 342 415 521   P. Bordwell, "Alienability and perpetuities" (1937).
M/B: Bordwell, <u>Alienability and Perpetuities</u>, 22 Iowa L. Rev. 437 (1937).

89 160 277 343 416 522   R.F. Fuchs, "The French law of collective labor agreements" (1932).
M/B: Fuchs, <u>The French Law of Collective Labor Agreements</u>, 41 Yale L.J. 1005 (1932).

90 161 278 344 417 523   M. Radin, "Fraudulent conveyances at Roman law" (1931).
M/B: Radin, <u>Fraudulent Conveyances at Roman Law</u>, 18 Va. L. Rev. 109 (1931).

91 162 279 345 418 524   M.S. Culp, "Process in actions against non-resident motorists" (1934).
M/B: Culp, <u>Process in Actions Against Non-resident Motorists</u>, 32 Mich. L. Rev. 325 (1934).

92 163 280 346 419 525   G.R. Farnum, "Admiralty jurisdiction and amphibious torts" (1933).
M/B: Farnum, <u>Admiralty Jurisdiction and Amphibious Torts</u>, 43 Yale L.J. 34 (1933).

93 164 281 347 420 526   B.R. Desenberg, "Torrens system of title registration" (1932).
M/B: Desenberg, <u>Torrens System of Title Registration</u>, 7 Notre Dame Law. 534 (1932).

94 165 282 348 421 527   G. May, "Experiments in legal control of sex expression" (1929).
M/B: May, <u>Experiments in Legal Control of Sex Expression</u>, 39 Yale L.J. 219 (1929).

95 166 283 349 422 528   J.C. Biggs, "Religious belief as qualification of a witness" (1929).
M/B: Biggs, <u>Religious Belief as Qualification of a Witness</u>, 8 N.C. L. Rev. 31 (1929).

96 167 284 350 423 529   J.J. Kenney, "Illegitimacy under the Children's Code" (1929).
M/B: Kenney, <u>Illegitimacy Under the Children's Code</u>, 14 Marq. L. Rev. 26 (1929).

EXERCISE 31.   INDEX TO LEGAL PERIODICALS: ARTICLES   (CONTINUED)

97 168 285 351 424 530   R.C. Clark, "Duties of the corporate debtor to its creditors" (1977).
M/B: Clark, <u>Duties of the Corporate Debtor to Its Creditors</u>, 90 Harv. L. Rev. 505 (1977).

98 169 286 352 425 531   M.E. Price, "First amendment and television broadcasting by satellite" (1976).
M/B: Price, <u>First Amendment and Television Broadcasting by Satellite</u>, 23 U.C.L.A. L. Rev. 879 (1976).

99 170 287 353 426 532   A.V. Lowe, "Right of entry into maritime ports in international law" (1977).
M/B: Lowe, <u>Right of Entry into Maritime Ports in International Law</u>, 14 San Diego L. Rev. 597 (1977).

100 171 288 354 427 533   R.N. Clinton, "Right to present a defense: an emergent constitutional guarantee in criminal trials" (1976).
M/B: Clinton, <u>Right to Present a Defense: An Emergent Constitutional Guarantee in Criminal Trials</u>, 9 Ind. L. Rev. 713 (1976).

LIBRARY EXERCISE 32.   INDEX TO LEGAL PERIODICALS: CASE NOTES AND COMMENTS.

INSTRUCTOR'S NOTE: The students are required to find the case comment[s] or note[s] on the following case using the Index to Legal Periodicals. For their answer, they are to cite the legal periodicals in which they can be found. No special form is required. If the student clearly shows that they have found the case comment[s] or note[s], then credit should be given.

1 172 289 355 428 534   1983   Grant v. Arizona Pub. Serv. Co. [652 P.2d 507]
25 Ariz. L. Rev. 505 (1983).

2 173 290 356 429 535   1984   Riley v. Northern Commercial Co. [648 P.2d 961]
1 Alaska L. Rev. 109 (1984).

3 174 291 357 430 536   1984   Sax v. Votteler [648 S.W.2d 661]
21 Hous. L. Rev. 295 (1984).

4 175 292 358 431 537   1983   State v. Berge [634 P.2d 947]
25 Ariz. L. Rev. 539 (1983).

5 176 293 359 432 538   1983   Sutter v. Groen [687 F.2d 197]
15 Conn. L. Rev. 617 (1983).
61 Wash. U.L.Q. 659 (1983).

6 177 294 360 433 539   1973   Baker v. Hamilton [345 F. Supp.345]
51 N.C. L. Rev. 1539 (1973).

7 178 295 361 434 540   1973   In re Lynch [503 P.2d 921]
61 Calif. L. Rev. 418 (1973).

8 179 296 362 435 541   1973   McKinney v. State [260 So. 2d 444]
44 Miss. L.J. 556 (1973).

9 180 297 363 436 542   1972   McMillen v. Klingensmith [467 S.W.2d 193]
24 Baylor L. Rev. 295 (1972).

10 181 298 364 437 543   1970   Appeal of McNeil [257 A.2d 835]
19 Kan. L. Rev. 153 (1970).

11 182 299 365 438 544   1971   Maddox v. Fortson [172 S.E.2d 595]
22 Mercer L. Rev. 473 (1971).

12 183 300 366 439 545   1973   Manson v. Edwards [345 F. Supp. 719]
71 Mich. L. Rev. 854 (1973).

13 184 201 367 440 546   67-68   Pierson v. Ray [87 S. Ct. 1213]
19 Syracuse L. Rev. 117 (1967).
1968 Wis. L. Rev. 275.

14 185 202 368 441 547   1968   Pinto v. Pierce [88 S. Ct. 192]
20 Ala. L. Rev. 355 (1968).

15 186 203 369 442 548   1969   Pittman v. State [434 S.W.2d 352]
23 SW. L.J. 405 (1969).

16 187 204 370 443 549   1969   Succession of Plunkett [213 So. 2d 793]
43 Tul. L. Rev. 900 (1969).

17 188 205 371 444 550   1967   Powers v. Temple [156 S.E.2d 759]
19 S.C. L. Rev. 896 (1967).

18 189 206 372 445 551   1967   Prentzler v. Schneider [411 S.W.2d 135]
32 Mo. L. Rev. 397 (1967).

EXERCISE 32. INDEX TO LEGAL PERIODICALS: CASE NOTES & COMMENTS   (CONTINUED)

19 190 207 373 446 552   1965   Fish v. State [159 So. 2d 866]
17 U. Fla. L. Rev. 639 (1965).

20 191 208 374 447 553   1965   Flesher v. United States [238 F. Supp. 119]
68 W. Va. L. Rev. 82 (1965).

21 192 209 375 448 554   1964   Fonte v. State [373 S.W.2d 445]
31 Tenn. L. Rev. 511 (1964).

22 193 210 376 449 555   1964   Foy v. Dayko [196 A.2d 535]
17 Ala. L. Rev. 154 (1964).

23 194 211 377 450 556   1965   Franklin v. Parker [223 F. Supp. 724]
18 Okla. L. Rev. 81 (1965).

24 195 212 378 451 557   1966   Frasier v. Pierce [398 S.W.2d 955]
20 Ark. L. Rev. 196 (1966).

25 196 213 379 452 558   1964   Swift v. Wimberly [370 S.W.2d 500]
31 Tenn. L. Rev. 264 (1964).

26 197 214 380 453 559   1964   System Meat Co. v. Stewart [122 N.W.2d 1]
49 Iowa L. Rev. 581 (1964).

27 198 215 381 454 560   1962   Texaco v. Goldstein [229 N.Y.S.2d 51]
12 De Paul L. Rev. 150 (1962).

28 199 216 382 455 561   1962   In re Thacher [10 N.Y.2d 439]
30 Fordham L. Rev. 537 (1962).

29 200 217 383 456 562   1963   Thome v. Thome [127 S.E.2d 916]
14 Mercer L. Rev. 449 (1963).

30 101 218 384 457 563   1962   Thompson v. Reedman [199 F. Supp. 120]
50 Geo. L.J. 626 (1962).
11 Kan L. Rev. 168 (1962).

31 102 219 385 458 564   1955   People v. Thompson [271 P.2d 507]
8 Ala. L. Rev. 383 (1956).
20 Alb. L. Rev. 99 (1956).
24 Fordham L. Rev. 460 (1955).
2 N.Y.L. Forum 112 (1956). (?)
31 N.Y.U. L. Rev. 847 (1956).
34 Tex. L. Rev. 939 (1956).
23 U. Chi. L. Rev. 532 (1956).

32 103 220 386 459 565   1957   People v. Horowitz [131 N.E.2d 715]
42 Cornell L.Q. 285 (1957).

33 104 221 387 460 566   1955   People v. Wilson [135 N.Y.S.2d 893]
24 Fordham L. Rev. 271 (1955).
31 N.D.L. Rev. 295 (1955).
3 St. Louis U.L.J. 211 (1954).

34 105 222 388 461 567   1956   Stone v. Dunn Bros. [80 So. 2d 802]
9 Vand. L. Rev. 874 (1956).

35 106 223 389 462 568   1956   Stuart v. Pilgrim [74 N.W.2d 212]
5 Drake L. Rev. 127 (1956).
41 Iowa L. Rev. 670 (1956).
31 Notre Dame Law. 724 (1956).

36 107 224 390 463 569   1957   Swigert v. Welk [133 A.2d 428]
26 Fordham L. Rev. 718 (1957-58).

EXERCISE 32. INDEX TO LEGAL PERIODICALS: CASE NOTES & COMMENTS (CONTINUED)

37 108 225 391 464 570   1956   Swift v. Beaty [282 S.W.2d 655]
24 Tenn. L. Rev. 625 (1956).

38 109 226 392 465 571   1982   Griffin v. Ocean Contractors, Inc.
[102 S. Ct. 3245]
68 A.B.A. J. 1663 (1982).
7 Mar. Law. 149 (1982).

39 110 227 393 466 572   1982   Hartman v. Shambaugh [630 P.2d 758]
12 N.M.L. Rev. 833 (1982).

40 111 228 394 467 573   1981   Hlodan v. Ohio Barge Line [611 F.2d 71]
6 Mar. Law. 87 (1981).

41 112 229 395 468 574   1982   McMinn v. Oyster Bay [445 N.Y.S.2d 859]
21 J. Fam. L. 174 (1982).

42 113 230 396 469 575   1982   Logan v. Zimmerman Brush Co. [102 S. Ct. 1148]
31 Emory L.J. 491 (1982).
96 Harv. L. Rev. 96 (1982).
1982 U. Ill. L. Rev. 831 (1982).

43 114 231 397 470 576   1952   Jawish v. Morlet [86 A.2d 96]
6 Vand. L. Rev. 137 (1952).

44 115 232 398 471 577   1952   Jersey Ins. Co. v. Roddam [56 So. 2d 631]
4 Baylor L. Rev. 534 (1952).

45 116 233 399 472 578   1954   Johnson v. Baltimore & O.R.R. [208 F.2d 633]
102 U. Pa. L. Rev. 675 (1954).
15 U. Pitt. L. Rev. 646 (1954).
1954 Wash. U.L.Q. 348.

46 117 234 400 473 579   54-55   Johnson v. Chicago, B. & Q.R.R. [66 N.W.2d 763]
43 Geo. L.J. 292 (1955).
39 Minn. L. Rev. 115 (1954).

47 118 235 401 474 580   1955   Johnson v. Safreed [273 S.W.2d 545]
9 Ark. L. Rev. 188 (1955).

48 119 236 302 475 581   1952   Joliet Contractors Ass'n v. NLRB [193 F.2d 833]
100 U. Pa. L. Rev. 1261 (1952).
62 Yale L.J. 116 (1952).

49 120 237 303 476 582   1950   Standfur v. Standfur [223 S.W.2d 111]
3 Baylor L. Rev. 102 (1950).

50 121 238 304 477 583   1982   Kaiser Steel Corp. v. Mullins [102 S. Ct. 851]
68 A.B.A. J. 347 (1982).

51 122 239 305 478 584   1981   Jain v. INS [612 F.2d 683]
47 Brooklyn L. Rev. 627 (1981).

52 123 240 306 479 585   1981   McClain v. Meier [637 F.2d 1159]
57 N.D.L. Rev. 495 (1981).

53 124 241 307 480 586   1951   State v. Crittenden [49 So. 2d 418]
11 La. L. Rev. 464 (1951).
25 Tul. L. Rev. 404 (1951).

EXERCISE 32. INDEX TO LEGAL PERIODICALS: CASE NOTES & COMMENTS   (CONTINUED)

54 125 242 308 481 587   1952   State v. Fowler [83 A.2d 67]
32 B.U. L. Rev. 101 (1952).
65 Harv. L. Rev. 690 (1952).
31 Neb. L. Rev. 492 (1952).

55 126 243 309 482 588   1946   NLRB v. Inter-City Advertising Co.
[154 F.2d 244]
32 Cornell L.Q. 287 (1946).
59 Harv. L. Rev. 990 (1946).

56 127 244 310 483 589   1947   NLRB v. Packard Motor Car Co. [157
F.2d 80]
33 Va. L. Rev. 214 (1947).

57 128 245 311 484 590   1946   National Surety Corp. v. City Bank and
Trust Co. [20 N.W.2d 559]
30 Marq. L. Rev. 74 (1946).

58 129 246 312 485 591   1946   Navarro v. Fiorita [62 N.Y.S.2d 730]
46 Colum. L. Rev. 1039 (1946).

59 130 247 313 486 592   1948   Neal v. State [192 P.2d 294]
97 U. Pa. L. Rev. 276 (1948).

60 131 248 314 487 593   1947   Neff v. Firth [47 A.2d 193]
51 Dick. L. Rev. 131 (1947).

61 132 249 315 488 594   1947   Neitsch v. Tyrrell [171 P.2d 241]
22 Wash. L. Rev. 144 (1947).

62 133 250 316 489 595   1980   MacDonald v. MacDonald [412 A.2d71]
59 Wash. U.L.Q. 328 (1981).

63 134 251 317 490 596   1980   Livingston v. Ewing [601 F.2d 1110]
10 N.M.L. Rev. 461 (1980).

64 135 252 318 491 597   1980-81   Lepis v. Lepis [416 A.2d 45]
12 Rutgers L.J. 1 (1980).
11 Seton Hall L. Rev. 545 (1981).

65 136 253 319 492 598   1980   Lau v. Nelson [601 P.2d 527]
55 Wash. L. Rev. 833 (1980).

66 137 254 320 493 599   1945   In re Cope's Estate [41 A.2d 617]
31 Va. L. Rev. 922 (1945).

67 138 255 321 494 600   1946   Corder v. Corder [189 S.W.2d 100]
24 Tex. L. Rev. 225 (1946).

68 139 256 322 495 501   1945   Corlew v. State [180 S.W.2d 900]
18 Tenn. L. Rev. 629 (1945).

69 140 257 323 496 502   1942   Hacker v. Nitschke [39 N.E.2d 644]
18 Notre Dame Law. 152 (1942).
90 U. Pa. L. Rev. 859 (1942).

70 141 258 324 497 503   1941   Hagerty v. Clement [196 So. 330]
3 La. L. Rev. 465 (1941).

71 142 259 325 498 504   1942   Hale v. Campbell [40 F. Supp. 584]
16 U. Cin. L. Rev. 176 (1942).

72 143 260 326 499 505   1941   Hancock v. Moore [146 S.W.2d 369]
19 Tex. L. Rev. 518 (1941).

73 144 261 327 500 506   1942   Haney v. Cheatham [111 P.2d 1003]
17 Wash. L. Rev. 53 (1942).

EXERCISE 32.   INDEX TO LEGAL PERIODICALS: CASE NOTES & COMMENTS   (CONTINUED)

74 145 262 328 401 507   1940   Hanley v. Central Sav. Bank [21 N.E.2d 213]
9 Brooklyn L. Rev. 346 (1940).

75 146 263 329 402 508   1937   Harper v. City of Wichita Falls [105 S.W.2d 743]
16 Tex. L. Rev. 104 (1937).

76 147 264 330 403 509   1938   Appeal of Harr [194 A. 395]
51 Harv. L. Rev. 931 (1938).
10 Ohio Opinions 107 (1938).
4 Ohio St. L.J. 103 (1937).
11 U. Cin. L. Rev. 544 (1937).

77 148 265 331 404 510   1937   Harris v. Harris [186 S.E. 29]
23 Va. L. Rev. 947 (1937).

78 149 266 332 405 511   1938   Estate of Harrison [70 P.2d 522]
51 Harv. L. Rev. 560 (1938).
12 S. Cal. L. Rev. 64 (1938).

79 150 267 33 406 512   1939   Hart v. McClusky [118 S.W.2d 1077]
17 Tex. L. Rev. 381 (1939).

80 151 268 334 407 513   78-79   Sherlock v. Stillwater Clinic [260 N.W.2d 169]
28 De Paul L. Rev. 249 (1978).
44 Mo. L. Rev. 589 (1979).
5 Wm. Mitchell L. Rev. 464 (1979).

81 152 269 335 408 514   1979   State v. Sobel [363 So. 2d 324]
7 Fla. St. U.L. Rev. 311 (1979).

82 153 270 336 409 515   1978   Sunday v. Statton Corp. [390 A.2d 398]
3 Vt. L. Rev. 129 (1978). (?)

83 154 271 337 410 516   1979   Suntide Inn Operating Corp. v. State ex rel. Oklahoma State Highway Commission [571 P.2d 1207]
3 Okla. City L. Rev. 749 (1979). (?)

84 155 272 338 411 517   79-80   Zweig v. Hearst Corp. [594 F.2d 1261]
29 De Paul L. Rev. 287 (1979).
19 Washburn L.J. 382 (1980).

85 156 273 339 412 518   1936   Kuhn v. Carlin Const. Co. [278 N.Y.S. 635]
36 Colum. L. Rev. 852 (1936).

86 157 274 340 413 519   1937   In re Kuntz' Will [290 N.Y.S. 867]
23 Va. L. Rev. 467 (1937).

87 158 275 341 414 520   1935   Laird v. Gulf Production Co. [64 S.W.2d 1080]
13 Tex. L. Rev. 242 (1935).

88 159 276 342 515 521   1936   In re Lalla's Estate [1 N.E.2d 50]
31 Ill. L. Rev. 277 (1936).
14 Chi.[-]Kent Rev. 360 (1936).

89 160 277 343 416 522   1931   Christian v. Canfield [155 A. 788]
5 U. Cin. L. Rev. 489 (1931).

90 161 278 344 417 523   1931   Cisler v. Ray [2 P.2d 987]
20 Calif. L. Rev. 97 (1931).

91 162 279 345 418 524   1933   City Ice & Fuel Co. v. McKee [57 S.W.2d 443]

EXERCISE 32.   INDEX TO LEGAL PERIODICALS: CASE NOTES & COMMENTS   (CONTINUED)

11 Tenn. L. Rev. 290 (1933).

92 163 280 346 419 525   1932   City of Houston v. Scanlan [37 S.W.2d 718]
32 Colum. L. Rev. 1443 (1932).
17 Minn. L. Rev. 341 (1933).
39 W. Va. L.Q. 183 (1933).
6 S. Cal. L. Rev. 315 (1933).

93 164 281 347 420 526   1931   City of El Paso v. Jackson [40 S.W.2d 845]
11 Or. L. Rev. 102 (1931).

94 165 282 348 421 527   1930   McHugh v. Mason [283 P. 184]
5 Notre Dame Law. 288 (1930).

95 166 283 349 422 528   23-30   McKee v. Suez [167 N.E. 720]
5 Notre Dame Law. 106 (1929).
5 Ind. L.J. 298 (1930).

96 167 284 350 423 529   1930   Estate of McLaughlin [275 P. 874]
18 Calif. L. Rev. 711 (1930).

97 168 285 351 424 530   1976   Long v. City of Weirton [214 S.E.2d 832]
78 W. Va. L. Rev. 278 (1976).

98 169 286 352 425 531   1978   Shevin v. Sunbeam Television Corp. [351 So. 2d 723]
11 Harv. C.R.-C.L. L. Rev. 432 (1976).

99 170 287 353 426 532   1976   Muncie Aviation Corp. v. Party Doll Fleet [519 F.2d 1178]
27 Mercer L. Rev. 1219 (1976).

100 171 288 354 427 533   76-77   Muzquiz v. San Antonio [528 F.2d 499]
47 Miss. L.J. 799 (1976).

LIBRARY EXERCISE 33. TEXTS AND TREATISES.

INSTRUCTOR'S NOTE: (a) Using the index (or a topic method if they are unable to locate a relevant index entry) to find relevant discussion in the designated text or treatise, students are required to answer the question given with their problem number. (b) The students are then required to cite the treatise or text on which their answer is based. Note that when a text or treatise is organized by sections running consecutively throughout the entire work, the relevant section should be cited; when a section is cited, the relevant page numbers should be added (e.g., § 52, at 102-03) to identify the specific portion of the section on which their answer is based (when necessary). Rule 15, 3.4. Students are directed to follow the rules for multiple page numbers containing repetitious digits stated in the instructions to Library Exercise 5.

The pages cited by the student may vary slightly from the ones stated in the answers below. Such variations should be permitted, provided the student complies with the rules for citing multiple pages. For example, for the first set of problems (1 128 250 301 426 551), pages "185-87" or "185, 187" may be cited.

The following Quick-Reference Abbreviations are particularly relevant to this exercise:

BOOK CITATION 1. IN ABSENCE OF SPECIAL RULES, CITE TEXTS, TREATISES, AND OTHER BOOKS BY THE AUTHOR'S LAST NAME AND AT LEAST THE AUTHOR'S FIRST INITIAL; THE TITLE; THE SERIAL NUMBER (IF ANY); THE PAGE, SECTION, OR PARAGRAPH (IF A SPECIFIC PART OF THE VOLUME IS CITED); THE EDITION (IF MORE THAN ONE); AND THE YEAR OF PUBLICATION. [BK 1]

BOOK CITATION 2. IN BRIEFS AND MEMORANDA, UNDERSCORE (ITALICIZE) THE TITLE OF THE BOOK. IN LAW REVIEW FOOTNOTES, PLACE THE AUTHOR'S NAME AND THE TITLE OF THE BOOK IN LARGE AND SMALL CAPITALS. [BK 4]

For problem numbers 1-25, 128-152, 250-274, 301-325, 426-450, 551-575, the students are to use the third edition (1982) of Perkins and Boyce's Criminal Law treatise.

1 128 250 301 426 551   How was the crime of mayhem defined under English common law? Was it a felony or misdemeanor?
(a) Mayhem, according to the English common law, is maliciously depriving another of the use of such of his members as may render him less able, in fighting, either to defend himself or to annoy his adversary. It is a felony.
(b) M/B: R. Perkins & R. Boyce, Criminal Law 239 (3d ed. 1982).

2 129 251 302 427 552   Was dueling a crime at common law?
(a) It is a misdemeanor at common law to fight a duel, to challenge another to a duel, intentionally provoke such a challenge, or knowingly to be the bearer of such a challenge.
(b) M/B: R. Perkins & R. Boyce, Criminal Law 243-44 (3d ed. 1982).

3 130 252 303 428 553   What elements make up the crime of common-law burglary?
(a) The breach, the entry, the dwelling "of another," the nighttime and buglarious intent.
(b) M/B: R. Perkins & R. Boyce, Criminal Law 246 (3d ed. 1982).

4 131 253 304 429 554   Can one be lawfully convicted for common-law arson if one intentionally burns down his own dwelling?
(a) No, common-law arson involves a disturbance of the "security of the dwelling house."
(b) M/B: R. Perkins & R. Boyce, Criminal Law 283, 285 (3d ed. 1982).

5 132 254 305 430 555   What is the common-law crime of "houseburning"?
(a) "Houseburning" is the common-law misdemeanor of intentionally burning one's own house.
(b) M/B: R. Perkins & R. Boyce, Criminal Law 285 (3d ed. 1982).

EXERCISE 33. TEXTS AND TREATISES   (CONTINUED)

6 133 255 306 431 556   What are the common-law elements of the crime of larceny?
(a) Personal property, of another, taken, by trespass, and carried away, with intent to steal.
(b)   M/B: R. Perkins & R. Boyce, Criminal Law 292 (3d ed. 1982).

7 134 256 307 432 557   What is an unlawful assembly?
(a) An unlawful assembly is a meeting of three or more persons with a common plan in mind which, if carried out, will result in a riot.
(b)   M/B: R. Perkins & R. Boyce, Criminal Law 481-82 (3d ed. 1982).

8 135 257 308 433 558   What does "reading the riot act" mean?
(a) "Reading the riot act" is a slang expression used to indicate an official command for rioters to disperse.
(b)   M/B: R. Perkins & R. Boyce, Criminal Law 485-86 (3d ed. 1982).

9 136 258 309 434 559   Under the treason provision in the United States Constitution, can a person be convicted of that crime if there is one witness to an overt act of treason even though there is no confession of guilt in open court?
(a) No.
(b)   M/B: R. Perkins & R. Boyce, Criminal Law 504 (3d ed. 1982).

10 137 259 310 435 560   What is the difference between the common-law crimes of perjury and false swearing?
(a) False swearing is what would be perjury except that it is not in a judicial proceeding but in some other proceeding or matter in which an oath is required by law.
(b)   M/B: R. Perkins & R. Boyce, Criminal Law 511 (3d ed. 1982).

11 138 260 311 436 561   What is the difference between the common-law crimes of escape and breach of prison?
(a) The distinguishing factor is the use of force required for breach of prison.
(b)   M/B: R. Perkins & R. Boyce, Criminal Law 559-67 (3d ed. 1982).

12 139 261 312 437 562   What is misprision of felony?
(a) Misprison of felony is concealment or non-disclosure of the known felony of another.
(b)   M/B: R. Perkins & R. Boyce, Criminal Law 572 (3d ed. 1982).

13 140 262 313 438 563   Under English common law, was compounding a misdemeanor punishable as a crime?
(a) Yes.
(b)   M/B: R. Perkins & R. Boyce, Criminal Law 578 (3d ed. 1982).

14 141 263 314 439 564   What did the common misdemeanor of maintenance involve?
(a) Maintenance was assistance in a suit or action in which the assistant had no interest of his own.
(b)   M/B: R. Perkins & R. Boyce, Criminal Law 582-84 (3d ed. 1982).

15 142 264 315 440 565   What are the requisites for a person's conviction as an accessory after the fact?
(a) A felony must have been committed by another and completed prior to the act of accessoryship. The accessory must not himself be guilty of that felony as a principal. He must do some act to assist the felon personally in his effort to avoid the consequences of his crime. This assistance must be rendered with guilty knowledge of the crime.
(b)   M/B: R. Perkins & R. Boyce, Criminal Law 748-49 (3d ed. 1982).

16 143 265 316 441 566   Was seduction a crime under the common law of England?
(a) No.
(b)   M/B: R. Perkins & R. Boyce, Criminal Law 462 (3d ed. 1982).

EXERCISE 33. TEXTS AND TREATISES   (CONTINUED)

17 144 266 317 442 567   To what crime does the phrase "infamous crime against nature" usually refer?
(a) Sodomy.
(b) M/B: R. Perkins & R. Boyce, Criminal Law 465-66 (3d ed. 1982).

18 145 267 318 443 568   At common law was it unlawful to throw a dead body into a river?
(a) Yes, a misdemeanor.
(b) M/B: R. Perkins & R. Boyce, Criminal Law 476 (3d ed. 1982).

19 146 268 319 444 569   Was an "affray" indictable at common law?
(a) Yes, a misdemeanor.
(b) M/B: R. Perkins & R. Boyce, Criminal Law 479 (3d ed. 1982).

20 147 269 320 445 570   Can a "riot" consist of two persons acting together in the commission of a crime by open force?
(a) No, at least three persons are required.
(b) M/B: R. Perkins & R. Boyce, Criminal Law 483 (3d ed. 1982).

21 148 270 321 446 571   What acts constitute the common-law crime of extortion?
(a) Collection of an unlawful fee by an officer under color of office.
(b) M/B: R. Perkins & R. Boyce, Criminal Law 442-48 (3d ed. 1982).

22 149 271 322 447 572   What elements are usually required for conviction of the offense of receiving stolen property under most statutes in the United States?
(a) 1. The property must be "received."
    2. It must have been stolen and must retain its character of stolen property at the time it is received.
    3. It must be received with "knowledge."
    4. Wrongful intent.
(b) M/B: R. Perkins & R. Boyce, Criminal Law 395 (3d ed. 1982).

23 150 272 323 448 573   Was bigamy a crime under the common law of England?
(a) No, it was not a crime but was punishable as an ecclesiastical offense.
(b) M/B: R. Perkins & R. Boyce, Criminal Law 456 (3d ed. 1982).

24 151 273 324 449 574   Under many modern statutes can a man be prosecuted for the crime of "seduction" even though the parties subsequently marry?
(a) No, many statutes provide that a subsequent marriage of the parties is a bar to prosecution.
(b) M/B: R. Perkins & R. Boyce, Criminal Law 462, 464, 1089 (3d ed. 1982).

25 152 274 325 450 575   What does the term "corpus delicti" mean?
(a) It means "body of the crime" and no criminal conviction can be based upon defendant's extrajudicial confession or admission unless there is other evidence tending to establish the corpus delicti.
(b) M/B: R. Perkins & R. Boyce, Criminal Law 140-42 (3d ed. 1982).

For Problems 26-50, 153-177, 275-299, 326-350, 451-475, 576-600, the students are to use the third edition (1985) of James and Hazard's Civil Procedure.

26 153 275 326 451 576   Did trial by jury largely begin as a trial by witnesses who judged facts within their knowledge?
(a) Yes.
(b) M/B: F. James & G. Hazard, Civil Procedure § 7.1, at 302 (3d ed. 1985).

27 154 276 327 452 577   What was the "local-action rule" of jurisdiction?
(a) The court of one jurisdiction would not entertain an action affecting real property located in another jurisdiction.
(b) M/B: F. James & G. Hazard, Civil Procedure § 2.30, at 103-04 (3d ed. 1985).

28 155 277 328 453 578   How is the "law of the case" different from res judicata?

EXERCISE 33. TEXTS AND TREATISES   (CONTINUED)

(a) The rules of res judicata apply between successive actions while the law of the case rule applies within one action regarding issues of law previously determined.
(b) M/B: F. James & G. Hazard, Civil Procedure § 11.5, at 593 (3d ed. 1985).

29 156 278 329 454 579   Is the use of remittitur to control verdicts likely to be overturned on constitutional grounds at this late date?
(a) No.
(b) M/B: F. James & G. Hazard, Civil Procedure § 7.21, at 396 (3d ed. 1985).

30 157 279 330 455 580   Does the weight of modern judicial authority hold that an amendment relates back to the time of the original pleading whenever the claim or defense asserted in the amendment arose out of the transaction or occurrence set forth or attempted to be set forth in the original pleading?
(a) Yes.
(b) M/B: F. James & G. Hazard, Civil Procedure § 4.16, at 219 (3d ed. 1985).

31 158 280 331 456 581   With what general problem does the case of Erie v. Tompkins deal?
(a) The law to be applied in a federal court when the case is not governed by the Constitution or a federal statute.
(b) M/B: F. James & G. Hazard, Civil Procedure § 2.34, at 116 (3d ed. 1985).

32 159 281 332 457 582   May a void judgment be attacked by a Rule 60(b) motion even if the motion is made more than one year after entry of the judgment?
(a) Yes.
(b) M/B: F. James & G. Hazard, Civil Procedure § 12.16, at 681-82 (3d ed. 1985).
Note: The students may have difficulty answering this question if they only consult section 12.14, at 677-78, which discusses whether an unintentional default judgment should be considered to be a void judgment and thus subject to relief under Rule 60(b). Both section 12.14 and 12.16 are cited in the index.

33 160 282 333 458 583   Under the common law and the codes, was a "variance" ground for objection to the admissibility of evidence outside the limits set by the pleadings?
(a) Yes.
(b) M/B: F. James & G. Hazard, Civil Procedure § 4.11, at 207-08 (3d ed. 1985).

34 161 283 334 459 584   What is the doctrine of forum non conveniens?
(a) A court has the discretionary power to decline to exercise jurisdiction whenever it appears that the cause before it may be more appropriately tried elsewhere.
(b) M/B: F. James & G. Hazard, Civil Procedure § 2.31, at 105 (3d ed. 1985).

35 162 284 335 460 585   What was the size of a jury at common law?
(a) 12 persons.
(b) M/B: F. James & G. Hazard, Civil Procedure § 8.12, at 452 (3d ed. 1985).

36 163 285 336 461 586   Which Federal Rule of Civil Procedure governs intervention?
(a) Rule 24.
(b) M/B: F. James & G. Hazard, Civil Procedure § 10.17, at 550 (3d ed. 1985).

37 164 286 337 462 587   At common law, the special verdict device emerged as a means by which the jury might protect itself from what danger?
(a) To protect the jury from liability for giving false judgment.
(b) M/B: F. James & G. Hazard, Civil Procedure § 7.4, at 312 (3d ed. 1985).

38 165 287 338 463 588   Do the Federal Rules of Civil Procedure provide a definition of "privileged" matter for discovery purposes?
(a) No.
(b) M/B: F. James & G. Hazard, Civil Procedure § 5.9, at 246 (3d ed. 1985).

EXERCISE 33. TEXTS AND TREATISES   (CONTINUED)

39 166 288 339 464 589   Is discovery permitted of insurance coverage under the Federal Rules of Civil Procedure?
(a) Yes.
(b) M/B: F. James & G. Hazard, Civil Procedure § 5.8, at 244 (3d ed. 1985).

40 167 289 340 465 590   Which Federal Rule of Civil Procedure governs interpleader?
(a) Rule 22.
(b) M/B: F. James & G. Hazard, Civil Procedure § 10.19, at 561 (3d ed. 1985).

41 168 290 341 466 591   When is a reply required under the Federal Rules of Civil Procedure?
(a) Only when the counterclaim is denominated as such.
(b) M/B: F. James & G. Hazard, Civil Procedure § 4.9, at 206 (3d ed. 1985).

42 169 291 342 467 592   For what was the common-law "demurrer to the evidence" used?
(a) To challenge the sufficiency of his adversary's evidence at trial to make out a case.
(b) M/B: F. James & G. Hazard, Civil Procedure § 7.4, at 308 (3d ed. 1985).

43 170 292 343 468 593   Under a 1934 Supreme Court decision, is the conditioning a new trial on the defendant's consent to an additur in federal court constitutional?
(a) No.
(b) M/B: F. James & G. Hazard, Civil Procedure § 7.21, at 397 (3d ed. 1985).

44 171 293 344 469 594   May the driver of a vehicle in which the plaintiff was riding when the collision occurred that caused the plaintiff's injury be compelled to submit to a physical examination under Rule 35?
(a) No.
(b) M/B: F. James & G. Hazard, Civil Procedure § 5.6, at 240 (3d ed. 1985).

45 172 294 345 470 595   Is impleader a proper device for a defendant to bring in someone he contends is really the one liable to the plaintiff?
(a) No.
(b) M/B: F. James & G. Hazard, Civil Procedure § 10.18, at 555 (3d ed. 1985).

46 173 295 346 471 596   Is an order allowing intervention immediately appealable?
(a) No.
(b) M/B: F. James & G. Hazard, Civil Procedure § 10.17, at 554 (3d ed. 1985).

47 174 296 347 472 597   Under the common law, did married women have the capacity to sue alone as a party?
(a) No.
(b) M/B: F. James & G. Hazard, Civil Procedure § 10.7, at 521 (3d ed. 1985).

48 175 297 348 473 598   Are federal venue rules cast in terms of the citizenship of the parties?
(a) No.
(b) M/B: F. James & G. Hazard, Civil Procedure § 2.10, at 66 (3d ed. 1985).

49 176 298 349 474 599   If venue in a federal court is improper and there is a district of proper venue, must the court in which the action was brought dismiss the action?
(a) No, the judge may transfer it.
(b) M/B: F. James & G. Hazard, Civil Procedure § 2.11, at 67-68 (3d ed. 1985).

50 177 299 350 475 600   Can parties to a lawsuit be compelled through discovery to identify each expert witness they expect to call at trial?
(a) Yes.

EXERCISE 33. TEXTS AND TREATISES   (CONTINUED)

(b) M/B: F. James & G. Hazard, Civil Procedure § 5.11, at 254 (3d ed. 1985).

For problem numbers 51-75, 101-102, 178-200, 201-224, 300, 351-375, 476-500, 501-525, the students are to use the fifth edition (1984) of Prosser & Keeton on The Law of Torts. How this work should be cited is not entirely clear. Compare, for example, the form used in 99 Harv. L. Rev. 809, 810, n.8 (1986) with the form used in 95 Yale L.J. 219, 224, n.18 (1985). The form used below follows the form used in the Yale Law Journal and the format used in the Library Exercise student instructions.

51 178 300 351 476 501   Under the Federal Tort Claims Act, is the local law of the place where the tort occurred applied?
(a) Yes.
(b) M/B: W. Keeton, D. Dobbs, R. Keeton & D. Owen, Prosser & Keeton on the Law of Torts § 131, at 1034 (5th ed. 1984).

52 179 201 352 477 502   Can the federal government be held liable for a claim arising out of abuse of process under the Federal Tort Claims Act?
(a) No.
(b) M/B: W. Keeton, D. Dobbs, R. Keeton & D. Owen, Prosser & Keeton on the Law of Torts § 131, at 1038 (5th ed. 1984).

53 180 202 353 478 503   In negligence cases, have most cases held insane persons liable for failure to conform to the standard of conduct required of a sane man?
(a) Yes.
(b) M/B: W. Keeton, D. Dobbs, R. Keeton & D. Owen, Prosser & Keeton on the Law of Torts § 32, at 177, § 135, at 1074 (5th ed. 1984).

54 181 203 354 479 504   Under the common law of England, if the victim of a tort died before he recovered in tort, did the victim's right of action "survive" or did it "die"?
(a) It died (or did not survive).
(b) M/B: W. Keeton, D. Dobbs, R. Keeton & D. Owen, Prosser & Keeton on the Law of Torts § 140, at 940 (5th ed. 1984). (?)

55 182 204 355 480 505   Are torts committed by the federal government immune under the Federal Tort Claims Act when they occur as a result of combatant activities of its military forces in time of war?
(a) Yes.
(b) M/B: W. Keeton, D. Dobbs, R. Keeton & D. Owen, Prosser & Keeton on the Law of Torts § 131, at 1037-38 (5th ed. 1984).

56 183 205 356 481 506   Have American courts consistently held (in absence of legislation) that there is no liability for "escape" of fire where the defendant was not negligent?
(a) Yes.
(b) M/B: W. Keeton, D. Dobbs, R. Keeton & D. Owen, Prosser & Keeton on the Law of Torts § 77, at 544 (5th ed. 1984).

57 184 206 357 482 507   If a tiger, which X keeps as a house pet, escapes and bites Y, will X be strictly liable for the damage done?
(a) Yes, the tiger is ferocious by nature.
(b) M/B: W. Keeton, D. Dobbs, R. Keeton & D. Owen, Prosser & Keeton on the Law of Torts § 76, at 542 (5th ed. 1984).

58 185 207 358 483 508   What interest is protected by permitting recovery for batteries?
(a) Freedom from intentional and unpermitted contacts with the plaintiff's person.
(b) M/B: W. Keeton, D. Dobbs, R. Keeton & D. Owen, Prosser & Keeton on the Law of Torts § 9, at 39 (5th ed. 1984).

59 186 208 359 484 509   When did the action of trespass first emerge?
(a) The thirteenth century.
(b) M/B: W. Keeton, D. Dobbs, R. Keeton & D. Owen, Prosser & Keeton on the Law of Torts § 6, at 29 (5th ed. 1984).

EXERCISE 33. TEXTS AND TREATISES   (CONTINUED)

60 187 209 360 485 510   What is the basic difference or distinction between trespass and trespass on the case?
(a) The distinction between the two lay in the immediate application of force to the person or property of the plaintiff, as distinguished from injury through some obvious and visible secondary cause.
(b) M/B: W. Keeton, D. Dobbs, R. Keeton & D. Owen, Prosser & Keeton on the Law of Torts § 6, at 29 (5th ed. 1984).

61 188 210 361 486 511   From what action did the tort of false imprisonment descend?
(a) Trespass.
(b) M/B: W. Keeton, D. Dobbs, R. Keeton & D. Owen, Prosser & Keeton on the Law of Torts § 11, at 47 (5th ed. 1984).

62 189 211 362 487 512   Could the common-law action of trespass be maintained without proof of any actual damage?
(a) Yes.
(b) M/B: W. Keeton, D. Dobbs, R. Keeton & D. Owen, Prosser & Keeton on the Law of Torts § 13, at 75 (5th ed. 1984).

63 190 212 363 488 513   When may a private citizen arrest without a warrant?
(a) To prevent a felony or breach of the peace which is being committed, or reasonably appears about to be committed, in the person's presence.
(b) M/B: W. Keeton, D. Dobbs, R. Keeton & D. Owen, Prosser & Keeton on the Law of Torts § 26, at 153 (5th ed. 1984).

64 191 213 364 489 514   When was negligence recognized as a separate tort?
(a) Not until the earlier part of the nineteenth century.
(b) M/B: W. Keeton, D. Dobbs, R. Keeton & D. Owen, Prosser & Keeton on the Law of Torts § 28, at 160 (5th ed. 1984).

65 192 214 365 490 515   Must there be actual loss or damage before a cause of action based upon negligence is stated?
(a) Yes.
(b) M/B: W. Keeton, D. Dobbs, R. Keeton & D. Owen, Prosser & Keeton on the Law of Torts § 30, at 165 (5th ed. 1984).

66 193 215 366 491 516   Does a jury determine the existence of the "duty" element of a negligence cause of action?
(a) No, it is a question of law to be determined by the court.
(b) M/B: W. Keeton, D. Dobbs, R. Keeton & D. Owen, Prosser & Keeton on the Law of Torts § 37, at 236 (5th ed. 1984).

67 194 216 367 492 517   What does the phrase "res ipsa loquitur" mean and when did it first appear in judicial arguments?
(a) "The thing speaks for itself;" the phrase first appeared in cases of injuries to passengers at the hands of carriers, the offspring of an argument of Baron Pollock in an 1863 case.
(b) M/B: W. Keeton, D. Dobbs, R. Keeton & D. Owen, Prosser & Keeton on the Law of Torts § 39, at 243 (5th ed. 1984).

68 195 217 368 493 518   What is the "sine qua non" rule?
(a) The defendant's conduct is not a cause of the event, if the event woud have occurred without it.
(b) M/B: W. Keeton, D. Dobbs, R. Keeton & D. Owen, Prosser & Keeton on the Law of Torts § 41, at 266 (5th ed. 1984).

69 196 218 369 494 519   Who has the burden, according to the great majority of courts, to plead and prove contributory negligence?
(a) The defendant.
(b) M/B: W. Keeton, D. Dobbs, R. Keeton & D. Owen, Prosser & Keeton on the Law of Torts § 65, at 451 (5th ed. 1984).

70 197 219 370 495 520   Can unmarried consorts, such as live-in lovers, who are financially dependent on the deceased for support recover for wrongful death under modern wrongful death statutes?
(a) No.

EXERCISE 33. TEXTS AND TREATISES   (CONTINUED)

(b) M/B: W. Keeton, D. Dobbs, R. Keeton & D. Owen, Prosser & Keeton on the Law of Torts § 127, at 947 (5th ed. 1984).

71 198 220 371 496 521   What is the essence of a private nuisance claim? In other words, with what does a private nuisance interfere?
(a) Use and enjoyment of land.
(b) M/B: W. Keeton, D. Dobbs, R. Keeton & D. Owen, Prosser & Keeton on the Law of Torts § 87, at 619 (5th ed. 1984).

72 199 221 372 497 522   Are loud noises sufficient to constitute an actionable private nuisance if they adversely affect a hypersensitive individual?
(a) No, only if substantial and unreasonable to a normal person.
(b) M/B: W. Keeton, D. Dobbs, R. Keeton & D. Owen, Prosser & Keeton on the Law of Torts § 88, at 627-28 (5th ed. 1984).

73 200 222 373 498 523   What is the traditional definitional difference between "libel" and "slander"?
(a) Libel originally concerned written or printed words, slander was of oral character.
(b) M/B: W. Keeton, D. Dobbs, R. Keeton & D. Owen, Prosser & Keeton on the Law of Torts § 112, at 786 (5th ed. 1984).

74 101 223 374 499 524   Who first recognized a separate tort based upon the right to privacy?
(a) Warren and Brandeis in their 1890 Harvard Law Review article. [also acceptable: New York]
(b) M/B: W. Keeton, D. Dobbs, R. Keeton & D. Owen, Prosser & Keeton on the Law of Torts § 117, at 849-50 (5th ed. 1984).

75 102 224 375 500 525   As originally developed, what are the elements of a cause of action for malicious prosecution?
(a) 1. A criminal proceeding instituted or continued by the defendant against the plaintiff.
     2. Termination of the proceeding in favor of the accused.
     3. Absence of probable cause for the proceeding.
     4. "Malice" or a primary purpose other than that of bringing an offender to justice.
(b) M/B: W. Keeton, D. Dobbs, R. Keeton & D. Owen, Prosser & Keeton on the Law of Torts § 119, at 871 (5th ed. 1984).

For problem numbers 76-87, 103-114, 225-236, 376-387, 401-412, and 526-537, the students are to use the third edition (1984) of McCormick on Evidence. For purposes of this exercise, cite this work to (1) Charles McCormick as the author, (2) use "McCormick on Evidence" at the title, and (3) indicate parenthetically that the third edition was edited by Edward Cleary. See USOC Rule 15.1 and 15.2.

76 103 225 376 401 526   Do most courts reject proof of an actor's character for care given through expert testimony?
(a) Yes.
(b) M/B: C. McCormick, McCormick on Evidence § 189, at 555 (E. Cleary 3d ed. 1984).

77 104 226 377 402 527   When the existence and scope of a partnership have been proved, is a statement of a partner made in the conduct of the business of the firm allowed as evidence of an admission of the partnership?
(a) Yes.
(b) M/B: C. McCormick, McCormick on Evidence § 267, at 791-92 (E. Cleary 3d ed. 1984).

78 105 227 378 403 528   Traditionally, were contemporary entries in a family Bible admissible (as an exception to the hearsay rule) to prove family history or pedigree even though the author may not be identifiable?
(a) Yes.
(b) M/B: C. McCormick, McCormick on Evidence § 323, at 903 (E. Cleary 3d ed. 1984).

EXERCISE 33. TEXTS AND TREATISES   (CONTINUED)

79 106 228 379 404 529   Will courts take judicial notice of historical facts, such as when a war ended?
(a) Yes.
(b) M/B: C. McCormick, McCormick on Evidence § 330, at 926 (E. Cleary 3d ed. 1984).

80 107 229 380 405 530   Under the common-law exception to the hearsay rule, what four elements had to be shown to use regularly kept business records to prove the facts recited in them?
(a) (1) the entries must be original entries made in the routine of a business, (2) the entries must have been made upon the personal knowledge of the recorder or of someone reporting to him, (3) the entries must have been made at or near the time the transaction recorded, and (4) the recorder and his informant must be shown to be unavailable.
(b) M/B: C. McCormick, McCormick on Evidence § 306, at 872 (E. Cleary 3d ed. 1984).

81 108 230 381 406 531   Is lack of religious belief generally available as a ground to impeach the credibility of a witness?
(a) No.
(b) M/B: C. McCormick, McCormick on Evidence § 34, at 73, or § 49, at 113-14 (E. Cleary 3d ed. 1984).

82 109 231 382 407 532   Will a party's refusal to furnish handing examplars serve as a basis for drawing an adverse inference based on an admission by conduct?
(a) Yes.
(b) M/B: C. McCormick, McCormick on Evidence § 271, at 804-05 (E. Cleary 3d ed. 1984).

83 110 232 383 408 533   When did the term res gestae come into common usage in discussing the admissibility of spontaneous statements accompanying material acts or situations?
(a) In the early 1800's.
(b) M/B: C. McCormick, McCormick on Evidence § 288, at 835 (E. Cleary 3d ed. 1984).

84 111 233 384 409 534   Is it an accurate statement concerning the burden of proof to say that even though a party is required to plead a fact, that party is not required to prove that fact if his averment is negative rather than affirmative in form?
(a) No.
(b) M/B: C. McCormick, McCormick on Evidence § 337, at 949 (E. Cleary 3d ed. 1984).

85 112 234 385 410 535   Will courts take judicial notice of the scientific principles on which radar is based even though those principles are not commonly known among the public?
(a) Yes.
(b) M/B: C. McCormick, McCormick on Evidence § 330, at 925 (E. Cleary 3d ed. 1984).

86 113 235 386 411 536   Was a clergyman-penitent privilege recognized at common law?
(a) Probably not.
(b) M/B: C. McCormick, McCormick on Evidence § 76.2, at 184 (E. Cleary 3d ed. 1984).

87 114 236 387 412 537   Is evidence of payment or offers to pay medical expense of an injured person ordinarily admissible to prove liability for the injury?
(a) No.
(b) M/B: C. McCormick, McCormick on Evidence § 275, at 818 (E. Cleary 3d ed. 1984).

EXERCISE 33.   TEXTS AND TREATISES   (CONTINUED)

For problem numbers 88-100, 115-127, 237-249, 388-400, 413-425, and 538-550, the students are to use Cunningham, Stoebuck, and Whitman's The Law of Property (1984).

88 115 237 388 413 538   Does the English rule give a possessor of land the absolute right to withdraw underground percolating water as he wishes for whatever purposes he wishes as long as he does not maliciously injure others?
(a)   Yes.
(b)   M/B: R. Cunningham, W. Stoebuck, & D. Whitman, The Law of Property § 7.5, at 427 (1984).

89 116 238 389 414 539   With regard to surface water, what is the essential idea of the "common enemy doctrine?
(a)   A landowner is privileged to use any and all methods to get rid of surface water and is not liable to his neighbors for flooding them. The surface water is considered an outlaw or common enemy.
(b)   M/B: R. Cunningham, W. Stoebuck, & D. Whitman, The Law of Property § 7.6, at 430 (1984).

90 117 239 390 415 540   For purposes of the law of trespass, does an ownership of land carry rights extending downward indefinitely?
(a)   Yes.
(b)   M/B: R. Cunningham, W. Stoebuck, & D. Whitman, The Law of Property § 7.2, at 412 (1984).

91 118 240 391 416 541   Is title insurance a contract of indemnity?
(a)   Yes.
(b)   M/B: R. Cunningham, W. Stoebuck, & D. Whitman, The Law of Property § 11.14, at 821 (1984).

92 119 241 392 417 542   Is the following statute a "race" type, a "notice" type, or a "notice-race" type of recording act: "Every conveyance not recorded is void as against any subsequent purchaser or mortgagee in good faith and for valuable consideration . . . whose conveyance is first duly recorded"?
(a)   "Notice-race" type.
(b)   M/B: R. Cunningham, W. Stoebuck, & D. Whitman, The Law of Property § 11.9, atr 776 (1984).

93 120 242 393 418 543   What is the general distinction between a nuisance and a trespass?
(a)   The general distinction between a nuisance and a trespass is that the trespass flows from a physical invasion and the nuisance does not.
(b)   M/B: R. Cunningham, W. Stoebuck, & D. Whitman, The Law of Property § 7.2, at 413 (1984).

94 121 243 394 419 544   Dictum in what American judicial decision is the source of the "correlative rights" doctrine for the use of percolating underground water?
(a)   Dictum in Bassett v. Salisbury Manufacturing Co.
(b)   M/B: R. Cunningham, W. Stoebuck, & D. Whitman, The Law of Property § 7.5, at 428 (1984).

95 122 244 395 420 545   Where does a proper "metes and bounds" description of land end up?
(a)   The last line returns to the point of the beginning.
(b)   M/B: R. Cunningham, W. Stoebuck, & D. Whitman, The Law of Property § 11.2, at 724 (1984).

96 123 245 396 421 546   How long does title insurance last?
(a)   It lasts indefinitely so long as the owner of his heirs, devisees, or corporate successors continue to hold the land.
(b)   M/B: R. Cunningham, W. Stoebuck, & D. Whitman, The Law of Property § 11.14, at 822 (1984).

97 124 246 397 422 547   In order to run to the covenantee's grantee, must the burden of a real covenant "touch and concerns" some estate in land?

EXERCISE 33.   TEXTS AND TREATISES   (CONTINUED)

(a) Yes.
(b) M/B: R. Cunningham, W. Stoebuck, & D. Whitman, The Law of Property § 8.15, at 470 (1984).

98 125 247 398 423 548   Do title insurance policies ordinarily exclude laws and governmental ordinances unless they appear on the public records?
(a) Yes.
(b) M/B: R. Cunningham, W. Stoebuck, & D. Whitman, The Law of Property § 11.14, at 824 (1984).

99 126 248 399 424 549   What is the "American" doctrine of rights to percolating underground water sometimes called?
(a) The reasonable use doctrine or correlative rights doctrine.
(b) M/B: R. Cunningham, W. Stoebuck, & D. Whitman, The Law of Property § 7.5, at 428 (1984).

100 127 249 400 425 550   Have recent cases recognized a duty of a title insurer to make a title search and report the defects found to the insured?
(a) Yes.
(b) M/B: R. Cunningham, W. Stoebuck, & D. Whitman, The Law of Property 11.14, at 823 (or 823-24) (1984).

LIBRARY EXERCISE 34. RESTATEMENTS OF THE LAW.

INSTRUCTOR'S NOTE: The specific directions are listed depend on the specific problem number assigned. The directions are given with the problem numbers below. The following two Quick-Reference Abbreviations are relevant to this exercise:

RESTATEMENT CITATION 1. FOLLOW THE SPECIAL USOC FORM FOR CITING RESTATEMENTS OF THE LAW. [RESTAT 1]
RESTATEMENT CITATION 3. IN MEMORANDA AND BRIEFS, CITE RESTATEMENTS IN ORDINARY ROMAN TYPE. IN LAW REVIEW FOOTNOTES, CITE THE NAME OF THE RESTATEMENT IN LARGE AND SMALL CAPITALS. [RESTAT 3]

For problems 1-17, 101-117, 201-217, 301-317, 401-417, 501-517, the students are to use the Restatement (Second) of Trusts (1959). Using the index in Volume 2, the students are required to find the section[s] (in Vol. 1 or 2) that answer[s] or govern[s] the question or subject listed with their problem number. (a) They are to cite the section[s] and (b) using the Appendix (Vol. 3), they are to list the "Cross References" to "Digest System Key Numbers" (West) for the section[s].

1 101 201 301 401 501   Is an equitable charge a trust?
(a)   M/B: Restatement (Second) of Trusts § 10 (1959).
(b)   Trusts 1
      Wills 821(1), 826(2)

2 102 202 302 402 502   Can an interest that has ceased to exist be held in trust?
(a)   M/B: Restatement (Second) of Trusts § 75 (1959).
(b)   Trusts 10, 37

3 103 203 303 403 503   Does an infant have the legal capacity to administer a trust?
(a)   M/B: Restatement (Second) of Trusts § 91 (1959).
(b)   Infants 6

4 104 204 304 404 504   Duty of trustee to keep the trust property separate.
(a)   M/B: Restatement (Second) of Trusts § 179 (1959).
(b)   Trusts 221, 283(1)

5 105 205 305 405 505   Can a trust be created without notice to or acceptance by the beneficiary?
(a)   M/B: Restatement (Second) of Trusts § 36 (1959).
(b)   Trusts 39

6 106 206 306 406 506   Is a receiver appointed by a court a trustee?
(a)   M/B: Restatement (Second) of Trusts § 16B (1959).
(b)   Receivers 69

7 107 207 307 407 507   Duty of a trustee to keep and render clear and accurate accounts.
(a)   M/B: Restatement (Second) of Trusts § 172 (1959).
(b)   Trusts 289

8 108 208 308 408 508   Liability of a successor trustee for a breach of trust committed by a predecessor trustee.
(a)   M/B: Restatement (Second) of Trusts § 223 (1959).
(b)   Trusts 243, 294

9 109 209 309 409 509   Amount which a trustee can properly lend on a mortgage upon real property.
(a)   M/B: Restatement (Second) of Trusts § 229 (1959).
(b)   Trusts 222

10 110 210 310 410 510   Can a trust be a "charitable trust" when the trust property is devoted to a private use?
(a)   M/B: Restatement (Second) of Trusts § 376 (1959).
(b)   Charities 10

EXERCISE 34. RESTATEMENTS OF THE LAW   (CONTINUED)

11 111 211 311 411 511   Are the duties of a trustee of a charitable trust similar to the duties of a trustee of a private trust?
(a)   M/B: Restatement (Second) of Trusts § 379 (1959).
(b)   Charities 33
      Corporations 49(2)

12 112 212 312 412 512   Does a resulting trust terminate if the legal title to the trust property and the entire beneficial interest become united in one person?
(a)   M/B: Restatement (Second) of Trusts § 410 (1959).
(b)   Trusts 63 3/4

13 113 213 313 413 513   Is consideration necessary for the creation of a charitable trust?
(a)   M/B: Restatement (Second) of Trusts § 352 (1959).
(b)   Charities 4, 40

14 114 214 314 414 514   If a trustee of a resulting trust repudiates the trust to the knowledge of the beneficiary, can the beneficiary then be barred by laches from enforcing the trust?
(a)   M/B: Restatement (Second) of Trusts § 409 (1959).
(b)   Trusts 365(4)

15 115 215 315 415 515   Does the Attorney General have the power to enforce a charitable trust?
(a)   M/B: Restatement (Second) of Trusts § 391 (1959).
(b)   Charities 49, 50

16 116 216 316 416 516   Is a charitable trust invalid if it is created for an "illegal purpose," such as inducing a crime?
(a)   M/B: Restatement (Second) of Trusts § 377 (1959).
(b)   Charities 10

17 117 217 317 417 517   Doctrine of cy pres applies to charitable trusts when there has been a failure of the purpose of the trust.
(a)   M/B: Restatement (Second) of Trusts § 399 (1959).
(b)   Charities 37, 48(2)

For problems 18-26, 118-126, 218-226, 318-326, 418-426, 518-526, the students are to use the Restatement (Second) of Torts (1965). The students are required to Locate Volume 1, (covering §§ 1 to 280). Using the index in the back of Volume 1, they are to find the section[s] that answer[s] or govern[s] the question or subject listed with their problem number. (a) They are to cite the section[s], and (b) using the Appendix volume covering that section, they are to list the "Cross References" to "Digest System Key Numbers" (West) for the section[s].

18 118 218 318 418 518   Special liability of a common carrier or other public utility for gross insults made by its servants.
(a)   M/B: Restatement (Second) of Torts § 48 (1965).
(b)   Carriers 283(3, 4)
      Innkeepers 10.2
      Master and Servant 306

19 119 219 319 419 519   Ways of committing a trespass to chattel.
(a)   M/B: Restatement (Second) of Torts § 217 (1965).
(b)   Trespass 6 et seq.

20 120 220 320 420 520   Privilege to enter land in possession of another person based upon private necessity.
(a)   M/B: Restatement (Second) of Torts § 197 (1965).
(b)   Trespass 26

21 121 221 321 421 521   Self-defense by use of reasonable force to defend oneself against negligent conduct.
(a)   M/B: Restatement (Second) of Torts § 64 (1965).
(b)   Negligence 105

EXERCISE 34. RESTATEMENTS OF THE LAW   (CONTINUED)

22 122 222 322 422 522   Privilege to enter land in another person's possession to abate a private nuisance.
(a) M/B: Restatement (Second) of Torts § 201 (1965).
(b) Nuisance 20
     Trespass 26

23 123 223 323 423 523   What constitutes confinement for purposes of determining whether the tort of false imprisonment has occurred.
(a) M/B: Restatement (Second) of Torts § 36 (1965).
(b) False Imprisonment 6

24 124 224 324 424 524   Ways of committing conversion.
(a) M/B: Restatement (Second) of Torts § 223 (1965).
(b) Trespass 4 et seq.

25 124 225 325 425 535   Trespass to land may occur by the failure to remove things tortiously placed on the land.
(a) M/B: Restatement (Second) of Torts § 161 (1965).
(b) Trespass 10 et seq.

26 126 226 326 426 526   Privilege of distraint of chattels for rent.
(a) M/B: Restatement (Second) of Torts § 273 (1965).
(b) Liens 18½
     Trover and Conversion 23

For problems 27-37, 127-137, 227-237, 327-337, 427-437, 527-537, the students are to use the Restatement (Second) of Torts (1965). They are to locate Volume 2 (covering §§ 281 to 503). Using the index in the back of Volume 2, they are to find the section[s] that answer[s] or govern[s] the question or subject listed with their problem number. (a) The students are required to cite the section[s], and (b) using the Appendix volume covering that section, they are required to list the "Cross References" to "Digest System Key Numbers" (West) for the section[s].

27 127 227 327 427 527   Definition of a trespasser.
(a) M/B: Restatement (Second) of Torts § 329 (1965).
(b) Negligence 33(2)

28 128 228 328 428 528   Obstruction of a highway which thereby prevents a third person from rendering aid to prevent physical harm.
(a) M/B: Restatement (Second) of Torts § 328 (1965).
(b) Highways 200

29 129 229 329 429 529   Definition of a licensee.
(a) M/B: Restatement (Second) of Torts § 330 (1965).
(b) Negligence 32(2) et seq.

30 130 230 330 430 530   Master's duty to protect an endangered or hurt employee.
(a) M/B: Restatement (Second) of Torts § 314B (1965).
(b) Master and Servant 85 et seq.
     Negligence 8

31 131 231 331 431 531   Definition of an invitee.
(a) M/B: Restatement (Second) of Torts § 332 (1965).
(b) Negligence 32(2.3) et seq.

32 132 232 332 432 532   Liability for intentionally preventing aid necessary to prevent physical harm to third persons.
(a) M/B: Restatement (Second) of Torts § 326 (1965).
(b) Negligence 1 et seq.

33 133 233 333 433 533   Custodian's duty of control of dangerous persons from harming others.
(a) M/B: Restatement (Second) of Torts § 319 (1965).

EXERCISE 34. <u>RESTATEMENTS OF THE LAW</u> (CONTINUED)

(b) Negligence 1 <u>et</u> <u>seq</u>.

34 134 234 334 434 534   Intentional infliction of emotional distress causing bodily harm.
(a) M/B: Restatement (Second) of Torts § 312 (1965).
(b) Damages 49

35 135 235 335 435 535   Possessor of land defined.
(a) M/B: Restatement (Second) of Torts § 328E (1965).
(b) Negligence 28 <u>et</u> <u>seq</u>.

36 136 236 336 436 536   Liability of possessor of land for dangerous natural conditions in private rights of way.
(a) M/B: Restatement (Second) of Torts § 349 (1965).
(b) Easements 64
    Highways 199
    Municipal Corp. 801(1) <u>et</u> <u>seq</u>.
    Negligence 35

37 137 237 337 437 537   Unintentional infliction of emotional distress causing bodily harm.
(a) M/B: Restatement (Second) of Torts § 313 (1965).
(b) Damages 49

For problems 38-50, 138-150, 238-250, 338-350, 438-450, 538-550, the students are to use the <u>Restatement (Second) of Agency</u> (1958). Using the index in Volume 2, the students are required to find the section[s] (in Vol. 1 or 2) that answer[s] or govern[s] the question or subject listed with theirr problem number. (a) They are to cite the section[s], and (b) list the "Cross References" to "Digest System Key Numbers" (West) for the section[s].

38 138 238 338 438 538   Statement of the fellow servant rule.
(a) M/B: Restatement (Second) of Agency § 474 (1958).
(b) Master and Servant 159-202.

39 139 239 339 439 539   Admissibility in evidence of statements of agents as to their authority.
(a) M/B: Restatement (Second) of Agency § 285 (1958).
(b) Principle and Agent 122

40 140 240 340 440 540   Definition of a "servant."
(a) M/B: Restatement (Second) of Agency § 2(2) <u>or</u> § 220 (1958).
(b) Master and Servant 1, 5 <u>or</u> 1, 5, 88, 137, 315-324

41 141 241 341 441 541   Definition of "ratification."
(a) M/B: Restatement (Second) of Agency § 82 (1958).
(b) Principal and Agent 163

42 142 242 342 442 542   Termination of agency powers by disloyal conduct of the agent.
(a) M/B: Restatement (Second) of Agency § 112 (1958).
(b) Principal and Agent 45

43 143 243 343 443 543   Definition of a "fellow servant."
(a) M/B: Restatement (Second) of Agency § 475 (1958).
(b) Master and Servant 159, 181, 196

44 144 244 344 444 544   Definition of "authority."
(a) M/B: Restatement (Second) of Agency § 7 (1958).
(b) Principal and Agent 92(1), 96

45 145 245 345 445 545   Liability of principal (master) for a servant's leaving the principal's instrumentality in a dangerous situation while pursuing a private purpose.
(a) M/B: Restatement (Second) of Agency § 240 (1958).
(b) Automobiles 193(1)
    Master and Servant 304

EXERCISE 34. RESTATEMENTS OF THE LAW   (CONTINUED)

46 146 246 346 446 546   Definition of "affirmance."
(a) M/B: Restatement (Second) of Agency § 83 (1958).
(b) Principal and Agent 167, 169 (1, 2)

47 147 247 347 447 547   Release as a defense of an agent against a principal.
(a) M/B: Restatement (Second) of Agency § 419 (1958).
(b) Release 4

48 148 248 348 448 548   Definition of "apparent authority."
(a) M/B: Restatement (Second) of Agency § 8 (1958).
(b) Principal and Agent 99-115

49 149 249 349 449 549   Laches as a defense available to the agent against his principal.
(a) M/B: Restatement (Second) of Agency § 421A(d) (1958).
(b) Judgment 695
     Principal and Agent 78(1, 2 1/4), 79(1)

50 150 250 350 450 550   Assault on a servant by other servants as affected by the fellow servant rule.
(a) M/B: Restatement (Second) of Agency § 487 (1958).
(b) Master and Servant 202

For problems 51-68, 151-168, 251-268, 351-368, 451-468, 551-568, the students are to use the Restatement (Second) of Conflict of Laws (1971). Using the index in Volume 2, the students are to find the section[s] (in Vol. 1 or 2) that answer[s] or govern[s] the question or subject listed with their problem number. (a) The students are to cite the section[s], and (b) using the Appendix (Volume 3), they are to list the "Cross References" to "Digest System Key Numbers" (West for the section[s] of the Restatement (Second).

51 151 251 351 451 551   Contribution and indemnity among tortfeasors.
(a) M/B: Restatement (Second) of Conflict of Laws § 173 (1971).
(b) Contribution 5

52 152 252 352 452 552   Foreign nation decrees enjoining an act; recognition in the United States.
(a) M/B: Restatement (Second) of Conflict of Laws § 102 (1971).
(b) Judgment 823

53 153 253 353 453 553   Contractual liability of partners.
(a) M/B: Restatement (Second) of Conflict of Laws § 295 (1971).
(b) Partnership 2

54 154 254 354 454 554   Requisites of a valid judgment.
(a) M/B: Restatement (Second) of Conflict of Laws § 92 (1971).
(b) Judgment 5 et seq.

55 155 255 355 455 555   Statute of Frauds.
(a) M/B: Restatement (Second) of Conflict of Laws § 141 (1971).
(b) Frauds, Statute of 120

56 156 256 356 456 556   Joint torts.
(a) M/B: Restatement (Second) of Conflict of Laws § 172 (1971).
(b) Torts 2

57 157 257 357 457 557   Termination of corporate existence.
(a) M/B: Restatement (Second) of Conflict of Laws § 299 (1971).
(b) Actions 17
     Corporations 592

58 158 258 358 348 558   Law controlling escheat of land.
(a) M/B: Restatement (Second) of Conflict of Laws § 243 (1971).
(b) Property 6

EXERCISE 34. RESTATEMENTS OF THE LAW   (CONTINUED)

59 159 259 359 459 559   Construction of a will devising land.
(a) M/B: Restatement (Second) of Conflict of Laws § 240 (1971).
(b) Wills 436

60 160 260 360 460 560   Trespass to foreign land.
(a) M/B: Restatement (Second) of Conflict of Laws § 87 (1971).
(b) Courts 7

61 161 261 361 461 561   Equitable interests in land.
(a) M/B: Restatement (Second) of Conflict of Laws § 235 (1971).
(b) Property 6

62 162 262 362 462 562   Recognition and enforcement of erroneous judgments in other states.
(a) M/B: Restatement (Second) of Conflict of Laws § 106 (1971).
(b) Judgments 819

63 163 263 363 463 563   Subject matter of conflict of laws.
(a) M/B: Restatement (Second) of Conflict of Laws § 2 (1971).
(b) Action 17

64 164 264 364 464 546   Domicil of a minor.
(a) M/B: Restatement (Second) of Conflict of Laws § 22 (1971).
(b) Domicile 1, 5

65 165 265 365 465 565   Transfer of chattel by an executor or administrator.
(a) M/B: Restatement (Second) of Conflict of Laws § 332 (1971).
(b) Executors and Administrators 86

66 166 266 366 466 566   Nationality and citizenship.
(a) M/B: Restatement (Second) of Conflict of Laws § 31 (1971).
(b) Courts 11

67 167 267 367 467 567   Meaning of the term "shareholder."
(a) M/B: Restatement (Second) of Conflict of Laws § 303 (1971).
(b) Corporations 170

68 168 268 368 468 568   Liability of majority shareholder.
(a) M/B: Restatement (Second) of Conflict of Laws § 306 (1971).
(b) Corporations 216

For problems 69-80, 169-180, 269-280, 369-380, 469-480, 569-580, the students are to use the Restatement (Second) of Property (1977). Using the index in Volume 2, the students are to find the section[s] (in Vol. 1 or 2) that answer[s] or govern[s] the question or subject listed with their problem number. (a) The students are to cite the section[s], and (b) using the "Table of Cross References" to "Digest System Key Numbers" (West) in the back of Volume 2, they are to list the references. The students are instructed to cite only the section and not the cite comments to a section.

69 169 269 369 469 569   Tenant's obligation to pay rent.
(a) M/B: Restatement (Second) of Property § 12.1 (1977).
(b) Landlord and Tenant 181 et seq.

70 170 270 370 470 570   Assumption of a lease by a trustee in bankruptcy.
(a) M/B: Restatement (Second) of Property § 20.2 (1977).
(b) Bankruptcy 255

71 171 271 371 471 571   Bankruptcy proceedings as a default under a lease.
(a) M/B: Restatement (Second) of Property § 20.1 (1977).
(b) Landlord and Tenant 101½

72 172 272 372 472 572   Definition of retaliatory action by landlord.
(a) M/B: Restatement (Second) of Property § 14.8 (1977).
(b) Landlord and Tenant 134(5), 150(1), 200.5, 275

73 173 273 373 473 573   Validity of an agreement to make a lease.

EXERCISE 34.   RESTATEMENTS OF THE LAW   (CONTINUED)

(a) M/B: Restatement (Second) of Property § 2.5 (1977).
(b) Landlord and Tenant 22(1-5)

74 174 274 374 474 574   Rejection of lease by landlord's trustee in bankruptcy.
(a) M/B: Restatement (Second) of Property § 21.2 (1977).
(b) Bankruptcy 255
     Landlord and Tenant 101½

75 175 275 375 475 575   Restraints on alienation generally.
(a) M/B: Restatement (Second) of Property § 15.2 (1977).
(b) Landlord and Tenant 76
     Perpetuities 6(17)

76 176 276 376 476 576   Time factor for the restoration of property.
(a) M/B: Restatement (Second) of Property § 12.3 (1977).
(b) Landlord and Tenant 160

77 177 277 377 477 577   Rejection of a lease by the tenant's trustee in bankruptcy.
(a) M/B: Restatement (Second) of Property § 21.1 (1977).
(b) Bankruptcy 255
     Landlord and Tenant 101½

78 178 278 378 478 578   What constitutes a paramount title.
(a) M/B: Restatement (Second) of Property § 4.1 (1977).
(b) Landlord and Tenant 121 et seq.

79 179 279 379 479 579   Tenant's share of a condemnation award.
(a) M/B: Restatement (Second) of Property § 8.2 (1977).
(b) Eminent Domain 82, 95, 136, 148

80 180 280 380 480 580   Capacity and authority to enter into a landlord-tenant tenant relationship.
(a) M/B: Restatement (Second) of Property § 1.3 (1977).
(b) Landlord and Tenant 1

For problems 81-90, 181-190, 281-290, 381-390, 481-490, 581-590, the students are to use the Restatement (Second) of Contracts (1979). Using the index in Volume 3, the students are to find the section[s] (in Vols. 1-3) that answer[s] or govern[s] the question or subject listed with their problem number. (a) The students are to cite the section[s], and (b) using the Appendix to the 2nd Restatement (Vol. 6), they are to list the "Cross References" to "Digest System Key Numbers" (West) for the section[s]. They are specifically directed not to cite comments or illustrations for their answer.

81 181 281 381 481 581   Effect of the death of the offeree.
(a) M/B: Restatement (Second) of Contracts § 48 (1979).
(b) Contracts 20

82 182 282 382 482 582   Assignment of option contracts.
(a) M/B: Restatement (Second) of Contracts § 320 (1979).
(b) Assignments 18

83 183 283 383 483 583   Enforceability of promises that tortiously interfere with the performance of a contract.
(a) M/B: Restatement (Second) of Contracts § 194 (1979).
(b) Contracts 113(4)

84 184 284 384 484 584   What constitutes an interest in land for purposes of the Statute of Frauds.
(a) M/B: Restatement (Second) of Contracts § 126 (1979).
(b) Frauds, Statute of 116(5)

85 185 285 385 485 585   Rules governing bidding and acceptance of bids at auctions.

EXERCISE 34. RESTATEMENTS OF THE LAW   (CONTINUED)

(a) M/B: Restatement (Second) of Contracts § 28 (1979).
(b) Auctions and Auctioneers 7

86 186 286 386 486 586   Whether a liquidated damage provision in a contract prevents issuance of an injunction or an order requiring specific performance of a contract.
(a) M/B: Restatement (Second) of Contracts § 361 (1979).
(b) Injunctions 17, 57-63
     Specific Performance 58

87 187 287 387 487 587   Ancillary restraints on competition.
(a) M/B: Restatement (Second) of Contracts § 188 (1979).
(b) Contracts 115-118

88 188 288 388 488 588   Punitive damages for breach of contract.
(a) M/B: Restatement (Second) of Contracts § 355 (1979).
(b) Damages 89(2)

89 189 289 389 489 589   Revocation of divisible offers.
(a) M/B: Restatement (Second) of Contracts § 47 (1979).
(b) Contracts 19

90 190 290 390 490 590   Acceptance of an offer by silence.
(a) M/B: Restatement (Second) of Contracts § 69 (1979).
(b) Contracts 22(1)

For problems 91-100, 191-200, 291-300, 391-400, 491-500, 591-600, the students are to use the Restatement (Second) of Judgments (1980). Using the index in Volume 2, the students are required to find the section[s] (in Vol. 1 or 2) that answer[s] or govern[s] the question or subject listed with their problem number. (a) The students are to cite the section[s], and (b) using the Appendix (Vol. 3), they are to list the "Cross References" to "Digest System Key Numbers" (West) for the section[s]. They are specifically instructed not to cite illustrations or comments to the section.

91 191 291 391 491 591   Effective date of a final judgment for res judicata purposes.
(a) M/B: Restatement (Second) of Judgments § 14 (1980).
(b) Judgment 580, 663

92 192 292 392 492 592   Whether incapacity generally is a sufficient ground to avoid a judgment entered in a contested action.
(a) M/B: Restatement (Second) of Judgments § 72 (1980).
(b) Judgment 346

93 193 293 393 493 593   General rules governing relief from a judgment obtained by fraud or duress.
(a) M/B: Restatement (Second) of Judgments § 70 (1980).
(b) Judgment 372-376

94 194 294 394 494 594   Does irregularity in the content of the notice of an action render the notice inadequate if action notice of an action has been given?
(a) M/B: Restatement (Second) of Judgments § 3 (1980).
(b) Judgment 17(9)

95 195 295 395 495 595   Whether a subsequent action by a bailor is precluded by a prior action by the bailee against a third party for interference with ownership or destruction of the property that is the subject of the bailment?
(a) M/B: Restatement (Second) of Judgments § 52 (1980).
(b) Judgment 697

96 196 296 396 496 596   Rules governing arbitration awards.
(a) M/B: Restatement (Second) of Judgments § 84 (1980).
(b) Arbitration 75-82

EXERCISE 34. RESTATEMENTS OF THE LAW   (CONTINUED)

97 197 297 397 497 597   Effects of a criminal judgment in a subsequent civil action.
(a) M/B: Restatement (Second) of Judgments § 85 (1980).
(b) Judgment 559, 648

98 198 298 398 498 598   When a default judgment will be excused.
(a) M/B: Restatement (Second) of Judgments § 67 (1980).
(b) Judgment 140, 141, 143(1-18)

99 199 299 399 499 599   Relief from a judgment based on a mistake of law or fact.
(a) M/B: Restatement (Second) of Judgments § 71 (1980).
(b) Judgment 362-371

100 200 300 400 500 600   Standing to seek relief.
(a) M/B: Restatement (Second) of Judgments § 64 (1980).
(b) Judgment 382

LIBRARY EXERCISE 35. UNITED STATES CONSTITUTION.

INSTRUCTOR'S NOTE: This exercise requires the students to cite the federal constitutional provision that governs the subject matter listed with their problem number. They are specifically instructed to include the relevant clause (if appropriate). The students are also told that if the subject matter is governed by more than one provision, they may cite any one of them for their answer. The following Quick-Reference Abbreviations are relevant to this exercise:

    CONSTITUTION CITATION 1. CITE THE U.S. CONSTITUTION BY ARTICLE, SECTION, AND, IF APPROPRIATE, BY CLAUSE. ABBREVIATE "UNITED STATES" TO "U.S." AND "CONSTITUTION" TO "CONST." [CON 1]
    CONSTITUTION CITATION 2. CITE AMENDMENTS BY ROMAN NUMBER. ABBREVIATE "AMENDMENT" TO "AMEND." DO NOT CAPITALIZE "AMEND." [CON 2]
    CONSTITUTION CITATION 3. IN MEMORANDA AND BRIEFS, CITE CONSTITUTIONS IN ROMAN TYPE. IN LAW REVIEW FOOTNOTES, CITE THE NAME OF THE CONSTITUTIONS IN LARGE AND SMALL CAPITALS. [CON 3]

1 177 262 385 498 509 Right to bear arms
M/B: U.S. Const. amend. II.

2 178 263 386 499 510 Qualifications of senators
M/B: U.S. Const. art. I, § 3, cl. 3.

3 179 264 387 500 511 Quartering soldiers
M/B: U.S. Const. amend. III.

4 180 265 388 401 512 President of the Senate
M/B: U.S. Const. art. I, § 3, cl. 4, OR M/B: U.S. Const. amend XII.

5 181 266 389 402 513 Full Faith and Credit
M/B: U.S. Const. art. IV, § 1.

6 182 267 390 403 514 Unreasonable searches
M/B: U.S. Const. amend. IV.

7 183 268 391 404 515 Runaway slaves
M/B: U.S. Const. art. IV, § 2, cl. 3.

8 184 269 392 405 516 Cruel punishments
M/B: U.S. Const. amend. VIII.

9 185 270 393 406 517 Admission of new states
M/B: U.S. Const. art. IV, § 3, cl. 2.

10 186 271 394 407 518 Bail
M/B: U.S. Const. amend. VIII.

11 187 272 395 408 519 Privileges and immunities
M/B: U.S. Const. art. IV, § 2, cl. 1, or M/B: U.S. Const. amend. XIV, § 1.

12 188 273 396 409 520 Original jurisdiction of Supreme Court
M/B: U.S. Const. art. III, § 2, cl. 2.

13 189 274 397 410 521 Punishment of treason
M/B: U.S. Const. art. III, § 3, cl. 2.

14 190 275 398 411 522 Powers reserved to states
M/B: U.S. Const. amend. X.

15 191 276 399 412 523 Income tax
U.S Const. amend. XVI.

16 192 277 400 413 524 Women suffrage
M/B: U.S. Const. amend. XIX.

17 193 278 301 414 525 Power of Congress to tax
M/B: U.S. Const. art. I, § 8, cl. 1.

EXERCISE 35.   UNITED STATES CONSTITUTION   (CONTINUED)

18 194 279 302 415 526   Post Offices
M/B: U.S. Const. art. I, § 8, cl. 7.

19 195 280 303 416 527   Patents
M/B: U.S. Const. art. I, § 8, cl. 8.

20 196 281 304 417 528   Unreasonable seizures
M/B: U.S. Const. amend. IV.

21 197 282 305 418 529   Copyrights
M/B: U.S. Const. art. I, § 8, cl. 8.

22 198 283 306 419 530   Naturalization
M/B: U.S. Const. art. I, § 8, cl. 4.

23 199 284 307 420 531   Postal roads
M/B: U.S. Const. art. I, § 8, cl. 7.

24 200 285 308 421 532   Bankruptcy
M/B: U.S. Const. art. I, § 8, cl. 4.

25 101 286 309 422 533   Habeas corpus
M/B: U.S. Const. art. I, § 9, cl. 2.

26 102 287 310 423 534   Congress' power to borrow
M/B: U.S. Const. art. I, § 8, cl. 2.

27 103 288 311 424 535   Bill of attainder
M/B: U.S. Const. art. I, § 9, cl. 3.

28 104 289 312 425 536   Repeal of 18th Amendment
M/B: U.S. Const. amend. XXI.

29 105 290 313 426 537   Coinage
M/B: U.S. Const. art. I, § 8, cl. 5, or M/B: U.S. Const. art. I, § 10, cl. 1.

30 106 291 314 427 538   Ex post facto laws
M/B: U.S. Const. art. I, § 9, cl. 3, or M/B: U.S. Const. art. I, § 10, cl. 1.

31 107 292 315 428 539   Commander in Chief
M/B: U.S. Const. art. II, § 2, cl. 1.

32 108 293 316 429 540   Titles of nobility
M/B: U.S. Const. art. I, § 9, cl. 8.

33 109 294 317 430 541   Weights and measures
M/B: U.S. Const. art. I, § 8, cl. 5.

34 110 295 318 431 542   Suits against states - restriction
M/B: U.S. Const. amend. XI.

35 111 296 319 432 543   Slavery prohibited
M/B: U.S. Const. amend. XIII, or M/B: U.S. Const. amend. XIII, § 1.

36 112 297 320 433 544   Counterfeiting
M/B: U.S. Const. art. I, § 8, cl. 6.

37 113 298 321 434 545   Preference of ports
M/B: U.S. Const. art. I, § 9, cl. 6.

38 114 299 322 435 546   Amendment of the Constitution
M/B: U.S. Const. art. V.

39 115 300 323 436 547   Delivery of fugitives
M/B: U.S. Const. art. IV, § 2, cl. 2.

EXERCISE 35. UNITED STATES CONSTITUTION   (CONTINUED)

40 116 201 324 437 548 Just compensation for taking
M/B: U.S. Const. amend. V.

41 117 202 325 438 549 18-year-old voting
M/B: U.S. Const. amend. XXVI, or M/B: U.S. Const. amend. XXVI, § 1.

42 118 203 326 439 550 Provision for a Navy
M/B: U.S. Const. art. I, § 8, cl. 13.

43 119 204 327 440 551 Regulation of commerce with Indians
M/B: U.S. Const. art. I, § 8, cl. 3.

44 120 205 328 441 552 Letters of Marque and Reprisal
M/B: U.S. Const. art. I, § 8, cl. 11.

45 121 206 329 442 553 Presents from foreign states
M/B: U.S. Const. art. I, § 9, cl. 8.

46 122 207 330 443 554 Tax on exports from states
M/B: U.S. Const. art. I, § 9, cl. 5.

47 123 208 331 444 555 Establishment of religion
M/B: U.S. Const. amend. I.

48 124 209 332 445 556 Supremacy Clause
M/B: U.S. Const. art. VI, cl. 2.

49 125 210 333 446 557 Freedom of the press
M/B: U.S. Const. amend. I.

50 126 211 334 447 558 Pardons
M/B: U.S. Const. art. II, § 2, cl. 1.

51 127 212 335 448 559 Petitioning for redress
M/B: U.S. Const. amend I.

52 128 213 336 449 560 Legislative power vested in Congress
M/B: U.S. Const. art. I, § 1.

53 129 214 337 450 561 Right to assemble peaceably
M/B: U.S. Const. amend. I.

54 130 215 338 451 562 Freedom of speech
M/B: U.S. Const. amend. I.

55 131 216 339 452 563 Probable cause for warrants
M/B: U.S. Const. amend. IV.

56 132 217 340 453 564 Unusual punishments
M/B: U.S. Const. amend. VIII.

57 133 218 341 454 565 Trial by jury - $20
M/B: U.S. Const. amend VII.

58 134 219 342 455 566 Speedy and public trial
M/B: U.S. Const. amend. VI.

59 135 220 343 456 567 President - oath of office
M/B: U.S. Const. art. II, § 1. or M/B: U.S. Const. art. II. § 1, cl. 7 or 8.

60 136 221 344 457 568 Double jeopardy
M/B: U.S. Const. amend. V.

61 137 222 345 458 569 Excessive fines
M/B: U.S. Const. amend. VIII.

62 138 223 346 459 570 Confrontation of witnesses

EXERCISE 35.   UNITED STATES CONSTITUTION   (CONTINUED)

M/B: U.S. Const. amend. VI.

63 139 224 347 460 571   Equal protection of laws
M/B: U.S. Const. amend. XIV, § 1.

64 140 225 348 461 572   Involuntary servitude abolished
M/B: U.S. Const. amend. XIII. or M/B: U.S. Const. amend. XIII, § 1.

65 141 226 349 462 573   Free exercise of religion
M/B: U.S. Const. amend. I.

66 142 227 350 463 574   President's power to make treaties
M/B: U.S. Const. art. II, § 2, cl. 2.

67 143 228 341 464 575   Right to assistance of counsel
M/B: U.S. Const. amend. VI.

68 144 229 342 465 576   Commerce clause
M/B: U.S. Const. art. I, § 8, cl. 3.

69 145 230 343 466 577   President's duty to receive ambassadors
M/B: U.S. Const. art. II, § 3.

70 146 231 344 467 578   Right to assistance of counsel
M/B: U.S. Const. amend. V.

71 147 232 345 468 579   Commerce clause
M/B: U.S. Const. art. II, § 1, cl. 4 or 5.

72 148 233 346 469 580   President's duty to receive ambassadors
M/B: U.S. Const. art. I, § 10, cl. 3.

73 149 234 347 470 581   Witness against oneself
M/B: U.S. Const. art. II, § 1, cl. 1.

74 150 235 348 471 582   President - at least 35 years old
M/B: U.S. Const. art. II, § 3.

75 151 236 349 472 583   Nomination of ambassadors
M/B: U.S. Const. art. II, § 2, cl. 2.

76 152 237 350 473 584   Guarantee of republican form of government
M/B: U.S. Const. art. IV, § 4.

77 153 238 351 474 585   Debts of the Confederacy not to be paid
M/B: U.S. Const. amend. XIV, § 4.

78 154 239 352 475 586   Right to vote - race not to disqualify
M/B: U.S. Const. amend. XV. or M/B: U.S. Const. amend. XV, § 1.

79 155 240 353 476 587   Death of President (amendment)
M/B: U.S. Const. amend. XX, § 4.

80 156 241 354 477 588   Impartial jury in criminal trials
M/B: U.S. Const. amend. VI.

81 157 242 355 478 589   Representatives - at least 25 years old
M/B: U.S. Const. art. I, § 2, cl. 2.

82 158 243 356 479 590   House of Representatives sole power to impeach
M/B: U.S. Const. art. I, § 2, cl. 5.

83 159 244 357 480 591   Senators - at least 30 years old
M/B: U.S. Const. art. I, § 3, cl. 3.

84 160 245 368 481 592   Treason - two witnesses
M/B: U.S. Const. art. III, § 3, cl. 1.

EXERCISE 35.   UNITED STATES CONSTITUTION   (CONTINUED)

85 161 246 369 482 593   President's State of the Union address
M/B: U.S. Const. art. II, § 3.

86 162 247 370 483 594   States prohibited from laying tonnage duties
M/B: U.S. Const. art. I, § 10, cl. 3.

87 163 248 371 484 595   Revenue bills originate in the House of Representatives
M/B: U.S. Const. art. I, § 7, cl. 1.

88 164 249 372 485 596   Expulsion of a member from Congress
M/B: U.S. Const. art. I, § 5, cl. 2.

89 165 250 373 486 597   Senators - must be a citizen for 9 years
M/B: U.S. Const. art. I, § 3, cl. 3.

90 166 251 374 487 598   Representatives - must be a citizen for 7 years
M/B: U.S. Const. art. I, § 2, cl. 2.

91 167 252 375 488 599   Senate's sole power to try impeachments
M/B: U.S. Const. art. I, § 3, cl. 6.

92 168 253 376 489 600   Habeas corpus may be suspended during rebellions
M/B: U.S. Const. art. I, § 9, cl. 2.

93 169 254 377 490 501   Congress' power to make all "necessary and proper" laws
M/B: U.S. Const. art. I, § 8, cl. 18.

94 170 255 378 491 502   Two-thirds vote for impeachment
M/B: U.S. Const. art. I, § 3, cl. 6.

95 171 256 379 492 503   Congress' power to declare war
M/B: U.S. Const. art. I, § 8, cl. 11.

96 172 257 380 493 504   President limited to two terms
M/B: U.S. Const. amend. XXII. or M/B: U.S. Const. amend. XXII, § 1.

97 173 258 381 494 505   Poll tax prohibited as a qualification of electors
M/B: U.S. Const. amend. XXIV. or M/B: U.S. Const. amend. XXIV, § 1.

98 174 259 382 495 506   Voting shall not be denied on account of sex
M/B: U.S. Const. amend. XIX. or M/B: U.S. Const. amend. XIX, cl. 1.

99 175 260 383 496 507   Slavery prohibited
M/B: U.S. Const. amend. XIII. or M/B: U.S. Const. amend. XIII, § 1.

100 176 261 384 497 508   Debts prior to adoption of the Constitution valid
M/B: U.S. Const. art. VI. or M/B: U.S. Const. art. VI, cl. 1.

LIBRARY EXERCISE 36. UNITED STATES TREATIES & OTHER INTERNATIONAL AGREEMENTS.

INSTRUCTOR'S NOTE: For this exercise, the students are to cite the agreement that is printed at the volume and page of <u>United States Treaties and Other International Agreements</u> listed for their respective problem numbers. Reasonable variations in the shortened name of the treaty or agreement and the name of the country should be permitted. Some of the more likely variations have been noted. The following Quick-Reference Abbreviations are particularly relevant to this exercise:

    TREATY CITATION 1. ORDINARILY, CITE TREATIES AND OTHER INTERNATIONAL AGREEMENTS BY NAME, THE DATE OF SIGNING (UNLESS THE DATE OR YEAR IS INCLUDED IN THE NAME OF THE AGREEMENT), THE PARTIES, AND THE SOURCES IN WHICH IT CAN BE FOUND. [TREAT 1]
    TREATY CITATION 2. FOR THE CITED NAME, USE THE POPULAR NAME OF THE TREATY. OTHERWISE, USE A SHORTENED VERSION OF ITS NAME AND SUBJECT MATTER. USE ONLY THE FIRST FORM THAT APPEARS ON THE TITLE PAGE. [TREAT 2]
    TREATY CITATION 3. IF THE TREATY WAS SIGNED ON A SINGLE DATE, USE THAT DATE. WHEN IT WAS SIGNED BY THREE OR FEWER PARTIES ON DIFFERENT DATES, CITE THE FIRST AND LAST DATES OF SIGNING. TREATIES WITH MORE THAN THREE SIGNATORIES SHOULD BE CITED TO THE DATE ON WHICH THE TREATY WAS OPENED FOR SIGNATURE, APPROVED, OR ADOPTED. [TREAT 3]
    TREATY CITATION 4. INDICATE THE NAMES OR THE PARTIES WHEN THERE ARE LESS THAN FOUR. OTHERWISE, THE PARTIES' NAMES NEED NOT BE GIVEN. THE NAMES OF THE SIGNATORIES MAY BE SHORTENED. [TREAT 4]
    TREATY CITATION 5. TREATIES TO WHICH THE UNITED STATES IS A PARTY SHOULD BE CITED EITHER TO THE <u>STATUTES AT LARGE</u> (PRIOR TO 1950) OR U.S. TREATIES AND <u>INTERNATIONAL AGREEMENTS</u> (SINCE 1950) AND ONE STATE DEPARTMENT SOURCE. A PARALLEL CITATION TO AN INTERNATIONAL TREATY SERIES SHOULD BE ADDED WHEN THE UNITED STATES IS A PARTY TO A MULTILATERAL AGREEMENT. [TREAT 5]

1 112 225 345 470 502   1   760
M/B: Health and Sanitation Agreement, Sept. 15, 1950, United States-Ecuador, 1 U.S.T. 760, T.I.A.S. No. 2147.

2 113 226 346 471 503   2   13
M/B: Emergency Relief Assistance Agreement, Jan. 6, 1951, United States-Yugoslavia, 2 U.S.T. 13, T.I.A.S. No. 2174.

3 114 227 347 472 504   2   1554
M/B: Oil Shale Study Agreement, Aug. 16, 1950, United States-Brazil, 2 U.S.T. 1554, T.I.A.S. No. 2296.

4 115 228 348 473 505   3   379
M/B: Technical Cooperation Agreement, Feb. 26, 1951, United States-Israel, 3 U.S.T. 379, T.I.A.S. No. 2401.

5 116 229 349 474 506   28   437
M/B: Rural Education Agreement, Dec. 29, 1975, United States-Bolivia, 28 U.S.T. 437, T.I.A.S. No. 8475.

6 117 230 350 475 507   3   3767
M/B: Technical Cooperation Agreement, Feb. 2, 1952, United States-Pakistan, 3 U.S.T. 3767, T.I.A.S. No. 2506.

7 118 231 351 476 508   4   939
M/B: Cultural Relations Agreement, Apr. 9, 1953, United States-Federal Republic of Germany, 4 U.S.T. 939, T.I.A.S. No. 2798.
Note: "United States-West Germany" would also be correct.

8 119 232 352 477 509   30   757
M/B: Low-Income Family Housing Agreement, Mar. 4, 1977, United States-Portugal, 30 U.S.T. 757, T.I.A.S. No. 9218.

9 120 233 353 478 510   5   453
M/B: Military Assistance Agreement, Apr. 23, 1954, United States-Nicaragua, 5 U.S.T. 453, T.I.A.S. No. 2940.

10 121 234 354 479 511   5   2010

EXERCISE 36. UNITED STATES TREATIES & OTHER INT'L AGREEMENTS (CONTINUED)

M/B: Technical Cooperation Agreement, Sept. 1, 1954, United States-Guatemala, 5 U.S.T. 2010, T.I.A.S. No. 3068.

11 122 235 355 480 512   5   2143
M/B: Economic Aid Agreement, Oct. 11, 1952, United States-Yugoslavia, 5 U.S.T. 2143, T.I.A.S. No. 3075.

12 123 236 356 481 513   6   507
M/B: Surplus Agricultural Commodities Agreement, Jan. 18, 1955, United States-Pakistan, 6 U.S.T. 507, T.I.A.S. No. 3184.

13 124 237 357 482 514   6   2023
M/B: Surplus Agricultural Commodities Agreement, June 14, 1955, United States-Austria, 6 U.S.T. 2023, T.I.A.S. No. 3267.

14 125 238 358 483 515   6   2843
M/B: Tin Concentrates Agreement, Sept. 9, 1955, United States-Thailand, 6 U.S.T. 2843, T.I.A.S. No. 3327.

15 126 239 359 484 516   6   5715
M/B: Surplus Agricultural Commodities Agreement, Nov. 10, 1955, United States-Israel, 6 U.S.T. 5715, T.I.A.S. No. 3429.

16 127 240 360 485 517   7   161
M/B: Civil Uses of Atomic Energy Cooperation Agreement, Feb. 3, 1956, Untied States-Korea, 7 U.S.T. 161, T.I.A.S. No. 3490.

17 128 241 361 486 518   7   2234
M/B: Consular Officers Free Entry Privileges Agreement, May 21, 1956, United States-Yugoslavia, 7 U.S.T. 2234, T.I.A.S. No. 3622.

18 129 242 362 487 519   7   2383
M/B: Civil Uses of Atomic Energy Cooperation Agreement, June 13, 1956, United States-New Zealand, 7 U.S.T. 2383, T.I.A.S. No. 3626.

19 130 243 363 488 520   8   33
M/B: Imported Aircraft Airworthiness Certificates Agreement, Aug. 6-Dec. 14, 1956, United States-France, 8 U.S.T. 33, T.I.A.S. No. 3736.
Note: "Certificates of Airworthiness Agreement" is also correct.

20 131 244 364 489 521   8   2447
M/B: Uranium Reconnaissance Agreement, Dec. 26, 1957, United States-Brazil, 8 U.S.T. 2447, T.I.A.S. No. 3964.

21 132 245 365 490 522   9   131
M/B: Military Bases Agreement, Jan. 27, 1958, United States-Philippines, 9 U.S.T. 131, T.I.A.S. No. 3985.
Note: "Manila Air Station Agreement" would also be correct.

22 133 246 366 491 523   10   1
M/B: Air Transport Services Agreement, Jan. 14, 1959, United States-Japan, 10 U.S.T. 1, T.I.A.S. No. 4158.

23 134 247 367 492 524   10   2087
M/B: Reciprocal Trade Agreement, Dec. 30, 1959, United States-Switzerland, 10 U.S.T. 2087, T.I.A.S. No. 4379.

24 135 248 368 493 525   10   3014
M/B: Somaliland Technical Cooperation Agreement, Dec. 24, 1959, United States-Italy, 10 U.S.T. 3014, T.I.A.S. No. 4392.

25 136 249 369 494 526   29   4183
M/B: Defense Areas and Facilities Agreement, Dec. 14, 1977, United States-Antigua, 29 U.S.T. 4183, T.I.A.S. No. 9054.

26 137 250 370 495 527   11   1330

EXERCISE 36. UNITED STATES TREATIES & OTHER INT'L AGREEMENTS   (CONTINUED)

M/B: Tracking Stations Agreement, Apr. 12, 1960, United States-Mexico, 11 U.S.T. 1330, T.I.A.S. No. 4466.

27 138 251 371 496 528   29   2975
M/B: Rural Education Agreement, Aug. 30, 1977, United States-Bolivia, 29 U.S.T. 2975, T.I.A.S. No. 8994.

28 139 252 372 497 529   12   1390
M/B: Emergency Relief Assistance Agreement, Aug. 3, 1961, United States-Chile, 12 U.S.T. 1390, T.I.A.S. No. 4862.

29 140 253 373 498 530   12   3181
M/B: Peace Corps Program Agreement, Dec. 29, 1961, United States-Sierra Leone, 12 U.S.T. 3181, T.I.A.S. No. 4922.

30 141 254 374 499 531   27   2019
M/B: Criminal Matters Mutual Assistance Treaty, May 25, 1973, United States-Switzerland, 27 U.S.T. 2019, T.I.A.S. No. 8302.

31 142 255 375 500 532   13   1227
M/B: Peace Corps Program Agreement, May 23, 1962, United States-Ethiopia, 13 U.S.T. 1227, T.I.A.S. No. 5067.

32 143 256 376 401 533   13   2711
M/B: Investment Guaranties Agreement, Dec. 1, 1961, United States-Ivory Coast, 13 U.S.T. 2711, T.I.A.S. No. 5242.

33 144 257 377 402 534   14   251
M/B: Friendship, Establishment, and Navigation Treaty, Feb. 23, 1962, United States-Luxembourg, 14 U.S.T. 251, T.I.A.S. No. 5306.

34 145 258 378 403 535   14   1547
M/B: Investment Guaranties Agreement, Oct. 2, 1963, United States-Morocco, 14 U.S.T. 1547, T.I.A.S. No. 5456.

35 146 259 379 404 536   26   687
M/B: Consular Relations Convention, Apr. 15, 1974, United States-Bulgaria, 26 U.S.T. 687, T.I.A.S. No. 8067.

36 147 260 380 405 537   15   1982
M/B: Educational Exchange Agreement, Aug. 20, 1963, United States-Paraguay, 15 U.S.T. 1982, T.I.A.S. No. 5675.

37 148 261 381 406 538   29   501
M/B: Science and Technology Research Agreement, Mar. 29, 1977, United States-Egypt, 29 U.S.T. 501, T.I.A.S. No. 8830.

38 149 262 382 407 539   16   1183
M/B: Ascension Island Tracking Station Agreement, July 7, 1965, United States-United Kingdom, 16 U.S.T. 1183, T.I.A.S. No. 5864.
Note: "United Kingdom of Great Britain and Northern Ireland" is also correct.

39 150 263 383 408 540   17   570
M/B: Tracking stations Agreement, Apr. 14, 1966, United States-Spain, 17 U.S.T. 570, T.I.A.S. No. 6003.

40 151 264 384 409 541   17   1412
M/B: Oceanographic Research Agreement, Sept. 26, 1966, United States-Tunisia, 17 U.S.T. 1412, T.I.A.S. No. 6101.
Note: "Mediterranean Marine Sorting Center Agreement" is also correct.

41 152 265 385 410 542   18   384
M/B: Civic Action Military Assistance Program Agreement, Apr. 14, 1967, United States-Indonesia, 18 U.S.T. 384, T.I.A.S. No. 6247.

42 153 266 386 411 543   18   1257

EXERCISE 36. UNITED STATES TREATIES & OTHER INT'L AGREEMENTS   (CONTINUED)

M/B: Cotton Textiles Trade Agreement, June 30, 1967, United States-Turkey, 18 U.S.T. 1257, T.I.A.S. No. 6276.

43 154 267 387 412 544   18   2503
M/B: Cotton Textiles Trade Agreement, Sept. 29, 1967, United States-Portugal, 18 U.S.T. 2503, T.I.A.S. No. 6349.

44 155 268 388 413 545   19   4568
M/B: Geodetic Survey Agreement, Jan. 17, 1968, United States-Mali, 19 U.S.T. 4568, T.I.A.S. No. 6446.

45 156 269 389 414 546   19   5836
M/B: Tracking Station Agreement, July 9, 1968, United States-New Zealand, 19 U.S.t. 5836, T.I.A.S. No. 6539.
Note: "Baker-Nunn Camera Tracking Station Agreement" is also correct.

46 157 270 390 415 547   19   7809
M/B: Remote Sensing Earth Resources Agreement, Dec. 20, 1968, United States-Mexico, 19 U.S.T. 7809, T.I.A.S. No. 6613.
Note: "Remote Sensing Earth Survey Research Agreement" or "Earth Resources Agreement" would also be correct.

47 158 271 391 416 548   20   334
M/B: King Crab Fisheries Agreement, Jan. 31, 1969, United States-Union of Soviet Socialist Republics, 20 U.S.T. 334, T.I.A.S. No. 6635.
Note: "United States-Soviet Union" or "United States-U.S.S.R." would also be correct.

48 159 272 392 417 549   28   2167
M/B: Rural Cooperative System Agreement, Apr. 28, 1976, United States-Colombia, 28 U.S.T. 2167, T.I.A.S. No. 8538.

49 160 273 393 418 550   20   3017
M/B: Okinawa Tracking Station Agreement, Sept. 25, 1969, United States-Japan, 20 U.S.T. 3017, T.I.A.S. No. 6778.

50 161 274 394 419 551   21   403
M/B: Meat Imports Trade Agreement, Jan. 30, 1970, United States-Ireland, 21 U.S.T. 403, T.I.A.S. No. 6823.

51 162 275 395 420 552   28   8877
M/B: Rural Health Services Agreement, Sept. 30, 1976, United States-Egypt, 28 U.S.T. 8877, T.I.A.S. No. 8775.

52 163 276 396 421 553   21   2495
M/B: Weather Stations Agreement, Oct. 7, 1970, United States-Trinidad and Tobago, 21 U.S.T. 2495, T.I.A.S. No. 6991.

53 164 277 397 422 554   28   7259
M/B: Rural Access Roads Agreement, Sept. 20, 1976, United States-Bolivia, 28 U.S.T. 7259, T.I.A.S. No. 8714.

54 165 278 398 423 555   2   383
M/B: Technical Cooperation Agreement, Dec. 29, 1950, United States-Paraguay, 2 U.S.T. 383, T.I.A.S. No. 2176.

55 166 279 399 424 556   2   1599
M/B: Agriculture Agreement, July 30, 1951, United States-Panama, 2 U.S.T. 1599, T.I.A.S. No. 2302.
Note: "Agricultural Agreement" is also correct.

56 167 280 400 425 557   3   530
M/B: Aviation Agreement, Jan. 5, 1946, United States-Egypt, 3 U.S.T. 530, T.I.A.S. No. 2410.

57 168 281 301 426 558   3   2927

EXERCISE 36. UNITED STATES TREATIES & OTHER INT'L AGREEMENTS   (CONTINUED)

M/B: Passport Visa Requirements Agreement, Jan. 21, 1952, United States-Spain, 3 U.S.T. 2927, T.I.A.S. No. 2471.
Note: "Passport Visa Agreement" is also correct.

58 169 282 302 427 559   3   3942
M/B: Passport Visas Agreement, Mar. 31, 1952, United States-Monaco, 3 U.S.T. 3942, T.I.A.S. No. 2528.

59 170 283 303 428 560   4   116
M/B: Economic Cooperation Agreement, Jan. 13, 1953, United States-Italy, 4 U.S.t. 116, T.I.A.S. No. 2769.

60 171 284 304 429 561   4   1563
M/B: Technical Cooperation Program Agreement, Apr. 14, 1953, United States-Lebanon, 4 U.S.T. 1563, T.I.A.S. No. 2821.
Note: "Technical Cooperation Agreement" is also correct.

61 172 285 305 430 562   5   317
M/B: Technical Missions Agreement, Jan. 21, 1954, United States-Japan, 5 U.S.T. 317, T.I.A.S. No. 2923.

62 173 286 306 431 563   5   1387
M/B: Technical Cooperation Agreement, June 23, 1954, United States-Nicaragua, 5 U.S.T. 1387, T.I.A.S. No. 3008.
Note: "Agricultural Technical Cooperation Agreement" is also correct.

63 174 287 307 432 564   5   2263
M/B: Defense Use of Azores Facilities Agreement, Sept. 6, 1951, United States-Portugal, 5 U.s.T. 2263, T.I.A.S. No. 3087.
Note: "Azores Defense Facilities Agreement" is also correct.

64 175 288 308 433 565   28   5471
M/B: Educational Programs Agreement, Nov. 19, 1975, United States-Panama, 28 U.S.T. 5471, T.I.A.S. No. 8647.

65 176 289 309 434 566   6   2721
M/B: Atomic Energy Agreement, June 15, 1955, United States-United Kingdom, 6 U.S.T. 2721, T.I.A.S. No. 3322.

66 177 290 310 435 567   6   2897
M/B: Cooperative Health and Sanitation Program Agreement, Apr. 25, 1955, United States-Costa Rica, 6 U.S.T. 2897, T.I.A.S. No. 3332.

67 178 291 311 436 568   6   5739
M/B: Medium and Small Industry Technical Cooperation Agreement, Oct. 28, 1955, United States-Chile, 6 U.S.T. 5739, T.I.A.S. No. 3432.

68 179 292 312 437 569   28   3694
M/B: Technology Transfer and Manpower Development Agreement, Apr. 22, 1976, United States-Egypt, 28 U.S.T. 3694, T.I.A.S. No. 8595.

69 180 293 313 438 570   7   2047
M/B: Economic Development Agreement, June 23, 1956, United States-Afghanistan, 7 U.S.T. 2047, T.I.A.S. No. 3606.

70 181 294 314 439 571   7   3467
M/B: Special Economic Assistance Agreement, June 17, 1954, United States-Jordan, 7 U.S.T. 3467, T.I.A.S. No. 3723.

71 182 295 315 440 572   8   26
M/B: Surplus Agricultural Commodities Agreement, Jan. 7, 1957, Untied States-Republic of Korea, 8 U.S.T. 26, T.I.A.S. No. 3733.

72 183 296 316 441 573   8   2343
M/B: Education Commission Agreement, Nov. 5, 1957, United States-Brazil, 8 U.s.T. 2343, T.I.A.S. No. 3949.

EXERCISE 36.   UNITED STATES TREATIES & OTHER INT'L AGREEMENTS   (CONTINUED)

73 184 297 317 442 574   9   601
M/B: Publications Agreement, May 30, 1958, United States-Poland, 9 U.S.T. 601, T.I.A.S. No. 4040.

74 185 298 318 443 575   10   13
M/B: Surplus Agricultural Commodities Agreement, Nov. 24, 1958, United States-Turkey, 10 U.S.T. 13, T.I.A.S. No. 4161.

75 186 299 319 444 576   10   1237
M/B: Special Economic Assistance Agreement, June 23, 1959, United States-Iceland, 10 U.S.T. 1237, T.I.A.S. No. 4260.

76 187 300 320 445 577   25   3090
M/B: Agricultural Commodities Agreement, Nov. 23, 1974, United States-Pakistan, 25 U.S.T. 3090, T.I.A.S. No. 7971.

77 188 201 321 446 578   27   4039
M/B: Nutrition Development Agreement, Oct. 23, 1975, United States-Chile, 27 U.S.T. 4039, T.I.A.S. No. 8426.

78 189 202 322 447 579   11   1401
M/B: Turks and Caicos Islands Oceanographic Research Station Agreement, May 12, 1960, United States-United Kingdom, 11 U.S.T. 1401, T.I.A.S. No. 4478.

79 190 203 323 448 580   12   1127
M/B: Cultural Exchange Agreement, June 20, 1961, United States-Iran, 12 U.S.T. 1127 T.I.A.S. No. 4824.
Note: "Cultural Exchange Commission Agreement" is also correct.

80 191 204 324 449 581   12   1703
M/B: Amity and Economic Relations Treaty, Apr. 3, 1961, United States-Viet-Nam, 12 U.S.T. 1703, T.I.A.S. No. 4890.

81 192 205 325 450 582   12   3081
M/B: Cotton Textiles Agreement, Oct. 16, 1961, United States-Japan, 12 U.S.T. 3081, T.I.A.S. No. 4908.

82 193 206 326 451 583   13   97
M/B: Agricultural Commodities Agreement, Nov. 9, 1961, United States-Syrian Arab Republic, 13 U.S.T. 97, T.I.A.S. No. 4944.
Note: "United States-Syria" is also correct.

83 194 207 327 452 584   13   2452
M/B: Shellfish Sanitary Practices Agreement, Oct. 24, 1962, United States-Japan, 13 U.S.T. 2452, T.I.A.S. No. 5207.
Note: "Shellfish Sanitary Shipment Processing Agreement" is also correct.

84 195 208 328 453 585   27   2353
M/B: Agricultural Commodities Agreement, June 9, 1976, United States-Honduras, 27 U.S.T. 2353, T.I.A.S. No. 8313.

85 196 209 329 454 586   14   397
M/B: Investment Guaranties Agreement, Apr. 19, 1963, United States-Greece, 14 U.S.T. 397, T.I.A.S. No. 5331.

86 197 210 330 455 587   14   2222
M/B: Investment Guaranties Agreement, Dec. 30, 1963, United States-China, 14 U.S.T. 2222, T.I.A.S. No. 5509.

87 198 211 331 456 588   15   153
M/B: Tracking Stations Agreement, Jan. 29, 1964, United States-Spain, 15 U.S.T. 153, T.I.A.S. No. 5533.

88 199 212 332 457 589   15   1439
M/B: Cotton Textiles Trade Agreement, July 17, 1964, United States-Greece, 15 U.S.T. 1439, T.I.A.S. No. 5618.

EXERCISE 36.   UNITED STATES TREATIES & OTHER INT'L AGREEMENTS   (CONTINUED)

89 200 213 333 458 590   27   975
M/B: Technical Cooperation Agreement, Mar. 4, 1975, United States-Iran, 27 U.S.T. 975, T.I.A.s. No. 8235.

90 101 214 334 459 591   26   2905
M/B: Agricultural Commodities Agreement, Oct. 14, 1975, United States-Jordan, 26 U.S.T. 2905, T.I.A.S. No. 8197.

91 102 215 335 460 592   26   1674
M/B: Economic Cooperation Agreement, May 13, 1975, United States-Israel, 26 U.S.T. 1674, T.I.A.S. No. 8127.

92 103 216 336 461 593   17   2171
M/B: Cotton Textiles Trade Agreement, Nov. 21, 1966, United States-Pakistan, 17 U.S.T. 2171, T.I.A.S. No. 6153.

93 104 217 337 462 594   18   558
M/B: Cotton Textiles Trade Agreement, June 2, 1967, United States-Mexico, 18 U.S.T. 558, T.I.A.S. No. 6265.

94 105 218 338 463 595   18   1268
M/B: Scientific Cooperation Agreement, June 19, 1967, United States-Italy, 18 U.S.T. 1268, T.I.A.S. No. 6280.

95 106 219 339 464 596   18   2510
M/B: Investment Guaranties Agreement, Sept. 29, 1967, United States-Swaziland, 18 U.S.T. 2510, T.I.A.S. No. 6350.

96 107 220 340 465 597   19   5211
M/B: Investment Guaranties Agreement, June 27, 1968, United States-Grenada, 18 U.S.T. 5211, T.I.A.S. No. 6516.

97 108 221 341 466 598   19   5900
M/B: Scientific Cooperation Agreement, July 17, 1968, United States-Tunisia, 19 U.S.T. 5900, T.I.A.S. No. 6543.

98 109 222 342 467 599   23   3501
M/B: Extradition Treaty, Jan. 21, 1972, United States-Argentina, 23 U.S.T. 3501, T.I.A.S. No. 7510.

99 110 223 343 468 600   26   800
M/B: Technical Cooperation Agreement, Feb. 13, 1975, United States-Saudi Arabia, 26 U.S.T. 880, T.I.A.S. No. 8072.

100 111 224 344 469 501   20   2720
M/B: Space Cooperation Agreement, July 31, 1969, United States-Japan, 20 U.S.T. 2720, T.I.A.S. No. 6735.

LIBRARY EXERCISE 37. UNITED STATES STATUTES AT LARGE.

INSTRUCTOR'S NOTE: Using the identifying information given for their problem number, the students are required to find the statute in United States Statutes at Large. For their answer, they are to cite the statute to Statutes at Large. For purposes of this exercise, no reference should be made to the United States Code nor should the subsequent history of the statute (e.g., amendment, repeal, etc.) be given. The Memo/Brief and Law Review forms are the same for this exercise. The following two Quick-Reference Abbreviations are particularly relevant to this exercise:

FEDERAL STATUTORY CITATION 1. CITE STATUTES IN THE STATUTES AT LARGE BY NAME, PUBLIC LAW NUMBER OR, PRIOR TO THE 85TH CONGRESS, CHAPTER NUMBER, PAGE, AND YEAR OF ENACTMENT UNLESS IT IS INCLUDED IN THE NAME OF THE STATUTE. [FS 1]

FEDERAL STATUTORY CITATION 2. USE THE FULL DATE OF ENACTMENT TO CITE UNNAMED FEDERAL STATUTES IN THE STATUTES AT LARGE. [FS 2]

1 128 210 322 411 590   86 Stat. 117, Pub. L. No. 92-269
Act of Apr. 6, 1972, Pub. L. No. 92-269, 86 Stat. 117.

2 129 211 323 412 591   85 Stat. 391, Pub. L. No. 92-140
Act of Oct. 15, 1971, Pub. L. No. 92-140, 85 Stat. 391.

3 130 212 324 413 592   84 Stat. 1660, Pub. L. No. 91-600
Library Services and Construction Amendments of 1970, Pub. L. No. 91-600, 84 Stat. 1660.

4 131 213 325 414 593   84 Stat. 450, Pub. L. No. 91-351
Emergency Home Finance Act of 1970, Pub. L. No. 91-351, 84 Stat. 450.

5 132 214 326 415 594   90 Stat. 2407, Pub. L. No. 94-503
Crime Control Act of 1976, Pub. L. No. 90-503, 90 Stat. 2407.

6 133 215 327 416 595   82 Stat. 1345, Pub. L. No. 90-634
Renegotiation Amendments Act of 1968, Pub. L. No. 90-634, 82 Stat. 1345.

7 134 216 328 417 596   90 Stat. 529, Pub. L. No. 94-294
Beef Research and Information Act, Pub. L. No. 94-294, 90 Stat. 529 (1976).

8 135 217 329 418 597   80 Stat. 268, Pub. L. No. 89-495
Act of July 5, 1966, Pub. L. No. 89-495, 80 Stat. 268.

9 136 218 330 419 598   79 Stat. 653, Pub. L. No. 89-171
Foreign Assistance Act of 1965, Pub. L. No. 89-171, 79 Stat. 653.

10 137 219 331 420 599   78 Stat. 437, Pub. L. No. 88-428
Act of Aug. 14, 1964, Pub. L. No. 88-428, 78 Stat. 437.

11 138 220 332 421 600   77 Stat. 55, Pub. L. No. 88-38
Equal Pay Act of 1963, Pub. L. No. 88-38, 77 Stat. 56.

12 139 221 333 422 501   89 Stat. 679, Pub. L. No. 94-126
Act of Nov. 12, 1975, Pub. L. No. 94-126, 89 Stat. 679.

13 140 222 334 423 502   75 Stat. 146, Pub. L. No. 87-66
Old Series Currency Adjustment Act, Pub. L. No. 87-66, 75 Stat. 146 (1961).

14 141 223 335 424 503   74 Stat. 197, Pub. L. No. 86-503
Act of June 11, 1960, Pub. L. No. 86-503, 74 Stat. 197.

15 142 224 336 425 504   73 Stat. 470, Pub. L. No. 86-234
Act of Sept. 8, 1959, Pub. L. No. 86-234, 73 Stat. 470.

16 143 225 337 426 505   72 Stat. 89, Pub. L. No. 85-381
Act of Apr. 16, 1958, Pub. L. No. 85-381, 72 Stat. 89.

17 144 226 338 427 506   71 Stat. 441, Pub. L. No. 85-172
Poultry Products Inspection Act, Pub. L. No. 85-172, 71 Stat. 441 (1957).

EXERCISE 37.   UNITED STATES STATUTES AT LARGE   (CONTINUED)

18 145 227 339 428 507   72 Stat. 614, Pub. L. No. 85-660
Act of Aug. 14, 1958, Pub. L. No. 85-660, 72 Stat. 614.

19 146 228 340 429 508   69 Stat. 183, ch. 190
Act of June 28, 1955, ch. 190, 69 Stat. 183.

20 147 229 341 430 509   68 Stat. 177, ch. 269
District of Columbia Business Corporation Act, ch. 269, 68 Stat. 177 (1954).
Note: "Act of June 8, 1954, chp. 269, 68 Stat. 177" is also correct.

21 148 230 342 431 510   67 Stat. 581, ch. 485
Act of Aug. 14, 1953, ch. 485, 67 Stat. 581.

22 149 231 343 432 511   66 Stat. 163, ch. 477
Immigration & Nationality Act, ch. 477, 66 Stat. 163 (1952).

23 150 232 344 433 512   65 Stat. 175, ch. 298
Fur Products Labeling Act, ch. 198, 65 Stat. 175 (1951).

24 151 233 345 434 513   91 Stat. 445, Pub. L. No. 95-87
Surface Mining Control and Reclamation Act of 1977, Pub. L. No. 95-87, 91
Stat. 445.

25 152 234 346 435 514   63 Stat. 377, ch. 288
Federal Property and Administrative Services Act of 1949, ch. 288, 63 Stat.
377.

26 153 235 347 436 515   62 Stat. 286, ch. 373
Act of June 2, 1948, ch. 373, 62 Stat. 286.

27 154 236 348 437 516   61 Stat. 419, ch. 316
Act of July 24, 1947, ch. 316, 61 Stat. 419.

28 155 237 349 438 517   60 Stat. 427, ch. 540
Act of July 5, 1946, ch. 540, 60 Stat. 427.

29 156 238 350 439 518   59 Stat. 10, ch. 19
Act of Mar. 2, 1945, ch. 19, 59 Stat. 10.

30 157 239 351 440 519   88 Stat. 1978, Pub. L. No. 93-618
Trade Act of 1974, Pub. L. No. 93-618, 88 Stat. 1978.

31 158 240 352 441 520   58 Stat. 671, ch. 359
Act of July 1, 1944, ch. 359, 58 Stat. 671.

32 159 241 353 442 521   56 Stat. 351, ch. 404
Act of June 11, 1942, ch. 404, 56 Stat. 351.

33 160 242 354 443 522   55 Stat. 255, ch. 214
Act of June 21, 1941, ch. 214, 55 Stat. 255.

34 161 243 355 444 523   54 Stat. 897, ch. 721
Act of Sept. 16, 1940, ch. 721, 54 Stat. 897.

35 162 244 356 445 524   53 Stat. 812, ch. 191
Act of June 7, 1939, ch. 191, 53 Stat. 812.

36 163 245 357 446 525   52 Stat. 447, ch. 289
Revenue Act of 1938, ch. 289, 52 Stat. 447.

37 164 246 358 447 526   50 Stat. 487, ch. 472
Act of July 9, 1937, ch. 472, 50 Stat. 487.

38 165 247 359 448 527   51 Stat. 4, ch. 3
Act of Dec. 6, 1937, ch. 3, 51 Stat. 4.

EXERCISE 37. UNITED STATES STATUTES AT LARGE   (CONTINUED)

39 166 248 360 449 528
Act of Aug. 27, 1935, ch. 748, 49 Stat. 891.

49 Stat. 891, ch. 748

40 167 249 361 450 529
Act of Mar. 10, 1934, ch. 71, 48 Stat. 451.

48 Stat. 451, ch. 71

41 168 250 362 451 530
Act of June 30, 1932, ch. 324, 47 Stat. 448.

47 Stat. 448, ch. 324

42 169 251 363 452 531
Act of June 17, 1929, ch. 26, 46 Stat. 19.

46 Stat. 19, ch. 26

43 170 252 364 453 532
Act of Apr. 23, 1928, ch. 407, 45 Stat. 444.

45 Stat. 444, ch. 407

44 171 253 365 454 533
Act of Feb. 8, 1927, ch. 75, 44 Stat. 1059.

44 Stat. 1059, ch. 75

45 172 254 366 455 534
Act of Feb. 24, 1925, ch. 302, 43 Stat. 965.

43 Stat. 965, ch. 302

46 173 255 367 456 535
Act of Sept. 18, 1922, ch. 323, 42 Stat. 847.

42 Stat. 847, ch. 323

47 174 256 368 457 536
Act of June 4, 1920, ch. 227, 41 Stat. 759.

41 Stat. 759, ch. 227

48 175 257 369 458 537
Act of May 29, 1917, ch. 23, 40 Stat. 101.

40 Stat. 101, ch. 23

49 176 258 370 459 538
Act of Feb. 8, 1917, ch. 34, 39 Stat. 900.

39 Stat. 900, ch. 34

50 177 259 371 460 539
Act of June 4, 1914, ch. 103, 38 Stat. 384.

38 Stat. 384, ch. 103

51 178 260 372 461 540
Act of Apr. 9, 1912, ch. 75, 37 Stat. 81.

37 Stat. 81, ch. 75

52 179 261 373 462 541
Act of Feb. 13, 1911, ch. 43, 36 Stat. 898.

36 Stat. 898, ch. 43

53 180 262 374 463 542
Act of Mar. 10, 1908, ch. 76, 35 Stat. 40.

35 Stat. 40, ch. 76

54 181 263 375 464 543
Act of Mar. 19, 1906, ch. 957, 34 Stat. 70.

34 Stat. 70, ch. 957

55 182 264 376 465 544
Act of Apr. 28, 1904, ch. 1761, 33 Stat. 451.

33 Stat. 451, ch. 1761

56 183 265 377 466 545
Act of Jan. 30, 1903, ch. 338, 32 Stat. 786.

32 Stat. 786, ch. 338

57 184 266 378 467 546
Act of Feb. 1, 1900, ch. 7, 31 Stat. 3.

31 Stat. 3, ch. 7

58 185 267 379 468 547
Act of May 17, 1898, ch. 339, 30 Stat. 416.

30 Stat. 416, ch. 339

59 186 268 380 469 548
Act of Mar. 3, 1897, ch. 372, 29 Stat. 621.

29 Stat. 621, ch. 372

60 187 269 381 470 549
Act of Mar. 2, 1895, ch. 162, 28 Stat. 704.

28 Stat. 704, ch. 162

61 188 270 382 471 550

27 Stat. 557, ch. 202

EXERCISE 37.   UNITED STATES STATUTES AT LARGE   (CONTINUED)

Act of Mar. 3, 1893, ch. 202, 27 Stat. 557.

62 189 271 383 472 551   26 Stat. 209, ch. 647
Act of July 2, 1890, ch. 647, 26 Stat. 209.

63 190 272 384 473 552   25 Stat. 672, ch. 171
Act of Feb. 16, 1889, ch. 171, 25 Stat. 672.

64 191 273 385 474 553   24 Stat. 20, ch. 81
Act of May 3, 1886, ch. 81, 24 Stat. 20.

65 192 274 386 475 554   23 Stat. 34, ch. 63
Act of June 3, 1884, ch. 63, 23 Stat. 34.

66 193 275 387 476 555   22 Stat. 566, ch. 133
Act of Mar. 3, 1883, ch. 133, 22 Stat. 566.

67 194 276 388 477 556   21 Stat. 5, ch. 11
Act of June 2, 1879, ch. 11, 21 Stat. 5.

68 195 277 389 478 557   20 Stat. 87, ch. 146
Act of May 31, 1878, ch. 146, 20 Stat. 87.

69 196 278 390 479 558   19 Stat. 219, ch. 1
Act of Dec. 18, 1876, ch. 1, 19 Stat. 219.

70 197 279 391 480 559   18 Stat. 291, ch. 1
Act of Dec. 15, 1874, ch. 1, 18 Stat. 291.

71 198 280 392 481 560   90 Stat. 729, Pub. L. No. 94-329
International Security Assistance and Arms Export Control Act of 1976, Pub. L. No. 94-329, 90 Stat. 729.

72 199 281 393 482 561   16 Stat. 188, ch. 207 (CCVII)
Act of July 7, 1870, ch. 207, 16 Stat. 188.

73 200 282 394 483 562   15 Stat. 125, ch. 186 (CLXXXVI)
Act of July 20, 1868, ch. 186, 15 Stat. 125.

74 101 283 395 484 563   14 Stat. 3, ch. 8 (VIII)
Act of Feb. 10, 1866, ch. 8, 14 Stat. 125.

75 102 284 396 485 564   91 Stat. 685, Pub. L. No. 95-95
Clean Air Act Amendments of 1977, Pub. L. No. 95-95, 91 Stat. 685.

76 103 285 397 486 565   84 Stat. 794, Pub. L. No. 91-378
Act of Aug. 13, 1970, Pub. L. No. 91-378, 84 Stat. 794.

77 104 286 398 487 566   77 Stat. 473, Pub. L. No. 88-234
Act of Dec. 23, 1963, Pub. L. No. 88-234, 77 Stat. 473.

78 105 287 399 488 567   76 Stat. 556, Pub. L. No. 87-669
Act of Sept. 19, 1962, Pub. L. No. 87-669, 76 Stat. 556.

79 106 288 400 489 568   75 Stat. 401, Pub. L. No. 87-164
Act of Aug. 25, 1961, Pub. L. No. 87-164, 75 Stat. 401.

80 107 289 301 490 569   74 Stat. 397, Pub. L. No. 86-618
Color Additive Amendments of 1960, Pub. L. No. 86-618, 74 Stat. 397.

81 108 290 302 491 570   73 Stat. 420, Pub. L. No. 86-192
Act of Aug. 25, 1959, Pub. L. No. 86-192, 73 Stat. 420.

82 109 291 303 492 571   72 Stat. 957, Pub. L. No. 85-793
Act of Aug. 28, 1958, Pub. L. No. 85-793, 72 Stat. 957.

83 110 292 304 493 572   71 Stat. 607, Pub. L. No. 85-282

EXERCISE 37. UNITED STATES STATUTES AT LARGE   (CONTINUED)

Act of Sept. 4, 1957, Pub. L. No. 85-282, 71 Stat. 607.

84 111 293 305 494 573   71 Stat. 81, Pub. L. No. 85-53
Act of June 13, 1957, Pub. L. No. 85-53, 71 Stat. 81.

85 112 294 306 495 574   70 Stat. 411, ch. 476
War Orphans' Educational Assistance Act of 1956, ch. 476, 70 Stat. 411.

86 113 295 307 496 575   69 Stat. 264, ch. 279
Act of July 7, 1955, ch. 279, 69 Stat. 264.

87 114 296 308 497 576   68 Stat. 961, ch. 1074
Act of Aug. 30, 1954, ch. 1074, 68 Stat. 961.

88 115 297 309 498 577   66 Stat. 579, ch. 669
Act of July 11, 1952, ch. 669, 66 Stat. 579.

89 116 298 310 499 578   65 Stat. 189, ch. 303
Act of Aug. 14, 1951, ch. 303, 65 Stat. 189.

90 117 299 311 500 579   64 Stat. 773, ch. 906
Act of Sept. 7, 1950, ch. 906, 64 Stat. 773.

91 118 300 312 401 580   63 Stat. 621, ch. 486
Act of Aug. 19, 1949, ch. 486, 63 Stat. 621.

92 119 201 313 402 581   63 Stat. 157, ch. 176
Act of June 7, 1949, ch. 176, 63 Stat. 157.

93 120 202 314 403 582   64 Stat. 832, ch. 946
Budget and Accounting Procedures Act of 1950, ch. 946, 64 Stat. 832.

94 121 203 315 404 583   65 Stat. 131, ch. 275
Defense Production Act Amendments of 1951, ch. 275, 65 Stat. 131.

95 122 204 316 405 584   66 Stat. 634, ch. 755
Act of July 15, 1952, ch. 755, 66 Stat. 634.

96 123 205 317 406 585   68 Stat. 495, ch. 553
Act of July 20, 1954, ch. 553, 68 Stat. 495.

97 124 206 318 407 586   69 Stat. 533, ch. 572
Act of Aug. 5, 1955, ch. 572, 69 Stat. 533.

98 125 207 319 408 587   70 Stat. 668, ch. 742
Act of July 26, 1956, ch. 742, 70 Stat. 668.

99 126 208 320 409 588   71 Stat. 45, Pub. L. No. 85-45
Act of June 1, 1957, Pub. L. No. 85-45, 71 Stat. 45.

100 127 209 321 410 589   73 Stat. 61, Pub. L. No. 86-32
Act of May 26, 1959, Pub. L. No. 86-32, 73 Stat. 61.

EXERCISE 38.   UNITED STATES CODE ANNOTATED

INSTRUCTOR'S NOTE: For this exercise, the students are required to find the title and section cited with their problem in West's United States Code Annotated. They are to use the "Notes of Decisions" in the main part of the volume to (a) answer the question asked. They also must (b) cite the case on which their answer is based. They are specifically instructed not to include the subsequent history of the case in their citation. They are to find any needed additional information for their citation by consulting the case in the relevant reporter. They are also specifically instructed to cite U.S. Supreme Court actions to United States Reports only and not to abbreviate any words in the Memo/Brief form except as specifically provided in Rule 10.2.1(c). If a student provides a different answer or different case authority, check to see whether the relevant United States Code Annotated volume has been recently reissued with changes affecting the listed answer below.

1 191 207 387 454 514   Under 5 U.S.C. § 553, does a court decision holding that a Board of Parole's rules were invalid on the ground that they were adopted improperly have the effect of retroactively invalidating past Board determinatins upon the merits of particular parole cases?
Note 5. Retroactive effect of court determinations   Pickus v. U. S. Bd. of Parole, 1974, 507 F.2d 1107, 165 U.S.App.D.C. 284.
Richard Pickus et al., Appellees, v. United States Board of Parole, Appellant, United States Court of Appeals, District of Columbia Circuit   Oct. 11, 1974
(a) No.
(b) M/B: Pickus v. United States Board of Parole, 507 F.2d 1107 (D.C. Cir. 1974).
     LR: Pickus v. United States Bd. of Parole, 507 F.2d 1107 (D.C. Cir. 1974).

2 192 208 388 455 515   Under 5 U.S.C. § 705, is it an abuse of discretion for a district court to suspend a private antitrust action pending a determination by the Federal Communications Commission of the propriety of a defendant television network's acquisition of a station when the principal issue in the action is whether the acquisition would violate the antitrust laws and the same facts will be reviewed in the administrative proceeding?
Note 11. Communications   Chronicle Pub. Co. v. National Broadcasting Co., C.A. Cal. 1961, 294 F.2d 744.
Chronicle Publishing Co., Appellant, v. National Broadcasting Company, Inc., a corporation, et al., Appellees   United States Court of Appeals Ninth Circuit   July 25, 1961
(a) No.
(b) M/B: Chronicle Publishing Co. v. National Broadcasting Co., 294 F.2d 744 (9th Cir. 1961).
Note: NBC for National Broadcasting Co. is also correct.

3 193 209 389 456 516   Under 5 U.S.C. § 8332, is work with the Civil Works Administration and the Work Projects Administration during the Depression creditable toward retirement from civil service employment?
Note 4. Particular service as creditable   Adelstein v. Macy, D.C.N.Y.1967, 265 F.Supp. 171.
David Adelstein et al., Plaintiffs, v. John W. Macy, Jr., et al., Defendants   United States District Court E.D. New York   Jan. 25, 1967
(a) No.
(b) M/B: Adelstein v. Macy, 265 F. Supp. 171 (E.D.N.Y. 1967).

4 194 210 390 457 517   Under 7 U.S.C. § 1366, when a producer challenges a decision of a review committee upholding the action of a county committee, who has the burden of proof as to fact issues raised by the producer?
Note 22. Burden of proof   Jones v. Hughes, C.A.Ark.1968, 400 F.2d 585.
C. B. Jones, Fred W. Koch, and John H. Simpson, Marketing Quota Review Committee, United States Department of Agriculture, Agricultural Stabilization and Conservation Service, Appellants, v. Lawson Hughes, Appellee. United States Court of Appeals Eighth Circuit   Sept. 16, 1968
(a) The producer.
(b) M/B: Jones v. Hughes, 400 F.2d 585 (8th Cir. 1968).

5 195 211 391 458 518   Under 8 U.S.C. § 1182, were American Indians excluded by the immigration laws?

EXERCISE 38. UNITED STATES CODE ANNOTATED   (CONTINUED)

Note 22. Indians U. S. ex rel. Diabo v. McCandless, D.C.Pa.1927, 18 F.2d 282, affirmed 25 F.2d 71.
United States ex rel. Diabo v. McCandless (District Court, E. D. Pennsylvania. March 18, 1927.)
(a) No.
(b) M/B: <u>United States ex rel. Diablo v. McCandless</u>, 18 F.2d 282 (E.D. Pa. 1927).
    LR: United States <u>ex rel</u>. Diablo v. McCandless, 18 F.2d 282 (E.D. Pa. 1927).

6 196 212 392 459 519   Under 8 U.S.C. § 1284, is an alien seaman seeking shore leave from his vessel entitled to an administrative hearing on the determination that he is a mala fide seaman?
Note 31. Hearing U. S. ex rel. Wei Yan Mun v. Shaughnessy, D.C.N.Y.1950, 89 F.Supp. 743.
United States ex rel. Wei Yan Mun v. Shaughnessy et al. United States District Court S. D. New York April 4, 1950
(a) No.
(b) M/B: <u>United States ex rel. Wei Yan Mun v. Shaughnessy</u>, 89 F. Supp. 743 (S.D.N.Y. 1950).
    LR: United States <u>ex rel</u>. Wei Yan Mun v. Shaughnessy, 89 F. Supp. 743 (S.D.N.Y. 1950).

7 197 213 393 460 520   Under 8 U.S.C. § 1445, is an alien wife of a citizen of the United States required to make a declaration of intention to become a citizen in connection with her application for citizenship?
Note 136. Wife of citizen U. S. v. Shapiro, D.C.Cal.1942, 43 F.Supp. 927.
United States v. Shapiro District Court, S. D. California, Central Division March 30, 1942
(a) No.
(b) M/B: <u>United States v. Shapiro</u>, 43 F. Supp. 927 (S.D. Cal. 1942).

8 198 214 394 461 521   Under 10 U.S.C. § 802, can a person accused of a public offense select the tribunal by which he is tried when he is subject to concurrent jurisdiction of military and civil courts?
Note 58. Concurrent jurisdiction of military and civil courts Ex parte Sumner, 1942, 158 S.W.2d 310, 143 Tex.Cr.R. 238.
Ex parte Sumner, Court of Criminal Appeals of Texas Jan. 28, 1942
(a) No.
(b) M/B: <u>Ex parte Sumner</u>, 143 Tex. Crim. 238, 158 S.W.2d 310 (1942).
    LR: <u>Ex parte</u> Sumner, 143 Tex. Crim. 238, 158 S.W.2d 310 (1942).

9 199 215 395 462 522   Under 10 U.S.C. § 1552, are military officers entitled to back pay when their original discharge is illegal?
Note 23. Illegal discharges Hamlin v. U. S., 1968, 391 F.2d 941, 183 Ct.Cl. 137.
James L. Hamlin v. The United States United States Court of Claims March 15, 1968
(a) Yes.
(b) M/B: <u>Hamlin v. United States</u>, 391 F.2d 941 (Ct. Cl. 1968).

10 200 216 396 463 523   Under 12 U.S.C. § 86, which establishes a penalty for charging usurious interest, is it a valid defense to the action if it is shown that the defendant sold and assigned the note before maturity in good faith and that it was acting merely as the assignee's agent in collecting it?
Note 113. Defenses First Nat. Bank v. Miltonberger, 1382, 51 N.W. 232, 33 Neb. 847.
First Nat. Bank of North Bend v. Miltonberger (Supreme court of nebraska Jan. 27, 1892.)
(a) No.
(b) M/B: <u>First National Bank v. Miltonberger</u>, 33 Neb. 847, 51 N.W. 232 (1892).
    LR: First Nat'l Bank v. Miltonberger, 33 Neb. 847, 51 N.W. 232 (1892).

11 101 217 397 464 524   Under 12 U.S.C. § 1713, is it within the province of the district court to decide whether a moratorium on a FHA mortgage is in the best interests of the government which is seeking to foreclose the mortgage?

EXERCISE 38.   UNITED STATES CODE ANNOTATED   (CONTINUED)

Note 8. Moratorium   U. S. v. Sylacauga Properties, Inc., C.A. Ala.1963, 323 F.2d 487.
United States of America, Appellant, v. Sylacauga Properties, Inc., Appellee   United States Court of Appeals Fifth Circuit   Oct. 1, 1963
(a)   No.
(b)   M/B: <u>United States v. Sylacauga Properties, Inc.</u>, 323 F.2d 487 (5th Cir. 1963).
Note: Inc. may be omitted from the citation.

12 102 218 398 465 525   Under 15 U.S.C. § 1, does the fact that the defendant unethically enticed away plaintiff's employees and sought to oppress its own employees whom it presumed had bought stock in its business rival, the plaintiff, in and of itself constitute a violation [of Section 1 of the Sherman Act]?
Note 336. Unethical practices   American Banana Co. v. United Fruit Co., C.C.N.Y.1908, 160 F. 184, affirmed 166 F. 261, 92 C.C.A. 325, affirmed 29 S.Ct. 511, 213 U.S. 347, 53 L.Ed. 826, 16 Ann.Cas. 1047.
American Banana Co. v. United Fruit Co. (Circuit Court, S. D. New York   March 4, 1908.)
(a)   No.
(b)   M/B: <u>American Banana Co. v. United Fruit Co.</u>, 160 F. 184 (C.C.S.D.N.Y. 1908).

13 103 219 399 466 526   Under 15 U.S.C. § 2, will a court sanction as lawful block buying under a motion picture license agreement when the pictures were separately priced and each picture was to be sold to the highest duly qualified bidder on a theatre by theatre basis without other conditions?
Note 110. Block buying   U. S. v. Paramount Pictures, D.C.N.Y.1946, 66 F.Supp. 323, affirmed in part and reversed in part on other grounds 68 S.Ct. 915, 334 U.S. 131, 92 L.Ed. 1260.
United States v. Paramount Pictures, Inc., et al.   District Court, S. D. New York   June 11, 1946
(a)   Yes.
(b)   M/B: <u>United States v. Paramount Pictures, Inc.</u>, 66 F. Supp. 323 (S.D.N.Y. 1946).
Note: Inc. may be omitted from the citation.

14 104 220 400 467 527   Under 15 U.S.C. § 13, are retail price fluctuations changing market conditions within the meaning of subsection (c) of Section 13?
Note 61. Changing market conditions   Bargain Car Wash, Inc. v. Standard Oil Co. (Ind.) C.A.Ill.1972, 466 F.2d 1163.
Bargain Car Wash, Inc., an Illinois corporation, Plaintiff-Appellant, v. Standard Oil Company (Indiana), an Indiana corporation, and the American Oil Company, a Maryland corporation, Defendants-Appellees   United States Court of Appels, Seventh Circuit   Aug. 17, 1972
(a)   No.
(b)   M/B: <u>Bargain Car Wash, Inc. v. Standard Oil Co.</u>, 466 F.2d 1163 (7th Cir. 1972).
Note: Inc. may be omitted from the citation.

15 105 221 301 468 528   Under 15 U.S.c. § 15, is it proper for a Court of Appeals to review the excessiveness or inadequacy of a damage verdict in an antitrust case?
Note 556. Damages   National Wrestling Alliance v. Myers, C.A.Iowa 1963, 325 F.2d 768.
National Wrestling Alliance, Appellant, v. Harold C. Myers, Appellee   United States Court of Appeals Eighth Circuit   Dec. 19, 1963
(a)   No.
(b)   M/B: <u>National Wrestling Alliance v. Myers</u>, 325 F.2d 768 (8th Cir. 1963).

16 106 222 302 469 529   Under 15 U.S.C. § 45, can a court properly review an advisory opinion of the Federal Trade Commission when the same course of action which was the subject of the advisory opinion is also the subject of a cease and desist order issued by the Commission?
Note 350. Advisory opinions   Floersheim v. Weinburger, D.C.D.C.1972, 346 F.Supp. 950.

EXERCISE 38. UNITED STATES CODE ANNOTATED   (CONTINUED)

Sydney N. Floersheim, an individual trading and doing business as Floersheim Sales Company, Plaintiff, v. Caspar N. Weinburger, et al., Defendants United States District Court, District of Columbia Feb. 29, 1972
(a) No.
(b) M/B: Floersheim v. Weinburger, 346 F. Supp. 950 (D.D.C. 1972).

17 107 223 303 470 530   Under 15 U.S.C. § 22, are venue and personal jurisdiction virtually congruent?
Note 125. Jurisdictions Pacific Tobacco Corp. v. American Tobacco Co., D.C.Or.1972, 338 F.Supp. 842.
Pacific Tobacco Corp., an Oregon corporation dba Pacific Tobacco Company, Plaintiff, v. The American Tobacco Company, Inc., a Delaware corporation, American Brands, Inc., a New Jersey corporation, et al., Defendants United States District Court, D. Oregon Jan. 27, 1972
(a) Yes.
(b) M/B: Pacific Tobacco Corp. v. American Tobacco Co., 338 F. Supp. 842 (D. Or. 1972).

18 108 224 304 471 531   Under 15 U.S.C. § 77q, is it a violation of the securities fraud provisions for a corporation to lend its credit to another corporation to enable that corporation to make purhcases of stock?
Note 24. Loans Securities and Exchange Commission v. Fifth Ave. Coach Lines, Inc., D.C.N.Y.1968, 289 F.Supp. 3.
Securities and Exchange Commission, Plaintiff, v. Fifth Avenue Coach Lines, Inc., Victor Muscat, Edward Krock, Thomas A. Bolan, Roy M. Cohn, Defendants United States District Court S. D. New York July 26, 1968
(a) No.
(b) M/B: SEC v. Fifth Avenue Coach Lines, 289 F. Supp. 3 (S.D.N.Y. 1968).
     LR: SEC v. Fifth Ave. Coach Lines, 289 F. Supp. 3 (S.D.N.Y. 1968).

19 109 225 305 472 532   Under 15 U.S.C. § 78j, does a showing of plaintiff's contributory negligence justify dismissal of a complaint when the complaint is based on fraud rather than negligence?
Note 64. Negligence Carroll v. First Nat. Bank of Lincolnwood, C.A.Ill.1969, 413 F.2d 353, certiorari denied 90 S.Ct. 552, 396 U.S. 1003, 24 L.Ed.2d 494.
Carroll et al., Plaintiffs-Appellants, v. First National Bank of Lincolnwood, Defendant-Appellee United States Court of Appeals Seventh Circuit June 27, 1969
(a) No.
(b) M/B: Carroll v. First National Bank, 413 F.2d 353 (7th Cir. 1969).
     LR: Carroll v. First Nat'l Bank, 413 F.2d 353 (7th Cir. 1969).

20 110 226 306 473 533   Under 15 U.S.C. § 78p, should the "first in, first out rule" be applied to short-swing speculation in corporate securities?
Note 94. First in, first out, rule Smolowe v. Delendo Corporation, C.C.A.N.Y.1943, 136 F.2d 231, 148 A.L.R. 300, certiorari denied 64 S.Ct. 56, 320 U.S. 751, 88 L.Ed. 446.
Smolowe et al. v. Delendo Corporation et al. Circuit Court of Appeals, Second Circuit June 8, 1943
(a) No.
(b) M/B: Smolowe v. Delendo Corp., 136 F.2d 231 (2d Cir. 1943).

21 111 227 307 474 534   Under 15 U.S.C. § 79k, must a reorganization plan have a provision providing a means of bringing about a fair and equitable distribution of voting power?
Note 129. Necessity for provision In re Interstate Power Co., D.C.Del.1947, 71 F.Supp. 164.
In re Interstate Power Co. et al. District Court, D. Delaware April 10, 1947
(a) Yes.
(b) M/B: In re Interstate Power Co., 71 F. Supp. 164 (D. Del. 1947).
     LR: In re Interstate Power Co., 71 F. Supp. 164 (D. Del. 1947).

22 112 228 308 475 535   Under 15 U.S.C. § 714b, does the Commodity Credit Corporation have the power to subject its property to a warehouseman's lien for storage?
Note 6. Lien, property subject to U. S. v. Edgerton & Sons, C.A.Conn.1949, 178 F.2d 763.

EXERCISE 38. UNITED STATES CODE ANNOTATED   (CONTINUED)

United States v. Edgerton & Sons, Inc. United States Court of Appeals Second Circuit Dec. 18, 1949
(a) Yes.
(b) M/B: United States v. Edgerton & Sons, 178 F.2d 763 (2d Cir. 1949).

23 113 229 309 476 536   Under 15 U.S.C. § 1052, is "Travelers' insurance" a generic term?
Note 154. Travelers' Insurance Travelers Ins. Mach. Co. v. Travelers' Ins. Co. of Hartford, Conn., 1911, 134 S.W. 877, 142 Ky. 523, modified on other grounds 136 S.W. 154, 143 Ky. 216.
Travelers' Ins. Mach. Co. v. Travelers' Ins. Co. of Hartford, Conn. (Court of Appeals of Kentucky Feb. 14, 1911)
(a) Yes.
(b) M/B: Travelers' Insurance Machine Co. v. Traveler's Insurance Co., 142 Ky. 523, 134 S.W. 877 (1911).
    LR: Travelers' Ins. Mach. Co. v. Traveler's Ins. Co., 142 Ky. 523, 134 S.W. 877 (1911).

24 114 230 310 477 537   Under 15 U.S.C. § 1114, is the name, "Telicon," a colorable imitation of the name, "Telechron," for trademark infringement purposes?
Note 69. Imitation Telechron, Inc. v. Telicon Corp., C.A.Del.1952, 198 F.2d 903.
Telechron, Inc. v. Telicon Corp. United States Court of Appeals Third Circuit Sept. 9, 1952
(a) Yes.
(b) M/B: Telechron, Inc. v. Telicon Corp., 198 F.2d 903 (3d Cir. 1952).

25 115 231 311 478 538   Is § 1125 of Title 15 of the United States Code intended to prevent the mere act of copying another's label?
Note 75. Copying another's label Bogene Inc. v. Whit-Mor Mfg. Co., D.C.N.Y.1966, 253 F.Supp. 126.
Bogene Inc., Plaintiff, v. Whit-Mor Manufacturing Co. Inc., Defendant United States District Court S. D. New York March 15, 1966
(a) No.
(b) M/B: Bogene Inc. v. Whit-Mor Manufacturing Co., 253 F. Supp. 126 (S.D.N.Y. 1966).
    LR: Bogene Inc. v. Whit-Mor Mfg. Co., 253 F. Supp. 126 (S.D.N.Y. 1966).

26 116 232 312 479 539   Under 16 U.S.C. § 803, what is the primary purpose of subsection (d) of this section (which requires the licensee to establish an amortization reserve account to reflect excess earnings of a hydroelectric project)?
Note 7. Amortization reserves Alabama Power Co. v. Federal Power Commission, C.A.Ala.1973, 482 F.2d 1208.
Alabama Power Company, Petitioner, v. Federal Power Commission, Respondent United States Court of Appeals, Fifth Circuit July 31, 1973
(a) To prevent a licensee from distributing "excess" profits to its shareholders and to require such excess profits to be set aside in an amortization reserve account to be used in event the government recaptures the project.
(b) M/B: Alabama Power Co. v. FPC, 482 F.2d 1208 (5th Cir. 1973).

27 117 233 313 480 540   Under 17 U.S.C. § 106, can owners of a number of copyrighted works combine their copyrights through an agreement which would otherwise violate the antitrust laws in order to preserve their property rights under this section?
Note 23. Antitrust violations Alden-Rochelle, Inc., v. American Society of Composers, Authors and Publishers, D.C.N.Y.1948, 80 F.Supp. 888.
Alden-Rochelle, Inc., et al. v. American Soc. of Composers, Authors and Publishers et al. United States District Court S. D. New York July 19, 1948
(a) No.
(b) M/B: Alden-Rochelle, Inc. v. American Society of Composers, Authors, & Publishers, 80 F. Supp. 888 (S.D.N.Y. 1948).
    LR: Alden-Rochelle, Inc. v. American Soc'y of Composers, Authors, & Publishers, 80 F. Supp. 888 (S.D.N.Y. 1948).
Note: "American Society of Composers" or "ASCAP" are also correct.

EXERCISE 38. UNITED STATES CODE ANNOTATED   (CONTINUED)

28 118 234 314 481 541   Under 17 U.S.C. § 107, is the use of citations copied from a previously copyrighted work in support of a new text on the same subject a "fair use" under the copyright laws when the new text is in no part copied from the earlier work and is supplemented with other citations?
Note 18. Use of citations to support own work   Edward Thompson Co. v. American Law Book Co., N.Y. 1903, 122 F. 922, 59 C.C.A. 148, 62 L.R.A. 607.
Edward Thompson Co. v. American Law Book Co. (Circuit Court of Appeals, Second Circuit   July 1, 1903.)
(a)   Yes.
(b)   M/B: Edward Thompson Co. v. American Law Book Co., 122 F. 922 (2d Cir. 1903).

29 119 235 315 482 542   Under 18 U.S.C. § 113, is a person a principal for purposes of this section if he is present and encourages the assault and battery?
Note 9. Principals   U. S. v. Ricketts, C.C.Dist.Col.1804, Fed. Cas.No.16,158.
United States v. Ricketts   Circuit Court, District of Columbia   June Term, 1804
(a)   Yes.
(b)   M/B: United States v. Ricketts, 27 F. Cas. 806 (C.C.D.C. 1804) (No. 16,159).

30 120 236 316 483 543   Under 18 U.S.C. § 203, must the prosecution prove a specific criminal intent, in terms of a conscious purpose of wrongdoing or evil motive?
Note 6. Knowledge and intent   U. S. v. Quinn, D.C.N.Y.1956, 141 F.Supp. 622.
United States of America v. T. Vincent Quinn, Martin Schwaeber and James D. Saver.   United States District Court S. D. New York   April 25, 1956
(a)   No.
(b)   M/B: United States v. Quinn, 141 F. Supp. 622 (S.D.N.Y. 1956).

31 121 237 317 484 544   Under 18 U.S.C. § 371, in order to sustain a conviction for violation of the conspiracy and white slavery statute, is it necessary that the victim of the transportation be innocent of prior sexual misconduct?
Note 435.   ____   Wright v. U. S., C.A.Ga.1957, 243 F.2d 569, certiorari denied 78 S.Ct. 45, 355 U.S. 831, 2 L.Ed.2d 43.
Geneva Carolyn Anthony Wright, Appellant, v. United States of America, Appellee   United States Court of Appeals Fifth Circuit   April 22, 1957
(a)   No.
(b)   M/B: Wright v. United States, 243 F.2d 569 (5th Cir. 1957).

32 122 238 318 485 545   Under 18 U.S.C. § 474, would a trial court be abusing its discretion in a counterfeiting prosecution if it refused to grant a mistrial when the prosecutor referred to the defendant's arrest for counterfeiting title certificates and driver's licenses in his opening statement?
Note 24. Mistrial   Koran v. U. S., C.A.Fla.1969, 408 F.2d 1321, certiorari denied 91 S.Ct. 1603, 402 U.S. 948, 29 L.Ed.2d 118.
Mortimer Norman Koran, Appellant, v. United States of America, Appellee
United States Court of Appeals Fifth Circuit   Jan. 27, 1969
(a)   No.
(b)   M/B: Koran v. United States, 408 F.2d 1321 (5th Cir. 1969).

33 123 239 319 486 546   Under 18 U.S.C. § 494, is the forgery of a note for the purpose of deceiving a national bank examiner a violation of this section?
Note 12. Notes   Cross v. North Carolina, N.C.1889, 10 S.Ct. 47, 132 U.S. 131, 33 L.Ed. 287.
Cross v. North Carolina   Error to the Supreme Court of the State of North Carolina   November 11, 1889
(a)   No.
(b)   M/B: Cross v. North Carolina, 132 U.S. 131 (1889).

34 124 240 320 487 547   Under 18 U.S.C. § 1001, does the entry of a plea of nolo contendre to a charge of receiving money from a federal savings and loan association with the intent to defraud justify disbarment of an attorney?

EXERCISE 38. UNITED STATES CODE ANNOTATED   (CONTINUED)

Note 189. Disbarment Bar Ass'n of Baltimore City v. Snyder, 1975, 331 A.2d 47, 274 Md. 534.
The Bar Association of Baltimore City v. Alvin I. Snyder Court of Appeals of Maryland Feb. 3, 1975
(a) Yes.
(b) M/B: Bar Association v. Snyder, 274 Md. 534, 331 A.2d 47 (1975).
     LR: Bar Ass'n v. Snyder, 274 Md. 534, 331 A.2d 47 (1975).

35 125 241 321 488 548   Under 18 U.S.C. § 1005, is the offense of making false entries in bank officer's reports separate and distinct from the offense of making earlier false entries in the books of the bank for purposes of the (statute of) limitations period?
Note 124. Limitations Hargreaves v. U.S., C.C.A.Cal.1935, 75 F.2d 68.
Hargreaves v. United States Circuit Court of Appeals, Ninth Circuit Jan. 21, 1935
(a) Yes.
(b) M/B: Hargreaves v. United States, 75 F.2d 68 (9th Cir. 1935).

36 126 242 322 489 549   Under 18 U.S.C. § 1341, does the fact that the defendants proceeded in good faith under the advice of a lawyer constitute an impregnable wall of defense against a charge of mail fraud?
Note 146. Good faith Linden v. U. S., C.A.Md. 1958, 254 F.2d 560.
Jerome D. Linden, Robert R. Baylis, Classified Business Director, Inc., and Directory Listings, Inc., Appellants, v. United States of America, Appellee United States Court of Appeals Fourth Circuit April 9, 1958
(a) No.
(b) M/B: Linden v. United States, 254 F.2d 560 (4th Cir. 1958).

37 127 243 323 490 550   Under 18 U.S.C. § 1461, is a defendant entitled to an acquittal in a prosecution for mailing obscene matter when he does not know that the matter might be characterized as obscene?
Note 176. Acquittal Rosen v. U. S. N.Y.1896, 16 S.Ct. 434, 161 U.S. 29, 40 L.Ed. 606.
Rosen v. United States Error to the Circuit of the United States for the Southern District of New York January 27, 1896
(a) No.
(b) M/B: Rosen v. United States, 161 U.S. 29 (1896).

38 128 244 324 491 551   Under 18 U.S.C. § 1709, is the issue of whether disclosure of stolen mail by a postal employee was voluntary or forcible a question to be decided by the court or for the jury?
Note 32. Questions for the court U. S. v. Abeln, C.A.Ky.1965, 353 F.2d 91.
United States of America, Plaintiff-Appellee, v. Melvin J. Abeln, Defendant-Appellant United States Court of Appeals Sixth Circuit Nov. 12, 1965
(a) Question for the court.
(b) M/B: United States v. Abeln, 353 F.2d 91 (6th Cir. 1965).

39 129 245 325 492 552   Under 18 U.S.C. § 2113, would evidence showing that the defendant was arrested near the scene of the burglary at 4 a.m. and was wearing clothing containing particles of debris similar to that in the bank that had been burglarized be sufficient to sustain a conviction of aiding and abetting a burglary of a bank?
Note 178. Clothing Davis v. U. S., C.A.Miss.1969, 409 F.2d 1095.
Clifford H. Davis, Appellant, v. United States of America, Appellee United States Court of Appeals Fifth Circuit April 14, 1969
(a) Yes.
(b) M/B: Davis v. United States, 409 F.2d 1095 (5th Cir. 1969).

40 130 246 326 493 553   Under 18 U.S.C. § 2312, will a court of appeals order that a transcript of a closing argument be furnished at government expense when the defendant asserts possible error based upon an alleged prejudicial comment by the prosecutor in that argument?
Note 214. Transcript U. S. v. McElrath, C.A.Tenn.1967, 377 F.2d 508.
United States of America, Plaintiff-Appellee, v. John Drew McElrath, Defendant-Appellant United States Court of Appeals Sixth Circuit May 19, 1967

EXERCISE 38. UNITED STATES CODE ANNOTATED   (CONTINUED)

(a) Yes.
(b) M/B: United States v. McElrath, 377 F.2d 508 (6th Cir. 1967).

41 131 247 327 494 554   Under 18 U.S.C. § 2388, formerly section 33 of Title 50, can a person be criminally prosecuted and convicted for his failure to subscribe for liberty bonds?
Note 46. Failure to subscribe for liberty bonds U. S. v. Pape, D.C.Ill.1918, 253 F. 270.
United States v. Pape (District Court, S. D. Illinois, S. D. August 17, 1918.)
(a) No. (So long as he did not endeavor to induce others to do likewise.)
(b) M/B: United States v. Pape, 253 F. 270 (S.D. Ill. 1918).

42 132 248 328 495 555   Under 18 U.S.C. § 3182, is the choice of the method by which extradition proceedings are commenced optional in the demanding state?
Note 143. Method of extradition People ex rel. Gilbert v. Babb, 1953, 114 N.E.2d 358, 415 Ill. 349, 40 A.L.R.2d 1142.
People ex rel. Gilbert v. Babb, Sheriff Supreme Court of Illinois May 20, 1953
(a) Yes.
(b) M/B: People ex rel. Gilbert v. Babb, 415 Ill. 349, 114 N.E.2d 358 (1953).
    LR: People ex rel. Gilbert v. Babb, 415 Ill. 349, 114 N.E.2d 358 (1953).

43 133 249 329 496 556   Under 18 U.S.C. § 3231, do state courts have jurisdiction over the crime of receiving stolen property belonging to the United States?
Note 90. Receiving stolen property Ex parte Groom, 1930, 287 P. 638, 87 Mont.377.
Ex parte Groom Supreme Court of Montana May 3, 1930
(a) Yes.
(b) M/B: Ex parte Groom, 87 Mont. 377, 287 P. 638 (1930).
    LR: Ex parte Groom, 87 Mont. 377, 287 P. 638 (1930).

44 134 250 330 497 557   Under 18 U.S.C. § 4161, is a prisoner entitled to "good time" credit for the time he was at liberty (without incident) under an erroneous discharge on a write of habeas corpus procured by him?
Note 23. Erreoneous discharge, time under Hunter v. McDonald, C.C.A.Kan.1947, 159 F.2d 861, certiorari denied 67 S.Ct. 1735, 331 U.S. 853, 91 L.Ed. 1861.
Hunter, Warden, v. McDonald Circuit Court of Appeals, Tenth Circuit Feb. 18, 1947
(a) No.
(b) M/B: Hunter v. McDonald, 159 F.2d 861 (10th Cir. 1947).

45 135 251 331 498 558   Under 19 U.S.C. § 482, do custom authorities waive the right to search persons crossing the border by not searching every person who crosses the border?
Note 31. Waiver Witt v. U. S., C.A.Cal.1961, 287 F.2d 389, certiorari denied 81 S.Ct. 1904, 366 U.S. 950, 6 L.Ed.2d 1242.
Ruth Etta Witt, Appellant, v. United States of America, Appellee United States Court of Appeals Ninth Circuit Feb. 16, 1961
(a) No.
(b) M/B: Witt v. United States, 287 F.2d 389 (9th Cir. 1961).

46 136 252 332 499 559   Under 19 U.S.C. § 1202, can the uncontradicted testimony of a single, competent, and credible witness be sufficient to discharge the plaintiff's burden of proof in a customs classification case?
Note 124. Burden of proof Haan v. U. S., 1971, 332 F.Supp. 182, 67 Cust.Ct. 104, C.D. 4260.
Vilem B. Haan et al. v. United States United States Customs Court, First Division Aug. 27, 1971
(a) Yes.
(b) M/B: Haan v. United States, 332 F. Supp. 182 (Cust. Ct. 1971).

EXERCISE 38.   UNITED STATES CODE ANNOTATED   (CONTINUED)

47 137 253 333 500 560   Under 46 U.S.C. § 1304, is a "Himalaya" clause void if it attempts to exempt completely noncarriers from liability for negligence?
Note 145.   Himalaya clause   Grace Line, Inc. v. Todd Shipyards Corp., C.A.Cal.1974, 500 F.2d 361.
Grace Line, Inc., Plaintiff-Appellee, v. Todd Shipyards Corporation, Defendant-Appellant   United States Court of Appeals, Ninth Circuit   May 20, 1974
(a)   It means the price that would have been received had the item been placed on the market.
(b)   M/B: <u>Grace Line v. Todd Shipyards Corp.</u>, 500 F.2d 361 (9th Cir. 1974).
<u>Note</u>:   Inc. may be included in the citation after "Line."

48 138 254 334 401 561   Does 46 U.S.C. § 682 provide the exclusive remedy (payment of wages) when a seaman is discharged?
Note 18.   Exclusiveness or remedy   The Heroe, D.C.Del.1884, 21 F. 525.
The Heroe   (District Court, D. Delaware   August 11, 1884)
(a)   No.
(b)   M/B: <u>The Heroe</u>, 21 F. 525 (D. Del. 1884).

49 139 255 335 402 562   Under 21 U.S.C. § 333, is the taxing of costs in a criminal case discretionary with the district court?
Note 63.   Costs   U. S. v. Bodine Produce Co., D.C.Ariz.1962, 206 F.Supp. 201.
United States of America, Plaintiff, v. Bodine Produce Co., Inc., a corporation, Defendant   United States District Court D. Arizona   May 24, 1962
(a)   Yes.
(b)   M/B: <u>United States v. Bodine Produce Co.</u>, 206 F. Supp. 201 (D. Ariz. 1962).

50 140 256 336 403 563   Under 21 U.S.C. § 844, is the question whether in a prosecution for illegal possession of narcotics the defendant was insane one to be decided by the court or the jury?
Note 28.   _____   Martin v. U. S., 1960, 284 F.2d 217, 109 U.S.App.D.C. 83.
Donald E. Martin, Appellant, v. United States of America, Appellee   United States Court of Appeals District of Columbia Circuit   June 23, 1960
(a)   For the jury.
(b)   M/B: <u>Martin v. United States</u>, 284 F.2d 217 (D.C. Cir. 1960).

51 141 257 337 404 564   Under 21 U.S.C. § 960, when a search of the defendant at the border is permissible, does the fact that warnings as to the defendant's constitutional rights are not given until after a controlled substance is found require a reversal of a conviction of illegal importation?
Note 8.   Advice of rights   U. S. v. Briones, C.A.Tex.1970, 423 F.2d 742, certiorari denied 90 S.Ct. 2270, 399 U.S. 933, 26 L.Ed.2d 804.
United States of America, Plaintiff-Appellee, v. Antonio M. Briones, Defendant-Appellant   United States Court of Appeals, fifth Circuit   March 13, 1970
(a)   No.
(b)   M/B: <u>United States v. Briones</u>, 423 F.2d 742 (5th Cir. 1970).

52 142 258 338 405 565   Under 21 U.S.C. § 374, are inspectors required to give <u>Miranda</u> warnings advising managers of food warehouses of their rights prior to conducting an administrative inspection when the managers are not in custody?
Note 11.   Advice of rights   U. S. v. Thriftimart, Inc., C.A.Cal.1970, 429 F.2d 1006, certiorari denied 91 S.Ct. 188, 400 U.s. 926, 27 L.Ed.2d 185, rehearing denied 91 S.Ct. 453, 400 U.S. 1002, 27 L.Ed.2d 454.
United States of America, Plaintiff-Appellee, v. Thriftimart, Inc., a corporation, dba Smart & Final Iris Co., Gil P. Stewart, Wm. Todd, Sr., and Robert D. Jensen, individuals, Defendants-Appellants   United States Court of Appeals, Ninth Circuit   July 7, 1970
(a)   No.
(b)   M/B: <u>United States v. Thriftimart, Inc.</u>, 429 F.2d 1006 (9th Cir. 1970).
<u>Note</u>:   Inc. may be omitted from the citation.

53 143 259 339 406 566   Under 28 U.S.C. § 1291, is an order denying a motion for a default judgment an appealable order?

EXERCISE 38. UNITED STATES CODE ANNOTATED   (CONTINUED)

Note 144. Default judgment, grant or denial   McNutt v. Cardox Corp.,
C.A.Ky.1964, 329 F.2d 107.
S. H. McNutt, Jr., and Alice H. McNutt, dM/B:bM/B:a partners Under the Firm
Name of Nehi Bottling Company, Plaintiffs-Appellants, v. Cardox Corporation,
Defendant-Appellee   United States Court of Appeals Sixth Circuit   march 26,
1964
(a) No.
(b) M/B: <u>McNutt v. Cardox Corp.</u>, 329 F.2d 107 (6th Cir. 1964).

54 144 260 340 407 567   Under 28 U.S.C. § 1291, to what is a court of appeals
limited in reviewing a Public Utilities Commission's administrative orders?
Note 363. Admisitrative orders   D. C. Transit System, Inc. v. Public
Utilities Commission, 1961, 292 F.2d 734, 110 U.S.App.D.C. 241.
D. C. Transit System, Inc., Appellant, v. Public Utilities Commission of the
District of Columbia, Appellee   United States Court of Appeals District of
Columbia Circuit   May 18, 1961
(a) Limited to questions of law (and the commission's findings of fact are
conclusive unless it appears that the findings are unreasonable, arbitrary, or
capricious).
(b) M/B: <u>D.C. Transit System v. Public Utils. Comm'n</u>, 292 F.2d 734 (D.C.
Cir. 1961).
     LR: D.C. Transit Sys. v. Public Utils. Comm'n, 292 F.2d 734 (D.C. Cir.
1961).
<u>Note</u>: PUC is also correct.

55 145 261 341 408 568   Under 28 U.S.C. § 1331, do foreign corporations have
the right to bring actions against U.S. citizens in federal district courts
for causes of action arising under the laws of the United States?
Note 193. Foreign corporations   Sortex Co. of North America, Inc. v. Mandrel
Industries, Inc., D.C.Mich.1964, 225 F.Supp. 877.
Sortex Company of North America, Inc., Plaintiff, v. Mandrel Industries, Inc.,
Defendant   United States District Court W. D. Michigan, S. D. Jan. 7, 1964
(a) Yes.
(b) M/B: <u>Sortex Co. of North America v. Mandrel Industries</u>, 225 F. Supp. 877
(W.D. Mich. 1964).
     LR: Sortex Co. of N. Am. v. Mandrel Indus., 225 F. Supp. 877 (W.D. Mich.
1964).

56 146 262 342 409 569   Under 28 U.S.C. § 1331, what is the test for
jurisdiction of an action challenging a condemnation proceeding where there
are no personal rights involved and an injunction is not sought?
Note 271. Condemnation   Coffman v. City of Wichita, Kan., D.C.Kan.1958, 165
F.Supp. 765, affirmed 261 F.2d 112.
G. V. Coffman et al., Plaintiffs, v. The City of Wichita, Kansas, a municipal
corporation, Defendant   United States District Court D. Kansas   march 14, 1958
(a) Pecuniary amount
(b) M/B: <u>Coffman v. City of Wichita</u>, 165 F. Supp. 765 (D. Kan. 1958).

57 147 263 343 410 570   Under 28 U.S.C. § 1332, has it been held that the
determination of citizenship is a mixed question of law and fact?
Note 797. Mixed fact and law questions   Julien v. Sarkes Tarzian, Inc.,
C.A.Ind.1965, 352 F.2d 845.
Carmen Julien, Plaintiff-Appellant, v. Sarkes Tarzian, Inc. and Helene Lewis,
as Administratrix of the Estate of Chalmer H. Lewis, Jr., Deceased,
Defendants-Appelless   United States Court of Appeals Seventh Circuit   Oct. 21,
1965
(a) A mixed question of law and fact (but mainly of fact).
(b) M/B: <u>Julieu v. Sarkes Tarzian, Inc.</u>, 352 F.2d 845 (7th Cir. 1965).

58 148 264 344 411 571   Under 28 U.S.C. § 1332, does a federal court
necessarily have jurisdiction to award <u>attorney fees</u> when it has jurisdiction
over a minority stockholder's derivative action?
Note 874. Attorney fees   Angoff v. Goldfine, C.A.Mass.1959, 270 F.2d 185.
Jules E. Angoff et al., Appellants, v. Bernard Goldfine et al., Appellees
United States Court of Appeals First Circuit   Sept. 10, 1959
(a) Yes.
(b) M/B: <u>Angoff v. Goldfine</u>, 270 F.2d 185 (1st Cir. 1959).

EXERCISE 38. UNITED STATES CODE ANNOTATED   (CONTINUED)

59 149 265 345 412 572   For purposes of 28 U.S.C. § 1335, is the United
States considered a citizen of all states when it is a party?
Note 45. Citizenship of parties Kent v. Northern California Regional Office
of Am. Friends Service Committee, C.A.Cal.1974, 497 F.2d 1325.
Roger Kent et al., Plaintiffs-Appellees, v. The Northern California Regional
Office of the American Friends Service Committee et al., Defendants-Appellants
United States Court of Appeals, Ninth Circuit   May 10, 1974
(a)   No.
(b)   M/B: <u>Kent v. Northern California Regional Office of American Friends
Service Commission</u>, 497 F.2d 1325 (9th Cir. 1974).
      LR: <u>Kent v. Northern Cal. Regional Office of Am. Friends Serv. Comm.</u>,
497 F.2d 1325 (9th Cir. 1974).
Note: The name of the appellee may be shortened because of its unusual
length.

60 150 266 346 413 573   Under 28 U.S.C. § 1341, is it proper for a federal
court to enjoin the collection of an illegal state tax when that tax has
clearly punitive qualities and presents such a heavy burden that to decline
equitable relief would be to deny judicial review altogether?
Note 55. Punitive tax   Denton v. City of Carrollton, Ga., C.A.Ga.1956, 235
F.2d 481.
H. W. Denton and International Union of Electrical, Radio and Machine Workers,
CIO, v. City of Carrollton, Georgia, et al.   United States Court of Appeals
Fifth Circuit   July 20, 1956
(a)   Yes.
(b)   M/B: <u>Denton v. City of Carrollton</u>, 235 F.2d 481 (5th Cir. 1956).

61 151 267 347 414 574   Under 28 U.S.C. § 1346, is the United States liable
for negligence of its agents if it were to fail to warn herders in an area of
anticipated radioactive fallout of planned atomic detonations known to involve
substantial danger?
Note 348. Radioactive fallout   Bulloch v. U. S., D.C.Utah 1957, 145 F.Supp.
824.
Caroline N. Bulloch, McRae N. Bulloch and Kern Bulloch, Executors of the
Estate of David C. Bulloch, McRae N. Bulloch and Kern Bulloch, Plaintiffs, v.
United States of America, Defendant   United States District Court D. Utah,
Central Division   Oct. 26, 1956
(a)   Yes.
(b)   M/B: <u>Bulloch v. United States</u>, 145 F. Supp. 824 (D. Utah 1956).
Note: The U.S.C.A. erroneously lists the date as "1957."

62 152 268 348 415 575   Under 28 U.S.C. § 1346, when a person and his team of
mules are in plain view in an open pasture, would it be actionable negligence
for a member of the U.S. military to fly a helicopter, which was making a loud
noise, directly at and over the person and animals at a height of thirty-five
feet?
Note 350. Sonic boom and loud noises   Long v. U. S., D.C.S.C.1965, 241
F.Supp. 286.
Olin S. Long, Plaintiff, v. The United States of America, Defendant   United
States District Court W. D. South Carolina, Greenwood Division   May 14, 1965
(a)   Yes.
(b)   M/B: <u>Long v. United States</u>, 241 F. Supp. 286 (W.D.S.C. 1965).

63 153 269 349 416 576   Under 28 U.S.C. § 1391, in a tenant's action against
a landlord for treble damages for rent overcharges pursuant to the Housing and
Rent Act, would a district court have venue jurisdiction over the parties if
the landlord was a resident of the district in which the federal district
court was sitting?
Note 188. Housing and Rent Act, actions under   Fields v. Washington,
C.A.N.J.1949, 173 F.2d 701.
Fields v. Washington   United States Court of Appeals Third Circuit   April 1,
1949
(a)   Yes.
(b)   M/B: <u>Fields v. Washington</u>, 173 F.2d 701 (3d Cir. 1949).

EXERCISE 38.   UNITED STATES CODE ANNOTATED   (CONTINUED)

64 154 270 350 417 577   Under 28 U.S.C. § 1391, do the norms prescribed for determining venue for commercial corporations apply with equal validity to charitable corporations?
Note 234.   Charitable corporations   Weinberg v. Colonial Williamsburg, Inc., D.C.N.Y.1963, 215 F.Supp. 633.
Ruth Weinberg and Milton S. Weinberg, Plaintiffs, v. Colonial Williamsburg, Incorporated, and Williamsburg Restoration, Incorporated, Defendants   United States District Court E. D. New York   Jan. 24, 1963
(a) Yes.
(b) M/B: <u>Weinberg v. Colonial Williamsburg, Inc.</u>, 215 F. Supp. 633 (E.D.N.Y. 1963).

65 155 271 351 418 578   Under 28 U.S.C. § 1441, is an action to determine ownership of land and federal tax liens properly removable from a state to a federal court when the plaintiff claims payment under the Soil Bank Act and names the Department of Agriculture as a party?
Note 280.   Soil Bank Act   Wood v. DeWeese, D.C.Ky.1969, 305 F.Supp. 939.
Haynes R. Wood, Plaintiff, v. H. C. DeWeese and Juanita (Wuanita) DeWeese; Taylor DeWeese, Administrator of the Jerome R. DeWeese; Paul Ingram dM/B:bM/B:a Morgantown Feed Mill; Weedman Motor Co.; U. S. Internal Revenue Service; U. S. Department of Agriculture; Andy Funk and Morgantown Deposit Bank, Defendants   United States District Court W. D. Kentucky, Bowling Green Division   Nov. 14, 1969
(a) Yes.
(b) M/B: <u>Wood v. DeWeese</u>, 305 F. Supp. 939 (W.D. Ky. 1969).

66 156 272 352 419 579   Under 28 U.S.C. § 1441, is there a presumption against jurisdiction in federal court upon removal from a state court?
Note 400.   Presumptions   Cudney v. Midcontinent Airlines, D.C.Mo 1951, 98 F.Supp. 403.
Cudney v. Midcontinent Airlines, Inc.   United States District Court E. D. Missouri, E. D.   June 13, 1951
(a) Yes.
(b) M/B: <u>Cudney v. Midcontinent Airlines</u>, 98 F. Supp. 403 (E.D. Mo. 1951).

67 157 273 353 420 580   Under 28 U.S.C. § 1447, does a federal court have teh power, on removal of a case from state court, to discharge a testamentary trustee?
Note 83.   Trustees   In re Gray's Estate, C.C.A.Ind.1933, 66 F.2d 367.
In re Gray's Estate.   Old Nat. Bank of Evansville v. Union Trust Co. of Indianapolis et al.   Circuit Court of Appeals, Seventh Circuit   Aug. 1, 1933
(a) No.
(b) M/B: <u>In re Gray's Estate</u>, 66 F.2d 367 (7th Cir. 1933).
    LR: <u>In re</u> Gray's Estate, 66 F.2d 367 (7th Cir. 1933).

68 158 274 354 421 581   Under 28 U.S.C. § 1447, is the issue whether causes of action have been improperly joined a matter for decision by a federal court after the case has been removed from state court?
Note 246.   Joinder of causes   Booth v. Merchants Nat. Bank of Brownsville, C.C.A.Tex.1938, 100 F.2d 478.
Booth v. Merchants Nat. Bank of Brownsville, Tex., et al.   Circuit Court of Appeals, Fifth Circuit   Dec. 29, 1938
(a) Yes.
(b) M/B: <u>Booth v. Merchants National Bank</u>, 100 F.2d 478 (5th Cir. 1938).
    LR: Booth v. Merchants Nat'l Bank, 100 F.2d 478 (5th Cir. 1938).

69 159 275 355 422 582   Under 28 U.S.C. § 1652, in a federal court, does the law of the state where an auctioneer's sale and contract of a sale were consummated determine the legal consequences of the auction sale?
Note 334.   Auctions   In re Philadelphia Penn Worsted Co., C.A.Pa.1960, 278 F.2d 661.
Matter of Philadelphia Penn Worsted Company, Bankrupt   Barney Cramer and Harvey Mencoff, Co-partners Trading as Advanced Textile Company, Appellants   United States Court of Appeals Third Circuit   May 23, 1960
(a) Yes.
(b) M/B: <u>In re Philadelphia Penn Worsted Co.</u>, 278 F.2d 661 (3d Cir. 1960).
    LR: <u>In re</u> Philadelphia Penn Worsted Co., 278 F.2d 661 (3d Cir. 1960).

EXERCISE 38. UNITED STATES CODE ANNOTATED   (CONTINUED)

70 160 276 356 423 583   Under 49 U.S.C. § 782, does the right to intervene
extend to a lienholder of a vehicle when that vehicle may be subject to
forfeiture as a result of its use in narcotics violations?
Note 14.   Intervention   U. S. v. One 1961 Cadillac Hardtop Auto,
D.C.Tenn.1962, 207 F.Supp. 693.
United States of America v. One 1961 Cadillac Hardtop Automobile, Serial No.
61J028918, Grace Cunningham, Intervenor, and Rogers and Company, Inc.   United
States District Court E. D. Tennessee, S. D.   Aug. 9, 1962
(a)   Yes.
(b)   M/B: <u>United States v. One 1961 Cadillac Hardtop Automobile</u>, 207 F. Supp.
693 (E.D. Tenn. 1962).
      LR: <u>United States v. One 1961 Cadillac Hardtop Auto.</u>, 207 F. Supp. 693
(E.D. Tenn. 1962).

71 161 277 357 424 584   Under 28 U.S.C. § 2111, would an erroneous denial of
a motion to quash process be a ground for reversal when the defendant appears
and is not prejudiced by the alleged defect in the process?
Note 463.   Process   Southern Oil Corporation v. Waggoner, C.C.A.Tex.1921, 276
F. 487, certiorari denied 42 S.Ct. 382, 258 U.S. 626, 66 L.Ed. 798.
Southern Oil Corporation v. Waggoner   (Circuit Court of Appeals, Fifth Circuit
November 22, 1921)
(a)   No.
(b)   M/B: <u>Southern Oil Corp. v. Waggoner</u>, 276 F. 487 (5th Cir. 1921).

72 162 278 358 425 585   Under 28 U.S.C. § 2201, was the existence of a cause
of action always essential to a bill for declaratory judgment?
Note 200.   Cause of action, existence of   Maryland Casualty Co. v. Hubbard,
D.C.Cal.1938, 22 F.Supp. 697
Maryland Casualty Co. v. Hubbard et al.   District Court, S. D. California,
Central Division   March 22, 1938
(a)   No.
(b)   M/B: <u>Maryland Casualty Co. v. Hubbard</u>, 22 F. Supp. 697 (S.D. Cal. 1938).

73 163 279 359 426 586   Using the notes to 28 U.S.C. § 2243, determine
whether at common law a prisoner could traverse the return of a writ of habeas
corpus and demand an issue on the legality of his commitment?
Note 192.   Common law   In re Kaine, C.C.N.Y.1852, Fed.Cas.No.7,598.
In re Kaine   Circuit Court, S. D. New York   July 9, 1852
(a)   No.
(b)   M/B: <u>In re Kaine</u>, 14 F. Cas. 84 (C.C.S.D.N.Y. 1852) (No. 7598).
      LR: <u>In re Kaine</u>, 14 F. Cas. 84 (C.C.S.D.N.Y. 1852) (No. 7598).

74 164 280 360 427 587   Under 28 U.S.C. § 2243, should notice be given to the
prosecuting officer when a prisoner is discharged on a habeas corpus writ for
an invalid sentence?
Note 519.   Notice   Biddle v. Thiele, C.C.A. Kan.1926, 11 F.2d 235.
Biddle, Warden, v. Thiele   (Circuit Court of Appeals, Eighth Circuit   January
13, 1926)
(a)   Yes.
(b)   M/B: <u>Biddle v. Thiele</u>, 11 F.2d 235 (8th Cir. 1926).

75 165 281 361 428 588   Under 28 U.S.C. § 2254, must a state defendant
exhaust his remedies on a claim concerning pretrial publicity before seeking
federal habeas corpus by either seeking a state habeas corpus proceeding or
assigning it as error on appeal?
Note 483.   Publicity   Bowring v. Cox, D.C.Va.1970, 320 F.Supp. 688.
Larry Grant Bowring v. J. D. Cox, Superintendent of the Virginia State
Penitentiary (formerly C. C. Peyton)   United States District Court, W. D.
Virginia, Roanoke Division   Dec. 31, 1970
(a)   Yes.
(b)   M/B: <u>Bowring v. Cox</u>, 320 F. Supp. 688 (W.D. Va. 1970).

76 166 282 362 429 589   Under 46 U.S.C. § 971, does an ordinary ship mortgage
constitute a maritime lien?
Note 20.   Mortgages   Bard v. The Silver Wave, D.C.Md.1951, 98 F.Supp. 271.

EXERCISE 38. UNITED STATES CODE ANNOTATED   (CONTINUED)

Bard v. The Silver Wave   United States District Court D. Maryland, Admiralty Division   May 23, 1951
(a)   No.
(b)   M/B: United States ex rel. Dunham v. Quinlau, 327 F. Supp. 115 (S.D.N.Y. 1971).
       LR: United States ex rel. Dunham v. Quinlau, 327 F. Supp. 115 (S.D.N.Y. 1971).

77 167 283 363 430 590   Under 28 U.S.C. § 2255, should the United States be a respondent in a proceeding on a motion in the nature of a writ of error coram nobis attacking a federal conviction?
Note 95.   Respondent   U. S. ex rel. Bogish v. Tees, C.A.Pa.1954, 211 F.2d 69.
United States ex rel. Bogish v. Tees   United States Court of Appeals, Third Circuit   March 9, 1954
(a)   Yes.
(b)   M/B: United States ex rel. Bogish v. Tees, 211 F.2d 69 (3d Cir. 1954).
       LR: United States ex rel. Bogish v. Tees, 211 F.2d 69 (3d Cir. 1954).

78 168 284 364 431 591   Under 28 U.S.C. § 2255, does the fact that the petitioner is not represented by nor informed of his right to counsel at the time a juvenile court waives jurisdiction over him entitle him to post-conviction relief?
Note 376.   Juvenile court proceedings   Mordecai v. U. S., D.C.D.C.1966, 252 F.Supp. 694.
Linton R. Mordecai, Jr., Plaintiff, v. United States of America, Defendant   United States District Court District of Columbia   March 8, 1966
(a)   No.
(b)   M/B: Mordecai v. United States, 252 F. Supp. 694 (D.D.C. 1966).

79 169 285 365 432 592   Does § 2283 of Title 28 of the United States Code preclude the issuance of an injunction in an action to restrain a state court prosecution for the unauthorized practice of law when the United States intervenes on behalf of the plaintiffs because it considers such relief vital to the national interest?
Note 155.   National interest   Sobol v. Perez, D.C.La.1968, 289 F.Supp. 392.
Richard B. Sobol, Gary Duncan and Isaac Reynolds, Plaintiffs, v. Leander H. Perez, Sr., Leander H. Perez, Jr., District Attorney for the Twenty-Fith Judicial District of Louisiana, and Eugene E. Leon, Judge of the Twenty-Fifth Judicial District of Louisiana, Defendants   United States District Court E. D. Louisiana, New Orleans Division   July 22, 1968
(a)   No.
(b)   M/B: Sobol v. Perez, 289 F. Supp. 392 (E.D. La. 1968).

80 170 286 366 433 593   Under 28 U.S.C. § 2284, is there an issue of sovereign immunity when a suit is brought to enjoin the enforcement of state legislative apportionment statutes?
Note 103.   Sovereign immunity   Lisco v. McNichols, D.C.Colo.1962, 208 F.Supp. 471, reversed on other grounds 84 S.Ct. 1459, 377 U.S. 713, 12 L.Ed.2d 632, on remand 232 F.Supp. 797.
Archie L. Lisco, and all Other Registered Voters of the denver Metropolitan Area, State of Colorado, Similarly Situated, Petitioners, v. Stephen L. R. McNichols as Governor of the State of Colorado, Tim Armstrong as Treasurer of the State of Colorado, George Baker as Secretary of the State of Colorado, the State of Colorado and the General Assembly Thereof, Respondents   United States District Court D. Colorado   Aug. 10, 1962
(a)   No.
(b)   M/B: Lisco v. McNichols, 208 F. Supp. 471 (D. Colo. 1962).

81 171 287 367 434 594   Under 28 U.S.C. § 2674, is the burden of proof upon the defendant in New York if the defense is assumption of risk?
Note 147.   Eisenhower v. U. S., D.C.N.Y.1963, 216 F.Supp. 803, affirmed 327 F.2d 663, certiorari denied 84 S.Ct. 1915, 377 U.S. 991, 12 L.Ed.2d 1044.
Leslie Andre Eisenhower, a/k/a Leslie Andre and Leslie Y. Ford, Plaintiff, v. United States of America, Defendant   United States District Court E. D. New York   May 6, 1963
(a)   Yes.
(b)   M/B: Eisenhower v. United States, 216 F. Supp. 803 (E.D.N.Y. 1963).

EXERCISE 38.   UNITED STATES CODE ANNOTATED   (CONTINUED)

82 172 288 368 435 595   Under 28 U.S.C. § 2674, is the alleged lightening of mink by mutation as a result of disturbance by military aircraft too conjectual and speculative damage to support an award?
Note 195. Conjectural or speculative   Wildwood Mink Ranch v. U. S., D.C.Minn.1963, 218 F.Supp. 67.
Wildwood Mink Ranch, a Minnesota corporation, Plaintiff, v. The United States of America, Defendant   United States District Court D. Minnesota, Third Division   March 8, 1963
(a) Yes.
(b) M/B: <u>Wildwood Mink Ranch v. United States</u>, 218 F. Supp. 67 (D. Minn. 1963).

83 173 289 369 436 596   Under 29 U.S.C. § 158, is an employer's rule of dress prohibiting the wearing of multiple union badges an unfair labor practice?
Note 68. Dress, rules of   Serv-Air, Inc. v. N. L. R. B., C.A.Okl.1968, 395 F.2d 557, certiorari denied 89 S.Ct. 121, 393 U.S. 840, 21 L.Ed.2d 112.
Serv-Air, Inc., Petitioner, v. National Labor Relations Board, Respondent   United States Court of Appeals Tenth Circuit   Jan. 19, 1968
(a) Yes.
(b) M/B: <u>Serv-Air, Inc. v. NLRB</u>, 395 F.2d 557 (10th Cir. 1968).

84 174 290 370 437 597   Under 29 U.S.C. § 158, is it illegal for an employer, engaged in collective bargaining, to offer a unilateral draft of the contemplated agreement, though such action results in shaping the terms finally agreed upon by the parties?
Note 493. Draft of proposed agreement   F. W. Means & Co. v. N. L. R. B., C.A.Ill.1967, 377 F.2d 683.
National Labor Relations Board v. P. Lorillard Co.   Circuit Court of Appeals, Sixth Circuit   Feb. 14, 1941
(a) No.
(b) M/B: <u>NLRB v. P. Lorillard Co.</u>, 117 F.2d 921 (6th Cir. 1941).

85 175 291 371 438 598   Under 49 U.S.C. § 1486, may improper venue for review of the Board's orders be waived if an objection is not seasonably asserted?
Note 10. Venue   Eastern Air Lines, Inc. v. C. A. B., 1965, 354 F.2d 507, 122 U.S.App.D.C. 375.
Eastern Air Lines, Inc., and National Airlines, Inc., Petitioners, v. Civil Aeronautics Board, Respondent   United States Court of Appeals District of Columbia Circuit   Nov. 29, 1965
(a) Yes.
(b) M/B: <u>Eastern Air Lines v. CAB</u>, 354 F.2d 507 (D.C. Cir. 1965).

86 176 292 372 439 599   Under 29 U.S.C. § 160, must the Board conduct a de novo hearing into every unfair labor practice case involving a refusal to bargain?
Note 490. De novo hearing   N. L. R. B. v. Clement-Blythe Companies, C.A.S.C.1969, 415 F.2d 78.
National Labor Relations Board, Petitioner, v. Clement-Blythe Companies, a joint venture, Respondent   United States Court of Appeals Fourth Circuit   Sept. 9, 1969
(a) No.
(b) M/B: <u>NLRB v. Clement-Blythe Cos.</u>, 415 F.2d 78 (4th Cir. 1969). <u>Note</u>: "Companies" is also correct.

87 177 293 373 440 600   Under 49 U.S.C. § 1653, is the decision of the Secretary of Transportation authorizing use of federal funds for the construction of an expressway through a public park entitled to a presumption of regularity?
Note 16. Presumptions   Citizens to Preserve Overton Park, Inc. v. Volpe, Tenn.1971, 91 S.Ct. 841, 401 U.S. 402, 28 L.Ed.2d 136, on remand 335 F. Supp. 873.
Citizens to Preserve Overton Park, Inc., et al., Petitioners, v. John A. Volpe, Secretary, Department of Transportation, et al.   401 US 402, 28 L Ed 2d 136, 91 S Ct 814   March 2, 1971
(a) Yes.
(b) Citizens to Preserve Overton Park, Inc. v. Volpe, 401 U.S. 402 (1971).

EXERCISE 38. UNITED STATES CODE ANNOTATED (CONTINUED)

88 178 294 374 441 501   Under 45 U.S.C. § 2, is it the duty of a rail carrier to establish reasonable repair points along its line?
Note 50. Establishment of repair points   U. S. v. Atchison, etc., R. Co., D.C.Cal.1908, 167 F. 696.
United States v. Atchison, T. & S. F. Ry. Co. (District Court, N. D. California   December 1, 1908)
(a)   Yes.
(b)   M/B: United States v. Atchison, Topeka & Santa Fe Railway, 167 F. 696 (N.D. Cal. 1908).
      LR: United States v. Atchison, T. & S.F. Ry., 167 F. 696 (N.D. Cal. 1908).

89 179 295 375 442 502   Under 29 U.S.C. § 186, can an employer be a beneficiary of an employee benefit pension trust established under this section?
Note 97. Employers   Dohrer v. Wakeman, Wash.App.1975, 539 P.2d 91.
George F. Dohrer, Appellant, v. Clyde Wakeman et al., Respondents, and Robert Phair et al., Defendants   Court of Appeals of Washington, Division 1   Aug. 11, 1975
(a)   No.
(b)   M/B: Dohrer v. Wakeman, 14 Wash. App. 157, 539 P.2d 91 (1975).

90 180 296 376 443 503   Under 29 U.S.C. § 203, are telegraph lines that extend through several states instruments of "commerce" for purposes of this section?
Note 71. Telegraph lines   Western Union Telegraph Co. v. Lenroot, N.Y.1945, 65 S.Ct. 335, 323 U.S. 490, 89 L.Ed. 414.
Western Union Telegraph Co. v. Lenroot, Chief of Children's Bureau, United States Department of Labor   Certiorari to the Circuit Court of Appeals for the Second Circuit   January 8, 1945
(a)   Yes.
(b)   M/B: Western Union Telegraph Co. v. Lenroot, 323 U.S. 490 (1945).
      LR: Western Union Tel. Co. v. Lenroot, 323 U.S. 490 (1945).

91 181 297 377 444 504   Under 29 U.S.C. § 203, is actual physical contact with goods produced for interstate commerce essential to bring a laborer within coverage of this section?
Note 88. Physical contact with goods   Chambers Const. Co. v. Mitchell, C.A.Neb.1956, 233 F.2d 717.
Chambers Construction Company, a Corporation, and L. H. Chambers, Appellants, v. James P. Mitchell, Secretary of Labor, United States Department of Labor, Appellee   United States Court of Appeals Eighth Circuit   June 5, 1956
(a)   No.
(b)   M/B: Chambers Construction Co. v. Mitchell, 233 F.2d 717 (8th Cir. 1956).
      LR: Chambers Constr. Co. v. Mitchell, 233 F.2d 717 (8th Cir. 1956).

92 182 298 378 445 505   In an action for overtime compensation under 29 U.S.C. § 216, does the fact that the employees participated in making a false record by working before and after they punched their time cards reflecting on their credibility as witnesses?
Note 169. Witnesses-Credibility   Feldman v. Roschelle Bros., D.C.N.Y.1943, 49 F.Supp. 247.
Feldman v. Roschelle Bros. Inc.   District Court, S. D. New York   Dec. 29, 1942
(a)   Yes.
(b)   M/B: Feldman v. Roschelle Brothers, 49 F. Supp. 247 (S.D.N.Y. 1942).

93 183 299 379 446 506   Under 29 U.S.C. § 464, has the legality of union trusteeships been largely a question for the court to determine?
Note 84. Questions for court   Jolly v. Gorman, C.A.Miss. 1970, 428 F.2d 960, certiorari denied 91 S.Ct. 588, 400 U.S. 1023, 27 L.Ed.2d 635.
J. D. Jolly et al., Plaintiffs, Granville Sellers and Herbert Ishee, Plaintiffs-Appellants, v. Walter Gorman, Individually and as Trustee of, and International Woodworkers of America, AFL-CIO, and Masonite Corporation, Defendants-Appellees   United States Court of Appeals, Fifth Circuit   June 30, 1970
(a)   Yes.

EXERCISE 38.   UNITED STATES CODE ANNOTATED   (CONTINUED)

(b)   M/B: Jolly v. Gorman, 428 F.2d 960 (5th Cir. 1970).

94 184 300 380 447 507   Under 30 U.S.C. § 28, must a prospector take some precaution to protect his location notice from destruction?
Note 143.   Destruction   Hagan v. Dutton, 1919, 181 P.578, 20 Ariz. 476.
Hagan v. Dutton et al.   (Supreme Court of Arizona   June 14, 1919)
(a)   Yes.
(b)   M/B: Hagan v. Dutton, 20 Ariz. 476, 181 P. 578 (1919).

95 185 201 381 448 508   Under 31 U.S.C. § 191, are receiver's fees and payment of administration expenses entitled to priority over a debt due the United States in the distribution of an insolvent estate?
Note 204.   Receiver's fees   Lerman v. Lincoln Novelty Co., 1941, 21 S.2d 827, 130 N.J.Eq. 144.
Lerman v. Lincoln Novelty Co.   Court of Chancery of New Jersey   Aug. 12, 1941
(a)   Yes.
(b)   M/B: Lerman v. Lincoln Novelty Co., 130 N.J. Eq. 144, 21 A.2d 827 (1941).

96 186 202 382 449 509   Under 33 U.S.C. § 191, must a barge in tow give fog signals?
Note 9.   Tows   The G. K. Mellon, C.C.A.N.Y.1929, 30 F.2d 238.
The G. K. Mellon.   The John M. Worth.   Circuit Court of Appeals, Second Circuit   January 7, 1929
(a)   No.
(b)   M/B: The G.K. Mellon, 30 F.2d 238 (2d Cir. 1929).

97 187 203 383 450 510   Under 33 U.S.C. § 409, is a wharfinger's duty to remove a sunken vessel or reasonably warn vessels thereof limited to vessels sunk in the area of land under water actually owned by him?
Note 17.   Wharfinger's duty   The Cornell No. 20, D.C.N.Y.1934, 8 F.Supp. 431.
Cornell Steamboat Co. v. Robert Gladstone, Jr., Inc., et al.   District Court, S. D. New York   July 18, 1934
(a)   No.   (It intends to the immediate access to the wharf).
(b)   M/B: The Cornell No. 20, 8 F. Supp. 431 (S.D.N.Y. 1934).

98 188 204 384 451 511   Under 33 U.S.C. § 905, where neither the owner of the vessel nor demise charterer are personally liable to a longshoreman for unseaworthiness, is a longshoreman entitled to bring a libel proceeding in rem against the vessel?
Note 343.   Proceedings in personam or rem   Ramos v. Beauregard, Inc., C.A.Puerto Rico 1970, 423 F.2d 916, certiorari denied 91 S.Ct. 101, 400 U.S. 865, 27 L.Ed.2d 104.
Francisco Torres Ramos, Plaintiff, Appellant, v. Beauregard, Inc., et al., Defendants, Appellees   United States Court of Appeals, First Circuit   April 7, 1970
(a)   No.
(b)   M/B: Ramos v. Beauregard, Inc., 423 F.2d 916 (1st Cir. 1970).

99 189 205 385 452 512   Under 41 U.S.C. § 16, is the government entitled to recover freight charges paid on goods sold to it under a contract calling for "delivery f.o.b. supply office"?
Note 76.   Freight charges   Harper Mfg. Co. v. U.S., C.C.A.Ga.1925, 10 F.2d 150.
Harper Mfg. Co. v. United Staets   (Circuit Court of Appeals, Fifth Circuit December 22, 1925)
(a)   Yes.
(b)   M/B: Harper Manufacturing Co. v. United States, 10 F.2d 150 (5th Cir. 1925).
      LR: Harper Mfg. Co. v. United States, 10 F.2d 150 (5th Cir. 1925).

100 190 206 386 453 513   Under 45 U.S.C. § 56, do state courts have jurisdiction over actions for injuries sustained on board vessels on the high seas?
Note 74.   High seas   Larson v. Lewis-Simas-Jones Co., 1938, 84 P.2d 296, 29 C.A.2d 83.

EXERCISE 38. UNITED STATES CODE ANNOTATED (CONTINUED)

Larson v. Lewis-Simas-Jones Co. et al. District Court of Appeal, Fourth District, California Nov. 9, 1938
(a) Yes.
(b) M/B: Larson v. Lewis-Simas-Jones Co., 29 Cal. App. 2d 83, 84 P.2d 296 (1938).

LIBRARY EXERCISE 39. STATE STATUTES.

INSTRUCTOR'S NOTE: The students are required to find the statutory provision that sets the time period after which the action listed for their problem number cannot be brought (limitations of actions). For their answer, they are to cite the provision to the statutory compilation that they used to find their answer. The student in some instances may be citing the supplement in the parenthetical. Note that new versions of the state's statutes may have appeared and may be cited by the student. The student may also indicate the relevant subsection of the statute (not shown below). The students are allowed to use any version of the state statutes.

1 101 201 301 401 501 Alabama Equity of redemption (mortgages)
Ala. Code § 6-2-35 (19xx).

2 102 202 302 402 502 Alaska Libel
Alaska Stat. § 09.10.070 (19xx).

3 103 203 303 403 503 Arizona Foreclosure of a mechanic's lien
Ariz. Rev. Stat. Ann. § 33-998 (19xx).

4 104 204 304 404 504 Arkansas False imprisonment
Ark. Stat. Ann. § 37-201 (19xx).

5 105 205 305 405 505 California Libel
Cal. Civ. Proc. Code § 340 (West 19xx).
Cal. Civ. Proc. Code § 340 (Deering 19xx).

6 106 206 306 406 506 Colorado Foreclosure of mortgage after taking possession
Colo. Rev. Stat. § 38-40-114 (19xx).

7 107 207 307 407 507 Connecticut Libel
Conn. Gen. Stat. § 52-597 (19xx).

8 108 208 308 408 508 Delaware Wrongful death
Del. Code Ann. tit. 10, § 8107 (19xx).

9 109 209 309 409 509 Florida Trespass on real property
Fla. Stat. § 95.11 (19xx).
Fla. Stat. Ann. § 95.11 (West 19xx).

10 110 210 310 410 510 Georgia Breach of covenant restricting land use
Ga. Code § 3-717 (19xx).
Ga. Code Ann. § 3-717 (19xx).

11 111 211 311 411 511 Hawaii Slander
Hawaii Rev. Stat. § 657-4 (19xx).

12 112 212 312 412 512 Idaho Trover
Idaho Code § 5-218 (19xx).

13 113 213 313 413 513 Illinois Action to enforce contract to make a will (For prupuses of this exercise, the students are instructed not cite the name of the act nor the original section number--see USOC, at page 146.)
Ill. Ann. Stat. ch. 83, § 24e (Smith-Hurd 19xx).
Ill. Rev. Stat. ch. 83, § 24e (19xx).

14 114 214 314 414 514 Indiana Injury to real property
Ind. Code § 34-1-2-1 (19xx).
Ind. Code Ann. § 34-1-2-1 (Burns 19xx).

15 115 215 315 415 515 Iowa Paternity actions
Iowa Code § 675.33 (19xx).
Iowa Code Ann. § 675.33 (West 19xx).

16 116 216 316 416 516 Kansas Forcible entry and detention
Kan. Stat. Ann. § 60-506 (19xx).

EXERCISE 39. STATE STATUTES   (CONTINUED)

17 117 217 317 417 517   Kentucky Breach of contracts for sale of goods
Ky. Rev. Stat. § 355.2-725 (19xx).
Ky. Rev. Stat. Ann. § 355.2-725 (Baldwin 19xx).
Ky. Rev. Stat. Ann. § 355.2-725 (Bobbs-Marrill 19xx)

18 118 218 318 418 518   Louisana Land patents ("prescriptive period")
La. Pub. Lands Code § 5661 (West 19xx).

19 119 219 319 419 519   Maine Contract for sale of goods
Me. Rev. Stat. Ann. tit. 11, § 2-725 (19xx).

20 120 220 320 420 520   Maryland Libel
Md. Cts. & Jud. Proc. Code Ann. § 5-105 (19xx).

21 121 221 321 421 521   Massachusetts Action by creditor against executor of an estate
Mass. Gen. Laws Ann. ch. 197, § 9 (West 19xx).
Mass. Ann. Laws ch. 197, § 9 (Michie/Law. Co-op 19xx).

22 122 222 322 422 522   Michigan Malicious prosecution
Mich. Comp. Laws Ann. § 600.5805 (19xx).
Mich. Stat. Ann. § 27A.5805 (West 19xx).
Mich. Stat. Ann. § 27A.5805 (Callaghan 19xx).
Mich. Comp. Laws § 600.5805 (19xx).

23 123 223 323 423 523   Minnesota Libel
Minn. Stat. § 541.07 (19xx).
Minn. Stat. Ann. § 541.07 (West 19xx).

24 124 224 324 424 524   Mississippi Action on unwritten contracts
Miss. Code Ann. § 15-1-29 (19xx).

25 125 225 325 425 525   Missouri Libel
Mo. Ann. Stat. § 516.140 (Vernon 19xx).
Mo. Rev. Stat. § 516.140 (19xx).

26 126 226 326 426 526   Montana False imprisonment
Mont. Code Ann. § 27-2-204 (19xx).

27 127 227 327 427 527   Nebraska Libel
Neb. Rev. Stat. § 25-208 (19xx).

28 128 228 328 428 528   Nevada Slander
Nev. Rev. Stat. § 11.190 (19xx).

29 129 229 329 429 529   New Hampshire Willful trespass
N.H. Rev. Stat. Ann. § 539:8 (19xx).

30 130 230 330 430 530   New Jersey Contracts not under seal
N.J. Stat. Ann. § 2A:14-1 (West 19xx).
N.J. Rev. Stat. § 2A:14-1 (19xx).

31 131 231 331 431 531   New Mexico Injury to a person's reputation
N.M. Stat. Ann. § 37-1-8 (19xx).

32 132 232 332 432 532   New York Redemption from a mortgage
N.Y. Civ. Prac. Law § 212 (McKinney 19xx).

33 133 233 333 433 533   North Carolina Flase imprisonment
N.C. Gen. Stat. § 1-54 (19xx).

34 134 234 334 434 534   North Dakota Questioning validity of municipal bonds
N.D. Cent. Code § 21-03-47 (19xx).

35 135 235 335 435 535   Ohio Recovery of personal property
Ohio Rev. Code Ann. § 2305.09 (Baldwin 19xx).
Ohio Rev. Code Ann. § 2305.09 (Page 19xx).

EXERCISE 39.   STATE STATUTES   (CONTINUED)

36 136 236 336 436 536   Oklahoma Oral contract
Okla. Stat. tit. 12, § 95 (19xx).
Okla. Stat. Ann. tit. 12, § 95 (West 19xx).

37 137 237 337 437 537   Oregon Waste
Or. Rev. Stat. § 12.080 (19xx).

38 138 238 338 438 538   Connecticut Action on oral contract
Conn. Gen. Stat. § 52-581 (19xx).

39 139 239 339 439 539   Rhode Island Wrongful death action brought by beneficiaries
R.I. Gen. Laws Ann. § 10-7-3 (19xx).

40 140 240 340 440 540   South Carolina False imprisonment
S.C. Code Ann. § 15-3-550 (Law. Co-op. 19xx).

41 141 241 341 441 541   South Dakota Recovery of gambling losses (Use S.D. Compiled Laws Annotated)
S.D. Comp. Laws Ann. § 21-6-1 (19xx).
Note: § 21-6-2 may also be cited.

42 142 242 342 442 542   Tennessee Libel
Tenn. Code Ann. § 28-3-104 (19xx).

43 143 243 343 443 543   Wisconsin Seduction
Wis. Stat. § 893.58 (19xx).
Wis. Stat. Ann. § 893.58 (West 19xx).

44 144 244 344 444 544   Utah Civil action for seduction
Utah Code Ann. § 78-12-29 (19xx).

45 145 245 345 445 545   Vermont Injuries sustained in skiing
Vt. Stat. Ann. tit. 12, § 513 (19xx).

46 146 246 346 446 546   Virginia Suit to avoid a gift
Va. Code § 8.01-253 (19xx).

47 147 247 347 447 547   Washington Slander
Wash. Rev. Code Ann. § 4.16.100 (19xx).

48 148 248 348 448 548   West Virginia Action to recover on a contract under seal
W. Va. Code § 55-2-6 (19xx).

49 149 249 349 449 549   Wisconsin Assault
Wis. Stat. § 893.21 (19xx).
Wis. Stat. Ann. § 893.21 (West 19xx).

50 150 250 350 450 550   Wyoming Trespass on real property
Wyo. Stat. § 1-3-105 (19xx).

51 151 251 351 451 551   Alabama Libel
Ala. Code § 6-2-39 (19xx).

52 152 252 352 452 552   Alaska Battery
Alaska Stat. § 09.10.070 (19xx).

53 153 253 353 453 553   Arizona Libel
Ariz. Rev. Stat. § 12-541 (19xx).

54 154 254 354 454 554   Arkansas Assault
Ark. Stat. Ann. § 37-201 (19xx).

55 155 255 355 455 555   California False imprisonment
Cal. Civ. Proc. Code § 340 (West 19xx).
Cal. Civ. Proc. Code § 340 (Deering 19xx).

EXERCISE 39. STATE STATUTES   (CONTINUED)

56 156 256 356 456 556 Colorado Restraint of trade and commerce involving void contracts
Colo. Rev. Stat. § 6-4-106 (19xx).

57 157 257 357 457 557 Connecticut Action on a tort
Conn. Gen. Stat. § 52-577 (19xx).

58 158 258 358 458 558 Delaware Waste
Del. Code Ann. tit. 10, § 8112 (19xx).

59 159 259 359 459 559 Florida Slander
Fla. Stat. § 95.11 (19xx).
Fla. Stat. Ann. § 95.11 (West 19xx).

60 160 260 360 460 560 Georgia Action on a promissory note
Ga. Code § 3-705 (19xx).
Ga. Code Ann. § 3-705 (19xx).

61 161 261 361 461 561 Hawaii Libel
Hawaii Rev. Stat. § 657-4 (19xx).

62 162 262 362 462 562 Idaho Recovery of possession of personal property (Replevin)
Idaho Code § 5-218 (19xx).

63 163 263 363 463 563 Illinois Seduction (For purposes of this exercise, the students are instructed not cite the name of the act nor the original section number--see USOC, at 146.)
Ill. Ann. Stat. ch. 83, § 5 (Smith-Hurd 19xx).
Ill. Rev. Stat. ch. 83, § 5 (19xx).

64 164 264 364 464 564 Indiana Contracts not in writing
Ind. Code § 34-1-2-2 (19xx).
Ind. Code Ann. § 34-1-2-2 (Burns 19xx).

65 165 265 365 465 565 Iowa Paternity actions
Iowa Code § 675.33 (19xx).
Iowa Code Ann. § 675.33 (West 19xx).

66 166 266 366 466 566 Kansas Contract in writing
Kan. Stat. Ann. § 60-511 (19xx).

67 167 267 367 467 567 Kentucky Malicious prosecuticn
Ky. Rev. Stat. § 413.140 (19xx).
Ky. Rev. Stat. Ann. § 413.140 (Baldwin 19xx).
Ky. Rev. Stat. Ann. § 413.140 (Bobbs-Merrill 19xx)

68 168 268 368 468 568 Louisiana Actions for arrearages of alimony
La. Civ. Code Ann. art. 3538 (West 19xx).

69 169 269 369 469 569 Maine Assault and battery
Me. Rev. Stat. Ann. tit. 14, § 753 (19xx).

70 170 270 370 470 570 Maryland Contracts under seal
Md. Cts. & Jud. Proc. Code Ann. § 5-102 (19xx).

71 171 271 371 471 571 Massachusetts Contracts under seal
Mass. Gen. Laws Ann. ch. 260, § 1 (West 19xx).
Mass. Ann. Laws ch. 260, § 1 (Michie/Law. Co-op 19xx).

72 172 272 372 472 572 Michigan Libel
Mich. Comp. Laws Ann. § 600.5805 (19xx).
Mich. Stat. Ann. § 27A.5805 (West 19xx).
Mich. Stat. Ann. § 27A.5805 (Callahan 19xx).
Mich. Comp. Laws § 600.5805 (19xx).

73 173 273 373 473 573 Minnesota False imprisonment

EXERCISE 39.   STATE STATUTES   (CONTINUED)

Minn. Stat. § 541.07 (19xx).
Minn. Stat. Ann. § 541.07 (West 19xx).

74 174 274 374 474 574   Mississippi Libel
Miss. Code Ann. § 15-1-35 (19xx).

75 175 275 375 475 575   Missouri False imprisonment
Mo. Rev. Stat. § 516.140 (19xx).
Mo. Ann. Stat. § 516.140 (Vernon 19xx).

76 176 276 376 476 576   Montana Libel
Mont. Code Ann. § 27-2-204 (19xx).

77 177 277 377 477 577   Nebraska Malicious prosecution
Neb. Rev. Stat. § 25-208 (19xx).

78 178 278 378 478 578   Nevada Waste
Nev. Rev. Stat. § 11.190 (19xx).

79 179 279 379 479 579   New Hampshire Trespass to the person
N.H. Rev. Stat. Ann. § 508:4 (19xx).

80 180 280 380 480 580   New Jersey Tortious injury to real property
N.J. Rev. Stat. § 2A:14-1 (19xx).
N.J. Stat. Ann. § 2A:14-1 (West 19xx).

81 181 281 381 481 581   New Mexico Unwritten contracts
N.M. Stat. Ann. § 37-1-4 (19xx).

82 182 282 382 482 582   New York Wrongful death
N.Y. Est., Powers & Trusts Law § 5-4.1 (McKinney 19xx).

83 183 283 383 483 583   North Carolina Libel
N.C. Gen. Stat. § 1-54 (19xx).

84 184 284 384 484 584   North Dakota Action for no-fault insurance benefits
N.D. Cent. Code § 26-41-16 (19xx).

85 185 285 385 485 585   Ohio Trespass to real property
Ohio Rev. Code Ann. § 2305.09 (Baldwin 19xx).
Ohio Rev. Code Ann. § 2305.09 (Page 19xx).

86 186 286 386 486 586   Oklahoma Libel
Okla. Stat. tit. 12, § 95 (19xx).
Okla. Stat. Ann. tit. 12, § 95 (West 19xx).

87 187 287 387 487 587   Oregon Action to cancel a land patent
Or. Rev. Stat. § 12.040 (19xx).

88 188 288 388 488 588   Wisconsin Replevin (wrongful taking or detention of personal property)
Wis. Stat. § 893.19 (19xx).
Wis. Stat. Ann. § 893.19 (West 19xx).

89 189 289 389 489 589   Rhode Island Slander
R.I. Gen. Laws § 9-1-14 (19xx).

90 190 290 390 490 590   South Carolina Assault
S.C. Code Ann. § 15-3-550 (Law. Co-op. 19xx).

91 191 291 391 491 591   South Dakota Action on a real property contract (Use S.D. Complied Laws Annotated)
S.D. Comp. Laws Ann. § 21-51-1 (19xx).

92 192 292 392 492 592   Tennessee Personal tort actions
Tenn. Code Ann. § 28-3-104 (19xx).

EXERCISE 39.   STATE STATUTES   (CONTINUED)

93 193 293 393 493 593   Texas Paternity suits
Tex. Fam. Code § 13.01 (19xx).

94 194 294 394 494 594   Utah Action for mesne profits of real estate
Utah Code Ann. § 78-12-23 (19xx).

95 195 295 395 495 595   Vermont False imprisonment
Vt. Stat. Ann. tit. 12, § 512 (19xx).

96 196 296 396 496 596   Virginia Distress for rent
Va. Code § 55-230 (19xx).

97 197 297 397 497 597   Washington Breach of contract for sale under the Washington Uniform Commercial Code
Wash. Rev. Code Ann. § 62A.2-725 (19xx).

98 198 298 398 498 598   West Virginia Recognizance of bail
W. Va. Code § 55-2-11 (19xx).

99 199 299 399 499 599   Wisconsin False imprisonment
Wis. Stat. § 893.21 (19xx).
Wis. Stat. Ann. § 893.21 (West 19xx).

100 200 300 400 500 600   Wyoming Recovery of real estate
Wyo. Stat. § 1-3-103 (19xx).

LIBRARY EXERCISE 40. CODE OF FEDERAL REGULATIONS.

INSTRUCTOR'S NOTE: Each answer for this exercise follows a basic format:

   30 C.F.R. § 57.2 (19xx).

   Note that the title number is given first, then the proper abbreviation of the Code (C.F.R.), followed by the section number and date. Because C.F.R. is revised each year, the date used by the student ordinarily will be this year's date or the preceding year.

   The following Quick-Reference Abbreviation is the one relevant to this exercise:

   ADMINISTRATIVE CITATION 2. CITE THE CODE OF FEDERAL REGULATIONS (C.F.R.) BY TITLE, SECTION, AND YEAR. [AD 2]

LIBRARY EXERCISE 41. FEDERAL ADMINISTRATIVE DECISIONS.

INSTRUCTOR'S NOTE: The students are to cite the decision that begins on the page listed below in the designated volume of Federal Trade Commission Decisions in proper form. They are instructed to cite only the F.T.C. volume. The following Quick-Reference Abbreviation is particularly relevant to this exercise:

   ADMINISTRATIVE CITATION 4. CITE ADMINISTRATIVE CASES BY THE FULL REPORTED NAME OF THE FIRST-LISTED PRIVATE PARTY OR THE OFFICIAL SUBJECT-MATTER TITLE. OMIT ALL PROCEDURAL PHRASES. [AD 4]

1 168 224 342 437 586   91   751
In the Matter of Jay Norris Corp., et al. May 2, 1978.
Jay Norris Corp., 91 F.T.C. 751 (1978).

2 169 225 343 438 587   2   202
Federal Trade Commission v. Winsted Hosiery Co. January 29, 1920
Winsted Hosiery Co., 2 F.T.C. 202 (1920).

3 170 226 344 439 588   3   345
Federal Trade Commission v. Federal Press, Inc., and C. W. Parker.
March 30, 1921.
Federal Press, Inc., 3 F.T.C. 345 (1921).

4 171 227 345 440 589   89   531
In the Matter of Alexander's, Inc. May 31, 1977.
Alexander's, Inc., 3 F.T.C. 531 (1977).

5 172 228 346 441 590   5   257
Federal Trade Commission v. Charles D. Daum, Thomas J. Rogers and Harry Spritzer, Partners, Styling themselves the Daum, Rogers, Spritzer Company. November 1, 1922.
Charles D. Daum, 5 F.T.C. 257 (1922).

6 173 229 347 442 591   6   267
Federal Trade Commission v. Samuel Blum. September 26, 1914.
Samuel Blum, 6 F.T.C. 267 (1923).

7 174 230 348 443 592   7   426
Federal Trade Commission v. Durable Pure Silk Fashioned Hosiery, Inc. September 26, 1914.
Durable Pure Silk Fashioned Hosiery, Inc., 7 F.T.C. 426 (1924).

8 175 231 349 444 593   8   400
In the Matter of Samson Rosenblatt. February 13, 1925.
Samson Rosenblatt, 8 F.T.C. 400 (1925).

EXERCISE 41.   FEDERAL ADMINISTRATIVE DECISIONS   (CONTINUED)

9 176 232 350 445 594   9   391
In the Matter of Rosenbush & Solomon, Inc. November 6, 1925.
Rosenbush & Solomon, Inc., 9 F.T.C. 391 (1925).

10 177 233 351 446 595   10   265
In the Matter of Keystone Silver, Inc., Formerly Keystone Metal Spinning &
Stamping Company. July 7, 1926.
Keystone Silver, Inc., 10 F.T.C. 265 (1926).

11 178 234 352 447 596   11   181
In the Matter of Hanford F. Smith. June 30,1927.
Hanford F. Smith, 11 F.T.C. 181 (1927).

12 179 235 353 448 597   12   303
In the Matter of Marsay School of Beauty Culture, O. C. Miller, A. J. Weber
and Ignatius Barnard. Jan. 16, 1929.
Marsay School of Beauty Culture, 12 F.T.C. 303 (1929).

13 180 236 354 449 598   89   255
In the Matter of Las Animas Ranch, Inc., et al. Apr. 22, 1977.
Las Animas Ranch, Inc., 89 F.T.C. 255 (1977).

14 181 237 355 450 599   14   361
In the Matter of Adiel Vandeweghe and David Feshback. Jan. 27, 1931.
Adiel Vandeweghe, 14 F.T.C. 361 (1931).

15 182 238 356 451 600   15   385
In the Matter of Philadelphia Hosiery Mills. Dec. 14, 1931.
Philadelphia Hosiery Mills, 15 F.T.C. 385 (1931).

16 183 239 357 452 501   16   393
In the Matter of Arrow-Hart & Hegeman, Inc., and the Arrow-Hart & Hegeman
Electric Company. July 6, 1932.
Arrow-Hart & Gegeman, Inc., 16 F.T.C. 393 (1932).

17 184 240 358 453 502   17   101
In the Matter of Jacob Gennet. Oct. 31, 1932.
Jacob Gennet, 17 F.T.C. 101 (1932).

18 185 241 359 454 503   18   151
In the Matter of Paul Case. Jan. 18, 1934.
Paul Case, 18 F.T.C. 151 (1934).

19 186 242 360 455 504   19   187
In the Matter of Old Hickory Mills et al. Aug. 6, 1934.
Old Hickory Mills, 19 F.T.C. 187 (1934).

20 187 243 361 456 505   20   468
In the Matter of A. McLean & Son. June 21, 1935.
A. McLean & Son, 20 F.T.C. 468 (1935).

21 188 244 362 457 506   21   637
In the Matter of Prince Matchabelli Perfumery, Inc. Dec. 10, 1935.
Prince Matchabelli Perfumery, Inc., 21 F.T.C. 637 (1935).

22 189 245 363 458 507   90   328
In the Matter of Zayre Corp. Oct. 27, 1977.
Zayre Corp., 90 F.T.C. 328 (1977).

23 190 246 364 459 508   23   849
In the Matter of Montebello Distillers, Inc. Nov. 13, 1936.
Matebello Distillers, Inc., 23 F.T.C. 849 (1936).

24 191 247 365 460 509   24   697
In the Matter of Grantie Arts, Inc. Feb. 16, 1937.
Granite Arts, Inc., 24 F.T.C. 697 (1937).

EXERCISE 41. FEDERAL ADMINISTRATIVE DECISIONS   (CONTINUED)

```
25 192 248 366 461 510      25    1019
```
In the Matter of May Hosiery Mills, Inc. Sept. 26, 1937.
May Hosiery Mills, Inc., 25 F.T.C. 1019 (1937).

```
26 193 249 367 462 511      26     852
```
In the Matter of United Woolen Mills. Mar. 2, 1914.
United Wollen Mills, 26 F.T.C. 852 (1938).

```
27 194 250 368 463 512      27     994
```
In the Matter of John B. Arata. Sept. 20, 1938.
John B. Arata, 27 F.T.C. 994 (1938).

```
28 195 251 369 464 513      28    1176
```
In the Matter of Grand Gaslight, Inc. Mar. 21, 1939.
Grand Gaslight, Inc., 28 F.T.C. 1176 (1939).

```
29 196 252 370 465 514      29     590
```
In the Matter of Zo-Ro-Lo, Inc. Aug. 12, 1939.
Zo-Ro-Lo, Inc., 29 F.T.C. 590 (1939).

```
30 197 253 371 466 515      30     647
```
In the Matter of Jean Ferrell, Inc. Mar. 9, 1940.
Jean Farrell, Inc., 30 F.T.C. 647 (1940).

```
31 198 254 372 467 516      31     742
```
In the Matter of Imogene Shepherd, Ltd. Aug. 14, 1940.
Imogene Shepherd, Ltd., 31 F.T.C. 742 (1940).

```
32 199 255 373 468 517      32     686
```
In the Matter of E. B. Hall, Trading as E. W. Hall. Feb. 5, 1941.
E.B. Hall, 32 F.T.C. 686 (1941).

```
33 200 256 374 469 518      33    1234
```
In the Matter of Continental Premium Mart. Sept. 5, 1941.
Continental Premium Mart, 33 F.T.C. 1234 (1941).

```
34 101 257 375 470 519      34     921
```
In the Matter of Folding Furniture Works, Inc., also doing Business as Coast to Coast Distributiors and Manufacturers and National Mercantile Reporters. Mar. 23, 1942.
Folding Furnitute Works, Inc., 34 F.T.C. 921 (1942).

```
35 102 258 376 471 520      35     569
```
In the Matter of Chicago Technical College. Oct. 12, 1942.
Chicago Technical College, 35 F.T.C. 569 (1942).

```
36 103 259 377 472 521      36     577
```
In the Matter of John F. Trommer, Inc. Apr. 28, 1943.
John F. Trommer, Inc., 36 F.T.C. 577 (1943).

```
37 104 260 378 473 522      37     440
```
In the Matter of Gladys H. Peiser. Sept. 21, 1943.
Gladys H. Peiser, 37 F.T.C. 440 (1943).

```
38 105 261 379 474 523      38     279
```
In the Matter of Philip R. Park, Inc. and Philip R. Park, Harrison H. Havner, John S. Hunt and Philip E. Iversen. April 20, 1944.
Philip R. Park, Inc., 38 F.T.C. 279 (1944).

```
39 106 262 380 475 524      39     425
```
In the Matter of David Jacobs and Allied News-Photo Service Corp., Etc. Nov. 4, 1944.
David Jacobs, 39 F.T.C. 425 (1944).

```
40 107 263 381 476 525      40     484
```
In the Matter of Scotchf Woolen Mills. May 1, 1945.

EXERCISE 41. FEDERAL ADMINISTRATIVE DECISIONS   (CONTINUED)

Scotch Woolen Mills, 40 F.T.C. 484 (1945).

41 108 264 382 477 526   41   177
In the Matter of Henry Lankenau, Richard Lankenau, and Harry Lankenau, Trading as Lankenau Company. Sept. 25, 1945.
Henry Lankenau, 41 F.T.C. 177 (1954).

42 109 265 383 478 527   42   165
In the Matter of South Coast Fisheries, Inc. Mar. 25, 1946.
South Coast Fisheries, Inc., 42 F.T.C. 165 (1946).

43 110 266 384 479 528   43   623
In the Matter of McKinley-Rossevelt, Inc. et al. June 25, 1947.
McKinley-Roosevelt, Inc., 43 F.T.C. 623 (1947).

44 111 267 385 480 529   44   878
In the Matter of Jack Field. May 25, 1948.
Jack Field, 44 F.T.C. 878 (1948).

45 112 268 386 481 530   45   502
In the Matter of Witol, Inc., National Products Outlet, Inc., and William Witol. Feb. 16, 1949.
Witol, Inc., 45 F.T.C. 502 (1949).

46 113 269 387 482 531   46   755
In the Matter of Englishtown Cutlery, Ltd. et al. Apr. 4, 1950.
Englishtown Cutlery, Ltd., 46 F.T.C. 755 (1950).

47 114 270 388 483 532   47   449
In the Matter of Martin W. Pretorius and Marie Joyce Doing Business as Martin W. Pretorius and as Pretorius Approved Products. Oct. 24, 1950.
Martin W. Pretorius, 47 F.T.C. 449 (1950).

48 115 271 389 484 533   48   999
In the Matter of Ronell Fashions, Inc. et al. Mar. 17, 1952.
Ronell Fashions, Inc., 48 F.T.C. 999 (1952).

49 116 272 390 485 534   49   1284
In the Matter of Phillips, Inc. et al. Apr. 7, 1953.
Phillips, Inc., 49 F.T.C. 1284 (1953).

50 117 273 391 486 535   50   555
In the Matter of Pillsbury Mills, Inc. Dec. 21, 1953.
Pillsbury Mills, Inc., 50 F.T.C. 555 (1953).

51 118 274 392 487 536   51   734
In the Matter of Permanent Stainless Steel, Inc., and Pressed Steel Car Company, Inc. (Now known as U.S. Industries, Inc.). Feb. 14, 1955.
Permanent Stainless Steel, Inc., 51 F.T.C. 734 (1955).

52 119 275 393 488 537   52   619
In the Matter of Joseph Carmel, Inc., et al. Jan. 5, 1956.
Joseph Carmel, Inc. 52 F.T.C. 619 (1956).

53 120 276 394 489 538   53   466
In the Matter of Fred Benioff Co., et al. Nov. 7, 1956.
Fred Benioff Co., 53 F.T.C. 466 (1956).

54 121 277 395 490 539   54   769
In the Matter of Crown Zellerbach Corp. Dec. 26, 1957.
Crown Zellerbach Corp., 54 F.T.C. 769 (1957).

55 122 278 396 491 540   55   1337
In the Matter of Ward Laboratories, Inc., et al. Mar. 4, 1959.
Ward Laboratories, Inc., 55 F.T.C. 1337 (1959).

56 123 279 397 492 541   56   862

EXERCISE 41.   FEDERAL ADMINISTRATIVE DECISIONS   (CONTINUED)

In the Matter of Mannie Feigenbaum, Inc., et al. Feb. 9, 1960.
Mannie Feigenbaum, Inc., 56 F.T.C. 862 (1960).

57 124 280 398 493 542   57   841
In the Matter of Eversharp, Inc., et al. Sept. 30, 1960.
Eversharp, Inc., 57 F.T.C. 841 (1960).

58 125 281 399 494 543   58   576
In the Matter of Asheville Textiles Corp. et al. Apr. 12, 1961.
Asheville Textiles Corp., 58 F.T.C. 576 (1961).

59 126 282 400 495 544   59   780
In the Matter of Seymour Lustig Doing Business as Seymour Lustig. Oct. 10, 1961.
Seymour Lustig, 59 F.T.C. 780 (1961).

60 127 283 301 496 545   60   694
In the Matter of Transair, Inc., et al. Apr. 5, 1962.
Transair, Inc., 60 F.T.C. 694 (1962).

61 128 284 302 497 546   61   534
In the Matter of Lanolin Plus, Inc. Sept. 12, 1962.
Lanolin Plus, Inc., 61 F.T.C. 534 (1962).

62 129 285 303 498 547   62   1215
In the Matter of Van-R, Inc., et al. Apr. 24, 1963.
Van-R, Inc., 62 F.T.C. 1215 (1963).

63 130 286 304 499 548   63   1164
In the matter of Coro, Inc. et al. Nov. 6, 1963.
Coro, Inc., 63 F.T.C. 1164 (1963).

64 131 287 305 500 549   64   629
In the Matter of Stauffer Laboratories, Inc., et al. Feb. 7, 1964.
Stauffer Laboratories, Inc., 64 F.T.C. 629 (1964).

65 132 288 306 401 550   65   225
In the Matter of Santa's Playthings, Inc., et al. Apr. 3, 1964.
Santa's Playthings, Inc., 65 F.T.C. 225 (1964).

66 133 289 307 402 551   66   655
In the Matter of Rainbow Crafts, Inc., et al. Sept. 11, 1964.
Rainbow Crafts, Inc., 66 F.T.C. 655 (1964).

67 134 290 308 403 552   67   744
In the Matter of Topps Chewing Gum, Inc. Apr. 30, 1965.
Topps Chewing Gum, Inc., 67 F.T.C. 744 (1965).

68 135 291 309 404 553   68   281
In the Matter of Peter Pan Yarn Corp. et al. July 28. 1965.
Peter Pan Yarn Corp., 68 F.T.C. 281 (1965).

69 136 292 310 405 554   69   667
In the Matter of William H. Rorer, Inc. May 9, 1966.
William H. Rorer, Inc., 69 F.T.C. 667 (1966).

70 137 293 311 406 555   90   406
In the Matter of Grand Spalding Dodge, Inc. Oct. 25, 1977.
Grand Spaulding Dodge, Inc., 90 F.T.C. 406 (1977).

71 138 294 312 407 556   71   817
In the Matter of Adrian Thal, Inc. et al. June 12, 1967.
Adrian Thal, Inc., 71 F.T.C. 817 (1967).

72 139 295 313 408 557   72   875
In the Matter of Schneider & Falk, Inc., et al. Nov. 24, 1967.
Schneider & Falk, Inc., 72 F.T.C. 875 (1967).

EXERCISE 41. FEDERAL ADMINISTRATIVE DECISIONS   (CONTINUED)

73 140 296 314 409 558   73   835
In the Matter of Max Adelman Furs, Inc. et al. May 7, 1968.
Max Adelman Furs, Inc., 73 F.T.C. 835 (1968).

74 141 297 315 410 559   74   324
In the Matter of Vanity Fair Mills, Inc. July 25, 1968.
Vanity Fair Mills, Inc., 74 F.T.C. 324 (1968).

75 142 298 316 411 560   75   803
In the Matter of Seymour Feldman, Inc., et al. May 14, 1969.
Seymour Feldman, Inc., 75 F.T.C. 803 (1969).

76 143 299 317 412 561   76   502
In the Matter of Morris Wasserman Fur Corp., et al. Oct. 30, 1969.
Morris Wasserman Fur Corp., 76 F.T.C. 502 (1969).

77 144 300 318 413 562   76   464
In the Matter of Jack Exell, et al. Oct. 23, 1969.
Jack Ezell, 76 F.T.C. 464 (1969).

78 145 201 319 414 563   77   906
In the Matter of Manis & Steve Furs, et al. July 2, 1970.
Manis & Steve Furs, 77 F.T.C. 906 (1970).

79 146 202 320 415 564   77   456
In the Matter of Hirschman Fur Corp., et al. Apr. 16, 1970.
Hirschman Fur Corp., 77 F.T.C. 456 (1970).

80 147 203 321 416 565   78   1428
In the Matter of Eastern Detective Academy, Inc., et al. June 30, 1971.
Eastern Detective Academy, Inc., 78 F.T.C. 1428 (1971).

81 148 204 322 417 566   91   869
In the Matter of Performance Sailcraft Inc. May 2, 1973.
Performance Sailcraft, Inc., 91 F.T.C. 869 (1971).

82 149 205 323 418 567   79   518
In the Matter of Compace Vacuum Centers, Inc., et al. Sept. 30, 1971.
Compace Vacuum Centers, Inc., 79 F.T.C. 518 (1971)

83 150 206 324 419 568   79   667
In the Matter of Mattel, Inc. Nov. 1, 1971.
Mattel, Inc., 79 F.T.C. 667 (1971).

84 151 207 325 420 569   80   653
In the Matter of Broadway-Hale Stores, Inc. April 13, 1972.
Broadway-Hale Stores, Inc., 80 F.T.C. 653 (1972).

85 152 208 326 421 570   94   236
In the Matter of Mack Trucks, Inc. Aug. 1, 1979.
Mack Trucks, Inc., 94 F.T.C. 236 (1979).

86 153 209 327 422 571   81   567
In the Matter of Tallman Piano Stores, Inc., et al. Oct. 5, 1972.
Tallman Piano Stores, Inc., 81 F.T.C. 567 (1972).

87 154 210 328 423 572   81   344
In the Matter of B. Altman & Co. Sept. 13, 1972.
B. Altman & Co., 81 F.T.C. 344 (1972).

88 155 211 329 424 573   82   391
In the Matter of Avnet, Inc. Feb. 16, 1973.
Avnet, Inc., 82 F.T.C. 391 (1973).

89 156 212 330 425 574   82   1025

EXERCISE 41.   FEDERAL ADMINISTRATIVE DECISIONS   (CONTINUED)

In the Matter of Seekonk Freezer Meats, Inc., et al.   March 15, 1973.
Seekonk Freezer Meats, Inc., 82 F.T.C. 1025 (1973).

90 157 213 331 426 575   83   696
In the Matter of General Mills, Inc.   Oct. 5, 1973.
General Mills, Inc., 83 F.T.C. (1973).

91 158 214 332 427 576   84   748
In the Matter of Holiday Magic, Inc., et al.   Oct. 15, 1974.
Holiday Magic, Inc., 84 F.T.C. 748 (1974).

92 159 215 333 428 577   84   547
In the Matter of Sterling Drug, Inc., et al.   Oct. 1, 1974.
Sterling Drug, Inc., 84 F.T.C. 547 (1974).

93 160 216 334 429 578   85   237
In the Matter of Weaver Airline Personnel School, Inc., et al.   Feb. 13, 1975.
Weaver Airline Personnel School, Inc., 85 F.T.C. 237 (1975).

94 161 217 335 430 579   85   207
In the Matter of Duofold, Inc.   Feb. 10, 1975.
Duofold, Inc., 85 F.T.C. 207 (1975).

95 162 218 336 431 580   86   860
In the Matter of Lear Siegler, Inc.   Oct. 6, 1975.
Lear Siegler, Inc., 86 F.T.C. 860 (1975).

96 163 219 337 432 581   86   425
In the Matter of Spiegel, Inc.   Aug. 18, 1975.
Spiegel, Inc., 86 F.T.C. 425 (1975).

97 164 220 338 433 582   87   68
In the Matter of Parker Advertising, Inc.   Jan. 12, 1976.
Parker Advertising, Inc., 87 F.T.C. 68 (1976).

98 165 221 339 434 583   87   299
In the Matter of Fox & Lenkofsky, Inc., et al.   Feb. 24, 1976.
Fox & Lenkofsky, Inc., 87 F.T.C. 299 (1976)

99 166 222 340 435 584   88   279
In the Matter of kane-Miller Corp., et al.   Sept. 1, 1976.
Kane-Miller Corp., 88 F.T.C. 279 (1976).

100 167 223 341 436 585   88   546
In the Matter of Leonard F. Proter, Inc., et al. - Docket 8964; Indian Arts & Crafts, Inc., et al. - Docket 8965; J.L. Houston, Inc. et al. - Dokcet 8966; Western Novelty Co., et al. - Docket 8967; Herman Krupp t/a Oceanic Trading Company - Docket 8968; Heinz Lange t/a Northwest Arts and Crafts - Docket 8969.   Oct. 19, 1976.
Leonard F. Porter, Inc., 88 F.T.C. 546 (1976).

LIBRARY EXERCISE 42.   FEDERAL RULES OF CIVIL PROCEDURE.

INSTRUCTOR'S NOTE: Using the current Federal Rules of Civil Procedure, the students are required cite the current rule provision[s] that govern[s] or answer[s] the subject or question listed with their problem number. Current rules can be found in West's *Federal Rules* pamphlet, Moore's *Federal Rules* pamphlet, and numerous other sources. Note that the students are specifically include the relevant subdivision of the rule in their answer, when appropriate, and that they are not required to answer the question posed.

1 126 292 348 459 513   General rule stating that opposing affidavits may be served not later than one day before a hearing unless the court permits otherwise.
Fed. R. Civ. P. 6(d).

2 127 293 349 460 514   Number of days within which a responsive pleading must be filed after service of an amended pleading.
Fed. R. Civ. P. 15(a).

3 128 294 350 461 515   Must a motion for a more definite pleading be made before a responsive pleading is filed?
Fed. R. Civ. P. 12(e).

4 129 295 351 462 516   Number of days service by mail adds to the period computed from time of service.
Fed. R. Civ. P. 6(e).

5 130 296 352 463 517   Requirement that if a party intends to raise an issue concerning the law of a foreign country, he must include a such notice in his pleading.
Fed. R. Civ. P. 44.1.

6 131 297 353 464 518   Time when requests for jury instructions may be made to the court.
Fed. R. Civ. P. 51.

7 132 298 354 465 519   Do the rules allow for the submission of special verdicts to the jury?
Fed. R. Civ. P. 49(a).

8 133 299 355 466 520   May alternate jurors replace disqualified jurors after the jury retires to deliberate?
Fed. R. Civ. P. 47(b).

9 134 300 356 467 521   Is there a time limit on the correction of clerical mistakes in a judgment or order?
Fed. R. Civ. P. 60(a).

10 135 201 357 468 522   Must the complaint be filed at the commencement of a civil action?
Fed. R. Civ. P. 3.

11 136 202 358 469 523   Time period after the entry of a judgment or order a motion for relief from that judgment or order may be filed when the basis of the motion is fraud?
Fed. R. Civ. P. 60(b).

12 137 203 359 470 524   When a supersedeas bond becomes effective.
Fed. R. Civ. P. 62(d).

13 138 204 360 471 525   When requests for admissions may be served on the plaintiff and the defendant.
Fed. R. Civ. P. 36(a).

14 139 205 361 472 526   Must the complaint be served with the summons?
Fed. R. Civ. P. 4(d).

15 140 206 362 473 527   Time period within which motions for a new trial must be served after entry of a judgment.

EXERCISE 42. FEDERAL RULES OF CIVIL PROCEDURE   (CONTINUED)

Fed. R. Civ. P. 59(b).

16 141 207 363 474 528   Are averments of time in pleadings considered to be material?
Fed. R. Civ. P. 9(f).

17 142 208 364 475 529   Time when objections to jury instructions must be made.
Fed. R. Civ. P. 51.

18 143 209 365 476 530   Time period an answer to a cross-claim must be filed. Fed. R. Civ. P. 12(a).

19 144 210 366 477 531   Number of days notice that must be given before taxation of costs.
Fed. R. Civ. P. 54(d).

20 145 211 367 478 532   Time when motions to strike from pleadings may be filed.
Fed. R. Civ. P. 12(f).

21 146 212 368 479 533   Upon the death of a public officer who is a party to a pending action, is his successor automatically substituted?
Fed. R. Civ. P. 25(d)(1).

22 147 213 369 480 534   Rules are to be construed to secure just, speedy, and inexpensive determination of every action.
Fed. R. Civ. P. 1.

23 148 214 370 481 535   Number of forms of action under the Federal Rules of Civil Procedure.
Fed. R. Civ. P. 2.

24 149 215 371 482 536   When does the clerk issue the summons?
Fed. R. Civ. P. 4(a).

25 150 216 372 483 537   When the period of time prescribed or allowed under the Rules is less than seven days, are Saturdays and Sundays counted in the computation?
Fed. R. Civ. P. 6(a).

26 151 217 373 484 538   May the court strike a pleading if a party fails to furnish a more definite statement as required by the court?
Fed. R. Civ. P. 12(e).

27 152 218 374 485 539   Is service required on parties in default for failure to appear in the suit?
Fed. R. Civ. P. 5(a).

28 153 219 375 486 540   Time period within which a motion for relief from a judgment or order must be made when the motion is based on newly discovered evidence.
Fed. R. Civ. P. 60(b).

29 154 220 376 487 541   Time when a judgment or order becomes effective according to the Rules.
Fed. R. Civ. P. 58(b).

30 155 221 377 488 542   Number of times a pleading may be amended, if any, as a matter of course before a responsive pleading is served.
Fed. R. Civ. P. 15(a)

31 156 222 378 489 543   Time period within which an answer to a notice of condemnation must be filed.
Fed. R. Civ. P. 71A(e).

EXERCISE 42.   FEDERAL RULES OF CIVIL PROCEDURE   (CONTINUED)

32 157 223 379 490 544   May a party amend a pleading at any time with the written consent of the adverse party or by leave of court?
Fed. R. Civ. P. 15(a).

33 158 224 380 491 545   Manner for service of the complaint and summons upon an infant or an incompetent person under the Rules.
Fed. R. Civ. P. 4(d)(2).

34 159 225 381 492 546   Time period within which a response to requested admissions must be made.
Fed. R. Civ. P. 36(a).

35 160 226 382 493 547   Are U.S. marshals authorized by the Rules to serve process?
Fed. R. Civ. P. 4(c).

36 161 227 383 494 548   Must the summons be signed by the clerk before it is served?
Fed. R. Civ. P. 4(b).

37 162 228 384 495 549   Number of days within which an objection must be served after a subpoena duces tecum calling for the inspection and copying of documents has been served.
Fed. R. Civ. P. 45(d)(a).

38 163 229 385 496 550   Number of days notice that must be given before a motion to dissolve or modify a temporary restraining order.
Fed. R. Civ. P. 65(b).

39 164 230 386 497 551   Must a reply to an answer to be filed under the Rules? Fed. R. Civ. P. 7(a).

40 165 231 387 498 552   When does a temporary restraining order granted without notice automatically expire?
Fed. R. Civ. P. 65(b).

41 166 232 388 499 553   Is a new demand for a jury trial necessary when an action has been removed from a state court to a federal court if such a demand has been made in the state court prior to removal?
Fed. R. Civ. P. 81(c).

42 167 233 389 500 554   Is Columbus Day considered a "holiday" for purposes of the Rules?
Fed. R. Civ. P. 77(c).

43 168 234 390 401 555   Should the time of inspection be included in a request for production and inspection of documents?
Fed. R. Civ. P. 34(b).

44 169 235 391 402 556   How soon after the commencement of an action may interrogatories (to parties) be served on the plaintiff?
Fed. R. Civ. P. 33(a).

45 170 236 392 403 557   Number of days within which answers to interrogatories to parties must be furnished.
Fed. R. Civ. P. 33(a).

46 171 237 393 404 558   Is handing a document to the attorney of a party sufficient service when the Rules permit service to be made upon a party's attorney?
Fed. R. Civ. P. 5(b).

47 172 238 394 405 559   Items that a summons must contain.
Fed. R. Civ. P. 4(b).

48 173 239 395 406 560   May a party amend his pleadings during trial or after judgment to conform with the proof?

EXERCISE 42. FEDERAL RULES OF CIVIL PROCEDURE   (CONTINUED)

Fed. R. Civ. P. 15(b).

49 174 240 396 407 561   In an action against the United States or an officer or agent thereof, number of days a United States Attorney has to file an answer after service of the complaint upon him.
Fed. R. Civ. P. 12(a).

50 175 241 397 408 562   Time period within which a motion to review the taxation of costs must be made.
Fed. R. Civ. P. 54(d).

51 176 242 398 409 563   Do the Rules apply to civil suits in admiralty cases? Fed. R. Civ. P. 1.

52 177 243 399 410 564   Service of a summons, notice, or order on a party who is not an inhabitant of the state or who cannot be found within the state.
Fed. R. Civ. P. 4(e).

53 178 244 400 411 565   Service of summons and complaint upon the United States.
Fed. R. Civ. P. 4(d)(4).

54 179 245 301 412 566   Does failure to make proof of service affect the validity of service under the Rules?
Fed. R. Civ. P. 4(g).

55 180 246 302 413 567   Are "demurrers" for insufficiency of pleading permitted?
Fed. R. Civ. P. 7(c).

56 181 247 303 414 568   Are averments in a pleading (to which a responsive pleading is required) admitted if they are not denied in the responsive pleading?
Fed. R. Civ. P. 8(d).

57 182 248 304 415 569   What a pleading which sets forth a claim for relief should contain.
Fed. R. Civ. P. 8(a).

58 183 249 305 416 570   May a party set forth two or more statements of a claim or defense alternatively or hypothetically in one count or defense?
Fed. R. Civ. P. 8(e)(2).

59 184 250 306 417 571   Is a specific negative averment in a pleading necessary to raise the issue of capacity of a party to be sued?
Fed. R. Civ. P. 9(a).

60 185 251 307 418 572   Must every pleading have a caption?
Fed. R. Civ. P. 10(a).

61 186 252 308 419 573   Must every pleading of a party be signed by at least one attorney of record representing that party?
Fed. R. Civ. P. 11.

62 187 253 309 420 574   Rule providing for interpleader.
Fed. R. Civ. P. 22.

63 188 254 310 421 575   Is misjoinder of a party a ground for dismissal of an action?
Fed. R. Civ. P. 21.

64 189 255 311 422 576   When an applicant will be permitted to intervene as a matter of right.
Fed. R. Civ. P. 24(b).

65 190 256 312 423 577   When a defense of lack of jurisdiction over the person is waived.

EXERCISE 42. FEDERAL RULES OF CIVIL PROCEDURE   (CONTINUED)

Fed. R. Civ. P. 12(h)(i).

66 191 257 313 424 578   Provision permitting the court to strike scandalous matter from a pleading.
Fed. R. Civ. P. 12(f).

67 192 258 314 425 579   Rule provision permitting the filing of a supplemental pleading setting forth transactions which have happened since the date of the pleading sought to be supplemented.
Fed. R. Civ. P. 15(d).

68 193 259 315 426 580   Rule permitting class actions.
Fed. R. Civ. P. 23.

69 194 260 316 427 581   Principal rule regulating third-party practice.
Fed. R. Civ. P. 14.

70 195 261 317 428 582   Requirement of a short and plain statement of the claim showing that the pleader is entitled to relief.
Fed. R. Civ. P. 8(a).

71 196 262 318 429 583   Rule governing summary judgment.
Fed. R. Civ. P. 56.

72 197 263 319 430 584   Must notice be given to the adverse party before a preliminary injunction is issued?
Fed. R. Civ. P. 65(a)(1).

73 198 264 320 431 585   Relation back of amendments.
Fed. R. Civ. P. 15(c).

74 199 265 321 432 586   Allegations to be included in the complaint based upon a derivative action by a shareholder.
Fed. R. Civ. P. 23.1.

75 200 266 322 433 587   Substitution of a party's representative when a party becomes incompetent.
Fed. R. Civ. P. 25(b).

76 101 267 323 434 588   Disability of a judge.
Fed. R. Civ. P. 63.

77 102 268 324 435 589   Penalties for filing affidavits in bad faith in conjunction with a summary judgment motion.
Fed. R. Civ. P. 56(g).

78 103 269 325 436 590   Pleading the occurrence of conditions precedent.
Fed. R. Civ. P. 9(c).

79 104 270 326 437 591   Motions for judgment on the pleadings after the pleadings are closed.
Fed. R. Civ. P. 12(c).

80 105 271 327 438 592   Requirement that special damages be pleaded specifically.
Fed. R. Civ. P. 23(e).

81 106 272 328 439 593   Notice of a proposed dismissal of a class action must be given to all members of the class.
Fed. R. Civ. P. 47(a).

82 107 273 329 440 594   Examination of prospective jurors by the court or the parties (or their attorneys).
Fed. R. Civ. P. 47(a).

83 108 274 330 441 595   The circumstances constituting fraud must be pleaded with particularity.

EXERCISE 42.   FEDERAL RULES OF CIVIL PROCEDURE   (CONTINUED)

Fed. R. Civ. P. 9(b).

84 109 275 331 442 596   Expenses to be paid by a party improperly failing to admit the genuineness of any document as requested under Rule 36.
Fed. R. Civ. P. 37(c).

85 110 276 332 443 597   Actions brought by or against the members of an unincorporated association.
Fed. R. Civ. P. 23.2.

86 111 277 333 444 598   Malice may be pleaded generally.
Fed. R. Civ. P. 9(b).

87 112 278 334 445 599   Requirement that a pleading setting forth a claim for relief include a short and plain statement of the grounds upon which the court's jurisdiction is based.
Fed. R. Civ. P. 8(a).

88 113 279 335 446 600   In pleading in response to a preceding pleading, a party must set forth affirmatively the defense of an injury by a fellow servant. Fed. R. Civ. P. 8(c).

89 114 280 336 447 501   Pleadings should be so construed as to do substantial justice.
Fed. R. Civ. P. 8(f).

90 115 281 337 448 502   Existence of another adequate remedy does not preclude a declaratory judgment in cases where it is appropriate.
Fed. R. Civ. P. 57.

91 116 282 338 449 503   Motion for a judgment notwithstanding the verdict.
Fed. R. Civ. P. 50(b).

92 117 283 339 450 504   By whom service of process may be made.
Fed. R. Civ. P. 4(c).

93 118 284 340 451 505   Harmless errors not inconsistent with substantial justice.
Fed. R. Civ. P. 61.

94 119 285 341 452 506   Parties may stipulate that the jury will consist of less than twelve members.
Fed. R. Civ. P. 48.

95 120 286 342 453 507   By whom subpoenas may be served.
Fed. R. Civ. P. 45(c).

96 121 287 343 454 508   When actions pending before the court involve a common question of law, the court may order all the actions consolidated.
Fed. R. Civ. P. 42(a).

97 122 288 344 455 509   In pleading in response to a preceding pleading, a party must set forth affirmatively the defense of laches.
Fed. R. Civ. P. 8(c).

98 123 289 345 456 510   Court may appoint an interpreter for the taking of testimony.
Fed. R. Civ. P. 43(f).

99 124 290 346 457 511   When a motion for directed verdict may be made.
Fed. R. Civ. P. 50(a).

100 125 291 347 458 512   Discovery of the existence of insurance agreements which may satisfy part or all of a judgment entered in the action permitted.
Fed. R. Civ. P. 26(b)(2).

LIBRARY EXERCISE 43. LEGISLATIVE HISTORY OF FEDERAL STATUTES.

INSTRUCTOR'S NOTE: This exercise requires the students to use the appropriate volume of West's United States Code Congressional and Administrative News to find a statute in that volume by consulting the index or popular name table. The students are supplied with the approximate year of enactment. There are three parts to the student's answer. (a) For this part, the students are required to cite the statute to the Statutes at Large using proper USOC form. The students, however, are instructed not to include a reference to the United States Code or to the subsequent history of the statute for this part of the exercise. (b) For this part, the students must state the bill or resolution number of the enacted legislation, e.g., H.R. 9564. No particular form is required for their answer to this part. (c) For this part, the student is required to cite the committee report identified with their problem number. If that report has been reprinted in the legislative history section of U.S. Code Congressional and Administrative News, the students are instructed to include a parallel reference to that source in their citation. Indicate missing page numbers for purposes of this exercise by a "___." Note that the first session of Congress occurs in odd-numbered years and the second session occurs in even-numbered years.

The following Quick-Reference Abbreviations are relevant to this exercise:

FEDERAL STATUTORY CITATION 1. CITE STATUTES IN THE STATUTES AT LARGE BY NAME, PUBLIC LAW NUMBER OR, PRIOR TO THE 85TH CONGRESS, CHAPTER NUMBER, PAGE, AND YEAR OF ENACTMENT UNLESS IT IS INCLUDED IN THE NAME OF THE STATUTE. [FS 1]

FEDERAL STATUTORY CITATION 2. USE THE FULL DATE OF ENACTMENT TO CITE UNNAMED FEDERAL STATUTES IN THE STATUTES AT LARGE. [FS 2]

LEGISLATIVE HISTORY CITATION 5. CITE CONGRESSIONAL REPORTS AND DOCUMENTS BY NUMBER, CONGRESS, SESSION, PAGE, AND DATE. DO NOT INCLUDE A PART OF THE REPORT OR DOCUMENT NUMBER THAT IDENTIFIES THE CONGRESS. ADD A PARALLEL CITATION TO THE UNITED STATES CODE CONGRESSIONAL AND ADMINISTRATIVE NEWS WHENEVER POSSIBLE. [LH 5]

1 158 255 328 453 572   Housing Act of 1964   H.R. Rep. No. 1265
(a) Housing Act of 1964, Pub. L. No. 88-560, 78 Stat. 769.
(b) S. 3049
(c) H.R. Rep. No. 1703, 88th Cong., 2d Sess. ___, reprinted in 1964 U.S. Code Cong. & Ad. News 3416.

2 159 256 329 454 573   Oil Pollution of the Sea (1966)   S. Rep. No. 1479
(a) Act of Sept. 1, 1966, Pub. L. No. 89-551, 80 Stat. 372
(b) H.R. 8760.
(c) S. Rep. No. 1479, 89th Cong., 2d Sess. ___, reprinted in 1966 U.S. Code Cong. & Ad. News,

3 160 257 330 455 574   Age Discrimination in Employment (1967)   H.R. Rep. No. 805
(a) Age Discrimination in Employment Act of 1967, Pub. L. No. 90-202, 81 Stat. 602
(b) S. 830.
(c) H.R. Rep. No. 805, 90th Cong., 1st Sess. ___, reprinted in 1967 U.S. Code Cong. & Ad. News 2213

4 161 258 331 456 575   Wilderness Act (1964)   H.R. Rep. No. 1538
(a) Wilderness Act, Pub. L. No. 88-577, 78 Stat. 890 (1964).
(b) S. 4.
(c) H.R. Rep. No. 1538, 88th Cong., 2d Sess. ___, reprinted in 1964 U.S. Code Cong. & Ad. News 3615

5 162 259 332 457 576   Committee on Opportunities for Spanish Speaking People (1969)   H.R. Rep. No. 699
(a) Act of Dec. 30, 1969, Pub. L. No. 91-181, 83 Stat. 838.
(b) S. 740.
(c) H.R. Rep. No. 699, 91st Cong., 1st Sess. ___, reprinted in 1969 U.S. Code Cong. & Ad. News 2696.

EXERCISE 43. LEGISLATIVE HISTORY OF FEDERAL STATUTES   (CONTINUED)

6 163 260 333 458 577   Merchant Marine Act of 1970   S. Rep. No. 1080
(a) Merchant Marine Act of 1970, Pub. L. No. 91-469, 84 Stat. 1081.
Note: "Act of Oct. 21, 1970," is also correct.
(b) H.R. 15424
(c) S. Rep. No, 1080, 91st Cong., 2d Sess. ___, reprinted in 1970 U.S. Code Cong. & Ad. News 4188.

7 164 261 334 459 578   Revenue Act of 1971   S. Rep. No 437
(a) Revenue Act of 1971, Pub. L. No. 92-178, 85 Stat. 497.
(b) H.R. 10947.
(c) S. Rep. No. 437, 92d Cong., 1st Sess. ___, reprinted in 1971 U.S. Code Cong. & Ad. News 1918.

8 165 262 335 460 579   Ocean Shipping Act of 1978   S. Rep. No. 1260
(a) Ocean Shipping Act of 1978, Pub. L. No. 95-483, 92 Stat. 1607.
(b) H.R. 9998.
(c) S. Rep. No. 1260, 95th Cong., 2d Sess. 1, reprinted in 1972 U.S. Code Cong. & Ad. News 4331.

9 166 263 336 461 580   Vietnam Era Veterans' Readjustment Assistance Act of 1972   S. Rep. No 988
(a) vietnam Era Veterans' Readjustment Assistance Act of 1972, Pub. L. No. 92-540, 86 Stat. 1074.
(b) H.R. 12828
(c) S. Rep. No 988, 92d Cong., 2d Sess. ___, reprinted in 1972 U.S. Code Cong. & Ad. News 4331.

10 167 264 337 462 581   Comprehensive Employment and Training Act of 1973   H.R. Rep. No. 659
(a) Comprehensive Employment and Training Act of 1973, Pub. L. No. 93-203, 87 Stat. 839.
(b) S. 1559.
(c) H.R. Rep. No. 659, 93rd Cong., 1std Sess. ___, reprinted in 1973 U.S. Code Cong. & Ad. News 2935.

11 168 265 338 463 582   Foreign Assistance Act of 1966   H.R. Rep. No. 1651
(a) Foreign Assistance Act of 1966, Pub. L. No. 89-583, 80 Stat. 795.
(b) H.R. 15750.
(c) H.R. Rep. No. 1651, 89th Cong., 2d Sess. ___, reprinted in 1966 U.S. Code Cong. & Ad. News 2887.

12 169 266 339 464 583   Employee Retirement Income Security Act of 1974   S. Rep. No. 127
(a) Employee retirement Income Security Act of 1974, Pub. L. No. 93-406, 88 Stat. 829.
(b) H.R. 2.
(c) S. Rep. No. 127, 93d Cong., 1st Sess. ___, reprinted in 1974 U.S. Code Cong. & Ad. News 4838.

13 170 267 340 465 584   Handicapped Childrens' Education (1975)   S. Rep. No. 168
(a) Education For All Handicapped Children Act of 1975, Pub. L. No. 94-142, 89 Stat. 773.
(b) S. 6.
(c) S. Rep. No. 168, 94th Cong., 1st Sess. 1, reprinted in 1975 U.S. Code Cong. & Ad. News 1425.

14 171 268 341 466 585   Postal Revenue and Federal Salary Act of 1967   S. Rep. No. 801
(a) Postal Revenue and Federal Salary Act of 1967, Pub. L. No. 90-206, 81 Stat. 613.
(b) H.R. 7977.
(c) S. Rep. No. 801, 90th Cong., 1st Sess. ___, reprinted in 1967 U.S. Code Cong. & Ad. News 2258.

15 172 269 342 467 586   Copyrights Act (1976)   H.R. Rep. No. 1476
(a) Copyrights Act, Pub. L. No. 94-553, 90 Stat. 2541 (1976).
(b) S. 22.

EXERCISE 43. LEGISLATIVE HISTORY OF FEDERAL STATUTES   (CONTINUED)

Note: "Act of Oct. 19, 1976, Pub. L. No. 94-553, 90 Stat. 2541" is also correct.
(c) H.R. Rep. No 1476, 94th Cong., 2d Sess. 1, reprinted in 1976 U.S. Code Cong. & Ad. News 5659.

16 173 270 343 468 587   Housing and Urban Development Act of 1968 H.R. Rep. No. 1585
(a) Housing and Urban Development Act of 1968, Publ. L. No. 90-448, 82 Stat. 476.
(b) S. 3497.
(c) H.R. Rep. No. 1585, 90th Cong., 2d Sess. ___, reprinted in 1968 U.S. Code Cong. & Ad. News 2873.

17 174 271 344 469 588   International Development and Food Assistance (1977) H.R. Rep. No. 240
(a) International Development and Food Assistance Act of 1977, Pub. L. No. 95-88, 91 Stat. 533.
(b) H.R. 6714.
(c) H.R. Rep. No 240, 95th Cong., 1st Sess. 1, reprinted in 1977 U.S. Code Cong. & Ad. News 748.

18 175 272 345 470 589   Middle Income Student Assistance Act (1978)   H.R. Rep. No. 951
(a) Middle Income Student Assistance Act, Pub. L. No. 95-566, 92 Stat. 2402 (1978)
(b) S. 2539.
(c) S. Rep. No 546, 91st Cong., 1st Sess. ___, reprinted in 1978 U.S. Code Cong. & Ad. News 5314.

19 176 273 346 571 590   Federal Contested Election Act (1969)   S. Rep. No. 546
(a) Federal Contested Election Act, Pub. L. No. 91-128, 93 Stat. 284 (1969).
(b) H.R. 14195.
(c) S. Rep. No 546, 91st Cong., 1st Sess. ___, reprinted in 1959 U.S. Code Cong. & Ad. News 1456.

20 177 274 347 472 591   Bankruptcy - Student Loans (1979)   S. Rep. No. 230
(a) Act of Aug. 14, 1979, Pub. L. No. 96-56, 93 Stat. 387.
(b) H.R. 2807.
(c) S. Rep. No. 230, 96th Cong., 1st Sess. 1, reprinted in 1979 U.S. Code Cong. & Ad. News 936.

21 178 275 348 473 592   Lotteries Transportation of Materials to Foreign Countries (1979)   H.R. Rep. No. 230
(a) Act of Oct. 23, 1979, Pub. L. No. 96-90, 93 Stat. 698.
(b) H.R. 1301.
(c) H.R. Rep. No. 45, 96th Cong., 1st Sess. 1, reprinted in 1979 U.S. Code Cong. & Ad. News 1645.

22 179 276 349 474 593   Newspaper Preservation Act (1970)   H.R. Rep. No. 1193
(a) Newspaper Preservation Act, Pub. L. No. 91-353, 84 Stat. 466 (1970).
(b) S. 1520.
(c) H.R. Rep. No. 1193, 91st Cong., 2d Sess. ___, reprinted in 1970 U.S. Code Cong. & Ad. News 3547.

23 180 277 350 475 594   Disqualification of Former Government Employees and Officers (1979)   H.R. Rep. No. 115
(a) Act of June 22, 1979, Pub. L. No. 96-28, 93 Stat. 76.
(b) S. 869.
(c) H.R. Rep. No. 115, 96th Cong., 1st Sess. 1

24 181 278 351 476 595   Suspension of Duties on Metal Waste and Scrap (1978) S. Rep. No. 1243
(a) Act of Oct. 24, 1978, Pub. L. No. 95-508, 92 Stat. 1774.
(b) H.R. 12165.

EXERCISE 43. LEGISLATIVE HISTORY OF FEDERAL STATUTES   (CONTINUED)

(c) S. Rep. No. 1243, 95th Cong., 2d Sess. 1, reprinted in 1978 U.S. Code Cong. & Ad. News 3891.

25 182 279 352 477 596   Emergency Loan Guarantee Act (1971)   H.R. Rep. No. 379
(a) Emergency Loan Gurantee Act, Pub. L. No. 92-70, 85 Stat. 178 (1971)
(b) H.R. 8432.
(c) H.R. Rep. No 379, 92d Cong., 1st Sess. ___, reprinted in 1971 U.S. Code Cong. & Ad. News 1270.

26 183 280 353 478 597   Small Business Act (1977)   H.R. Rep. No. 1
(a) Act of Aug. 4, 1977, Pub. L. No. 95-89, 91 Stat. 553.
(b) H.R. 692.
(c) H.R. Rep. No. 1, 95th Cong., 1st Sess. 1, reprinted in 1977 U.S. Code cong. & Ad. News 821.

27 184 281 354 479 598   Federal Rules of Criminal Procedure Amendments (1977)   S. Rep. No. 354
(a) Act of July 30, 1977, Pub. L. No. 95-78, 91 Stat. 319.
(b) H.R. 5864.
(c) S. Rep. No. 354, 95th Cong., 1st Sess. 1, reprinted in 1977 U.S. Code Cong. & Ad. News 527.

28 185 282 355 480 599   Ports and Waterways Safety Act of 1972   S. Rep. No. 724
(a) Ports and Waterways Safety Act of 1972, Pub. L. No. 92-340, 86 Stat. 424.
(b) H.R. 8140.
(c) S. Rep. No 724, 92d Cong., 2d Sess. ___, reprinted in 1972 U.S. Code Cong. & Ad. News 2766.

29 186 283 356 481 600   Voting Rights Act of 1965   H.R. Rep. No. 439
(a) Voting Rights Act of 1965, Pub. L. No. 89-110, 79 Stt. 437.
(b) S. 1564.
(c) H.R. Rep. No 439, 89th Cong., 1st Sess. ___, reprinted in 1965 U.S. Code Cong. & Ad. News 2437.

30 187 284 357 482 501   Emergency Medical Services Systems Amendments of 1979   S. Rep. No. 102
(a) Emergency Medical Services Services Medical Services Systems Amendments of 1979, Pub. L. No. 96-142, 93 Stat. 1067.
(b) S. 497.
(c) S. Rep. No 835, 92d Cong., 2d Sess. ___, reprinted in 1972 U.S. Code Cong. & Ad. News 4573.

31 188 285 358 483 502   Consumer Product Safety Act (1972)   S. Rep. No. 835
(a) Consumer Product Safety Act, Pub. L. No. 92-573, 86 Stat. 1207 (1972).
(b) S. 3419.
(c) S. Rep. No. 835, 92d Cong., 2d Sess. ___, reprinted in U.S. Code Cong. & Ad. News 4573.

32 189 286 359 484 503   Social Security Act - Disability Determination (1957)   H.R. Rep. No. 277
(a) Act of July 17, 1957, Pub. L. No. 85-109, 71 Stat. 308.
(b) H.R. 6191.
(c) H.R. Rep. No. 277, 85th Cong., 1st Sess. ___, reprinted in 1957 U.S. Code Cong. & Ad. News 1374.

33 190 287 360 485 504   Vessels - Construction Subsidy (1960)   H.R. Rep. No. 1715
(a) Act of July 7, 1960, Pub. L. No. 86-607, 74 Stat. 362.
(b) H.R. 10644.
(c) H.R. Rep. No. 1715, 86th Cong., 2d Sess. ___, reprinted in 1960 U.S. Code Cong. & Ad. news 2787.

34 191 288 361 486 505   Health Programs Extension Act of 1973   H.R. Rep. No. 227
(a) Health Programs Extension Act of 1973, Pub. L. No. 93-45, 87 Stat. 91.

EXERCISE 43. LEGISLATIVE HISTORY OF FEDERAL STATUTES   (CONTINUED)

(b) S. 1136.
(c) H.R. Rep. No. 337, 93rd Cong., 1st Sess. ___, reprinted in 1973 U.S. Code Cong. & Ad. News 1464.

35 192 289 362 487 506   National Banking Laws - Clarification (1959) S. Rep. No. 730
(a) Act of Sept. 8, 1959, Pub. L. No. 86-230, 73 Stat. 457.
(b) H.R. 8159.
(c) S. Rep. No 730, 86th Cong., 1st Sess. ___, reprinted in 1959 U.S. Code Cong. & Ad. News 2232.

36 193 290 363 488 507   Temporary Unemployment Compensation (1958) S. Rep. No. 1625
(a) Temporary Unemployment Compensation Act of 1958, Pub. L. No. 85-441, 72 Stat. 171.
(b) H.R. 12065.
(c) S. Rep. No. 1625, 85th Cong., 2d Sess. ___, reprinted in 1958 U.S. Code Cong. & Ad. News 2582.

37 194 291 364 489 508   Colorado River Basin Salinity Control Act (1974) S. Rep. No. 906
(a) Colorado River Basin Salinity control Act, Pub. L. No. 93-320, 88 Stat. 266 (1974).
(b) H.R. 12165.
(c) S. Rep. No. 906, 93d Cong., 2d Sess. ___, reprinted in 1974 U.S. Code Cong. & Ad. News 3327.

38 195 292 365 490 509   Public Debt Limit Act (1962)   S. Rep. No. 1221
(a) Act of Mar. 13, 1962, Pub. L. No. 87-414, 76 Stat. 23.
(b) H.R. 10050.
(c) S. Rep. No. 1221, 87th Cong., 2d Sess. ___, reprinted in 1962 U.S. Code Cong. & Ad. News 1498.

39 196 293 366 491 510   Lead-Zinc Producers (1963)   S. Rep. No. 239
(a) Act of July 22, 1963, Pub. L. No. 88-75, 77 stat. 92.
(b) H.R. 3845.
(c) S. Rep. No. 239, 88th Cong., 1st Sess. ___, reprinted in 1963 U.S. Code Cong. & Ad. News 771.

40 197 294 367 492 511   Energy Policy and Conservation Act (1975)   H.R. Rep. No. 340
(a) Energy Policy and Conservation Act, Pub. L. No. 94-163, 89 Stat. 871 (1975).
(b) S. 622.
(c) H.R. Rep. No. 340, 94th Cong., 1st Sess. 1, reprinted in 1975 U.S. Code Cong. & Ad. News 1762.

41 198 295 368 493 512   Energy Policy and Conservation Act (Amendment) (1979)   H.R. Rep. No. 510
(a) Act of Nov. 30, 1979, Pub. L. No, 96-133, 93 Stat. 1053.
(b) S. 1971.
(c) H.R. Rep. No. 510, 96th Cong., 1st Sess. 1, reprinted in 1979 U.S. Code Cong. & Ad. News 2055.

42 199 296 369 494 513   Pipeline Safety Act of 1979   S. Rep. No. 182
(a) Pipeline Safety Act of 1979, Pub. L. No. 96-129, 93 Stat. 989.
(b) S. 411.
(c) S. Rep. No. 182, 96th Cong., 1st Sess. 1, reprinted in U.S. Code Cong. & Ad. News 1971.

43 200 297 370 495 514   Electric and Hybrid Vehicle Research (1976)   H.R. Rep. No. 439
(a) Electric Hygrid Vehicle Research, Development, and Demonstration Act of 1976, Pub. L. no. 94-413, 90 Stat. 1260.
(b). H.R. 8800.
(c) H.R. Rep. No. 439, 94th Cong., 1st Sess. 1, reprinted in 1976 U.S. Code Cong. & Ad. News 2315.

EXERCISE 43.   LEGISLATIVE HISTORY OF FEDERAL STATUTES   (CONTINUED)

44 101 298 371 496 515   Export Administration Act of 1979   S. Rep. No. 169
(a) Export Administration Act of 1979, Pub. L. No. 96-72, 93 Stat. 503.
(b) S. 737.
(c) S. Rep. No. 169, 96th Cong., 1st Sess. 1, reprinted in 1979 U.S. Code Cong. & Ad. News 1147.

45 102 299 372 497 516   Speedy Trial Act Amendments Act of 1979   S. Rep. No. 212
(a) Speedy Trial Act Amendments Act of 1979, Pub. l. No. 96-43, 93 Stat. 327.
(b) S. 961.
(c) S. Rep. No. 212, 96th Cong., 1st Sess. 1, reprinted U.S. Code Cong. & Ad. News 805.

46 103 300 373 498 517   State Veterans' Home Assistance (1977)   S. Rep. No. 166
(a) State Veterans' Home Assistance Improvement Act of 1977, Pub. L. No. 95-62, 91 Stat. 262.
(b) H.R. 3695.
(c) S. Rep. No. 166, 95th Cong., 1st Sess. 1, reprinted in 1977 U.S. Code Cong. & Ad. News 434.

47 104 201 374 499 518   National Consumer Cooperative Bank Act (1978) S. Rep. No. 1211
(a) National Consumer Cooperative Bank Act, Pub. L. No. 95-351, 92 Stat. 499 (1978).
(b) H.R. 2777.
(c) S. Rep. No. 795, 95th Cong., 2d Sess. 1, reprinted in 1978 U.S. Code Cong. & Ad. News 1302.

48 105 202 375 500 519   Airline Deregulation Act of 1978   H.R. Rep. No. 1211
(a) Airline Deregulaltion Act of 1978, Pub. L. No. 95-504, 92 Stat. 1705.
(b) S. 2493
(c) H.R. Rep. No. 1211, 95th Cong., 2d Sess. 1, reprinted in 1978 U. S. Code Cong. & Ad. News 3737.

49 106 203 376 401 520   Tribally Controlled Community College Assistance (1978)   H.R. Rep. No. 1211
(a) Tribally Controlled Community College Assistance Act of 1978, Pub. L. No. 95-471, 92 Stat. 1325.
(b) S. 1215.
(c) H.R. Rep. No. 1558, 95th Cong., 2d Sess. 1, reprinted in 1978 U.S. Code Cong. & Ad. News 2987.

50 107 204 377 402 521   Cigarettes Distribution Racketeering (1978) S. Rep. No. 962
(a) Act of Nov. 2, 1978, Pub. L. No. 95-575, 92 Stat. 2463.
(b) S. 1487
(c) S. Rep. No. 962, 95th Cong., 2d Sess, 1, reprinted in 1978 U.S. Code Cong. & Ad. News 5518.

51 108 205 378 403 522   St. Lawrence Seaway Development Corp. (1957) H.R. Rep. No. 473
(a) Act of Jly 17, 1957, Pub. L. No. 85-108, 71 Stat. 307.
(b) H.R. 5728.
(c) H.R. Rep. No. 473, 85th Cong., 1st Sess. ___, reprinted in 1957 U.S. Code Cong. & Ad. News 1363.

52 109 206 379 404 523   Diplomatic Relations Act (1978)   S. Rep. No. 1108
(a) Diplomatic Relations Act, Pub. L. No. 95-393, 92 Stat. 808 (1978).
(b) H.R. 7819.
(c) S. Rep. No. 1108, 95th Cong., 2d Sess. 1, reprinted in 1978 U.S. Code Cong. & Ad. News 1941.

53 110 207 380 405 524   Federal Hazardous Substances Labeling (1960) H.R. Rep. No. 1961

EXERCISE 43. LEGISLATIVE HISTORY OF FEDERAL STATUTES   (CONTINUED)

(a) Federal Hazardous Substances Labeling Act, Pub. L. No. 86-613, 74 Stat. 372 (1960).
(b) S. 1283.
(c) H.R. Rep. No. 1861, 86th Cong., 2d Sess. ___, reprinted in 1960 U.S. Code Cong. & Ad. News 2833.

54 111 208 381 406 525   Labor-Management Reporting Act of 1959   H.R. Rep. No. 741
(a) Labor-Management Reporting and Disclosure Act of 1959, Pub. L. No. 86-257, 73 Stat. 519.
(b) S. 1555.
(c) H.R. Rep. No. 741, 86th Cong., 1st Sess. ___, reprinted in 1959 U.S. Code Cong. & Ad. News 2424.

55 112 209 382 407 526   Nurse Training Act of 1964   S. Rep. No. 1378 56 113
(a) Nurse Training Act of 1964, Pub. L. No. 88-581, 79 Stat. 907.
(b) H.R. 11241.
(c) S. Rep. No. 1378, 88th Cong., 2d Sess. ___, reprinted in 1964 U.S. Code Cong. & Ad. News 3669.

56 113 210 383 408 527   District Courts - Jurisdiction (1958)   S. Rep. No. 1830
(a) Act of July 25, 1958, Pub. L. No. 85-554, 72 Stat. 415.
(b) S. 1991.
(c) S. Rep. No. 651, 87th Cong., 1st Sess. ___, reprinted in 1962 U.S. Code Cong. & Ad. News 3099

57 114 211 384 409 528   Manpower Development and Training Act of 1962 S. Rep. No. 651
(a) Manpower Development and Training Act of 1962, Pub. L. No. 87-415, 76 Stat. 23.
(b) S. 1991
(c) S. Rep. No. 651, 87th Cong., 1st Sess. ___, reprinted in 1962 U.S. Code Cong. & Ad. News 1502.

58 114 212 385 410 529   National Foundation on the Arts and Humanities (1965)   H.R. Rep. No. 618
(a) National Foundation on the Arts and the Huminaties Act of 1965, Pub. L. No. 89-209, 79 Stat. 845.
(b) S. 1483.
(c) H.R. Rep. No. 618, 89th Cong., 1st Sess. ___, reprinted in 1965 U.S. Code Cong. & Ad. News 3186.

59 115 213 386 411 530   Interstate Commerce - Seat Belts (1963)   S. Rep. No. 665
(a) Act of Dec. 13, 1963, Pub. L. No. 88-201, 77 Stat. 361.
(b) H.R. 134.
(c) S. Rep. No. 665, 88th Cong., 1st Sess. ___, reprinted in 1963 U.S. code Cong. & Ad. News 1136.

60 117 214 387 412 531   Tax Treatment Extension Act of 1977   S. Rep. No. 746
(a) Tax Treatment Extension Act of 1977, Pub. L. No. 95-615, 92 Stat. 3097 (1978).
(b) H.R. 9251.
(c) S. Rep. No. 746, 95th Cong., 2d Sess. ___, reprinted in 1978 U.S. Code Cong. & Ad. News 7612.

61 118 215 388 413 532   Communication Act Amendments of 1978   S. Rep. No. 580
(a) Communication Act Amendments of 1978, Pub. L. No. 95-234, 92 Stat. 33.
(b) H.R. 7442.
(c) S. Rep. No. 580, 95th Cong., 1st Sess. 1, reprinted in 1977 U.S. Code Cong. & Ad. News 109.

EXERCISE 43.   LEGISLATIVE HISTORY OF FEDERAL STATUTES   (CONTINUED)

62 119 216 389 414 533   Airports - Federal Grants (1964)   H.R. Rep. No. 1002
(a) Act of Mar. 11, 1964, Pub, L. No. 88-280, 78 Stat. 158.
(b) S. 1153.
(c) H.R. Rep. No. 1002, 88th Cong., 1st Sess. ___, reprinted in 1964 U.S. Cong. & Ad. News 2063.

63 120 217 390 415 534   Federal Reserve Banks - Gold Reserves (1965) S. Rep. No. 65
(a) Act of Mar. 3, 1965, Pub. L. No. 89-3, 79 Stat. 5
(b) H.R. 3818.
(c) S. Rep. No. 65, 89th Cong., 1st Sess. ___, reprinted in 1965 U.S. Code Cong. & Ad. News 1353.

64 121 218 391 416 535   Appalachian Regional Development Act of 1965 H.R. Rep. No. 51
(a) Appalachian Regional Development Act of 1965, Pub. L. No. 89-4, 79 Stat. 5.
(b) S. 3.
(c) H.R. rep. No. 51, 89th Cong., 1st Sess. ___, reprinted in 1965 U.S. Code Cong. & Ad. News 1373.

65 122 219 392 417 536   Elementary and Secondary Education Act of 1965 S. Rep. No. 146
(a) Elementary and Secondary Education Act of 1965, Pub. L. No. 89-10, 79 Stat. 27.
(b) H.R. 2362
(c) S. Rep. No. 146, 89th Cong., 1st Sess. ___, reprinted in 1965 U.S. Code Cong. & Ad. News 1446.

66 123 220 393 418 537   Excise Tax Reduction Act of 1965   S. Rep. No. 324
(a) Excise Tax Reduction Act of 1965, Pub. L. No. 89-44, 79 Stat. 136.
(b) H.R. 8371.
(c) S. Rep. No. 324, 89th Cong., 1st Sess. ___, reprinted in 1965 U.S. Code Cong. & Ad. News 1690.

67 124 221 394 419 538   Back Pay Act of 1966   S. Rep. No. 1062
(a) Back Pay Act of 1966, Pub. L. No. 89-380, 80 Stat. 94.
(b) S. 1647.
(c) S. Rep. No. 1062, 89th Cong., 2d Sess. ___, reprinted in 1966 U.S. Code Cong. & Ad. News 2097.

68 125 222 395 420 539   Uniform Time Act of 1966   H.R. Rep. No. 1315
(a) Uniform Time Act of 1966, Pub. L. No. 89-387, 80 Stat. 107.
(b) S. 1404.
(c) H.R. Rep. No. 1315, 89th Cong., 2d Sess. ___, reprinted in 1966 U.S. Code Cong. & Ad. News 2111.

69 126 223 396 421 540   Small Business Act - Revolving Funds (1966)   H.R. Rep. No. 1348
(a) Act of May 2, 1966, Pub. L. No. 89-409, 80 Stat. 132.
(b) S 2729.
(c) H.R. Rep. No. 1348, 89th Cong., 2d Sess. ___, reprinted in 1966 U.S. Code Cong. & Ad. News 2186.

70 127 224 397 422 541   Marine Resources and Engineering Development Act of 1966   H.R. Rep. No. 1025
(a) Marine Resources and Engineering Development Act of 1966, Pub. L. No. 89-454, 80 Stat. 203.
(b) S. 944.
(c) H.R. Rep. No. 1025, 89th Cong., 1st Sess. ___, reprinted in 1966 U.S. Code Cong. & Ad. News 2262.

71 128 225 398 423 542   Bail Reform Act of 1966   H.R. Rep. No. 1541
(a) Bail Reform Act of 1966, Pub. L. No. 89-465, 80 Stat. 214.
(b) S. 1357.

EXERCISE 43.   LEGISLATIVE HISTORY OF FEDERAL STATUTES   (CONTINUED)

(c) H.R. Rep. No. 1541, 89th Cong., 2d Sess. ___, reprinted in 1966 U.S. Code Cong. & Ad. news 2293.

72 129 226 399 424 543   Saline Water Conversion Program (1967)   S. Rep. No. 219
(a) Act of June 24, 1967, Pub. L. No. 90-30, 81 Stat. 78.
(b) H.R. 6133.
(c) S. Rep. No. 1541, 89th Cong. 2d Sess. ___, reprinted in 1966 U.S. Code Cong. & Ad. News 2293.

73 130 227 400 425 544   Military Selective Service Act of 1967   H.R. Rep. No. 267
(a) Military Selective Service Act of 1967, Pub. l. No. 90-40, 81 Stat. 100.
(b) S. 1432.
(c) H.R. Rep. No. 267, 90th Cong., 1st Sess. ___, reprinted in 1967 U.S. Code Cong. & Ad. News 1308.

74 131 228 301 426 545   Mental Health Amendments of 1967   S. Rep. No. 294
(a) Mental Health Amendments of 1967, Pub. L. No. 90-31, 81 Stat. 100.
(b) S. 1432.
(c) H.R. Rep. No. 267, 90th Cong., 1st Sess. ___, reprinted in 1967 U.S. code Cong. & Ad. News 1308.

75 132 229 302 427 546   Interest Equalization Tax Extension Act of 1967 H.R. Rep. No. 68
(a) Interest Equalization Tax Extension Act of 1967, Pub. l. No. 90-59, 91 Stat. 145.
(b) H.R. 6098.
(c) H.R. Rep. No. 68, 90th Cong., 1st Sess. ___, reprinted in 1967 U.S. Code Cong. & Ad. news 1414.

76 133 230 303 428 547   Omnibus Crime Control and Safe Streets Act of 1968   S. Rep. No. 1317
(a) Omnibus Crime Control and Safe Streets Act of 1968, Pub. L. No. 90-351, 82 Stat. 197.
(b) H.R. 5037
(c) S. Rep. No. 1097, 90th Cong., 2d Sess. ___, reprinted in 1968 U.S. code Cong. & Ad. News 2112.

77 134 231 304 429 548   Postal Employees - Embezzlement (1968)   S. Rep. No. 1317
(a) Act of July 5, 1968, Pub. L. No. 90-384, 82 Stat. 292.
(b) H.R. 17024.
(c) S. Rep. No. 1317, 90th Cong., 2d Sess. ___, reprinted in 1968 U.S. Code Cong. & Ad. News 2112.

78 135 232 305 430 549   Aircraft Noise Abatement (1968)   S. Rep. No. 1353
(a) Act of July 21, 1968, Pub. L. No. 90-411, 82 Stat. 395.
(b) H.R. 3400.
(c) S. Rep. No. 1353, 90th Cong., 2d Sess. ___, reprinted in 1968 U.S. Code Cong. & Ad. News 2688.

79 136 233 306 431 550   Air Carriers - Ownership & Control (1969)   S. Rep. No. 185
(a) Act of Aug. 20, 1969, Pub. L. No. 91-62, 83 Stat. 103.
(b) S. 1373.
(c) S. Rep. No. 1353, 90th Cong., 2d Sess. ___, reprinted in 1969 U.S. Code Cong. & Ad. News 1098.

80 137 234 307 432 551   Securities - Institutional Investors Study (1969)   H.R. Rep. No. 501
(a) Act of Oct. 20, 1969, Pub. L. No. 91-94, 83 Stat. 141.
(b) S. 1373.
(c) S. Rep. No. 185, 91st Cong., 1st Sess. ___, reprinted in 1969 U.S. Code Cong. & Ad. News 1098.

EXERCISE 43. LEGISLATIVE HISTORY OF FEDERAL STATUTES   (CONTINUED)

81 138 235 308 433 552   Educational Television and Radio Amendments of 1969
H.R. Rep. No. 466
(a) Educational Television and Radio Amendments of 1969, Pub. L. No. 91-97, 83 Stat. 146.
(b) S. 1242.
(c) H.R. Rep. No. 466, 91st Cong., 1st Sess. ___, reprinted in 1969 U.S. Code Cong. & Ad. News 1200.

82 139 236 309 434 553   Naturalization - Waiting Period (1969)   S. Rep. No. 534
(a) Act of Dec. 5, 1969, Pub. L. No. 91-136, 83 Stat. 283.
(b) H.R. 3666.
(c) S. Rep. No. 534, 91st Cong., 1st Sess. ___, reprinted in 1969 U.S. Code Cong. & Ad. News 1440.

83 140 237 310 435 554   Egg Products Inspection Act (1970)   H.R. Rep. No. 1670
(a) Egg Products Inspection Act, Pub. L. No. 91-597, 84 Stat. 1620 (1970)
(b) H.R. 19888.
(c) H.R. Rep. No. 1670, 91st Cong., 2d Sess. ___, reprinted in 1970 U.S. Code Cong. & Ad. News 5242.

84 141 238 311 436 555   Seamen's Service Act (1970)   S. Rep. No. 1424
(a) Seamen's Service Act, Pub. L. No. 91-603, 84 Stat. 1674 (1970).
(b) H.R. 15549.
(c) S. Rep. No. 1424, 91st Cong., 2d Sess. ___, reprinted in 1970 U.S. Code Cong. & Ad. News 5347.

85 142 239 312 437 556   Clean Air Amendments of 1970   H.R. Rep. No. 1146
(a) Clean Air Amendments of 1970, Pub. L. No. 91-604, 84 Stat. 1676.
(b) H.R. 17255.
(c) H.R. Rep. No. 1146, 91st Cong., 2d Sess. ___, reprinted in 1970 U.s. Code Cong. & Ad. News 5356.

86 143 240 313 438 557   Federal-Aid Highway Act of 1970   H.R. Rep. No. 1554
(a) Federal-Aid Highway Act of 1970, Pub. L. No. 91-605, 84 Stat. 1713.
(b) H.R. 19504
(c) H.R. Rep. No. 1554, 91st Cong., 2d Sess. ___, reprinted in U.S. Code Cong. & Ad. News 5392.

87 144 241 314 439 558   Emergency Energy Conservation Act of 1979   H.R. Rep. No. 373
(a) Emergency Energy Conservation Act of 1979, Pub. L. No. 96-102, 93 Stat. 749.
(b) S. 1030.
(c) H.R. Rep. No. 373, 96th Cong., 1st Sess. 1, reprinted in 1979 U.S. Code Cong. & ad. News 1764.

88 145 242 315 440 559   Railroad Retirement - Annuities (1971)   S. Rep. No. 206
(a) Act of July 2, 1971, Pub. L. No. 92-46, 85 Stat. 101.
(b) H.R. 6444.
(c) S. Rep. No. 206, 92d Cong., 1st Sess. ___, reprinted in 1971 U.S. Code Cong. & Ad. News 1211.

89 146 243 316 441 560   Health Care Benefits - Dependents (1971)   H.R. Rep. No. 351
(a) Act of July 29, 1971, Pub. L. No. 92-58, 85 Stat. 157.
(b) S. 421.
(c) H.R. Rep. No. 351, 92d cong., 1st Sess. ___, reprinted in 1971 U.S. Code Cong. & Ad. News 1211.

90 147 244 317 442 561   Emergency Loan Guarantee Act (1971)   H.R. Rep. No. 379
(a) Emergency Loan Guarantee Act, Pub. L. No. 92-70, 85 Stat. 178 (1971).
(b) H.R. 8432.

EXERCISE 43. LEGISLATIVE HISTORY OF FEDERAL STATUTES   (CONTINUED)

(c) H.R. Rep. No. 379, 92d Cong., 1st Sess. ___, reprinted in 1972 U.S. Code Cong. & Ad. News 2351

91 148 245 318 443 562   Atomic Energy Commission - Licenses (1972)   H.R. Rep. No. 1027
(a) Act of June 2, 1972, Pub. L. No. 92-46, 85 Stat. 101.
(b) H.R. 14655
(c) H.R. Rep. No. 379, 92d Cong., 1st Sess. ___, reprinted in 1971 U.S. Code Cong. & Ad. News 1211.

92 149 246 319 444 563   Education Amendments of 1972   H.R. Rep. No. 554
(a) Education Amenedmnts of 1972, Pub. L. No. 92-318, 86 Stat. 235.
(b) S. 659.
(c) H.R. Rep No 554, 92d Cong., 1st Sess. ___, reprinted in H.R. Rep. No. 554, 92d Cong., 1st Sess. ___, reprinted in 1972 U.S. Code Cong. & Ad. News 2452.

93 150 247 320 445 564   Civil Defense - Extension (1972)   S. Rep. No. 941
(a) Act of Aug. 2, 1972, Pub. L. No. 92-36, 86 Stat. 503.
(b) S. 3772.
(c) S. Rep. No. 941, 92d Cong., 2d Sess. ___, reprinted in 1972 U.S. Code Cong. & Ad. News 2883.

94 151 248 321 446 565   Juvenile Delinquency Prevention Act (1972)   S. Rep. No. 1003
(a) Juvenile Delingquecy Prevention Act, Pub. L. No. 92-381, 86 Stat. 532 (1972).
Note: "Act of Aug. 14, 1972" is also correct.
(b) H.R. 15635.
(c) S. Rep. No. 1003, 92d Cong., 2d Sess. ___, reprinted in 1972 U.S. Code Cong. & Ad. News 2934.

95 152 249 322 447 566   Economic Stabilization Amendments of 1973   S. Rep. No. 63
(a) Interest Equalization Tax Extension Act of 1973, Pub. L. No. 93-28, 87 Stat. 27.
(b) S. 398.
(c) S. Rep. No. 63, 93d Cong., 1st Sess. ___, reprinted in 1973 U.S. Code Cong. & Ad News 1299.

96 153 250 323 448 567   Interest Equalization Tax Extension Act of 1973 S. Rep. No. 84
(a) Interest Equalization Tax Extension Act of 1973, Pub. L. No. 93-17, 87 Stat. 12.
(b) H.R. 3577.
(c) S. Rep. No. 84, 93d Cong., 1st Sess. ___, reprinted in 1973 U.S. Code Cong. & Ad. News 1245.

97 154 251 324 449 568   Older Americans Comprehensive Services Amendments of 1973   H.R. Rep. No. 43
(a) Older Americans Comprehensive Services Amendments of 1973, Pub. L. No. 93-29-87 Stat. 30.
(b) S. 50.
(c) H.R. Rep. No, 93d Cong., 1st Sess. ___, reprinted in 1973 U.S. Code Cong. & Ad. News 1327.

98 155 252 325 450 569   Crime Control Act of 1973   H.R. Rep. No. 249
(a) Crime Control Act of 1973, Pub. L. No. 93-83, 87 Stat. 197.
(b) H.R. 8152.
(c) H.R. Rep. No. 249, 93d Cong., 1st Sess. ___, reprinted in 1973 U.S. Code Cong. & Ad. News 1729.

99 156 253 326 451 570   Federal Prisoners - Extension of Confinement Limits (1973)   S. Rep. No. 418
(a) Act of Dec. 29, 1973, Pub. L. No. 93-209, 87 Stat. 907.
(b) H.R. 7352.

EXERCISE 43.   LEGISLATIVE HISTORY OF FEDERAL STATUTES   (CONTINUED)

(c) S. Rep. No. 418, 93d Cong., 1st Sess. ___, reprinted in 1973 U.S. Code Cong. & Ad. News 3017.

100 157 254 327 452 571   Federal Water Pollution Control Act Amendments (1973)   H.R. Rep. No. 680
(a) Act of Dec. 28, 1973, Pub. L. No. 83-20, 87 Stat. 906.
(b) S. 1776.
(c) H.R. Rep. No. 680, 93d Cong., 1st Sess. ___, reprinted in 1973 U.S. Code Cong. & Ad. News 3008.

EXERCISE 44.   UNITED STATES ATTORNEY GENERAL OPINIONS.

INSTRUCTOR'S NOTE: This exercise simply requires the students to find a United States Attorney General opinion from a known citation. All of the student answers should follow this pattern:

   x Op. Att'y Gen. xxx (19xx).

   The relevant Quick-Reference Abbreviation is:

   ADMINISTRATIVE CITATION 6. CITE ATTORNEY GENERAL OPINIONS BY VOLUME, PAGE, AND DATE. USE THE ABBREVIATION "Op. Att'y Gen." [AD 6]

LIBRARY EXERCISE 45. FORMULATING WESTLAW SEARCH REQUESTS.

INSTRUCTOR'S NOTE: This exercise is designed to introduce students to formulating WESTLAW search requests. The answers for each subpart are explained below.

(a) The students may list one of the following abbreviations for their answer, an individual state database, or a more specialized database (e.g., cta8):

   ne
   nw
   pac
   se
   so
   sw
   sct
   cta
   dct

   Note that the requests in this and the following subparts of this exercise may use capital letters, e.g., Fed or FED. Periods should not be used (nw, not n.w.). Note also that the instructions for Exercise 45 state that the student should assume that the databases stored in the WESTLAW computer are sufficient to meet the requirements of this exercise. For example, a student should answer "atl" for "155 A. 788" even though the computer only contains cases reported in the Atlantic Reporter, Second Series. An answer such as "p4" would be incorrect; typing p and the relevant page number would cause the computer to display a detailed coverage of the file.

(b) The search formulated by the student should be limited to the Title field. Considerable latitude should be given to the student regarding what part of the case name he includes and the connectors he uses. The requests should follow this basic pattern:

   title(hill & douglass)

   Note that the answer is incorrect if there is a space between "title" and the first parenthesis. Procedural phrases such as "in re" should probably be omitted from the query and abbreviations should be avoided (e.g., "hosp." for "hospital"). If a student uses two or more words together as part of the query, the student should either use quotation marks (e.g., "lalla's estate" or "long beach") to treat the words as a phrase or a connector between them (e.g., lalla's & estate, lalla's +3 estate, lalla's +s estate, etc.).

(c) The student should explain that the FIND function should be used. To do so, the student should either state that the FIND key should be pressed, followed by entering the citation or the following could be typed and entered:

   find321f.2d577
   fi 321 F.2d 577

   Spacing and punctuation are optional.

(d) If the students list only one word from Exercise 25 in their answer in addition to the word authority, the following format should be used:

   digest(authority & alibi)

   If the students list a phrase from Exercise 25 in their answer, the phrase should be enclosed in quotation marks:

   digest(authority & "account current")

   Note that the answer is incorrect if there is a space between "digest" and the first parenthesis. Note also that the following request is incorrect:

   digest(authority /p alibi)

438

EXERCISE 45. FORMULATING WESTLAW SEARCH REQUESTS   (CONTINUED)

(e) The search query formulated by the student should follow this basic pattern:

   waiv! estop! & date(after 1912)
   date(aft 1912) & waiv! estop!

Note that the "date after" or "date aft" must either <u>begin</u> or <u>end</u> the search request and that the date restriction should be connected to the remainder of the search query by an ampersand. Although it would not retrieve "waiving," "waive!" probably should be accepted as correct. Note also that there should be no space between "date" and "(aft 1912)."

(f) The search query should follow this basic pattern:

   judge(black) & 30k1133

The order of the items may be reversed. Note that no space should be left between "judge" and the parenthetical or between the WESTLAW Topic Number, the "k", and the key number.

(g) If the students list only one word from Exercise 25 in their answer in addition to the word <u>authority</u> and the word <u>influence</u>, one of the following formats should be used.

   alibi /p authority influence

   authority influence /p alibi

Note that authority and influence should not be connected by "&." If the students list a phrase from Exercise 25 in their answer, one of the following formats should be used:

   "account current" /p authority influence

   authority influence /p "account current"

Note also that the following search query would be incorrect because it would require that all three terms appear in the same paragraph:

   authority /p alibi /p influence

(h) The student should use a subject matter word with the title and section numbers in the search query:

   parole & 5 +s 553

The order of the items may be reversed:

   5 +s 553 & parole

The student may also use an "/s" connector instead of the "+s" connector shown in the above answers.

If the student uses more than one subject matter word, the words should be treated as a phrase or properly connected (+s, /s, &), unless they could stand alone as alternatives:

   28 +s 2243 & "habeas corpus" 46 +s 971 & maritime /s lien 21 +s 844 & narcotic drug

(i) The student should explain that the INSTA-CITE key should be pressed and that the citation should then be entered <u>or</u> the following could be typed:

   ic 197 N.E.2d 911
   ic 197ne2d911

Note that the student may or may not use spaces, periods, or capitals.

EXERCISE 45. FORMULATING WESTLAW SEARCH REQUESTS   (CONTINUED)

(j) The student should explain that either the SHEPARDIZE key should be pressed or sh should be entered.

LIBRARY EXERCISE 46. FORMULATING LEXIS SEARCH REQUESTS

INSTRUCTOR'S NOTE: The answers for each of the subparts are explained below.

(a) The search request formulated by the student should be limited to the NAME segment. Considerable latitude should be given with respect to what part of the case name the student includes and the connectors the student uses. The request should follow this basic pattern:

    name (hill and douglass)

Note that the requests in this and the following subparts of this exercise may use all capital letters or a combination of upper and lower case letters. One space must be left between "name" and the first parenthesis.

(b) The search request should utilize the CITE segment and the "pre/" proximity connector:

    cite (277 pre/6 177)

Note that the number in "pre/" may vary, but in any event it should not be less than three. Note also that one space msut be left between "cite" and the first parenthesis. The name of the reporter or one of its abbreviations should not be used by the students in their search request.

(c) The students should explain that the faster and more convenient method of retrieving the case listed for their problem number in part (a) of Exercise 7 is to use the LEXSEE service. To use that service, the student would type and then transmit:

    lexsee 207 fsupp 9

(d) The search request formulated by the student should follow this basic pattern:

    waiv! or estop! and court (ala) and date aft 1912
    waiv! or estop! and court (alabama) and date aft 1912

Parentheses may be added:

    (waiv! or estop!) and court (ala) and date aft 1912

Note that the order of the items may vary and that "waiv*" and "estop*" would be incorrect. Although it would not retrieve "waiving," "waive!" probably should be accepted as correct. Note that the court may also be indicated by "court (alabama)" or "court (ala.)" and that the full date must be used (not '12 or the like).

(e) A typical search request formulated as an answer to this subpart would be:

    zoning and writtenby (black or stone)

Note that the order of the items and names may be reversed and that "opinionby" is incorrect. Phrases should be listed without an internal connector. Only the last name of each justice should be used. Reserved words in a phrase should be enclosed in quotation marks.

(f) The search request formulated by the student should follow this basic pattern:

EXERCISE 46.   FORMULATING LEXIS SEARCH REQUESTS   (CONTINUED)

   5 w/10 553 or §533 and parole

Note that the above search request includes the section sign and number without a space between them and the number alone. One of the following variants below would also be correct:

   5 w/10 553 or §553 w/30 parole
   5 w/10 553 or §553 or § 533 and parole

The number used in the proximity connector may vary and a phrase may be used to describe the subject matter (e.g., habeas corpus).

(g) The student should explain that the AUTO-CITE key should be pressed and then the citation should be transmitted:

   135 US 100
   or 135 us 100

The student may type ac instead of using the AUTO-CITE key. Note especially that the student must leave a space between the volume number, the reporter, and the page number to be correct. The <u>United States Reports</u> citation, of course, will vary.

(h) To shepardize the case listed in Exercise 14, the student would type and transmit:

   sh 207 f2d 9
   or sh 207 F2d 9

The citation, of course, will vary, but, as indicated in the text, the proper abbreviation must be used (page 354). The student could also explain that the Shepard's service could be accessed through the SELECT SERV key.

The student then should explain that the display should be limited by typing and transmitting one of the following restriction:

   e,1,2

Note that "explained," "ex," or "Ex" are incorrect.

Notes

Notes

Notes

Notes

Notes

Notes

Notes

Notes

Notes

Notes

Notes

Notes

Notes

Notes

Notes